1-10

100

Design: Dorianne Dysart

Deadly Doctor Freud

The Murder of Emanuel Freud
and
Disappearance of John Freud

Paul Scagnelli, Ph.D.

Pinewood Publishing Company
P.O. Box 2417
Durham, NC 27715

Published by: Pinewood Publishing Co.
              P.O. Box 2417
              Durham, N.C. 27715-2417

All rights reserved. No parts of this book may be reproduced or transmitted in any form or by any means, electronic or mechanical, including photocopying, recording or any information storage or retrieval system, without written permission from the author, except for the inclusion of brief quotations in a review.

Copyright © by Paul Scagnelli

Library of Congress Catologing in Publication Data

Scagnelli, Paul, 1932-
    Deadly Dr. Freud : the murder of Emanuel Freud and the disappearance of John Freud / Paul Scagnelli.
        p. cm.
    Includes bibliographical references and index.
    ISBN 0-9638184-6-5
    1. Freud, Sigmund, 1856-1939—Mental, health. 2. Freud, Sigmund, 1856-1939—Family. 3. Jones, Ernest, 1879-1958—Mental health.
4. Psychoanalysts—Austria—Biography. 5 . Psychoanalysts—Canada—Biography. 1. Title. II. Title: Deadly Doctor Freud.

BF173.F85S23 1994   150.19'52
                               QBI93-1214

Library of Congress Catalog Card Number (CIP): 93-85705

1 2 3 4 5 6 7 8 9 10

Acknowledgments

I would like to express my love and gratitude to my wife, Elaine, for the sensitive listening and criticism, practical help, and great emotional support that she has given me over many years. To describe her adequately I would have to use Jackie Gleason's famous saying: she is simply The Greatest.

Also, I wish to acknowledge my countless debts and gratitude to the enormously talented and dedicated corps of Reference Librarians at the Perkins Library of Duke University. With untiring zeal and professionalism, they have helped me to locate most of the materials that appear in this book. Equal praise and gratitude should go to the excellent group of Reference Librarians at Duke's Lilly Library.

Finally, I wish to thank three brilliant women. Dorothea Dysart and Marilyn Helms assisted with some of the proofreading work. My special thanks to Dorianne Dysart for her help with cover design and especially her provocative abstract design that appears opposite the title page. (In my view, it encodes a crucial mystery concerning Freud's unconscious functioning.)

Table of Contents

Chapter 1	An Introduction to Clinical Infamy	page 1
Chapter 2	Freud's Childhood and Psychopathology	page 27
Chapter 3	Freud's Uncanny Acting-out of Fantasy Identifications	page 60
Chapter 4	Freud's Identification with 20 Murderers	page 108
Chapter 5	Freud's Mental Imbalance	page 158
Chapter 6	Name Magic, Death, and the Revenants	page 216
Chapter 7	1900: Freud's Madness, Revenge, and Dora's Case	page 287
Chapter 8	The Murder of Emanuel Freud	page 322
Chapter 9	The Disappearance of John Freud	page 407
Chapter 10	Freud Identifies with Satan	page 475
Chapter 11	Dr. Ernest Jones: Eminent Psychopath	page 503
Appendix A		page 540
Bibliography		page 543
Index		page 554
Order Forms		Final Page

Chapter One

An Introduction to Clinical Infamy

Freud's Criminal Heritage

In 1976 the eminent scholar Renée Gicklhorn dropped a hot chestnut into the hands of social scientists and the literary world. Following that event seventeen years ago, a small army of pro-Freud biographers has held its collective breath, hoping that a controversial issue would vanish and not have to be dealt with in print. That issue concerns extensive criminality in Sigmund Freud's early family life. Also, embarrassed researchers have wished to avoid exploring the manner in which influential Freudians covered up this topic for many decades, and how the factor of criminality might have influenced Freud's early development and personality structure.

The issue of criminality was first disclosed, and discussed in detail, in Gicklhorn's 1976 book *Sigmund Freud und der Onkeltraum* (Sigmund Freud and the Uncle Dream). The title refers to Freud's dream in *The Interpretation of Dreams* (1967, pp. 170-8) concerning his uncle Josef, a younger brother of his father, Jacob. In 1866 Josef received a ten-year prison sentence for his involvement in the counterfeiting of currency, which provoked scandalous publicity in Viennese newspapers. The sensitive boy, Sigmund, was then ten-years old and was shamed by this notoriety. Incredibly, the specific details about Josef's crime and sentence were lost to the modern world until Gicklhorn's book was published in a German edition.

Her reporting of this incident suggests that Viennese police authorities suspected that Sigmund's older half-brothers, Emanuel and Philipp—then living in Manchester, England—also were involved in counterfeiting activity, and perhaps Jacob Freud as well. Following Gicklhorn's exposé, another researcher uncovered indications that the father of Freud's wife, Martha

(Bernays), was once implicated in a counterfeiting scandal that led to a prison term. That raises the question of whether the Freud and Bernays families were brought together initially by mutual involvement in criminality. If so, this would contrast with romantic tales about the engagement periods of Sigmund and Martha, and their respective siblings, Anna and Eli Bernays, who preceded them in marriage.

Those huge biographies of Freud titled *The Life and Work of Sigmund Freud* (Jones, 1953, 1955, 1957) have omitted any mention of the subject of counterfeiting in relation to the extended Freud family, although this scandal was well-known in Vienna during the 1860s and later. Therefore, it is not surprising that recent works on Freud's life and career have not come to grips with Gicklhorn's material on criminality. Some authors have downplayed the topic by giving it only a sentence or two, thereby implying that it lacked substance. An exception is found in the German (1979) and English editions of Marianne Krüll's book *Freud and His Father*, published in America in 1986. It offers an entire section titled "The Counterfeit Money Affair" (pp. 164 ff.) and provides the English translation of an informative newspaper article from a Vienna newspaper of February 22, 1866. That lengthy article describes Josef's trial (pp. 243, 271), the specific accusations against him, and names a man (Herr Weiss) who may have been his accomplice.

Krüll's summary of Gicklhorn's official data contains persuasive information about criminality in the Freud family. Clearly, that new information should have prompted revisions of the standard picture of Freud's healthy development that was sold to us by Jones's first volume (1953). However, the American reading public and most Freud scholars probably are unaware of those new materials concerning criminality.

My impression is that Krüll's is the only work published in North America that has reviewed this topic adequately, and that her informative volume has faded into relative obscurity among book reviewers and clinical researchers. In rare instances when her work was cited by literary reviewers and critics, almost no mention has been made of this crucial topic (criminality) that she summarized. All of this makes me wonder whether a coverup, or benign neglect, is operating on the American literary scene. Consciously or otherwise, are we motivated by collective desires to avoid confronting painful information about our cultural heroes including Freud, Ernest Jones, Anna Freud, and other deities?

An illustrative case is a recent book by Paul Roazen whose previous works, particularly *Brother Animal* (1969), have exposed enormous flaws in Freud's character. That contrasts with his protective stance towards Freud in his more recent work *Encountering Freud* (1990) which provides five pages summarizing the contents of Krüll's *Freud and His Father*. He devoted considerable space (pp. 3-7) to Krüll's book due to his feeling that "little attention has been paid" to it. Roazen added that it was a valuable work consisting of "fascinating material that Krüll has assembled, partly on the basis of fieldwork of her own, about Freud's childhood and youth." While expressing admiration for her book, he noted that she had tracked down important data on Freud's early life: "both the people and the social circumstances, that constitute a real addition to the previous literature."

Having praised Krüll for the "fascinating material" uncovered in her book, Roazen failed to mention her detailed summary of Gicklhorn's data on criminality, and its possible influences on young Sigmund's recurrent obsessions with death-wishes, revengeful feelings, and his desire to shock society's moral sensibilities. It is astonishing that Roazen described various important features of Krüll's book, but totally neglected its crucial materials concerning criminality in the Freud families.

Roazen made no comments about Gicklhorn's claim that Sigmund's schoolmates teased him about newspaper reports of his uncle's arrest, trial, and sentencing (similar to Freud's admission that they teased him painfully about the connotations of his name). Although Krüll played down Gicklhorn's strong assertions that this family disaster had powerfully affected the boy's development, she acknowledged that he must have been aware of its serious consequences. Otherwise, in his associations to the uncle Josef dream thirty years later, he would not have remembered that his father's concern about Josef's arrest caused his hair to turn "grey from grief in a few days." Or was that a metaphor for Jacob's fear that he, and his sons in Manchester, were themselves in danger of imminent arrest?

Later chapters will express my admiration for psychologist Paul Vitz's book *Sigmund Freud's Christian Unconscious* (1988) which elucidates major aspects of Freud's personality and psychopathologies that other biographers have overlooked. However, even Vitz erred when, in one short paragraph (p. 38), he discounted the subject of criminality in the Freud families. First, he noted that uncle Josef was sentenced to prison for passing counterfeit money, and that this Freud scandal "was common public knowledge at the time, as it was carried in the Vienna newspapers." Then Vitz wrote that the police never found out who had printed the counterfeit bank notes, but "there is evidence to suggest that they strongly suspected Emanuel and Philipp, who were in England."

Although Vitz recognized that this public disgrace for the Freuds was at its peak during Sigmund's sensitive years, ages nine through fourteen, he made no attempt to explore how this painful embarrassment might have damaged the boy's emerging personality. Vitz's pallid conclusion about this dreadful affair is a grasping at straws: "It must have further weakened the status of the father's family in the eyes of Sigmund." Finally, Vitz remarked that Freud almost entirely evaded this affair in his dream book when citing the dream about uncle Josef, using the "most veiled and ambiguous terms, thus suggesting his embarrassment at the incident and his reluctance to be candid about it."

Unfortunately, Vitz did not ask what monumental deceptions and censorship were involved in both Freud's and Ernest Jones's failures "to be candid" about this same criminal enterprise. Surely, the family was publicly associated with the scandal during the 1860s, and for many decades thereafter. This is the first of many accusations, in this volume and my other manuscripts ready for publication, that Jones's massive biographies of Freud are so riddled with censorship and distortions that they cannot be trusted to give a valid, honest picture of Freud's life and the development of psychoanalysis

Since I have raised the issue of flagrant, ongoing distortions of the historical record of the lives and careers of Freud and his disciples, perhaps some readers will wonder whether they can trust Renée Gicklhorn's reporting of criminality in the Freud family. However, the idea that she falsely manipulated the data seems quite implausible, since she relied on newspaper articles and public documents that are readily available to scholars. It may be that Gicklhorn's potential critics have hesitated to subject her book to denigration regarding unfavorable materials about Freud, because scholars have accorded her previous research efforts on Freud's early family life widespread acceptance and respect. For example, Ellenberger's lengthy biographical chapter (1970) on Freud relied heavily on Gicklhorn's writings, as frequent referencing of her research articles in his endnotes indicates (pp. 550-70).

In recent years, Freud's biographers have not been openly critical of Gicklhorn's book on criminal activity in the Freud family. Instead, they have limited themselves to one strategy for coping with findings which seem to demand our rethinking of the "Freud fantasy" begun by Jones and perpetuated by his literary heirs. Instead of attacking her book, they have resorted to a "rule of silence" about it in their own works. Or, when they have mentioned it briefly, they have adopted the style of the fairy tale courtiers who assured the public that the emperor was not naked, saying: "Since we have all agreed tacitly that there is no real significance to Gicklhorn's new data about criminality in the Freud family, historians and clinicians should feel free to ignore the matter."

A Brief Biography

Some readers might not have had access to biographical materials about Freud, and would find it helpful to absorb some basic information about his life story. The present section will offer highlights of his life and career that provide an orientation toward later chapters. This overview will rely considerably on standard portrayals of Freud's life, like Jones's, but will incorporate information obtained from a broader investigation of Freud's history, along with my personal commentary about key events that will expose negative aspects of his life.

Sigmund Freud was born in 1856 in the small town of Freiberg, where his father, Jacob, and adult half-brothers, Emanuel and Philipp, worked in the wool trade. His mother, Amalia, was a beautiful girl of 19, the daughter of a rabbi, and she married Jacob when he was in his forties. Sigmund's early playmates, the children of Emanuel and his wife, were named John and Pauline. John was the older nephew of Sigmund and his greatest rival, in an intense love/hate relationship that was the template for all of Sigmund's ambivalent relationships with male friends and colleagues in adulthood.

Amalia was a working woman, so Sigmund was cared for by a nursemaid who made heavy demands on his development, but praised his great potentials. She was a Catholic woman who took the boy to church with her often and indoctrinated him in some aspects of her faith. The Freud family learned that she was stealing small items from them, and had her placed in jail for ten months, to the consternation of the boy who was so attached to her. This was stressful to him, and so was the death from illness of his baby brother, Julius, later followed by the birth of his sister Anna, another rival for his mother's affection.

When Sigmund was age four his family split up and left Freiberg, allegedly due to adverse economic conditions. Emanuel's family and Philipp emigrated to Manchester, England while Jacob's family stopped in Leipzig and then made Vienna a permanent home. In Vienna, Jacob's family expanded and lived on a subsistence level, yet Sigmund received a fine education and was often at the head of his class. At various times in his childhood there were remarkable prophecies that he would become a great man, and his mother believed this and favored him over her other children, especially his five sisters.

During adolescence, John Freud came from Manchester to visit Sigmund and his family briefly. At age 16 Sigmund made a summer's visit back to Freiberg where he stayed with old friends, the Fluss family, and became smitten with their lovely daughter, Gisela. However, she did not return his ardor, so he pretended that it was only her mother who attracted him. At age 17 he was accepted into medical school in Vienna, and at 19 he traveled to Manchester for his first visit with Emanuel's family.

Jones portrayed the Freuds of Vienna as repeatedly struggling with poverty, but that depiction is suspect when one lists their worldly possessions and luxuries. Sigmund could have gone through medical school on scholarships, but his "poor" father insisted on paying full price. Moreover, the lad loafed his way through medical school, taking double the usual time for completion of his studies, as if he were a rich man's son. (Jones offered no adequate explanation of monetary discrepancies, ignoring the mysterious point that Jacob's work in Vienna over decades was undeterminable and that the Freud's "golden goose" might have been connected with counterfeiting.)

In the early 1880s Sigmund worked in a neurological laboratory doing brain research. This was the period when he began his long engagement to Martha Bernays, and exhibited strange, depressed behavior towards her and her family members. This was also the era when he became fixated on cocaine, which he offered to others as a remedy for fatigue, various ailments, and impotence. He was enormously ambitious for wealth and fame and hoped to discover some novel application for cocaine. His enthusiastic prescribing of it led a number of persons to overdose and die, causing him to be labeled a "public menace" in Vienna. Many years later he was still using cocaine himself and had prescribed it for his ailing friend, Fleischl von Marxow, who died of an overdose.

In the 1880s Dr. Josef Breuer, a wealthy physician, became Freud's mentor and told him about the remarkable case of Anna 0. She was an hysteric patient with florid symptoms whom Breuer had treated, with some success, using a cathartic "talking cure." This planted the seeds for Freud's later discovery of psychoanalysis. Another event stimulating that discovery was his brief visit to Paris in 1885 where he studied with Dr. Jean Charcot and absorbed his ideas on hysteria and the uses of hypnosis in treating it. In April of 1886 Freud started a private practice in Vienna, and in September he married Martha Bernays. Late in the next year their child, Mathilde, was born followed by five siblings, the last being Anna in 1895.

When December of 1887 arrived, Freud began to treat patients, including hysterics, by using hypnosis and was on his way to becoming a "covert psychiatrist" and then the father of Psychoanalysis in the 1890s. In 1889 he began the treatment of Frau Emmy von N. and within the next two years applied the cathartic method (recall of childhood traumas, using hypnosis) to her case. In 1892 he started to treat hysteria while dispensing with hypnosis, relying on the patient's waking speech, and later emphasizing free association, dream analysis, and analysis of transference factors—with emphasis on sexual conflicts deriving from childhood. At that point Psychoanalysis was born and was greatly assisted by Freud's self-analysis of his allegedly minor mental problems, including a small amount of hysteria and some paranoid and obsessive-compulsive trends. A turning point occurred when he denied the reality of patients' sexual abuses in childhood, deciding that these were fantasies that needed to be psychoanalyzed.

By 1892 differences with Breuer had surfaced and led to a painful breakup within the next few years. However, the men collaborated in writing *Studies on Hysteria* (1895), featuring the case of Anna O. and several of Freud's cases. During the 1890s, the close relationship with Breuer was replaced by an intense friendship between Freud and Dr. Wilhelm Fliess, a surgeon of Berlin who concocted wild biological/psychological theories. The men met together frequently on holidays and engaged in a heavy correspondence. Pro-Freud authors often claim that many of Fliess's ideas were balmy (but fail to emphasize that Freud endorsed them heartily). During this decade, Freud suffered many strange physical and mental symptoms and Fliess became his personal physician who encouraged him in his theorizing and performed questionable surgery on him. Near the end of the decade, theoretical differences and concerns about plagiarism put increasing strains on their friendship, which finally disintegrated in the summer of 1900 at a mountain resort called Achensee. (Fliess claimed that Freud ranted and became destructive towards him, but Freud countered that those were Fliess's paranoid accusations.)

Near the end of 1899 Freud published *The Interpretation of Dreams*, exhibiting and analyzing his own dreams and the dreams of patients, and other persons. This book offered Freud's theory that the core factor in dreaming is wish-fulfillment, and indicated that an analysis of dream conflicts could assist psychoanalytic treatment of neuroses. This was followed by his popular work *The Psychopathology of Everyday Life* (on "Freudian slips," forgetting of names, etc.), and his book on unconscious factors in jokes and puns. Thereafter, he produced a steady torrent of books and articles on psychoanalytic topics, over many years.

From 1900 till 1914, Freud's growing eminence and the worldwide spread of Psychoanalysis progressed nicely, despite some setbacks. After the dream book appeared, a small group of Viennese disciples was drawn to Freud and his Cause—including Stekel, Adler, Sadger, etc.—and weekly meetings were held at Freud's home to discuss his newest writings on psychoanalysis, and those of participants. Freud attracted widespread attention due to his writings on the Unconscious; psychoanalytic treatment, theory, and case studies; and particularly his fanatic devotion to the topic of sexual factors in neuroses and normal development—his theories of the Oedipus complex, infant sexuality, etc. The vocal opposition to some of Freud's ideas (sexual ones, especially) by medical greybeards merely increased his renown throughout Europe, assisting the formation of psychoanalytic societies in Berlin, Munich, Zurich, Budapest, London, and various American cities. Freud's lively and colorful case studies—the Wolf-Man and the Dora case—attracted widespread interest, and the sexually sensational details of the latter case certainly helped to increase notoriety for Freud.

In March 1907 the charismatic Swiss psychiatrist, Carl Jung, paid his first visit to Freud's home in Vienna. Soon Jung became Freud's fervent disciple and assisted the Cause in many ways, finally becoming president of the international society. In 1909 Freud visited America with Jung and Sandor Ferenczi to give lectures at Clark University's twentieth anniversary celebration. Artful publicizing tactics caused Freud's theories to be reviewed favorably in many American newspapers (with questionable claims that psychoanalysis had cured countless patients in Europe), increasing Freud's fame as a "psychiatric" savior. This helped to strengthen and multiply analytic societies in America and Canada. Using his clinic position in Toronto as homebase, the analyst Ernest Jones was then traveling widely in America to foster the growth of these societies and the spread of psychoanalytic treatment.

However, this progress was slowed in the period 1910 through 1914. After Jung, a Christian, was elected president of the international body in 1910, Freud's faithful Jewish disciples in Vienna felt betrayed that he had not chosen one of them as his heir. In June 1911 Adler resigned from Freud's group and formed a competing organization to foster his own theories and style of treatment. In 1912 the creative analyst named Wilhelm Stekel resigned, along with some of his colleagues. During that year Freud began to have serious conflicts with Carl Jung and by January 1913 broke off private contacts with him. Following a bitter political struggle in 1913 and 1914, Jung severed all ties with the Cause in July 1914, just as World War I was starting.

The setbacks for Psychoanalysis from 1910 to 1914 were magnified by the chilling effects of the Great War. Immediately, Freud became a vociferous, militant supporter of Germany and Austria against the despised enemies, Britain, France, and later the United States. (His hatred for the USA was unfathomably intense.) Freud's sons enlisted in military service and two of them saw combat. Along with other Austrians, Freud and his family suffered badly during the war years, and near the war's end his fears and depression were intensified when his oldest son was wounded, captured, and placed in a prison camp that cut off correspondence with families. Near the end of the war, Freud's depression was increased by the serious illness of his wife. A year later his daughter, Sophie, died of the same illness, and in 1919 a letter from Manchester advised Freud of the strange disappearance of his nephew, John. (In October 1914 John's father, Emanuel, had died in a peculiar train incident at age 81.)

In 1920 Freud published *Beyond the Pleasure Principle* in which he set forth the dubious idea that a Death Instinct is dominant in mental life and in human affairs, generally. For Freud this was a revolutionary turnaround, since for decades he had been a fanatic proponent of the idea that Eros (the sexual or life instinct) is dominant in human life. Now he reversed himself by proclaiming that the death instinct will inevitably destroy all mankind, since it holds sway over the life instinct. (Most of his followers were very embarrassed by this reversal.) Eventually, his writings also supported the less controversial theory that the human mind consists of a balance among three entities called id, ego, and superego (conscience) and that conflicts among these entities underlie various mental disorders.

After the war was ended, Freud revived his efforts in making Psychoanalysis a worldwide movement, and new students came to study with him from all over the world, along with new patients from abroad seeking treatment. This upturn lasted until 1923 when the first signs of Freud's jaw cancer appeared, eventually requiring more than 30 jaw operations until his death in 1939. As in the period before the war, there were new defections of disciples in the twenties and beyond. His longterm ally, Otto Rank, defected in 1924, and his disciple, Karl Abraham, showed strong signs of defecting just prior to his strange death in 1925 (he choked on a fish bone). Much later, Freud had to contend with the defection of his beloved "son," Ferenczi, and his death in 1933. Almost all of his important followers, except Jones, eventually broke up with Freud. (Chapter eleven explores Jones's powerful tendencies toward criminality.)

During the twenties Freud's daughter, Anna, slowly took over direction of the movement, and began to steer psychoanalysis towards an emphasis on conscious factors in mental life, versus unconscious ones. She became the prophetess of "ego psychology," and engaged in prolonged struggles with dissidents like Melanie Klein—a radical thinker about the primacy of the unconscious mind. However, many of Freud's allies followed Anna into the realm of the Ego, and he did not seem to object to this new direction she imposed on his life's work. (Until her death in the 1980s, Ms. Freud assisted the growth of Psychoanalysis, especially in America, where its training programs and its specialized journals continued to flourish.)

In the years following the emergence of his cancer, most of Freud's writings became less professional in style than previously was the case. In 1925 he published a self-serving autobiography. Then in 1927 and 1928 he indulged his atheistic and anti-religious feelings via slim, opinionated works titled *The Future of an Illusion* and *Civilization and Its Discontents*. Next, in 1929 and 1930 he co-authored an extremely unprofessional work titled *Thomas Woodrow Wilson*, which alleged that President Wilson had been a madman who repeatedly identified himself with Jesus Christ. The book's psychologizing about Wilson is so distorted that it astonished many Freudians. Evidently, ways were found to suppress its publication until 1965, and some disciples have made the outrageous claim that it is a forgery that was not written by Freud. (See my long section in chapter nine.)

In 1933 Freud started writing *Moses and Monotheism* which was published in 1937. The Moses-book is a weird opus which offers many of Freud's bizarre revisions of the Bible and of Jewish history. In it he claims that Moses was not Hebrew but a princely Egyptian; that there were *two* men named Moses and that the first one was murdered by his disciples; and that the Jewish people have been brutalized historically mainly because they had murdered their God and refused to admit their crime! There are many currents of Freud's periodic episodes of near-psychosis in the Moses volume. It is relevant that this balmy epic was completed in 1936, the same year that Freud completed his uncanny letter to Romain Rolland concerning "A Disturbance of Memory on the Acropolis." In that piece Freud discussed an issue that had been bothering him for 32 years, namely a near-psychotic episode (labeled "depersonalization") which he had experienced in 1904 while visiting the Acropolis in Athens.

In 1929 Freud took Dr. Max Schur, a loyal analyst, as his personal physician. Schur treated his cancer for over ten years, and in September 1939 helped Freud to commit suicide by giving him an overdose of morphine. His death occurred in England where he spent the last few years of his life, after pressures from the Nazis had forced him to leave his home in Vienna to avoid internment in a concentration camp.

The most crucial issue that this biographical sketch has neglected concerns Freud's destructive impulses. That issue was not faced by Jones's volumes, but Max Schur's writings are more honest and direct about that subject. Although he idolized Freud, Schur admitted that from the earliest years of his life Sigmund was weighted down by fears of death and by deathwishes towards his male relatives, and other persons. Schur even acknowledged that Freud harbored a "Cain complex," pointing to the immense power of fratricidal impulses in him.

In contrast with Jones's total censorship of this event, Schur discussed Freud's strange behaviors towards a female client in 1895. This was the case of Emma Eckstein whose hysteric symptoms Freud had treated unsuccessfully for several years. In frustration, he then arranged to be present when Wilhelm Fliess performed a balmy nose operation on Emma to cure her neurosis. (This reflected Freud's endorsement of Fliess's weird "nasal neurosis" theory, which equated the nose with the vagina.) Following the first operation, Emma hemorrhaged badly and nearly died, with several repetitions of hemorrhaging and near fatality. She was left with a permanent disfigurement of her lovely face. Soon Freud decided that she was to blame for this calamity—due to her alleged masturbation and erotic feelings for her doctor which stimulated the bleeding—despite that Fliess accidentally left a large wad of gauze in the wound.

Dr. Schur did not discuss whether Freud's death-wishes were operative in the above fiasco that nearly cost Emma's life. In my unpublished manuscript *The Dark Side of Freud* I have discussed at length my reasons for believing that Freud's murderous feelings towards Emma were greatly to blame, partly because of her defiance towards him and also because she represented the nanny who "abandoned" him during the Freiberg days when she was jailed.

This brings us to the central issue of this book. It questions whether Freud harbored powerful death-wishes towards various people—murderous impulses that he sometimes, in periods of great stress, was unable to control. There is a real possibility that he actualized those impulses on some occasions.

Was Freud a Murderer?

As this book will show, there are many reasons why loyal Freudians would want to keep a lid on Renée Gicklhorn's data about criminality in the Freud family. In general, their intent is to suppress or ignore any material that could seriously harm Freud's reputation with the public and, particularly, with leading figures in the social sciences whose support is valuable to Psychoanalysis.

However, I suspect that there is a special unconscious reason why eminent psychoanalysts might wish to cover up Gicklhorn's data. Freud's supporters may harbor a gnawing concern that there are connections between criminal activities of the Freuds and the question of whether two of the most important persons in Sigmund's childhood—his half-brother Emanuel and nephew John—were secretly murdered, with Sigmund bearing a special responsibility for those deaths. I refer to the very strange death of 81 year-old Emanuel in 1914 when he mysteriously fell from a moving train in England, and the similarly bizarre end of Emanuel's son, John Freud, who disappeared from his English home in 1919, at age 64, and was never seen again.

My initial exposure to the thesis that Sigmund Freud had murdered his nephew came from a careful reading of Eric Miller's *Passion for Murder–The Homicidal Deeds of Dr. Sigmund Freud* (1984). I first read Miller's book in 1985, when I had already written a manuscript titled *The Fatal Freud* (unpublished) exploring Freud's destructive behaviors. My thesis was that he helped provoke various suicides, especially of his rivals, and was responsible for the deaths of patients in ways that suggest he was acting-out inner rage and urgent death-wishes.

Since I had investigated aspects of Freud's lethal potentials before reading Miller's book in late 1985, it should have been easy for me to give some credibility to his major thesis: that Freud had deliberately killed several people, including that hated boyhood rival, his nephew John. However, I did not afford credence to Miller's claim that Freud was an actual murderer. Initially, I resisted Miller's thesis for a simple reason. Although my unpublished writings had revealed a number of Freud's lethal behaviors, these were limited to times when he provoked certain persons to commit suicide and killed others by making intemperate prescriptions of drugs. But we cannot classify those acts as murder, even though murderous elements might exist as hidden aspects of Freud's motivations.

Allow me to summarize some central ideas in Miller's book, so that I can explain my additional reasons for rejecting his claims that Freud was a murderer. Miller argued that from his earliest childhood years Freud's behaviors, character, fantasies, and dreams had provided his biographers with many indications that his was a homicidal personality. In general, Freud had a secret obsession with the subject of murder. For example, Miller emphasized the topics of patricide and fratricide that permeated many of his works and surfaced in several of his key dreams (the *Non vixit* dream); the numerous identifications Freud made with literary murderers; and the recurrent and powerful death-wishes that he directed toward family members and other persons. In his book, he discussed these lethal factors in Freud's life and career and connected them with instances when he was responsible for killing certain people, including patients and friends, accidentally. Also, Miller cited the time when Freud's closest friend, Wilhelm Fliess, had accused him of planning to murder him, during the bitter breakup of their friendship in 1900, at a Tyrol resort.

Furthermore, Miller characterized some behaviors as covertly murderous, including instances in the 1880s when Freud encouraged people to overdose with cocaine, which caused the medical community to brand him a "public menace." Miller categorized as covert murders Freud's overdosing of his friend and colleague, Ernst Fleischl von Marxow, and his "incautious prescription" of a deadly dose of sulphonal to a patient called Mathilde. Also, Miller charged that Freud murdered his disciple, Victor Tausk, and claimed to have evidence for that accusation—contradicting the accepted belief that Tausk committed suicide while embroiled in a very depressing conflict with Freud. The most persistent accusation of covert murder involved Miller's charges concerning the mysterious disappearance of Freud's nephew, John Freud. He insisted that (p. 83) this had occurred circa 1873, when John was 18 and Sigmund was 17.

In addition to elaborating upon the preceding accusations, Miller discussed at length his claim that Freud provided many clues to the aforementioned covert murders in his own dreams and dream associations in *The Interpretation of Dreams*, and in other writings. While Helen Puner, in her biography of Freud (1949), made the lesser charge that Freud's dream book incorporated a hidden "confession of sins," Miller repeatedly expressed the more extreme viewpoint that we can interpret Freud's "masterpiece" as an ingenious confession of murder, similar to the self-accusing unconscious behaviors of criminals that Prof. Hanns Gross (the father of criminology) had already discovered in the 1880s.

On first reading Miller's book, I was surprised to find another writer, besides myself, who was so aware of Freud's lethal potentials. However, I still could not accept Miller's main thesis that Freud was a deliberate murderer who had killed Victor Tausk, and his nephew John Freud. Roazen's book *Brother Animal* (1969) seemed to offer convincing evidence that Tausk's death was a suicide (accompanied by a note), so I had no reason to accept Miller's claim that Freud "had him murdered" (1984, p. 255), nor that he is privy to unpublished research evidence that amply supports his accusation.

Certainly, I was skeptical about Miller's notion that John Freud had disappeared abruptly around 1873 and that this was because Sigmund had murdered him. Although Miller provided some interesting circumstantial evidence to support his claim that Sigmund had exterminated nephew John during their late adolescent years, his thinking placed undue emphasis on one episode that reflected Sigmund's lethal feelings towards John. That incident occurred several years before John's alleged disappearance when he visited Jacob's home in Vienna and evidently Sigmund maneuvered him into doing a duologue in front of his classmates. In this fragment of a play by Schiller, John had taken the role of Julius Caesar and Sigmund took the role of Brutus. One can readily agree with Miller's view—and that of Freud's physician, Max Schur (1972)—that this gambit expressed Sigmund's unending murderous hatred and rivalry toward John. Consider that Brutus had assassinated this emperor named Julius, also the name of Freud's hated younger brother for whom he harbored intense death-wishes. Miller implied that Sigmund's symbolic murder of John (by acting-out Schiller's play), laid the groundwork for the actual murder a few years later.

My primary reason for disbelief was that Miller gave insufficient evidence to support his claim about John Freud's disappearance. His assertion conflicts with evidence that John continued to reside with his family in Manchester until around 1919, as reported by Freud's biographer, Ronald Clark. However, Miller's evidence that John disappeared about 1873 included (pp. 83-4) a personal communication from Dr. Max Schur's widow, stating that John had disappeared when he was 18 years old. This generally confirms what her husband, Freud's friend and longterm physician, wrote in an article in *American Imago* (26: 303-23), when he remarked that John Freud "came to Vienna for a visit in 1870 . . and mysteriously disappeared in 1872."

According to Miller, John's disappearance in 1872 was supported by Freud family genealogy tables, including one kept by Freud's niece, Hella Freud. Also supporting it is a note penned by Fred Hartwig (said to be a relative of the Freud family) which Miller claimed he discovered in the Rylands Library in Manchester, England. Miller contended that the official census report at Manchester in 1881 lists all of Emanuel Freud's family members, and that: "Only John is missing." One could easily reply that perhaps John had moved out on his own to some other locality, at least for several years. But Miller countered with this sweeping statement: "Further independent research established the fact that John was also missing from all other records in England and Wales." (Of course, this ignored Scotland, European nations, Canada, etc.) Finally, Miller cited Emanuel Freud's naturalization papers in 1877, listing all his family members, except John.

Unfortunately, Marianne Krüll offered some brief and vague remarks (1986: pp. 129, 234-5, 270) which seem to support the idea that John Freud disappeared from his family home in Manchester during the 1870s, as Miller and Schur contended. She stated that the "Freud family tree" (kept in the Freud Archives) contains "a note to the effect that John disappeared when eighteen years old, but gives no further details." However, that comment seems misleading, for when one consults her book to study the "Jacob Freud Family Tree" (pp. 234-5), there is an alternative notation for John Freud which shows his birthdate as 8/13/1855 in Freiberg, but then states: "vanished after 1875 or in 1918." Thus, in her prior citation of that first note, Krüll wrote that it specified that John had disappeared "when eighteen," whereas this second note states "after 1875" (when he was age 20). Moreover, Krüll totally neglected to mention that the most important aspect of this alternative note had added: "or in 1918." Mysteriously, this second notation (whose authority is unknown) indicates that John Freud disappeared either after age 18 or at age 63, in 1918!

Krüll's final remark about this crucial and perplexing issue was that: "In any case, John's disappearance remains unexplained." To my mind, it is amazing—considering that Freud called young John his greatest rival and the template for all his later ambivalent relationships with men—that Krüll did not express her own astonishment that the hordes of Freud's biographers have not tried to clarify the following issues: 1. Did John disappear from the face of the earth in a sudden and unexplained manner?; 2. Did he disappear in the 1870s and/or circa 1918?; 3. What family or personal circumstances surrounded his disappearance, including mental health factors, occupation, address, relationships with others, and living habits?; 4. Did John disappear around 1918 due to a family argument, because he had stolen money from the family business, or because he had become senile and out of touch with reality—and then simply wandered off?

Allow me to explain what caused me to disbelieve Miller's and Max Schur's thesis that John Freud disappeared in the 1870s, and my strong skepticism that Freud had assassinated John when he was 18. To begin with, Miller himself acknowledged that on various occasions after 1874 Freud had written about John in the present tense, indicating that he was still alive (though Miller seemed to regard this as a ruse to throw us off the trail). In a letter dated October 9, 1875 to his friend, Silberstein, Freud mentioned his English nephew, John, and his business acumen, clearly indicating that John was still at home in England at age 20. Then in his letter to Fliess dated October 3, 1897 he referred to his nephew (John) "who is now living in Manchester and who visited us in Vienna when I was fourteen years old." In 1897 John would have been age 42, and it seems inconceivable that Freud would have concocted a blatant lie about John's presence in Manchester in 1897, if he had disappeared decades earlier. Indeed, why would Freud have told such a dangerous lie to Fliess, one that might have been exposed to his friend via various channels?

In *The Interpretation of Dreams* (1967) Freud made several references to the extreme importance of John Freud to his own personal development. For present purposes, the key reference is on page 265 where he mentioned his year-older nephew "who was *at present* living in England." (Emphasis mine.) Assuming that the original German text specifies the present tense as forcefully as this English translation does, it is obvious that Freud had told the entire world that John was still living in England in 1900.

Finally, in Clark's distinguished biography of Freud (1980) he recounted that in 1919 Freud received a letter from his relatives in England informing him that John Freud had suddenly disappeared. It seems quite strange that the unnamed English relative's letter apparently had nothing further to say about this matter. (Or did Clark withhold some important information from us?) Furthermore, it seems odd that Clark offered no intimation of Freud's emotional response to the news of John's mysterious disappearance, as if it had no impact on Freud at all, and as if Freud (and Clark) had no further curiosity about the ultimate fate of Sigmund's greatest rival. Most peculiar is the fact that Jones's biographies had nothing to say about the career and fate of John Freud, in the two final volumes.

When Miller reviewed materials indicating that John might have been alive in England decades after the 1870s, he neglected to present Freud's compelling letter to Fliess of October 3, 1897 and the letter in 1919 by Freud's English relative that Clark cited. This seemed to be a grave flaw in Miller's thesis that John had disappeared in the early 1870s, and prompted my skepticism about Miller's idea that Freud had murdered John when the latter was 18. The fact that Freud had referred to John as alive and kicking in his 1897 letter to Fliess, and more so in his dream book, made it clear to me that his nephew must still have resided in England at age 45 in 1900, when the dream book appeared. It was inconceivable to me that Freud would have dared to lie so publicly about a subject that many of his English relatives and their friends could readily have exposed as a falsehood.

Obviously, that reasoning likewise applies to Clark's reporting of the relative's letter advising Freud that John had just disappeared in early 1919, even though Clark's book with this datum was not published until 1980. If that information had been falsified in some manner, why would the Freud family in Manchester—or their relatives, and friends—have kept their silence about the matter? (Could a family conspiracy have been operative, pertaining to that old issue of criminality?)

Miller's claim that, after the 1870s, Freud had simply falsified the data about John's continued existence, was not at all convincing, nor was the corollary that John had been murdered at age 18. However, I must admit that there was a more compelling emotional basis for my rejection of Miller's thesis. Despite the fact that for several years before reading Miller's thesis I had been amassing data concerning the dark side of Freud's personality, and was convinced that he had a very noxious personality, I was emotionally incapable of giving real credence to Miller's ideas. That was because my initial training as a clinical psychologist at Duke University in the early 1960s had strongly championed the Freudian orientation, and during several years of indoctrination by persuasive mentors, Freud had become a great hero to me.

So completely had I absorbed the heroic legends which portrayed Freud as an incomparable humanitarian and ethical giant that, when first exposed to Miller's book, I was unable to consider the notion that Freud might have been a murderer. Even my own research about the dark side of his personality did not prepare me to take that additional step. The idea seemed bizarre, and made me experience a nauseous rejection in the weeks and months following my first reading of Miller's strange book. Besides all this, I was not favorably impressed by the level of scholarship in Miller's volume: his tendency to go off on tangents; to make what seemed like extreme and unproved claims; to assert that Freud had murdered Tausk without offering adequate evidence, and much more.

Did Freud "Arrange" for Murder?

Despite my previous remarks, in this book I will present compelling evidence, perhaps more persuasive than Miller's, that Sigmund Freud did arrange for the murders of two men. The core of my evidence will be found in chapters eight and nine, but my case against Freud will be made throughout this entire volume, buttressed by three additional manuscripts about Freud's life (mainly completed but unpublished). Their titles are *The*

Dark Side of Freud; Secret Sex Lives: Freud, Jung, and Jones; and *The Fatal Freud.*

Months after I had read and rejected the core of Miller's book, a colleague introduced me to Krüll's volume with its impressive section describing the role of counterfeit currency in the Freud families in Vienna and Manchester. That led to my immersion in Gicklhorn's work and to the data collection which eventually prompted me to write a long chapter in *The Dark Side of Freud* concerning the Freud's criminal activities. In turn, that caused me to ponder the peculiar demise of Emanuel Freud in 1914, when he allegedly fell from a moving train to his death, which Miller did not discuss at all!

An unsettling question began to haunt my mind. Was it plausible that Emanuel's unlikely accident was really a murder, a disguised killing that somehow was connected with that dangerous counterfeiting enterprise that had cost Josef Freud a ten-year prison sentence? Had Emanuel been maneuvered by someone, perhaps someone he knew, onto the platform connecting two railroad carriages, beaten on the head, and dumped onto the tracks? Or was there a less exotic reason for Emanuel's death that did not involve murder?

Unfortunately, the literature regarding his death was quite sparse. Krüll's book (p. 268) cited the official death certificate of the General Register's Office in London which recorded that he had died on October 17, 1914 at age 81. That was soon after the onset of World War I, in July and August of 1914. However, Krüll did not provide any information as to why Emanuel was riding that train between Manchester and Southport, how fast the train was moving when he fell, whether the accident occurred at night or in daytime hours, and whether there was damage to his head that was consistent with a severe blow—perhaps from a hammer.

Evidently, the official death record gave no indication that police interviewed passengers on the train to learn whether anyone could explain or describe Emanuel's falling. Had anyone seen him fall? If the fall occurred at night, perhaps fellow passengers were dozing and unaware of any pertinent circumstances? Probably the police had no reason to suspect foul play, so there might not have been a thorough investigation. Since the deceased was an old man, the simple assumption might have been that he died of natural circumstances that precipitated his accidental death. That is, perhaps he had decided to get a breath of fresh air by walking onto the platform where he then fainted, suffered stroke or heart attack, and fell to his death?

Krüll gave one additional bit of information (p. 264) concerning Emanuel's death. She cited this ambiguous conclusion from the death certificate filed in London: "Cause of death: accidental injuries received through falling from Manchester to Southport Express in which he was a passenger whilst in motion on date of death." Case closed.

Now let me return to the question that had been recurring in my mind for several months. Was it possible that Emanuel Freud had been murdered when he fell from that train in 1914, and was this related to the issue of counterfeiting? As I pondered that question, some alternative notions began to filter into consciousness. Soon I found myself downplaying the issue of counterfeiting, although it might have been a partial factor, in favor of the hypothesis that Sigmund Freud's psychopathologies were so severe that he could have been responsible for arranging Emanuel's death, at the instigation of powerful complexes held over from childhood.

At this point, I will not try to give a full explanation for the "case" which I eventually formulated to support this murder hypothesis (see chapter 8), but will briefly mention the ideas that influenced my thinking. First, the death machine happened to be a train. How many important persons (or less significant ones) can we name who died by falling from trains? Statistically, this is one of the most unlikely causes of death imaginable. Yet, one could argue that, in Freud's mind, trains were not unlikely instruments of murder—not at all.

In later chapters I will explore Freud's well-known train phobia. Here, it will suffice to say that trains made horrendous connections in Freud's mind with images of pain, torture, death, and souls burning in hell—and with primitive desires for revenge against Emanuel, Philipp, and John Freud. Moreover, in all of Freud's writings that I have read, I know of only one time when he expressed an unambiguous desire to kill someone, and that was connected with a train ride. Let me explain.

During Freud's balmy engagement to Martha, while he was consuming huge amounts of cocaine, he wrote her a letter in which he described an argument he had had with an unknown fellow on a train. Evidently, they had debated about whether a window should be open or closed. The debate became so intense that insults occurred, and Freud—acting like the conquistador that he wished to be—invited the man to do battle. What is even more revealing is that Freud told Martha that if the fellow had not backed down, he was quite ready to kill him. Moreover, there were other instances of Freud's arguments on trains, suggesting that trains triggered strong aggressive impulses in him.

As I continued to collect data on Freud's train phobia (travel anxiety), I learned that trains could produce the crippling "panic attacks" that Wilhelm Fliess once witnessed, and finally the underlying factor occurred to me. The core was Freud's fear of his murderous impulses, i.e. trains involved a concrete reflection of his childhood death-wishes towards male family members. (In chapter 8 much data is given about his fantasies, dreams, and anxieties concerning trains, and how train travel evoked his lethal feelings.) I began to realize that perhaps Freud chose a train as his instrument for killing Emanuel, because it compensated for a fantasized "murderous act" against himself involving a train, for which he held his older brother accountable—as discussed in chapters 2 and 8. In effect, Freud's use of a train to kill Emanuel would have been poetic justice and an instance of the unconscious mind's compulsion to employ The Law of Talion, which Freud discussed as a mechanism of neurotics and preliterate people. That ancient Law demands that when a person is murdered the punishment must fit the crime precisely. The murderer who used a spear must be impaled with a spear himself, or in this case, killed with a train.

Finally, I asked myself whether, in the period of Emanuel's death in 1914, there is evidence that Freud was in a depressed, semi-psychotic, and truly murderous frame of mind? An affirmative reply is found in chapter 8, concerning Sandor Ferenczi's description of Freud's psychotic symptoms in August of 1914. In mid-1914 Freud's "dreams of empire" for Psychoanalysis were rudely demolished. He had spent years grooming Carl Jung to lead the Cause and suddenly Jung had betrayed him, rejecting the core of his dogmas, and leaving Freud without a gentile champion to consolidate the worldwide dispersion of his work. That same era saw the painful defections of Stekel and Adler, so that Freud began to fantasize that he was the primal father in *Totem and Taboo*, cruelly murdered by his ambitious sons.

Several authors have suggested that Freud concocted that volume as an autobiographical fantasy, indicating that unconsciously he feared being murdered by his contentious disciples. Freud's recurrent fainting spells with Jung and others also have been interpreted as reflecting fear that he would be murdered by his disciples, and on occasion he expressed direct concerns that Jung and others wished to kill him. Clearly, he interpreted some of their behaviors as urgent death-wishes toward him.

Nobody has paid much attention to the other side of the coin, i.e. whether Freud's accusations against others indicated his own lethal impulses toward Jung and other unfaithful disciples. In that era he spent many days in Rome studying Michelangelo's statue of Moses, with whom he identified intensely. The article that he wrote about the statue, and published anonymously, gives an autistic description and interpretation of the Moses statue that reflects Freud's strange fantasies regarding murder.

In his article, Freud expressed the weird idea that he could read the sculptor's mind and then impute a peculiar intention that flies in the face of literal scripture and common sense. The statue of Moses holds stone tablets in its hands—he has not yet shattered the tablets, provoked by the disobedience of his followers. Only later would Moses' murderous rage lead to the slaughter of 3,000 disciples. Instead, Freud's essay argued that the bodily and facial appearance of the statue indicated that the moment of rage had passed, that Moses had calmed his anger, and that he would not break the tablets. Of course, this implied that the impending slaughter had been forestalled, and that Moses would restrain his lethal command. Apparently, it did not bother Freud that he was rewriting the Bible, so pressing were his needs to concoct a fantasy that would allow him to deny his murderous intentions toward Jung.

Even Ernest Jones had to admit that the 1914 essay represented a fantasy about Freud's heroic self-restraint. Jones acknowledged that the master was expressing his hope of restraining his own urgent impulses to murder and inflict revenge. But had this ploy been successful? Chapter 8 will explore this question and will show its relevance to Emanuel Freud's uncanny fall from a train in October 1914.

My study of the Freud/Jung letters and of Jung's autobiography convinced me that, during the period surrounding their breakup, Jung did harbor urgent death-wishes toward Freud. Surely, Freud was correct in believing that Jung was concealing strong unconscious desires to injure or kill him. These presumed threats could have stimulated Freud's murderous impulses to the point that they required concrete expression. A chapter in *Secret Sex Lives* will show that the breakup of these men provoked depressed and suicidal feelings in Jung for several years, along with behavior that some Freudians insist was overtly psychotic. In comparison, the dangers of Freud's flagrant psychosis were probably curtailed, and psychic pressures released, by his presumed arranging of Emanuel's death. I assume that Freud concocted a plan to murder Emanuel in a semi-psychotic episode during stressful days preceding the outbreak of World War I, and that it helped him to avoid a full-blown psychotic breakdown. Extensive data in my early chapters show that Freud struggled with near-psychotic episodes throughout his life, totaling fourteen or more such episodes.

The biography by Max Schur (1972), Freud's physician and friend, emphasized his powerful murderous impulses toward family members. Although Schur was a sensitive psychoanalyst, it never occurred to him to inquire whether Freud might have actualized those impulses on occasion, as proposed by Eric Miller and the present author. Nor did Schur acknowledge that Freud often struggled with suicidal urges, for that is contrary to the mystique which asserts that he was incomparably brave and would never resort to suicide.

On occasion Freud adopted a macho stance, insisting that only a coward would commit suicide. Therefore, Schur denied vehemently the testimony of Freud's previous physician, Dr. Felix Deutsch. Deutsch asserted that when cancer appeared in 1923 Freud tried to "delegate" his suicide (via drugs) to Deutsch, who would not comply. One wonders why Schur would have doubted Deutsch's claim so strongly, since in 1939 Freud successfully delegated his suicide by drugs to his obedient friend, Dr, Schur.

Certain acts like suicide and murder were ones that Freud implied that no civilized, sane man would perform, but which he committed himself. However, his disciples insist that he did not commit suicide, since he delegated its commission to another person. Perhaps some will protest that Freud did not commit murder, since I merely provide evidence that he "arranged for" murders by others, as discussed in the eighth chapter.

Several years ago, when I began to formulate the hypothesis that Freud might have killed his brother Emanuel, my discovery of published materials on his fluctuating severe psychopathology, and his pressing lethal potentials, stimulated that idea. These data are scattered liberally throughout the first ten chapters of this book. In particular, one item influenced my growing conviction that Freud was capable of planning a murder, an incident that Roazen (1975) and Brome (1983) discussed briefly. It occurred near the beginning of the 1930s and started when Ernest Jones learned that Dr. Isidor Sadger hoped to publish a Freud biography containing damaging material about the master.

This book could have greatly threatened Freud's reputations because Sadger, one of his earliest Viennese disciples, had maintained a relationship with Freud for several decades. It would not be surprising that he had garnered sordid secrets (even murderous ones) about Freud, for later chapters will expose Freud's vulnerabilities in many areas. Assuming that Sadger's book was to be an exposé of Freud's unsavory deeds (which Jones believed was the case), this new work could have been much more destructive of Freud's image than the embarrassing Freud biography published in 1924 by Sadger's nephew, Fritz Wittels.

In the early 1930s, Jones responded to the news about Sadger's impending biography by writing to one or more of Freud's Viennese followers, insisting that the publication be prevented. Jones advised that Sadger, in some covert manner, should be denounced to the Nazi authorities occupying Vienna so that he would be placed in a concentration camp. Apparently, this was accomplished, for Sadger died in a death camp. He was the only one of Freud's Viennese disciples to lose his life in a Nazi camp, suggesting that the plan formulated by Jones and others to block publication of his book was quite effective.

This is what I call the "administrative murder" of Isidor Sadger. Although Roazen's book mentioned only that Jones and some Viennese followers of Freud were involved in this lethal plan, I assume that Freud was deeply enmeshed in this affair and that he at least gave "a nod of assent." He was always the analytic power in Vienna, so it is inconceivable that this grave matter was not routed through him, perhaps with a shrewd use of "deniability." (Paul Federn was one of the correspondents about this issue, and he was always subservient to Freud on important matters.) In any case, this revolting incident helped to persuade me that Jones and Freud were capable of arranging for an attenuated form of murder, so it is plausible that in 1914 Freud arranged for his brother Emanuel's death.

Two Murders, At Least

The preceding section began with the remark that later chapters will provide data and analyses supporting my conviction that Freud arranged the murders of two men. Having commented briefly about the mysterious death of Emanuel Freud, I will offer some ideas about the second presumed victim, Emanuel's son, John. My second murder hypothesis is that John Freud's uncle Sigmund arranged for his disappearance in early 1919, when John was in his sixties, soon followed by his murder.

Again, I will argue that there were magical compensatory mechanisms at work in John's presumed murder. For example, at age four Sigmund had been devastated by the sudden, inexplicable, and horrendous disappearance of crucial persons in his life. These included his beloved nursemaid, his sexual molester, whose thefts of money had caused the Freuds to arrange her ten-month jail sentence. Then there was the vanishing of Sigmund's younger brother, Julius, who died of an illness in infancy. Also, there were the disappearances of the children John and Pauline; their parents, Emanuel and Marie, who lived a short distance from Sigmund's home; and the second half-brother, Philipp, who lived a house or two away. An overwhelming trauma for Sigi occurred when the Freud family broke up in 1859, Jacob and his immediate family traveling to Leipzig (later to Vienna) and all the others to Manchester, England.

In 1919 the four year-old child in Freud's unstable mind demanded revenge from John and his remaining family members. He held them accountable for the enormous pain he had suffered in 1859 when they inexplicably abandoned him, and for causing the sudden loss of his "primal mother," the perverse and seductive nanny. Indeed, so great was the pain of these disappearances that in Sigmund's adult years he described them as catastrophic, using the following grim words: " . . the loss in which the original catastrophe has involved my whole existence." Therefore, the Law of Talion demanded that family members in England should suffer the horror of John's inexplicable disappearance, to match Sigmund's original terror and confusion at age four. (The data and analyses pertaining to these murder hypotheses in chapters eight and nine will expand on the brief comments made so far.)

It should be emphasized that my two murder hypotheses differ from Eric

Miller's (1984) central idea in which he stated that Freud was responsible for the disappearance and murder of John Freud in about 1873, instead of 1919. It surprises me that he did not mention my primary murder hypothesis: that Freud arranged for the murder of Emanuel Freud in 1914. Perhaps the fascinating idea concerning John's possible disappearance in 1873, and the alleged long-term cover-up, captured Miller's imagination so strongly that he did not consider whether Freud had murdered Emanuel as well. In any case, my later analyses will suggest that their presumed murders in 1914 and 1919 were strangely interrelated in Freud's mind.

Although Miller and I agree that Freud probably arranged John's murder, we specify times of death that are 46 years apart. In my view, some of the psychological analysis that Miller gave to support his thesis is interesting and worth considering, but I have not tried to summarize his ideas. Curious readers might wish to obtain his book and review his complex interpretations. I would like to believe that my case for John's murder is stronger than Miller's, though some critics, comparing our data in detail, might not agree. Of course, Miller will retain the honor of being the first author to inform the public about lethal aspects of Freud's personality that may have been actualized in murderous behaviors.

The Great Falsifier

Most of the chapters in this book provide new information about Freud's severe psychopathology. In doing so, they dispute the notion propagated by Jones that Freud suffered only a mild form of mental disability and overcame it by self-analysis. This book, and my other works, emphasize the need to expose Jones's falsifications of historical data, and it is clear that his prestigious accounts of Freud's life, personality, and psychopathology differ widely from my own. The romanticized picture of Freud's life and mind depicted in more recent biographies stems largely from a heavy reliance on Jones's "official word."

In fact, his biographies are riddled with distortions, and suffer from crucial—often intentional—omissions of data. Unfortunately, recent authors have ignored occasions when the psychiatrist, Thomas Szasz (1976), referred to Jones as "the great falsifier," with good reason. But even Szasz detected only a fraction of the literary failings that support his characterization of Jones. The overall contents of my own works strengthen Szasz's accusation, particularly the ending of two chapters about Jones in *Secret Sex Lives* which list Jones's distortions and omissions of signal events in Freud's life that badly damage his reputation, and Jones's credibility as well. Some of that material is summarized in the eleventh chapter of the present book, which gives a brief history of Jones's life and his recurrent psychopathic behaviors.

In clinical circles, and in the literary world, not much has been known about Ernest Jones, and his public image has remained fairly solid, due to his worldwide recognition as Freud's biographer. Clinicians and the general public have not yet recognized that Jones placed a fine-meshed screen over his own sleazy behaviors by giving sparse and sometimes misleading accounts of himself in the voluminous Freud biographies. Likewise, his Pollyanna autobiography provides only a glimpse of the Jekyll side of Dr. Jones, and hardly an inkling of the vicious Mr. Hyde lurking in the shadows.

A number of authors who have written about Freud's life have commented about Jones, sometimes characterizing him as a pugnacious fellow who, though not an original thinker, was loyal to Freud and a tireless worker in spreading the doctrines of psychoanalysis. He has also been described as an extremely ambitious, ruthless, and angry man. Opponents feared his talent for public debate and his capacity to tear them to shreds with sharp words and persuasive arguments. It is a surprising lapse that none of these writers, that I know, has commented upon the fact that Freud's inner circle knew Jones as an incorrigible liar. In the early days of psychoanalysis, Jung pointed out Jones's persistent lying, but Freud minimized the problem forgivingly.

In Young-Bruehl's 1988 biography of Anna Freud, we learn that she often referred to Jones as "The Liar from Wales," though this did not stop her from choosing him as her father's biographer. In calling him an inveterate liar, she agreed with his mistress, Loe Kann, who characterized him as a persistent "fibber." One should wonder, considering Anna's compulsive concocting of mental "fairy tales" during her childhood and adolescence, whether she regarded Jones's lying as a prerequisite for manipulating the data that would appear, under her close supervision, in that monumental fairy tale and source of modern legends, Jones's biography of the master.

Perhaps some readers were troubled by my intimation that Jones was venal enough to commit murder, as his involvement in the "administrative murder" of Isidor Sadger suggested. After all, critics might argue, can anyone produce strong evidence that Jones was involved in serious criminal activity that might point to an underlying psychopathic problem? The affirmative reply is found throughout chapter eleven, focusing on the Welsh analyst's criminal tendencies. For example, it discusses Jones's admitted smuggling of a huge amount of currency past Austrian and Swiss border guards in 1919, probably as requested by Sigmund Freud. After reading chapter eleven, readers may be less skeptical about Szasz's forthright claim that Jones was "the great falsifier."

Although it is comforting that a famous clinician like Szasz expressed his disapproval of Jones's biographies of Freud, despite the prestige Jones acquired as long-term president of the British psychoanalytic society, I suspect that many more such critics will soon appear on the literary scene. It is encouraging that the perceptive scholar, Peter Swales, (in Spurling, 1989) has made scathing criticisms of Jones's skewed presentations. He deeply deplored that Jones, while "granted privileged access to all kinds of material on Freud's life" had repeatedly shown himself to be "guilty of historical disingenuousness" in his "highly partial use of that material . . " Swales concluded: "No doubt it will take some decades simply to rectify the radically erroneous portrait which—in being true to Freud at the expense of truth and history—such persons have been largely responsible for perpetrating."

Procedural Issues

Some readers love to become immersed in long books, and have ample time to do so. They will have no trouble absorbing the present work, chapter by chapter, without skipping any. However, many individuals today have enormous demands upon their time and might become discouraged by the length of this volume. To such persons, let me suggest that they might take a more casual approach to this book, treating it like an interesting murder-mystery. For maximum interest, they might try reading it in the following order: chapters 1 and 2, followed by chapters 7 through 12. After completing the 12th chapter, they might like to pause for a few weeks and then, if time permits, go back and read chapters 3 through 6, followed by a rapid rereading of chapters 8 and 9.

The above procedure will allow readers who are pressed for time to arrive fairly quickly at chapters 8 and 9. They are really the heart of this book and absorbing their contents, without too great a delay, should foster the illusion that the materials are not too forbidding and can be treated like a gripping murder-mystery. Even professionals who are masters of rapid reading techniques—psychologists, psychiatrists, social workers, etc—might enjoy the above reading procedure that I have suggested.

―――――――――――――

Allow me to mention here abbreviations and code terms for some book titles that will appear occasionally in this volume. At times I refer to *The Interpretation of Dreams*, as "the dream book" and *The Psychopathology of Everyday Life* as "the book on 'slips.'" Sometimes I use the term *Complete* to stand for *The Complete Letters of Sigmund Freud to Wilhelm Fliess* (1985). My own unpublished manuscript *The Dark Side of Freud* is often called *Dark Side*, and my manuscript *Secret Sex Lives: Freud, Jung, and Jones* is abbreviated as *Secret SL* or *SSL*. The brief titles *Fatal Freud* and *Name Magic* will be used for my unpublished manuscripts *The Fatal Freud: His Suicide Complex*, and *Falsifying of Data* and *Name Magic: In Murder, Madness, and the Normal Mind.*

Chapter Two

Freud's Childhood and Psychopathology

Introduction to the Toxic Early Years

Recent authors who have written that there is no compelling information in the newest version of the Freud/Fliess letters (1985) that might change our conception of Freud's personality (and pathologies) are doing a great disservice to the reading public. That wholly inaccurate viewpoint might serve to persuade young scholars and clinicians that they don't need to bother reading that massive volume for themselves and can rely on snatches of information and summaries provided by writers on Freud's life. Nothing could be farther from the truth if they hope to achieve honest, objective understanding of Freud's life and his bizarre relationship with Wilhelm Fliess.

My advice is that each seeker of truth should buy a copy of that volume and read it while making extensive marginal notes, and detailed notes on front and back blank pages, as I have done. With careful reading and note-taking, and with cross-referencing, they should be able to recognize the extensive degrees of psychopathology that existed in the personalities of Freud and Fliess, and to assess many of the ways that Freud's toxic childhood contributed to his severe mental imbalance.

In *Dark Side* I have presented a long chapter titled "Freud's Watergate Scandal." It gives my analysis of the hatchet job (censorship) which Anna Freud and her clique performed on the earlier volume of the Freud/Fliess letters titled *Origins of Psycho-Analysis* (1954) to prevent the public from obtaining reams of data that would have damaged her father's reputation.

Because of public pressures, much of that suppressed data now appears in the 1985 version of the letters. But my analysis in *Dark Side* indicates the high probability that many crucial letters are still "missing" from the 1985 volume and that the public has not been made aware of the basis for that deception.

However, the 1985 version of the Freud/Fliess letters provides data that does enable us to become aware of sexual traumas which Freud suffered in early childhood that can help to explain the severe psychopathology he suffered in his adult years. First, there is the sexual molestation he experienced at about age three by his nursemaid. Also, we'll see that there is a real possibility that, at an earlier age, he was induced to perform perverse sexual acts by one or more adult members of his family. All of this will be found relevant to serious mental imbalance in Freud—to various "splits" in personality, death anxiety, depression, delusional thinking, compensatory megalomania—and to his lifelong obsessions with sexuality, incest, and mental healing.

Ernest Jones' initial chapter (1953) on Freud's childhood provides hardly any basis for comprehending his later pathologies (there is no hint of sexual molestations, which is also true of the Jung autobiography's suppression of *his* sexual molestation in childhood). Readers who had suspicions about Freud's deep psychopathology and wished to understand how it was connected to childhood traumas had to await accounts of the Freiberg years that were clarified by data from the Freud/Fliess letters of 1985. That infusion of new data is found in the important books written by Krüll (1986) and Vitz (1988).

The valuable chapters which those two authors have written about Freud's childhood years have served as a background for much of what appears in the present chapter. But many of their interesting details and speculations about the Freiberg years have not been repeated here, since the present chapter focuses mainly upon childhood factors that seem relevant to aspects of later psychopathology—including Freud's inducements of others to commit suicide and his murderous behaviors concerning Emanuel and John Freud.

Contrary to Jones and most other analysts who endorsed Freud's claim that he'd suffered only a mild hysteria that was allegedly overcome by his "heroic" self-analysis, the psychologist Vitz (1988) has employed data from the 1985 version of the Freud/Fliess letters to support a more malignant diagnosis. (Now we'll see why Freud wanted desperately to destroy those letters.) Vitz cited evidence (pp. 141 ff.) that Freud suffered "from various psychological pathologies," including aspects of ego splitting (as in some hysterias) and from a borderline personality disorder. With regard to this ego splitting in Freud—pertaining to his huge number of identifications with famous real and fictional men in attempts to create an idealized identity—Vitz related this to the breaking up of consciousness into two or more separate centers. (In Chapter 4 many aspects of Freud's dualistic nature will be discussed.)

Concerning the issue of splitting, Vitz noted that it is found in the "borderline character disorder" and the "multiple personality syndrome," the latter often arising from sexual molestation in childhood. That is, the sexually abused child attempts to counter the grotesque identity imposed upon him by his victimization by continually struggling to formulate new, fragile identities, as Freud seemed to do throughout his life. Vitz indicated (p. 146) how a variety of Freud's symptoms can be matched with criteria supporting a diagnosis of "borderline personality" shown in the official DSM-III psychiatric diagnostic descriptions. For example, he cited Freud's considerable uncertainty of identity; his emotionally changeable evaluations of other persons; his substance abuse (cocaine, cigar smoking, alcohol in adolescence); and his recurrent affective changes.

It is instructive that in 1985 the present author formulated this same diagnosis of Freud's personality (301.83 Borderline Personality Disorder) while reading the Freud/Fliess letters (1985). It's my guess that Ms. Anna Freud previously had tried to suppress much of the data in that volume, because she realized that, once having assimilated the taboo data, many clinicians would formulate that same diagnosis of her father's psychopathology.

I should note that some disagreement exists between Vitz and myself on this issue. He has softened his diagnosis by stating that Freud's was an attenuated form of this disorder called "borderline personality" in modern times. Thus, he did not acknowledge as applicable to Freud that this disorder allows for incidences of brief reactive psychosis, i.e. periods of extreme stress may induce transient psychotic symptoms. In my opinion, what prevented him from recognizing the applicability of this to Freud was Vitz' general lack of awareness of many horrendous aspects of "the dark side of Freud" that are revealed in this book and in my companion volumes. Another difference with Vitz is my view that in Freud's complicated character structure the borderline personality disorder was coexistent with a cyclothymic disorder, as recognized by DSM-III "in some cases." This would account for his hypomanic episodes, including manic periods of work activity which sometimes preceded bouts of depression.

Those brief comments about severe psychopathology in Freud will serve as background for our examining the ego-damaging stresses which he suffered during his first three years in Freiberg. As awesome as those stresses will seem, we should remind ourselves that biographers may still be unaware of additional intense pressures impinging upon young Sigmund and his family members due to covert criminal activities that perhaps already were influencing family life in the Freiberg era.

The Setting in Freiberg

Young Sigmund Freud spent the first three years of his life in the small Moravian town called Freiberg located about 150 miles northwest of Vienna, near the Polish border of Austria. Today it is part of Czechoslovakia and at the time of Freud's official birthday in May 1856 the Czech influence was strong, along with Roman Catholicism. Freiberg then had a population of 4,500 with only about 135 Jewish citizens (3%).

During the Freiberg years he and his parents lived on the upper floor of a two-story house at 117 Schlossergasse (his birthplace) which was owned by a locksmith named Herr Zajic. There were two large residential rooms upstairs, one used by Jacob Freud, his wife Amalia and their children, while the Zajic family lived in the room alongside theirs. Herr Zajic had his locksmith's workshop on the first floor where Sigmund sometimes played in his third year.

Not much is known about the work activities of Jacob Freud during the Freiberg years. The impression one gets is that he was a trader in woolen goods and that his work required him to travel fairly often. It's not clear, but Jacob (then in his forties) might have been in business at times with his eldest sons Emanuel and Philipp who were Sigmund's half-brothers in their early twenties. The younger fellow, Philipp, about the same age as Jacob's young wife Amalia, lived in a house that was across the street from his father's house. The oldest son Emanuel, with his wife Maria and their two children (John and Pauline), lived in a house that was only a few minutes' walk from Jacob's home. During his third year there were various boys that Sigmund played with, but his nephew John Freud was by far his most constant companion and rival amongst them.

Vitz has commented (p.5) that although Jacob and his small family lived in one room this does not mean that they were poor. Evidently, the family was able to afford a nursemaid on a fairly regular basis. Also, there is documented evidence that Amalia traveled with the nanny and Sigmund to a spa, which does not suggest poverty. Vitz characterized Jacob's family in Freiberg as lower-middle-class and struggling. However, I would caution that we don't know whether criminal activity was generating funds that needed to be kept hidden from societal awareness.

The psychopathic Nanny

The most significant factor in Freud's early life (which he tried to hide from the public and the world of science) is that he was cared for by a Catholic nanny who turned out to be a thief and *who sexually molested* him.

There are several ways that this woman's psychopathic behaviors induced serious psychopathology in young Sigmund, as will soon be discussed.

Nobody can be absolutely certain, as yet, concerning the name and identity of this nursemaid. Until recently, most scholars have assumed that she was a Czech woman named Monica Zajic, a close relative of Herr Zajic the locksmith. The researcher Sajner discussed this woman's identity with a well-informed relative of Herr Zajic. Apparently Sajner became convinced that the crucial nursemaid of young Sigmund was Monica Zajic (though there may have been other temporary nannies for brief periods).

Recently Krüll (1986) has cited a spa record from the time when Sigmund was about age one which shows that Amalia Freud was accompanied by a nursemaid named Resi Wittek. In my view, Krüll made a weak argument in claiming that Resi was Freud's crucial nanny, on the basis of this spa document. For even if she had been his nanny at age one (perhaps briefly?), this does not indicate that she was still his nanny during his third year when the sexual molestation presumably occurred—as well as various thefts which caused the Freuds to send the nursemaid off to prison.

To cut this debate short, let me mention that in *Dark Side* I've discussed at length why I believe that Monica Zajic was Sigmund's pivotal nursemaid, though it seems to me that Resi Wittek might also have been a somewhat important caretaker of his. My suggestion is that both of these women were compressed into a dual image of the nursemaid in his unconscious mind, and in Chapter 15 I cited one of Freud's dreams which seems to encode the name "Resi." However, that dream does not thereby provide an overwhelming reason for believing that Resi was the key nanny in his childhood, for in *Dark Side* I've offered evidence that the name Monica was encoded unconsciously in Freud's adult writings and in some of his dreams.

One could claim that young Sigmund was, in effect, sexually molested by his own mother, so powerful was the maternal influence that this nursemaid had upon his pliable mind. If so, we can see that his Oedipus theory originated from personal events in his own early childhood. Also, we see that Freud's fanatic writings on childhood sexuality likewise had an autobiographical underpinning (as did many of his other writings, according to Peter Swales). Is all this relevant to the question of scientific objectivity regarding Freud's dogma about sexuality?

A convincing discussion was offered by Vitz to show that very often Sigi's mother Amalia was physically and emotionally unavailable to him, thereby increasing greatly the strength of the nursemaid's maternal influence. Vitz noted that during Sigi's first three years "his mother was busy with two pregnancies and two births, and had a sick child who died during this time, while Sigmund was put in the charge of his nanny." During this period when baby Julius died of enteritis at age six months, and later with the pregnancy relating to sister Anna, it seems that only the nursemaid was available to help the hardpressed Amalia. Vitz remarked that Jacob was at work elsewhere in town "and often traveled in the surrounding area buying wool."

As an indication of Amalia's relative unavailability to Sigmund during the first 32 months of his life, Vitz remarked that she became pregnant soon after his birth and quite soon after Julius' birth, indicating that she breastfed her sons for only a short time after each of them was born. Therefore, assuming that Sigmund was nursed by his mother only for a brief time, that increases the probability that Monica acted as a wet nurse, thereby strengthening the bond between them. Moreover, in Schur's biography he noted that in Freiberg the Freud women often worked together in a warehouse in the garment district while a maid cared for their children. This was a simple physical factor that kept Amalia away from her son and made him more accessible to his nanny's influence.

All of this suggested to Vitz that "Sigmund would have been almost exclusively with the nanny for many weeks during his earliest years." In addition, it seems plausible that the death of Amalia's second baby, Julius, would have induced a lengthy depression in her. This would have further decreased her emotional availability to Sigmund and enhanced the role of the nanny as his surrogate mother. Apparently, Amalia had named baby Julius after her brother (Julius Nathanson), about a year older than she, who lived in Vienna. With this naming, perhaps she hoped magically to extend her brother's lifetime via the name she gave to her son, considering that this brother had been suffering from tuberculosis when her baby was born. Ironically, the date of her brother's death occurred exactly a month before the death of baby Julius, so this name magic was in vain. Losing a beloved brother and her baby with the same name, almost simultaneously, must have elicited a depression of considerable severity and duration in Amalia—with significant effects upon her eldest son.

It seems realistic that these malignant events would have greatly provoked Sigmund's anxieties about death, induced a covert depression in him, and caused him to cling fiercely to his nanny for emotional support. Now it is clear why Vitz has posited that this nanny "filled the maternal vacuum" during this crucial time of Sigmund's childhood and that she became, not merely a second mother to him, but his primary mother. Indeed, this perverse woman became the foundation stone of Sigmund's personality and of his budding psychopathology as evidenced by his lifelong unconscious pursuit of her "image" in his dreams, writings, and female relationships.

Soul-murder by a Nanny

Over the last ten years, television "talk shows" have exhibited dozens of adults, mainly women, who were vilely forced by their fathers to endure incest. Anyone who has listened to the pitiful, tearful accounts by these women of the incestuous acts perpetrated by their fathers could easily recognize the deep depression still existing in these women. In terms of the lasting feelings of degradation, betrayal, confusion, and low self-esteem suffered by these women, it is not overly dramatic to say that each of them suffered a "murder of the soul" due to these incestuous assaults.

Likewise, one can say that Sigmund Freud was subjected to soul murder by his "primary mother," his nanny, during his third year in Freiberg. It is Vitz' position, and I agree with him, that her sexual abuse of this precocious, sensitive boy engendered a serious "split" in his ego functioning. Sadly, that was not the only severe and lasting ego splitting that occurred to young Sigmund during that Freiberg era, as we shall learn later. But first we need to explore, as best we can, what perversions were inflicted upon Sigmund and ask why his nanny performed such bizarre acts with a helpless child.

During the heat of Freud's famous self-analysis in 1897, his letters to Fliess of October 3, 4, and 15 provide the basic data about his nanny's sexual molestation of him. In the first of those letters he indicated that she had been the "prime originator" of his neurosis, although his wording requires clarification. In previous letters he had explained to Fliess his belief (firm during those days but later revised) that neuroses were caused by his adult patients having been sexually molested during their childhoods. So, when he referred to *his own case* (twice) and called his nanny the "prime originator," there is no doubt that he believed that she had sexually abused him. And he told Fliess what were the newly revived memories that supplied the basis for that belief.

In Freud's letter penned on October 4 he advised Fliess that his recent analysis of one of his dreams had elicited further recollections about the nanny's sexual abuse of him. He wrote that: "she was my teacher in sexual matters and complained because I was clumsy and unable to do anything." Freud then related this to the issue of neurotic impotence and to his "present impotence as a therapist," also remarking that he'd concurrently imagined the skull of a small animal which in the dream he had thought was a "pig."

He did seem aware that this skull of a pig represented himself, but he related it only to concerns that he'd been "a little blockhead." He was not aware that the skull pertained to his lifelong fears of death, which were closely connected to his participation with nanny in perverse sexual acts. That is, sex with "mama" inexorably leads to being *murdered by "Father."* Also, Freud did not notice that this disgusting "pig" symbolized his buried feelings of shame and degradation for those early perversions with nanny, along with his self-hatred and low self-concept that required compensatory bursts of megalomania throughout his lifetime.

In the preceding letters, Freud did not mention to Fliess what specific sexual acts were involved in his nanny's molestation of him. Krüll has discussed (p. 121) her assumption that this may have involved her manipulating or stroking his penis as a way of helping him to fall asleep, and she cited from Freud's writings his recognition that "unscrupulous nurses put crying children to sleep by stroking their genitals." Vitz cited (p. 133) historical data indicating that it was not uncommon, in various cultures, for adults to stroke the penises of little boys to quiet them. He chose another remark from Freud's writings which noted that it was quite common for children's genitals to be caressed "by fond relations," or even parents.

If writers continue to interpret Freud's language concerning sexual abuse by his nanny as implying only some mild stroking of his penis to quiet him, they will simply reveal their own fearfulness about critical human behaviors—especially sexual ones pertaining to father-figures. It should be obvious that Freud was not referring to some relatively bland activities, like those mentioned above, when he advised Fliess that nanny had been his *teacher in sexual* matters and had complained when he was clumsy and ineffective. Concerning this information, Vitz seemed ready to get down to brass tacks by stating bravely that: "However, it may refer also to something explicitly sexual." Unfortunately Vitz immediately dropped this hot potato and turned to historical considerations, avoiding any discussion of what perversions might have been involved in the sexual abuse of young Sigmund!

First, let's examine the language that Freud used. He said that nanny was teaching him about sexual activities and that she complained when he was clumsy and ineffective. Where have we encountered that kind of wording before, if not in countless sex manuals and sexy novels? These are words describing, in many instances, a woman who hopes to receive pleasure from her erogenous zones administered by a lover who is inexpert and groping. Therefore, it is not far-fetched to believe that nanny was trying to teach the boy to give her pleasure, perhaps by having him stroke her clitoris and breasts, although she might also have taught him to masturbate himself. Did Krüll and Vitz forget that even in the 1800s sexologists like Krafft-Ebing had written about the explicit unnatural acts of sexual psychopaths, including nursemaids and governesses who taught young children in their care to perform varieties of perverse acts for their own pleasure? That data suggests the possibility that Sigmund's nanny might even have taught him to engage in oral sex, focusing upon her clitoral region and his penis.

Is all this merely the product of my fevered imagination, or is there very good reason to entertain that latter possibility concerning oral sex between Sigmund and his nanny? In fact, that is suggested by some very important material in the Freud/ Fliess letters that Krüll and Vitz seem to have overlooked. This topic will be reviewed in a later section that discusses Freud's strange allegations that many infants (who later became his adult patients) had been subjected to oral sex in the earliest months of their lives, as revealed by his clinical research.

In those same few letters to Fliess in October 1897 Freud provided additional items of information about his primal nursemaid. In simple terms he described her as elderly, clever, and ugly. (Perhaps that ugliness was an unconscious reference to her sexual perverseness.) He added that she had told him a great deal about God Almighty and had instilled in him a high opinion of his own capacities. Also, he suggested that he might have reason to be grateful to this woman "who provided me at such an early age with the means for living and going on living." After making that statement, he remarked that the "old liking" for her was again breaking through into consciousness. That statement that she had provided him with "the means for living" seems to hint that she had suckled him as a wet nurse, in my opinion.

Later, he told Fliess that he'd consulted his mother about this nanny, and she remembered the nursemaid and described her as a very clever older woman who was always taking him off to church with her. Amalia said that when he would return from these outings he'd preach to his parents about God. Furthermore, she remarked that the Freuds had discovered that this woman was a thief who was stealing from their family (which will be discussed later).

In his dream book, Freud made a brief mention of this nursemaid. His remarks about her expressed both ambivalence and deep love, but he totally suppressed even a hint that she had sexually molested him. Of course, he censored that data, because he knew that clinicians would have raised many searching, troubling questions about this man had they known about his early molestation, and he never expected that the truth would emerge via the eventual publication of his private letters to Fliess. In the dream book, he casually noted that his nanny had been sharp and efficient and that her words to him could be harsh if he did not achieve her standards of cleanliness. But his final thought was affectionate, as follows: "It is reasonable to suppose that the child loved the old woman who taught him these lessons, in spite of her rough treatment of him." (Sadly, that does not mean his unconscious mind forgave her for the betrayal of his trust when she used him to satisfy her lustful needs.)

At this point we need to ask whether there were special reasons for her molesting this boy. One speculation that has been offered is that perhaps she was anti-Semitic and abused the lad as a reflection of her hostility towards Jews. That's possible, but there is no strong evidence to support that idea. It's true that she frequently took the boy to church with her, but we can't be sure she did that to lay the foundation for his later conversion to Catholicism and/or as a reflection of any hostility to Judaism.

Who knows? Perhaps she went to church frequently to confess her psychopathic urges and acts, in hope of keeping them under control, and took the boy with her simply because she was in charge of him. On the other hand, if she had been his wet nurse during his second year of life, maybe her suckling of the boy had aroused sexual feelings towards him which she found hard to suppress in his third year, when he may have begun to express sexual curiosity. And there is another possibility, concerning the well-known fact that adults who molest children often were sexually abused themselves in childhood. It's possible that nanny was acting-out her own childhood abuse using Sigmund as a victim, or was obtaining partial revenge for sexual abuse that she had suffered either in childhood or as a young maid. (In those days even very young maids were subject to sexual harassment by their masters or their sons.)

Traumatic Losses

The preceding material suggests that this nanny had forged very powerful bonds with Sigi. At times, she could be demanding of high standards of cleanliness with him and used harsh words to enforce her demands. But, softer moments occurred when she performed lovingly as his wet nurse. Also she took care of him during periods when his mother was depressed. From his own statements it seems clear that the boy was not cowed by Monica's occasional "rough treatment" of him, and that her attentiveness and pride in his rapid development had engendered his genuine feelings of love for her.

That she had affectionate feelings for the lad and took pride in his precocious intellectual development can be inferred from one of Freud's remarks to Fliess. He reported that this nanny had instilled in him "a high opinion of my own capacities." Jones has written that, on more than one occasion in Freud's childhood, persons with supposed prophetic abilities had told his family that he would become an eminent or famous man. One of these was a peasant woman, leading to suspicions that this was none other than his proud nanny expressing her conviction that Sigi would become a great man. Perhaps this was the beginning of his later "pathological ambition," originating in a matrix of bizarre sexuality and megalomanic prophecies? In any case, it seems clear that the perverse nanny had forged strong bonds with her "son" by permitting peculiar sexual indulgences and by convincing him of his potential intellectual brilliance. (Indeed, she proved to him his sexual precocity by showing that he could pleasure a grown woman.)

However, there were several evil serpents slithering around in this Eden known as Freiberg. For nanny's psychopathic urges were not limited to child sexual abuse: she was also a thief and apparently had Faginesque tendencies to teach children to steal for her. In Freud's letter to Fliess dated October 4, 1897 he remarked that his dream concerning thoughts about a "pig" (himself) had stimulated a chain of memories about his nanny. He discovered that she had made him steal zehners (ten-kreuzer coins with small value) "to give them to her."

Later, he asked his mother to tell him more about this nanny, and that's when Amalia described the nursemaid as a clever person who was always taking him to church. She added that when she had been pregnant with his younger sister Anna, the family had discovered that nanny was a thief. Shiny new kreuzers, zehners, and various toys that had been given to him were found in her possession, so his brother Philipp summoned a policeman and "she then was given ten months in prison."

When Freud heard from his mother this account of the nursemaid's theft, he decided to recant his confession that he'd helped the old woman to steal. He wrote Fliess that his previous memory must have been mistaken and that his mother's account meant that only the nanny had been involved in theft. This was not a convincing denial of his previous confession and suggests that Freud was eager to absolve himself of exhibiting felonious tendencies at an early age.

Freud remarked to Fliess that he then had asked himself a searching question. Logic told him that if this nanny had disappeared so suddenly from his life upon being carted off to jail, then shouldn't it be possible "to demonstrate the impression" this momentous event had made upon his young mind? While pondering this question the corresponding scene emerged from his unconscious into awareness. He noted that for 25 years this crucial scene occasionally had appeared in his conscious memory without his being able to understand its significance. Now, during self-analysis he recognized that it pertained to the traumatic loss of his nanny in childhood.

He told Fliess that in that recurrent childhood scene his mother Amalia was nowhere to be found, and he was crying in utter despair. Then his adult brother Philipp unlocked a wardrobe (*Kasten*) for him, and when the boy did not find his mama inside it he cried even harder. Finally, his crying was relieved when his beautiful mother walked into the room through a doorway.

In later editions of *The Psychopathology of Everyday Life,* Freud interpreted this scene using a sexual emphasis. He said that the boy (himself) felt concern that his mother's pregnancy with sister Anna might take Amalia away from him, as had happened with the loss of the nursemaid, and that Philipp was "involved" with both of these events. That interpretation merely implies that birth and death (separation) are twin concepts relating to this scene, failing to stipulate the boy's primitive death anxiety. What Freud wrote to Fliess in 1897 gives a better approach to understanding that his fears of death and murder were the basic underlying issues concerning this scene.

Focusing upon this same pivotal scene, Freud wrote to Fliess in late 1897 that at last he had deciphered its true meaning. He realized that it was related to his anguish over the sudden loss of his nanny, and that he must have asked Philipp to open the wardrobe due to a fear that his mother had disappeared inside it. That is, he was afraid that Amalia had vanished permanently "just as the old woman had a short time before." Freud reasoned that he must have heard that his nanny had been locked up "and therefore must have believed that my mother had been locked up too." Thus, the boy firmly believed that his nanny had been "boxed up" (*eingekastelt*), because his brother Philipp was always fond of using such puns. Freud added that in this recurrent scene, the fact that he'd turned to Philipp for help proved "that I was well aware of his share* in the disappearance of the nurse."

It is easy to recognize that this child's guilty horror at the sudden loss of his nanny, along with his misinterpretation of his brother's pun, caused him to believe that his angry kinsmen had invoked retribution for her financial and sexual crimes by killing her and placing her body in a wooden "box," i.e. a coffin. Perhaps this primitive death anxiety had been coalesced by his earlier awareness that this is what they had done to baby Julius, i.e. they put his body into a wooden box (coffin) in order to rid themselves of this squalling child (as Sigi had desired). Now fate had paid him back for this death-wish against Julius by arranging for the boxing-up of nanny.

This death anxiety in the boy had stimulated another primitive fear of death that must have provided the template for countless lethal fantasies that dominated his adult years. Since it's likely that he regarded himself as the nanny's "partner in crime" (sex and thievery), one would expect that his primal sense of justice demanded that someday his male relatives would seek his death, as well. (Partly, this resulted from a grieving wish that his own death would enable him to rejoin nanny—the core of a suicide "complex.") The notion that his male relatives someday would kill him may have provided the defensive core for numerous death-wishes against them in adulthood, as reported by Schur. More likely, those death-wishes against his male relatives were stoked by powerful feelings of *revenge* that they had cruelly torn nanny away from him, abandoned her to an uncertain fate, or even had killed her.

As horrible as it was for this boy suddenly to be wrenched away from

---

*Probably, Sigi afforded Emanuel greater blame, since he was the oldest and most powerful brother.

his "primary mother's" bosom, considering his grave misconceptions about this event, even worse for his unsettled mind was the timing of this event. It seems that once she was whisked away from his home for thievery, probably he never saw her again. Thus, Vitz (1988) has given persuasive reasons for believing that the time when Sigmund's immediate family left Freiberg (for a temporary home in Leipzig) was in early June of 1859, when he had just reached age three. Further arguments were offered by Vitz to the effect that Sigmund's loss of his nanny probably occurred in the days just preceding his family's departure from Freiberg, not giving him any chance to see her again after her incarceration was ended.

Now it has become obvious that Freud did not exaggerate at all when he described his family's departure from Freiberg as an emotional catastrophe for him. In his letter to Fliess of December 3, 1897 his comment that they would soon use train travel to meet in Breslau evoked his recollection that this city had played an important role in his childhood memories. He told Fliess that at age three, when his family had moved from Freiberg to Leipzig, they had passed through the Breslau station. At that Breslau station, Freud remarked, for the first time he'd seen *gas flames* (station lights) and they had reminded him "of spirits burning in hell"—which he then connected with his persistent travel or train anxiety (phobia).

Earlier, I stated my view that Freud's persistent train (travel) anxiety was a reflection of his unconscious desire to murder his male kinsmen, and now we learn that the first instance of that train phobia occurred when he traveled aboard that train leaving Freiberg at age three. This was the train that forever separated him from his beloved nursemaid, and the gas flames in Breslau that reminded him of souls burning in hell were inextricably connected with his belief that she'd been murdered by his kinsmen—especially Emanuel and Philipp. For she was the originator of his neuroses who, he told Fliess, had "told me a great deal about God Almighty and hell." The Jews do not believe in concepts of heaven or hell, so it's likely that the boy got all of his ideas about souls in hell from his nanny's teachings about religious matters.

Obviously, this young boy had fully absorbed this Catholic woman's explanations of the "afterlife," consisting of heaven for good persons and an eternity of "souls burning in hell" for bad ones. Partly, that horrific image of souls burning in hell at Breslau was a reflection of his feeling that he and his perverse nanny were being punished for their sins. But that hellish image, in its relationship to his budding train phobia, was also a sign of the boy's revengeful wishes that his male kinsmen someday would meet such a horrendous fate themselves. Apparently, his germinal fantasy was that he would find ways to murder them (for having murdered her) and that each of them would become a soul burning in hell eternally. If this is correct, it has great relevance to the idea that he arranged for Emanuel's murder in

1914 using a train as his instrument of retribution, and also is relevant to his identification with Satan.

In the preceding materials we have uncovered the primary catastrophic stresses that produced the fault lines for Freud's tendency towards ego splitting in his later years. These stresses included the depressed unavailability of his mother and the transfer of emotional bonds to a nanny with strong psychopathic tendencies; sexual molestation by this primal mother; participation in her petty thefts at his family's expense; the sudden loss of this woman, which the child interpreted in terms of murder and death, evoking his lifelong death anxieties and death-wishes; and the sudden loss of his idyllic home, friends, and extended family in Freiberg with the concomitant need to adapt to new, strange environments in Leipzig and Vienna.

Krüll's analysis of "the departure from Freiberg" (1986, pp. 140-47) provides many ideas that coincide (and many that disagree) with my preceding analysis. She stated that the sudden move from Freiberg had provoked feelings of desolation in the boy and "a diffuse sense of outrage" (p. 147). However, she believed that later his suppressed rage was towards his father Jacob, not mentioning that he had just as strong reasons for feelings of rage and betrayal concerning both of his older brothers. Since Emanuel was the eldest and most vigorous son, the leader, the boy must have harbored immense feelings of rage towards him for the family's decision to "eliminate" his nanny, and for Emanuel's decision to break up the family and whisk away to far-off England his primary playmates, little John and Pauline (the latter was Sigmund's age).

Krüll considered the popular notion that the Freuds left Freiberg due to an economic downturn in Moravia in 1859, and she provided persuasive evidence that this economic thesis was not supported by real facts. Then she examined some other vague explanations that have been offered for their departure from Freiberg, and these also seemed to have little merit, in my opinion.

Although she did not present her thesis in a forceful manner, Krüll also considered the possibility that criminal activity might have prompted the Freud's sudden departures from Freiberg. She mentioned that Renée Gicklhorn's recent research has suggested that "Jacob and his sons may have become involved in a venture that was to lead to the arrest in 1865 of Josef, Jacob's brother, for possession of counterfeit money." Krüll added that if Emanuel and Philipp went to England to join the counterfeiters in some capacity, it's likely that Jacob knew about this, and he may have sold his Freiberg business to bankroll their criminal activities. There was an implication here that the Freuds may even have left Freiberg with anxious concern that the Moravian police authorities were only a step behind them.

Krüll has offered this thesis about criminality as another reason (p. 142) why Sigmund "was so shaken by the train journey; in my view, the adults, and his parents in particular, must also have displayed agitated, perhaps even panicky, behavior." Later, Krüll asserted her belief (p. 146) that the adults accompanying the boy on that train ride from Freiberg "were in a state of anxiety or even panic, and that no explanation for this was given to Sigmund." If so, the boy may have absorbed their feelings of intense fear, helping to stoke his baleful fantasy about souls burning in hell at the Breslau station. (Later, we'll see that perhaps there was another reason for him to harbor a primitive fear about the city of Breslau, relating to the issue of insanity.)

Earlier Sexual Molestations?

During the first nine months of 1897 Freud was vigorously pursuing his self-analysis. At the same time he was using data from his patients' analyses to obtain laborious confirmations of his theory about the primal origins of the neuroses (the hysterias), and even of some psychotic disorders. What had not been recognized until the Freud/Fliess letters appeared in print is that Freud formulated a strong central position emphasizing "paternal etiology." Repeatedly, he claimed (offering many clinical anecdotes) that fathers had been the most frequent sexual abusers of his adult neurotic patients, and that they had molested their own offspring during early childhood. More than that, Freud insisted in numerous letters to Fliess that his uncoverings of early memories showed that the fathers were perverts who had molested their children in *infancy*—prior to 18 months and often during the first 12 months—by inducing these infants to suck on their penises.
For example, in his letter to Fliess of February 8, 1897 he asserted that hysterical headaches (with sensations of pressure on top of the head and temples) were characteristic of "scenes" that emerged during analysis reflecting that the infants' heads had been held still by their fathers "for the purpose of actions in the mouth." The preceding description was another of Freud's references to fathers who allegedly had induced their young children (taking advantage of strong sucking responses) to perform oral sex. In this context, Freud made the astonishing announcement that his own father, Jacob, (then recently deceased) had been one of these revolting pedophiles! He wrote that: "Unfortunately, my own father was one of these perverts and is responsible for the hysteria of my brother . . . and those of several younger sisters."

The above accusation that Jacob Freud was a pervert who had sodomized at least one of his sons and several of his daughters appeared at the end of Freud's letter of February 8, 1897. No further information appeared there concerning an obvious unmentioned question that Freud left hanging in the air: had his father likewise provoked young Sigmund to oral sex during infancy? Eight months passed before Freud addressed that question in his letter of October 3, 1897. There he referred to his father when he stated that: "I can only indicate that the old man plays no active part in my case."

At that point, he cited his new awareness that he'd been sexually molested by his nanny in childhood, and he used this as his weak reason for claiming that Jacob had not molested him. His suspect, unclear rationalization seemed to be that since nanny had sexually abused him, that was a sufficient basis for explaining his neuroses. Ergo, he did not need to consider whether the pervert Jacob (who still had not been absolved of sodomizing several of his other children) had been a second and earlier molester of Sigi. In conclusion, Freud tried to maintain the fragile position that almost all neuroses, including those of his siblings, were caused by oral sex induced by fathers prior to age 18 months, exempting only his own case!

Apparently, Freud's dodging of his own paternal molestation was occasioned by his recognition that it would not be seemly and dignified for Fliess or other clinicians to learn that the Father of Psychoanalysis had been sodomized by his own father. That was not the heroic beginning that Freud envisioned for himself in the many grand legends that he and his disciples would concoct to glorify him. So, he eliminated this likelihood of an earlier molestation by Jacob, rather arbitrarily. Similarly, his daughter Anna and her clique totally suppressed this information about Jacob's molestations of his children from the earlier versions of the Freud/Fliess letters, although later she was forced to capitulate and allowed the taboo data to appear in the 1985 version of the letters.

Now we need to consider whether Freud became the champion of concepts involving childhood sexuality because, not only had he been sexually molested by his own "primary mother," his nanny, but also by one or more of the male adults in his own family. While it seems obvious that Jacob might have been the male molester that Freud's theory of paternal etiology demanded, it's also true that his half-brothers Emanuel and Philipp were old enough to represent alternate father-figures to young Sigmund. So, either or both of these half-brothers might also have been sodomizers of their baby brother.

Earlier, we learned that Sigmund had suspected that Philipp (close to Amalia's age) had made his mother pregnant with sister Anna. That now leads us to wonder whether Philipp would have allowed his sexual impulses to be directed towards other family members as well, including young Sigmund. In his writings, Freud mentioned that one of his boyhood friends in Freiberg had indoctrinated him in sexual matters, and that his name was Philipp. Isn't it quite possible, therefore, that there were two Philipps who had done this, one masking the other, and that the second Philipp was Sigmund's brother?

There is also the possibility that Emanuel had subjected Sigmund (in infancy) to oral sex, or at least that Freud fantasized that this had happened. Jones' biographies indicate that Sigmund secretly disparaged his old, bumbling father, Jacob, and sometimes expressed the wish that Emanuel had been his father. This wish probably coalesced a powerful fantasy that Emanuel *was* his father, thereby leading to the corollary that Emanuel had sodomized him in infancy (as indicated by Freud's theory of the paternal etiology of neuroses).

Jones remarked (1953, p. 9) that when Freud was 19 his half-brother Emanuel told him that the family really had consisted of three generations, indicating that Jacob "should be Sigmund's grandfather." Jones added that Sigmund found this remark "illuminating," because it "evidently accorded with his own early feelings." As explained by Jones, young Sigmund had paired off the two older people, Jacob and his nanny, which made it likely that his mother Amalia and Philipp were paired sexually, since they were about the same age. However, Jones overlooked that Amalia and Emanuel were born less than two years apart, making it just as likely that Sigmund harbored the wish and fantasy that he'd been fathered by his virile eldest brother, Emanuel. This likely fantasy that Emanuel was his father would have been fostered by Freud's lifelong insecurities about the actual date and circumstances of his birth, which will be discussed later as an additional ego stress.

Presently, that is all that will be said about Freud's male relatives who may have molested him during infancy, or even during that slightly later period when he was sexually abused by his nursemaid. Returning to the correspondence with Fliess about his theory that sexual abuses of his patients in early childhood had caused their adult mental disorders, in his letter of January 11, 1897 he made an enthusiastic offering of a "red-hot" idea, as he called it. That idea was that the cause of a "confusional psychosis" (amentia) might be that the sufferer had been subjected to sexual abuse prior to the 16th or 18th month, and perhaps much earlier than that. One may wonder whether Freud formulated this new theory about the origins of some psychoses partly due to his suspicions about the infantile roots of his own fluctuating episodes of psychosis in adulthood (which I've posited were aspects of his psychopathology).

Since Freud believed that sexual abuses of young children could generate ego splits of such severity that even psychoses could occur, eventually he must have become aware that he and his patients had been subjected to a kind of soul murder. So, it is instructive that in one of his letters he implied having the feeling that sexually abused children had, in effect, been murdered. In a letter to Fliess of April 6, 1897 he used a French phrase to convey the idea that he'd be glad to stop his theorizing about child sexual abuse—if only the murderers would stop their killings of these children.

It seems that in the unconscious mind of Sigmund Freud the tortured child in him believed that his adult male relatives had murdered him in at least two ways. First, they had subjected him to "murderous" sexual molestations in infancy that provoked his vulnerabilities to psychotic episodes. Second, they had "murdered" his beloved nanny, thereby causing her to be forever separated from him. Since they had been his murderers, wasn't he justified in harboring powerful death-wishes towards them, and in fantasizing that someday he should arrange the murder of at least one of them?

A Maelstrom of Sexuality

The preceding materials should convince many readers that, during his first three years in Freiberg, young Sigmund Freud had been thrown into a hothouse of sexuality, with regard to erotic factors existing within his household. It seems obvious that he was subjected to sexual abuse by his psychopathic nanny. Also, it seems likely that he was molested by his father and perhaps by his elder brothers, as well. Moreover, there are additional sexual factors in this Freiberg era that need to be considered.

Before proceeding it should be acknowledged that some persons may be skeptical that Jacob Freud actually molested young Sigmund. Vitz has noted (p. 131) that both Krüll and Marie Balmary (1982) have studied this issue, and they concluded independently that Jacob Freud probably did molest some of Sigmund's siblings and perhaps Sigmund also, and the present writer concurs. However, Vitz decided that he did not think Jacob "seduced" young Sigmund. Though he thought the validity of that molestation "is still possible," Vitz noted "that Freud's comments about his own father primarily implicate Jakob with respect to Freud's siblings, not himself." (In my view, that seems a weak basis for Vitz's skepticism about Jacob Freud's probable guilt concerning Sigmund.)

The notion that the Freud household was a hotbed of sexuality is partly derived from the ways that Freud, as a boy, perceived various events. For example, his childhood belief that Jacob and the nanny were paired sexually provides a hint that he could have observed his father and nanny engaged in sexual intercourse together. The possibility that they might have been involved together in sexual dalliances is not farfetched considering that previous material has suggested that both of them had difficulty restraining psychopathic sexual impulses with children. Perhaps Sigmund observed them in sexual intercourse on an afternoon when he was napping and presumed to be fully asleep, in the same room with them, not forgetting that the Freuds all shared one room and that Amalia sometimes worked in a warehouse away from home.

The conclusion drawn by several writers that Amalia and Philipp were involved in an affair derives from her age similarity with this stepson, the great disparity between her age and Jacob's age, and that Sigmund had sexually paired his mother with Philipp and believed that he'd made her pregnant. Krüll has suggested (pp. 124-8) that Sigmund might have observed Amalia and Philipp while they were actually involved in an affair and that perhaps Jacob sent his sons to England, partly due to the old man's desire to separate young Philipp from the beautiful Amalia.

Krüll believes that several of Freud's boyhood dreams and dream associations indicate that there may have been strong erotic feelings between Amalia and Philipp. It was noted by Krüll that Freud's famous dream and associations about people with birds' beaks point "uniquivocally to a sexual relationship between Philipp and" his young stepmother. In this dream Sigmund saw his: "beloved mother, with a peculiarly peaceful, sleeping expression on her features, being carried into the room by two (or three) people with birds' beaks and laid upon the bed."

The above dream evoked terror in Sigmund, who awoke screaming and tearful, interrupting his parents' sleep. In his associations to the dream he remarked that the tall, beaked figures were derived from illustrations that he'd seen in Phillipson's Bible, and he thought they had been falcon-headed gods from an Egyptian funerary relief. Freud's analysis of the dream made him recall a boy he had played with called Philipp, who taught him the vulgar term for sexual intercourse. Also, he realized that the expression on his mother's face, in the dream, was similar to the visage of his ailing grandfather as he lay in a coma just before his death. Therefore, this indicated that in the dream his mother was dying, and he woke up greatly anxious until his real mother had awakened, enabling him to confirm that she was not dead.

Krüll's interpretation is that in this dream the child, in effect, observed sexual intercourse and that "Philipp and Amalie were the chief actors in this scene." Thus, Philipp's concealed sexual activity (with Amalia) in the dream is revealed when his name, in the dream associations, is applied to the boy who told Sigi about sexual intercourse. Notice that Philipp's name also is encoded in the name "*Philipp*son." (In the context of the powerful death theme in the dream, the encoding "Philipp's son"–from "Philippson"– might have related to the boy's suspicion that Philipp had fathered the deceased baby Julius.)

Apparently, Krüll believed that the lovely Amalia's comatose expression in the dream indicated that Sigmund once had actually observed her with an orgasmic expression on her face, lying on a bed with Philipp. Perhaps that is true, but Krüll ignored that the dream specifies that she was carried onto her love bed by as many as three people. If we acknowledge that same number, this suggests that she was laid on the bed by three tall men: Philipp, Emanuel, and Jacob. This could indicate that Sigmund had spied upon his mother when, at different times, she had intercourse with each man separately, or even that the boy had observed the four adults involved in a group sexual activity. Either of those possibilities would have been very confusing, troubling, and stressful for the boy to assimilate, especially if he connected them with nanny's molestations of him and his guilty feelings about those acts.

Before ending this section, there is another key issue that I need to mention so that my sensitive readers will not decide that I am backing away from a crucial topic involving murder. In the first chapter I proposed two murder theses, i.e. that Freud had "arranged" for the murders of Emanuel and John Freud in 1914 and 1919, respectively. In the present section we've seen that young Sigmund also had ample reasons to harbor powerful death-wishes towards his half-brother Philipp. However, I have not had anything to say about the possibility that—if he arranged the murders of Emanuel and John—he might also have done so with regard to Philipp's death. Let me explain my reluctance to suggest this additional murder hypothesis, at the present time.

All that I will write, for now, concerning my hesitation about this matter is that I know nothing about Philipp's death except for its date and location (August 29, 1911 in Manchester). Therefore, I know nothing about Philipp's death at age 77 that should provoke suspicion that he might have met an untimely or peculiar demise. Krüll remarked (p. 176) that the official death record "simply states that he was a former traveler in fancy goods." (One would like to know whether the cause of death was specified on the death certificate?)

Krüll has provided (pp. 173-78) only a small amount of data about Philipp's life in England. She cites his marriage to Bloome Frankel of Birmingham in 1873, and that the names of their two children were Pauline (Poppy) and Morris. The marriage certificate indicates that he was a jeweler. However, Krüll wrote that: "It is odd how little information there is about Philipp." (She noted that the unpublished family correspondence might give an explanation of why so little is known about this man.)

Should we be suspicious that so little is known about Philipp Freud's years in Manchester, considering Gicklhorn's data about counterfeiting in the Freud family? Maybe so. We do know that during their engagement period in the early 1880s Freud wrote a letter to Martha in which he referred to Philipp as "Mr. Robinson." Was that a joke of some sort, or was this an alias of his elder half-brother? The latter possibility makes us recognize that aliases are often used by persons who participate in criminal enterprises.

Nanny and Nephew John

Since John Freud's mysterious disappearance in 1919 has been interpreted by me as one indication that Freud arranged to murder his kinsman and greatest rival, one would expect that factors might be uncovered in the Freiberg years pointing to murderous impulses so powerful and tenacious that they generated a bizarre killing almost 60 years later. That is what I propose to show, and Freud—the great publicist about childhood sexuality—would be proud to learn that later I will focus upon an intense sexual factor from his early childhood that could help explain his psychotic destructiveness in 1919 toward John Freud. But, first, I'd like to discuss some general factors from his conflicted boyhood relationship with John and seemingly minor sexual issues often addressed by other authors—mutual masturbatory activity and the question of a possible "rape" or "seduction" of Sigmund's young niece, Pauline.

Jones wrote (1953, p.8) that ample evidence indicates that nephew John was the most important person in Freud's early childhood, next to his parents. In that judgment, the Great Falsifier deliberately omitted to mention that Freud's nanny was even more important than his parents, so that he would not have to acknowledge the central role of her sexual molestation and other critical influences on Sigmund. In any case, Jones is correct that John had an immense influence upon Sigmund's early and later development, even if that conceals the larger picture.

It was Freud who wrote that in Freiberg the two boys had been constant companions. Affection and hostility had alternated, with much bickering and physical fighting between them, and Sigi, the younger by nine months and physically weaker—often found himself losing these quarrels. Jones remarked that this aroused feelings in Sigmund that were far stronger than usual. In his writings Freud wrote that his later martial ideals may have arisen from these early battles in Freiberg with John. Jones added that: "When Freud came to review his childhood he repeatedly indicated how his ambivalence towards John had conditioned the development of his character." Freud also commented that his childish relationship with John had determined all his "later feelings in intercourse with persons of my own age." So great and permanent was John's influence that Freud stated that his nephew "had many incarnations" in later relationships. Referring to John's influence upon his ambivalences with other persons he wrote that: "An intimate friend and a hated enemy have always been indispensable to my emotional life; I have always been able to create them anew . ."

There were unusual reasons why John probably evoked feelings of confusion and envy in Sigmund. Since John was the older and stronger boy, he should have been the uncle. Ironically, their positions were reversed (which might also have been rankling to John, stoking *his* hostilities and rivalry). Also, Sigmund secretly wished (and perhaps believed) that he and John shared the same father, Emanuel. Therefore, it must have angered the younger boy that John, not he, was able to live with this man—and that Emanuel took John with him to England, leaving Sigmund behind in Austria with Jacob, whom he regarded with hidden contempt as an old, cowardly Jew. (That disapproval of the old man arose most strongly when the boy learned that his father had endured an anti-Semitic slur from a gentile who also knocked his hat into a gutter, with passive acceptance of these insults by Jacob.)

Various authors including Jones, Bernfeld, and Swales have suggested that Freud had a long-term "problem" with onanism (a masturbation complex that also afflicted analyst Georg Groddeck). Probably, this was a fixation suffered by many analysts, and even quite healthy persons, so there is perhaps no reason to make much of it in Freud's case. However, Krüll believes (p. 121) that young Sigmund might have been taught to masturbate by his nanny but later was punished for masturbating by his parents. If so, she believes he must have suffered violent conflicts about the act: "for the combination of active stimulation by adults with threats of castration for self-stimulation must have utterly confused him."

Krüll believes it is quite possible (p. 129) that Sigmund and John played homosexual games with one another, such as mutual stroking of their penises. Vitz has referred to (p. 137) various kinds of evidence suggesting that the boys engaged in masturbatory play. And Vitz feels there is good evidence to believe that John initiated Sigmund into masturbation. Jones hinted at their mutual masturbation when he wrote (1953, p.8) that "there are indications that their mutual play was not always entirely innocent."

Now it is time to turn to the question of Sigmund's "rape fantasy" involving Pauline Freud, John's younger sister who was about six months younger than Sigmund. Jones remarked that in the Freiberg era she had "some emotional significance" for Sigmund. Jones added that: "In the screen memory that Dr. Bernfeld unraveled, an amorous attachment to her is manifest, and beyond that an unconscious fantasy of her being raped by John and himself together." Furthermore, Jones noted that Freud had admitted that he and John used to inflict cruel treatment on the little girl, which Jones assumed had an erotic component, even if an unconscious one.

Various analytic authors have followed Jones' lead by dismissing the preceding memory as merely involving Sigmund's fantasy of rape. Later, I'll discuss why I believe that it was much more cruel than that, and had an explicit sexual content. In order to pursue that thought, let me now provide a summary of this Screen Memory material which Freud tried to palm off as a memory belonging to someone else, not himself, until Dr. Bernfeld exposed this fakery.

This Screen Memory described a green meadow with a great number of yellow dandelions and nearby two women were chatting in front of a cottage door, a peasant woman and a children's nurse. Three children were playing in the tall grass, one of them being the author between the age of two and three. The two other children were his year older male cousin, and his sister who was about the author's age. The children were picking the yellow flowers and holding bunches of them in their hands, the little girl holding the best bunch. Suddenly, as if by mutual agreement, the two boys "fall on her and snatch away her flowers. She runs up the meadow in tears and as a consolation the peasant-woman gives her a big piece of black bread." Seeing this, the boys ask for bread too and are given some by the same woman, who cuts the loaf with a long knife. The bread tastes delicious—and the scene ends.

It seems apparent that this was a disguised and distorted memory of Freud's relating to the Freiberg era, as Bernfeld claimed (1946). Thus, the three children were Sigi and his two "cousins," John and Pauline, and the two women were probably a composite image of the nursemaid, Monica Zajic. If so, the primary question is this: why did Freud exert such a great deal of psychic energy to falsify this matter, and to try hiding from his readers that this was an elaboration of one of his own early memories? My answer is that this memory encodes a number of shameful secrets, along with his feelings of murderous anger relating to those destructive sexual events in his early life. (Similarly, his attempt to impose a comparable deception in the case of his "aliquis slip" analysis, and anonymity regarding his Moses article in 1914, pertain to his hiding of murderous anger in those writings.)

The shameful secrets that are encoded in this Screen Memory all concern the sexual molestation of young children. Jones has written that when the two boys jump on the little girl to snatch her flowers, this represents a fantasy of "defloration" or rape. Much more likely, but in the same vein, is that both of these boys had been sexually molested by the nursemaid encoded in this memory, and then in turn they had "progressed" from mutual masturbation to performing together an actual sexual molestation of young Pauline. For it's well-known that those who are abused are apt to become abusers. Their abuse of Pauline might only have involved a touching (with or without penetration) of her genitals, although at age four John might have been able to perform a rudimentary version of intercourse, as well.

The great anger that is found in that dreamlike memory of Freud's pertains to the rapacious, sadistic hostility that is directed towards the little girl by the two boys. As others have noted, the long knife in this memory pertains to a sadistic threat of castration. It represents Freud's murderous anger concerning castration threats felt by him, because he had engaged in sexual activities with his nanny. There is also an ironic element of nurturance in this memory—the giving of bread—since the nanny slyly exercised her sexual molestations within a context of loving concern. Also suppressed in this memory is Freud's intense anger that he and John both had been molested by the nursemaid, i.e. that his stronger, older nephew was a rival who had had a longer sexual relationship with nanny than he'd had.

Concerning the latter point, Vitz has examined a good deal of relevant data and concluded (1988, p. 137) that John had been "seduced" by his own nanny and that Monica Zajic at one time was the nursemaid for John and Pauline. Employment records of the Freiberg period show that Monica Zajic, at one time, was the nursemaid within Emanuel Freud's household. However, the close proximity and living arrangements between the families of Emanuel and Jacob indicate that she might very well have cared for John and Pauline, along with Sigmund, on many occasions. In any case, I'm in agreement with Vitz about the likelihood that she had molested John Freud.

Since the evidence is persuasive that she molested Sigmund, it's probable that while she was caring for John she would have expressed her perverse sexuality with him also. During the boys' masturbatory play with one another, they must have compared notes and revealed to one another the sexual secrets about nanny that she had induced them to conceal from their parents. When Sigmund learned (or inferred) that John was involved sexually with Monica, probably over a longer time than he'd experienced with her, his rivalrous feelings towards his nephew would have evoked extremely angry and resentful emotions in him. No doubt this provides the crucial reason why John exercised such an enormously powerful and persistent influence over Freud and all his later relationships with men, which otherwise is not explainable by the childhood fights and rivalry that millions of other boys have experienced without such dramatic aftereffects. It was this intense, bizarre sexual rivalry in childhood that evoked murderous feelings towards John that were finally gratified by Sigmund in 1919.

The Breslau Station

The stresses mentioned so far during the childhood of Sigmund Freud have been mainly severe pressures involving sexuality, castration anxiety, and fears of death in the mind of this sensitive and precocious child. However, the preceding materials also hinted at problems of mental imbalance within Freud's family that could have threatened the boy's sense of security. For example, we learned that Jacob Freud was molesting his own children, and it's possible that one or more of Freud's elder half-brothers had molested him in infancy, all of which suggests the presence of mental disorders in the male adults in Freud's family.

Recall that Freud had notified Fliess that Jacob was a pervert who had molested his own brother (presumably Alexander Freud) and several of his sisters, thereby provoking their neuroses. This indicates that Sigmund and four of his six siblings (not counting the deceased Julius) were all sufferers of mental disorders, along with Jacob's illness and perhaps imbalance suffered by one or both of the elder brothers. It is also possible that criminal activities in the extended Freud family point to mental problems among the male members. Considering all this pathology in his family, one could guess that Freud harbored some peculiar suspicions that baby Julius might have died due to revolting sexual abuses of him involving "actions in the mouth" of such intensity that strangulation occurred.

There is no clear evidence for mental disorder in Freud's mother Amalia. Two of her granddaughters described her in her older years as being tyrannical, very self-centered, and sometimes exhibiting explosive behaviors (a "tornado"), but also she was seen as clever and as having a keen sense of humor. That does not tell us enough to suggest any clear-cut syndrome or a specific diagnostic category. However, going back to the early days of her marriage, one wonders why this beautiful young girl decided to marry a bumbling, nearly impecunious graybeard who was twice her age. Does this point to an unresolved oedipal problem (incestuous urges) in this girl who married a man who was old enough to be her father? An affirmative answer to that question may be indicated by the fact that she married a man named Jacob and that this was also the name of her father, and her paternal grandfather ("name magic").

Did Freud grow up harboring an additional mental stress—that he and his siblings were prone to the hellish possibility that hereditary factors would make them succumb to insanity? In the Jones biography (1953, p. 4) he admitted to having just such a "neuropathological taint," as Freud described it. He connected this concern with one of the two brothers of his father, namely his uncle Abae (who apparently was close to Jacob's age, perhaps a year or so younger). Freud noted that this uncle had four children, only one of whom was mentally healthy. Of the other three, one was a hydrocephalic imbecile, another was a male who became insane at age 19, and his sister who became insane at age 20.

What is fascinating and provocative is that this uncle Abae and his insane offspring lived at Breslau, suggesting that Sigi's memory of souls burning in hell at the Breslau station at age three was partly determined by the strong possibility that insanity might occur to himself or to his immediate family members. Indeed, in his rage at his father and elder half-brothers for their "murder" of nanny, perhaps Sigmund's arrival at the Breslau station caused him to wish them some hellish form of madness, or provoked his suspicion that they were already insane. This assumes that this sensitive boy, so precocious in his understanding of language, had overheard his parents on some occasion discussing fearfully the insanity "infecting" Abae's children, with anxious concern that this plague of madness would overtake their own children. (If Abae had married early, as Jacob did, it's possible that his children at Breslau had already become psychotic when Sigmund was age three and that he'd heard about the mental problems of these cousins who lived not very far from Freiberg.)

If I'm right that a pressing fear of insanity was another important mental stress in Sigmund's childhood, one would expect that signs of this stress also had appeared in his adult years. In *Dark Side* I have discussed various signs of Freud's fears of insanity in his mature years, but at this point I'll briefly mention only one of them. In the Freud/Jung letters are found a brief correspondence between Jung's wife Emma and Freud, in the period just preceding his breakup with Jung. In that clandestine exchange of letters with Emma Jung she became quite bold and presumed to lecture Freud on certain matters. At one point, he thought she had cast aspersions on the development of his children, and he reacted in a quite strange and extreme manner. Freud's defensive and somewhat paranoid response reflected his fear that perhaps she had pointed accurately to his children's vulnerability to severe mental instability, though it's likely she had not meant to hint at an outcome of that kind.

Authors who wish to explore the possibility that Breslau continued to hold important, special meanings for Freud into adulthood might want to examine all the ramifications of his "congress" with Fliess at Breslau in December of 1897. I don't have space here to analyze possible significances of that meeting, nor connections with his recent awareness then of having been molested by his nanny. (See his provocative letter of December 22, 1897.) In any case, my suggestion is that this congress took place at Breslau as an unconscious reflection of Freud's boyhood concerns that Breslau had strong connections with his vulnerability to insanity.

The Hebrew/Christian Split

In his book *Sigmund Freud's Christian Unconscious* (1988) Vitz has discussed a number of serious ego splits in Freud's mind, but the focus of his attention is on a complex schism in the religious portion of Freud's personality. At the beginning of his book, Vitz noted that the standard view of Freud's religious life (taken from many of his writings) was that he was a lifelong "natural atheist" and an unremitting enemy of religion, particularly of Christianity, but of Judaism also. In several works Freud explained that all religions are variants of obsessional neuroses whose doctrines are merely illusions—projections of infantile needs by persons who are unable to face harsh realities, especially suffering and death.

The major thesis of Vitz is that "in a state of curious coexistence with this standard image of Freud the atheist (and anti-Christian), there is another side of Freud." Vitz' book presents a great deal of new evidence showing that Freud was not simply an atheist or agnostic, but that there was a rather peculiar schism in his religious feelings that are traceable to connections with his Freiberg nanny's teaching. Vitz wrote that: "Freud was deeply ambivalent about Christianity; such ambivalence requires at least two strong opposing psychological forces." (1988, p. 2) Accordingly, Vitz' book developed the idea that Freud harbored a lifelong identification and attraction for Christianity, countered by—as a significant secondary emphasis of Vitz' work—"Freud's little-known, unconscious hostility to Christianity, which is reflected in his curious preoccupation with the Devil, Hell, and related topics such as that of the Anti-Christ." These very substantial Christian (and anti-Christian) portions of Freud's psyche should help to clarify his great ambivalence about religion, Vitz noted, and increase our understanding of "major aspects of Freud's personality."

In Vitz' lengthy description and analysis of Freud's period of early maturity (1882-1900), he provided numerous examples from Freud's private letters showing his deep religious preoccupations, which often expressed positive unconscious tendencies in him concerning religion. For example, Vitz pointed to Freud's "Easter-Pentecost complex" manifested by his frequent references to God, the Bible, Easter, and the Christian holiday of Pentecost (Whitsunday) in his personal letters to various persons. (Vitz argued that Freud's fixation on Pentecost may have been related to the loss of his nanny at that time of year.) In Freud's correspondence with his fiancée Martha Bernays, Vitz detected a general and striking religious quality with numerous religious references sprinkled throughout, including many that are specifically Christian in nature. Thus, on two occasions he extended "fond Pentecost greetings" to Martha, which prompted Vitz to remark: "For a secular Jew to have written this to his decidedly Jewish fiancée is most peculiar indeed."

Throughout several chapters of his book, Vitz provided additional evidence that Freud harbored powerful religious concerns and feelings, including many that can be regarded as pro-Christian. Briefly summarizing some of the evidence of Freud's hidden pro-Christian feelings, Vitz wrote: "Fond Pentecost greetings, longings for Rome, both conscious and unconscious desires for conversion, and enjoyment of ambiguous Christian literature were expressed by Freud time and time again. Yet these secret desires were held back from any kind of direct fulfillment." (Were those secret religious desires held back because they were connected with profane and incestuous sexual desires relating to nanny, his primal mother?)

Vitz' fourth chapter titled "Freud and the Devil: Literature and Cocaine" offers rather remarkable evidence for an unconscious split in Freud regarding Christianity and shows that the side of him that was hostile to Christianity was involved with demonic themes that "were deeply connected to his personal motivation." Thus, Vitz revealed that Freud was preoccupied with literature whose themes were centrally concerned with Satan, with Heaven and Hell, or "with hostility to Rome as a symbol of Catholicism." In contrast to extensive data indicating Freud's positive attraction to Christianity and its God, much of the world's literature to which he was attracted suggests, as Vitz noted, that "a very important part of Freud sided with Satan against God and Heaven and Christ, and sided with the enemies of the Church." (The present volume's tenth chapter deals with the complexities of Freud's Satanic pacts.)

It was noted by Vitz that Velikovsky (1941) was the first author to suggest that Freud had entered into some sort of Satanic pact and that Bakan's book *Sigmund Freud and the Jewish Mystical Tradition* (1958) provided considerable material about Freud's Faustian pact with the devil (which most analytic writers about Freud completely ignore). Vitz was quite aware of biographical material proving that Freud, to some extent, had identified himself with Satan and made these comments: "The exact nature of Freud's relations with the Devil still remains uncertain, and perhaps must always remain so; the same is true of his identification with the Anti-Christ." However, Vitz asserted that much evidence exists that there was a "split," to some degree, in Freud's personality and that a significant portion of his psyche "was involved in a neurotic fantasy pact with the Devil."

Then Vitz remarked that the question of Freud's ultimate allegiance—whether with God or with Satanic forces—is "a very central one." Though he was frank in being "unable to decide what Freud's final psychological commitment was," Vitz stated the hope and belief that Freud's diabolical identification and "pathological past" had not prevented him, in the end, from choosing "the side of the angels." The present author disagrees with the hesitant, simplistic vote of confidence that Vitz so generously gave to Freud on the question of "doing good versus doing evil." That question is complicated by the fact that there were at least two Sigmund Freuds and that a ruthless, murderous figure (Mr. Hyde) was hidden subtly within the dark side of Freud's personality where his diabolical forces resided. That demonic figure in Freud definitely was not on the side of the angels and was capable of great destructiveness towards his enemies, real and imagined.

Freud was a very clever devil concerning these matters. He tried to convince his pliant disciples that even his identification with Satan, which he acknowledged explicitly on two occasions, had a positive and humane aspect to it which enabled him to create brilliant psychological theories and achieve insights that benefited mankind. Thus, he implied that it was his Satanic self that enabled him to delve deeply into the unconscious mind (Hell) to obtain precious gifts for humanity. Of course, there were some elements of truth in that but also significant falsehoods. Unfortunately, he failed to tell the whole story and acknowledge that his Satanic self, during periods when he was psychotically depressed, could become an enraged and murderous fellow who brutally acted-out the horrible conflicts from early childhood that Freud never managed to resolve via his vaunted self-analysis.

Chapter Three will reveal Vitz' awareness that Freud harbored dozens of identifications, including ones that can be categorized as Biblical Characters, Military Heros, Literary Figures, etc. What Vitz failed to notice is that an extremely important segment of Freud's identifications can be categorized as *Murderers* (including ones who perpetrated patricide and fratricide). Of these identifications that Freud made with murderers, the most lethal one historically is Satan—famous as the destroyer of human flesh but especially of countless human souls. Freud discussed the figure of Satan in psychological terms as symbolizing the murderous rage hidden within our unconscious personality structures. In later chapters of this book we'll see that this covert murderous rage within Sigmund Freud sometimes did not remain symbolic, and that his Satanic self became the destroyer of actual human souls, along with "near misses" like his patient Emma Eckstein whom he almost killed by arranging a bizarre, botched nose operation, ostensibly to cure her neurosis.

In his analysis of the complex religious split within Freud's personality Vitz has implied that its origins can be found during his first three years in Freiberg in Sigi's relationship with his Catholic nanny. Recall that this demanding woman who had been his primal mother often took him to church with her and taught him so much information about the doings of God Almighty, of heaven and hell, that he frequently was inspired to preach related sermons to his parents. The strength of this early Catholic influence was magnified by the fact that there were no synagogues in Freiberg in that era to which the boy might be taken to receive competing stimuli. Also, it seems that the Freuds were non-religious Jews who did not even observe Jewish holidays in their home.

Although Freud's mother came from a religious family, she did not seem to maintain an interest in her faith. However, there are indications that Sigmund's father did have a pietistic streak and was conversant with sacred Hebrew writings. Consider that Freud was a precocious reader (probably reading at age four) and that his autobiographical writings indicate that his earliest readings were in the Bible. Therefore, it's likely that when his father taught him at home in the pre-adolescent days that he directed the lad's readings towards the stories of Hebrew biblical characters with whom Sigmund eventually identified himself so intensely.

The preceding material suggests the origin of the religious split in Freud that Vitz has discussed in detail. During his first three years the boy's mind was inundated by rather primitive Christian images, concepts, and feelings which he absorbed from his primary mother, his nanny. Surely, this was the affective source of Freud's later identification with Jesus which Vitz and a few other authors have mentioned briefly, and for which I have offered considerable evidence in *Dark Side*. But this powerful Christian influence that permeated the bottom layer of Freud's psyche was countered by his father's later direction of his readings towards the Hebrew scriptures. Here was the beginning of the religious split in Freud which can be characterized by both the divergences and similarities between his strange identifications with the competing figures of Moses and Jesus. These were two of the schismatic images in Freud's mind which, in the style of Jekyll and Hyde, was constantly being pulled apart by the opposing dualistic forces, identifications, and images that will be analyzed in the next two chapters.

In Freud's letter to Fliess dated October 4, 1897 he told of that dream in which he saw the skull of a "pig," but he related this to a wish that, like Goethe, he might find a skull on the Lido to enlighten him. This image of the skull he related indirectly to a dream image, or perhaps an actual memory, of his nanny in Freiberg who "washed me in reddish water in which she had previously washed herself." Freud stated that the interpretation of this was "not difficult," but he did not explain it, seeming to imply that it had a sexual meaning, i.e. the reddish water pertained to menstruation and to their sexual acts together.

Vitz remarked that several of his Catholic acquaintances had responded to the fact that Freud's nanny was a devout Catholic by suggesting that it was likely that she had performed a secret baptism on young Sigi (considering that she did not need to perform this ritual in a church and that it could have been done in ten seconds). Various convincing reasons were given by Vitz as to why she might have performed this act (pp. 18-19). Concerning Freud's memory that she had washed him in red water, the eminent psychologist Robert R. Holt suggested to Vitz that this imagery could have meant that the nanny had secretly baptized Sigmund's head with water, while telling him that he'd been "washed in the blood of the Lamb." (Freud's description of the pig's head compared it with the head of a sheep!) Vitz noted that after Freud mentioned the reddish water he used the term *experimenta crucis*—the test of the cross—which offers an obvious connection with Christ's suffering on the cross. Moreover, the name Goethe (which Freud cited) is structurally similar to the "gotha element" of the place's name where Christ was crucified, called *Golgotha*, which means "the place of *a skull*."

The pieces of this puzzle fit together so amazingly well that Vitz concluded: "All of this implies that when he wrote that his nanny washed him in 'water in which she had previously washed herself,' Freud was referring to his covert baptism." The present author agrees wholeheartedly, and must emphasize that Freud continued to repress all of this crucial self-understanding in the throes of his greatly overrated self-analysis.

But, why were these images of nanny's covert baptizing of him emerging from Freud's unconscious mind in October of 1897? There are various reasons for this re-emergence of the forbidden nursemaid in 1897 that I could mention, but I'll refer only to two of them here. First, in *Secret SL* I have discussed that in that era Freud's sister-in-law Minna had become a governess (not unlike a nanny) in his household and that she eventually took the supportive role with him of his Freiberg nanny, along with the covert and illicit sexual role formerly held by Monica Zajic. (In terms of Freud's propensity to use "name magic" to resurrect lost figures—emphasized in Chapter Six—the names Minna and Monica were structural and psychic equivalents for him.) Second, in that period of 1897 it's likely that Freud was struggling covertly with the idea of accepting an overt baptism, i.e. of becoming a convert to Christianity to accelerate his promotion to a full professorship, a career-enhancing strategy that had been used successfully by many other eminent Jews in those days. (Instead, as we shall see later, Freud used a clever form of bribery to attain his ambitious goal.)

Let's think carefully about Vitz' thesis that in October 1897 memories began to emerge from Freud's unconscious mind concerning his nanny's covert baptizing of him in childhood. Although Freud did not understand their religious significances in 1897, this does not mean that the boy Sigi failed to perceive or suspect that nanny's special washing of him had involved the ritual called baptism which she may have explained to him on other occasions. Consider that he was involved with her in other illicit acts (sex and thefts) which he realized must be withheld from his parents' awareness. Likewise, he may have perceived, if somewhat vaguely, that she had involved him in this strange ritual and that "making him a Christian" would have angered his parents, so this was another matter that needed to be kept secret from them. Then, when the family suddenly had her put in prison, the shock of this loss probably caused the boy to blot out his conscious memories of their illicit acts together, including the covert baptism.

All of this suggests that young Sigmund, immersed in the concrete and magical world of the preschool child, had become a covert Christian when he was preaching those sermons about God's doings to his bemused parents. Isn't it possible that his peculiar identification with Jesus had already started then, and that Sigi's sermons represented his version of the precocious boy Jesus' sermons to his astonished elders? My suggestion is that young Freud, shocked by the sudden loss of his primal mother and his Eden called Freiberg, coalesced a compensatory fantasy about being Jesus, which he hoped would enable him someday to resurrect his dead nanny and restore her to him.

This unconscious fantasy of being his nanny's beloved hero called Jesus enabled Sigmund to concoct strange ideas that he would someday become a world-famous healer of the sick, the focal point of a global movement constituting a "new religion" (as Fromm has described Psychoanalysis), allowing him to achieve great honor and reverence. In its emulation of Jesus, however, this unconscious fantasy demanded that someday Freud's disciples would betray and desert him and that eventually his downfall would occur when his kinsmen would demand that he should be destroyed (murdered or exiled) because of his blasphemous ideas and acts. One must recognize the likelihood that all of these unconscious ideas pertaining to a Jesus identification actually became elements of self-fulfilling prophecies in the life of this messianic wizard, Sigmund Freud.

The present section has already introduced us to the idea that Freud had made powerful conflicting identifications with both Jesus and Satan which apparently were connected with deep feelings pertaining to his nanny and the rage which he felt about her loss—feelings that eventually precipitated murderous behaviors towards his own kinsmen. Concerning similar matters Jones wrote (1953, p. 13) that: "Freud has taught us that the essential foundations of character are laid down by the age of three and that later events can modify but not alter the traits then established." Jones blithely recounted that this was the same age when Sigmund "was taken away or, when one thinks of the circumstances, one might almost say torn away from" his childhood home. Then Jones pretended that he would summarize the "problems" faced by Sigi in his first three years and how these influenced his later development.

But, guess what Jones decided about these matters? It is astonishing that he claimed that Sigi's early "problems"—such as the horrendous loss of his nanny—had hardly any negative effects upon his later development and merely acted as a spur for his self-understanding and for his magnificent ability to cope with reality! Of course, in stating this silly notion about the idealized Freud (Dr. Jekyll), what Jones had slyly omitted from his historical account of Freud's early childhood was almost all of the grim data that are presented in this present chapter. In essence, Jones alleged that Freud was a psychic anomaly whose first three years of life had no important negative influences upon his later development. The Great Falsifier strikes again.

One final look should be taken at the possibility that Sigmund's early problems had produced significant effects upon aspects of his later development. We need to ponder that his earliest religious influences concerning Christianity and Judaism came to him from his devout nanny and pious father Jacob, and that both of these august persons were sexual molesters of children. Thus, Sigmund's initial encounters with the two major religions in his life were imbued with experiences involving hypocrisy, betrayal of his trust, perversion, and resultant feelings of suppressed rage in him. Can we doubt that all of this has a great deal to do with Freud's fanatic public hostility towards religion in his adult years?

Chapter Three

Freud's Uncanny Acting-out of Fantasy Identifications

Freud's Double Birthdate

The focus of this chapter will be upon Freud's fantasy identifications, which his biographers (except for Vitz) have failed to recognize can provide important clues to Freud's very unstable sense of identity and to crucial aspects of his hidden psychopathology. In fact, most authors have given tacit endorsement to Jones' false position that Freud made only a handful of these fantasy identifications, primarily with Biblical figures like Moses and Josef (the dream master) and military heros like Hannibal, Alexander, and Napoleon—and that generally Freud's identifications, while interesting, were rather inconsequential with regard to his inner life.

Instead, this writer proposes that the large majority of Freud's biographers have downplayed the issue of his fantasy identifications as an unconscious way of protecting his inflated reputation, reminiscent of their suppression of information about criminality in the Freud family (Gicklhorn's data). Indeed, they have failed to acknowledge that Freud was engaged in amazing and almost promiscuous uses of these identifications. In fact, in this chapter more than 100 of these identifications by Freud will be listed. Also, I'll show that he acted-out aspects of his fantasy identifications in a considerable number of these cases, often in very strange ways. When we connect that finding (about acting-out) with a mass of data showing that he made bizarre identifications with more than 20 murderers—including literary characters and real historical figures—this will have obvious relevance to my hypotheses concerning the probable murders of Emanuel

Freud in 1914 and John Freud in 1919.

Before discussing Freud's fantasy identifications, let's consider the fact that there have been two birthdates attributed to Freud, since this may suggest an important psychic determinant for the copiousness of these identifications. In Jacob Freud's family Bible, his son's birth was recorded, using his Hebrew name of Schlomo, on May 6, 1856 (the correlative date on the Jewish calendar was Rosch Hodesch Iyar 5616). However, in 1931 when the town council of Freiberg (now called Pribor) placed a special plaque on the house where Freud was born, it was discovered that the "real" date of birth was *March* 6, 1856. In Jones' biography (p.1) he accepted that the March 6th date actually had appeared on the register in 1931, but explained this discrepancy by claiming that the recording clerk in 1856 must have made a clerical error! (Considering that 20% or more of firstborn children have been conceived "prematurely"—before marriage—one imagines that this same excuse of a "clerical, error" has been offered in millions of such cases.)

Leslie Adams' article (1954) concerning the mystery of Freud's true birthday relates that in 1931 when Freiberg's town council suddenly announced that the local archives showed that Freud had been born on March 6, 1856 this proclamation was annoying to Sigmund Freud. In a coy manner, he expressed his resentment that someone was trying to make him two months older than he actually was, stating that he'd obtained the May 6th date from his mother "who ought to know best."

Freud failed to mention that his mother might have lied a bit about this embarrassing issue, since she and Jacob Freud had been married in Vienna on July 29, 1855 and, if Sigi's birthdate had been March 6th, then he had been born only seven months and six days after their wedding day. Adams remarked that if the March 6th date were accurate then Freud "was probably the child of a prenuptial conception, thus opening the door to all the confused motives of hope and fear of a doubting folly in a youth with intense ambition and a compulsive imagination." Adams' tortuous language failed to mention that the following questions would then emerge: 1. did that old man Jacob Freud seduce the young girl, Amalia?; 2. instead, had Emanuel seduced her and later asked his father to bear the responsibility of marrying her, since Emanuel was already married, with children?; 3. did the question of his true birthdate present Freud with a perverse sexual mystery that reverberated with his childhood molestation by nanny, causing sexuality to become the fanatic underpinning of his later intellectual and career development?

This enterprising author named Adams—whom I suspect of being a loyal Freudian—claimed that he'd done some detective work and had proved "beyond all possible question or dispute" that Freud had been born on May

6, 1856. He indicated that the Freiberg clerk had not made a clerical error in 1856, while recording Freud's birthdate on the official register. Instead, Adams alleged that the presumed expert who had examined the entry and informed Ernest Jones about this matter, along with all the town council members in 1931 who examined the entry, had made a rather foolish but understandable error by misreading Freud's birthdate on the official register. Adams stated that he had ordered an expert named Mr. Nähnadl to examine the entry. This savant had advised Adams that the birth month was written with the old spelling *May* instead of *Mai*, so that it was fairly easy to confuse this word with *März* (March)—except that no umlaut had been placed over this word, which the spelling of *März* requires.

Perhaps Adams' preceding explanation, and his tale of the missing umlaut, will convince most readers that he has offered the correct solution to this mystery about Freud's double birthdate. However, I must admit to considerable skepticism that Adams' explanation of this matter is "indisputable." For the last 20 years I have been making careful studies of the "fudging" of Freud documents by members of the Freudian elite, so Adams will have to excuse me for considering the possibility that in 1931 the Freiberg town council members might have correctly read Freud's birthdate as *März*, and that sometime after that examination the birth register could have been altered by a forger to safeguard the reputations of Freud and his parents. (Readers familiar with forging techniques will decide for themselves how simple it would have been to totally expunge an umlaut, without leaving an observable trace of any tampering.)

In Adams' article he tried to convince readers that he had taken extraordinary efforts to confirm that May 6, 1856 was the true birthdate of Freud that appeared on the official register of births in Freiberg. Adams noted that the expert he had sent to that city, Mr. Nähnadl, had the title of official genealogist of the kehilah of Prag (a Jewish communal organization). Moreover, Adams stated that he had sent this alleged expert to make: "repeated trips to Freiberg for me and for four years [he] applied the resources of his vast special knowledge and local acquaintance to the situation . . . "

At that point varied suspicions were aroused in my mind about Adams' allegation that Mr. Nähnadl had needed to make repeated trips to Freiberg over a span of *four years* to establish that Freud's birthdate was May 6, 1856! Was that a gross exaggeration by Adams—a bit of overkill—to sway our minds into accepting his opinion on this matter? If Adams is correct that the question of an alternate birthdate for Freud was raised by the members of Freiberg's town council in 1931 due to their simple misreading of the month of Freud's birth, couldn't a corrective reading have been accomplished by this so-called expert in one brief trip to Freiberg? (He could have taken several photographs of the notation, magnified these photos to ensure clarity, etc.)

Again, I would like to raise the possibility that someone might have tampered with Freud's birth notation after it had been examined by the presumed expert who informed Ernest Jones that the date was listed as March 6, 1856, causing Jones to mention this date in the Freud biography. That is, it seems questionable that Jones' informant and the members of the Freiberg town council in 1931 all would have failed to perceive what Adams implied was an obvious fact: that the record is "clearly written" in an excellent German script "and plainly says 'May 6.'" If forgery has not occurred, it still seems likely that this was not the obvious sort of error that Adams implied it was, since so many thoughtful persons allegedly made the same "error" involving a presumed misreading.

That last point needs to be emphasized, since I will be arguing momentarily that Freud probably inspected that same Freiberg record when he became sixteen and perhaps made the same misreading error, causing him to suspect that his family Bible's notation and his mother's assertions were false and that his true birthdate was March 6th. From this point onward, moreover, I will no longer be arguing with Adams about the possibility that Freud's original birth record in Freiberg might have been written as March 6, 1856. The more important probability is that Freud had strong doubts himself about this issue and harbored gnawing suspicions that his true birthdate was March 6th, thereby raising serious questions in his mind about the real identity of his biological father.

Adams himself has stated (1954) that Freud had considerable doubts about the date of his birth, as reflected in some of his dream-thoughts. We are then directed by Adams to Freud's letter of March 15, 1898 to Fliess in which he mentioned his budding ideas on the neuroses and stated that he needed to find a literary source in which he could learn more about the Oedipus legend (since he was just formulating his theory of the Oedipus complex). Adams noted a crucial dream that Freud had about one month later (cited in his collective works) which is concerned with the date of his parents' marriage and of his own birth, including a "cross-examination" of his father about these issues. The associations to this dream indicate, Adams remarked, that Freud had been reading Sophocles' *Oedipus* which evoked thoughts about the hero's failure to understand the mystery of his birth (not forgetting that Freud identified with Oedipus intensely). Adams noted that Freud pondered the burning desire of Oedipus "to trace at last the secret of my birth"—"to fathom all the secret of my birth"—"burst out what will, I seek to know my birth!"

Considering again that Freud harbored a powerful and well-known fantasy identification with the tragic hero Oedipus, we see now that at least two factors had consolidated that identification. The hero's intercourse with his mother was matched by Freud's sexual contact with his primal mother (his nanny); and both men had painful, gnawing doubts about the questions of their own births. (Later, we'll consider whether the hero's murder of his father was matched by Freud's killing of a symbolic father, his brother Emanuel.)

Since Adams has already cited one dream by Freud (not appearing in the dream book) which points to the theme of painful doubts about his birth, allow me to cite another of his dreams that seems pertinent to the same topic. In the sixth chapter of the dream book, in a section which attempts to explain "absurd dreams," (but fails), one of these is just such a dream by Freud himself which focuses upon some uncanny comparisons between the years 1851 and 1856, the latter being the year of Freud's birth.

The first line of that dream reads: "I received a communication from the town council of my birthplace concerning the fees due for someone's maintenance in the hospital in the year 1851, which had been necessitated by an attack he had had in my house." To summarize the dream's contents, Freud felt amusement in the dream about this charge, because he was not yet alive in 1851, and although the charge might have related to his father, he also seemed exempt because he was already dead (Jacob F. was already dead in 1899 when the dream occurred, having died in 1896). In the dream, Freud then walked into the next room to tell this to his *dead* father who "was lying on his bed . ." To Freud's surprise, his dead father then recalled that in 1851 he had once gotten drunk and had to be locked up or detained. Freud told his father: "So you used to drink as well?" And he asked Jacob: "Did you get married soon after that?" Then Freud calculated that he was born in 1856 "which seemed to be the year which immediately followed the year in question" (strangely, 1856 seemed to follow immediately after 1851).

I will not attempt to set forth Freud's analysis of this dream, since it is largely a mass of rationalizations which attempt to conceal the core meanings of the dream, i.e. his painful anxieties about his double birthdate and *how this related to the date of his parents' wedding date*. That is why, in the dream, he asked his father to tell him the date of his marriage, albeit in a subtle manner.

Both this dream and Freud's associations to it encode numerous hidden worries that he had about his birthdate and the circumstances of his conception and birth. The idea of birth is conveyed in the dream by the word "birthplace," by the words "I was not yet alive in 1851," and by the words "I was born in 1856." Moreover, there are various paradoxes in the dream concerning Freud's birthdate, including that he was born in 1856 yet this seemed exactly the same as if he'd been born in 1851! In his associations he wrote that: "The most blatant and *disturbing* absurdity in the dream resides in its treatment of the date 1851, which seemed to me not to differ from 1856 . ." (Emphasis added.)

It seems quite obvious that this merging and equivalence of two separate years, one of them being Freud's birth year, was symbolism concerning his awareness that March and May were two months (both beginning with the letter "m") that had claims to being his true birth month. In the dream, the fact that these two months (masquerading as years) seemed capable of merging together relates not only to the question of which one was his true birth month, but also suggests that sometime he'd inspected the official birth register in Freiberg and had realized that it was difficult to decide whether his birth entry specified March or May. The merging of the two birth months (years) in the dream seems to represent Freud's wish that only one birth month had been applicable to him, i.e. that the question of unsure paternity did not exist in his life.

In the dream, Freud walked into a room and saw his dead father lying on a bed, yet the dream's internal magic made his dead father appear to be perfectly alive and able to communicate in a normal manner. This image of the dead/alive father lying on his bed secretly relates to the question of Freud's anxieties about his conception and birth, since it is a kind of replay of the famous dream he had in childhood (cited in Chapter Two) concerning the men with bird beaks who carried his mother onto her bed. In that dream young Sigmund saw his mother lying on her bed as if she were dead, but she was really alive (which he confirmed by waking fearfully from the dream, and then by arousing her from sleep). Thus, the image of the dead/alive father lying on his bed (in the 1899 dream) corresponds with the dead/alive mother lying on her bed in the childhood dream.

In effect, the image of the father lying on his bed in the 1899 dream is a "screen" for the image of Amalia lying on her bed in a comatose state in the childhood dream. My previous analysis of the latter image indicated that it reflected Sigi's concern and anger that his mother had had sexual relations with several men, thereby giving uncertainty to his own paternity. Concerning the dream of 1899, suffused with anxieties about the circumstances of his birth, his associations state that the dream-thoughts concealed a very "embittered and passionate polemic" against the image of his father, but he stated that this fatherly image was only "a show-figure" masking or screening someone else. This latter shadowy figure was someone "who was as a rule treated as sacred . ." according to Freud's comments.

Most readers will agree that the unconscious mind (the child's mind in all of us) regards the mother as its most sacred object. However, Freud dodged that obvious interpretation by claiming that the sacred person concealed in his 1899 dream was a composite of two venerable colleagues who had been critical of his analytic work and theories. If one endorses the idea that this hidden sacred figure in the dream was his mother Amalia, we can recognize that in 1899 Freud was still suffering from anguish and uncertainty about the circumstances of his birth and that he harbored extremely angry feelings towards his mother and father about this subject, which he was still repressing.

This dream of 1899 raises questions about drunkenness, which is an implicit accusation by Freud that he'd been conceived when someone in a drunken state had seduced or raped his mother, who also might have been drunk at the time (he feared). This relates to his return visit to Freiberg at age sixteen when he fell madly in love with Gisela Fluss and, when his affection was not returned by her, indulged in a wild, drunken binge in public that made him sick to his stomach. At that point, passionate feelings became connected with the drunken state in Freud's psyche, and this connection probably exists in the dream of 1899. (His drunken binge in Freiberg was revealed in one of his letters in that era to his friend Silberstein.)

Readers may wonder that a surprising coincidence occurs in the dream of 1899, so filled with birth concerns, since it conveys an embarrassing notice from the town council of Freiberg which somewhat correlates with the Freiberg town council's actual announcement in 1931 about Freud's dual birthdate. My explanation for this coincidence is a bit circuitous, yet I believe it is sound. It starts with the assumption that both of Freud's aforementioned dreams indicate that from childhood onward he harbored nettling suspicions about his paternity, the circumstances of his birth, and his true birthdate. (I believe these suspicions derived from his having observed his mother, and perhaps Jacob at other times, in adulterous behaviors.)

In a boy as proud and sensitive as Sigi, these doubts and suspicions about his paternity (fostered by the ambivalent wish that Emanuel was his true father) would have created great psychological stress. With this crucial issue preying upon his mind, it is reasonable to believe that when he visited Freiberg at age sixteen he was impelled to visit the office that kept the official registry of births. There he must have seen for himself that the official record showed that he was born on March 6, 1856 (even if this was a misreading of the date).

Then in 1899 when he had nearly completed his dream book, he must have been hoping and fantasizing that the book would bring him some measure of fame in Austria, if not worldwide. Indeed, it's likely that he fantasized that some day Freiberg might dedicate a plaque to honor him, for in a much earlier letter to Fliess he mentioned the hope that some day a plaque would be dedicated to him for mastering the interpretation of dreams. Therefore, his dream of 1899 seems to have reflected his ambivalent recognition that some day the town council of Freiberg might check his birthdate in the official register, in order to honor him in some manner. In that eventuality, someone might then discover and announce that March 6, 1856 appeared as his birthdate on the official register, to the embarrassment of himself and his parents.

In disguised form these concerns became embedded in the dream of 1899. Then in 1931 they became actualized when Freud's fame made it reasonable for Freiberg's town council to decide that a commemorative plaque with his birthdate should be affixed to the house where he was born, requiring that his actual birthdate should be obtained from the official records. When it was discovered and announced that his true birthdate was two months earlier than previously believed, the opening sentence of the dream of 1899 and the dream's thinly veiled birth concerns seemed to acquire almost a quality of premonition or of remarkable coincidence, which when examined is really not so uncanny at all.

Previously, I noted that the dream of 1899 appears in the dream book's section pertaining to absurd dreams (1967, pp. 461-496). It's my opinion that those 36 pages are permeated with Freud's great anxieties about the mystery of his birth. It would take too many pages here to defend that thesis fully, but I must mention that the very next dream by Freud himself which he cited four pages later ("Goethe's Attack on Herr M.") is a disguised analogue of the prior dream about the years 1851 versus 1856. The Goethe dream mentions that Goethe died in 1832, but it says that Freud "was not quite sure, however, what year we were actually in . ." This ambiguity about years again conceals Freud's great concerns about his birthdate, and since his brother Emanuel was born in 1832 (by some accounts of his birth year), this hides Sigmund's suspicions that Emanuel was his real father and should have been attacked (by Sigi in the role of Goethe) for abandoning him in childhood—not forgetting that Freud identified strongly with Goethe. (A fuller re-interpretation of this dream will be given in a later volume.)

Preceding both of the aforementioned dreams Freud provided a fragment of his lengthy dream about Count Thun. This dream fragment mentions Freud's conversation with a cab-driver and that he ordered the man to drive him to a railway station, telling the driver: "Of course I can't drive with you along the railway line itself." In his associations Freud said that he was identifying this cab-driver with his (unnamed) brother, whom I claim was a composite of Alexander Freud and Emanuel Freud, particularly the latter. The hidden theme of this fragment is Sigi's anger that in 1859 Emanuel "abandoned him," so that the boy was unable to travel with him and had to take that dreadful train ride to Leipzig without having the cherished company of this yearned-for "father" (Emanuel). With this interpretation in mind, it immediately becomes clear that this dream fragment again relates to Freud's birthdate and to concerns that Emanuel was his real father; to his hidden rage that Emanuel "abandoned" him after jailing nanny; and to primitive wishes that his brother should be attacked by "Goethe" and punished (demoted) in connection with a severe penalty connected with train travel. (Consider his death in 1914 via that uncanny train "accident," and that this dream fragment meshes with the murderous train sequence in Freud's dream concerning his presumably lethal Hollthurn patient cited in the next chapter.)

While giving his associations to this dream fragment, Freud mentioned an evening when he was present with a group of revelers at the home of a "hospitable and witty lady." Apparently, the group was having fun trying to solve riddles and Freud was embarrassed (was "a rather ludicrous figure"), because he "had heard two riddles which I had been unable to solve."

Freud presented these two riddles to his readers, which I will not repeat here, for it will suffice to say that they were like brief poems which had very similar wordings. Each riddle had a one-word solution whose connotations generate some striking connections with one another, and those solutions are the words "Ancestry" and "Progeny." It should be emphasized—or even shouted—that Freud acknowledged that he was not able to solve these riddles at the party, though their solutions were known to everyone else there.

We see that Freud's associations to this dream fragment (involving his anger towards Emanuel) covertly portray him in his identification with Oedipus, trying to solve the riddle given to the hero by the murderous Sphinx (a part of his own personality, presumably). It will be seen by readers for themselves that Freud's attempts to explain the significance of these riddles at the party were quite inadequate and futile, since he failed to recognize their relations to his deep anxieties about his clouded paternity. His failure to obtain the solution to the first riddle, "Ancestry," means that his true ancestry—the mystery of his birth—would forever remain hidden from him. Likewise, his progeny could never be certain of their ancestry either, which points to the second solution as being inter-connected with the first one. Here we see that Freud again unwittingly identified himself with Oedipus, the patricidal figure who struggled to unravel the mystery of his own birth and paternity.

I have stated that the entire section of Freud's dream book that is devoted to absurd dreams is laden with his anxieties concerning the mystery of his birth. Perhaps that was his unconscious mind's painful, bitter way of saying that he was a ridiculous bastard whose lofty pretensions were made absurd by the fact that he did not know the identity of his real father. Such feelings must have generated suppressed, murderous rage in Sigmund Freud as hinted by the very first dream which he offered in his long section on absurd dreams. He claimed that this was the dream of one of his patients, but later chapters will support my claim that many of the dreams which he attributed to patients were really dreams of his own. However, it doesn't really matter too much whose dream this was, since it was (in the last analysis) selected by Freud to introduce this section that is permeated by his hidden rage towards his father figure, Emanuel, for having "abandoned" him.

In this first absurd dream, the "patient" dreamed that: "His father had met with a grave calamity. He had been traveling by the night train, which had been derailed. The carriage seats were forced together and his head was compressed from side to side." In the brief remaining portion of this dream, the dreamer then saw his (dead) father lying in bed. (Compare this with Freud's dream of 1899, when he saw his dead father lying in bed.) The dreamer was surprised by the calamitous accident that had befallen his father, since he'd already been dead for six years. The final sentence of the dream was: "How clear his eyes were!"

Are we justified in wondering whether this dream (if Freud were the dreamer) had given an unconscious prediction of Emanuel's uncanny death in 1914? Or did the mere "selection" of this dream of one of his patients confirm that Freud secretly wished for the death of Emanuel via a train "accident"? Considering that the father in this dream was killed by a forceful compressing of his head and that during birth infants suffer a similar compression of their heads, this dream seems to encode hidden themes of murdering a father in connection with grave concerns about birth. If so, this dream serves as a strangely appropriate introduction to this section on absurd dreams which conceals so many items about the mystery of Freud's birth, and his suppressed rage towards his mother and half-brother Emanuel. (Notice that the compression that occurs in this dream seems pertinent to the body compression which occurs in the Hollthurn dream during the "switch" from one train carriage to another as discussed in the next chapter, again suggesting that the present dream was one dreamt by Freud.)

A major thrust of recent pages is that Freud undoubtedly had great doubts about the date and circumstances of his birth, and his paternity. In Vitz' discussion (1988, p. 219) of some related issues, he mentioned that various factors had undermined Freud's respect for his father Jacob and also may "have raised doubts about his own paternity. Who was his father? This is a question he apparently never psychologically resolved."

If Vitz and I are correct about this issue, one senses that the basis for young Sigmund's identification with Jacob Freud had been permanently damaged by his anger at his father's cowardice (the hat incident) and especially by Sigmund's failure to know who his real father was. Apparently, this led to a remarkable attempt at compensation in which Freud allowed himself to identify with a huge number of men, often ones who were famous and heroic. In my opinion, the difficulty of identifying with Jacob, and not being sure of the identity of his real father, were two of the prime factors stoking Freud's proliferation of fantasy identifications. However, my prolonged study of this issue has led me to conclude that perhaps the earliest and most powerful source of this unconscious "project" to create numerous fantasy identifications was Sigmund's loss of his nanny and the perpetual desire to find some way to recapture her love by identifying with heroic or famous figures, particularly Jesus and other Biblical characters. More will be said about that later.

The sexual molestation by nanny also may have provoked this widespread identification "project." From an early age onward, great shame about perverse sexuality may have stoked unconscious feelings of self-hatred that caused Sigi to attempt escaping from his despised self by creating a host of alternate self-images via these magical fantasy identifications, ones that were more acceptable and soothing to his battered ego. In later chapters we'll see that Freud concealed enormous amounts of hatred for countless people, surely as a projection of the hidden self-hatred and shame that gnawed away like a ravenous rat at the core of his being. And this brings us to a point where we need to begin examining Freud's numerous fantasy identifications to discover what they can teach us about hidden aspects of his personality.

Freud's Fantasy Identifications

Earlier, I noted that Ernest Jones had fostered the false impression that the master had made only a small number of fantasy identifications, largely involving Biblical and military heroes. That inaccurate view of Jones was tacitly adopted, in the decades following publication of the Jones biographies, by additional Freud biographers who failed to sense the crucial significance of these fantasy identifications for providing evidence of Freud's deeper psychopathology. However, there have been a few authors who have paid special attention to Freud's identifications, and their work will now be reviewed.

The most notable of these authors is Paul Vitz whose recent book (1988) investigated Freud's multiple identifications (pp. 145ff.) in the context of demonstrating that "he suffered from reduced (but still noticeable) aspects of borderline character disorder with narcissistic elements." Vitz pointed out Freud's habitual tendency to identify with certain heroes "who often took on the function of alter-egos for Freud." This tendency was viewed by Vitz "as a seeking of idealized identities, with each hero serving to help focus and define one aspect of Freud's fractured ego . ." That is, the various parts of Freud's somewhat fragile ego "anxiously sought to provide a new identity better than his father could provide." Furthermore, Vitz was aware that at times these fantasy identifications had a pathological basis and often were expressions of Freud's "narcissistic grandiosity." Also, he remarked that these identifications "captured different parts of Freud's ego—different spirits (or demons) of Freud's personality." By emphasizing the demonic aspects of some of these identifications, Vitz exhibited a tenuous awareness that deeply pathological processes were sometimes operating here. Unfortunately, Vitz then strenuously denied this deep psychopathology in Freud, as he also used denial to ignore that murderous potentials were acted-out via some of these fantasy identifications.

The writings of Vitz about Freud's identifications offer a landmark in understanding Freud's disturbed personality, since he tied these identifications to a diagnosis of borderline personality disorder. In simpler terms, Vitz' work is important merely because he provided his readers with an awareness of how extensively Freud had indulged in these fantasy identifications, citing 28 of them in just one paragraph. (These will serve as the first 28 identifications in my list of more than 100 of them that will be mentioned in this section.)

Vitz began his list of Freud's fantasy identifications by citing some of the famous military heroes with whom he is known to have identified, including: Alexander the Great, William the Conqueror, Napoleon, and the latter's general named Masséna. Next, he listed renowned figures who were part of Freud's "anti-Rome ego," including: Hannibal, Oliver Cromwell, Garibaldi, and Ulrich von Hutten. Then there were Biblical figures who were part of "his complex Jewish identity": Moses, Jacob, and Josef (master of dreams). Also, certain of these fantasy figures were "part of his pro-Christian or ambivalent Christian self": Jesus Christ, Scipio (Africanus), St. Paul, Franz Brentano, and Romain Rolland. Some identification figures were aspects of "his anti-Christian identity," including Satan (the Devil), Oedipus, the anti-Christ, Faust, Frollo, "and perhaps Leonardo and Goethe belong here." Finally, Vitz cited five scientific, professional, or artistic models with whom Freud identified, including Brücke, Charcot, Fleischl von Marxow, Fliess, and Schnitzler.

Another author who recently has made some valuable comments about Freud's fantasy identifications is Anzieu (1986) in his volume about Freud's self-analysis. Anzieu offered a number of the same identifications that appear on Vitz' list but also gave his readers thirteen new ones which, when added below to the 28 offered by Vitz, will bring our running total to 41. The following literary characters were offered by Anzieu, usually with ample discussion of each one: Aeneas, Julian Boufflers, Leo Vincey, Gargantua, Gulliver, and Hercules. In a small group of authors Anzieu included: Dante, Emile Zola, and J.J. David. Finally, there was a group of four other renowned men starting with two German-Jewish politicians: Eduard Lasker, Ferdinand Lassalle, Johann Winckelmann, and Ignatius Loyola.

As we continue to expand the list of Freud's fantasy identifications, the following group of sixteen literary characters and real persons is remarkable because they were murderers—or, in some cases, were suspected murderers, including: Macbeth, Hamlet, Cain (brother of Abel), Brutus, Don Juan, Fiesco, The Moor of Tunis called Muley Hassan (hired assassin), Franz Moor, Karl Moor, St. Sigismund, Josef—the Military Messiah, Jekyll/Hyde, and a patient of Freud who worried that he killed during amnesic states (the Hollthurn dream's patient). Also, there was the unnamed man who was accused of trying to kill his father (Freud paid all his legal fees); along with Freud's patient named Fanny Moser who was accused of killing her rich husband; and Freud's murderous colleague, the psychoanalyst named Dr. Otto Gross. These additional sixteen identifications bring our running total to 57 such figures. (In the entire next chapter, Freud's identifications with murderers will be examined, and we'll see that four names should be included in this lethal category that already have appeared among the first 41 names on our list—indicating that the total number of Freud's murderous identifications was at least 20.)

To the preceding group of Freud's identifications that pertain to murder will now be added a more generalized group of 44 identifications that have been cited by various authors, including myself. (The names of some of the authors who have cited these 41 identifications and those citing the previous list of sixteen, will be shown in Appendix A.) Here is an unstructured list of these 41 identifications, which will bring our running total to 98: Zeus, Siegfried, Pope Julius, G. Lessing, F. von Schiller, Copernicus, Darwin, Galileo, Kepler, Newton, Adam (Biblical), King Solomon, Homer, Horace, Julius Freud, Charlemagne, Columbus, Dr. Lecher, Monica Zajic, Resi Wittek, King Lear, Solomon Almoli (master of dreams), God/Jahweh, Victor Tilgner, A. von Freund, Emanuel Freud, Victor Adler, Alfred Adler, Wilhelm Stekel, G.T. Fechner, Robinson Crusoe, Jupiter, Prometheus, Shakespeare, Socrates, D.P. Schreber, Karl L. Börne, Adolph Fischof, General "M" (Freud followed his career for many years), Woodrow Wilson (negative identification), and Admiral Dewey.

The final group of Freud's further identifications comprises 34 figures that the present author has compiled during the past twenty years, and these will bring our final total to 132 such identifications. These include literary figures and real persons that the present writer has hypothesized represented irrational identifications of Freud—as discussed in *Dark Side*, *Secret SL*, and other unpublished writings of mine. Here are the identifications of Freud that are included in this final group: F.A. Mesmer, Michelangelo, Sige and Hystera (Hebrew Gnostic dieties), Jung, Nietzsche, Schopenhauer, Heine, Juno, Anna O., Ananke (deity of fate or death), Dr. Paul Flechsig, Sigi (mythological relation of Odin and Thor), Daedalus, Mars, Josef Breuer, Signorelli, Sigmund Exner, Max Schur, Otto Weininger, Otto Rank, Emma Eckstein, Josef Paneth, Josef Popper, Josef Freud (uncle), N. Bergasse, Lou

Andreas Salomé, Minna Bernays, Martha Freud, Anna Freud (daughter), Julius Wagner-Jauregg (negative identification), Amalia Freud, N. Weiss, Jacob Freud (negative identification), and John Freud.

Origins of Freud's Excessive Identifications

The preceding list of already published identifications by Freud represents an astonishing total, and there are probably more of these published identifications that my literary research has failed to uncover. If readers are kind enough to credit a modest portion of the identifications that my personal efforts have disclosed (though these will await future publications of mine for explanations of each one), that will bring the total of Freud's identifications to at least 100.

The questions we'll return to now are why Freud's psyche generated such a huge number of these fantasy identifications, and does this tell us anything about the issue of hidden currents of psychopathology in him. None of my readers will be surprised that we need to return to the earliest years of childhood in order to find satisfactory answers to those questions.

One of the most prestigious researchers on infant development is René Spitz, whose detailed observations of infants have provided us with a persuasive theory of how the earliest processes of identification are essentially involved in the formulation of the conscience (superego). Placing emphasis upon the sixth month of life and thereafter, Spitz' observations have disclosed what Sagan (1988) calls "a veritable orgy of identification" in young children. Referring to the period between six and eighteen months, it is Spitz' impression (1958) that "the wish to identify is so strong and plays such a major role in object relations . . . that the child identifies indiscriminately with any behavior of the love object he is able to appropriate."

According to Spitz, in this early period it appears that the mechanism of identification passes "through a phase of nondifferentiation. It is indulged in by the child for identification's sake, as it were." Moreover, this global identification mechanism is used for both object relations and mastery, "for defense as well as attack." Indeed, Spitz suggests that the young child's indiscriminate manner of appropriating everything contained by the love object ("things, gestures, inflections, actions, attitudes, etc.") could help explain the hidden source of identification with the aggressor.

That Freud himself engaged in an orgy of identifications, starting in childhood and proceeding into his adult years, suggests that most, if not all, of his fantasy identifications were rooted in infantile identification processes. One might say that a substantial portion of Freud's psyche was fixated at the level of these promiscuous infantile identification processes occurring around the eighteenth month of life. That was near the era when he suffered the twin catastrophes of being sexually molested by his nanny and then finding that this primary love object was lost to him forever, eliciting a maelstrom of murderous, revengeful feelings in the betrayed child. Concerning those murderous feelings in Sigi at ages two and three, it is reasonable to assume that severe injury to his capacity to identify with his nurturer provided an inadequate amelioration of his tendency to identify with aggressors—which in later years might have helped to generate his bizarre identifications with a wide variety of murderers.

The research of Rosalind Gould (1972) has distinguished three basic modes of identification that operate within the infantile era, all of them having critical effects upon the development of conscience. These basic modes are: identification with the nurturer; identification with the aggressor; and identification with the victim (the capacity to have empathy for those who are harmed or victimized). It appears that identification with the nurturer and the aggressor have essential characteristics that are in conflict and that it is the task of the developing conscience to mediate and resolve such conflicts. In the case of young Sigi Freud it seems that momentous and lasting distortions occurred in these early identification processes centering around his inability to trust and count on the love received from his primary love object (his nanny). This is relevant to the remarkable fact that in the earliest decades of theorizing about mental development Freud insisted quite irrationally that relationships with the father are central in the child's early psychic life, with hardly any mention of maternal influences!

The preceding paragraphs suggest that there were serious gaps or lacunae (and distortions) in the identification processes and conscience-formation of young Sigmund Freud, in the first few years of his troubled life. These problems laid the groundwork for severe psychopathology which he tried to "cure" with his self-analysis and his formulation of the insights of psychoanalysis. Emphasis should be given to the point that these difficulties in Sigi's early years occurred during the childhood era which Selma Fraiberg (1959) has described as "the magic years," when the child indulges in amazing varieties of "magical thinking." Again, it can be said that a large portion of Freud's psyche remained fixated at this magical level; that in adulthood he displayed a strange split between rational thought and magical ideation; and that his excessive uses of fantasy identifications can be regarded both as a psychological defense against fears of being harmed or destroyed and a sometimes creative device for achieving mastery that was nevertheless rooted in magical thinking and often contaminated by it. In stressing that the adult Freud was covertly immersed in magical ideation of many kinds, this writer disagrees with Jones and his followers who have tried to foster the hoax that their master did not have a strong magical side and merely indulged in occasional superstitions.

The next few chapters and later sections of this book (along with major portions of *Dark Side*) will reveal the gross extent to which Freud indulged surreptitiously in many kinds of magical thinking including number magic, name magic, death magic, birthday magic, etc. It is not hard to argue that these strains of magical thought and feeling in the adult Freud were the direct result of the catastrophes that were associated with his Freiberg nanny, and that distortions in his magical ideation were causally related to his destructive urges. These included his need to precipitate suicides in many persons; to his presumed murderous behaviors involving Emanuel and John Freud; and to behaviors which caused the deaths of various other persons (the cocaine deaths, von Marxow's and his patient Mathilde's deaths, etc.) and the near-killing of his psychoanalytic patient Emma Eckstein.

In *Dark Side* I have explained in detail why I believe Freud made a powerful and bizarre identification with Emma Eckstein, the woman who became his first actual psychoanalytic patient. Various factors involving magical ideation (name magic in particular) enabled Freud unconsciously to equate Emma Eckstein with his Freiberg nanny, who had "promised" that Sigi would become a great man but then seemed to betray him by "abandoning" him. Freud's peculiar analytic treatment of Emma discloses residues of his infantile desires to punish nanny for her betrayal, to use Emma to confirm the nursemaid's expectations of his greatness, and to tie a resurrected "nanny" to him irrevocably.

Ergo, his strange program of nose surgery on Emma provided punishment by bringing her close to death several times with huge outpourings of her blood and subjected this pretty woman to facial disfigurement for life. He kept secret from public scrutiny that eventually he made her a "minor analyst" (the second psychoanalyst in history) but continued to treat her himself for many years. By these means he tied her to him and made certain that Emma—as the magical reincarnation of his nanny (there were others)—would not be able to betray or abandon him ever again. Coincidentally, the analytic treatment of Emma/nanny served as the cornerstone case upon which the inflated reputation of Psychoanalysis, as a great healer of mental illness, was founded. One might say that the case of Ms. Eckstein enabled Freud to kill many birds with one stone—considering that her magical surname means "cornerstone."

Sigi's Project of Fantasy Identifications

As already noted, Jones' biography (1953) had precious little to say about Freud's fantasy identifications, probably because the Welsh analyst feared that discussing this area of Freud's psyche in some detail would open up obvious questions about the master's psychopathological vulnerabilities. Jones implied that Freud's fantasy identifications were largely restricted to a "militaristic phase" that he passed through in childhood and adolescence which generated hero worship for a few famous warriors including Hannibal, Alexander, Oliver Cromwell, William the Conqueror, Napoleon, and the latter's general called Masséna (whom Freud erroneously believed was born on his birthdate, 100 years earlier). Although Jones was candid enough to admit that Freud cherished "dreams of becoming a great general himself," he fudged the data by claiming that Freud's military ardor had faded and died by his early twenties. He managed to "forget" that in his late fifties Freud, in the early years of WWI, generated rabid militaristic passions against America, England, and their allies. (Only when it became clear that his side would lose the war did Freud slyly adopt a moralistic, pacifist position while proclaiming loudly that war was a disgraceful business naturally opposed by a humanitarian like himself.)

It's interesting that Jones accepted Freud's explanation for his militaristic phase and those few martial identifications, namely that those aggressive factors could be traced back to the angry battles that Sigi had with his nephew John. For this seems relevant to the hypothesis that in 1919, when Freud and his compatriots lost WWI, he may have found an irrational way to punish his English kinsman by arranging his disappearance and death. (In this context, Jones remarked blandly that in 1870 the boys performed a playlet together with Sigmund taking the role of Brutus opposite John's portrayal of Caesar—though Jones chose to ignore that Sigmund was expressing murderous feelings towards John via that scenario.)

Readers will be amused that Jones failed to list and emphasize another obvious category of Freud's fantasy identifications—his religious ones—which probably preceded his martial identifications developmentally. Despite his claim to an almost omniscient comprehension of Freud's complex personality, Jones merely gave brief notice to Freud's attraction to the figures of Moses and Josef (interpreter of dreams) and failed to list and discuss the master's identifications with Jesus, Satan, the anti-Christ, Cain, Adam, Jacob, King Solomon, St. Paul and others. Jones chose to ignore all of this religious ferment in Freud's psyche in hope of portraying him exclusively as a scientific atheist. Although he acknowledged Freud's admission that he'd been greatly influenced by his childhood readings of the Bible, Jones insisted that Freud must have meant this in an ethical or historical sense and was devoid of any belief in God (not to mention Satan!). Of course, Vitz' book (1988) has gone a long way towards exposing Jones' pretenses about Freud having been a totally nonreligious person.

This writer offers the thesis that young Sigi commenced his unconscious "project of fantasy identifications" at around age three in reaction to his nanny's fanatic absorption in religious matters. Earlier, I suggested that perhaps his first fantasy identification was with the figure of Jesus Christ, hoping to obtain love and approval from his nanny by identifying with her greatest hero. I suggested that he acted-out that identification by his precocious preaching of Christian ideas to his parents in the Freiberg era, thereby emulating the story of Jesus' precocious religious instructions to his elders which charmed and amazed them (according to scripture).

Considering the various catastrophic events relating to nanny that occurred in Freiberg, it's likely that another great religious identification was then born within Freud's ravaged psyche to counterbalance the Jesus identification, namely an unconscious identification with Satan (the devil). That this period of Sigi's life—around age three—can readily generate such unconscious identifications with the devil in the minds of very troubled children is seen in Selma Fraiberg's book *The Magic Years* (1959). She tells about the youngster named Stevie (pp. 141-5) who suffers a temporary split in his psyche by generating an evil, devilish "imaginary companion" (called Gerald) whom Fraiberg describes as if he were the fantasied embodiment of Satan. One can speculate that this same splitting occurred in the psyche of Sigi Freud at age three at the birth of his unconscious identification with Satan. However, the child called Stevie managed eventually to overcome and dissolve his internal devil, but there is good reason to believe that Freud never succeeded in exorcizing this demon and that his identification with both Jesus and Satan continued powerfully into his late adult years. In later chapters we'll see that Freud's identification with Satan did not consist only of unconscious factors, but also contained compelling conscious elements that his disciples have tried to "explain away."

Probably all of Freud's fantasy identifications with religious figures owe their genesis to various reactions he had to his nanny's fanatic preoccupation with religion, to her encouragements that he should become a powerful and famous man, and to his murderous rage about the circumstances of her loss to him (her sudden jailing, perceived by him as her death). In general terms, it's quite possible that all of his scores of fantasy identifications owe their genesis to his intense, lifelong fixation on his nanny in relation to her abrupt disappearance. The proliferation of these fantasy figures implies his magical belief that he could resurrect significant dead persons almost at will, allowing him to hope unconsciously that some day her reincarnation might also be possible. The extensiveness and incredible persistence of his unconscious fixations on her into his adult years is discussed in detail in *Dark Side*. Although several writers have posited that Freud's identification with Hannibal/Rome had been generated by his relationship with his Catholic nanny, it seems surprising that none of these writers has considered the thesis that all of Freud's identifications were tied to his nanny-fixation, as has now been proposed.

Emphasis should be given to the fact that Freud harbored identifications with figures who were such polar opposites as Jesus Christ and Satan, signifying a deep split in Freud's psyche and both real and symbolic wars between good and evil that were waged perpetually within his dark, brooding soul. We know that it is not unusual for mental asylums to house one or more patients who harbor delusions that they are Jesus (see *The Three Christs of Ypsilanti*) and others who believe that they are Satan. However, it's a bit unusual for the same unbalanced person to identify intensely with both Jesus and Satan simultaneously, as Freud did. The best known modern example of this is the famous American murderer Charles Manson, who announced his roles both as the healer Jesus and the destroyer Satan. (See Bugliosi's *Helter Skelter*.)

There are additional interesting similarities between Manson and Freud which suggest that both men suffered from borderline personality disorders. Both of them were subject to prolonged cocaine abuses and to various excesses involving the topic of sexuality, and both men concealed painful uncertainties about the identities of their actual fathers. Both men indulged dramatically in "name magic" and other magical ideation and were regarded as charismatic healers who seemed to have hypnotic influences over their followers. In different ways, each of these overly ambitious men developed small cults of disciples to initiate their great "programs" that were suffused with megalomanic, paranoid goals. In both men the childhood relationship with the mother was both traumatic and highly sexualized—regarding Freud's sexual relationship and cruel break with his "primary mother" (nanny) and Manson's eroticized relationship with his young mother (who was a teenage prostitute). It remains to be seen whether these two men shared one final characteristic, concerning Manson's clear penchant for using other persons to commit murders for him. The latter point relates to my hypothesis that Freud did the same to dispatch Emanuel and John Freud.

There were numerous infantile, megalomanic, and perverse motivations encoded within Freud's scores of fantasy identifications with power figures from the ranks of deities, mythological characters, Biblical and military heroes, literary and scientific geniuses, great healers, and eminent murderers (along with many lesser persons who held special meanings for him). For example, one finds the theme of "perverse oppositionality" not only between figures within a particular category (Jesus versus Satan), but also between two or more major categories of identification—famous healers (Jesus, Charcot, Breuer, Meynert, etc.) versus a long list of famous murderers.

In his massive, erudite volume (1986) which attempts to explain Freud's self-analysis, Anzieu has commented on some of these fantasy identifications in ways that reveal another type of perverse oppositionality in the master's psyche. Anzieu observed that some of these identifications involved heroes and power figures who seem to be "winners" but really can be seen as "losers" and victims, which is described as Freud's covert identification with persons who were badly victimized. (Most likely, the latter point relates to his having been brutally victimized at age three in the relationship with his nanny and with the abrupt loss of her and his Freiberg family.)

Early in Anzieu's discussion of these matters (pp. 200-1), he noted that "identification with the victim" is implicit in a list of heroes enumerated in Freud's commentary on one of his dreams. Soon thereafter, Anzieu remarked about weird ambivalences in some of Freud's identifications, i.e, often "they were also masochistic identifications" (heroes who were doomed to fail). Reinforcing this view was Anzieu's claim (p. 335) that: "as often with Freud a heroic or megalomanic identification is matched by a masochistic identification with the victim." Here, Anzieu suggested various similarities of life experiences between Freud and the victimized literary character Julian Boufflers (in a short story by Meyer) which caused Freud to identify with this literary "loser," including that both men had been rejected by fathers who disdained their intellectual capabilities (once Jacob Freud had remarked angrily that Sigi would not amount to anything in life). And later Anzieu asserted (p. 396) that Freud had "experienced a heroic-masochistic identification" with the misunderstood and unhappy writer, J.J. David.

Concerning Freud's famous group of four Rome dreams (p. 429) Anzieu stated that: "The dominant feature of those dream . . .was a series of heroic-masochistic identifications with historical figures like Hannibal, Winckelmann and Masséna, who first achieved glory but eventually failed." I shall not go into the details' here, but will say that Freud's writings make clear that he equated Hannibal with Winckelmann, the renowned archaeologist and art historian of the 1700s, since both men's fame was tied to their intense fixations on the city of Rome, which Freud shared with them. Both Grinstein (1968) and Vitz (1988) have found obvious similarities between the lives of Winckelmann and Freud, which helped to solidify Freud's identification with this erudite Prussian whose career and fame were greatly enhanced by his decision to "conquer" Rome artistically by moving his residence to that city (similar to Hannibal's wish to conquer Rome militarily).

Grinstein seems to have sensed that there was a lethal component in Freud's identification with Hannibal and Winckelmann and their desires to conquer Rome. One can guess that Freud fantasized that if he had the courage to vanquish Rome—to overcome his well-known Rome phobia and "enter" the city—that he might then become vulnerable to one of the lethal punishments inflicted upon Hannibal and Winckelmann for their similar desires. In the case of Hannibal, his irrational and protracted failure to enter

Rome was connected with his suicide. In the case of Winckelmann, after he had conquered Rome he went to Vienna in 1768 where Empress Maria Theresa showered expensive presents on him. Later, he seemed to suffer a nervous breakdown in connection with his strange decision to visit his Prussian homeland. Then, while spending some time in Trieste for mysterious reasons, he was murdered there in June 1768 by a fellow traveller named Archangeli. Grinstein noted that if Freud compared himself with Winckelmann (which obviously he did) "then he may have felt that he too would be murdered after he had 'conquered' Rome." All of this is relevant to my claims, later in this book, that Freud was burdened irrationally by two interrelated complexes involving suicide and murder. These complexes probably were connected with Freud's homosexual urges and guilt—especially with regard to his passionate feelings for Wilhelm Fliess—since Winckelmann was recognized by many authors as a homosexual, and Hannibal was also believed to be a homosexual, in a relationship with his brother Hasdrubal (McGrath, 1986, p.66).

In Freud's dream book he wrote about his fixation on Rome and stated that "the wish to go to Rome had become in my dreamlife a cloak and symbol for a number of .. passionate wishes." But he did not admit frankly to his readers what "passionate wishes" were encoded here. Possibly, they included desires to regain a sexual nexus with his primary mother (nanny); to join her emotionally by converting to Catholicism; and to murder the kinsmen whom he feared were his ancient competitors for her sexual favors (Emanuel and John Freud).

Several writers including K. Grigg have postulated that Freud's frenetic desire to conquer and "enter" Rome pertained to his sexual desires concerning nanny, i.e. that Rome largely was a symbol for his primary mother and her fanatic Catholicism. However, it's my view that this equation does not fit the simple oedipal one involving unconscious desires to murder the father (Jacob), since in this case young Sigi perceived that his strongest rivals for the favors of his nursemaid were brother-figures—Emanuel and John. This is pertinent to my thesis that in the decade prior to 1920 Freud arranged for the murders of both these men. There is also this issue to consider: Freud's punitive suicidal tendencies were so persistent that he needed relief by transforming his suicidal impulses occasionally into homicidal ones, i.e. by indulging the murderous impulses connected with his Cain complex.

Apparently, Freud's identifications with Hannibal and Winckelmann provide us with clues to both his suicidal and murderous complexes. His identification with Hannibal relates to his intense childhood hatreds towards brothers and nephew and his wishes to destroy and wreak revenge upon the Christian worlds of Vienna and Rome that had treated him and his family with contempt for being Jews and criminals (regarding the highly publicized counterfeiting affair that soiled his family's reputation in Vienna). In turn, the identification with Winckelmann pertains to Freud's great childhood fears that he would be murdered by his kinsmen for various sexual sins, generating unconscious impulses to kill his own brethren to prevent them from killing him (as they had "killed" nanny). This correlates with a theme often found in the annals of famous murderers: 'I killed to prevent myself from being killed.'

Although Anzieu (1986) is a writer who sensed that complex perverse motives are encoded in many of Freud's fantasy identifications, that author backed away from the implication that profound psychopathological factors often are encoded in these identifications. Of course, that is partly because Anzieu did not come to grips with the fact that Freud had identified with a large number of murderers, and the possible implications of that finding. At one point, Anzieu wrote (p.400) about Freud that: "identification with the victim or the patient (the failed artist, the unrecognized writer, the depressive, the paralytic, the impotent) was just as important for Freud as identification with the creative genius . ." Concerning such highly negative identifications Anzieu perhaps meant to imply that they served largely to increase Freud's empathic understanding of sick and degraded people, ignoring that the greater lesson was that such identifications revealed the deep sickness concealed in Freud's soul, which Jung proclaimed as a final, bitter accusation against the master. In this manner, Anzieu ignored and covered-up the basic import of Freud's remarkable identifications with hysterics, madmen, and murderers,

Freud's Acting-out of Identifications

This section will explore the issue of Freud's acting-out of many fantasy identifications in ways that often were profound, unconscious, and quite compulsive, although there also were a few instances when he seemed to be conscious of acting-out the superficial aspects of his identifications with famous men. Our study of this acting-out should prove interesting in itself, but it is directed towards what may appear to be a macabre purpose. For if we become convinced that Freud often was compelled to act-out his fantasy identifications, this will become relevant to a burning question posed by the next chapter. That chapter will review Freud's numerous identifications with famous murderers, and the logical question will become this one: if the present section can provide numerous persuasive instances when Freud acted-out various identifications in relatively benign ways, is it likely that he acted-out in lethal ways his identifications with many murderers, especially with regard to his pressing patricidal impulses?

Quite a few writers have noticed that Freud had a propensity for acting-out or "living out" (Sulloway's term) various elements of his fantasy identifications, but none of those authors seemed aware of how extensive this inclination was in Freud, nor some of the hidden implications of this tendency. An incomplete list of those authors includes McGrath (1986), Sulloway (1979), Robert (1976), Vitz (1988), Shengold (1979), and Swales (1983, 1984).

Sulloway's studies of Freud's fantasy identifications with military and religious figures convinced that scholar that, to a surprising extent, Freud acted-out elements of the stories involving his heroes. In a section which Sulloway titled "Freud's Personal Myth of the Hero," (pp. 476 ff.) he observed that: "Freud's entire life followed the classic hero-path so closely as to suggest his conscious (or unconscious) living out of heroic expectations." Unfortunately, Sulloway did not mention the megalomanic and regressive aspects of this tendency in Freud, and indicated only some beneficial features, ignoring very harmful ones. Accordingly, he made the questionable judgment that this heroic pattern—which Adler would have called "neurotic superiority striving"—was deeply ingrained in Freud at an early age, "and that he cultivated it as a highly effective life-strategy in later years." Contradicting Jones' view that Freud's identifications with military heroes ended in the late teen years, Sulloway remarked accurately that he continued to "live out" heroic identifications with great warriors and famous leaders even "in his role as a neurologist and later as a psychoanalyst."

Without doubt, McGrath (1986) is the most helpful author in providing specific examples of Freud's tendency to act-out aspects of the life stories of his fantasy identifications. Although the material in this vein presented by McGrath is persuasive, it is unfortunate that his series of examples is a relatively short one, comprised basically of Hannibal, Faust, Moses, Brutus, Josef (the master of dreams), and Karl Moor. In any case, I'll summarize what McGrath had to say about Freud's acting-out of his identifications with some of those heroic figures.

Evidently, McGrath was aware (as various other writers have been) that the major way that Freud imitated his hero Hannibal was in terms of Freud's "Rome phobia." As a basis for comparison, the Carthaginian general won a great victory over the Romans at Lake Trasimene but then mysteriously failed to take the next logical step by laying siege to Rome and conquering it. Instead, he camped with his army in a town near Rome for months and later committed suicide, giving rise to the notion that his failure to enter Rome reflected a "Rome phobia." In a somewhat similar fashion, Freud in his late 30s and 40s made many trips to Italy with the primary intention of visiting Rome, but then held back from entering the city until he was forced to acknowledge his own "Rome phobia." Not until his famous dream book had been published did he enter Rome (1901) for the first time, which he called "the high point of my life."

In studying Freud's letters to Fliess, McGrath discovered another striking instance of his unconscious imitation of Hannibal's military activities. Early in 1897, Freud decided to take a meandering trip through Italy in search of "absolute beauty," at a time when he was in the throes of his self-analysis. However, McGrath noted that his actual trip in Italy was determined by unconscious conflicts concerning Hannibal rather than his intended pursuit of classical beauty. Without realizing it Freud chose a specific route that was tied to his identification with Hannibal (who was connected, as noted earlier, with the ancient nanny). McGrath remarked that Freud's route was via San Gimignano, Siena, Perugia, Assissi and Ancona, and that these cities "had relatively little to offer the tourist in search of classical beauty" (unless one equates the primary mother with classical beauty?). Moreover, Freud traveled near Lake Trasimene, the place where Hannibal had enjoyed his most famous victory over the Romans. Shortly thereafter, according to McGrath, Freud "realized that on this journey he had quite literally been following in Hannibal's footsteps."

Freud affirmed this imitation of Hannibal in the dream book (1967, p. 229) while discussing his travels in Italy during 1897 when he passed by Lake Trasimene, then saw the Tiber river "and sadly turned back when I was only fifty miles from Rome." At that point, while Freud was making plans to by-pass Rome again in the next year's trip to Italy, he made a mental comparison between Hannibal's and Winckelmann's hesitant desires to enter Rome. Suddenly, he realized: "I had actually been following in Hannibal's footsteps."

However, Freud did not clarify for himself or his readers *why* his fantasy identification with Hannibal had caused him, *compulsively* and unawares, to retrace the footsteps of his hero. The clue that we need to solve this riddle is in the sentences just preceding the above material when Freud cited "incidentally" (p. 228) that he understood the Czech language in his early childhood. He stated that: "A Czech nursery rhyme, which I heard in my seventeenth year, printed itself on my memory so easily that I can repeat it to this day, though I have no notion what it means."

But in terms of his unconscious conflicts, most of my readers will know what it means. These seemingly gratuitous references to the Czech language and a Czech nursery rhyme had made unconscious connections with Sigi's Czech nanny who eroticized him and was "murdered" by his family, leaving him with lifelong feelings of sexual fixation, depression, suicidal urges, and especially desires for revenge. (Revenge was pivotal with regard to nanny and Hannibal.) Ergo, the Czech nanny and the calamitous train journey *away from her* in 1859 needed to be reversed in 1897, in the form of Freud's Italian journey towards the forbidden city of Rome—which represented nanny and his forbidden (Oedipal) love for her. It's no accident, therefore, that soon after Freud returned from that Italian journey in 1897 his psyche was able to release his repressed memories of this nanny, and her sexual "instruction" of him (as disclosed initially in the letters to Fliess of October 3rd and 4th). Also released from repression was the memory of Jacob Freud's sexual abuse of his children, with the original intimation that Sigi might have been sexually abused by his father (letter of September 21, 1897). It should be noted that Freud's four dreams about Rome occurred just prior to the 1897 journey in Italy, and that those dreams are suffused with hidden references to his nanny, which I have discussed in *Dark Side*.

Probably, there are good reasons why all of this was connected in Freud's mind with a retracing of Hannibal's journey, considering the ancient stories about this hero's having been involved in homosexuality and incest with his brother Hasdrubal, certainly an excellent example of "forbidden love" that correlated with the forbidden love in Freud's childhood. Moreover, it seems relevant that medieval poets often used wordplay to suggest that beautiful Roma, with its breast-like hills, was strikingly symbolic of forbidden love. For a reversal (a mechanism signifying "the forbidden") of the city's name Roma comes close to producing the Italian word for love, "amore"—which in itself has a forbidden quality, since its encoding "more" is similar to the Italian word for death, "morte." Also, the underground layer of this city, the catacombs, suggests that death underlies its beautiful, love-inducing exterior.

Taking the view of Freud that phobias have a sexual origin, we can now surmise from the preceding word-play that the Rome phobias of Hannibal and Freud might have had (partly) a sexual basis. Concerning the authors who have posited that Rome symbolized Freud's nanny, we can assume that his desire to "enter" Rome had a castrative, Oedipal fear attached to it which reminded him that Hannibal's and Winckelmann's desires for Rome were followed by their suicide and murder, respectively. (Did the name of Shakespeare's hero Romeo signify forbidden love for that author?)

Freud wrote that his creation of the famous dream book was tied emotionally to the death of his father in October 1896. Perhaps so, but we should now suspect that the dream book was also generated by the aforementioned journey in 1897 that enabled him to unrepress the bitter memories of his nanny's "murder" by his brothers, along with a renewal of his primitive desires for revenge against them. Notice that Freud's first mention to Fliess that he was thinking about writing the dream book occurred in his letter of May 16, 1897, just preceding the summer's trip through Italy during which he retraced Hannibal's footsteps. Furthermore, the motto which Freud eventually chose as a preface to the dream book reeks with feelings of revenge, and makes an indirect but compelling reference to

Hannibal. In fact, one might say that Freud's choice of that motto was a symbolic imitation of the oath which Hannibal took in childhood which later impelled him to seek the destruction of Rome (which for Freud symbolized the authorities of his childhood, his elder brothers and his nanny).

The motto chosen by Freud for his dream book was taken from Virgil's Aeneid and reads: "If I cannot bend heaven, then I will arouse hell!" For some people this will hint at a secret devil's pact, but specifically this was a horrific, vengeful oath spoken by the Goddess Juno. Her rage against the hero Aeneas (due to abandonment of the woman Dido followed by her suicide) made Juno summon the Furies (demons) from hell, intending to prevent him from founding the city of Rome. It should be noted that in the older Greek mythology the primary function of the Furies was to massively punish anyone who had murdered a relative—not forgetting that Sigi had blamed his brothers for "killing" the woman whom he considered his dearest relative, his primary mother (nanny). Thus, the dream book can be seen as motivated partly by Freud's primitive life-strategy: to use his work to obtain the power and wealth that would someday enable him to enjoy a special revenge against his authoritative brother-figures (Emanuel and John), who had "killed" *him* via the Freiberg catastrophe. In this vengeful quest, he was also loosely acting-out his identification with the Biblical Josef who, during childhood, was almost murdered by his elder brothers, and who in turn nearly frightened them all to death with the ironic revenge to which he subjected them when he'd become all-powerful as the prime minister of Egypt. (In 1897 vengeful feelings in Freud also might have been provoked by the death of Josef Freud in Vienna, in March of that year.)

But how do we know that the vengeful figure of Hannibal is connected with Juno's words of revenge in the motto that Freud chose as the preface for his dream book? In the Aeneid the poet Virgil had the unhappy woman Dido express her desire for vengeance against Aeneas (founder of Rome) with this line: *Exoriare aliquis nostris ex ossibus ultor*. A loose translation of the Latin is: "Let there arise from my bones an avenger!" Various classical scholars have observed that Virgil wrote that line as an ironic "prophecy" that it was Hannibal who would rise from Dido's ancestral line to inflict a terrible vengeance upon Rome, especially since she was the mythical founder and queen of Carthage.

By the way, in Freud's book on "slips" that line by Dido became the focus of his analysis of the forgetting of the word *aliquis* (in that same quotation) by a young man whom Freud allegedly met on a holiday. Swales has shown (1982) convincingly that Freud lied about this matter and that the young man was really Freud himself. A close reading of this *aliquis* analysis reveals that this forgetful young man (Freud) had a psyche that was permeated by desires for revenge. Like Dido, he predicted that a new generation of his people would arise who "would inflict vengeance on the oppressors." This supports the idea that Freud's motto for the dream book is intimately connected with his fantasy identification with Hannibal and with young Sigi's primitive desire for revenge against the brothers who "abandoned" him and "murdered" his nanny.

Freud's identification with the figure of Faust, or Dr. Faustus, was also discussed by McGrath with regard to the times when Freud had acted-out elements of the Faust story, particularly as that tale was presented in Goethe's plays about Faust. Before we review McGrath's ideas, it should be noted that in the 16th century in Germany there was an alchemist, astrologer, and necromancer named Johan Faust whose clouded life history provided some of the ideas underlying the literary versions of the Faust story that have appeared in novels, plays, and operas. The most famous literary accounts contributing to a complex Faust legend were various "Faust-books" of the 1500s and 1600s, a drama about Faust by Christopher Marlowe (1590), Goethe's plays about Faust In the 1700s, and the novel *Doktor Faustus* (1947) by Thomas Mann.

Using the plays by Goethe as his guide, McGrath at first took a global approach in describing how Freud had acted-out his identification with Faust. He wrote (p. 91) that Freud was guided in his life by a Faustian model: "The hero of Goethe's drama personified the scientist who approached nature.." by plumbing nature's depths as if pursuing "an erotic quest." The implication is that Freud's obsession with sexuality in his work was partly imitative of Faust's erotic orientation (which did not exclude sodomy, by some accounts).

McGrath remarked that Freud's journey south into Italy in 1897 was somewhat imitative of Goethe's *Faust* in which "the hero undertook a similar journey." For both Freud and Faust these represented voyages of discovery into the unconscious mind. Also, McGrath cited Freud's epigram 'Where id was shall be ego,' as if this intellectual quest were similar to a project of land reclamation. Indeed, Freud said that analytic therapy was a cultural labor comparable to the draining of the *Zuider Zee*, McGrath noted that at the end of one of Goethe's plays the venerable Faust looked toward the sea while thinking about his last great project, the draining of the Zuider Zee. Here again we see that Faust had served as a model for Freud's analytic research. McGrath remarked that: "Faust's efforts to harness the power of the sea and reclaim the land along the Dutch coast ran parallel to his efforts to win control at last over the emotional forces which had for so long ruled his life."

Faust's great quest was to understand his own unconscious mind via a journey into his troubled psyche (hell or id), which Freud tried to imitate by his 1897 journey in Italy and by his self-analysis. With that 1897 journey, he imitated both Hannibal and Faust, and himself—regarding his painful journey away from nanny in 1859. Parenthetically, when Freud referred to the Zuider Zee this was his use of name magic to symbolize the most important "Z" in his life, namely Monica Zajic, and later I'll discuss that often he used place names (Rome) to make unconscious references to her. (Here, Zee equals "sea," a mother symbol.)

Unfortunately, McGrath has noted only the instances when Faust and Freud were involved in culturally uplifting enterprises, which ignores the dark sides of their megalomanic personalities. The Faust legend includes stories about an anti-hero who was continually in rebellion against authority; who held religion in great contempt and consorted with the devil and demons who served him; who indulged in black magic and magical thinking as an escape from sterile rationalism (and reality); and was widely regarded as a sodomist who indulged in "the most dastardly forms of lewdness." In Marlowe's drama, Faust went to Rome where he made himself invisible and played nasty tricks on the pope. Later, at the German emperor's court he conjured up "the true substantial bodies" of Alexander the Great and his paramour; and later did the same with Helen of Troy whom he took as his own mistress.

It was said that the historical Faust, on more than one occasion, had referred to the devil as his "crony" or "brother-in-law," signifying his great intimacy with Satan that later became a firm element of the literary tradition. Goethe's plays portray Faust's extended and complex relationship with the devil (Mephistopheles) and continue the tradition that Faust was involved in a pact with the devil. What McGrath has ignored, along with the great majority of Freud biographers, is that Freud consolidated his fantasy identification with Faust by making an uncanny imitative identification with Satan, and by making several explicit pacts with the devil. Freud openly acknowledged his fantasy identification with Satan to his own Viennese disciples on at least two occasions (though he did not confess the pacts he'd made), all of which is covered in my tenth chapter.

The subject of Freud's identification with Satan and indulging in Satanic pacts seems to be under a firm taboo by Freud biographers, perhaps because this topic can expose indications of his recurrent periods of deep depression, madness, and murderous inclinations. However, Velikovsky, Bakan, Vitz, and Swales have offered some material about this general area in their writings. In an article reinterpreting some of Freud's dreams, Velikovsky (1941) was the first writer to briefly raise the idea that Freud had engaged in a Satanic or Faustian pact. Then, in his fascinating book about Freud's ties to the Jewish mystical and Gnostic traditions, David Bakan

(1958) provided extensive biographical materials showing Freud's identification with the devil and his indulgence in Satanic pacts. Subsequently, many authors have referred to numerous segments of Bakan's book, but they have taken great pains to ignore or suppress his lengthy discussions about Freud's identification with the devil! Vitz (1988) is not one of these authors and has cited the writings of both Velikovsky and Bakan in elaborating his own ideas about Freud's Satanic pacts in two excellent chapters concerning "Freud and the Devil."

Vitz' book reflects awareness that Freud's identification with Faust had caused him to imitate the medieval necromancer when this Viennese doctor formulated his identification with the devil and the concomitant Satanic pacts. But Vitz offered a quite specific example of Freud's acting-out of his identification with Faust (as portrayed in Goethe's work), an example which Vitz credited to the research of Peter Swales. This has to do with the fact that Freud first took cocaine, at age 27, on the night of April 30, 1884, an evening called *Walpurgisnacht* that is as well-known in some European regions as Halloween is in America.

This arcane evening called *Walpurgisnacht*—associated with witches and Satanic rites—is celebrated (by adults, not children) in many parts of Europe, and in rural areas it is dreaded by superstitious people. Vitz pointed out that in taking cocaine in liquid form as a 'brew' *on that uncanny evening*, Freud was acting-out his identification with Faust. Specifically, Vitz stated that: "In doing this, Freud, who took the drug in liquid form (as a 'brew') was clearly imitating Faust in his pact with Mephistopheles." It occurred to Vitz that this imitation might have been "primed" by the fact that in 1884 Goethe's play *Faust* was "the talk of Vienna" after a series of performances at the Burgtheater. (Vitz offered some other interesting evidence that Freud's cocaine behavior was imitative of Faust, but it is too complicated to summarize here.)

Since Vitz and Swales have emphasized this connection between Freud's initial imbibing of a cocaine brew and his identification with Satan, I will add that these factors were also connected with Freud's revengeful and murderous impulses (his supposedly "accidental" killings of various people with cocaine). In a later chapter, and in *Dark Side*, I will explain that "cocaine" had a quite magical, lethal significance in Freud's psyche, in terms of name magic. It is germane that this substance's name encodes the name of Cain with whom Freud identified as the world's first murderer and as the originator of fratricide (pertaining to my thesis about the deaths of Emanuel and John).

Having made a thorough study of literary references in Freud's work, Vitz concluded (p. 107) that Goethe's Faust was the literary work that was most frequently cited in Freud's writings. Vitz added that "it was the piece of literature that most powerfully influenced him throughout his life." So it should not be surprising that Freud—so susceptible to acting-out his fantasy identifications—would have imitated Faust's pacts by concluding one or more Satanic pacts of his own.

Historically, it was Velikovsky (1941) who first suggested that Freud had entered a devil's pact of some sort. Later, Bakan (1958) posited that Freud's "pact" with the devil was basically a metaphor, or a psychological strategy which Freud used to suspend superego functions so that he could explore his unconscious mind. This seemed to imply that the devil was not real for Freud. Vitz challenged that rationalized view (p. 150) by writing: "But there are sound reasons to believe that there was much more to Freud's dealings with the Devil than Bakan's purely 'psychological' interpretation would suggest—that they started earlier, and had deeper, more complex, and less rationalistic roots." Various arguments and data were provided by Vitz to support "an interpretation of Freud's pact that is more specific and more extensive than Bakan's thesis ... " Thus, Vitz asked his readers to consider that Freud might have signed an actual blood pact with the devil, and explained why he felt that Freud might even have concluded two pacts with the devil at different times in his life (p. 156).

In the fifth chapter I will explore the dualistic (Jekyll/ Hyde) nature of Freud's personality that biographers have not yet recognized, to any great extent. In line with that idea of duality, this writer believes that both Bakan and Vitz are partly correct in their argument with one another. My tenth chapter discloses that Freud did view the devil as a metaphor in much of his mature thinking, but that the primitive side of his nature (Mr. Hyde) caused him, at times, to regard Satan as *a reality* whose deadly intentions needed to be diverted by the negotiation of "pacts." This was connected with Freud's lifelong horrendous belief in various death years (the fear that he would surely die at ages 40, 43, 51, etc.) along with his childish fixations on number magic and Fliess's "periodicity theory" (which stimulated Freud's anxieties about death).

It was interesting for me to read Vitz' thesis that Freud had concluded two Satanic pacts, since I had formed a similar notion (two *or* more pacts) several years before reading Vitz' ideas. In my tenth chapter this view of mine is discussed in terms of Freud's famous explanation (in the book on "slips") of why he "casually" chose the number 2,467—which I expose as relating to a covert Satanic pact, and to Freud's murderous feelings about his brother Emanuel. Also, I explain why it's likely that his bizarre fixation on his new telephone number, near the turn of the century, was also reflective of a hidden devil's pact which he hoped would considerably extend his life.

Since we are investigating ways that Freud might have acted out his identification with Faust, let's consider that a traditional motif in the Faust legends is of Faust's conjuring and materializing a whole series of ancient heroes, including Alexander the Great. Doesn't this suggest that Faust harbored identifications with a long list of power-figures, just as Freud did? And isn't it possible that Faust's tendency towards making power-identifications helped to stimulate Freud's tendency, imitatively?, Let's not ignore that Alexander was one of Freud's heroes as well, and that he persuaded his father to give the name Alexander to his younger brother.

Finally, we need to ponder the most prominent behaviors associated with the dark side of Faust: his continual rebellion against authority; great contempt for religion; indulgences in magical thinking; and preoccupations with "the most dastardly forms of lewdness." One can guess that throughout his lifetime the great necromancer and analyst of Vienna was imitating, to some degree, all those questionable behaviors of Faust. Persons who reflexively insist that an attribution of lewdness to Freud is slanderous nonsense concocted by his enemies are requested to read my proposed volume *Secret Sex Lives: Freud, Jung, and Jones*, before deciding finally whether Freud was a "covert pervert"—along with Jones and Jung.

Many writers have observed that Freud harbored an intense fantasy identification with Moses. However, it appears that McGrath (1986) may be the only author with a clear recognition that Freud had a tendency to act-out aspects of Moses' life story, just as he did with the life of the Biblical Josef (master of dreams). Evidently, Freud was attracted to both of those men, because they were awesome power-figures who started out as humble Jews but then became great men by their associations with the pharaohs of Egypt . Similarly, Freud nurtured a fantasy (which he divulged to Fliess) that he would someday become a great man by healing a relative of the Russian Czar, thereafter becoming wealthy and influential as the Czar's favorite physician.

It was McGrath's view that one of the hidden motives of Freud in writing *The Interpretation of Dreams* was to become the leader of the Jews by liberating their minds via the enlightening contents of that book—thereby imitating Moses' role as the leader and enlightener of the Jews of his era. McGrath argued that while Freud was finishing the book in 1899 his mind was flooded with allusions to Egypt (and Moses), as seen in his letters to Fliess, and that he even referred to his manuscript as "the Egyptian dream book." According to McGrath, those Egyptian allusions pertaining to the final pages of the book "provided an appropriate context for the Moses image which hovered before him in his final self-transformation." More significantly, McGrath observed that: "The most important sense in which Freud acted-out the role of Moses in completing *The Interpretation of Dreams* involved the nature and purpose of its concluding chapter." That final chapter gave him a chance to present a new set of principles to guide his future disciples, "and here he recapitulated the role of Moses as lawgiver to his recently liberated people."

Allow me to reinforce McGrath's view that the final chapter of Freud's dream book represented his acting-out of the role of Moses as the lawgiver and savior of his followers. Several years before I read that idea by McGrath, I had hypothesized (while reading the Freud/Fliess letters) that Freud unconsciously regarded the essence of his "Egyptian dream book" as the equivalent of Moses' journey out of Egypt towards the Promised Land. For in Freud's letter dated August 6, 1899 he described the conceptual structure of his new dream book as having been modeled on "an imaginary walk" that began in the woods. At the start of this walk was "the dark forest of authors (who do not see the trees, hopelessly lost on wrong tracks." On this imaginary walk, Freud led the reader through a concealed pass, representing his specimen dream about Irma's injection, with "its peculiarities, detail, indiscretions, bad jokes.." Then suddenly, on this imaginary walk, the high ground was reached and the question became: "which way do you wish to go now?"

It occurred to me that the image of Moses leading the hopelessly misguided Israelites down into that miraculous passage in the Red Sea (compare with the Zuider Zee) and then onto high ground towards enlightenment and freedom is reflected in Freud's above wording. Here we recognize his retracing of Moses' fateful journey, reminding us of Freud's retracing in 1897 of Hannibal's route towards his great victory at Lake Trasimene. Probably, his fantasied retracing of both of those heroes' journeys were unconscious attempts to heal the effects of Sigi's catastrophic journey away from his nanny in 1859. Especially for a physician in his forties, there is a good deal of grandiosity in these imitations that should at least raise the question of a considerable mental imbalance.

The first chapter mentioned Freud's bizarre essay of 1914 concerning Michelangelo's statue of Moses, a topic that needs to be reconsidered since it represents a rather disturbed example of his acting-out of the identification with Moses. McGrath has noted (1986) that Freud published his 1914 essay anonymously—"presumably because it was so self-revelatory"—and added that: "The theme of imposing emotional control was central in Freud's interpretation of the statue . ." Several authors, including myself, have claimed that Freud was obsessed with the wrathful visage and posture of the Moses statue, because in that era he was struggling to control his murderous feelings towards Jung while their relationship was slowly dissolving.

Clark has noted (1980, pp. 358-9) that after 1901 Freud visited the Moses statue on many occasions, but that it was only in *September 1913* that he became utterly obsessed by it. Freud wrote that the statue became like a "love child" to him, and that every day "for three lonely weeks" in September 1913 he stood in front of the statue studying it avidly. Was he referring to his own possible illegitimacy with that term "love child" and when he wrote about his Moses essay: "Not until much later did I legitimize this nonalytic child."? When he returned to Vienna he read various art books about the statue hoping to find even a weak excuse for believing that Michelangelo had intended that his Moses would withhold his wrath, and would not break the stone tables nor indulge in angry behaviors leading to the slaughter of his disciples. When he was unable to find any clue that the sculptor intended this revision of Biblical history, Freud took the next "illogical" step, responding to the depth and pressure of his own identification with Moses. Making a daring revision of history on his own, he wrote in his essay that his "analysis" of the statue's posture revealed to him that this Moses did not break the tables nor unleash wrath against his disciples.

Clark was correct in writing (p. 359) that Freud's essay on the Moses statue reveals nothing about Michelangelo but "implies quite a lot about Freud." My own position about Freud's strange behavior is this. Since the primitive, infantile part of his mind believed that he was Moses, it gave him permission to revise Moses' actions almost any way that he wished (even though the rational side of Freud must have known that this was only a powerful fantasy). Then, having changed Moses' actions in his own mind, Freud was able to act-out this new version of history by writing about it in his 1914 essay, as if all of this were perfectly rational and deserving of acceptance by others. (However, his insecurity about this matter was seen in his publishing the essay anonymously.)

This is the same psychological strategy that Freud followed in writing his peculiar history about Moses in the 1930s, titled *Moses and Monotheism*. That balmy, embarrassing volume amounts to Freud's acting-out of his omnipotent identification with Moses—or even Moses and Jahweh. Since he believed himself to be Moses, Freud was able to change some vital aspects of Moses' life story in that book. Notice that he changed key significances of Moses' name, just as Freud changed his own given name (from Sigismund to Sigmund) in his teen years. Impelled by his own childish wish to be a member of royalty (favorite of the Czar), he changed Moses' history and made him a true member of the Pharaoh's family. In doing so, he firmly denied that Moses was a Jew, relating to Freud's secret wish to be a gentile that becomes quite apparent in Vitz' book (1988). Contrary to the Biblical account, he claimed that Moses had been killed by his disciples, correlating with Freud's great fears that his own disciples wished to kill him, especially Jung (and with Sigi's Freiberg fears that his brothers wished to kill him).

One writer who seemed somewhat aware of Freud's penchant for acting-out the lives of his fantasy identifications was M. Robert (1976). She wrote that: "Freud lived on terms of natural intimacy with the great figures of the Bible; they were so much a part of his inner life that he felt himself to be by turns Joseph, Jacob, and Moses." Commenting on her statement, McGrath added that what is comparable to Freud's conscious imitation of Joseph appears in a letter he wrote to Jung while they were still allies. McGrath noted that in that letter Freud "compared himself to Moses and suggested that Jung, like Joshua, would lead the Children of Israel into the promised land . ." This points to another acting-out of the Moses identification, and McGrath added that: "Freud also seemed to act-out the role of Moses on other occasions in his later life."

Finally I will cite another astonishing instance when Freud acted-out his identification with Moses, which has escaped the attention of McGrath and other authors. First, we should note that the Biblical story of Moses cites various occasions when he was strongly vexed with the immoral behaviors of his Jewish countrymen, and he is portrayed as openly denouncing them for their sins. It's my view that Freud imitated Moses' denunciations by vicious rebukes that Freud made against the Jews near the end of *Moses and Monotheism*. In effect, he charged that they were the worst kinds of criminals and murderers, seeming almost to resurrect the claims of Christian bigots of former years that the Jews were responsible for the murder of the Christian deity!

Freud cloaked his "Mosaic" denuciation of the Jews in a weak psychological analysis in which he asserted that the desire to kill God has festered in the unconscious minds of all human beings, but that Christians have admitted and atoned for their crime by acknowledging their responsibility for the death of Jesus Christ. In this context, Freud made a brutal accusation against the Jews that they stubbornly refuse to admit the analogue of their ancient "murder of God" (relating to his thesis of the killing of the totemic primal father in prehistory).

Bluntly put, Freud indicated that the Jews were the murderers of God/Moses (the primal father-figure) and implied that this was the source of their great travail throughout the ages. In effect, his denunciation included the advice that the Jews should confess their former murder of God, the ancient father, to allow for the early stages of psychic healing.

There are various interpretations that can be made of this partial Mosaic imitation by Freud, his denuciation of the Jews for their sins (particularly, as murderers of the primal father). One of the interpretations is that this reveals his animosity towards his own people and a covert desire to be a Christian, relating to materials by Vitz and by Father Dempsey which suggest that Freud secretly wished to convert to Christianity. Another interpretation is that Freud's accusation (near the end of his life) amounts to a projection of his former murder of a father-figure in 1914, relating to the strange death of his eldest brother, Emanuel. If so, the secret heart of the dream book was Freud's covert confession that he had urgent wishes to commit parricide (murder of kinsmen), and the heart of his final book—the Moses travesty—was that he had *actually committed* that foul crime.

Numerous authors have written about Freud's strong fantasy identification with the Biblical Josef, the great prime minister of the Pharaoh in Genesis. It has been noted that there were many likenesses that Freud might have used to connect himself with Josef. For example, both men had fathers named Jacob and the Biblical patriarch was a shepherd, which is similar to Jacob Freud's work in the wool trade. The Biblical Josef was placed in Pharaoh's prison for 13 years, whereas Freud's uncle named Josef was given a ten-year sentence in the Austrian Emperor's prison for an offense relating to currency counterfeiting. Both Freud and the Bible's Josef were eldest sons of their fathers' second wives, and both men were their mothers' favorites. There is good reason to believe that both men were badly spoiled by their parents in childhood, and that both suffered from megalomania and pathological ambition.

The Biblical Josef suffered from a murderous attack by his elder brothers, and apparently Freud nurtured a childhood belief that his eldest brothers wished to murder him. Also, Josef was violently separated from his older brothers in childhood, whereas young Sigi experienced a catastrophic separation from his older brothers in 1859. The Hebrew myths describe Josef as having a charming, effeminate manner, and Freud was said to have a slight build and effeminate characteristics. Young Josef was subjected to a very aggressive sexual intimidation from an older woman (Potifphar's wife), and Sigi was sexually molested by his nanny. There are other similarities between Josef and Freud that might be mentioned, and some of these can be found in Shengold's essay "Freud and Joseph" (1979).

Authors like McGrath (1986) and Sulloway (1979, p. 478) have been quite aware that the primary way that Freud acted-out his fantasy identification with the Biblical Josef, the ancient world's "master of dreams," involved Freud's strenuous efforts to achieve fame as master of dreams in the modern era. However, readers who are sticklers for detail might feel let down, since it seems that Freud did not attempt to imitate Josef's exact approach to dreams, i.e. using dreams to prophesy precise aspects of future events. Or did Freud initially hope to accomplish a similar predictive feat with dreams, later downgrading his interpretations of dreams towards less spectacular clinical uses involving elucidation of emotional conflicts?

Emphasis should be given to the fact that Josef became famous by employing dream interpretations to foretell important future happenings—using dreams of two fellow inmates in prison to predict precise aspects of their destinies, and later using Pharaoh's dreams to make accurate predictions concerning seven years of economic abundance, followed by seven years of famine. Is there any shred of evidence suggesting that perhaps Freud hoped to imitate Josef's awesome prophetic powers with dreams? The eminent historian Sulloway's research (1979, p. 321) shows that long before the middle 1890s, when Freud began to recognize that dreams had a psychoanalytic application, he had an avid interest in dreams and various ways of interpreting them. Indeed, Freud had been a copious dreamer even in his early years and had filled up notebooks with his own dreams during his medical school days (the 1870s) "and perhaps even earlier." Sulloway added that: "In these notebooks he had systematically analyzed dreams as possible portents of the future." Ergo, isn't it likely that this young man Freud was trying to imitate Josef's prophetic powers with dreams in order to achieve the sudden fame and fortune that his hero had attained? (This is another example of the hidden, ubiquitous magical thinking that never left Freud's mind.)

Freud's fantasy identification with Napoleon's general named Masséna can also be regarded as an acting-out of the earlier identification with the Biblical Josef, abetted by both Freud's penchant for name magic and birthday magic. Freud mistakenly assumed that Masséna was a Jew and thought that his surname was a variant of the Hebrew name Manasseh. In Freud's mind, that caused the general to become a magical equivalent of the eldest son of Josef in Egypt, whose name was Manasseh and by tradition was the founder of the tribe of Israel. The identification with this general was also assisted by Freud's identification with Napoleon, and by the fact that Masséna shared Freud's birthday (though he was born about a century earlier).

Several comments were made by Schur (1972), Freud's personal physician for many years, that birthdays had various magical significances for the master throughout his lifetime. Often they were associated with his strong fears of dying, perhaps relating to ambivalent feelings about both his paternity and his dual birthdate—May 6th versus March 6th. In *Dark Side* I have discussed in detail that the number he once chose to explain his theory of psychic determinism—2,467—was reflective of a rather bizarre Satanic pact that was very frightening to him. When he was age 43, the preceding number was laden with death fears tied to the additional number of years of life then "allotted" to him (24), since 24 and 43 equals 67! And this number 24 also symbolized the catastrophic events that had occurred to him between ages 2 and 4 when his nanny had been jailed/murdered. All of these numerical fantasies by Freud compelled him to "arrange events" so that he was placed in jail on his 24th birthday. (I assume that this involved an unconscious compulsion, in league with birthday magic.)

Jones mentioned (1953, p.55) that in 1880 Freud was undergoing compulsory military training. Because he failed to attend eight military sessions in succession, he was sentenced by the commanding general for being absent without leave and spent his 24th birthday in a military jail. This enabled him to act-out his identifications with his nanny and his uncle Josef, both of whom spent long periods in prison. With regard to the latter name, Josef, we can guess that this self-imposed jailing by Freud on his 24th birthday likewise enabled him to act-out the identification with his hero, the Biblical Josef, and Jesus as well, since both spent time in prison. Since the imprisonments of both these heroes preceded their glorious triumphs, especially Jesus' victory over death, it is plausible that Freud would act-out his identifications with both men by having himself put in jail briefly—in the era just preceding his orgiastic cocaine binges. He used those binges to counter his own death fears and to express his hatred and rage towards humanity via his "accidental" cocaine killings.

Attention has been called by McGrath (p. 57) to the possibility that occasionally Freud might have effected conscious actings-out of his Josef identification. McGrath supported that viewpoint by mentioning Samuel Rosenberg's citation of an incident in which: "Freud concealed two Egyptian statuettes in Karl Abraham's briefcase in a manner similar to that of the Biblical Joseph who had had his silver goblet concealed in the sack of his brother Benjamin, when he came to Egypt to get grain." Concerning this strange imitation by Freud of the Biblical Josef, McGrath commented that here "Freud consciously moved in Joseph's footsteps" and that his early dream of the Egyptian "bird-beaked figures reveals that he had begun moving in those footprints as a child."

Whether or not the preceding imitation of Josef was conscious, it deserves further discussion for it probably was laden with horrific meaning for Freud and his older brother Emanuel. This imitation occurred in December of 1907, and was mentioned by Karl Abraham in his letter to Freud dated December 21, 1907. This was a few days before Christmas, which must have stimulated Freud's thoughts and feelings about Emanuel whose birthday was on Christmas day (birthday magic, again). That Freud secretly had slipped two Egyptian statuettes into Abraham's briefcase, which the latter discovered when he arrived home, did not involve a simple Christmas gift but has an ominous portent that is relevant to my thesis that Freud continued to harbor a murderous grudge against his older brother. Let me explain this by discussing the significance of Josef having secretly slipped a silver goblet into his brother Benjamin's sack when he came to Egypt with his older brothers to obtain additional grain.

In the story of Josef and his brothers, the first phase involved the murderous rage towards the hero by his ten older brothers which caused them to plot his death by throwing him naked into a pit. Later, they relented and sold him to slave traders who took him in bondage to Egypt where eventually he became prime minister to Pharaoh, after having solved the riddle of Pharaoh's dreams. The second phase of the story occurred during the great famine which Josef had predicted, when nine of his older brothers came to Egypt to buy grain and did not recognize Josef when they were brought before this potentate as suspected spies from Canaan. In a later scene, Josef sent his brothers back to their old father Jacob in Canaan after secretly slipping his awesome silver goblet (a symbol of his prophetic powers) into his brother Benjamin's sack of grain. This was a cruel (but justified) trick which caused the brothers—greatly frightened for their lives— to be hauled before Josef as thieves. After giving them a final test of their motives and of their repentant feelings, he forgave his brothers and heaped treasures on them—thus taking a subtle revenge by lording over them, as his childhood dreams predicted someday he would.

It's my contention that in December 1907 Freud imitated the above silver goblet scenario, because at that late date, when he was age 51, he was still gripped by a grotesque desire to obtain revenge upon Emanuel by arranging for his murder. At age 51 Freud was suffering from an intense fear that he would die in that year, for Schur (1972) has explained that age 51 was the most monumental of the death ages that terrified Freud. Ergo, he attempted to ameliorate that death fear by displacing it magically via his archaic death wish against Emanuel, whom he still blamed for "abandoning" him in 1859 and for jailing/murdering his beloved nanny. Like Josef in Egypt, he still desired to obtain a cruel revenge against his eldest brother for having "killed" him in childhood by the suffering inflicted on Sigi.

But Josef softened *his* need for revenge, since his older brothers passed a special test and showed true repentance, whereas Emanuel Freud was not able to do anything to assuage his young brother's hidden and irrational desire for revenge against him (which may have been consummated in 1914 via murder). Was there any special reason why Freud chose Karl Abraham as his surrogate for Emanuel while acting-out his imitation of the scenario about Josef's goblet? In December 1907 Freud and his new disciple were in the earliest days of their relationship, so it is doubtful that he'd already learned anything about Abraham's behaviors or background that made him an appropriate surrogate for Emanuel in this goblet scenario.

But consider that Emanuel was regarded by Sigmund as a great father-figure, since the latter had clearly expressed the wish in earlier years that Emanuel, not Jacob, had been his real father. Therefore, we detect another example of unconscious name magic in Freud's life allowing Karl Abraham to serve unconsciously as a father-figure and as representative for Emanuel Freud. Consider that the name Abraham symbolizes the greatest father-figure in Jewish history, the patriarch of Genesis whom some persons suspect harbored a powerful wish to murder his own son (but was dissuaded from doing so by "the voice of God").

In the previous chapter I offered the thesis that the Freiberg catastrophe (nanny in the chest or coffin) had generated young Sigmund's fantasy that his older brother desired to murder him. If so, that corrosive fantasy (which perhaps paved the way for two murders in 1914 and 1919) may have been stoked by Freud's early embracing of his fantasy identification with the Biblical Josef. The suggestion here is that Sigmund progressively acted-out Josef's knowledge of the murderous intentions of his older brothers by attributing the same lethal intention to his older "brothers" Emanuel and John, the latter having acted as a brother-figure for Sigi while stimulating immense feelings of "sibling rivalry" and revenge.

Evidently, Freud regarded the land of Egypt as symbolic of the underworld, or the unconscious mind. Shengold has indicated (1979) that Josef's "conquering" of Egypt signified that he had become the master of the unconscious mind (via his mastery of dreams). These trains of thought suggest that this was another way that Freud acted-out his identification with Josef, i.e. by becoming the explorer and master of unconscious functioning while developing a keen understanding of dream interpretation and the "structure" of dreams. (By the way, medieval allegorists often assumed that in Genesis the land of Egypt symbolized humanity's lack of freedom and ignorance, which can be interpreted as references to the unconscious mind and repression.)

McGrath's suggestion that perhaps at times Freud made conscious imitations of his identification with the Biblical Josef brings us to a letter which Freud wrote to the famous novelist Thomas Mann in November 1936. In May of that year Mann had given a lecture in Vienna titled "Freud and the Future" to help celebrate the master's 80th birthday. A meeting was then arranged between Freud and Mann, and they had a long talk focusing on Josef and Moses, since Mann was then writing his Josef series of books and Freud was about to publish his Moses book.

In his lecture at Vienna in 1936 Mann discussed the concept of identification and noted that in his novel *Joseph in Egypt* the primary theme concerned life as a succession of moving in others' footsteps (fantasy identifications with others). Also, his novel had stressed that this concept of identification could pertain to the "living out" of mythical identifications and themes, which Mann felt could play a large role in shaping the lives of individual human beings. In general terms, Mann remarked that this concept might even have applied to Freud's own life.

Freud's letter to Mann dated November 29, 1936 referred to that motif of the "living out" of fantasy identifications stated in Mann's previous lecture. He'd been thinking about that topic, Freud remarked, because he had just finished reading Mann's new book about "the Joseph legend." Freud implied that he wished to make a reply to Mann's emphasis in his lecture and to suggest a new theory that might support it. He stated that he'd been pondering whether there was some historical figure "for whom the life of Joseph was a mythical prototype, allowing us to detect the phantasy of Joseph as the secret daemonic motor behind the scenes of his complex life." Disingenuously, he added: "I am thinking of Napoleon I."

Freud supported his theory with certain alleged "facts." He claimed that Napoleon unconsciously nurtured lifelong feelings of murderous rivalry towards his eldest brother, named Joseph, and that eliminating Joseph (by becoming Joseph himself) must have been Napoleon's strongest childhood emotion. (This indicated that a mixture of sibling rivalry and name magic had effected a "mythical identification.") Also, he claimed that Napoleon probably married a young widow because her name was Josephine (name magic, again) consolidating his connections with his brother and with the Biblical Joseph.

Furthermore, Freud suggested that Napoleon's famous expedition to Egypt was an acting-out of his identification with Josef in Genesis. Freud wrote about Napoleon's Egyptian campaign: "Where else could one go but Egypt if one were Joseph and wanted to loom large in the brothers' eyes?" Then Freud seemed to imply that when Napoleon "took care of his brothers," by making them kings and princes of various countries, he was acting-out the Biblical Josef's eventual largesse towards the brothers whom he'd forgiven for attempting to kill him and selling him into slavery. Finally, Freud argued that near the end of his career Napoleon abandoned his Joseph myth by repudiating his wife Josephine, which provoked the start of his decline and acts of self-destruction that ruined him.

Most readers will recognize easily that Freud's letter to Mann indicates his conscious awareness that Napoleon and he had been compelled to act-out their fantasy identifications with the Biblical Josef. That Freud was consciously aware of at least some of his own imitative tendencies concerning Josef is reflected in the dream book (1967, p.522) when he wrote that the name of Josef played a great part in his dreams, and that his ego easily hid behind people with that name "since Joseph was the name of a man famous in the Bible as an interpreter of dreams."

In M. Robert's review (1976) of Freud's preceding letter to Thomas Mann about Napoleon's imitations of Josef, she was well aware "that Freud was actually speaking of himself in his subtle analysis of an extraordinary destiny" and, in doing so, was resuming the confession that he had hidden "between the lines" of his dream book. I agree with her that Freud was making a subtle confession about himself in his analysis of the primary reason for Napoleon's fixation on Josef (which amounted to a projection of Freud's murderous conflicts concerning his oldest brother Emanuel).

Notice Freud's claim that Napoleon felt "an elemental, unfathomably deep hostility" for his oldest brother Joseph "for which in later life the expressions 'death wish' and 'murderous intent' may be found appropriate." Actually, Freud gave a rather weak explanation for why Napoleon developed a desire to murder his eldest brother, which hints that this was largely a projection of Freud's desire to kill Emanuel. In any case, it seems clear that Freud was making a veiled confession that he once shared Napoleon's (alleged) burning desire to kill the older brother. Freud indicated that the Corsican general had used reaction-formations to reverse this hatred, turning it into love for the older brother, which probably was also true of Freud's adult feelings for Emanuel—affectionate feelings that glossed over lethal ones. One suspects that Freud's real confession here, dimly sensed by M. Robert, is that his underlying murderous hatred for his eldest brother finally broke through (in 1914).

Now let's turn to Freud's fantasy identification with the Biblical Jacob, and his acting-out behaviors relating to that figure. Various authors including McGrath (1986) have written about Freud's identification with the Biblical Jacob, which was fostered by Freud's susceptibility to name magic. That is, given his identification with Josef, we notice that both men had fathers named Jacob. Also, Krüll (1986) suggested that Jacob Freud probably identified with the Biblical Jacob himself and secretly encouraged Sigi to identify with Josef. If so, perhaps the boy's next step was to identify with the classic image of Jacob, as a more powerful and attractive version of his lowly Viennese father (whom he felt was a coward).

My contention is that Freud became the master of dreams, generally, as an imitation of Josef, but that his imitative identification with the Biblical Jacob was the most potent reason for his development of the wish-fulfillment theory of the origin of dreams. This contention that Freud was acting-out his identification with the Biblical Jacob when he created his special version of the wish-fulfillment theory of dreams will require me now to provide some background to support my viewpoint.

Some of Freud's modern disciples would like us to adopt the fiction that Freud was the sole creator of the wish-fulfillment theory of dreams. This shabby legend has been greatly weakened by Ellenberger (1970) and by Sulloway (1979), the latter pointing out that in the dream book the master had cited seven modern authorities on dreaming, especially Griesinger, who had anticipated him on the idea of wish-fulfillments in dreams. Sulloway noted that the psychiatrist Wilhelm Griesinger in a work dated 1861 had asserted that dreams and psychoses share the common factor of being "the imaginary fulfillment of wishes." In his 1979 book Sulloway seemed to concede that Freud did not owe a huge debt to Griesinger for this wish theory by assuming graciously that Freud first read the latter's work on dreams several years after developing his own theory. That generous assumption by Sulloway is one he might decide to retract, if he gets a chance to read my sixth chapter's discussion about Freud's probable plagiarism of Josef Popper's crucial dream-conflict theory.

I do not doubt that Freud was influenced by the writings of those modern authorities while he was formulating his own expanded wish-fulfillment theory of dreams in mid-1896 (when he first attempted to analyze the landmark dream called "Irma's injection"). However, it's my thesis that in 1896 there was another great authority on wish-fulfillments in dreams who had a more potent influence on Freud's thinking because of the master's irrational identification with him. I'm referring to the Biblical Jacob, although most of my readers may be quite unaware that ancient Jacob had propounded such a theory, tacitly. Indeed, Freud did not mention this, nor have his modern disciples done so—which seems a very strange omission or blind spot by Freud and his biographers.

Yes, Freud did acknowledge in the dream book (1967, p. 167) that there was one man in antiquity who had anticipated his idea of deriving dreams from wishes—a physician named Herophilus who lived under Ptolemy I. But how did Freud "forget" that the Biblical Jacob had also propounded, in his own quiet way, a wish-fulfillment interpretation of dreams? Isn't it strange that Freud honored this Egyptian physician (as he honored an *Egyptian Moses*), while failing to acknowledge the ancient wisdom of his own people?

In Genesis the story of Josef tells us that this shepherd boy became involved in intense sibling rivalry (Adler's concept) with his elder brothers, who hated him because he was the obvious favorite of their father Jacob. (Evidently, they feared that someday he would steal their father's "blessing"—magical power—as Jacob had contrived to do himself with *his* rivalrous brother.) This brings us to Josef's two dreams which caused his brothers' hatred to become so murderous that eventually they sold him into slavery.

The Bible makes clear that Josef's first dream revealed that he wished to have dominion over his eleven brothers, and that its symbolism was easily understood by them. In this dream Josef and his brothers were binding sheaves in a field, and suddenly his sheaf stood upright, while their sheaves gathered around it and bowed down to his sheaf. Naturally, his brothers became enraged by the obvious meaning of this dream. In Josef's second dream, the sun, moon, and eleven stars were bowing down to Josef! When Jacob heard the contents of this dream, he rebuked him and said: "Shall I and your mother and your brothers indeed come to bow ourselves to the ground before you?"

Obviously, the patriarch Jacob did not regard dreams as utter ideational nonsense, instead employed a symbolic approach to their interpretation, and recognized that wishes often were at the core of dreams. He was an excellent Freudian dream interpreter in the surety with which he analyzed Josef's dream and exposed it as a wish-fulfillment involving power-strivings (Adler's theme, again). In my view, there is ample evidence here that Freud, even in his childhood, could have begun vaguely to formulate his wish-fulfillment theory of dreams on this template, as an acting-out of his identification with the Biblical Jacob.

But is any evidence available to suggest that in 1896, at the time of the Irma Dream's analysis and the formulation by Freud of the wish-fulfillment theory, an imitation of ancient Jacob had become prominent in Freud's psyche? Indeed, in Eissler's work (1971, p. 183) he recounts that Freud was reading a novel *Niels Lyhne* that deeply impressed him, at the exact time that he was developing his wish-fulfillment theory of dreams. And this book by J.P. Jacobsen "clearly speaks of the wish fulfillment of dreams," according to Eissler (although Freud "neglected" to use this reference in his bibliography). Notice that name magic might have been operating in Freud's suppression of this author's name, Jacobsen, which is easily translated as "Jacob's son." Thereby, it provoked Freud's fantasy that he, as Jacob's son (with its dual meaning), had the right to "steal" the wish-fulfillment theory from his ancient patriarch.

Accordingly, in 1896 Freud was inspired to "steal his father's blessing" (ancient Jacob's wish theory), at the same time that he was impelled to "steal" (plagiarize) another crucial aspect of his dream theory from an old man named Josef—none other than Josef Popper, the sage of Vienna. In chapter six I will explain why I feel sure that Freud did steal that critical dream concept from Josef Popper (whose surname can be translated loosely as "papa" or "father"), although Freud cleverly denied that he had committed this key act of plagiarism. By the way, both of those conceptual thefts by Freud can be regarded as his acting-out of the Biblical Jacob's famous stealing of his father's blessing (the story of the wolf in sheep's clothing).

Probably, all of the above material is related to the fact that in mid-1896 Freud was making regular visits to the deathbed of his father Jacob, who died in October 1896. This must have fit together, ironically and allegorically, with images of the Biblical Jacob's visit to his father's deathbed at the time of that stealing of a special, magical gift from the blinded old man. If so, the time became just right for Freud's stealing of conceptual "dream gifts" from two men named Jacobsen and Josef Popper. (We should ponder Freud's dream about his dead father indicating "it is necessary to close the eyes.")

The story of the shepherd Jacob's changing of his name perhaps was imitated by Freud, in one way or another. In that famous legend Jacob wrestled all night with an angel (or demon) who finally conceded defeat and gave him a special gift by changing his name to the great "power name," Israel. Freud's changing of his name was somewhat less dramatic. He'd been born with the name Sigismund and was known by that name at school through most of his adolescent years. Clark noted (1980, p. 36) that in mid-1875 at age 19 he began to sign his letters with the name Sigmund in his regular correspondence with his friend Silberstein. A guess was made by Clark (and others) that this name change at age 19 was prompted by the fact that "Sigismund" was the favorite name in Vienna "for abuse in anti-Semitic jokes." If so, that was only one motive for Freud's name change.

Authors with a knowledge of name magic among the ancient Hebrews and orthodox Jews in the present era have suggested that Freud's changing of his name might correlate with their belief that it is health-inducing to change the names of persons who are very sick. Perhaps that was partly Freud's motive as well, since he changed his name at age 19, which was the same age when one of his male first-cousins living in Breslau was declared insane. The number 19 was a highly charged and magical one for Freud, as seen by some quite strange reasons he had for choosing and living for 45 years at Berggasse 19. (See my discussion of this matter in *Dark Side*.)

If I'm correct that, to some extent, Freud's changing of his name Sigismund to Sigmund was an unconscious imitation of the Biblical Jacob's appropriation of a great power-name, we should note that Freud's name change involved a suppression of the middle element "is." My view is that this represented a shortened version of the name Israel, or "Is." This further extended his identification with the patriarch Jacob while attempting magically to expropriate his strength, fame, and the privilege of purloining his wish-fulfillment theory of dreams without fear of psychic retribution for this plagiarism.

There is another interesting way that Freud probably made an unconscious imitation of the Biblical Jacob. In the story of Jacob, a murderous hatred existed between Jacob and his twin brother Esau, because Jacob had contrived to steal their father's "blessing." (It's magical powers are related to the fact that these characters were viewed as humble humans, and at other times as mythological demi-gods by allegorists.) Later, Jacob escaped from Esau's wrath by fleeing into exile to work with his kinsman named Laban, who did not worship the God of Jacob's father but became a godlike, father-figure to Jacob. For 20 years Jacob worked hard for Laban, married his daughters Leah and Rachel (in a polygamous family), and grew prosperous by acquiring many animals and servants. Finally, Jacob decided to return to his homeland to make a fearful reconciliation with Esau, and covertly slipped away from Laban's domain, because he feared that Laban (like

Pharaoh later, in Moses' story) would not willingly permit Jacob and his people to be free of his domination. Soon after Jacob and his family left Laban's territory, Laban and his men stormed after them. And after catching up with Jacob, Laban furiously accused him of disloyalty and of an offense that would demand a fatal punishment—the stealing of Laban's household gods (which were symbolic of his power and authority).

Jacob vigorously denied this accusation, not realizing that he, as head of his household, was responsible for this thievery (analogous to unconscious theft). For he did not recognize, consciously, that the household gods (graven idols) had been stolen by Rachel, who cleverly concealed them from Laban's search of her tent by placing them in a camel's saddle and *sitting* on them (mental suppression). This was a later version of Jacob's stealing of his father's "blessing" with the help of a scheming female (Rebekah), which points to Jacob's propensity for thievery by shrewd manipulations—again, the wolf in sheep's clothing. With regard to the effects of name magic in Freud's life and the name Rebekka, new data (Krüll, 1986, pp. 96-7) suggests that Jacob Freud had a third, little-known wife named Rebekka; it seems that the Freuds and their friendly biographers have tried to conceal the existence of this woman, and in my later works I will suggest the probable, embarrassing identity of this woman.

As is true of many repetitive episodes in the Old Testament, the story about the stealing of Laban's household gods (small statues) is a precursor of the alleged stealing of Josef's magical silver cup (the Grail story?) by his kinsmen—which we have seen that Freud imitated by covertly placing small Egyptian statues in the briefcase of Karl Abraham. Now we can see that Freud's action may be regarded as a composite of the previous two Bible anecdotes: the stealing of Josef's cup and the stealing of Laban;s gods. So we need to ask whether there were any other ways that Freud might have imitated the expropriation of Laban's gods.

My view is that there are at least two ways that Freud effected imitations of the stealing of these "profane" gods, by Jacob. The first way involved Freud's compulsion to make fantasy identifications with gods that are regarded as profane by religious Jews. These included Freud's fairly well-known identifications with Jesus, Zeus, Jupiter, and Juno. To this list I've added his probable identifications with Ananke (goddess of fate or death), Sigi (kinsman of Odin and Thor), Mars, and Sige (the Hebrew Gnostic deity whose lower form is called Hystera).* The second way that Freud imitated Jacob's thefts of valuable properties owned by others related to recurrent accusations throughout Freud's lifetime that he plagiarized the work of other people (Neitzsche, Schopenhauer, Janets, and many others), about which

---

*The latter name's similarity to "hysteria" is obvious, and must have had profound effects on Freud's imitative tendencies.

his followers have made numerous unconvincing denials. This issue of plagiarism is discussed repeatedly in my four volumes about Freud.

The fifth chapter will list a series of balmy "scientific" notions that Freud championed during his lifetime, which show that his useful creative ideas often were struggling mentally with currents of madness that had covert connections with his childhood conflicts or with factors pertaining to his irrational fantasy identifications. It's my guess that his imitation of the shepherd Jacob's wish-fulfillment theory of dreams—which received high critical acclaim in some clinical quarters—encouraged Freud to imitate another "scientific achievement" that may be credited to the shepherd Jacob, extending this fantasy to quite bizarre lengths in defiance of reasonable scientific credibility.

The anecdote about Jacob that I believe Freud continually was imitating pertains to the story of how Jacob outwitted Laban by using a trick to siphon off great numbers of his cattle, sheep, and goats. At the outset, Jacob struck a deal with Laban whereby he would no longer receive wages for his work tending Laban's flocks, but would be allowed to keep all new animals that were striped, spotted, or mottled (which seemed to favor Laban, since speckled coloration was said to be unusual in those days). Although Laban used deceit by removing all speckled and black animals from the herds right after making this contract, Jacob used a deceit of his own.

While Laban's strongest animals were breeding, Jacob set poplar rods in front of their eyes that had been peeled to achieve a streaked or speckled effect. Thus, it was said that the animals bred in front of these ("magical") rods brought forth numerous striped, speckled, and spotted offspring (relating to the belief that females, at the time of conception, could be influenced by visual impressions in ways affecting the color of the offspring). In this sly manner, Jacob's flocks were greatly increased, and Laban's were correspondingly decreased.

My thesis is that Freud imitated the preceding story about Jacob with regard to the master's lifelong championing of the Lamarckian theory, to the consternation and embarrassment of most of his followers. In one of its simplest versions, that theory claims that unique sensory impressions or traumas received by female animals during conception can somehow induce corresponding genetic effects, thereby seeming to correspond with the "theory" employed by Jacob to produce dramatic effects which increased the frequency of speckled animals in Laban's herds.

Freud accepted this Lamarckian doctrine in many ways, even endorsing Ferenczi's bizarre idea that global traumatic events (Example: the Ice Age) in early history had produced deep mental effects in human beings that were then somehow transmitted unconsciously to all future generations. Even after decades of scientific research had thoroughly discredited the Lamarckian hypothesis, Freud continued stubbornly to believe in it—in itself a sign that it had irrational roots in his mind that perhaps went back to his childhood immersion in the Bible stories with his lost nanny.

Clark has noted (1980, p. 524) that both in the Moses book and *Totem and Taboo* the inheritance of acquired characteristics, basic Lamarckianism, was central to Freud's arguments and "was held to account for the continuation of guilt in Jewish history, transmitted through generations of descendants." Similarly, Sulloway has remarked (1979, pp. 440-1) that in Jones' biography the Welsh analyst "psychoanalyzed Freud's Lamarckian gullibility" by relating it to his learning from the Bible in childhood that God punishes the iniquity of the fathers by afflicting their offspring in successive generations (per Freud's belief that mainly guilt and fear are transmitted in this manner).

Of course, I'm amenable to Jones' idea that the Bible was a major source of Freud's Lamarckianism, in the manner described. However, I must add my thesis that Freud's compulsive and magical endorsement of the notion that Jacob had manipulated acquired characteristics to alter Laban's flocks (to attain great wealth) was another Biblical source of his irrational Lamarckianism. This accords with a statement by Freud in his autobiography that: "My deep engrossment in the Bible story . . . had, as I recognized much later, an enduring effect upon the direction of my interest." More explicitly, one might add, the Bible provided Freud with many rational *and* magical ideas that generated profound influences upon his major "scientific works"—which many of his disciples today are loathe to acknowledge.

I believe that there were various other ways that Freud acted-out his identification with the stories of Jacob and his son Josef. However, there is not enough space here to mention all of them, so allow me to mention briefly only one other key imitation of Jacob that I've discussed extensively in *Secret Sex Lives*. That has to do with the well-known allegation that Freud lived a quite unconventional sexual life, despite all the suppression of data that has enabled biographers to portray the master of sexuality as a kind of puritan saint who did not have sex till he was age 30, never sexually abused his patients (in imitation of his own sexual abuse in childhood), never involved his patients in sex with him to obtain special favors from them, etc.—which is at odds with material in *Secret SL.*.

That well-known gossip about Freud's unconventional sexual life derives largely from an accusation by Carl Jung, which implied that Freud lived for years in a *menage á trois* with his wife Martha and her younger sister Minna. All that I will say about that accusation here is that I believe that it is probably true (despite daughter Anna Freud's insistence that this charge is "impossible" and that this three-cornered situation could not have existed, since she had no conscious knowledge of it). In *Secret Sex Lives* I explain that there were many powerful factors in Freud's mind that favored the formation of such a covert, unconventional relationship—which also existed in the lives of many of Freud's ardent disciples in Europe who probably were imitating him. One of those factors pertains to Freud's imitation of the family life of the Biblical Jacob, which is analyzed in some detail in my later work. In the meantime, readers can figure out for themselves a good deal about Freud's probable sexual imitation of the shepherd Jacob by immersing themselves in the relevant pages of Genesis.

Concerning the long list of Freud's fantasy identifications presented at the beginning of this chapter, there are many others I could cite whose life stories (real or fictional) provided elements that Freud apparently acted-out. In most such cases, the imitations by Freud did not seem to be as extensive as with the ones already discussed above, although some of this additional acting-out is quite remarkable and will be discussed in my later writings. One additional instance of Freud's imitations of a fantasy identification figure that did provide extensive material has to do with his unconscious identification with Jesus Christ, especially during the years 1882 to 1886. That material about Freud's strange identification with Jesus, particularly in relation to name magic, is quite complex and requires more than 10 pages of *Dark Side* for a full explanation. Therefore, I hope that Paul Vitz will find my discussion of Freud's Jesus identification interesting and plausible, since it seems quite relevant to his ideas about Freud's "Christian unconscious."

Chapter Four

Freud's Identifications with 20 Murderers

This chapter will examine in considerable detail Freud's fantasy identification with literary characters and real persons who were murderers (as well as some individuals who were strongly suspected of being murderers). A provisional list of some of these 20 figures is as follow: Macbeth; Oedipus; Hamlet; Brutus; Don Juan; Moses; Cain; Satan; the anti-Christ; Fiesco; the Moor of Tunis (Muley Hassan); Franz Moor; Karl Moor; Fanny Moser; and Otto Gross. This chapter's final section is devoted to the claim of Freud's dearest friend, Wilhelm Fliess, that in 1900 Freud formulated a plan to murder him at a resort area called Achensee in the Tyrol mountains (with relevance to his acting-out of a mythic identification).

Some Literary Murderers

Kurt Eissler is an ardent disciple and defender of Freud who seems always ready to portray him as a shining knight with impeccable character traits (no matter how strong the contradictory evidence might be, on any occasion). So it is amusing to observe Eissler's wording (1971, p. 281) when confronted by evidence that Freud had identified himself with the villainous murderer Macbeth. Totally ignoring the fact that Freud had identified himself with many literary characters who were murderers, and making it seem that this was the solitary instance when he had done so, Eissler wrote: "It is puzzling to read that he twice quoted Macbeth, in a way that strongly suggests his identification with that most culpable and wicked of Shakespearean characters." Eissler's slippery rationalizing of this issue did mention that a severe guilt reaction probably was at the core of Freud's identification with Macbeth. However, he evaded the possibility that

Freud's murderous feelings (fully discussed by Max Schur) had engendered those guilt feelings and the identification with Macbeth. Instead, Eissler ingeniously implied that this guilt in Freud arose as a response to his "genius"—a troubled awareness that he had "disturbed the peace of the world"—with no hint about how this could be applicable to Macbeth's guilt feelings.

Eissler noted that the first time that Freud identified himself with the murderous Macbeth was in a letter of August 6, 1878 which he wrote to his friend Wilhelm Knopfmacher, whom he sent copies of his earliest published research papers on neurological topics, long before disturbing the world's peace (which Eissler ignored). Jokingly, he referred to his simple published research as his "collected works," and then predicted boastfully that many more of his works would soon appear, in a long series. He wrote that new research papers "keep appearing in my prescient mind, which is startled by them like Macbeth by the ghosts of the English kings: 'What! Will the line stretch out to the crack of doom?'" At that time he'd not decided between zoology and medicine, and in his next line Freud "joked" that he had moved into another laboratory where he was preparing himself for his "real profession." Quoting the humorist Wilhelm Busch, he described his real profession as "the flaying of animals or torturing of human beings," stating ambivalently that he found himself increasingly in favor of the former. Concerning this "joke," notice that the murderous sadism in young Freud (age 22) was almost palpable, and that it seemed to be connected symbolically with the issue of patricide, via his quoting of Macbeth's guilt-ridden remark.

Concerning Macbeth's guilty remark about the ghosts of English kings, psychoanalysts assert that kings symbolize our primal father-figures, so we can interpret Macbeth's startled comment as reflecting his guilt about the killing of an actual king (Duncan) and his unconscious desire to murder a series of father-figures. In identifying with Macbeth's lethal remark, Freud likewise revealed to us his hidden wish to murder a long series of father-figures in his own life (which becomes evident when one studies Schur's data about Freud's recurrent parricidal urges). Since all of this occurred (in that 1878 letter) in the context of Freud's desire for an infinite number of publications, we can surmise that his pathological ambition was closely connected with the wish to defeat and annihilate a long list of father-figures (including Emanuel).

In the pages that follow we'll see that Freud identified himself with an entire series of literary figures who, like Macbeth, harbored pressing patricidal urges, including Oedipus, Hamlet, Brutus, and Don Juan—as well as Schiller's characters called Franz Moor, Karl Moor, and the vicious nobleman, Fiesco. Let's start our discussion with Oedipus and later we'll review the other literary characters on this list.

Diverse sources have cited Freud's identification with the tragic hero Oedipus. When we remember that young Sigi had been involved in sexual activity with his primal mother (nanny), and that this had enduring effects upon his psyche, it is understandable that this sexual similarity should have helped coalesce an identification with Oedipus in this Viennese lad. However, we can also suspect that a similarity in patricidal urges helped to trigger this identification, recalling that the hero "unwittingly" (unconsciously, one might say) murdered his own father—who happened to be a king and therefore a primal father-figure. And we should not forget that Sigi harbored fears in early childhood that his kinsmen wished to kill him (as an extension of fears that they had killed nanny), which provides another similarity with the hero's story in which his parents ordered that the infant Oedipus should be killed. That order was provoked by a prophecy that when the babe had grown to adulthood he would murder his father, the king—which might be called a self-fulfilling prophecy if one accepts the power of unconscious functioning.

A number of writers, including Holland and Trosman (1972) noted that Freud bore a strong identification with Hamlet, and Krüll (1986, p. 63) has argued that in important respects Freud's "own history resembled that of Hamlet." The plausibility of the thesis that Freud identified with Hamlet is strengthened by the fact that he inserted the notion that Hamlet was himself a "little Oedipus" in his earliest announcement of the Oedipus complex theory. That occurred in his crucial letter to Fliess dated October 15, 1897 in which he cited the jailing of nanny (his first sex partner), and then firmly articulated his new theory: that being in love with the mother and jealous of the father was "a universal event in childhood." Also, he stated that this triangle had occurred in his own life, and then unconsciously equated himself with Hamlet by claiming that the Oedipus complex was the underlying, hidden factor in Hamlet's personality, i.e. the unconscious desire to murder his own father (the dead king whose ghost haunted his mind).

First, it should be emphasized that Freud identified himself with the mentally unstable prince Hamlet who killed King Claudius, the father-figure named Polonius, and his two courtiers, Rosencrantz and Guildenstern. Moreover, Freud's claim that Hamlet wished to murder his own father is based upon a very tenuous premise, as it was explained to Fliess in that key letter (and later in the dream book). Instead, what is suggested is that Freud was projecting his own ferocious desire to murder father-figures (like Emanuel) onto Shakespeare's famous character, Hamlet. Evidently, that awesome patricidal urge had been stimulated, at that same time in October 1897, when Freud had learned from his mother the repressed details of the jailing of his beloved nanny by his elder brothers circa 1859.

In a previous chapter, I have already mentioned Freud's identification with another lethal Shakespearean character, namely Brutus. That he killed the great king Julius Caesar provides the basis for saying that this is another example of Freud's identifying himself with a patricidal figure (though others prefer to stress that he identified himself with a democratic hero who disposed of a tyrant). Young Freud acted-out his identification with Brutus by playing the role twice in school plays. On one of those occasions, his nephew John played the role of Caesar, suggesting that Sigmund was satisfying patricidal and "fratricidal" wishes simultaneously. That fratricidal wishes were involved is also suggested by equating via name magic the names of Julius Caesar and Freud's hated (deceased) brother, Julius.

And now we need to consider Freud's presumed identification with another literary character, the notorious "lady killer" called Don Juan, especially as he is portrayed in Mozart's opera about Don Giovanni. The thesis that Freud bore a peculiar identification with Don Juan has been argued in detail by Marie Balmary in her book *L'home aux statues. Freud et al faute cachée du père* (1979). The core of her idea is that Freud repeatedly attended and was fixated on the Mozart opera, as a reflection of his identification with the figure of Don Juan, especially the scene in which the statue of the Commander—representing a father-figure whom the Don had killed—dragged him down into the fires of hell. (Notice that this makes a convincing correlation with data about Freud's identification with Faust and Satan, with regard to the issue of hellfire.)

Balmary supported her contention that Freud was identified with Don Juan, and was particularly fixated on the scene in which a statue destroyed him, by citing evidence that Freud seemed regularly to effect a partial acting-out of this identification. She remarked that in his customary late dining behaviors in the apartment at Berggasse 19 Freud displayed rather strange mannerisms. In his late dinners with Martha, he typically enforced a doleful silence so that he could gaze with a transfixed stare upon his newest piece of statuary that was placed in front of his dinner plate. It's interesting that Balmary regarded this as an acting-out of Freud's fantasy identification with Don Juan, though she did not seem aware of evidence that he had imitated many other fantasy identification figures.

Furthermore, she did not stress the possibility that Don Juan's prodigious sexual conquests reflected a secret devil's pact (consonant with his being dragged into hellfire), since these pacts were most often entered to obtain sexual conquests, fortune and fame, or extensions of life—all of which provides solid reasons for Freud's identification with the Don, in my view. (See *Secret SL* for a review of the sexual details.) Concerning the central point of this section, it should be emphasized that the Mozart opera portray Don

Juan as the murderer of an obvious father-figure (whose spirit later animated the revengeful statue of the Commander). Here was another major factor (patricide) that compelled Freud to identify with Mozart's portrayal of the arrogant, lascivious Don Juan. Concerning Balmary's thesis that Freud was involved emotionally with a huge, revengeful statue (the Commander), let's recall data which revealed his bizarre emotional preoccupation with Michelangelo's statue of Moses—whose murderous, revengeful qualities Freud tried to soften. (Was that done to save Freud's disciples, or to salvage a Viennese analyst with immense patricidal urges, the master himself?)

Some Biblical Murderers

Since the name of Moses has been mentioned again, it's time to consider Freud's identification with a series of Biblical figures who can be regarded as murderers: Moses, Cain, Satan, and the anti-Christ. Although some religious persons might be offended by my saying that Moses was a murderer, there is little doubt that he did commit one murder and, evidently, was forgiven by Jehovah for this sin. Recall that before Moses led the Jews out of Egypt he was enraged, on one occasion, by an Egyptian overseer who had beaten a Jewish slave. This provoked Moses to slay the bully and to hide his corpse by burying him in the sand. There is good reason to suspect that Freud had identified, in particular, with this murderous side of Moses when we recall his peculiar behaviors with Michelangelo's statue of Moses. With those behaviors he attempted to deny, and even reverse, the deadly aspect of Moses' nature (as a magical attempt by Freud to control his own lethality).

Turning now to the figure of Cain, the possible murder of Emanuel Freud in 1914 raises pressing questions about both patricide and fratricide in Freud's unconscious mind (since his eldest brother was unquestionably a father-figure for Sigmund). The latter crime, fratricide, relates to Freud's unconscious identification with the archetypal killer named Cain—and I have already suggested that this identification via name magic helped to stoke his fixation on that sometimes lethal substance, *cocaine*. It is Max Schur's biography (1972) of Freud that provides the clearest evidence that he was involved unconsciously in an identification with the Biblical Cain, although Schur simply discusses Freud's horrendous fratricidal urges as involving "a Cain complex," on many pages of his informative book.

In the story of Cain and Abel a peculiar element was God's refusal of Cain's food offering, which enraged Cain and led to the murder of his brother Abel. One wonders whether, to some extent, this provoked actings-out by Freud pertaining to his persistent irrational complaints about food, to his occasional fears that he would starve to death, and to his murderous wishes that others would die of starvation. For example, on one occasion he expressed his recurrent bitter hatred for America and its people by wishing that some day all Americans would die due to starvation. These data bring to mind Balmary's claim about Freud's peculiar eating habits at his dinner table, mentioned above. Of course, such weird complaints and behaviors about food suggests the continuing effects of a severe disturbance in the relationship with the primary nurturer, the nanny.

Freud's identification with Cain probably was connected mentally with his identifications with Jacob and Josef, since all of their stories are prominent in the book of Genesis and all three stories have sibling rivalry (Adler) and fratricidal urges as strong underlying themes. That latter theme is blatant in Cain's story, but it becomes more attenuated in the stories of Jacob and then of Josef. In the story of Josef, his brothers' attempted fratricide was ultimately forgiven by the hero Josef. In the story of Jacob, his own murderous rivalry with his twin brother was overcome via the healing power of the magical name (Israel) that an unknown deity (his dark side) gave to Jacob after he had struggled to defeat his own murderous nature. Ergo, Freud may have tried to curtail his own fratricidal urges by changing his name at age 19, and by altering the motive of the Moses statue, though it is doubtful that either of those stratagems or his self-analysis were ultimately effective in controlling his lethal impulses towards Emanuel and John Freud.

As we now proceed with our review of Freud's identifications with Biblical murderers, little will be said here about his uncanny identifications with Satan and the anti-Christ. His identification with Satan, whom religionists regard as the arch murderer of body and soul, was mentioned in earlier pages and is also covered extensively in my tenth chapter. Freud's identification with the book of Revelation's ominous figure, the anti-Christ (often regarded as a counterpart of Satan), has been cited by Vitz (1988) and will also be discussed extensively in a future work of mine (including the possibility that Freud attempted to make eerie actings-out of his identification with this "beast").

Four of Schiller's Murderers

Two of the gory plays of the renowned German dramatist Friedrich Schiller, titled *Fiesco* and *The Robbers*, provided four central characters—all murderers—with whom Freud developed strong identifications. Next to Goethe, Schiller was the playwright and poet for whom Freud displayed the greatest affinity over his long lifetime. The valuable book by McGrath (1986) offers convincing evidence that Freud's mind generated identifications with the major characters of *Fiesco*, namely the treacherous nobleman with that name and his brutal henchman Muley Hassan, and with the main characters of *The Robbers*, the fratricidal and patricidal brothers named

Franz and Karl von Moor.

To help readers understand Freud's identifications with the figures of Fiesco and Muley Hassan (the Moor of Tunis), a very brief summary of *Fiesco* will now be given, one that fails to specify many violent and erotic aspects of its tangled plot. The play centers upon a time of great civil unrest in the city-state of Genoa in the 1500s. The rule of the old, kindly Duke of Genoa (Andreas Doria) is threatened by competing forces that hope to unseat him, and one of the most diabolical of the schemers is the nobleman Fiesco who pretends to be a friend of the Duke while he plots to depose him and snatch the reins of power. Fiesco is described as a man who is filled with dignified pride "and deceitfulness."

In an early scene Fiesco has a discussion with a vile murderer called Muley Hassan who calls himself an honest man, but then tries to kill Fiesco by stabbing him with a dagger. Fiesco disarms the killer and forces him to name the enemies who had employed him to commit the assassination (for a paltry sum of money). Despite his contempt for the Moor, Fiesco then hires him to do his own dirty work at a large annual salary. This sly rascal states that he is ready to do any vicious crime, but prefers not to do any honest work.

Fiesco then hatches a plot to enflame the public against the family of the ruling Duke of Genoa. He pretends that the Duke's family is trying to kill him using the Moor as their assassin, and feigns apprehending this killer again while the latter fakes a second murder attempt, this time in public view. To make this second version of intended murder and apprehension appear authentic, Fiesco requires the Moor to deny his guilt while being tortured (on a very painful machine) by the criminal tribunal until the second degree of torture has been reached. Then he is allowed to "confess," with the assurance that Fiesco will obtain a pardon for him. After this entire deception has been completed, Fiesco is hailed as a benevolent hero by the citizens when he generously pardons the Moor.

Then Fiesco concocts additional plots and begins to gloat when he sees that the balance of power is tipping in his direction. As he contemplates victory and his coming dukedom, he calls himself the greatest man in Genoa while pondering his "fateful ambition." Next, he arranges for mercenaries to be smuggled into the city to assist in a revolution, and the Moor responds to this knavery by saying "We two will pull the state in pieces, and sweep away the laws . . ." To curry favor with his master, he reveals that he has become a double agent and that Fiesco's enemies have instructed him to poison Fiesco's wife. Hearing this news, Fiesco replies angrily: "Fellow, thy villainy deserves a gallows of its own . . ." To this the Moor respond: "The Moor has done his work—the Moor can go." (This line, and the Moor's previous ordeal of torture, are connected closely with Freud's Dream of

Dishonesty, in which he expressed innocence concerning a presumed theft; then walked through a hall that reminded him of an Inferno with torture machines on which a friend was being "stretched out;" then was told he could leave but finally that he could *not* go—which he correlated with that remark by Muley Hassan, i.e. he had done his duty, and "can go.")

Later, Fiesco terminates the Moor's services and hints that he should leave Genoa. In another scene, the old Duke of Genoa exhibits an act of kindness towards Fiesco, who almost has second thoughts about deposing him (indicating that he is slightly ambivalent about his "patricidal" urges). But the plotting cannot be reversed, and in the final act many fearful acts occur as the revolution erupts. In one scene, under cover of night, Fiesco tries to murder one of his enemies, not knowing that his own wife has disguised herself by wearing the man's cloak and hat. He impales her on his sword and later is horrified to learn that his ruthless ambition had made him the unwitting murderer of his beloved wife. In another scene, the Moor is brought before Fiesco for trial, because he had tried to set fire to a convent, during the rebellion. Enraged at this insane act, Fiesco orders that the Moor be taken away and hanged at the church door. The Moor's response shows that Satan is his true master: "Well, if it must be so, the devil may make ready for an extra guest."

The final scene is set in the harbor of Genoa after the revolt has succeeded and Fiesco has been made the new Duke of Genoa. However, one of his co-conspirators begs him to give up the hated dukedom and his immense ambitions, and when Fiesco refuses he is pushed off a dock into the sea, sinks like a stone, and drowns.

In his book reinterpreting many of Freud's dreams, Grinstein (1968) has discussed the play *Fiesco* and specified that its main themes were the tragic consequences of intense ambition and the aggression of man against woman. That is partly correct, but Grinstein failed to emphasize the play's most compelling theme: that many power-driven persons, especially men, are willing to employ even murder to attain their goals, including revenge. (This correlates with a central theme of Genesis in which God portrays power-striving men as essentially treacherous liars and murderers, starting with Adam and Cain.) In fact, there are many murderers in Schiller's play, and prominent among these are the Moor and his master Fiesco.

A number of Grinstein's ideas about how this play relates to Freud's Dream of Dishonesty (the hall with torture machines), and to his basic psychological makeup, are highly questionable. However, I am in full agreement with his ideas that due to many similarities between Fiesco and the Moor "they may be considered as psychologically equated," and that probably Freud was identified with both men. By the way, that notion of the equivalence of Fiesco and his henchman is akin to the literary thesis that

Othello and Iago, for instance, can be regarded as two sides of the same person—and there are interesting parallels between those figures of Shakespeare and with Schiller's duo.

Grinstein cited the following similarities between Fiesco and the Moor: both men "have little regard for loyalty or conscience, are fundamentally dishonest, are ambitious . . .and both ruthlessly disregard the feelings of others in the pursuit of their personal wishes." Moreover, Grinstein noted that the Moor always was ready to commit any crime for whatever price he was offered, while Fiesco was also a ruthless criminal, though on a grander scale. Also, Grinstein observed that both men exhibit serious defects in relating to love objects and would change their loyalties readily to serve personal ambitions, i.e. they were unscrupulous Machiavellian manipulators. Eventually, both men were punished by death for their murderous wishes against father- figures.

Without reservations I can endorse Grinstein's idea that Freud's associations to his Dream of Dishonesty indicate clearly his identification with the murderous Moor in Schiller's play. Grinstein's thoughts on this matter hinted that name magic had helped to precipitate Freud's identification with Schiller's Moor. Grinstein emphasized that Freud's remark about being born with a mass of black hair, prompting his mother to call him "little Moor," indicated his identification with the evil Moor of Schiller's play who was an "unscrupulous, untrustworthy, dishonest figure who spies, bears tales, and readily shifts his allegiance." That identification was further confirmed, Grinstein noted, by Freud's prefatory comments that in the dream *he* was "apparently charged with dishonesty." According to Grinstein: "The theme of dishonesty is the common denominator of the dream and the drama, especially in connection with the characterization of the Moor." (Grinstein, 1968).

Grinstein pointed to key similarities between the play and Freud's Dream of Dishonesty. In the dream, a servant declares Freud to be a respectable person, while in the play the Moor announces (to Fiesco) that he is an honest man. (Was Freud's mind very troubled about criminality in his family?) The dream features torture machines which reminded Freud of a hellish Inferno, while the Schiller play features the torturing of the Moor on a wheel to extract a devious confession from him. Near the end of the dream, Freud was told that he "could go," which meshes with the Moor's words that he'd done his dishonest work and "can go." To these points we should add that Freud's dream makes clear allusions to hellfire, which correlates with the Moor's admission at his hanging that he is ready to descend into hellfire and also reminds us of Freud's pacts with Satan, as well as his connection with Don Juan's descent into hellfire.

Evidently, Grinstein was convinced (and so am I) that Freud had identified himself with the Moor and that his Dream of Dishonesty was closely correlated with the contents of Schiller's play whose themes involved dishonesty, inflated ambition, and treachery. Therefore, it is rather astonishing that Grinstein should write that when Freud's dream assured him he was a respectable person "his associations indicate that for some reason he considered himself dishonest." Those words—"for some reason"—seem unworthy of a man with Grinstein's impressive psychoanalytic credentials, for they suggest that he wished to deny (as if preposterous) Freud's implied self-accusation concerning dishonesty and the underlying issues concerning his identifications with *two* manipulative murderers. This should remind us of Eissler's use of denial about Freud's identification with the brutal murderer Macbeth.

With a similar ring of denial Grinstein asked: "Why should Freud feel identified with the Moor?" His first answer to that question seemed to lay down an ethnic smokescreen by suggesting that Freud's affinity for the Moor was based upon their similar suspicions about the motives of Christians. Seeking deeper reasons for Freud's identification with the Moor, he then noted the dynamic unity between the Moor and Fiesco and placed emphasis on Fiesco's ruthless ambition. Then, pointing to Freud's identification with Fiesco, Grinstein compared the latter's ambitious goals with Freud's desire to become a professor, while ignoring that Freud's pathological ambition aimed at much higher prizes than anything Vienna or Genoa could offer: a worldwide empire.

Grinstein also suggested that Freud shared with Fiesco some wishes of a patricidal nature which could have made him fear that someday he'd be killed (like Fiesco) by a father-figure or his representative. (This should remind us of Balmary's thesis that unconsciously Freud feared being killed by a revengeful statue representing a father-figure.) In any case, Grinstein made these murderous wishes of Freud seem quite remote and pallid by calling them "ancient parricidal wishes." That wording implied that these were Freud's vaguely hostile fantasies, rather than the actively murderous kind that had impelled the Moor and Fiesco to wreak destructiveness against their victims.

In explaining how Freud's identification with Fiesco can help us to understand the former's psychological makeup, Grinstein mentioned Fiesco's "inadvertent" killing of his wife in a murderous attack. Grinstein asserted that: "With this act the hero's aggression against all women . . . breaks out to the fullest extent. We may suspect that Freud's unconscious feelings of anger towards his mother (or nurse) could find expression in his identification with this hero." Again, Grinstein's wording seems intent on persuading us that Freud's destructive impulses towards women were neutralized or buried deeply in the unconscious mind where they could do no harm.

If so, why didn't Grinstein reflect upon Freud's killing of Mathilde (the sulphonal patient) in its possible relationships to his roles in the surgical butchery of Emma Eckstein, which nearly cost her life several times, and the death of Freud's patient Margit Kremzir? Since Fiesco killed his wife, why didn't Grinstein consider Freud's possibly hostile and revengeful feelings towards *his* wife, as indicated by Helen Puner's (1947) claim that their marriage "died" in early middle-age. (She wrote that Freud would not even trust her with the raising of their children, in the event that he should die before she expired!)

To his credit, Grinstein did offer a variety of additional ways that Freud's Dream of Dishonesty and its associations made solid connections with the themes of Schiller's play *Fiesco*. He pointed, for example, to common issues concerning great ambition, forbidden aggressive and incestuous wishes towards a woman, and hostile feelings leading to fears of drastic punishment in Freud's unconscious mind. Unfortunately, Grinstein greatly diluted these issues in their possible application to Freud by his brief and sometimes vague presentation. It is instructive that Anzieu (1986, pp. 320-1) asserted, with regard to *Fiesco*, that "A parallel can easily be drawn between several of the play's themes and Freud's own problems"—which he lists as including problems with ambition, homicidal rivalry towards father and brother figures, betrayal of others, contempt for women, and fears of punishment.

My basic disagreement with Grinstein is that his discussion of the above issues seemed only to distract readers from the most important factor of all. For the truth is that Freud identified himself here with not just one, but two, despicable murderers—the Moor and Fiesco. Not only did he add to the long list of literary murderers with whom he had identified himself, but for the first time he revealed his identification with a conscience-less *professional criminal*. This might cause us to wonder whether his strong identification with Schiller's evil Moor reflects his similar identification with another professional criminal in his own family—his uncle Josef—though he artfully denied this in his dream book.

In the Dream of Dishonesty and its associations Freud revealed that he felt that he was a dishonest man, though Grinstein apparently has concluded (like all good Freudians) that there cannot be any substantial truth in the self-accusation by the master's unconscious mind. (How "loyal" can one be?) Actually, Freud's vague feelings of dishonesty in connection with this dream amount to a smokescreen, similar to the dream of Irma's injection. As with the famous dream about Irma, the Dream of Dishonesty and its associations make only token and vague charges of dishonesty against Freud. It is only via a thorough analysis of the closely related play *Fiesco* that we learn of Freud's identifications with two murderers and that the authentic charge against him (that is both concealed and revealed by the dream) is the charge of intense psychopathic tendencies that do not exclude murder. Now we recognize that the accusations by several authors that the dream book constitutes a secret "confession" by Freud perhaps involves more dramatic charges than previously believed, pointing to a variety of vile crimes including murder.

In his identification with the Moor and Fiesco, Freud revealed many negative aspects of his personality that his followers will simply shrug off and refuse to acknowledge. He told us that he was an unscrupulous, untrustworthy liar and scoundrel—a dishonest, murderous fellow who was capable of spying on others, carrying deceitful tales, and was able to shift allegiances readily to achieve his own selfish ends. Moreover, with regard to the dualistic interplay between Fiesco and the Moor, Freud's identifications with both of those rascals hints broadly at the Jekyll/Hyde structure of his own psyche. However, he seemed to disclose that there was an ample measure of evil in *both* sides of his divided nature.

The second play by Schiller which reflects Freud's identifications with two additional murderers is *The Robbers*, which Schiller wrote when he was only age nineteen and is filled with adolescent bravado, anti-authoritarianism, blood and gore, madness, intimations of incest, and especially flagrant themes of patricide and fratricide. The play's core is the ferocious rivalry that consumes two brothers of a noble family. The older brother Karl Moor is portrayed as handsome and vigorous, while the younger brother Franz Moor is depicted as a wily villain who was born ugly and deformed. The rivalry centers upon their struggle for the inheritance of the vast estate of their old father, Count Maximilian Moor, and their shared love for a beautiful cousin named Amelia who acts as a compassionate nurse to their ailing father. A very condensed version of the play follows.

In the first act, Franz uses deceit to get his aged father to disinherit Karl for his irresponsible vagabond behaviors, which causes Karl to organize a band of debtors who live with him as their captain in the Bohemian forest, in the style of Robin Hood. They become a band of robbers, but initially Karl seems motivated by idealism, for he gives his share of the loot to orphans and other needy persons. Later, the robbers begin to murder and plunder, and even Karl commits murders "in the name of justice." At one point, their rash acts lead to a great fire in a city, killing many innocent adults and children and causing Karl to feel extremely guilty.

At the Moor castle, the old Count is remorseful about his lost son Karl, and in this context the play retells the Biblical tale of Jacob and his lost son

Josef. Franz tries to drive his father into madness and death by convincing him that Karl had died in battle while cursing the old man for abandoning him. The old count falls into a comatose state and Franz entombs him in a dungeon. He proclaims himself the new ruler, and exclaims that his reign will be marked by horrible cruelty and fear. Then he tries repeatedly to seduce Amelia, although she is pure and is his brother's fiancée. In the forest, Karl is told that his father is dead and he blames himself. In a melancholy scene at night he recites verses which allow him to play the roles of Brutus' and Caesar's ghosts in a duologue that reeks with images of patricide. Then he learns that his father is still alive, i.e. although old Moor had been thrust into a coffin by Franz and left to starve, a compassionate servant had brought food and kept him alive. At this point, Franz has ordered a servant to find Karl in the forest and kill him; likewise, Karl orders his robber band to storm the castle in order to murder Franz and sop up his blood.

That night Franz is at the brink of madness, has nightmares, and hears "voices" calling him a murderer. Though he had always scoffed at religion, he asks to see a clergyman named Fra Moser who tells him that the unpardonable sins that God will never forgive are patricide and fratricide. After hearing those dreadful words, Franz runs berserk and strangles himself!

In the concluding scene, Karl frees his father from the dungeon, but his guilty feelings are so overwhelming that he cannot be comforted by the presence of Amelia and his father. Instead, he shouts out to them that he and his robber band have become vile murderers, and in a frenzied state he screams that his father and Amelia must be killed. Hearing this grotesque speech old Moor collapses and dies. Karl then spews out his guilty feelings to Amelia, and she begs him to kill her rather than leaving her again. In his unbalanced state of mind, he stabs her to death and calls her a "sacrificed angel." As the play ends Karl gives himself up to the justice of a lawful tribunal.

Several writers including McGrath (1986) have recognized that this macabre play *The Robbers* had a profound effect upon Freud's mind, over many years. To begin, we see that this play incorporates the scene featuring the ghosts of Caesar and Brutus which Freud acted-out twice during his school years, one of those times being at age 14 when he played Brutus and his nephew John (visiting from England) played Caesar's ghost. Freud's fixation on this play is also supported by McGrath's report of a letter that Freud wrote to his friend Silberstein. In mid-1873 Freud wrote his friend that he had just attended two different performances of *The Robbers* within two weeks, and at two different theaters.

McGrath wrote (pp. 66, 68 ff.) that this play by Schiller "occupied a unique place in Freud's psychic world," and that a careful analysis of the play indicates "why it became a vehicle for the powerful feelings involved in Freud's 'family complex.'" For example, the play incorporates significant references to the Biblical stories about Jacob and his son Josef, which relates to the given name of Jacob Freud (and to his son Sigmund, who was identified with the dream master named Josef). Although McGrath did not specify Freud's great vulnerability to name magic, he wrote insightfully: "The drama's portrayal of the beautiful young Amalia caring for the old father provided a framework into which Freud could easily fit his own family story of an old father with a young wife much desired by the brothers." (p. 69).

In his lengthy analysis of how this play relates to Freud's "family complex" and political ideas, McGrath argued forcefully that Freud identified himself with both brothers, Franz and Karl Moor. Regarding the identification with the ugly younger brother Franz, McGrath (p. 80) mentioned a time when Freud used some of Franz' language from the play to emphasize that he equated himself with this ugly, treacherous fellow (and apparently felt doomed to play that role of a miscreant who eventually commits suicide.). Also, notice that Freud and Franz Moor were alike in their pathological ambitiousness; their murderous feelings towards a brother and father-figure; and their vulnerabilities to psychosis and self-destructiveness. At times, each heard hallucinatory "voices" (Freud's "voices" called his name during his sojourn in Paris). Also, both of them had strong "incestuous" feelings towards maternal figures named Amelia (Amalia).

Additionally, McGrath emphasized that Franz Moor was portrayed as a man who gained success "in his ruthless quest for power by making use of the various scientific and rational advances" of his era—which also seems applicable to Freud. In the play, Franz displayed a "scornful rejection of religious faith" as well as a diligent use of medical knowledge in attaining his pernicious goals. To many persons, the similarities between Franz and Freud will seem quite provocative ones.

Earlier in this volume, it was noted that Freud's perverse dualistic nature sometimes allowed him to make fantasy identifications with persons whose characters or lives seemed strikingly in opposition to one another. Examples of this were his identifications with both Jesus Christ and Satan. Likewise, Freud in his student years identified with Scipio Africanus, the Roman general who defeated Hannibal at his "Waterloo." McGrath has affirmed (1988, p. 46) Freud's strange identification with this Roman general, remarking that "he quite consciously identified with the very man who defeated Hannibal"—based upon work by Gedo and Wolff (1976) whose research on Freud's early letters revealed that he often used the name

"Cipio" in writing to his friend Silberstein. They believed that, via this nickname, Freud was showing his identification with Scipio (Africanus)—this being another example of name magic to effect an identification. Having reviewed these materials, it will not seem far-fetched when McGrath claimed (p. 82) that Freud, in addition to identifying with Franz Moor, also harbored a "phantasized identification with Karl Moor."

As was the case with his identifications with Franz Moor and the murderous Moor in *Fiesco*, Freud's name in early childhood—the Moor—helped mediate his identification with Karl Moor. That Freud and Karl Moor had affectionate desires for women named Amelia (Amalia) and that both were motivated, in young manhood, by political/revolutionary feelings helped to cement Freud's identification with this handsome "hero." We should wonder if Karl's connections with a band of robbers could have been related in Freud's mind with his associations with his Uncle Josef and half-brothers in Manchester, concerning their presumed band of counterfeiters.

Moreover, the unfolding action in *The Robbers* reveals that (similar to Freud's two-sided self) Karl Moor has a dualistic nature and that his Mr. Hyde-self is a murderous one. In his self-righteous mood he ruthlessly slew men whom he regarded as unjust, and at other times he exhibited lapses that allowed his band to send innocent children and adults to their fiery deaths. Of course, a large undercurrent of madness was lurking in Karl, as shown by the horrendous verbal outburst that ended his father's life (patricide), by his intention to kill Franz (fratricide), and by his macabre murder of his fiancée Amelia. Also, recall that Karl, at one point, took the conflicting roles of both Brutus and Caesar as a reflection of his deeply dualistic nature, which offers another reason why Freud identified with this covertly insane killer. Previously, it was noted that Fiesco and his accomplice (the Moor) can be regarded as symbolic and opposing halves of one dualistic personality, which is also true of Karl and Franz. This provides another reason why Freud identified himself with all four of these lethal characters.

Some Real Persons (Plus Zeus)

Now that we've reviewed some of Freud's identifications with literary characters who were murderers, it's time to discuss some real persons in his life who had lethal potentials. One of the four main patients of his that he described in *Studies on Hysteria* (1895) he gave the pseudonym Frau Emmy von N., and only in recent years her real name has been exposed as Frau Fanny Moser (used hereafter). She was the offspring of a wealthy Swiss family who in 1870 at age 23 married an old widower name Heinrich Moser—age 65 and all of 42 years her senior—who owned a huge fortune with businesses spread through Europe and Asia. Four years later he died, and when his adult children from his first marriage learned that he'd left his entire estate to his young widow, they charged that he'd been crassly manipulated and murdered by her, via poisoning. Although an autopsy cleared her of that accusation, there was still reason for deep suspicion, since poison often is hard to detect (even today, and more so in that primitive era). In newspapers and salons throughout Europe this affair was famous for years, especially because Fanny was reputed to be the richest woman in Europe, and at least some gossip must have disclosed that she developed rather bizarre behaviors after the questionable death of her fatherly husband.

Fanny suffered mental agonies for many years after Heinrich's death, and she hopped from one doctor and sanitarium to another. Finally, in 1889 she went to Vienna to be treated by Dr. Josef Breuer for an amazing variety of tics, delusions, fearsome hallucinations and phobias. After six weeks with Breuer she was passed on to Freud, whom her daughters described as Breuer's chief assistant. After seven weeks of extensive treatments with Freud, she returned to her vast estate in Switzerland where he later visited her for a few days, and the next year she returned to Vienna for an additional two-month treatment until she developed antagonism and distrust towards Freud. In the *Studies*, he exaggerated his therapeutic success with her but admitted that "it was not a lasting one." Fanny continued for many years thereafter to fall ill in similar ways, and to seek out new doctors.

In the *Studies* Freud's extensive discussion of Fanny Moser's case was very dramatic and used his highest novelist's skills to make this the centerpiece of his offerings (which probably he hoped would rival Breuer's dramatic and exciting account of the famous case of Anna O., which preceded Freud's case). Fanny's case was the young Dr. Freud's first detailed case history in a lifetime series of such case presentations, and there's no doubt that he chose her case for his honor because he knew it would give him maximum notoriety with rich women throughout Europe as a "provocative" sex-doctor who was willing to massage his female patients' bodies— as he "advertised" he did with her during their late *evening* sessions. A lengthy chapter in *Dark Side* gives my strong criticisms of Freud's (prepsychoanalytic) "treatments" of Fanny, and I argue that his work, and the manner of his reporting of it, was unprofessional and unethical, to such a great extent that I'm amazed that biographers have failed to make strong criticism of this case.

In *Dark Side* I've argued that, despite Freud's lofty remarks about confidentiality, he sought notoriety with Fanny's case, because this would advertise to the world that young Dr. Freud (age 33) had such a huge professional reputation and sexy bedside manner that he had attracted as a patient, from far-off Switzerland, the richest woman in Europe. His case presentation gave so many informative details about Fanny's life, wealth, and the murder charge, that the cognoscenti of Europe should have had no trouble deducing "Emmy N.'s" true identity—as he desired. Besides slyly breaching confidentiality, he engaged in an outrageous scam in the way that he used hypnosis with Fanny. Freud had the audacity to admit, using somewhat oblique wording, that he employed a post-hypnotic suggestion against Fanny's best interests, then implied this was just a little "joke."

Freud's case presentation was very reluctant to acknowledge that Fanny sometimes exhibited behaviors that were quite bizarre and even flagrantly psychotic, so that he could maintain that she was merely an hysteric and could discuss her in terms of his theories and treatment of hysteria. In *Dark Side* I have discussed her psychotic tendencies and behaviors as indicating a diagnosis of Borderline Disorder with transient psychotic episodes in a client with guilty feelings about murderous desires and impulses. If I'm correct about this diagnosis, it is probably no coincidence that Freud should have chosen her as his first major case presentation, since this same diagnosis seems to have great applicability to Freud himself.

Although his report about Fanny offered many opportunities for him to discuss her symptoms and guilty feelings in relation to factors involving her husband's death, or his possible murder, Freud failed to touch upon any of this material. His evasive approach implied that there was no reason at all to wonder whether murderous behavior, or merely the charge of murder, had provoked her bizarre symptoms, when obviously there were good reasons to consider those issues—as I have done in *Dark Side*. Instead, he argued cleverly that he believed that she was not a liar and was a thoroughly honest and saintly woman, which implied that she never could have committed a murder (even to gain incomparable wealth and enormous power). In fact, he praised her alleged virtues so vociferously that one has to become suspicious of his motives, and hers as well.

In *Dark Side* I have discussed evidence indicating that Freud developed a fantasy identification with Fanny Moser, and I will not review all of that same material here. However, I will provide some of it by giving my analysis of his first historical instance of a "motivated forgetting." Freud's letter to Fliess dated August 26, 1898 cited his very first analysis of this sort, his forgetting of the name Julius Mosen, and in his letter of September 27th he gave a second example, his famous forgetting of the name Luca Signorelli. The latter became famous with clinicians because he used it as his first such analysis in *The Psychopathology of Everyday Life*, not telling his readers that he had totally suppressed his earliest example, his forgetting of the name Julius Mosen. If his letters to Fliess had not been published in recent years, despite his heated opposition to the project, the Julius Mosen example probably would have remained suppressed forever, and we'll soon learn why Freud desired that outcome.

For the first time Freud broached the subject of the motivated forgetting of personal names in his August 26th letter to Fliess. To introduce his forgetting and later recalling of the name of the poet Julius Mosen, Freud wrote: "You know how one can forget a name and substitute part of another one for it; you could swear it was correct although invariably it turns out to be wrong." He then stated that recently such a lapse had occurred to him in his forgetting of the name of the poet Julius Mosen who wrote *Andreas Hofer*, and here he quoted the first four words of that heroic poem: "Zu Mantua in Banden." Then he remarked that he'd known that the forgotten name "must be something with an *au*" (ending with the suffix *au*), such as the names Lindau or Feldau. But eventually he had remembered that the forgotten poet's name was Julius Mosen, and later he remarked to Fliess that: "the 'Julius' had not slipped my memory." This indicated that earlier he'd forgotten the surname Mosen, but had *not* forgotten the given name Julius (which was also the name of his deceased brother).

Without offering supporting evidence Freud mentioned to Fliess that he had "proved" the following ideas: (1) that he'd repressed the name Mosen "because of certain connections;" (2) that infantile material was involved in this repression; (3) that the substitute names (Lindau, Feldau) in the foreground of consciousness "were formed, like symptoms from both groups of material." He boasted that his analysis has explained everything "with no gaps left." Finally, he remarked to Fliess that he would never be able to expose his analysis of this memory lapse to the public, implying that he would not be willing to provide public disclosure of matters that were very embarrassing to him.

What personal matters could be so threatening to Freud that they required eternal censorship? Something sexual or unethical? How about murder? My thesis, in fact, is that an analysis of the preceding lapse of memory will reveal Freud's identification with the alleged murderess Fanny Moser, along with deep anxieties about his own "murder complex." As we'll soon see, there are numerous indications that both the forgetting of Julius Mosen's name, and its interaction with the famous forgetting of the name Signorelli, are connected with just such a murder complex in Freud's unconscious mind. Parenthetically, readers may wish to know that my analysis of the Mosen lapse is greatly in contrast with McGrath's analysis (pp. 292-4) which focuses on various political emphases in Freud's life.

In my analysis of how Freud's lapse about Julius Mosen relates to his hidden murder complex, the following factors need consideration:

1. The name Julius (above) relates to Freud's brother against whom he expressed his earliest murderous feelings, as admitted by Freud and discussed in Schur's biography. But the name Julius also represents Freud's murderous feelings towards his bullying nephew John, mediated by the

name Julius Caesar. It was in Freud's *Non vixit* dream, in which he expressed his lethal desires so freely, that the name Julius referred to Julius Caesar, in terms of the dream's associations. Furthermore, nephew John played that role opposite Sigmund's portrayal of Brutus in their enactment of the patricidal/fratricidal duologue featuring those Roman characters in Schiller's play *The Robbers*.

2. Having noted above that the name Julius Mosen had a hidden connection in Freud's mind with *The Robbers*, we must stress that a significant character in that play is the cleric, Fra Moser. His surname is identical with that of Fanny Moser. (Note that Fra Mosen suggests *Frau* Moser.) It was Fra Moser who denounced patricide and fratricide (as leading surely to hellfire in The Last Judgment) to Franz Moor—the insane murderer with whom Freud identified. Notice that the surnames of Fra Moser and Fanny Moser connect strongly with the poet's name Mosen, and with key elements of Franz Moor's surname, which was Freud's childhood nickname as well. All of this suggests Freud's identifications with Fanny Moser, Fra Moser, and Julius Mosen mediated by his identifications with Franz and Karl Moor (with the help of name magic and his childhood name "the Moor.") By these complex connections, we see that Julius Mosen's name was fixated in Freud's mind with many factors pertaining to patricide, fratricide, a cleric who denounced both those types of murder, and an alleged murderess—all parts of Freud's murder complex.

3. When Freud struggled to remember the surname of Julius Mosen, he surmised that the missing name must contain the syllable *au*—like the final portions of the surnames Lindau and Feldau. This provides another clue that the poet's name Mosen was strongly associated in Freud's mind with the surname of Fanny Moser (an alleged murderess of a wealthy father-figure), since she inherited from her husband a vast estate called Au (which Freud once visited). Ergo, Fanny was the very person who owned "something with an *au*," as Freud had stated it to Fliess. That she possibly had obtained this grand estate via "patricide" makes a connection with the huge estate which Franz Moor obtained briefly via "patricide" in *The Robbers*. Also, the chemical symbol for gold is "au," which further hints at Freud's identification with Fanny Moser (who owned an "au"), since his mother's childhood name for him was "*golden Sigi*." Concerning the thesis that Freud's citing of "au" referred covertly to Fanny's estate, it should be noted that the initial syllables of Lindau and Feldau are German words whose meanings are consonant with the pastoral qualities of Fanny's sprawling estate, as I have discussed in *Dark Side*.

4. When Freud briefly discussed his Mosen lapse, he referred to the opening words of a revolutionary poem about Andreas Hofer, the defiant Hannibal-like hero who opposed Napoleon's power and was executed in

Mantua—"Zu Mantua in Banden." Surely, Freud knew that Mantua was also famous as the birthplace of another great man, namely the Roman poet Virgil, author of the *Aeneid*, from which Freud took the defiant words of the motto for his dream book (If I cannot bend heaven, then I will arouse hellfire!). Unconsciously, this motto referred to young Sigi's murderous wishes towards his male kinsmen for "killing" his nanny—the desire to pitch them into hellfire—harking back to the train ride in 1859 when he saw "hellfire" at Breslau as he sped away from her forever. (Notice that the city of Breslau is also something with an "au.") Thus, the Mosen lapse contains covert connections with the bedrock of his murderous rage, his lost nanny. It's possible that her name Monica Z. is encoded, as a *reversal*, in the first two words of the poem, i.e. "Z. Mantua" equals Z. Monica. Notice that this city's name has a structure (m-n-a) that is quite similar to the structure of "Monica." Her name lends itself to being equated with the name of yet another city—Monaco—and in *Dark Side* I've explained how a significant item about Monaco in Freud's book on "slips" made complex unconscious connections with her name. Likewise, some writers have claimed that Rome symbolized her identity for Freud, and Kanzer (1979) noted that he once correlated her identity with the city of Alhama (whose last three letters encode her work as a wetnurse (*Amme*, in German).

5. The second memory lapse that Freud mentioned to Fliess was his forgetting of the name of the painter Signorelli, whom Freud described as having painted "the *Last Judgment* in Orvieto, the greatest I have seen so far." The dramatic theme of that painting, the human suffering and hellfire involved in God's final judgment, connects with the second item above: Franz Moor's nightmare about the last judgment and Fra Moser's response that at the final judgment only the sins of patricide and fratricide would not be forgiven by the Lord. Thus, it is Freud's murder complex, his guilt about patricidal/fratricidal feelings and his great unconscious fears of the "last judgment" by God, that underlies both the Mosen and the Signorelli memory lapses. Likewise, his infantile rage about his lost nanny is encoded in the Signorelli example when we regard that name as involving this cryptic sentence: Sig ignore(s) elli. The first element refers to his childhood name, and "Elli" refers to the awesome wetnurse who symbolized death in the Norse myths about Odin, Thor, and *Sigi*. The aforementioned sentence indicates that Freud, during his self-analysis, was still "ignoring" or failing to deal with his murderous feelings about his lost nanny. Zilboorg (1967) has remarked accurately that Freud spent his entire lifetime "trying to undo the catastrophe that befell him in his childhood," that his murderous wishes relating to the Freiberg years made him feel that he deserved to die, and therefore that he harbored a horrendous fear of the Day of Judgment.

6. Finally, we should notice that the poet's name Mosen incorporates

most of the name Moses, with whom Freud identified intensely. Since the figure of Moses is embedded in the memory lapse regarding Julius Mosen, the special meaning that this Biblical character had in Freud's psyche provides an additional indication that a murder complex permeated the Mosen lapse. This refers to his bizarre behavior with the Moses statue in 1913 when he tried autistically to revise Moses' murderous anger, in hope of controlling his own lethal impulses. (Consider that the Moses encoding in Fanny Moser's surname probably helped to mediate Freud's identification with her.)

My extensive research into Freud's identifications reveals that, though the instances were exceptional, he seemed to engage in very rapid acts of identification with some persons. One example of this was his instant depression and identification with Victor Tilgner when he learned about the latter's sudden death, as reported in Schur's biography. Another instance of what seems like Freud's rapid identification was with a young man who may have indulged patricidal impulses for apparently "justifiable" reason. This episode was reported in Jones' biography (III, p. 88) while he covered important events in Freud's life that occurred during the year 1922.

In November 1922 "the son of an old servant of Freud's shot his father, thought not fatally," while the old man allegedly "was in the act of raping the youth's half-sister." Evidently, Freud made a rapid identification with this young man, although *he did not know him personally,* for Freud paid *all* the legal expenses himself! This largesse was extraordinary for Freud, and makes one wonder about his personal motives. Despite attempts by some writers to make him seem like a philanthropist, they have offered little evidence to undermine my strong impression that he was quite tightfisted, and Eissler (1971) has emphasized that Freud did not exhibit irrational needs to rescue persons in trouble.

Jones tried to explain Freud's behavior in the previous case by writing that "his humanitarian nature was always moved by sympathy with juvenile delinquents." That is a weak assertion, because I don't recall any other instance in Jones' three massive volumes which confirmed that Freud was a champion of juvenile delinquents. Is it possible that Freud identified with the young would-be murderer of a father in this case, partly because it was said the old man tried to rape his son's half-sister, which perhaps correlated in Freud's psyche with his accusation that his own father had sexually molested his own sisters?

Another peculiar aspect of Freud's behavior in this case is that, though he did not know this patricidal youth personally, he wrote a memorandum to the court "saying that any attempt to seek for deeper motives would only obscure the plain facts." So the man who was the master of searching for ulterior motives insisted that, though unseemly patricidal urges might have surfaced under an investigation, no such inquiry should be made and "the eyes should remain closed," one might say (per the words of his dream about Jacob's death). Another professor also wrote a memo to the court saying that the excitement had caused a "short circuit" in the youth's mind that caused temporary insanity, which was accepted by the court, allowing the defendant to be freed quite readily.

Does anyone beside myself smell a decaying fish hidden behind Freud's "charity" in the above matter? Is it possible that Ernest Jones smelled it too, at least unconsciously? Consider this interesting sequence in Jones's book. Thirteen lines preceding the material about the son who shot his old father, Jones wrote about a rumor circulating in psychoanalytic circles in 1922 that the analyst Max Eitingon secretly had made a huge financial donation to the "cause." At an after-dinner speech Jones amused his audience by explaining why it would be difficult to maintain secrecy about the name of the generous donor. Jones cited two notable proverbs: "Charity begins at home" and "Murder will out." Humorously, he suggested that condensation and displacement should be applied to these two proverbs in order to rearrange matters and conclude that first "Murder begins at home"—which he called "a fundamental tenet of psychoanalysis"—and second that "Charity will out."

When we consider the sequencing of those provocative materials, it seems plausible that Jones suspected, in the case of Sigmund Freud's lethal impulses towards his kinsman, that: 'Murder begins at home.' And didn't Jones secretly fear and expect that someday writers would begin to see through and beyond his tendentious version of Freud's life and that 'Murder will out'? If so, he might also have suspected that people would eventually begin to question Freud's "charity" in paying the legal expenses of that patricidal young man with whom he identified so readily.

The second chapter of one of Roazen's books (1969) about Freud is titled "Zeus." In that chapter we learn (p. 49) that Freud made a comparison of himself with the Greek god Zeus that hints at his fantasy identification with this deity. Likewise, in the book on "slips" there is material (pp. 281-20) about Zeus that connects with Freud's family situation and makes more likely his unconscious identification with the Greek god.

In the *Psychopathology of Everyday Life* Freud discussed an error he made in writing that Zeus had castrated (i.e. equivalent of murdered) his father Kronos and dethroned him. Later, he realized that he had mixed up the generations involved by "erroneously carrying this atrocity a generation forward"—since it was Kronos who castrated his father Uranus. (In a footnote, he noted that Zeus did castrate his father, but in another version of the myth.) Then Freud cited another error he had made in his writings by mixing up the generations of the famous Barca family of ancient Carthage, the family of Hannibal with whom he identified so strongly—by confusing the name of his hero's brother with that of the father. With frankness Freud admitted that the latter error had occurred in a context involving his dissatisfaction with Jacob Freud's "cowardice," and in relation to his early fantasies and wishes that his brother Emanuel should have been his father instead of old Jacob.

Then Freud remarked that memories of his brother Emanuel had generated "my error in advancing by a generation the mythological atrocities of the Greek pantheon," i.e. of Zeus's "killing" of his father. For he recalled Emanuel telling him: "you really belong not to the second but to the third generation in relation to your father" (a rather confusing statement, actually). Concerning his "generation errors" relating to those three sources—Zeus, Hannibal (himself in disguise), and the Freud family—Freud admitted that "the same theme is at the bottom of all three examples I have given," saying that these errors were derived from "repressed thoughts connected with my dead father." He indicated slyly that this repressed material pertained to "an unfriendly criticism of my father." But when we emphasize his identification with Zeus who, in effect, killed his father, it will seem more likely that Freud was hiding monumental patricidal urges from his readers' awareness.

We can guess that connected in Freud's mind with those three generation errors was his ancient rage about his clouded paternity, and the issue of whether his birthday really occurred in March rather than May. For while discussing those three generation errors, he inserted gratuitously an error made when he changed the name of Schiller's birthplace from Marbach to Marburg. Of course, he identified strongly with Schiller and this error shows that unconsciously he wished to elevate himself by correlating Schiller's birthplace with his own (since the second syllable of Marburg and Freiberg are essentially equivalents). Again, it should be emphasized that birthplaces and birthdates were magical in Freud's psyche due to his bastardy anxieties. Furthermore, emphasis should be given to the common element in both place names, Marburg and Marbach, namely the first syllable Mar, which signified the German word for the month of March (März), which he secretly believed was his true month of birth. It seems plausible that this Schiller "slip" was connected conceptually with those three "generation errors" and with Freud's murderous rage towards father-figures. All of this relates to Freud's identifications with Schiller's patricidal characters: Franz Moor, Karl Moor, the Moor of Tunis, and Fiesco.

Freud's associations to the Hollthurn dream in his famous dream book revealed that this dream was tied to his identification with one of his male patients with a neurosis who tortured himself with the fear (1967, p. 293) that he would kill everyone he met. According to Freud that analysis was successful and showed that this obsession was based on an impulse to murder his rather strict father. Before this the patient had spent all his time imprisoned in his own home due to fear that he might murder someone in an amnesic state. Walking through streets was a burden due to a compulsion to make certain where everyone disappeared to, for fear that he might have killed some person not accounted for (recall Sigmund's anguish about many persons who "disappeared" in his childhood). Freud stated that a "Cain" fantasy or complex lay behind this patient's strange fears, implying that fratricidal urges were also present here (p. 495). Whenever the patient read about unsolved murders in newspapers, he worried that he might be the wanted murderer, so he made up alibis in case the police wished to question him sometime.

Freud claimed that this patient (who might have been Freud himself, in my view) had high morals and education and that his obsessions about murder had surfaced "shortly after the death of his parents." His impulse to kill his father was expressed consciously at age seven, but had originated much earlier in his childhood (after a nanny disappeared, perhaps?). Freud wrote that he was quite right to shut himself up in his room because a person who felt he "was capable of wanting to push his own father over a precipice from the top of a mountain" should also not be trusted with the lives of persons who were not his relatives. According to Freud, this man's hostile impulses against his father, dating back to childhood, had involved a sexual situation. Freud added provocatively: "In so far, therefore, as I was identifying myself with him, I was seeking to confess to something analogous." (Should this remind us that Freud accused his father of molesting his own children?)

Of course, Freud did explain how his identification with this patient suffering from obsessions about murder and patricidal impulses was connected with his Hollthurn dream, and I will get to that point momentarily. But first I'd like to express my view that this dream may have had some "prophetic" qualities concerning Freud's murderous impulses towards father-figures, and that possibly it predicted his murder of Emanuel Freud many years later via that strange "train accident." We'll soon see why I wonder about this, after reviewing a summary of the Hollthurn dream.

Near the turn of the century, during the night of July 18-19, Freud was asleep on a train as it pulled into the city of Marburg (in the Austrian province of Styria) when he had this uncanny dream, which I'll now report in condensed form. In his sleep he heard a conductor announce "Hollthurn, ten minutes," with "Hollthurn" being a substitute for the name Marburg. This word made Freud (in his dream) think of holothurians (sea slugs). His dream thoughts then turned to the Tyrol region and brave men who fought in vain against the ruler of their country. Still asleep, he wished to get out of the train onto the platform, but hesitated and saw women with baskets of fruit on the platform, holding up their fruit invitingly. Then—in a flash—he was in another compartment where the seats were so narrow "that one's back pressed directly against the back of the carriage." This surprised him, but he thought: "I MIGHT HAVE CHANGED CARRIAGES WHILE I WAS IN THE SLEEPING STATE."

Still dreaming, in this new carriage he saw an English brother and sister and a row of books, including a volume by Adam Smith and *Matter and Motion* by Clerk-Maxwell. The man asked his sister whether she had forgotten a book by Schiller. It seemed that the books belonged alternatively to them and to Freud, and he wanted to intrude in their conversation in a confirmatory manner—when he woke up and saw that his train was stopped at the Marburg station. Later, while writing down the dream he remembered an additional piece of it that he had tried to suppress. In the dream he had spoken in English to the brother and sister, and referring to a particular book, said that it was written by . . .(author's name not given). On a much later page of his discussion, Freud revealed that the suppressed name of this author had been none other than *Johann F. Schiller*.

In a later discussion of this dream (1967, p. 557) Freud admitted that he'd left this dream "almost uninterpreted on account of its gross indecency." Let me suggest that what he wished to hide from us were not merely sexual indecencies but ugly material having to do with his "murder complex" regarding his relatives. He did make it quite clear that in the dream he bore very hostile, revengeful feelings towards the English brother and sister. But he failed to mention what would seem to be obvious to most readers—that they represented his English kinfolk in Manchester, including John, Emanuel, and Pauline Freud. These were the people who had enraged Sigi in 1859 when they took a train ride away from him, "abandoning" him after having "killed" his beloved nanny. Nanny appears in several places in the dream, as well. She is encoded as the disguised wetnurses who hold their breasts (fruit) up to him, which caused him to regress instantly to the infantile state in the dream. Thus, the compartment (carriage) into which he was whisked magically was a baby carriage, and this explains why it became so narrow (like a womb) that his back was forced against the rear end of this "carriage." And he changed carriages in a sleeping state, because that is a common occurrence with a baby who has thoroughly wet or soiled one carriage, if a second, clean carriage is available.

The train ride in this dream refers indirectly to a time in childhood when a moving carriage, with its sleep-inducing qualities, served as a baby carriage for Sigmund–that catastrophic train ride in 1859 that destroyed his Freiberg world with nanny, and fixated murderous rage against his Manchester kinsmen. Freud's lethal rage against the English brother and sister sharing his compartment in the dream is not hard to ascertain, because he indicated in his associations that he took "fearful vengeance" against them, implying that he used harsh words and insults in a quarrel with them. The crux of that quarrel was that they refused to open the window of the compartment in a "ruthless" manner, and Freud soon felt that he was suffocating. This sequence bears a close resemblance to an event which actually occurred to Freud on a train in the early 1880s (mentioned earlier). He wrote Martha that a man on the train had argued with him about whether a window should be opened and so enraged him that Freud reported that he was on the verge of killing the man, and would have done so gladly. Surely, an infantile complex had been triggered here, and that incident became the template for his *murderous* rage against the couple in his dream, which may have been satisfied finally with Emanuel's "train accident" in 1914 and later with John's disappearance in 1919. (Notice that Freud's "patient" worried that he had murdered people who "disappeared" from his sight.)

There are other indications of Freud's "murder complex" hidden in the Hollthurn dream. His reference to the Tyrol region and valiant men who "fought in vain against the superior power of the ruler of their country" makes obvious connections with the hero Andreas Hofer in Julius Mosen's poem. Thus, we see that all the murderous associations relating to the Mosen lapse are secretly embedded within the Hollthurn dream, including Schiller's four murderers with whom Freud identified, as he also identified with his murderous patient. Freud remarked (p. 557) that his suppression of Schiller's name in the garbled message that he penned as an addendum* to the dream's content had probably been exposed to greatest mental resistance, and therefore was the most important part of the dream. Again, it's likely that this had concealed Freud's murder complex from public view and that he'd become identified with Schiller's killers. In his associations to the dream, again he made the error of stating that Schiller was born at Marburg (instead of Marbach), which means that all the lethal potentials of the aforementioned "Marburg lapse" were encoded within this complex dream. The great importance of Marburg is seen by the fact that this was the actual station which Freud's train was pulling into while he was having the

---

*His *reference to the Tyrol region might have predicted his murder plan against Fliess in the Tyrol (Achensee) in 1900.- Later I'll explain that this addendum, citing grammatical "errors," hinted at his 2467 errors in the dream book, symbolizing murderous intentions.*

Hollthurn dream, and that the dream tried to conceal this by substituting the name Hollthurn for Marburg.

In his discussion of the dream (pp. 494-5) Freud pointed to the capitalized material (I MIGHT HAVE CHANGED CARRIAGES IN A SLEEPING STATE) as having only one possible explanation. To him this sentence implied that he must have left the carriage in a sleeping or "twilight state," indicating a gap in his memory that was caused by a kind of temporary amnesia. Freud then correlated this implied amnesic state in his dream with the fears of his patient who believed that during amnesic states he murdered people, indicating that one meaning of the dream was that it accused him of identifying with the murderous impulses of this man (including patricidal ones). But Freud did not acknowledge that this was related to the loss of his nanny and to desires for murderous revenge against his kinsmen, nor did he admit to his readers how all of this was connected with his well-known "train phobia," which made him worry obsessively that relatives and friends (like Fliess) might be killed in train accidents! (Does one sense a relationship to Emanuel's death?)

There are a number of Freud's dreams which, when "properly interpreted," reveal the depth of his murder complex. These include the *Non vixit* dream, the Dream of Dishonesty (torture machines), the dream of self-dissection (which refers to self- analysis and murder), the Irma dream, and the Hollthurn dream. These dreams suggest that Freud harbored wishes to kill various victims in different ways: burning them up (hellfire), torturing some to death, poisoning others, slicing them to ribbons with knives, pushing them off mountains, subjecting them to injuries on trains, etc. The Hollthurn patient's desire to push his father off a mountain reminds us that after Freud's breakup with Fliess this man who was Freud's dearest friend and personal doctor (father-figure) claimed that at their final bitter meeting at a mountain resort Freud had planned to kill him by pushing him off a precipice. In the next chapter we'll see that Freud's brief psychotic break in 1904 while he stood atop the Acropolis in Athens was probably related to feelings of guilt pertaining to his desire to kill Fliess and others by pushing them off great heights.

In his discussion of the Hollthurn dream Freud alleged that he had "cured" this murder-obsessed patient. Presumably, this cure occurred in the 1890s, and clinicians like myself who have studied his work in that era will find it hard to believe that he cured *any* patient in those muddled years. Perhaps his claim that the patient with intense murder fantasies was cured reflected a wish-fulfillment by Freud that someday his own murder complex would be cured by his ongoing self-analysis. It's interesting that after he "cured" this patient, he had a long overnight *train ride* into the provinces with him, to visit his relatives, and described their train ride as very entertaining, with windows wide open. Perhaps this reflected Freud's hope that the cure of his own murder complex might be accomplished by a magical train ride that reversed the agonies of the train ride in 1859 that took him away from his beloved nanny.

Finally, we need to ask why this dream began as it did. Recall that Freud was aboard an actual train that was pulling into the city of Marburg when his dream transformed the city's name to Hollthurn (which is not the name of a real place). Was there a murderous intent in this by the imp controlling Freud's dream? Remember that he thought at once of "holothurians," which are slimy sea slugs, which implied that Marburg itself was changed magically into a lowly sea slug. If Marburg had been a man whom Freud detested, this destruction of his identity by the imp would certainly imply a murderous intent. Indeed, in the book on "slips" Freud revealed that Herr Marburg was a business friend of his father who was connected with "an annoying story" and whose name he tried to suppress from his own and his readers' awareness while analyzing the Hollthurn dream.

Perhaps this apparent frankness by Freud was another attempt to deceive his readers about his immense hatred for a man named Marburg, who exposed Freud's sexual indulgences to public ridicule (depending on the timing of events in relation to this dream). For the Italian analyst Dr. Edoardo Weiss, in his book about Freud's career, noted that there was once a Prof. Marburg who became a thorn in Freud's backside. Evidently, this Marburg had known Freud personally and, according to Weiss, he made him the subject of much gossip by exposing him as a "Casanova" (Don Juan, per Balmary). Similarly, in *Secret SL* I have offered a long discussion about an eminent neurologist, Dr. Moses Starr, who subjected Freud to public ridicule when he revealed at a conference covered by New York newspapers that he had been Freud's colleague during their school days in Vienna and indicated that Freud's life then was *not* conducted on a high moral plane.

Some Additional Killers

David Bakan's work (1958) has shown that many of Freud's concepts and theories were grounded in his immersion in writings pertaining to the Jewish mystical tradition, which seems consonant with his fantasy identifications with characters in Genesis and his frequent acting-out of those Biblical connections. Also, Bakan cited various factors in Freud's life and personality which suggest that he had incorporated the messianic role which the Jews have nurtured for centuries, with Moses being the original Messiah and Freud carrying that messianic role forward via his identification with Moses.

Bakan wrote (p. 170) that "Freud's whole effort in the creation of psychoanalysis may be viewed as Messianic . . ." He also pointed to certain unusual factors in Freud's life and stated that: "The view that Freud conceived of himself as a Messiah in the spirit of Jewish mysticism is supported by otherwise puzzling biographical facts in Freud's life." He noted that Freud once wrote that he often felt as if he had inherited all the passion of his ancestors when they defended their temple and wished that he "could joyfully cast away my life in a great cause." However, Bakan claimed that Freud had not just identified with Moses as the Jewish messiah, but also had identified himself with a powerful figure in the history of Jewish thought called Messiah- ben-Joseph.

There were two images of the messiah that developed in the history of Jewish mysticism, that of the warrior and military hero being the first of these images. It was the warrior-messiah, who was portrayed as having great strength (and horns on his head!), who would defeat all of the Jews' enemies and obtain vengeance for them as well as political independence. This was the Messiah-ben-Joseph who would pave the way for the second messiah, a spiritual one (the Messiah-ben-David), who would rule after redemption had been achieved. Bakan argues that Freud's strong military interests showed that probably he had identified with the great warrior, Messiah-ben-Joseph. He noted that Freud had identified with Josef, the master of dreams by following in his footsteps, and Bakan concluded: "In addition, however, we believe that he followed the fuller significance attached to the name of Joseph as the warrior Messiah who would redeem the Jews." (Again we see here the tracks of Freud's unconscious involvement in name magic.)

Freud's obsession with Rome was viewed by Bakan as evidence for his hidden fantasy identification with the Messiah-ben-Joseph. For in the history of the Jewish tradition, Rome was said to be the legendary dwelling place of the warrior Messiah "and the place where the Messiah will reveal himself." It was believed that the military Messiah dwelled in concealment at the gates of Rome waiting for the time of redemption, and this image reminds us of Hannibal, the Semitic general who waited so long outside the gates of Rome. (Bakan noted that the dream book tells of one of Freud's dreams in which he sees a gateway that somehow is associated with Rome.) It's plausible that this identification with the warrior-messiah was why Freud seemed to view his initial visit to Rome as the necessary first step towards fame and fortune. If so, perhaps this was an acting-out of his identification with the military Messiah's connection to Rome.

Finally, we return to the issue of murder, and we must ask ourselves whether Freud's presumed identification with the warrior-messiah has a particular relation to his flagrant lethal impulses. Bakan wrote that Freud's identification with the military Messiah "catches in metaphor several critical aspects of Freud's personality." Without realizing the full implications of his statement, Bakan then told us an awesome factor pertaining to this aggressive Messiah-ben-Joseph: "The military Messiah, blessed by Moses, can violate one of the strongest taboos among the Jews, the commandment against killing . . ." Ergo, this messiah also was presumably free even to *murder* as he saw fit to do so, and one must wonder how the power of his incorporated image might have influenced Freud to do likewise. Was this one of the continuing sources of his murder complex?

Bakan tried to escape from the logical implications of the preceding ideas by emphasizing that the military messiah was also permitted to overcome the taboo against having thoughts of aggression involving bloodshed. With this ploy he evaded any question of whether Freud at times had indulged irrationally his "freedom to murder." Bakan merely noted that Freud's identification would have allowed him to have thoughts of killing oppressors which were forbidden to others. With this evasive emphasis on murderous ideation rather than actions, Bakan remarked that Freud's ego was free to tolerate "murderous thoughts" and that this enabled him to theorize about death wishes against others, "particularly the father, . . . in the fundament paradigm of the Oedipus complex." Bakan implied that all of society benefitted from Freud's freedom to think freely about murdering others, without wondering whether this vengeful, hate-filled man maintained adequate controls over impulses to murder his male family members, and some other people as well.

In conclusion, Bakan wrote about Freud that "the military ethos may well have been one of the primary sources of his enormous energy." However, one might ask whether this was one of the important sources of his murder complex, as well. Did Freud's murder complex feed not only upon his fantasy identifications with the many murderers we have cited, but also with the series of aggressive military figures with whom he identified as aspects of his ruthless conquistador image? It's likely that the answer to this question should be an affirmative one.

There is good reason to believe that Freud nurtured a fantasy identification with St. Sigismund, and we'll soon recognize that this saint can be regarded as an infamous murderer, albeit a repentant one. McGrath (1988, pp.42-3) has written some informative material about the probable role of St. Sigismund in Freud's psychic life, and many of my ideas on this subject are grounded in McGrath's account of the matter.

McGrath began his exposition of the meaning of the name "Sigismund" in Freud's life by noting that some writers have assumed that he was named after Sigismund I, a famous king of Poland who defended the religious rights of the Jews. A more likely possibility, according to McGrath, is that the name Sigismund had meanings for the Freud family that were both Czech and

Catholic in orientation. Although his Hebrew name was Schlomo (signifying Solomon), it's likely that his parents gave him the name Sigismund as a partial adaptation to naming practices of the local Catholic culture in Freiberg in which the first names given to children typically were names of saints. This is relevant to the fact that St. Sigismund was a patron saint of Bohemia, bordering on their Moravian community; also his relics are kept in Prague; and his saint's day is well known to the Czech people as May 1. McGrath remarked that the Freuds probably had picked this saint's name for their son "because they wanted a name with positive connotations for the surrounding culture, and because his feast day, coming just before Freud's birth on May 6, had suggested it to them."

In his usual insightful manner, McGrath remarked that there were deeply psychological connotations of the name Sigismund which derived from the life story of St. Sigismund, a tale that was popular in Czechoslovakia. Earlier in his life this saint was king of the Franks in the 6th century and his first wife died after bearing him a son, call Sigeric. (We can imagine that Freud suspected that both father and son were called "Sigi" in early childhood just as he was, solidifying his identification with this story.) After a while the king remarried and his new queen became hostile towards her stepson, Sigeric, and undermined him by telling the king that Sigeric was plotting to murder him and make himself the monarch. Urged on by the queen's machinations, Sigismund had his young son strangled to death while he slept, but later began to show great remorse for this murder. Over a long period of time he wept and fasted, and due to his deep repentance and the holy life he led, the public eventually began to regard him as a saint.

Obviously McGrath is correct in writing that the above story constitutes an intense Oedipal drama which "surrounded Freud's very name," one that involved a lethal patriarch, an unreliable second wife, and a son who was potentially patricidal. It's easy to assume that Freud knew this story about St. Sigismund and that, via name magic, it is another factor helping to consolidate his strong identification with Oedipus and his eventual formulation of the theory of the Oedipus complex. McGrath is right in saying that Freud probably had heard this story about St. Sigismund on at least one occasion, considering "the importance of names for Freud," and adding that Freud once wrote: "A man's name is a principal component of his personality, perhaps even a portion of his soul."

The previous chapter showed that Freud had strong tendencies, both conscious and unconscious, to employ name magic as an important basis for his acting-out of a number of his fantasy identifications. Chapter six will greatly add to data indicating that Freud was very vulnerable to name magic, as he was to number magic, and also to name-compulsions which caused him to act-out the hidden connotations of some of his own personal names (which included Schlomo, Sig, Sigi, Sigismund, Sigmund, Freud, "the Moor," Cipio, "golden Sigi," etc.), and perhaps some names of persons with whom he identified. We'll also see that Freud spent time with special "name books" studying the traditional meanings of personal names inscribed in those books, as he revealed in his correspondence with Fliess. When McGrath noted that personal names had considerable importance for Freud, I think that he did not suspect how immense this magical name factor was in Freud's psychic life. For in many ways Freud fit the picture of Stekel's (1911) patients who were involved in name-compulsions which caused them unawares to act-out the hidden connotations of personal names in rather uncanny ways.

That is why I feel confident that McGrath was right in assuming that Freud knew the preceding story about St. Sigismund. He would have been driven to find out everything relating to his own name because of the hold that name magic had on his mind. Furthermore, I feel sure that Freud's susceptibility to name magic would have provoked him to consolidate an unconscious fantasy identification with St. Sigismund and his murderous potentials (just as I suspect that he made an unconscious identification with King Solomon, pertaining to his name Schlomo, and then acted-out factors pertaining to "wisdom" and to "sexuality," as the latter pertains to the "Song of Solomon"). These viewpoints of mine lead to an obvious question. Did Freud have urges with his own sons to act-out St. Sigismund's murderous behaviors regarding his son, Sigeric?

Actually, Freud's presumed shame about such matters did not keep him from writing that he did bear death-wishes towards his own sons. During World War I Freud was an enthusiastic supporter of Germany and the Axis powers against England and American, and his three sons served in Germany's armed forces. It was during those years that Freud had dreams about them which he acknowledged had revealed his death wishes towards his sons, perhaps having some relevance to his identification with St. Sigismund's behavior toward his son. Roazen wrote (1969, p. 112) about Freud that: "He certainly harbored death wishes against his own sons, as he himself recorded . . ." That Roazen (in his popular book about Freud contra Tausk) had made this information widely available to the American public greatly annoyed Dr. Eissler who then wrote peevishly that Roazen should have congratulated Freud's bravery in revealing these death wishes towards his sons. Since Eissler's intentions always seemed to be directed towards defending Freud's reputation, it did not occur to him to ask what reasons might be found to explain Freud's wishes that his sons should be killed (reminding us of his death-wishes toward his other male relatives). Nor did it occur to Eissler that this self-disclosure by Freud might have had less to do with bravery and more to do with his urgent need to confess his sins, consonant with the idea that his dream book is a covert confession of that sort.

Previous pages have recorded the possibility that Freud may have changed his name, Sigismund, at age 19 partly in hope of mitigating his underlying madness, consonant with Hebrew beliefs that changes of names can have curative effects upon various illnesses. Now, a related possibility is that he also changed his name in hope of ridding himself of murderous potentials that the name Sigismund might have engendered towards his future sons, concerning associations to St. Sigismund's lethal behavior towards his son.

Finally, thought needs to be given to the duality in St. Sigismund's nature, a Jekyll and Hyde factor that pertains to his being both a saint and a murderer. This seems pertinent to the perverse duality in Freud's nature, for we have seen that he identified with Jesus versus Satan, Hannibal versus Scipio Africanus, etc. The next chapter will have a great deal to say about the dualities involved in Freud's character and in aspects of his life work.

———————————

It can be predicted that many psychoanalysts will vehemently deny my claim that Freud made a strong identification with Dr. Otto Gross, and even that there was a strong mutual identification operating between them. Their objections will relate to the fact that various astute clinicians have regarded Gross as a madman and murderer, and in fact he was probably one of the most disreputable psychoanalysts who ever lived. In this brief space I cannot give all my reasons for claiming that Freud had made a firm identification with Gross. However, in *Secret SL* a great deal of material supports the theses that Freud identified with Gross; that Gross was a key figure in early psychoanalysis whom loyal Freudians have tried to "disown" for many decades (sweeping him under the rug); and that Freud bears a heavy responsibility for some of the murders and other destructive acts that Gross committed, because he did not stop his murderous rampage but secretly condoned it (in my opinion). Moreover, I have explained that this cover-up extends to Gross' questionable relationship with Ernest Jones and that Jones suppressed most of this information from his massive biographies of Freud.

This flamboyant analyst Otto Gross (1877 to 1920) was probably the first psychiatrist (not excepting Jung or Abraham) to become a disciple of Freud and in Eissler's words: "he soon came to be considered by many as Freud's most eminent follower." In 1908 Freud wrote in a letter that Jung and O. Gross were the only analysts who were capable of making original contributions to psychoanalysis. Freud implied that Gross might not make those contributions, however, because of his "poor health." That was a hypocritical euphemism for a variety of horrendous personality defects, mental imbalances, and acting-out behaviors of the worst kind that Gross exhibited throughout his adult life.

To start with, at the turn of the century Gross was already addicted to cocaine, morphine, and opium. Except for brief periods he remained addicted to those drugs until his bitter death in 1920, and often tried to convince other persons to initiate drug usage—reminding us of Freud's campaign in the early 1880s to convince dozens of person to initiate cocaine usage, including his own family members. In 1907 Gross began to work at Kraepelin's psychiatric clinic in Munich, but then and for many years thereafter he spent most of his time at an infamous café as one of the leaders of a raunchy group of Bohemians, anarchists, drug users, thieves, and "free love" advocates. At a table in this café Gross performed countless psychoanalytic "treatments," of a quite intuitive nature, while he was "high" on one drug or another, and also acted as a "guru" for his band of Bohemians, teaching them a mixture of psychoanalysis, philosophical notions, anarchistic ideas, and sexual license. At times he sponsored and took part in sexual orgies held in a barn with animals, where the most grotesque acts of sexual degradation were practiced under the influence of alcohol and other drugs. Gross believed, and taught, that sexual immorality was the healthy state for neurotics, so he transformed his patients into gross immoralists in order to liberate their minds.

There was another bizarre form of treatment that Gross used regularly over the years. He felt that he could liberate his patients, especially confused and depressed females, by persuading them to commit suicide, which a number of them did under his Svengalian influence. In 1906 he provided poison to a disturbed woman named Lotte Chattemer, and she used it to kill herself. In 1910 he was involved in a sexual relationship with a young painter and anarchist named Sophie Benz. When she became mentally disturbed, he prescribed a heavy dose of cocaine for her which she used to kill herself. In that same era, he performed psychoanalysis with a childlike, näive woman named Regina Ullmann and made her pregnant. Then he refused to give her financial support and abandoned her. She reported that during her depressed state of mind he encouraged her to commit suicide by leaving poison near her, as if to tempt her.

On various occasions, those kinds of lethal behaviors towards women by Dr. Gross caused legal authorities to attempt his incarceration, but this clever con artist always found ways to dodge the bullet. He used the great prestige and the wealth of his father to assist him, despite his obviously venomous hatred for his indulgent father, and at other times he ducked into psychiatric institutions for treatment so that the law could be held at bay. In 1908 he was psychoanalyzed briefly by Jung, while hospitalized, and years later was analyzed by another renowned psychoanalyst, Wilhelm Stekel (after Stekel's break with Freud). Gross was given varying diagnoses by different authorities including schizophrenic, psychopath, megalomaniac, neurotic, etc., but for our purposes these diagnoses do not seem of paramount importance. Emphasizing the lethal outcomes of his above behaviors, and various indications in his life of hidden and overt hostility towards women, one can easily say that he was a murderer of women. He accomplished these killings by using various inducements to suicide, and then he rationalized this with absurd prattle about euthanasia, i.e. claiming to give his victims "freedom" from pain and suffering.

Readers are asked to keep in mind my claim that Freud identified with Otto Gross and his murderous ways, and that both of these analysts had powerful needs to induce suicide in other persons. For a major segment of this book (and a later one) will provide evidence that Freud repeatedly tried to induce suicide in various individuals including friends, patients, and colleagues. In effect, this becomes another factor in his murder complex which encompasses: identifications with many murderers; powerful death wishes towards family members and other persons; inducements to suicide; the "assault" on Emma Eckstein; the cocaine deaths in the early 1880s; bizarre behavior with the Moses statue in 1913; the Acropolis incident in 1904 (brief psychotic break); the Julius Mosen lapse and forgetting of the name Signorelli; several key dreams involving murder; the presumed killings of Emanuel and John Freud—and much more ahead.

While we are thinking about Otto Gross' inducements of vulnerable women to commit suicide, and my claim that Freud indulged in similar lethal activities, we should consider whether Freud ever effected a fantasy identification with a literary character who was infamous for inducing suicides. In 1919 Freud published his well-known essay "The 'Uncanny'" in which he discussed psychological sources in us which generate this strange feeling. It is noteworthy that at one point he remarked that in Hebrew the word "uncanny" signifies the demonic. Along the way, Freud summarized a rather bizarre story by Hoffman titled "The Sand-Man."

This tale involves a boy named Nathaniel whose mother tells him that the bogeyman called the Sand-Man is only a figure of speech, not a real person. However, the boy's *nanny* frightens him by saying that the Sand-Man is an evil old fellow who tears out the eyes of bad children who refuse to go to bed at night. He does this by throwing hot coals into a child's eyes and later plucks out his eyes and feeds them to his bird-beaked offspring. (Notice that the theme of bird-beaked people correlates uncannily with Freud's early dream about bird-beaked figures who carried his "dead" mother to bed.) The analysis of this story by Freud emphasized that the tearing out of eyes signifies castration and that the Sand-Man represents both a demon and the child's punitive father.

Since Freud remarked that demonic figures like the Sand-Man have evil powers like those of Mephistopheles (Satan), and since we also know that Freud identified intensely with Satan, the logical conclusion can be drawn that Freud identified with both Satan and the Sand-man. In discussing this story, Vitz (1988, p. 142) shrewdly noticed Freud's comment that many people may regard psychoanalysis as uncanny (demonic?), and he compared the Sand- Man's hypnotic stare with Freud's piercing gaze (cited by many colleagues) and his early uses of hypnotism. Vitz wrote: "One wonders whether Freud ever thought of himself as the Sand-Man." What is implied by Vitz' query is that perhaps Freud had made a fantasy identification with the Sand-man, which my first sentence above indicates is highly probable.

Assuming the correctness of this view, that Freud had made an unconscious identification with the Sand-Man, this also relates to my claim that Freud induced certain persons to commit suicide (as also reflected in his identification with Otto Gross). For in Vitz' summary of Hoffman's tale he wrote: "In the story, the Sand-Man's presence is fear-inducing; his hypnotizing stare can *bring his victims to suicide . . .*" (Emphasis added.) One might deduce that the enraged infantile part of Freud's mind was acting-out his identification with the Sand-man when he was involved in repeated efforts to impel other persons to commit suicide, as he did with his depressed colleague Victor Tausk. Therefore, it is particularly uncanny that Freud wrote this essay ("The 'Uncanny'") in 1919, and that this was the same year that Freud pushed Tausk over the edge, into oblivion. A major portion of chapter nine will be devoted to a summary of the horrendous relationship between Freud and Tausk which culminated in this disciple's grotesque suicide in 1919. For readers who like to make note of uncanny "coincidences," attention will be given to my claim that in that very same year, 1919, Freud "arranged" for his nephew John Freud to disappear from the face of the earth.

This brings me now to a correction that I need to acknowledge concerning a statement I made in my first chapter. There I indicated that the only writer who has preceded me with the thesis that Freud was a murderer is Eric Miller in his 1984 book *Passion for Murder (The Homicidal Deeds of Dr. Sigmund Freud)*. At this point, let me revise that viewpoint by suggesting that in 1969 Paul Roazen was the first author to imply strongly that Freud was a murderer. However, Roazen apparently did not have the *chutzpah* to make a direct, unambiguous charge of this sort against a "great man" in his dramatic volume *Brother Animal*, which gives a detailed account of the bitter relationship between Freud and his disciple Tausk. For once I am entirely in agreement with Eissler's words (1983, p.3) when he wrote: "Roazen's book is the story, not of suicide, not even of a manslaughter, but of a murder in which Freud is unmasked as the culprit." (Of course, ultimately Eissler insisted upon Freud's innocence by stating that: ". .Freud did not kill Tausk or hire anybody to do so . . .") But Eissler's preceding statement is correct when he remarked that Roazen's book can be interpreted easily as having charged Freud with the *de facto* murder of Victor Tausk.

The previous pages of this chapter have revealed Freud's fantasy identifications with 20 literary characters and real persons who were murderers, or were strongly suspected of that crime. In addition, Freud probably harbored an identification with Stevenson's famous duo, Dr. Jekyll and Mr. Hyde, consonant with the dualistic aspects of Freud's personality that will be covered in the next chapter and because of a bizarre episode involving Freud and Dr. Ludwig Jekels (Jekyll?) that will be discussed later. And in the next chapter I'll discuss a quite special figure from Greek mythology, again a murderer, with whom I believe Freud harbored a fantasy identification (in connection with his depersonalization episode on the Acropolis in 1904).

Concerning my thesis that in 1914 Freud arranged for the murder of Emanuel Freud—a monumental father-figure in his life—readers should note that 16 of the 20 lethal fantasy identifications previously discussed can be seen as having patricidal themes. These identifications include ones with Macbeth, Oedipus, Hamlet, Brutus, Don Juan, Fiesco, Franz Moor, Karl Moor, Fanny Moser, Zeus, the Hollthurn dream's patient, the son who shot his old father (for whom Freud paid all legal fees), Otto Gross, and the St. Sigismund story. With regard to Satan's murderous hatred towards the patriarchal Jahweh, the identifications with Satan and the anti-Christ also can be interpreted as having patricidal themes.

Concerning my second thesis that in 1918 Freud arranged for the disappearance and presumed murder of his *nephew* John Freud, some readers may feel a bit let down that I've not been able to find a fantasy identification by Freud with any important figure who murdered a *nephew*. Actually, in the next chapter the special figure from Greek mythology with whom I claim Freud probably identified was the murderer of his talented nephew, whom he killed due to motives of intense rivalry. This should remind us of the rivalrous feelings that made Freud so bitter towards his nephew John starting in their Freiberg years.

Now that readers have assimilated these materials about Freud's fantasy identifications with 20 murderers, they are in a position to decide for themselves the basic question posed at the end of the previous chapter.

Considering the numerous examples in chapter three showing that Freud had powerful tendencies to act-out his fantasy identifications repeatedly, is it quite plausible that he would have acted-out in some lethal manner his identifications with some of these 20 murderers? Many readers will agree with me that, in the context of Freud's murder complex discussed throughout this book, the stated question should receive an affirmative reply, particularly in relation to the deaths of Emanuel and John Freud.

In deciding whether Freud's identifications with so many murderers probably generated evil and destructive actions in his own life, it will be interesting to review his advice and warnings about fantasy identifications to a young man in 1913 (the year before Emanuel's presumed murder). McGrath refers (1986, pp. 313-20) to a long discussion in that year which Freud had with Hans Herzl, the son of the deceased Theodor Herzl (father of Zionism). Ignoring any awareness of his own hypocrisy, Freud cautioned young Herzl that intense ambitions were poisoning his life and that he needed finally to lay to rest the ghost of his dead father who was still very alive in his feelings. Freud warned Hans against following in his father's footsteps. He called the elder Herzl one of that dangerous breed of men who try to transform the magical aspects of people's dreams and fantasies into realities while manipulating them for their own political ends.

Freud designated this dangerous breed of men who manipulate the fantasy lives of other people (and themselves) as "robbers in the underground of the unconscious world," and he warned young Herzl to stay away from them "even if one of them was your father . . ." It is significant that Theodor Herzl probably harbored a fantasy of himself as the new Moses, as seen by a dream he had at age 12. McGrath noted that Freud viewed T. Herzl as a modern Moses, as suggested by Freud's Myops dream, and that one of his unpublished dreams indicates that Freud's fantasy identification with Moses was merged with his feeling that Herzl also was the new Moses. Ergo, Freud was unconsciously warning young Herzl against himself, as a man who used the magical aspects of many fantasy identifications (including Moses) for his own strange ends. However, McGrath did not seem to be aware of this factor and did not mention it.

McGrath wrote that Freud's fatherly advice to Hans Herzl "sprang in part from a feeling of having himself experienced the young man's problem." But McGrath attenuated this insight by adding that: "Freud too had wanted to see his father as Moses and had suffered from an inability to come to terms with his conflicted feelings about him." It would have been better if McGrath had emphasized his awareness that Freud wanted to be

Moses himself, and that this bizarre fantasy identification and scores of others that gripped his imagination, were obvious clues to Freud's awesome, unremitting psychopathology which his self-analysis hardly ameliorated at all. Instead, McGrath followed the path of many predecessors and whitewashed Freud's deep psychic problems by writing that his fantasy identifications "did help to point him towards the goal of high achievement..."

In his final lecture at Clark University in 1909 Freud noted that some people escape from reality by entering a life of fantasy. This includes the creation of fantasy identifications, and Freud noted that these involve wish fulfillments just as dreams do. He remarked that such fantasies "include a great deal of the true constitutional essence of the subject's personality as well as of those impulses which are repressed where reality is concerned." Well, what about a very troubled man whose "medical accidents" have killed many people, and who harbors fantasy identifications with a long series of murderers? Can one assume that the essence of his personality is likely to involve murder—a murder complex? And when Freud warned young Herzl about dangerous men who manipulate the magical aspects of fantasy identifications and dreams, wasn't he referring unconsciously to his own demonic nature?

The Plan to Murder Fliess

Having considered Freud's fantasy identifications with a very large number of murderers, now it is appropriate to inquire whether he ever actualized those murderous impulses of his in real life. Is there persuasive published evidence, for example, that Freud ever planned a murder or even that he made a physical attempt to murder anyone? Similarly, with regard to his fantasy identifications, has any knowledgeable scholar ever suggested that Freud might have become involved in murderous behaviors while effecting an irrational acting-out of his fantasy identification with some real or fictional murderer, such as the patricidal killers called Brutus or Oedipus?

This brings us to a review of a paper by Peter Swales (in Spurling, 1989) which provides compelling materials indicating that Freud probably devised a plan to murder Wilhelm Fliess in 1900, and perhaps made an actual attempt to murder him. This is pertinent to Fliess's claim that Freud tried to kill him during the final meeting of these two old friends, at a resort called Achensee in the Tyrol mountains—an alpine region connecting western Austria and Italy. It should be noted that Swales has written many biographical and conceptual essays about Freud and, as the foremost scholar about the life and works of Fliess, has spent many years preparing a biography of Fliess utilizing an extensive array of primary documents.

Early in his article about the Achensee affair Swales reviewed some of the key factors in the long-term relationship between Freud and the Berlin physician, Fliess. He noted that in the 1890s the two men met about every six months in numerous European cities for scientific talks pertaining to some of their common interests, particularly sexuality. Fliess provided biological insights that Freud incorporated into his budding psychoanalytic framework and, as Frank Sulloway (1979) has shown, contributed some basic concepts that Freud used in his theorizing—though many Freudians still deny vigorously Fliess's important conceptual influences on the master.

Swales has discussed in detail the key ideas concerning bisexuality that Fliess formulated in the late 1890s, concepts that Freud decided were essential for developing his own theories about the neuroses. As early as 1897, Fliess told Freud his new idea that each person harbors sexual characteristics of the opposite sex, and that this provides a powerful explanation for the origin of repression, for which Freud had not been able to find an adequate explanation. Fliess posited that the origin of repression occurs when the dominant sexual disposition forces all psychic material of a contrary nature into the unconscious mind, which immediately had a great impact on Freud's thinking.

A fairly thorough account was given by Swales of Freud's covetous feelings towards Fliess's theory of bisexuality during the period from 1897 till the early months of 1900. In those years there were strong indications that Freud was intent on stealing priority from Fliess (plagiarizing) regarding the bisexuality concept, but eventually Freud was force to recant and then pretended that an amnesic episode had cause him to "forget" that his friend was the originator of this idea! Many of the Freud/Fliess letters of that era make it obvious that Freud was greatly angered that Fliess had been the originator of the "psychic bisexuality" notion, and circa December 1899 Freud acknowledged that he might explode with envy concerning his friend's discoveries (by Fliess's account).

In my view, probably it was Freud's attempt to plagiarize the bisexuality concept that initiated the growing estrangement of the two men. Perhaps as an act of retaliation, Fliess suddenly expanded his own arcane theories in a manner that excluded any real significance for Freud's psychoanalytic theories and made them quite superfluous. Near the end of 1899 this growing division between the two men was further increased when Freud's "enemy," Dr. Breuer, became the physician of Fliess's mother-in-law and then further solidified his new role in Fliess's household when Breuer's daughter Margarethe (on May 27, 1900) married a protégé of Fliess's. In March of 1900 Freud angrily described this as a "Breuerization" of Fliess's home, which he obviously felt was shutting him out of Fliess's life permanently.

Although Swales did not make this next point explicitly, the preceding material suggests that by the summer of 1900 Freud was experiencing enormous feelings of anger, envy, and revenge in his relationship with Wilhelm Fliess. Given Freud's lifelong struggle with death-wishes towards others, it should not be surprising that murderous feelings towards Fliess became excessive in early August 1900 at Achensee, a final meeting during four or five vacation days that they spent together. For later it was Fliess's contention that Freud had formulated a plan to *kill him* at Achensee, as reported by Swales.

According to Swales, Fliess characterized Freud's behavior towards him at Achensee as manifesting "violence" and "personal animosity," allegedly relating to Freud's envious feelings. Evidently, the two men again debated the priority issue concerning the discovery of a universal latent bisexuality sometime during their Achensee meeting, and Freud must have become extremely angry. Indeed, Swales reported that Fliess later told some of his family members, and at least one friend, that "*Freud had a plan to murder him*" at Achensee (p. 311), and insisted adamantly that this murder plan was stimulated by Freud's envy.

In greater detail, Swales cited Fliess's assertion that "it was Freud's intention to lure him into a lonely mountainous region, then to push him over a precipice or into water below." Swales noted that Fliess could not swim and "was a man of very small stature," but that Fliess claimed he escaped Freud's murder plot because he'd had reason to suspect his destructive intentions. Swales remarked that he'd corroborated that Fliess had made those charges by consulting various knowledgeable sources, including Fliess's daughter and the son of Fliess's close friend, George Heinitz, in Berlin, and via indirect access to a niece of Fliess's. Apparently, all of these persons confirmed that Fliess had charged Freud with concocting a murder plan to be used at Achensee, though not all the parties agreed that Fliess had claimed that an actual murder attempt had been made. More will be said later about this seeming discrepancy.

It is Swales's opinion (and I agree with him) that Freud provided us with "a disguised account of the events at Achensee in *The Psychopathology of Everyday Life*—a work published exactly one year after the final meeting . ." Shrewdly, Swales noted that this book was "full" of references to Fliess, both "obvious" and "concealed"—as Freud announced in a letter to the Berlin physician. The disguised episode to which Swales referred will now be summarized.

While demonstrating the everyday occurrence of "symptomatic acts," Freud showed his readers that the casual draping of a man's cape on a chair had been "symptomatic" and unconsciously showed hostility to him and a desire to exclude his presence. The story began on Freud's summer vacation at a hotel, while he was alone waiting for an unnamed travelling companion to join him. He met a stranger who was equally lonely, so the two men went for walks together. During the afternoon of the third day, this young man suddenly told Freud that his wife would arrive that evening by train, urging Freud to eat supper without him since he would eat later when his wife arrived. Freud noted that now his psychological interest had become aroused: "for I had already been struck that morning by my companion's having declined my proposal for a longish expedition and how, during our short walk, he objected to taking a certain path as being too steep and dangerous."

In the hotel foyer the next morning, the man introduced Freud to his wife and invited him to have breakfast with them. A few minutes later the couple was seated at a table and Freud went to join them, but draped over the only extra chair was the fellow's heavy Loden-cape. The woman nudged her husband and informed him that thoughtlessly he'd "taken up the gentleman's seat." However, Freud claimed that the cape upon the chair represented an unconsciously motivated behavior that revealed the man's hostility—a symptomatic act signifying: "There's no room for you here, you're superfluous now."

After referring to the above anecdote, Swales provided various reasons for concluding that it was a disguised version of the Achensee meeting between Freud and Fliess in mid-1900. For example, he noted that for many years it was Fliess's custom to wear an unfashionable Loden-cape, like the fellow in the above story. Also, Fliess was expecting his wife Ida to join them at the end of the Achensee meeting, as the above man also awaited his wife, and Swales remarked that eventually Freud blamed Ida, to a great degree, for his breakup with Fliess and for helping Breuer to invade their household. Swales recognized that Freud's feeling of becoming "superfluous" in the Fliess's home was similar to the above fellow's feeling that he'd become "superfluous" at the breakfast table. Swales even hinted at name magic in Freud's mind, since the word superfluous (in German, *Überflussig*, or overflowing) provokes strong associations with the German word meaning "to flow," or *Fliessen*, which incorporates the name Fliess!*

For Swales the "clincher" in deciding that the above anecdote was a disguised version of the Achensee meeting rests upon the story's reference to a short walk and a proposed expedition, declined by the young stranger as being too steep and dangerous. This seems to match the account Fliess gave to his relatives of Freud's intention to lure him onto a dangerous path and push him over a precipice or into water.

In my opinion, Swales seized too quickly upon the anecdote's statement that since the young man had declined to walk on a steep, dangerous path (indicating that Fliess likewise had declined walking on a risky path) this showed that no attempt on Fliess's life actually had been made by Freud. For

---

*And that related German word (*Überflussig*) contains the provocative name Sig!

it may be true that Fliess declined to walk on the most dangerous of the paths, but that does not prove that a disguised attempt on his life had not already been managed earlier. It's true, of course, that Freud could not have made an open, blatant attempt to kill Fliess, otherwise Fliess would not have continued his dwindling correspondence with Freud for the two years following Achensee, but another possibility should be considered.

My above remarks tend towards the proposal that the following course of events could easily have occurred during the Achensee meeting, assuming that Freud went there with a simple murder plan in mind. My suggestion is that on the first or second day of hiking, the men walked a path together at a place that was moderately risky—perhaps near a descent into water (Fliess's nemesis). Assume that Freud maneuvered this little fellow, Fliess, into taking a slight lead, and then Freud managed "accidentally" to stumble forward over a small rock, pushing Fliess's body quite hard downwards, toward the water. But perhaps the canny Fliess had used a walking stick to catch himself, or luckily grabbed onto a sapling, stopping his downward course—and then found himself consoling a profusely apologetic Freud—who seemed sincerely "shaken" and contrite.

For months or even a few years thereafter Fliess might not have recognized that the above hypothetical scenario had been an actual murder attempt by his "beloved friend." In a state of mental ambiguity, slowly he might have confided to relatives and his closest friends that Freud at Achensee had harbored a murder plan which he attempted to enact, but with other persons who might not readily accept his "interpretation" of Freud's stumble he might have withheld his claim of a murder attempt—thereby explaining the discrepancy among the sources contacted by Swales.

What would have enabled Fliess eventually to recognize that Freud's presumed "stumble" had constituted a murder attempt? Swales provided some of the factors that would have provoked Fliess's eventual enlightenment, especially the Berliner's knowledge that Freud harbored urgent deathwishes towards countless persons and towards Fliess, in particular. Actually, in connection with those death-wishes, "Fliess was well aware Freud had entertained towards him" some intensely lethal feelings. Those deadly feelings served "the interests of denying him and robbing him of priority in the matter of bisexuality," which Freud exhibited towards Fliess at Achensee. Knowing Freud's personality in depth, was Fliess justified in suspecting he was capable of murdering to facilitate plagiarism of the bisexuality concept? Obviously, he was quite justified in that suspicion, though some critics dismiss this as reflecting his alleged paranoia.

Furthermore, it was emphasized by Swales that during Fliess's editing of the dream book, a year earlier, he had read of Freud's admission that he identified closely with a male patient suffering obsessional neurosis who was deluged by murderous feelings towards many different people. Freud wrote that the man was obsessed with a Cain fantasy and was even "capable of wanting to push his own father over a precipice from the top of a mountain." Swales noted that Fliess's friendship with Freud was fraternal but that analysts often regard him as a *father*-figure to Freud. So Swales concluded that "Freud's self-avowed identification with his patient could well have assumed a most sinister significance for Fliess in the Alpine context of Achensee." This could have been another reason why Fliess eventually decided that Freud's "stumbling" (or some other deadly ruse) had constituted an actual murder attempt at Achensee.

By the way, my thesis that perhaps Freud stumbled against Fliess on a risky path at Achensee is fostered by a recognition that Fliess's small size would have made it easy for him to be pushed downward, despite that Freud himself was only five feet and six inches tall, weighing about 130 pounds. Swales commented that Fliess's "very small stature as an adult was due to an illness in childhood that stunted his growth." (Probably, he was fond of wearing that Loden-cape, because it gave him a more impressive appearance than his near-dwarfish size allowed.)

Near the end of his essay Swales made some interesting points. He inquired as to why Freud bothered, in his anecdote about the cape-on-chair "symptom," to insert that superfluous material about the proposed expedition and the younger man's concerns about the steep and dangerous footpath. Reasoning quite incisively, Swales remarked that "the reference is redundant and obtrusive for it bears no logical relation to the thrust of Freud's anecdote about his later being rendered 'superfluous' by the wife's arrival."

That Freud did include this strangely unnecessary material, Swales observed, must eventually have convinced Fliess that Freud had the same idea in mind that he'd had himself—the issue of an impending murder attempt on that dangerous footpath! In effect, Freud could not help "confessing" to Fliess that his suspicion was correct by inserting the unnecessary self-disclosing data into his little anecdote, which Fliess must have recognized as a disguised version of the Achensee incident while reading Freud's book on "slips" a year later. If this was Freud's veiled confession to Fliess of a murder plan, he also provided Fliess with one of the self-serving motives—'you deserved to die for making me and my theories *superfluous*.' No wonder Swales observed that: "Here, unmasked, is quite a different Freud than the man portrayed by his biographers."

What other motive did Freud have for including that unnecessary material in his anecdote, seemingly designed to help Fliess comprehend that he'd planned to murder him at Achensee? Swales asserted that Freud did this deliberately, "writing specifically with the 'indignant' Fliess in mind as a future reader and thereby seeking to intimidate and belittle him." It was further claimed by Swales that Freud was trying to insinuate his superiority over Fliess, and with regard to intimidation Swales remarked that Freud tried "to subvert Fliess's peace of mind by practicing psychological warfare—he was 'gas-lighting' him." (This refers to the film in which Charles Boyer tried to drive his wife into insanity using sinister mind-games.) In a footnote (p. 321), Swales insisted that Freud was attempting to "mind-fuck" Fliess (rape of the mind)—evidently by showing him that he'd come close to being murdered and might become victimized at some later time, if he became a threat to Freud.

Now, briefly diverting from Swales's comments, let me suggest why Freud needed to intimidate Fliess in the preceding manner, and to explain the ways he probably thought Fliess could become a threat to him later. In *The Fatal Freud* I offer an entire chapter about Freud's vicious, manipulative relationship with the student Weininger and his friend Swoboda (Freud's patient). In Swales's essay he recounted that in 1906 Fliess made a public accusation that Freud was the "instigator in a plot to plagiarize him." This related to Fliess's well-founded claim that Freud assisted both those young men to produce writings that stole Fliess's basic concepts about bisexuality, which he'd not yet published, Weininger becoming the author of a famous book that plagiarized Fliess's discoveries. In my chapter emphasizing young Weininger's suicide, for which I claim that Freud was largely to blame, sound reasons are offered to support my deduction that Freud began his nefarious plot to plagiarize Fliess by making contact with Weininger *only a few days or weeks* following the Achensee debacle. This indicates that Freud's unfulfilled blood lust and revenge at Achensee immediately pressured him to obtain a measure of vengeance by quickly formulating the plagiarism plot with Weininger and Swoboda.

The sequence of events that I propose is the following. After failing to steal the bisexuality concept from Fliess by murdering him at Achensee, Freud's envy and need for revenge were still intense. In subsequent days or weeks, he initiated the conspiracy with Weininger and Swoboda, using them as surrogates in his plagiarism of Fliess's work, thereby obtaining an indirect revenge against his friend. During the next few years books were published by Swoboda and Weininger that plagiarized Fliess's ideas on bisexuality, and Fliess learned about Swoboda's work in the spring of 1904. On April 27, 1904 Fliess wrote to Freud accusing him of having assisted Swoboda's plagiarism. Then Fliess wrote Freud again on July 20, 1904 noting that he'd just discovered Weininger's book (published 1903), and he charged that this unstable young man also had plagiarized his work with assistance from Freud.

On July 23rd Freud replied that the deceased Weininger was a "burglar," allegedly had killed himself "out of fear of his criminal nature," but might have gotten the ideas about bisexuality from the general literature (rather than from Freud). On July 26th Fliess wrote again with more specific information, obtained from Freud's friend Dr. Oscar Rie (Fliess's kinsman), that Weininger had consulted Freud about his early manuscript. Immediately, Freud's next letter admitted his partial culpability, asserting that the harm done to Fliess by Weininger was "very slight" since the youth's book was a "shoddy piece of work," and complained that Fliess was bothering him about "such petty incidents."

Despite Freud's bravado in telling Fliess not to bother him about "petty incidents" like the plagiarizing of his bisexuality research, Freud must have felt quite threatened that Fliess could publicly damage his reputation by bringing a plagiarism lawsuit against him. It was indicated by Jones (I, p. 316) that Fliess fought back by publishing some of their correspondence, presumably their letters dealing with bisexuality. Jones noted (p. 315) that in one of Freud's letters: "He frankly confessed he must have been influenced by his wish to rob Fliess of his originality, a wish presumably compounded of envy and hostility." Also, Jones reported that near the end of 1905 "Fliess got a friend of his to publish a pamphlet attacking Weininger, Swoboda, and Freud." This was the kind of threat Freud knew that Fliess might become to him when he wrote that manipulative anecdote about the cape-on-chair in his book on "slips," attempting to intimidate Fliess by slyly informing him, in effect: 'Yes, I concocted a murder plan to kill you at Achensee, as you suspected. And if you try to threaten me about my plagiaristic intentions, I'll devise a *successful* murder plot against you, in future.'

However, Fliess was a brave little man who was willing to fight vigorously for his rights, and eventually this helped to provoke peculiar disorientation and a moderate psychotic episode in Freud in mid-1904, soon after their final exchange of letters about plagiarism. Swales stated (p. 303) that in June of 1904 Fliess asked Freud for a meeting in Vienna, presumably to discuss important issues concerning the plagiarisms by Weininger and Swoboda "but Freud fled the city two days before his arrival in order to avoid him." This fleeing from a confrontation with Fliess seems to relate to the very strange "holiday" trip, about that same time, that Freud took with his brother, Alexander. In a depressed mood—probably in August of 1904—they went first to Trieste, where Freud became obsessed with numerical delusions that seemed to pertain to Fliess's "number magic" (relating to his prediction of Freud's death at age 51, which Freud feared). Then they went to Athens where Freud stood near the Acropolis and suffered a brief mental breakdown in which he fantasized being split into two persons. A later chapter will provide further discussion of this mildly psychotic "Acropolis episode" and its relationship to Freud's parricidal intentions involving Fliess, Emanuel and John—and indications that Freud reenacted his desire to hurl his nephew to his death *from a precipice* at the Acropolis.

The information given on the last two pages helps to put the Achensee murder plan into a broader perspective which clearly links it with the balmy Acropolis episode of 1904. Thus, one can assume that Freud was in a moderately psychotic state of mind in the summer of 1900, when he concocted and presumably tried to implement his murder plan against Fliess. Similarly, as a fearful reaction to planning murder and plagiarism in 1900, he later experienced another moderate psychotic episode in the summer of 1904 at Trieste and Athens.

Judging it on its own terms, I'm already willing to give substantial credence to Swales's thesis that an Achensee murder plan devised by Freud was a reality (not Fliess's paranoid delusion). Furthermore, its credibility is greatly strengthened by making use of other historical perspectives. First, we need to look at the Achensee murder incident within the context of Freud's very disturbed behaviors throughout the entire year of 1900, as I have done exhaustively in a later chapter. Hopefully, most readers will be favorably impressed by my characterization of the year 1900 as "a year of madness and revenge" for Freud, after reading my descriptions of his deranged behaviors during that year of extremely intense stresses for him. In the early months of that year, his letters to Fliess admitted the episodes of madness and deep depression that were tormenting him, so it will not seem implausible that a moderate psychosis at Achensee, in mid-1900, prompted his formulation of a murder plan and probably an attempt to kill Fliess in some disguised manner.

Likewise, in chapter eight I've characterized the year 1914 as another year of madness and revenge for Freud, pertaining to plausible evidence that he concocted two murder plans in that year—one against Jung (that was canceled by the flow of events), and the second against Emanuel Freud starting in June and actualized in October via the train "accident" that killed him. I'm fairly confident that many readers will give considerable credibility to one or both of those presumed murder plans of 1914 and, in doing so, will sense that the recognition of either plan as a virtual reality thereby strengthens Swales's thesis about the Achensee affair.

A further reinforcement of Swales's thesis is provided by an interpretation that can be given to Freud's admission, in the dream book, that he closely identified with a male patient who wished to kill his father by hurling him off a precipice. My suggestion is that the incorporation of that remarkable item in the dream book perhaps supports the thesis that Freud did plan to kill Fliess at Achensee by pushing him from a precipice, for the following reason. In chapter eight I've described numerous peculiar behaviors and dreams of Freud's prior to October 1914 (when Emanuel died) that can readily be interpreted as being predictive of his intention to murder his brother. Apparently, this uncanny predictiveness of Freud's lethal intentions was a recurrent aspect of his unconscious functioning, so the aforementioned patricidal item in the dream book probably was predictive of Freud's intention to push Fliess (a father-figure) off a cliff, as Fliess seemed to think it was. Of course, Freud's apologists still assume that Fliess was wrong about this matter, since they continue to regard his accusation as reflective of a paranoid delusion.

Near the end of his essay Swales asked again whether it is "conceivable that Freud really *did* intend to murder Fliess?" To buttress Fliess's accusation Swales suggested that Freud's lethal behavior at Achensee was the result of his acting-out a fantasy identification with a patricidal hero, namely Oedipus. Swales wrote: "Recently I have argued that, in the summer of 1900, only a few weeks after their big quarrel, Freud sought to re-enact the mythical role of Oedipus by committing the crime of incest with the MOTHER—in Freud's case, with a mother-substitute in the form of his wife's sister, Minna Bernays." Here, Swales was referring to the "honeymoon" trip in Italy that Freud took with Minna immediately following the Achensee debacle, which is pertinent to my previous claim that Minna, a *governess* in Freud's home, was the surrogate for his primal mother of the Freiberg era, his seductive nanny. Swales added that "the other side of the Oedipal coin" was the "murder of the FATHER," or a father-figure in Freud's case, emphasizing that most analysts regarded Fliess as a "father symbol" for the master.

Citing his firm belief that Freud seduced Minna in the summer of 1900, it then became equally plausible to Swales that "while at Achensee a few weeks before, Freud entertained *serious fantasies* about murdering the primal FATHER incarnate in Fliess—that is to say, by pushing him over a precipice." At this point Swales reminded his readers that all the years of his life Freud had sought to pattern his life after heroes of myth and legend— "and the deed of murder, like that of incest, is permitted to those heroes."

Swales is the first author to make a resolute declaration that Freud probably was embroiled in murderous activity, on one occasion, in connection with an acting-out of murderous behaviors of a mythic hero with whom he'd effected a fantasy identification. One wonders what additional thoughts about Freud's homicidal potentials might appear in Swales's future writings after he absorbs the contents of this chapter concerning Freud's fantasy identifications with at least twenty murderers?

Now, I'd like to try buttressing Swales's thesis, in my own way, that Freud at Achensee was acting-out the lethal behavior of Oedipus. Let's recall that the myth specifies that Oedipus had to accomplish two remarkable killings before he could "return home" (Freiberg?) and capture his great sexual prize, the primal mother. First, he had to kill his own father (in a transference state), and then he had to kill the magical creature called the Sphinx.

Recall that the Sphinx was part-beast and partly human, a lethal creature who could speak fluently and posed a deadly riddle, killing myriad travellers who could not answer it correctly. The riddle was: 'what walks on four legs in the morning, two legs at noon, and three legs in the evening.' Oedipus defeated this killer by correctly answering "Man"—since the baby's early locomotion is on hands and knees; the mature person walks on two legs; and the old man walks on three "legs," including a cane.

There are several aspects of the above story that need emphasis. The Sphinx is a magical figure and a symbol of Death, but it riddles about Life— the course of *human development*. In doing so, its deadly riddle incorporates a hint of ancient number magic, utilizing the numbers four, two, and three. Finally, this tale specifies that Oedipus's victory over the creature (death/castration) occurs when it plummets from *a high precipice* to its death, paving the way for his incest with the primal mother.

My suggestion is that Freud's unconscious mind required compulsively that, in acting-out his fantasy identification with Oedipus, he needed to make an attempt to kill a father-figure and a person capable of representing the Sphinx. It was in the person of Wilhelm Fliess that both requirements were met, i.e. Freud fantasized that Fliess represented the Sphinx, at Achensee.

Elsewhere, I've suggested that for Freud his uncanny friend Fliess was a magical figure who represented the mythical creature called "the golden fleece" (since "Fliess" means "fleece" in German). This was the healing, life-giving side of Fliess. In Freud's dualistic thinking, the Berliner also represented the Sphinx, pertaining to the destructive death-inducing side of Fliess. For Fliess was regarded as a great healer in Berlin, but he claimed that his (magical) numerical computations could predict the exact year of a person's death, imposing the death sentence of age 51 upon his friend Freud! In Freud's view, all of Fliess's work was predicated upon death, a reaction to the early death of his sister Pauline and irrational desires to reverse death (here, a life symbol), but his predictions of persons' deaths also made him a formidable symbol of death for Freud.

Fliess's incredible uses of magical thinking (cloaked as a science) made him a magical person for Freud. Perhaps his physical stature was part of this picture, as well as his wearing of a cloak (as necromancers often wore). That is, Fliess was the size of many children, and young children are magical because much of their thought is still at a precausal level. Indeed, Fliess was of a near-dwarfish size, and in the history of necromancy dwarfs are seen as having magical properties. Ergo, as a magical person, Fliess was able to connect in Freud's mind with the magical creatures, the golden fleece and the Sphinx, who were symbols of life and death.

The unconscious equation between Fliess and the Sphinx is also suggested by the fact that the creature's famous riddle pertains to the course of man's development (infancy, maturity, senescence) and incorporates a strong hint of number magic. Consider Frank Sulloway's persuasive claim that Freud obtained from Fliess his initial clues to the anal-oral-phallic stages of human development. Moreover, Fliess was forever a "riddler" who posed strange conundrums (and "solved" them) about man's biological development using arcane equations that were merely number magic.

If I have now established the strong probability that Fliess, at Achensee, represented the Sphinx to our hero, Oedipus Freud, does this also suggest the way that Fliess was supposed to die to permit a full reenactment of the myth? In the ancient myth the Sphinx was destroyed by plummeting from a precipice. Was it only a coincidence that Fliess claimed that Freud had concocted a plan at Achensee to push him over a precipice? Was it the fantasy of Freud, or of Fliess, that the little magician from Berlin was a revenant of the Sphinx—or did both of those mentally unstable fellows suffer from the same mythic delusion?

In effect, did those presumably lethal events at Achensee help confirm the claim of the analyst Strachey that Freud and Fliess were involved in *folie à deux*—madness for two? Or, considering that we have no evidence as yet that Fliess had tendencies to enter fantasy identifications with mythic figures and then to act them out, but Freud did have powerful tendencies of that sort, isn't it more likely that it was Freud at Achensee who was involved in a singular form of murderous psychosis? Finally, which of the men evidenced a lifetime of murderous wishes towards others, and recurrent fears of being murdered? The answer to this "riddle" seems obviously to be that: Freud is our man.

Chapter Five

Freud's Mental Imbalance

Freud's and Breuer's Diagnoses of Freud's Psychopathology
If full consideration is to be given to the idea that Freud was impelled irrationally to "assist" the suicides of various persons, as later pages will confirm, and that he probably instigated the deaths of several other persons, including the murders of Emanuel and John Freud, then it will prove useful to explore additional evidences of mental imbalance in Freud in this chapter. The present chapter, and the next one, should help to dispel a myth that has been artfully maintained by the majority of Freud's biographers. That myth contends that Freud suffered only a modest degree of neurosis during his lifetime and that this minor brush with mental illness was largely dissipated by his self-analysis.

The fiction that Freud had experienced only minor mental illness was propagated initially by the master himself and was buttressed by propaganda within Jones's three-volume biography (though Jones once slipped and admitted that Freud had suffered from a "very considerable psychoneurosis"). Basically, the public image that Freud and Jones hoped to "sell" was that the father of psychoanalysis had struggled briefly with a moderate degree of hysteria and perhaps some obsessive-compulsive tendencies that never firmly took hold. Also, Freud alluded to some paranoid tendencies in himself in vague terms, and soon after his break with Fliess in the early 1900s he alleged that Fliess's serious charges against him (plagiarism and intent to murder) proved that his erstwhile bosom friend had retained severe elements of paranoia. Boastfully, Freud proclaimed that his own paranoid trends had been cured by his self-analysis (though he did not confess to his readers what kinds of paranoid delusions and fantasies he had once concocted, so that we might compare these with his scores of fantasy identifications and other evidences of magical thinking in him).

In an earlier era, when the writings of Freud and Jones were establishing that ludicrous fiction of the master's moderate and benign mental disorder, there was not yet an effective challenge to that myth. But an effective challenge finally occurred in 1985 with the publication of the relatively complete letters of Freud to Wilhelm Fliess written from 1887 to 1904. Those letters reveal numerous examples of the bizarre ideation of both Freud and his dearest friend Fliess pertaining to many topics, over an extensive period of time. A careful reading of those letters entitles us to conclude that both Freud and Fliess were afflicted with recurrent episodes of ambulatory psychosis, often in tandem, as seen most clearly in their mutual near-murderous surgery on Emma Eckstein's nose, which was based upon utterly quack ideas which both men embraced ardently.

Unfortunately, few members of the public have the time or expertise to read with painstaking carefulness the Freud/Fliess letters to convince themselves of many evidences of Freud's madness that lurk within those eerie pages. Moreover, the pro-Freud camp is still churning out propaganda designed to convince the public that, while Fliess often was quite insane, his friend Freud was merely humoring him and was not equally psychotic. In a recent article Sander Gilman (1988) offered some of the historical background of psychoanalysis that emphasized Fliess's insanity but downplayed Freud's severe mental illness. Gilman wrote: "It has been accepted that Fliess was a quack—he put forth absolutely mad views . . . " Later, Gilman added that Fliess's theories "appear to us as more than slightly mad." (Doesn't that wording imply that Fliess was psychotic?) Several pages later Gilman admitted that Fliess's quackery "was accepted by Freud," but Gilman seemed to emphasize Fliess's madness and to leave Freud's mental status as merely somewhat questionable (at least prior to the conclusion of his "heroic" self-analysis).

There are numerous reasons why Freud hoped to avoid publication of the Freud/Fliess letters in the 1930s by destroying them. Included in his unsavory motives is the fact that those letters reveal many indications of his severe mental imbalance in the period from 1887 to 1904 and hint that his murderous rage was tied to the act of sexual seduction by his Freiberg nanny. Furthermore, those letters to Fliess incorporated two expert clinical opinions indicating Freud's severe mental imbalance, opinions that Freud hoped would never be made public. Surprisingly, those diagnostic opinions were offered by Josef Breuer and Sigmund Freud himself.

In the early months of 1896 the slow estrangement between Freud and Josef Breuer had proceeded for more than two years when Freud wrote to Fliess (3/1/96) a startling diagnosis that Breuer had made of Freud's mental status. As I have discussed at length in *Dark Side*, there is good reason to believe that this painful diagnosis was a major hidden reason for the eventual break with Freud that Breuer probably initiated, indicating that this older and more experienced physician finally had recognized deep and perhaps dangerous mental instabilities in Freud. In that March letter to Fliess, Freud alluded to his great anger towards Breuer because of their theoretical differences. Then he remarked that their personal relationship had cast a "deep shadow" over his existence in Vienna, relating to Freud's concern that Breuer had become an obstacle to his "professional progress" (1985, p. 56), eventually leading to Freud's intention to relocate in another city and even to leave the practice of medicine. Freud complained that he could no longer do anything right for Breuer and that he had given up trying to please the man.

After having expressed that despair about Breuer in his March letter to Fliess, suddenly Freud revealed Breuer's grim diagnosis of his mental status, as follows: "According to him I should have to ask myself every day whether I am suffering from moral insanity or paranoia scientifica. Yet, I regard myself as the psychically more normal one." Freud used English words in writing the term, "moral insanity," which Breuer had applied to him, and we should note that this psychiatric term was introduced in England in the early 1800s to describe a puzzling form of madness in persons who may appear intellectually sound and normal to their peers, yet suffer serious hidden behavioral deviations (including perversions of natural feelings and moral inclinations). This disguised form of madness also relates to the vague psychiatric term "ambulatory psychosis," which may pertain even to some practicing judges, physicians, and scientists. It is interesting that Masson (1984, pp. 139-41) discussed that the term "ambulatory psychosis" seems to have considerable applicability to Fliess's mental status—as sometimes occurs with renowned scientists who appear normal to the outside world, while actually being quite psychotic. However, Masson did not mention that this term "ambulatory psychosis" might readily have applied to both Fliess and to Freud, as Breuer's diagnosis of "moral insanity" in Freud had implied.

Of course, Freud did not reveal in his March 1st letter to Fliess the list of his unusual covert behaviors that Breuer undoubtedly had offered in support of his diagnosis of Freud's madness. For as we've noted, Freud needed to pretend that it was Breuer who was psychotic and that he himself was the sane one. When we consider that moral insanity covers a wide range of behaviors, from theft and perverse sexual seductions to multiple homicides, we can imagine that Breuer had collected some alarming evidences of Freud's acting-out behaviors, and of his perverse tendencies. In *Dark Side* I have discussed a number of those items which Breuer knew about Freud that biographers have tended to suppress or ignore. By suppressing those items, these writers have perpetuated the myth that it was Freud who initiated the break, due to a key theoretical conflict with Breuer—alleging falsely that the latter's puritanism had caused him to downplay sexual factors regarding the neuroses.

As we begin our review of Freud's mental status, we have learned already that the renowned clinician who knew him earliest and best—his beneficent mentor Josef Breuer—came to regard Freud's psyche as being secretly undermined by psychosis. Readers may be asking themselves why the psychoanalytic elite has not emphasized publicly that Breuer regarded Freud as afflicted with moral insanity. Why, indeed? Moreover, the publication of the Freud/Fliess letters in 1985 revealed that on two separate occasions Freud alluded to his own vulnerability to psychosis, thereby offering substantial support for Breuer's grim diagnosis.

The first time that Freud acknowledged to Fliess that he was subject to periods of psychotic ideation was in his letter of November 29, 1895. In that letter Freud finally admitted that during the previous six months his frenetic and maniacal work on a bizarre "masterpiece" (now called the "Project for a Scientific Psychology," or simply "the Project") had been suffused with psychotic ideation. Freud's letter of May 25th reveals the beginnings of that maniacal activity, which was stoked by heavy doses of cocaine. Apparently, Freud hoped that this turgid "masterpiece" would make his reputation as the Newton of psychology by the creation of a lengthy and obtuse theory that linked mind and physical body via a vast array of quasi-magical symbols. This "Project" was, by and large, such an absurd effort that Freud eventually disowned it, and in his letter to Fliess dated November 29th he began to emerge from a psychotic haze and stated that he no longer understood the state of mind in which he had "hatched" this megalomanic enterprise. Then he apologized to his dear friend Fliess for having afflicted him with accounts of this harebrained project and stated: "to me it appears to have been a kind of madness."

And madness it was, despite efforts of various analytic writers to excuse it by claiming weakly that it was an extremely valuable achievement, because it allegedly held the seeds of some aspects of Freud's later dream theories. References to dream material in the "Project" are extremely brief and of highly questionable scientific value, but the Freudians urgently need to make a mountain of this mole hill to nullify Freud's admission of his madness. In *Dark Side* I have explored in detail Freud's bizarre activities in the days when he pursued this insane will-o-the-wisp called the "Project." (Probably, Freud's maniacal activity on the "Project" for many months helped to coalesce Breuer's awareness that his friend was suffering from an ambulatory psychosis, complicated by a steady ingestion of huge doses of cocaine.)

The second time that Freud referred to his own mental status in a manner suggesting that he had self-awareness that he had suffered from a brief period of madness was in his letter to Fliess of March 23, 1900. In that era Freud acknowledged that he had become extremely angry, frustrated, and depressed because the recent publication of his dream book had not led to the great fame and fortune that he'd been expecting. He admitted to Fliess that he had been suffering from "a deep inner crisis" which had aged him perceptibly, and he also referred to this depression as a "catastrophic collapse," which had caused his analytic patients to be perceived by him as "tormentors." Later in that letter he compared his suffering to the torment experienced by Christ—"it is my cross, I must bear it... my back has become noticeably bent"—as a reflection of his insane identification with Jesus.

Furthermore, he stated that he'd become deeply impoverished emotionally and that a great accumulation of troubles were weighing heavily upon his mind that emanated "from the natural habitat of madness." This reference to his madness he attributed as a diagnosis that *Fliess* might have made of Freud's mental status, but it is obvious that Freud also was regarding himself at tainted by psychotic affect and ideation during the early months of 1900. In *Dark Side* I have discussed whether this period of psychotic vulnerability might have caused Freud to harm any of his analytic patients, whom he called (1985, p.404) his tormentors and "*victims.*" It was during that era that a woman named Margit Kremzir might have become lethally victimized as a patient of Freud due to aspects of name magic that could have linked her irrationally with the man who had led to the social downfall of the Freud family in the 1860s (the counterfeiting fiasco). In April 1900 Freud analyzed Mrs. Kremzir for only 14 days and then dismissed her as a case of paranoia, after which she hanged herself in a hotel room in Vienna. In a later chapter we'll consider whether she represented an instance of his tendency to manipulate various persons into committing suicide.

For now, we will rely upon those well-informed diagnoses by both Breuer and Freud which seem to agree that the latter suffered from intermittent episodes involving psychotic ideation. However, in a later section we'll consider the viewpoints of more than 20 additional writers who have commented upon the question of what kinds of psychopathology were operative in Freud's psyche. At that point, we should be getting a good deal closer to the question of whether Freud's personality was a lethal one, or not—and the remainder of this chapter will provide data that is extremely relevant to that issue.

Freud's Periods of Severe Mental Imbalance

During the waning years of his life, Freud wrote pointedly about the *one* time that he had experienced depression. That was an absurd statement and a deliberate deception that he used to buttress the myth that he'd suffered only mild and infrequent mental disturbance during his lifetime. He did not anticipate that some day the Freud/Fliess letters would be published revealing numerous times when he was mired in depression, which was also exposed in the biography by Max Schur, his personal physician, which disclosed many intimate elements of his personal and mental life. Schur's volume revealed that during Freud's lifetime he suffered a wide variety of neurotic symptoms and numerous episodes of depression, including the times when he had completed some important book or article that had absorbed his energies and then became irrationally despondent. The psychoanalyst Zilboorg (1967) asserted correctly that Freud suffered from *a lifelong depression*, and that for more that 40 years of self-analysis he struggled in vain to undo the horrors of that Freiberg catastrophe involving the loss of his nanny and of his early family structure.

Various writers have cited one or more periods of crisis in Freud's life that involved severe mental instability. However, to the best of my knowledge, no author has offered a complete chronology of these episodes of mental crisis and imbalance, which I will soon attempt to provide. Krüll's book placed a special emphasis on his mental crisis of 1896-97 in a full section (1986, pp. 176-180) that analyzed complex life factors during those years. I am in general agreement with her thesis that the crisis of 1896-97 was partially a repetition of the early Freiberg "catastrophe" and that some of the pathological dynamics of those two crises were repeated "on many other occasions as well"—though she failed to specify most of those other periods of crisis and severe mental instability. There is some validity to her idea that the crisis of 1896-97 related to his father Jacob's death and was stimulated by "his feelings of rage and hatred against his father, secretly stored up for years." However, Krüll failed to see that this rage was not merely against his father Jacob but also towards other father-figures and brother-figures as well—including Emanuel, John, Philipp, Breuer, and Fliess. This expanded conception of his rage, and the tortuous ways that it was channeled, will help to prepare us for an understanding of how it was directed lethally against Emanuel and John Freud in later years, in connection with their mysterious deaths.

Vitz is another author who has commented about periods of serious mental instability in Freud's life. With that issue in mind, he referred to Freud's strange article (1911) about the florid paranoid psychosis of Dr. Paul Schreber, a paper that grossly distorted the case material due to Freud's hidden preoccupation with his own pathologies. Vitz mentioned a "curious autobiographical note" in Freud's case presentation, referring to the fact that Schreber "suffered from two distinct periods of mental crisis." The first of Schreber's psychotic crises was in 1884-85, and the second period began in

1893 and proceeded into 1895-1900. Vitz remarked that: "These two periods rather closely correspond to Freud's own periods of maximal psychological disturbance." The inference that Vitz drew here was that Freud had become identified with the madman Schreber, but sadly Vitz failed to notice whether Freud, in doing so, had pointed to his own rampant vulnerability to psychosis. (I'm in agreement with Vitz that those two periods were ones of intense psychological disturbance for Freud, but I would insist that there were later years that were equally crisis-laden, or moreso, including 1904, 1912-14, 1918-20, 1923, and portions of the 1930s.)

At this point, I'd like to offer an extended chronology of the periods of greatest mental instability in Freud's life, with at least brief comments on each of those painful eras. The first of these, of course, can be labeled "the Freiberg catastrophe," covering ages three to five. Those years incorporate the sexual molestation by nanny; her loss to Sigi via imprisonment; the loss of his extended family and the disruptive moves to both Leipzig and Vienna; and the adjustment to city life. Clark emphasized (1980, p. 17) Freud's intimation that he'd suffered a bitterly unhappy childhood, though one suspects that there must have been some happy times that he failed to recall.

The second period of severe mental stress in Freud's life was from ages nine to ten, and somewhat beyond, relating to the arrest of his uncle Josef in Vienna in June of 1865 for possession of counterfeit money, and his sentencing to ten years' imprisonment in February 1866. Josef's wife drafted annual petitions for clemency from 1866 to 1870, so it's likely that both of the Freud families in Vienna were kept in turmoil, shame, and depression about this matter with maximal effects on Sigmund's early teenage years, as Prof. Gicklhorn has described quite vividly (1976).

We can surmise that in the era of puberty, around age thirteen, Sigmund experienced a revival of feelings of depression and shame relating to the Freiberg catastrophe and to the more recent imprisonment of his uncle. Perhaps unconsciously he knew about the jailing of nanny and related it to uncle Josef's incarceration. One clue to his unsettled state of mind at age thirteen is found in the dream book (1967, pp. 237-8) in connection with his dream of the Three Fates, represented by three unnamed women who were standing in Freud's kitchen. His very first association to the dream pertained to the first novel he'd ever read, *at age thirteen*, which gives us an inkling of his disturbed mental state during puberty. For he had a vivid memory of the ending of this unspecified novel, whose hero's fate was to become submerged in a condition of madness and to repeatedly call out the names of the three women who had brought the greatest sorrow and happiness to his life.

In the second of his dream associations he revealed unawares that one of these three Fates represented his own wet-nurse (who had sexually molested him, we recall), and his story about the man who slyly implied his desire to have sexual relations with his own wet-nurse exposed Freud's concerns about the sexual involvement with his Freiberg nanny. As was often the case, Freud offered no compelling interpretation of this dream. However, it is probable that its core meaning involved his wish that it would not be his fate to succumb to madness, despite that his sexual molestation in infancy had made him vulnerable to psychosis. Evidently, that was a great fear that he struggled with during the third crisis period in his life, around age thirteen.

The fourth crisis period in Freud's life occurred at age 16 when he returned to Freiberg on a summer holiday and fell madly in love with Gisela Fluss, probably as an unconscious attempt to revive the connection with his lost nanny (as implied obliquely by Ernest Jones). During this Freiberg holiday in 1872 with the Fluss family, Sigmund also exhibited an unusual attraction for, and dependence upon, Gisela Fluss's mother. She tended his broken heart when Gisela ignored him, a rebuff that provoked a horrendous alcoholic binge by Sigmund. He remained deeply enamored of Gisela for decades thereafter (despite denials by Jones and other friendly biographers), as will be discussed in some detail in the next chapter in connection with his various bizarre, repetitive behaviors relating to Gisela and the man she married. In Krüll's book it is suggested (1986, p.177) that the episode with Gisela Fluss, when Sigmund was age 16, was an important crisis period in his life, and I've given a strong endorsement to Krüll's position.

In the years from 1873 to late March of 1881 Freud attended the University of Vienna as a medical student. The nearly eight years that this allegedly impoverished student took to complete his medical degree, almost twice the normal time required, has been rationalized by his apologists using various weak excuses. A more candid picture was given by Clark (1980, pp. 47-8) when he noted Freud's admission that he was "decidedly negligent" in pursuing his medical studies and that "his acquaintances regarded him as a loafer and doubted whether he would get through." It is my suspicion that Freud suffered serious recurrent emotional problems that interfered with his medical studies, and that the paucity of details about those years has kept historians in the dark about his mental status during that prolonged stay in medical school. (In his letters to Martha, there are also hints that he suffered a phobia about taking his final medical exams, and perhaps put them off repeatedly.)

It's plausible that Freud's medical studies were harmed by a profligate lifestyle that has been hidden from public scrutiny. This relates to damaging accusations by fellow trainees in neurology (Drs. Allen Starr and Bernard Sachs) who claimed that, at a slightly later period, Freud regularly engaged in what might be called "dissolute behaviors." In a *New York Times* article

Dr. Starr claimed that he had worked alongside Freud in a laboratory during an entire winter, and was well-informed about his unseemly style of life. In turn, Freud tried to deny this by claiming he'd never known Starr and attempted to ignore that, in those very early years, Starr had sent abstracts of Freud's initial clinical papers to be published in American journals! In a lengthy discussion about the controversy raised by Dr. Starr in my volume *Secret SL*, my final conclusions are in favor of the veracity of Drs. Starr and Sachs, contrary to the Freud biographers who have employed several distortions of the historical record to charge that these eminent neurologists simply desired to "smear" Freud's saintly reputation. In any case, I persist in a strong suspicion that Freud's eight years of medical school were probably rife with episodes of mental instability for him and deserve to be labeled tentatively as the fifth crisis period in his life (awaiting further explorations by clinical historians).

The period from 1882 to 1886 was the sixth period of mental crisis in Freud's life, and I have covered that era in some detail in *Dark Side*. Those were the years of his long, deeply disturbed period of engagement to Martha Bernay, when he exhibited repeated episodes of depression, rage, and rather balmy behaviors that caused Martha's mother to write him a critical letter urging him to "shape up," overcome his depression, and to stop acting like an infant. His excessive jealousy towards Martha, demanding that she should cease all relations with her beloved brother Eli, was a revival of his jealous feelings concerning his ancient nanny (Gisela, Martha, and Minna were *revenants* of his wet-nurse). This was also the era of his earliest and greatest cocaine excesses, during which he hooked many people on very heavy doses of this drug, leading to some deaths and to his being regarded by the medical world as a "public menace."

His own vulnerability to episodes of cocaine psychosis may have started in these years from 1882 to 1886. In *Dark Side* I have explained that this period generated various symptomatic behaviors relating to his identification with Jesus Christ, along with contrary ones pertaining to his Satan identification—particularly, his earliest involvements with Satanic pacts. This incorporates the era when, during his sojourn in Paris, he repeatedly *hallucinated* his own name (a recognized cocaine symptom today). Moreover, Freud at first believed that this name-hallucination was a remarkable E.S.P. phenomenon; and also he became obsessed with visiting the Notre Dame cathedral (which was symbolic of his persistent tie to the Catholic nanny who had sexually molested him in Freiberg). Refer to Vitz's book for considerable data about Freud's balmy obsession with the Notre Dame cathedral, in this era.

This sixth crisis period was also the one in which he became obsessed with Breuer's famous case of Anna O. It is my contention that Freud's fixation on this patient (who was a friend of Martha) was largely because the patient's strikingly dualistic personality resonated with Freud's dim awareness of his own dual nature, then manifesting itself in his conflicting identifications with Jesus and Satan. At the end of this period he married Martha and insisted that they should be the first occupants of a new, expensive apartment building called the House of Atonement. It was given that name because it was built on the site where more than 600 people had been burned to death in a raging, hell-like fire. Freud's eager occupancy of this "death house" was another of his bizarre symptomatic acts that pertained to his immense fears of death; to his murderous rage towards his Freiberg family members; to his fiery Satanic pacts; and to his stated desire to inflict a holocaust upon the entire world during an outburst of jealousy regarding Martha (a nanny surrogate).

In *Dark Side* I have proposed that the entire era of Freud's closest involvement with that mad physician Dr. Wilhelm Fliess, particularly 1892 to 1904, can be regarded as a period of severe mental instability for Freud. The biography by Dr. Schur and the Freud/Fliess letters have exposed a host of Freud's ailments and bizarre ideation during that era (and later). These problems include hypochondriasis, psychosomatic cardiac problems, migraine headaches, diarreah and spastic colon, psychosomatic backache, chronic sinus infections, bogus sciatica and fantasied smallpox, various digestive problems and lifelong constipation, and "peculiar" nose problems that required operations by Fliess. From time to time, Freud also suffered from recurrent depression and manic-like episodes, train and travel phobias, agoraphobia, a derealization episode, various hysteric and paranoid symptoms, homosexual urges towards Fliess and other sexual obsessions, a number of psychopathic behaviors (Ex. manipulating a patient to obtain a professorship, via a bribe, and accepting the gift of a villa!), a Rome phobia, fainting spells, an obsession with premature death, and bizarre ideas about numerology and "nasal neurosis" and "periodicity theory" (explained later). Gross has stated (1978, p.243) that "Freud was tormented by hatreds and by the guilts created by these thoughts," and these internal conflicts often surfaced during that very unstable period of his association with Fliess.

Actually, the Fliess era can be divided into at least three periods of severe mental instability for Freud. Ergo, the seventh crisis period in his life can be designated as the years 1895 to 1897 (a slight expansion of the period noted by Krüll). This period was marked by an intensification of the split with Breuer, which both depressed and enraged Freud. This supplied a partial motivation for his immersion in months of cocaine abuse and near sleepless nights, as he struggled to concoct the balmy "Project for a Scientific Psychology," which he hoped would bring instant fame and would cause Breuer to "crawl on his belly" in defeat—a phrase he confided to Fliess.

(Later, one of his perverse motives for creating the dream book was likewise to make Breuer "eat crow" for daring to withdraw his support and for diagnosing him as a case of "moral insanity"). Parenthetically, Freud's acknowledged madness in this era was conditioned partly by fears of death pertaining to his 40th birthday.

This seventh crisis period was marked by revival of his hatred and depression about feelings that his father Jacob had not been supportive of him (like Breuer's "failure"), for Jacob died in October of 1896. This era was one that rekindled repressed memories and feelings relating to his seduction by nanny, and presumably about Jacob's sexual molestation of him and of other younger siblings. His depressed and revengeful feelings about his lost nanny were channeled, in early 1895, into the quite psychotic nose surgery on Emma Eckstein (another revenant of nanny). This operation almost precipitated Emma's death on several occasions in bloody surgical encounters reminiscent of a recollection that Freud revived of a molestation scene involving nanny and *bloody water*. This crisis period also generated the remarkable dream of Irma's injection and its covert confessions about his murderous rage, which was connected to several deaths and near-deaths that he had caused in response to a complex set of irrational motivations. The array of symptoms listed previously *all* can be regarded as self-inflicted punishments for his perverse acts and motives, particularly his persistent desires for murderous revenge against his kinsmen and "friends."

The eighth crisis period ran from 1899 to 1901, and I have written about it in other parts of this volume and in *Dark Side*, so my comments will be brief about this era. Several great stresses were placed on Freud: anger and frustration about the public reception of his dream book; the growing split with Fliess; the "infiltration" of Breuer into the Fliess family, which Freud felt was greatly harmful to his relationship with Fliess. (Freud seemed to believe that Breuer was poisoning Mrs. Fliess's mind regarding his homosexual inclinations for Fliess.) Various perverse behaviors of Freud included his obvious manipulation of young Otto Weininger to plagiarize Fliess's work, leading to Weininger's suicide (discussed in a later chapter). Freud was similarly involved in questionable behavior regarding the suicide of his patient Margit Kremzir, covered in the next chapter. Also, Freud engaged in a florid "honeymoon" trip throughout Italy with his sister-in-law Minna (revenant of nanny), which he described in surprising detail in his letter to Fliess dated September 14, 1900.

As noted earlier, in early 1900 Freud acknowledged to Fliess that he was then wallowing in a period of depression and near-madness, and that he felt tormented by his patients. According to Fliess, the most bizarre behavior that Freud displayed in 1900 occurred during their trip together to Achensee, when Freud exposed an intention to murder Fliess by pushing him off a precipice after attempting to plagiarize his friend's novel theory of bisexuality. Near the end of 1900 Freud spent several months in a remarkable attempt to analyze an adolescent female with suicidal tendencies whom he called Dora. Some of Freud's most bizarre and destructive behaviors towards any patient were ones that he inflicted upon poor Dora, who was lucky that she fled Freud's treatment and escaped with her life, as will be discussed in detail in chapter seven.

The final year of the Fliess era was 1904, and that year also marks the ninth crisis period of Freud's life. In the summer of 1904 Fliess accused Freud of vindictively assisting Otto Weininger in the plagiarism of Fliess's work, stimulating great fear in Freud that Fliess would take legal action to destroy his reputation. Soon afterward Freud panicked and made a strange trip to Trieste, in the early stages of a psychotic episode. He then traveled to the Acropolis in Athens where his guilt-ridden, depersonalized behavior provided additional evidence of a brief psychotic break with reality. This crisis will be described later in this chapter, and in the next one.

An especially maddening era from 1911 to 1914 was the tenth crisis period in Freud's life. This period generated great stress for Freud concerning breaks with key followers, including Alfred Adler and Wilhelm Stekel. The worst of these breaks was with Carl Jung, whom Freud believed was the renowned gentile who would take the helm of his movement and persuade the Christian world to accept psychoanalysis as a worldwide "cause." Therefore, the growing schism with Jung provoked immense anxiety and rage in Freud, who felt that his lifework and identity were in danger of destruction. Indeed, his writings reflected great fear that he would be murdered by his disciples. (Reaction-formation?) All of this generated irrational compensatory acts by Freud including his personal involvements with the Moses statue in Rome, in hope of assuaging his monumental infantile rage, and his arranging to destroy his half-brother Emanuel in 1914 as a lethal surrogate for Jung. The year 1914 was one of intense depression for Freud, as revealed in the biography by his eldest son Martin (1957, p. 179). The start of WWI in that year was very stressful for Freud for various reasons, including that it constituted a massive threat to the orderly progress of his worldwide empire, as did the loss of Jung.

As the war years proceeded and the militant Freud (two of whose sons were in military service) became aware that he was on the losing side, the war became a growing burden for his mental stability. In the waning months of the war his eldest son Martin was in a prison camp and severe economic privation fell upon the Freud family, increasing the depression and other mental stresses suffered by Freud. The year 1918 was highlighted by Germany's humiliating defeat, and its immediate aftermath in 1919—when most Germans and Austrians, along with the Freud family, began to experience hunger pangs and horrible economic conditions—can be regarded as two of the bleakest years in Freud's life. In letters to Jones, he described the near-starvation diet of his family ("no meat, not enough bread, no milk, potatoes and eggs extremely dear"), and described his dire mental condition: "I can't remember a time of my life when my horizon was so thickly veiled by dark clouds . . ." Surely, a major part of Freud's pain was because he was humiliated and enraged that Germany/Austria had lost the war, as seen by his bitter and quixotic complaints against Pres. Wilson in a book he co-authored many years later to ventilate his venomous feelings.

So it seems obvious that the years 1918-1919 can qualify as the eleventh period of severe mental crisis in Freud's life. Partly as a perverse expression of his silent rage concerning the world that was crumbling around him, in this era he cruelly manipulated his mentally disturbed rival and colleague named Dr. Victor Tausk—an army veteran who returned from military service in a depressed and impoverished condition seeking analytic help from Freud—and soon helped to drive Tausk to a grotesque suicide. (A few years later he did the same with his disciple Herbert Silberer, as my later writings will describe.) It's my contention that in this same era Freud arranged for the disappearance and death of his greatest ancient rival, his English nephew John Freud, as he had also arranged for the death of John's father Emanuel in 1914 via a convenient train "accident." As a reflection of his murderous feelings in 1918-1919, Freud made a weird major revision of psychoanalytic doctrine by introducing the "death instinct theory" (which he largely plagiarized from his colleagues Drs. Stekel, Spielrein and Groddeck). As propounded by Freud, this death instinct theory incorporated subtle and perverse justifications for acts of murder (as subsequent material will explain), thereby reflecting the lethal impulses that were surging dangerously within Freud's psyche.

The years 1923-1925 constitute the twelfth period of great mental stress in Freud's life. In early 1923 he was given a firm diagnosis of cancer of the jaw and in April he endured a small operation (there were 33 surgeries over the next 16 years). The advent of his cancer, and the death of his young grandson, Heinz Rudolf (of milary tuberculosis) in June of 1923, generated recurrent depression in Freud. The legend of his heroic response to cancer was baldly contradicted by the insistence of his physician, Dr. Felix Deutsch, that Freud attempted to persuade him to assist in his suicide (euthanasia), which was eventually performed by Dr. Schur in 1939 at Freud's request. The great mental stress suffered by Freud in 1923 is also suggested by his strange intrusion into the case involving Philippe Daudet's *kidnapping* and *murder*. (Again, Freud's fixation on name magic is hinted by the names Philippe Daudet and Philipp Freud.)

Freud's mental imbalance in 1923 also is evidenced by his attempt to overcome his cancer by subjecting himself to an absurd "rejuvenation operation" on his testicles (the Steinach operation), which he believed could nullify the death instinct by stimulating the sexual instinct. Unconsciously, Freud might also have been using name magic to cure himself of being "nuts" (insane), by attempting partially to remove them surgically, i.e. his "nuts" or testicles (assuming his mastery of sexual slang in English).

Moreover, Freud claimed that in this twelfth crisis period he almost bled to death in an uncanny clinic accident, but it's likely that this was a symptomatic distortion of his. He claimed that he became unconscious while bleeding to death; that clinic personnel were strangely unavailable; and that his life was saved by an unusual clinic patient—an idiot dwarf who heroically came to his aid. Notice that a reversal of Freud's surname is "duerf," an approximation of the English word "dwarf," suggesting that this was another legend which he concocted with the help of name magic. Probably, this was a fantasied replay of his bloody interaction with the Freiberg nanny, and the bloody fiascos involving Emma Eckstein's brutal surgery in 1895.* Furthermore, there was extra stress in 1925 due to jaw operations, and perhaps by deep feelings triggered by the deaths of Josef Breuer and Karl Abraham, the latter after quite peculiar events involving the indirect return of Wilhelm Fliess into Freud's life when the nearly defunct Abraham chose Fliess as his final physician. (This weird event is discussed in a later volume.)

After 1925 there were additional years of great physical and mental stress for Freud relating to the vicissitudes of his jaw cancer. For example, 1928 was a particularly painful year for him with regard to his illness, and 1929 troubled him due to the cooling of the friendship with his devoted disciple, Ferenczi. And the years 1932-1934 probably can be regarded as the thirteenth period of mental crisis for the master. In 1932 the final break with Ferenczi occurred, followed in the next year by his peculiar death (see *The Fatal Freud*). In 1932 Freud had five jaw operations, the one in October being extensive. The spring of 1933 saw Freud's books being burned in a Nazi bonfire in Berlin, which may have triggered anxieties similar to those in 1914 that his identity and empire were being destroyed.

The year 1933 marked the onset of Nazi persecutions, which were as troubling to Freud and his family as they were to other Jews in Austria. He was advised by colleagues to flee from Austria, but he did not do so, largely because his illness engendered a lack of mobility. This era (1934) marked the beginning of work on one of his balmiest epics, the Moses book, which may have contained a covert "confession" that he had murdered his brother Emanuel (see chapter 8). In this period his old disciple Dr. Isidor Sadger attempted to arrange publication of a biography of Freud that was said to be

---

*During the 1895 surgery he was assisted by a near-dwarf—Fliess.

extremely damaging to the master's reputation (more harmful than the biography penned by Sadger's nephew, Fritz Wittels). This news infuriated Ernest Jones, and it appears that he ensured that the biography would not be published by arranging for the "administrative murder" of Sadger in a Nazi death camp as discussed in chapter 11. (It's likely that Freud was part of this plot to destroy his erstwhile friend, Sadger.)

The period 1938-1939 involved the final era of mental crisis for Freud. Austria was invaded by the Nazis in early 1938 and Freud's apartment received a menacing visit from the Gestapo. Eventually, the authorities granted the Freud family an exit permit, and they fled to England, with all the mental strains of a major relocation and the arranging of new doctors for Freud. In 1939 his health grew steadily worse, and then at age 83 he arranged for his *de facto* suicide via an overdose of morphine provided by Dr. Schur. Thus ended a life of perpetual stress and repeated emotional crises—ones that often were handled badly and with lethal consequences for other persons.

Some of Freud's Most "Peculiar" Ideas

During the first eight decades of this century, the public has become informed about ideas and theories by Freud that, by now, seem quite rational and reasonable to many persons. A brief list of these would include the theory of the Oedipus complex, which we've seen was probably contaminated by Freud's fantasy identification with Oedipus, by his sexual molestation by his primal mother, and by his desires to kill various father-figures in his life. Another of his major conceptions was his dream theory which proposed that dreams have significant hidden meanings that are wish-fulfillments—which may have been tainted and skewed by his peculiar identifications with the Biblical dream theorists Josef and Jacob and by dream "data" that is suffused with his personal distortions. Also, Freud was made famous by his idea that the core of neurosis involves unconscious fantasies that relate to complex sexual factors, and that the unconscious mind secretly dominates conscious functioning even in "normal" persons (although my later work will show that his theories were seriously compromised by his tendency to falsify data).

Several other of Freud's major ideas are regarded as being quite rational ones, even by severe critics of his thinking. For example, his emphasis upon various stages of early development (oral, anal, phallic, etc.), and that these can be fixated in ways that influence later personality and behaviors, is usually seen as a sensible notion even by many critics who insist that little scientific evidence is available to support it. The same can be said of his theoretical division of the mind into id, ego, and superego which presumably conflict with one another in specifiable ways in different forms of mental illness, and his emphasis upon repetition-compulsions in disturbed mental functioning (which is seen as a powerful factor in his own life, in chapter six).

Readers will have a difficult time assessing the degree of mental instability in Freud if they rely upon the seemingly reasonable theories and ideas mentioned above. Therefore, the remainder of this section will provide brief discussions of additional ideas that he either conceived or strongly endorsed that suggest far less rational roots within his psyche.

Many of Freud's most peculiar ideas that are not well-known have to do with the role of sexuality in psychopathology, and often these notions were contaminated by his great hostility towards father-figures, as shown below. After making a few months' visit to Charcot in Paris (1886), he realized that he could gain much scientific and public attention (which he'd craved since childhood) by placing an exaggerated emphasis upon sexuality in relation to hysteria, and the neuroses in general. This sensitive topic, sexuality, became an obsession with him, for he understood that fame is often preceded by notoriety. In the early 1890s and later, he championed the theory that masturbation was a crucial factor in hysteria and neurasthenia. Actually, he pulled his masturbation theory of mental illness "out of a hat" to attain rapid fame, knowing it could not be disproved (since almost everyone has masturbated, including pillars of the community, and it could also be found in legions of the mentally ill). Furthermore, he knew that his theory would receive support from widespread magical and guilt-ridden beliefs of the public and the medical world, in that era, that "self-abuse" was the cause of every evil from warts and cancer, to madness.

Did Freud create his earliest theory of mental illness—his masturbation theory—largely from the wellsprings of his own id, due to personal problems with compulsive masturbation? Krüll's book (1986, pp. 111-114) emphasized personal data that pointed to a strong masturbation complex in Freud's psyche, with apparent connections to castration anxieties and feelings of hatred for his father Jacob. If so, it's likely that an awareness of his potentials for psychosis made Freud give unconscious endorsement to the popular notion of a strong link between masturbation and severe mental illness, fearing that it was operative in his own psyche. This was perhaps the first example of his projecting his own psychopathology onto the entire world.

In 1894-1895, while still emphasizing the role of masturbation in generating neuroses, Freud became an ardent advocate of Fliess's balmy postulation of the "nasal reflex neurosis" and the idea that these alleged neuroses are caused by sexual factors pertaining to masturbation and to physical relationships between nose "spots" and the genitals! Likewise, Freud embraced the idea "that the condition of the heart depends upon the condition of the nose," and applied this claptrap to his own cardiac problems (hinting at a guilty connection with his masturbation). With enthusiasm, Freud endorsed nasal cauterizations, cocaine applied to nose spots, and elaborate surgery, as techniques for curing the (phantom) nasal neuroses. Pursuing this mad theorizing, he had Fliess operate on his nose at least twice, and also arranged for Fliess's catastrophic operation on the nose of Freud's first analytic patient, Emma Eckstein, which disfigured her lovely face permanently and almost cost her life—since Fliess "accidentally" left gauze in the wound, provoking massive hemorrhages.

In that same era (1895-1896) he suddenly created the theory that neuroses (especially hysteria) were caused by early sexual abuse of children, which reminds us of his molestation by nanny. However, later he claimed that such sexual abuse usually was committed by fathers, not excluding his father Jacob, in connection with the hysterias of Sigi's brother and sisters. Freud's father died in 1896, so he started to formulate this accusation against Jacob both at the time of his declining health and soon after his death, as hostile/dependent feelings were being revived in Sigmund. Although some of the "evidence" supporting Freud's sexual abuse theory might have been reasonable, much of its formulation may have been irrational and distorted, especially his claim that adult hysterics often were seduced at the ages of six months to eleven months of infancy. Apparently, he gave full credibility to the notion that said infants were forced into providing oral sex for their fathers, who had held their heads while effecting these incestuous acts. (One wonders how Freud could ever have provided substantial scientific evidence to support these assertions that would have satisfied any rational group of clinical authorities about them?)

In September 1897, about nine months after announcing it to Fliess, Freud abandoned the preceding seduction theory—for which he'd offered hardly any convincing clinical evidence—and abruptly he created a new theory positing that patients' early sexual *fantasies* (not real acts) were the kernels which generated later neuroses, again offering no sound clinical evidence to support this conceptual reversal. This new theory was perfect for Freud's purposes since, like the masturbation theory and the infant-seduction idea, it was basically incapable of eliciting scientific confirmation or disproof.

Another of Freud's peculiar theories about sexuality and mental illness belongs to the year 1893. In February of that year he announced to Fliess his grandiose idea for eventually wiping all neuroses from the face of the earth, not by finding cures but by providing a method for preventing them. This related to his earlier notion that most neuroses were caused by a lack of true orgasmic sexual fulfillment. Therefore, his grand idea for preventing neuroses was to enlist a worldwide army of respectable and unattached young women who would agree to provide free sexual intercourse for all the young men in the world! As a practical matter, in his letters to Fliess he stated that innocuous methods for preventing conception would first need to be developed, but it did not even occur to him (reflecting his urgent psychopathic tendencies) to consider the horrendous moral implications of such a plan. In *Secret SL* I've discussed this plan to mobilize a vast army of "respectable whores" as reflecting his covert accusation that all women are secret whores, consonant with ancient grievances against the nanny who "seduced" and "abandoned" him.

In a letter to Fliess in the mid-1890s, Freud revealed that he was then endorsing another kind of medical quackery called organotherapy. While visiting the town of Oderberg, he had seen a pubertal female with some vague physical symptoms, and he recommended that she should be brought to Vienna to afford her treatment with organotherapy. This was another pseudo-medical practice that he embraced impulsively in the hope of attaining fame and fortune overnight. In a footnote to the Fliess letters, Masson explained that: "Organotherapy is the treatment of disease by the administration of portions of certain animal organs or extracts thereof." One can guess that this endorsement of organotherapy in the 1890s laid the groundwork for Freud's quixotic decision in 1923 to suffer the Steinach operation on his testicles in the hope of reversing his jaw cancer.

During the mid-1890s Freud embraced enthusiastically Fliess's bizarre "periodicity theory" which these two men in concert spun out in a vast web of grandiose delusions. Fliess claimed that he'd discovered that a male 23-day cycle and a female 28-day cycle were the hidden cornerstones of human biology, and that the male cycle released a substance producing pleasure in both sexes, while the female cycle's substance produced unpleasure. Using this "knowledge" and a covert system of number magic and modified astrology, Fliess and Freud showed that complex, arcane calculations could be manipulated to predict the onset and disappearance of diseases in any person, the precise time of birth *and death*, various critical periods in life, and many other significant events. In Freud's long letter to Fliess of December 6, 1896 we find a particularly zany attempt by Freud to apply periodicity theory to his psychological concerns, including his notion that anxiety neurosis and neurasthenia were connected "with the existence of the two 23-day and 28-day substances." In that letter, and many others by Freud, he provided entire pages of ridiculous calculations which he used to help verify the magnificent edifice called "periodicity theory."

Freud was so impressed by Fliess's pseudo-scientific gibberish that he dubbed him "the Kepler of biology," and a close reading of their correspondence shows that Freud harbored very jealous feelings concerning his friend's alleged creative genius. Early in 1895, Freud became engaged frenetically in a grandiose project that he hoped would establish his own genius as superior to Fliess's and would humiliate Breuer for having diagnosed him as a case of moral insanity. After months of obsessive thought about this project—a megalomanic attempt to delineate a "unified field theory" interrelating brain physiology, normal and abnormal psychology, and neurology into one grand scheme using a blizzard of arcane symbols—he began writing this "Project for a Scientific Psychology" during near-sleepless nights while ingesting huge doses of cocaine. In a furious burst of manic activity he finished this work and mailed it to Fliess for his review and adulation, but in the next month Freud came to his senses and concluded that he'd "hatched" this project in a deranged state of mind. Ergo, he didn't bother to ask Fliess to return this weird manuscript, exhibiting his disaffection with this masterpiece that was supposed to establish his incomparable genius.

Ellenberger has noted (1970, p. 456) that in September of 1913 Freud and Jung finally broke off their stormy relationship, and soon thereafter the Swiss group of Freud's disciples abandoned his cause. In my view, it is no mere coincidence that in that same year Freud published his quixotic major work *Totem and Taboo* which, in my opinion, contains peculiar ideas that were projections of Freud's fears of being murdered, and his covert desires to murder other persons, including Jung and Emanuel Freud. In that volume Freud concocted another grandiose theory, this one being intended to interrelate neurotic symptoms in mental illness, social and cultural factors in the lives of primitive peoples, and the origins of civilization.

The central theory (or projected fantasy) proposed by Freud, as a partial outlet for his murderous rage towards Jung, is the story of the murder of the primeval father, which is an offshoot of the idea of the Oedipus complex. Freud posited that the patricidal wish in every modern male's Oedipal complex depends upon a patricidal template "inherited" from our preliterate ancestors, i.e. from one crucial event that occurred in the prehistory of mankind. Thus, eons ago men lived in hordes or clans under the complete domination of a powerful father who monopolized the females and exiled his rivalrous sons. (Was this a fantasy about Jacob Freud "exiling" his sons to Manchester?) United by homosexual feelings, these sons lived in a separate group, but eventually they rebelled against the father, then killed and ate him to satisfy their hatred.

According to Freud, that was the beginning of totemism in which a clan set up a sacred animal as a benevolent ancestor (the idealized father) which, at regular intervals they killed and devoured. Allegedly, after killing the primal father they did not dare to molest his women, as the result of "delayed obedience." Using this central thesis (or fantasy) in *Totem and Taboo*, Freud presumably "explained" the origins of two of the primary injunctions of all mankind, namely the patricide and incest prohibitions—the groundwork of morals, culture and religion.

Of course, there is no way to prove that this decisive patricidal event occurred in prehistory, and it is absurd to believe that its residues could be inherited by modern males (to fit with Freud's Lamarckian biases). Instead, Freud secretly projected himself into the role of the powerful father who was murdered, as an act of denial of his own intense desires to kill his friends (Jung, Adler) and kinsmen (Emanuel and John). This bizarre fantasy about totemism had roots that were similar to his *concurrent* fantasy about the Moses statue, which likewise allowed him to deny his wishes to murder Jung and Emanuel Freud. It is not surprising, therefore, that *Moses and Monotheism* provides fantasies about Moses that incorporate peculiar variations of Freud's previous ideas about totemism and the murder of the primal father (along with many other absurd notions). In my view, the Moses book allowed Freud to identify with the murdered Moses, thereby covertly denying that he had murdered Emanuel and John, while allowing him to make a secret "confession" of those very crimes—since Freud also identified the murdered Moses with his brother Emanuel, as I will explain in chapter 8.

A great surprise and embarrassment to Freud's followers came in 1920 with publication of *Beyond the Pleasure Principle*, which incorporates his strange death instinct theory. Previously, he had stressed the primacy of the life and sexual instincts (Eros), and the pleasure principle. As a stark reversal, in his 1920 volume he decided that he'd been wrong, all along, and postulated a dual classification of life instincts and death instincts, with the latter being more fundamental. Now he attributed great power to the aggressive and destructive instincts and proclaimed that "the goal of life is death." Evidently, he'd been writing those ideas in 1919, the very year when he'd manipulated Victor Tausk into embracing suicide and presumably arranged for the death of John Freud. Can we assume that his destructive impulses towards Tausk and John Freud had surged upwards in 1919, impelling him perversely to give his endorsement to some of the death instinct ideas that he plagiarized from other writers? (Later, I'll emphasize that his death instinct formulation contains a sly justification for acts of murder, which may be relevant to the deaths of Emanuel and John Freud.)

As we near the end of this brief review of Freud's peculiar ideation, readers should be reminded of Freud's lifelong adherence to the doctrine of Lamarckianism. His championing of that bankrupt notion is particularly quixotic if it is true, as I've contended, that he was secretly fixated on the Lamarckian thesis because of his identification with the story of the Biblical shepherd Jacob—who attained great wealth by adherence to a Lamarckian (magical) idea.

Freud was willing to carry his Lamarckian views to absurd lengths, as reported in Sulloway's book (1979, p. 387). In a letter to Ferenczi in 1915, Freud asserted that many kinds of mental illness in modern life were due to historic "acquired dispositions," i.e. they had resulted from primeval deprivations that had occurred during early instances of worldwide catastrophes. (Evidently, this was Freud's unconscious way of dealing with the "Freiberg catastrophe" that haunted him all his life.) Years later, Freud gave strong credibility to Ferenczi's zany Lamarckian theory that five catastrophic events in human prehistory were fully recapitulated in man's current sexual development! Likewise, in his *Introductory Lectures* Freud announced the theory that the fantasies of children and neurotics are a replay of historic events in the era of the primeval family of mankind. This theory "saved the day" for Freud when severely neurotic children were found to have only mild Oedipal histories, for their problems could be explained conveniently as deriving from ancient memory traces of severe privations meted out by the dreaded primeval father. In effect, Freud claimed that Lamarckian memory traces were sometimes the root causes of modern mental disturbances.

In this review of Freud's arcane history of ideas, we need to consider whether there were irrational factors involved in his insistence that Shakespeare's writings were not produced by the playwright and actor credited with those works, but that they were created by a member of British royalty. My suggestion is that this notion was generated by Freud's identification with this English genius, along with this Viennese doctor's fantasy and wish that he was a secret member of royalty himself, with relevance to his many fantasy identifications involving kings (Oedipus, Alexander, Napoleon, King Sigismund) and princes (Hamlet).

A goldmine of Freud's bizarre ideation also is found in the next chapter and in a later one that focuses upon his identification with Satan, and his repeated formulations of Satanic pacts in hope of extending his life. And there is a good deal of additional information about Freud's strangest ideas in my related volumes *Dark Side* and *Secret SL*. Probably, a great number and diversity of Freud's most peculiar ideas will be found in the huge Freud/Ferenczi correspondence which still awaits publication (still under censorship?), since Ferenczi had a reputation among early analysts for being a consistent generator of crackpot ideas, and because Freud was known to be quite *en rapport* with this disciple over many years. It's my suspicion, however, that many of the most damaging letters (concerning Freud's irrational ideas) will have been deleted from this correspondence before publication, which resonates with my strong arguments in *Dark Side* that extensive tampering may have occurred with both editions of the Freud/Fliess letters.

Additional Evaluations of Freud's Mental Health

The first section of this chapter provided information indicating that both Josef Breuer and Freud himself were aware that the latter suffered from severe psychopathology, in contrast with the "party line" of psychoanalysis that the master was afflicted merely with moderate forms of mental illness that were cured by his self-analysis. In this section, additional dissenting views about Freud's mental health will be offered in a series of brief summaries.

Even in the decade of the twenties, Maylan's pathography of Freud (1929) portrayed him as suffering from a severe mental disturbance, and explained this as emanating basically from destructive aspects of his "father complex" (his boyhood reaction to Jacob's alleged cowardice and business setbacks). Maylan explained the effects of this destructive father-fixation on Freud's personality and lifework. (More than fifty years later, Krüll returned to new analyses of these issues in her volume *Freud and His Father*.)

Another biographer of Freud in the 1920s was Fritz Wittels (1924), who had been a member of Freud's inner circle, along with his uncle Isidor Sadger. Wittels gave a very uncomplimentary account of Freud's personality and described him as a little king, who would brook no opposition to his ideas, and a crass manipulator of others. He wrote that Freud "has become a despot who will not tolerate the slightest deviation from his doctrine; holds councils behind closed doors . . (etc.)" This suggests that Freud eventually became the primal father of *Totem and Taboo*, who bullied his "sons" unmercifully while fearing that they would murder him. (On several occasions, he accused Jung of wishing to murder him, although Freud's recurrent fainting spells can be interpreted as a way of counteracting his own intense urges to murder Jung and others.)

Wittels was the third clinician, after Breuer and Freud, to imply strongly that Freud suffered from certain vulnerabilities to psychosis, namely megalomania. This was indicated when Wittels claimed that Freud suffered from a "Jehovah complex"—though he was not aware that this thesis is supported massively by Freud's fantasy identifications with many other deities including Jesus Christ, Satan, Zeus, Jupiter, etc. In a long paper that Wittels published in 1933 he made an abject renunciation of his previous critical remarks about Freud, but this may have been due partly to fear that he would be subject to vicious retaliation from Freud and his cohorts, including the "administrative murder" which befell his uncle Isidor Sadger as a way of suppressing his blistering biography. (See chapter 11.)

Wittels is not the only author who has made the serious claim that Freud suffered from megalomania. In 1955 Natenberg's book *The Case History of Sigmund Freud* discussed aspects of Freud's delusional thinking and his psychopathic tendencies, calling him "the cleverest charlatan the world has ever known." By Natenberg's account, not only was Freud a brilliant con artist, but he was also a fanatic and subject to megalomania. In fact, in his final paragraph Natenberg emphasized that his book about Freud was "the case history of a megalomaniac."

While we are still thinking about the topic of megalomania in regard to Freud, it is instructive that he once made an oblique confession that perhaps he was vulnerable to "sexual megalomania." In his letter to Karl Abraham of January 9, 1908 Freud confided that one of the crucial hidden meanings lurking within the dream of Irma's injection (Freud's landmark dream) was the issue of his "sexual megalomania" towards the three godmothers of his daughters. (Perhaps we can reinterpret this by saying that, in this confession, godmothers symbolize mother-figures, indicating that Freud's underlying "sexual megalomania" was towards his primal mother, the nanny who sexually molested him.)

Percival Bailey's biography of Freud (1965) is extremely annoying to his disciples, since it unmasks many spurious contentions about his "greatness" in an authoritative manner. Bailey had earned excellent credentials in both psychiatry and neurology, so Freud's partisans were nettled by Bailey's analysis which concluded that the master's early work in neurology was mediocre, raising many doubts about why he *really* abandoned his neurological work to infringe upon the field of psychiatry. In general, Bailey described Freud as a crass manipulator who excused his failures by invoking questionable charges of anti-Semitism and alleging the unfair hostility of his colleagues. Bailey denied that Freud was a great thinker, instead regarding him as an intriguing study in psychopathology and a weaver of fantastic (perhaps delusional) theories.

Erich Fromm's short biography of Freud (1959) portrayed him as a fanatic with a variety of neurotic vulnerabilities. Fromm viewed him as driven by the near-delusion that his mission was to create a cultural revolution and a worldwide movement with a covert religious and political substructure. (Similarly, Natenberg viewed Freud as a fanatic whose thinking was, at times, delusional.)

Martin Gross's excellent chapter (1978) on Freud's life and personality perceived him as being driven relentlessly by envy, malice, and deathwishes towards others. In Gross's view, his mental stability was made precarious by phobias, depression, cocaine abuse, numerous physical complaints, and by severe neuroses. Moreover, his ability to maintain loving relationships was continually eroded by ruthless ambition, competitiveness, jealousy, and hatred—making victims of Breuer, Fliess, Jung and others whom he saw as obstacles to immortality. Similar to Natenberg, Gross claimed that Freud projected much of his inner venom into his clinical theories and speculations, often attributing evil motives and complexes to patients, and all mankind, that belonged primarily to himself.

The eminent personality theorist Silvan Tomkins offered an extensive analysis of Freud's personality (1963) and, pursuant to Tomkins' writings on paranoia categorized Freud under the heading: "the paranoid posture." Relevant to this characterization is the fact that after Freud's breakup with Fliess he claimed that he (Freud) had overcome his paranoid ideation. To the contrary, Tomkins' analysis indicated that strong paranoid trends persisted thereafter in Freud, though he did not regard him as clearly psychotic. (If the 1985 edition of the Freud/Fliess letters had been available to him, perhaps Tomkins would have felt differently about Freud's psychotic potentials?)

Tomkins described Freud's "paranoid posture" as a war between the self and one's antagonists (consider his military fixation) and an attempt to inflate the self (megalomania?) so that others will be defeated, while the self remains protected. In this disorder, it is typical for the self to be over-valued in importance and for others to be correspondingly under-valued. Thus, the self defends itself against early childhood traumas not only by inflation but also by persistently hating, attacking, and derogating others. (Consider Freud's endless death-wishes.) Another major factor is the repeated sense of being betrayed by important persons—parents, siblings, friends, colleagues. Tomkins believed that Freud harbored intense feelings of having been betrayed by his mother (and nanny?), which surfaced between-the-lines in some of his writings on early child development, and that he regarded the births of each of his younger siblings as a betrayal of him. It is rather amazing that Tomkins accurately formulated some of the preceding judgments about Freud's personality, despite that Tomkins remained unaware that he had been sexually molested during infancy by a mother-figure.

Another important source of data about Freud's frequently pathological emotions and ideation is the huge biography (1972) by his personal physician, Dr. Max Schur. Although he was a psychoanalyst and an adoring disciple of Freud, Schur did not neglect the inclusion of much evidence about Freud's bizarre fears about death-ages (relevant to his urgent death wishes against kinsmen and others), as well as Freud's susceptibility to magical thought throughout his life, and many other indications of his unstable mental functioning. Although Schur often tried to minimize the significance of these factors in assessing Freud's possible psychopathology, readers need to study his volume earnestly and form their own independent conclusions.

Many of the ideas of Tomkins and Schur concerning destructive aspects of Freud's personality are relevant to Roazen's book *Brother Animal* (1969) which focused upon the triangular relationship involving Freud with his disciples Victor Tausk and Lou Andreas Salomé. Roazen's exhaustive research clarified Freud's destructive behaviors towards male followers who stimulated his rivalrous feelings and described his cruel treatment of Victor

Tausk and Herbert Silberer that contributed greatly to their suicides.

The analyst Choisy's book (1963) posited that a weakness of libido was central to Freud's personality. Also, she placed a heavy emphasis upon his covert death anxieties (likewise stressed by Schur at a later date). She described the many instances of fear of death in Freud's life and emphasized his repeated *denials* of his death concerns in his writings (at least until 1919 when he proposed the death instinct theory). For example, she saw his early view that fear of death is merely secondary to castration fears as one instance of such denial in him. Quite useful were her brief analyses of his other rationalizations about death that reflected his personal conflicts about the issue. Choisy cited his uses of four defense mechanisms in his life to mask a basic fear of death (sex, drugs, extreme rationalism, and *aggression*) and claimed that: "Freud used all of them lavishly . ." Being a loyal Freudian, however, she gave only a sketchy presentation of his uses of aggression to defend against death fears, and she seemed reluctant to specify the full extent of his mental instability—as was also the case with Schur.

An important book by Thornton (1983) was first published in Britain with the title *Freud and Cocaine*. Her central thesis commenced with new evidence that Freud did not cease ingesting huge amounts of cocaine in 1887, as was claimed by Jones, instead showing his renewed uses of the drug from 1892 to 1896 (and probably many years thereafter?). She analyzed strange behaviors by Freud and Fliess, focusing on Freud's long list of physical ailments and peculiar twists and dictates of his theories, and she correlated these factors with the progressive symptoms of a drug induced psychosis presumably suffered by both men. This is relevant to psychoanalyst James Strachey's astonished remark to Jones, after reading their suppressed correspondences that they had obviously been enmeshed in a shared web of madness, or *folie à deux*. Strachey's acknowledgment that both Freud and Fliess had suffered from some variety of psychosis is a more frank assessment than the recent one by Gilman (1988), who asserted the fact of Fliess's madness but then tried to downplay a similar diagnosis for Freud.

A novel way of denying the considerable severity of Freud's mental imbalance over many decades was reflected by Ellenberger's (1970, p. 447 ff.) attempt to romanticize the issue. He suggested that during his Fliess friendship Freud suffered from a "creative illness," similar to peculiar illnesses experienced by shamans, mystics, philosophers, and creative writers. Ellenberger was vague when he stated that this condition "can take the shape of depression, neurosis, psychosomatic ailments, or even psychosis." Thus, he alleged that Freud's condition was a very special and romantic one, and he did not specifically address whether Freud was subject to a fluctuating psychosis. Ellenberger described creative illnesses as not being long-lasting and connected that idea with his claim that Freud's serious imbalance had run its course by 1902, near the end of his self-analysis and the Fliess era. That allegation conflicts with my previous section which provides evidence of severe imbalances after 1902, and decades thereafter, and the awareness of various current experts that Freud continued his self-analysis throughout his entire lifetime.

The psychoanalyst Zilboorg's book (1967) about Freud's personality and career did not support the idea that Freud's mental illness ended circa 1902. Indeed, Zilboorg insisted that Freud suffered a lifelong depression ("depressive neurosis") relating to the "Freiberg catastrophe" (nanny), and that he exhibited a relative inability to sustain friendships and irrational fears of becoming impoverished (fear of losing nanny's breast?). This author claimed that religious concerns were at the center of his inner conflicts, and Zilboorg asserted that Freud had a great preoccupation with death (struggling between fear of death and desire to embrace it) and a great fear of the Day of Judgment specified in the Bible. (Did nanny's powerful influence never cease, one wonders?)

Kushner's book (1967) analyzed Freud's personality in terms of his six key obsessions (and four corollary ideas). For examples Kushner provided evidence that Freud had a covert obsession to prove that incest is a "natural instinct," not deserving of societal prohibition, rather than a pathological phenomenon. (If so, did he secretly hope to justify sexual acts with his primal mother?) Another hidden obsession in Freud's work, Kushner argued, was a wish to demonstrate that a desire to murder the father is a natural urge of mankind, using spurious anthropological data. (If Kushner is right, perhaps this was a weird attempt by Freud to justify his desires to kill various father-figures, including Emanuel Freud.)

A highly publicized book by Masson (1984) badly upset the analytical establishment by accusing Freud of horrendous malpractice (the surgery on Emma Eckstein), an egregious lack of courage about key theoretical issues, and gross deceptions involving falsifications of data. In general, Masson's charges seem to point to deep psychopathic tendencies in Freud (previously stressed by Natenberg). These assessments of Freud were particularly damaging to his reputations because Masson once was a member of the inner analytic circle close to Freud's daughter Anna, and because Masson was privy to research data about Freud's affairs that were not available to other authors. Later, Masson charged that a renowned journalist and author named Janet Malcolm had written about him, in relation to the formulation of his book concerning Freud, in ways that distorted the truth and grossly slandered his reputation, and that charge has provoked a famous lawsuit whose outcome is likely to alter the course of journalistic history.

Helen Puner's biography of Freud (1947) was one of the first to unmask a series of fictions about him, including the myth that his self-analysis was a heroic feat that "cured" him of his mental ills. Puner was one of the earliest authors to stress that his psyche was dominated by needs for revenge, by patricidal urges, and by immense feelings of ambition. Concerning his family life, she was frank in exposing strained aspects of his relationship with his wife, Martha. Not only did Puner discuss Freud's death-wishes towards others but also his fears that his disciples harbored murderously revengeful feelings about him. In her remarks about Freud's analysis of Hamlet (p. 225), she stated that this analyst projected his own patricidal urges onto the Dane, noting that Freud himself possessed the mind of *a murderer*. Probably, these damaging insights into Freud's disturbed, murderous personality were so threatening to Freud's reputation that the analytic elite was pressured into arranging for Jones to produce his tendentious biographies of Freud in the fifties, as an indication of the great influence historically of Puner's remarkable little book.

Her pioneering effort to expose numerous myths about Freud makes Puner's book important historically, in its own right, but also because unwittingly she helped to stimulate additional myths and distortions about Freud that Ernest Jones incorporated into his three-volume biography to protect and bolster Freud's reputation. However, when Puner began the process of exposing myths, distortions, and lies concerning Freud's life and personality she also gave encouragement to Ellenberger (1970) and Sulloway (1979) in their valuable efforts, to demythologize the life story of Freud—a project that still has a long way to go.

This review now will be concluded with a brief reminder about Vitz's book (1988) which stressed, like Zilboorg, that hidden religious factors are basic for understanding Freud's strange personality. Vitz's compelling analysis of Freud's personality also emphasized early sexual seduction (by nanny), along with connections between cocaine use and his identification with Satan (pacts with the devil) and numerous other fantasy identifications, as all of these related to "splitting" of Freud's personality. Vitz concluded that Freud's illness can be characterized as a Borderline Personality Disorder, though he disclaimed that he was ever psychotic. The present author agrees with Vitz's general thesis, but notes that this disorder sometimes is subject to fluctuating periods of psychosis, which I believe was the case with Freud in numerous "crisis periods" during his entire lifetime. Also, I have suggested that these admittedly imprecise classifications of mental illness are applicable to both Freud and Fliess: Borderline Personality Disorder; Ambulatory Psychosis; and even Moral Insanity (the term which Breuer applied to Freud).

The Acropolis Episode

In a later chapter I'll discuss my thesis that Freud, near the end of his life, employed *Moses and Monotheism* as a covert "confession" to reveal that he had displayed his godlike omnipotence (megalomania) by arranging for the murder of Emanuel Freud. In this section, I'll help support this thesis by stating that near his 80th birthday he wrote a small article titled "A Disturbance of Memory on the Acropolis" as both a covert confession of his madness and of his murderous ways, i.e. that he had arranged for the murders of Emanuel and his son John.

This section will provide an abbreviated version of my arguments and ideas about the "Acropolis episode" which Freud experienced during his visit to Athens in 1904—an uncanny occurrence during which, under the threat of immense fears about his desires to murder, or that he might be "executed" himself, he experienced a startling *splitting* of his personality into two persons. Various authors have written about this episode, and all have artfully minimized its significance and declined to acknowledge that it reveals dangerous psychotic processes that emerged temporarily from Freud's psyche in 1904. In chapter six, following my detailed presentation of the harrowing breakup with Fliess, I will provide additional information that is germane to my analysis of this Acropolis episode and Freud's brief article about it.

During 1936 Freud wrote that uncanny article about his 1904 Acropolis visit as an "open letter" to honor the 70th birthday of the French writer Romain Rolland, indicating that for 32 years he'd suppressed public exposure of the mind-boggling events that he'd experienced while making an initial visit to the Acropolis accompanied by his younger brother Alexander. It is ironic that the title of this article by Freud referred to "A Disturbance of Memory on the Acropolis," since that title cleverly evades the issue of an outbreak of psychosis. Also it is ironic and deceptive to call this an "open letter," since Freud's article attempted to conceal from Rolland, and the public, some crucial information that might have exposed his severe mental disorder in the late summer of 1904. Of course, we'll soon "fill in the blanks" that he hoped to conceal from Rolland and everyone else.

Freud began his paper by referring to "love of the truth," implying that his great honesty had prompted this article that required him to expose personal materials in order "to throw light upon unusual, abnormal or pathological manifestations of the mind." He added that: "During the last few years, a phenomenon of this sort, which I myself had experienced a generation ago, in 1904, and which I had never understood, has kept on recurring to my mind." So, Freud acknowledged that recollections of this weird Acropolis episode had been haunting his mind (for 32 years!), and later he admitted that thoughts about it "have troubled me so often . ." Near the end of this article, his explanation for this episode involving such strange ideation was that his massive guilt feelings in 1904 were connected to it, and he stressed as a corollary the weak claim that travel to Athens (a great luxury) had exposed his guilty superiority to his father's modest accomplishments in life. Thus, he tried to palm off the hypothesis that his peculiar ideation on the Acropolis (suppressing mention of his bizarre thoughts *in Trieste*) had resulted merely from an inner conflict between his "filial piety" and the sudden recognition that he'd surpassed his father's achievements. My correction to his hypothesis is that great guilt and fear regarding "murder and madness" had prompted this Acropolis balminess in 1904, and caused it to haunt Freud's psyche for 32 years thereafter, as we shall soon understand.

Describing that late summer trip with Alexander, Freud noted that it began in Trieste where, by a lucky series of events, they were suddenly given the chance to take a boat to Athens for a three day visit. However, while waiting briefly for this boat they were not joyous about their good fortune, but inexplicably exhibited "remarkably depressed spirits" and wandered around Trieste in a discontented and quite "gloomy state," which Freud characterized as "most strange." (We'll see later that he held back from Rolland, and the public, extremely crucial information about zany ideation that he experienced in Trieste, aside from his depressed condition there.)

Later that same day Freud and his brother arrived in Athens and soon were standing on a famous historical landmark, the Acropolis. While Freud stood among the temple ruins and cast his eyes upon the landscapes a surprising thought entered his mind: 'So all this really *does* exist, just as we learnt at school!' Actually, he stated that the person who expressed that thought was *sharply divided* from another person within his psyche who was astonished that his "other self" had ever doubted the real existence of Athens and the Acropolis.

To emphasize the stark contrast in ideation, his "first self" became astonished—under the impact of being forced to believe in an event, a place, whose reality "had hitherto seemed doubtful." Ergo, in this uncanny moment of his first visit to the Acropolis, Freud was confronted by a clear split between two parts of his psyche, his Self No. One and Self No. Two (just as Jung described frankly these two divided entities in himself, in his autobiography). Also, Freud wrote that his "first self," forced suddenly to revise its ancient disbelief when confronted by this glimpse of the real Acropolis, was like a person walking beside the Loch Ness in Scotland who had received a great shock. For suddenly this person saw, stranded on the shore, the famous sea-serpent "we've never believed in" and was forced to admit: "So it really *does* exist . ." (At this point, he specified that he was alluding to the famous Loch Ness "monster," as he called it.)

Having implied that Freud's underlying psychosis in 1904 is indicated by the splitting of his psyche which he experienced on the Acropolis, let me emphasize that his covert madness is also strongly connected with the metaphor of a concealed and dangerous serpent which he connected with that split within his mind. To understand Freud's covert madness in 1904, we need eventually to integrate three phases of discussion, each of which may conceal the theme of "dangerous serpents": 1. a symbolic arrival of scores of sea-serpents into Freud's memory at the onset of madness, that pertained to threats of severe denunciations of Freud by Fliess (provoking Freud's fears of being murdered, and desires to murder others, in the weeks preceding the trip to Trieste); 2. an *escalation* of the serpent theme on his arrival in Trieste, related to Freud's uncanny number magic and to fears that Fliess would soon arrange to castrate (kill) him; 3.the further outbreak of psychosis in Athens in connection with Freud's desire to kill Fliess and nephew John Freud, with the serpent being a covert symbol of those lethal desires. In a moment, I'll return to these serpentine factors, starting with the serpent's connection with the Acropolis episode—but first let me mention how Freud, in 1936, characterized the feelings of unreality and mind-splitting which he had experienced on the Acropolis in 1904.

In a brief and unsatisfactory discussion of his strange experiences on the Acropolis, Freud applied the terms "derealization" and "depersonalization" to them. About derealizations, he said that they are little understood, sometimes occur in normal people, and are seen as failures in mental functioning (abnormal structures) that are found frequently, in various mental diseases. Derealizations are found in two forms, he said: 1. the subject feels that a piece of reality is strange to him; 2. in depersonalizations he feels that a piece of his own self is strange to him. Per Freud, these phenomena are intimately interrelated; and, depersonalizations that are severe can result in "dual consciousness" or "split personality." Evidently, Freud manifested both of those factors during the Acropolis episode, though his degree of depersonalization was perhaps not fully expressed or described by him. He noted that derealizations have two major characteristics—a placing of emphasis upon defense (allowing the ego to disavow a painful issue); while also, there are accentuations of past memories or distressing experiences, sometimes allowing for falsifications of the past.

Although Freud seemed to acknowledge that these forms of derealization were applicable to him, concerning his behaviors during the Acropolis episode, he evaded the issue of whether he'd experienced a psychotic degree of these phenomena, while implying that his pathology had been quite moderate. Of course, he cleverly evaded the issue of why recurrent guilty memories of this episode had dogged him for 32 years, *if* only a moderate pathology had been involved. He was able to maintain this fiction of his moderate pathology in the summer of 1904 by not revealing to Rolland, and the public, the truly bizarre ideation regarding number and death magic that had embroiled his mind in Trieste and Athens, relating to his terrified reactions to Fliess's recent accusations about Freud's abetting of plagiarism. Indeed, those accusations promised, in effect, to destroy Freud's reputation and his professional identity.

Unfortunately, although Freud did state that "the depression at Trieste and the idea on the Acropolis, were intimately connected," he did not admit to his readers that the key connection between them was murder: his wish to murder Fliess, as well as Emanuel and John Freud. However, he acknowledged in a letter to Jung dated April 16, 1909—which he never expected would someday be published—that during his Trieste trip in 1904, and a bit later in Athens, he'd been pursued by various magical numbers relating to his fear of dying, and noted Fliess's hidden influence regarding these irrational fears. Indeed, Freud regarded Fliess as the master of number magic, and greatly feared Fliess's prediction that his "friend" would die at age 51.

Allow me now to give a brief summary of my ideas about Freud's summer trip to Trieste and Athens in 1904. And they will be explained in further detail later, following my review of Freud's extremely destructive, rivalrous acts towards Fliess which led him to manipulate an unstable (schizophrenic) lad, Otto Weininger, into plagiarizing Fliess's major work (thereby provoking Weininger's suicide). In any case, soon after Freud had received Fliess's letters in July 1904 accusing him of these vicious, rivalrous, and unethical behaviors, Freud "escaped" to Athens via Trieste, taking his brother Alexander along for company and emotional support.

This was a magical journey for Freud, during which he successively played the secret heroic roles of both Winckelmann (the "twin" of Hannibal, in Freud's mind) and Daedalus, the Greek hero—this journey being similar to Freud's unconscious re-enactment of Hannibal's role and travels, in the earlier era when Freud was still attempting unsuccessfully to overcome his Rome phobia. My suggestion is that in 1904 his trips to Trieste and the Acropolis at Athens constituted counter-phobic, symptomatic acts by which he tried to assuage his guilt about killing Weininger and desiring to kill other persons (Fliess, Emanuel, John, etc.), as well as his own fear of being murdered in Trieste. This was related to the fact that the homosexual Winckelmann had been murdered in Trieste, following a period of grave mental depression. Moreover, it is likely that Freud, in his intense identification with Winckelmann, associated the man with Winckelmann's fixation upon two sea-serpents (reminding us of the Loch Ness sea-serpent cited by Freud). This refers to Winckelmann's virtual obsession with the statue (and myth) of Laocoön, which earned him *fame* in the world of art criticism—a myth which pertains to the Trojan priest, and his sons, who were killed by two sea-serpents after warning the Trojans about the wooden horse at the seige of Troy. (Notice that these sea-serpents were involved with the killing of men.)

I've stated that Freud's trip to Trieste was counter-phobic, and I could easily cite other counter-phobic acts by him concerning death—becoming the first resident of the dreaded "house of death" or Suenhaus, the site where 600 souls had died, was one example; occupying N. Weiss's apartment right after his suicide was another instance; also the devil's pacts were counter-phobic concerning death. Ergo, in August 1904, gripped by fear that Fliess would murder him (a projection), Freud made that counter-phobic trip to the city where Winckelmann was murdered (Trieste). There he became deluged by depression and bizarre ideation about being pursued by Fliess's magical, murderous numbers, as a "heroic" way of trying to overcome his own murder fears, wishes, and associated guilt. Later, in Athens, his role was suddenly switched to his identification with the murderer named Daedalus, the mythic Greek hero whose killing of a *nephew* caused him to be exiled from Athens for the rest of his life, with the certainty of death if he should return. Therefore, Freud's "return" to Athens in his role of Daedalus was a counter-phobic act to overcome the fear that he would be killed there for having wished to kill his own *nephew*, John Freud. Let me now explain how details found in the story of Daedalus help to confirm these ideas, in conjunction with the theme of the deadly serpent that is incorporated in this myth, which relates to Freud's metaphor about the Loch Ness serpent.

A concise telling of the myth concerning Daedalus and Talos has been offered by Graves (1982, pp. 311-313). It starts with the claim that the magnificent blacksmith Daedalus belonged to the royal line of Athens and had received instruction in his craft from the goddess Athena herself. One of his apprentices was his nephew Talos, the son of his sister Polycaste, who in his twelfth year surpassed Daedalus in craftsmanship, evoking considerable jealousy in the master.

One day the precocious Talos picked up the jawbone of *a serpent* and discovered that he could employ it to cut a stick in half. So he used it as a model and made an iron copy of it, inventing the first saw in that manner. Later, Talos created many other inventions (the compass, the potter's wheel, etc.) and these secured his fame in Athens. Soon Daedalus became very rivalrous towards his nephew and claimed that he had invented the saw (plagiarism.). His intense jealousy increased to the point where he decided to murder Talos, and the temple of Athena was then woven into his lethal plan.

Daedalus led his nephew to the roof of Athena's temple *on the Acropolis* and pointed out distant sights to him. Then he suddenly pushed him over the edge to his death. (It was said that one of his motives was that he suspected Talos of having incestuous relations with his mother Polycaste—

which should have caught Freud's attention.) Next, the killer rushed to the foot of the Acropolis and stuffed Talos's corpse into a sack, intending to bury it secretly. When questioned by passers-by about blood stains seeping through the sack, he lied artfully by stating that the sack contained a *dead serpent*. But his crime was detected, and a lawful tribunal banished him from Athens for committing this murder.

A further segment of the myth of Daedalus tells about the time when he and his son Icarus were trapped in the Labyrinth in Crete, and Daedalus used bird feathers and wax to fashion huge wings so that he and his son could escape. Recall that he warned Icarus not to fly too high, fearing that the sun's heat would melt the wax, and as they flew off together he warned his son to follow him closely and not to set his own course. But Icarus disobeyed. He soared upward towards the sun, whereupon his wings disintegrated and he plummeted into the sea and drowned.

We can see that the Law of Talion was operating here, since the plummeting of Talos to his death from a great height (due to murder) was atoned by Icarus's plunge to his death from an even greater height. Rivalry between kinsmen is central to the first segment of this myth, and the moral of the latter segment is that a son may face death if covert rivalry prompts him to "surpass" his father (to go higher). Probably, Freud unconsciously had access to the latter portion of this myth when he explained that his bizarre ideation on the Acropolis was prompted by hidden conflicts about "surpassing his father." However, this also helps to confirm that he was acting-out the Daedalus myth unconsciously, although it was the first segment of the myth—relating to the murder of the rivalrous nephew, Talos—that must have been central to the peculiar ideation of his Acropolis episode of 1904.

That last conclusion is supported by numerous concordances between the myth and Freud's life history. First, we know that Freud nurtured a monumental rivalry with his own nephew (John) and that Sigmund harbored an intense desire to murder him (review the Brutus episode). Next, we see that Freud's mention of a *sea-serpent*, in relation to his very disturbed state of mind while standing on the Acropolis, makes a tight connection with Daedalus's presumed mental disturbance when he murdered his nephew *on the Acropolis*, and then deceitfully referred to him as a serpent. It seems clear that Freud's reference to the ever-hidden serpent at Loch Ness meshes nicely with the alleged serpent concealed in a sack by Daedalus. In fact, Freud's use of the metaphor of the dangerous, concealed serpent seems to symbolize the potent murderous forces that were forever concealed, but bubbling upwards in his unconscious mind. In a later chapter I'll discuss that, for Freud, the serpent symbolized murderous Satanic forces and fears of castration, and also I'll explain my thesis that just prior to the Trieste trip of 1904 his unbalanced mind was flooded by anxieties about legions of vengeful, castrative sea-serpents.

Concerning that murderous rivalry between Daedalus and Talos, in its presumed influences upon Freud's Acropolis episode, we should note that the trips to Trieste and Athens in 1904 were immediately preceded by the culmination of Freud's vicious acts of rivalry towards Wilhelm Fliess (also tied to Weininger's death). The outcome of that rivalry had raised intense wishes, fears, and guilt about murder in Freud's psyche, which helps explain his deranged ideation on the Acropolis, since this pertained to his identification with Daedalus and this hero's murder of his rivalrous nephew, on the Acropolis. (We can see that one of Freud's perverse motives in visiting the Acropolis in 1904 was to demonstrate his power and invulnerability by "returning to the scene of the crime" and getting away with it!)

There are other factors that point to Freud's fantasy identification with the Greek hero Daedalus. Several writers (Kanzer 1979, pp. 265, 298) have noted Freud's identification with Prometheus, the great creative hero of the Greeks, and it is clear that the immense creativity of Daedalus makes him the mythic counterpart of the daring Prometheus. Notice that Freud also identified with many other mythic and cultural heroes of Greece including Oedipus, Hercules, Aeneas, Zeus, Socrates, Homer, Philipp of Macedon, and Alexander. Taking these factors into consideration, probably it was no accident that Freud was accompanied to the Acropolis by his brother Alexander, whom Sigmund had named after the Greek conqueror. Perhaps Alexander Freud was there as "protection" for Freud in his fantasized role of Daedalus, since the latter hero had been eternally banished from Athens for the murder of Talos, under a threat of death. (In the next chapter I'll discuss my thesis that Freud also might have made fantasy identifications with the hero Jason—enamored of the Golden Fleece—and the hero Theseus, whose negligent behaviors caused his father, a king, to plunge to his death *from the Acropolis.*)

In considering Freud's probable identification with Daedalus, it should be emphasized that the Greek hero murdered his rival by pushing him from a height. One must wonder about the "coincidence" that Wilhelm Fliess made the accusation that Freud, in an enraged state of mind, was planning to push him off a precipice in 1900 when together they visited a resort at Achensee, as their relationship was starting to crumble due to Freud's rivalrous feelings. Perhaps a meaningful comparison can be made with my thesis that Emanuel Freud probably was *pushed*, by someone, from the platform of a speeding train in 1914. If these ideas do fit together into a pattern, one could guess that John Freud's disappearance in 1919 was connected with his being pushed from a height and that his corpse may have been stuffed into a sack (the serpent theme) before he was buried. (Although these are only conjectures, they are well-informed ones, psychologically.)

Earlier in this section, I proposed the idea that Freud's Acropolis incident encodes his murderous desires towards both John and Emanuel Freud, and that his preoccupations in 1936 with his much earlier psychotic episode in 1904 (revealed by that strange "letter" to Romain Rolland) reflect a covert confession that he'd actually arranged to murder those two kinsmen. But, so far, I've discussed the Acropolis episode only in terms of its probable connection with Freud's nephew, John (counterpart of the murdered nephew, Talos). Now it's time to consider how the figure of Emanuel Freud might have entered into the Acropolis episode.

In that 1936 article, Freud used the metaphor of the imaginary serpent at Loch Ness to symbolize the intense denial of reality (madness) that had gripped his mind on his 1904 visit to the Acropolis. With reference to the Daedalus myth, we've seen that its incorporation of an imaginary serpent pertains to the corpse of a rivalrous murdered nephew (Talos), in turn secretly referring to the rivalrous nephew (John) whom Freud desired to murder. Moreover, the fact that the Loch Ness metaphor refers to a dangerous serpent located in the British Isles also makes an indirect connection with nephew John Freud, whose home was located in an English city not too distant from Scotland, and Loch Ness. And we can discern another compelling metaphor of Freud's, in that same article, which exposes that his madness on the Acropolis was relevant to his wish to murder Emanuel Freud.

At one point in that article, Freud made an indirect connection of his denial of reality on the Acropolis by comparing this with: "the famous lament of the Spanish Moors '*Ay de mi Alhama*' ['Alas for my Alhama'], which tells how King Boabdil received the news of the fall of his city of Alhama." Notice that this was the Moorish King of Granada, in the 1400s, who knew that the fall of his key city Alhama meant the end of his rule (relevant to Freud's fear in 1904 that Fliess would soon ruin his reputation). As Freud remarked, this ancient king received the undesired information via letters brought by a messenger, but he would not let this reality "be true," and totally denied the bad news. Freud commented that this irrational king needed "to combat a feeling of powerlessness" so he demonstrated his absolute powers by *burning the letters* and by having the messenger murdered. (Consider that Freud burned his private letters and papers several times in his lifetime to prevent biographers from learning the true nature of his character and deeds.)

In a paper about Freud's trip to the Acropolis, Kanzer (1979, p. 265 ff.) observed that there was obviously "some inner link between Boabdil and Freud himself," and noted that this Semitic king had deposed his own father. Indeed, to some extent Kanzer seemed aware that Freud's mention of the king's despair at the loss of the city Alhama made a covert reference to Sigmund's sudden loss of the primal Freiberg scene and his key relationships in childhood, especially his loss of "a Catholic nurse ('Amme') . ." With these remarks, Kanzer came close to specifying that Freud, in his article, was employing hidden name magic, correlating his nanny (called 'Amme') with the name of the city Alhama. Let me endorse that idea by pointing to further name magic here, for the childhood name of Freud was "Moor," which correlates with the identity of the Moorish king, Boabdil, indicating that unconsciously it was Freud who murdered the offending "messenger."

Therefore, in Freud's reference to this Moorish monarch who suddenly lost his kingdom, like the Freiberg loss, his unconscious mind was telling us the underlying, earliest reason for his modest episode of psychosis on the Acropolis in 1904 and for his need to murder a particular "messenger." In covert language he was admitting that the loss of his nanny (Alhama)* at age three had thrown him into a lifelong vengeful depression. Also, this revealed that for decades thereafter, he'd maintained a burning desire to murder the messenger (his brother Emanuel) who had first informed him about his nanny's "downfall"—a reality about her loss to him that he continued to deny, as the cornerstone of his psychotic vulnerabilities.

There is another encoding of the identities of nanny and brother Emanuel in Freud's article on the Acropolis, again with a subtle indication of Freud's urgent desires to murder his eldest half-brother. In a megalomanic fashion, Freud compared himself and his brother Alexander—while they stood atop the Acropolis, thereby proving that he had attained a high standing in life—with the moment when the great Napoleon had stood in the Notre Dame cathedral for his coronation and indicated to his eldest brother Josef that their father would have been so proud of his glorious achievement.

First, in that gratuitous mention of Notre Dame, again Freud had made an unconscious reference to his Catholic nanny, reminding us that during his Paris visit with Jean Charcot his frequent visits to the Notre Dame cathedral exposed his unconscious fixation on his nursemaid (as previously discussed). Also, his mention of Napoleon reminds us of his fantasy identification with that power-figure. It is pertinent that Freud invented the notion that Napoleon had made his self-congratulatory remark to his *eldest brother Josef.* For in his 1930s letter to Thomas Mann, alleging that Napoleon had suffered from extensive name-compulsions regarding his fantasy identifications with the Biblical dream master, Josef, Freud "invented"

---

*Recall that Freud used various cities and other places to represent the nanny: Rome, Mantua, Monaco, Athens (perhaps), Notre Dame, the Zuyder Zee, Alhama, etc.

the claim that Napoleon harbored an unconscious, *murderous* hatred for his eldest brother, Josef. This fanciful concoction by Freud, that Napoleon secretly wished to murder his eldest brother, was simply a projection of Freud's covert burning desire to kill his eldest brother Emanuel, which was rightly juxtaposed with the image of nanny (Notre Dame) in this peculiar anecdote that he injected into the Acropolis paper. (Concerning Freud's hidden guilt about murderous urges in the Acropolis paper, as related to rage about his lost nanny and fears of the Day of Judgment, notice that the words Acropolis and Apocalypse have strong structural similarities, in English.)

In the above analysis I've stated that Freud's 1904 paper about his Acropolis episode encodes the notion (that was bubbling in Freud's unconscious mind) that the emperor Napoleon secretly desired to kill another member of the Bonaparte family (Josef). If so, logic can suggest another strong reason why Freud, in 1936, was stimulated to revive his memories about the Acropolis madness of 1904. Consider these points. Freud injected his comment about Napoleon into his paper in 1936, and there is no good reason to assume that he had thought about Napoleon in 1904, while experiencing the Acropolis episode initially. Actually, his talks and correspondence with Thomas Mann about Napoleon in the early 1930s most likely had provided a partial trigger for his inclusion of that Napoleon anecdote in the 1936 paper concerning the Acropolis episode.

Now let's follow some logical reasoning. First, I've said that the 1936 paper about the Acropolis episode encodes Freud's fantasy that Napoleon wished to kill a royal member of the Bonaparte family. Second, we know that Freud harbored a strong identification with Napoleon. Third, it becomes quite possible, therefore, that in 1936 Freud himself was struggling with an intense desire to murder a royal member of the Bonaparte family—a member of that famous family who happened to be a colleague of Freud. Consider that the Acropolis madness during the year 1904 was triggered by Freud's strong desire to murder Wilhelm Fliess (a colleague) who was threatening to destroy Freud's reputation via public disclosure of extremely unsavory behaviors by Freud—and perhaps a very similar motive for murder existed in 1936.

My suggestion, of course, is that in 1936 Freud may have been struggling with an intense desire to murder his psychoanalytic colleagues Princess Marie Bonaparte, a princess *of Greece* who was a direct descendant of the emperor Napoleon. In that same era, this influential and wealthy woman was utterly plaguing Freud by insisting that she would arrange for publication of his private letters to Wilhelm Fliess, which Freud feared would cause the eventual destruction of his reputation. He exerted great pressure on Marie Bonaparte, trying to manipulate her into relinquishing ownership of those letters which she had bought indirectly from the wife of Fliess, but Princess Bonaparte refused to give them up. There is no doubt that, like King Boabdil, Freud hoped to protect himself by "burning the letters" (his exact wording in the Acropolis article!), and there is good reason to suspect that he wished to effect this same destruction of letters by a further imitation of the mad Moorish king, i.e. by murdering the messenger (Marie Bonaparte). Anyone who doubts that, to prevent publication of the Fliess letters Freud would have arranged her murder (if he could have found a non-incriminating way to do so), should ponder the "administrative murder" of his colleague, Dr. Isidor Sadger, to prevent publication of his damaging biography of Freud in that same period of the 1930s. (Despite Freud's vehement objections, Princess Bonaparte did effect the initial—perhaps partial—publication of the Freud/Fliess letters.)

Readers do not have to agree with every idea that I have expressed about Freud's little paper concerning the Acropolis episode of 1904. Nevertheless, it should be clear by now that this strange episode, and the article written in 1936 to memorialize it, are secretly suffused by these central issues: murder and madness in relation to Freud. It should also be clear that Freud's article is largely a scam. Thus, he pretended to be a champion of truth who would willingly suffer public displeasure or contempt by revealing unpleasant information about himself, in order to clarify what he implied was a fairly modest and brief aspect of psychopathology that he'd suffered in 1904. But in doing this he withheld crucial information (his bizarre behaviors regarding number magic in Trieste and Athens, still to be described later), and probably distorted other data in order to protect his reputation, thereby abusing and offending his sacred duty to Science. This abuse of his scientific integrity will serve as an introduction to far greater offenses against the scientific ethic that are described in a long chapter titled "Freud Falsifies the Data," which appears in a later volume of mine.

Freud's Dual Personality

The Acropolis episode of 1904 has provided quite solid evidence that a hidden factor in Freud's personality concerns the issue of two contending selves in him, a kind of Jekyll versus Hyde syndrome. The notion of a dual personality in Freud should not be surprising in light of our previous review of his scores of fantasy identifications, a number of which seemed to be in opposition to each other. There is more to be said about this presumed dual personality in Freud, and in the remainder of this chapter we will explore this issue at some length.

When one considers influential authors and clinicians who have shown some awareness that Freud was plagued by a dual personality, it is reasonable to start with the master's dim recognition of his own condition.

In 1883, at age 27, he was mired in depression and abuses of cocaine during the roller-coaster period of his formal engagement to Martha Bernays. She provoked intense jealousy in him, because Martha stood as a replacement of the nanny who seemed to have abandoned or jilted him in Freiberg. In a letter to his beloved Martha on August 28, 1883 he complained that it wasn't easy for him to find any peace of mind that day, and that he could not bear anyone's company for very long, especially family members.

In a crucial sentence, he exclaimed: "I am really only half a person in the sense of the old Platonic fable which you are sure to know, and the moment I am not active my cut hurts me. After all, we already belong to each other, and if we are going to have a tussle . . . let it be at close quarters." The last part of that idea evoked the romantic notion that true lovers are halves of one entire person, but there is more to that idea than meets the eye. In stating that he was only half a person, in terms of Plato's fable, Freud was also admitting dimly that there were two competing selves vying within him, one of them being suppressed in an underground existence. Also, there may have been some recognition that his dual selves were intimately connected with the bisexuality that was struggling within him, for in later years he cited Plato's fable as being a precursor of Fliess's theory that bisexuality is the core of man's sexual nature. (Plato's fable posits that there are male and female halves of all human beings.)

Grotjahn has stated (1973, p. 444) that the letters between Freud and Ferenczi provide a deep insight into Freud's personality (although Jones would not publish any substantial portions of those letters in his three biographies, and this correspondence remains veiled in secrecy). A strong indication was given that Freud's self-analysis was uncovering evidence of his dual personality, in his letter to Ferenczi of February 22, 1915. For in that letter Freud referred to "that murderous firebrand and ever active devil in me (who has now become visible) . . " Evidently, this was the lethal Mr. Hyde-self that had emerged from Freud's dual personality, only a few months after the peculiar death of his brother Emanuel (whom I suggest that Freud had murdered). About the emergence of this Hyde-self circa early 1915, Freud tried to suppress this murderous self, stating that he would "bury him so deeply even from myself that I could regard myself as a peace loving man of science." Of course, that last idea implied that Freud knew that his dual personality was still controlled by the "murderous firebrand" and devil within himself and that he was not really a peaceful man of science—that science was used as a flimsy defense against his lethal impulses.

In the year 1897 Freud (at age 41) was near the peak of the crisis period of 1895-1897 when he wrote to Fliess on June 22, 1897 that he was in a period of intellectual paralysis and that every line of his writings was like torture. The results of his self-analysis made him feel like he was "in a cocoon, and God knows what sort of beast will crawl out." This was just a few months before his analysis spewed out his memories of nanny's sexual molestation of him, and memories of his sudden loss of her; and on August 18th his letter was filled with anxieties that *train accidents* might befall himself and others. Of course, these "train wrecks" symbolized his murderous rage and death wishes towards Emanuel and other family members in retaliation for "the Freiberg catastrophe" of 1859. (Recall Emanuel's lethal and inexplicable "train accident" in 1914.)

During that period of maximum stress in 1897, Freud's feeling that he was a beast that was about to emerge from a cocoon provides another symbolic reference to his dual personality and to his Jekyll/Hyde character. The metaphor that he employed reflects his conflicted personality consisting of two very different "selves"—the despicable worm (phallus) versus the beautiful butterfly (a female image). However, we see that the usually peaceful butterfly had been suppressed in his metaphor, and the implication is that a dangerous beast (Mr. Hyde) had taken its place. The moral seem to be that in Freud's divided personality even his Dr. Jekyll-self was suffused with unsuspected violent potentials, and that this dangerous division in himself was causally related to the sudden loss of his nanny in the Freiberg era.

Bakan's volume (1958, p. 135) cited Freud's fixation on a stone replication of the God called Janus (which reminds us of his fixation on the statue of Moses and of Balmary's report that Freud was fascinated successively by various statuettes that he took to his dinner table). The report of Freud's fixation on the Roman deity called Janus is particularly relevant to this section, since this god always was shown with two faces, each face gazing in opposite directions. This hints that Freud's interest in Janus was a projection of his own dual personality, which was often in conflict with itself.

The previous item is relevant to Freud's fantasy identifications with various figures who are known to have been characterized by dual personalities. For example, there is his identification with the playwright and poet Goethe and his creation Faust. Goethe's famous autobiography provides some clear indications of his dual personality, so it is not surprising that he projected that problem into the lecherous Faust. At one point, Faust acknowledged sadly that: "Two souls, alas, are housed within my breast."

Moreover, in Freud's identification with Moses there is the implication that he believed this Hebraic hero was a victim of dual personality. This can be interpreted from the fact that in *Moses and Monotheism* Freud championed the peculiar idea that historically there had been *two* leaders of the Jews called Moses, and that the original Moses had been murdered and replaced by the second Moses. Apparently, this idea of the two men called Moses was partly a projection of Freud's dual personality (along with his need to express murderous feelings towards important father-figures in his life and imagination). If I'm correct that Freud identified both himself and his brother Emanuel with the figure of Moses, it becomes easier to fathom why Freud harbored murderous feelings towards this fatherly hero, Moses.

Perhaps, at times, Freud suspected that he had more than two souls housed within his breast, as was probably also true of Faust. On his 80th birthday in 1936 he was given a special medal created by the sculptor Nemon, and this award (plus other fanfare) pleased Freud so much that he responded that he felt "as precious as a quintuplet." It's true that the Dionne quintuplets received much publicity in the 1930s and were in everyone's thoughts. But would any other eminent person have compared himself with a quintuplet, except for one whose underlying personality had been struggling for decades with numerous divisions and the dangers of psychic fragmentation?

Brief History of Dual Personality and Splitting

The comprehensive history of dynamic psychiatry by Ellenberger (1970, pp. 111 ff.) emphasizes that the period of 1775-1900 was one in which hypnotism became the main approach to the unconscious mind. That epoch also saw, as a primary feature, the evolution of a new model of the mind "based on the duality of conscious and unconscious psychism," which later included the notion of a "cluster of subpersonalities underlying the conscious personality." In the latter half of the 1800s the discoveries obtained by research with hypnosis, particularly in the treatment of hysterical patients, focused upon a special aspect of dualistic functioning—the autonomous activity of split-off fragments of the personality.

The late 1800s produced several outstanding theorists on hysteria and dual consciousness including Jean Charcot and Pierre Janet. In a famous lecture by Charcot in May 1885, he stressed that, via suggestion, groups of associated ideas can become embedded in the mind like parasites, which then become isolated from control by the rest of the ego and express themselves in corresponding motor acts. Concerning hysterical paralyses, Charcot asserted that they originated in a similar way, albeit spontaneously. According to Ellenberger (p. 149), that was the origin of the concept "that small, split-off fragments of the personality could follow an invisible development of their own and manifest themselves through clinical disturbances" (mental illness). In Janet's writings, he referred to this same phenomenon as subconscious *fixed ideas*. His extensive research with hypnosis and hysteria showed that such fixed ideas, excluded from consciousness, were like viruses in their capacity to develop secretly in an inaccessible corner of the personality. He declared that, operating subconsciously, they were able to provoke numerous physical ailments and all the varied disorders of hysteria and other mental diseases.

It was indicated by Janet that, in some cases, a complex system of these fixed ideas might occur and produce "dual consciousness." In later years, influenced by Janet, Jung referred to these subconscious fixed ideas as "complexes" and noted that usually (1963, p. 322) a split-off complex generates a personality, "as if the complex had a consciousness of itself." Concerning Janet's contention that hysterical symptoms are related to split-off parts of personality (generated by fixed ideas), his research demonstrated their origin in traumatic events of a subject's past life. Moreover, his work showed that the curing of these symptoms was possible via the uncovering and dissolving of these underground psychical systems.

Turning from Paris to Vienna, Josef Breuer's strongest exposure to dual consciousness in the early 1880s occurred with his famous treatment of a woman, allegedly an hysteric, whom he called Anna O. (actually Bertha Pappenheim). This young woman exhibited some remarkable examples of mind-splitting while Breuer worked with her. She lost the ability to speak German but retained an excellent command of English. During her "absences" (states of confused delirium) there were alterations of her entire personality, as she drifted into a state of autohypnosis which she called her "clouds." As an *absence* progressed, she became completely dissociated from her usual waking self, and afterwards had amnesia for what had occurred. Breuer discovered that hers was a case of hysterical double personality, and that by merely showing her an orange he could cause her to switch from her normal personality to what he labelled her "bad self." The splitting of mind was also indicated by her frequent hallucinations of events in her life that had occurred exactly 365 days earlier. (The extensive details of this case, and its treatments will not be given here.)

In later writings by Breuer, he claimed that the initial traumas precipitating hysterias can occur in states of mental abstraction which he labeled "hypnoid" states, marked by intense daydreaming related to sexual or sad thoughts. Although Breuer argued that hypnoid states formed the foundation of hysteria, he continued to accept the view of the French clinicians that the end result was likely to be dual consciousness and various forms of mind-splitting. Thus, the *Studies on Hysteria* (1895) emphasizes the concept of hypnoid states throughout, but also endorses the existence of mind-splitting in those scores of instances when such splits are mentioned. According to Jones (1953, p. 274), initially Breuer had favored the French idea that hysteria can be explained entirely by a congenital tendency towards a splitting of consciousness, from which he later derived his concept of hypnoid states. (The autohypnotic ability of Anna O. prompted him to conclude that sporadic hypnoid states were the principle causes of her hysterical mind-splitting.)

Concerning Freud's co-authorship of *Studies on Hysteria*, in that volume he acknowledged the concept of hypnoid states as viable and the pervasiveness of mind-splitting in the hysterias. Later, however, he repudiated the hypothesis that hypnoid states are crucial phenomena underlying the hysterias. Sulloway noted (1979, p. 65) that Freud's clinical research led to his claim "that defense against distressing ideas could induce a 'splitting of mind' independently of Breuer's mechanism of hypnoid states." At that point, however, Freud rejected Breuer's concept about hypnoid states while still acknowledging that mind-splitting occurred frequently in some of the forms of hysteria (which had been categorized as Hypnoid hysterias, Retention hysterias, and Defense hysterias).

According to Sulloway (p. 368), in the period from 1893-97 Freud's general notion of hysteria started with the ideas that repression (or "defense") was responsible for suppressing certain traumatic or incompatible ideas; that repression severed a traumatic idea from its affect; and thereafter that the displaced affect induced a "splitting of the mind" (while also generating other neurotic symptoms). However, his questionable abandonment of the seduction theory called this whole scheme into question when he decided suddenly that the early traumatic events of his patients were merely fictitious, i.e. were largely fantasies. At that juncture, he'd abrogated the theoretical structure which had explained the occurrence of dual personality and mind-splitting, and thenceforth (along with his disciples) tended to ignore these crucial phenomena in his theoretical writings.

The preceding historical survey shows that awareness of dual consciousness and mind-splitting was fairly intense in early psychoanalysis and then, after 1900, these factors were relegated to a theoretical limbo. Unfortunately, during two decades thereafter the subject of mind-splits and dual personality received only some small attention in the writings of Janet and of Carl Jung, and hardly anywhere else. Sulloway has noted (p. 435) that in 1911-12 Jung asserted that an individual's inability to assimilate the contents of the collective unconscious portion of the mind "leads to psychoneurosis through a 'splitting of the mind'..." In the first half of the 1900s, these topics generally have received little concern from clinicians, except for anecdotal kinds of interest in the related topic of multiple personality. Not until the last few decades has there been a modest revival of interest in the subject of mind-splitting by clinicians who have begun to realize that it can play a significant role in the syndrome called Borderline Personality Disorder. (Recall that Vitz and I agree that Freud belongs in this category of mental disorder, without ignoring that he suffered from hysterical, obsessive-compulsive, and paranoid tendencies, as well.)

Clinicians Aware of Freud's Splits

There are many writers about Freud's life and personality who have mentioned dualistic aspects of his personality, but none (except Vitz, to my knowledge) has done so in coherent ways that might lead to a more accurate diagnosis of his mental imbalance. It should not be surprising that numerous authors have reported upon dualisms in Freud's personality, considering that his 1936 article on the Acropolis episode gave such a blatant clue to his suppressed dual consciousness, i.e. his admission that his psyche was temporarily split into two conflicting halves, by his own observation. What is amazing, however, is that these authors generally have not cited the Acropolis article's striking data while offering their own limited evidences of dual personality in Freud. It's almost as if they have backed away from this essential information within the Acropolis episode, perhaps making it taboo, because it so flagrantly reveals a painful truth about their hallowed father-figure named Freud? However, it should prove interesting to find out what these writers have managed to tell us about relevant aspects of this uncomfortable topic as this pertains to Freud's personality.

A good place to start is with Zanuso's (1986) chapter titled "The Two Sides of Freud's Personality," which showed some awareness of the dualism problem but did not do justice to its depth and complexity. Numerous glaring contradictions and ambivalences in Freud's personality were discussed briefly by Zanuso, although that author seemed unaware that these might point to underlying "splits." For example, the early years of Freud's career and love life were discussed in terms of the contradiction in him between the "placid scientist" versus "a man of violent, sometimes uncontrollable passions . . ." No thought was given to his uses of Science as a defense against murderous rage. Mainly, Zanuso's analysis dwelt upon Freud's violent, jealous behaviors during his stormy engagement period with Martha (who was, in my view, a threatening replacement for his lost nanny but one he felt that he could eventually control and punish, retributively). Citing one of Freud's articles on the sexual inadequacies of engagements and later marital relations, the author noted how it was obvious that "Freud exploited the profound discrepancy between his emotions and his reason."

Zanuso emphasized the Janus-faced character and behaviors of Freud by stating: "There is not a single trait of his character, nor a decision he made nor an incident in his life, that cannot be interpreted in two different ways." Despite this striking characterization of the master's ambivalences, there was still no mention of "splits" in personality, and the author proceeded to examine Freud's repeated assertions that he was not ambitious, despite obvious signs of megalomania and many other contradictions of Freud's claims about his non-ambitious nature. (Indeed, massive evidence of his raging ambitiousness would cause many of us to regard it as quite pathological, though he tried ingenuously to deny this in his dream book.)

Another of Freud's repeated ambivalences that Zanuso discussed involved his see-saw pattern of relationships with Breuer, Fliess, Jung, and others. "His relationships tended to follow a pattern, cooling down after a period of total amity and ending in overt hostility." The author cited Freud's admission that this fragile pattern was based upon his ambivalent and rivalrous childhood relationship with his nephew John (not recognizing that the precarious relationship with nanny likewise was an essential, hidden factor in this ambivalence). Also, it was noted that Freud's self-analysis showed that: "his equally ambivalent relationship with his father was responsible for his initially docile and submissive attitude towards his teachers, which invariably changed into one of hostile antagonism."

Some other extreme contradictions in Freud's nature were noted by Zanuso. There was, for example, the conflict between the austere man of science and the bold and often quixotic conquistador and adventurer (which Freud seemed to admit were essential, perhaps psychopathic aspects of his temperament). The author contrasted the behaviors of the reserved Doctor Freud, a man who seemed to have utmost respect for the conservative customs of his day, with the covert Faustian daredevil "who conceals an unconventional, rebellious, impassioned and indomitable nature." Likewise, there was the methodical scientist, at times constrained by scientific discipline, versus the bold (sometimes wild, like Fliess) innovator who barely controlled his rambunctious, speculative nature. It was concluded that Freud's work reached unusual heights "precisely because it was nourished by this tension between contrasting values." Thus, Zanuso never considered whether a great price was demanded by Mr. Hyde (the devil within) for these alleged achievements—sometimes paid for by the unnatural deaths of various persons in Freud's life.

While reviewing some of Freud's inconsistent behaviors, Zanuso quoted a letter that Freud received in 1886, during his conflicted engagement period, from his intended mother-in-law (Emmeline Bernays), but the author seemed unaware that in making severe criticisms of Freud's behaviors and character she had unwittingly put her finger on one of the fundamental splits in his personality. First, she warned him to try to regain a sense of tranquillity "which at present is so entirely wrecked." With a sharp pen she criticized his frequent ill-humor and despondency "which borders on the pathological," and which she saw no good reason for him to indulge. She asked him first to become a sensible *man*, emphasizing the last word to contrast it with his incredibly infantile behaviors. With painful frankness, she wrote him: "At the moment you are like a spoilt *child* who can't get his own way and cries, in the belief that in that way he can get everything." In her final thoughts, she asked him not to mind that last sentence but insisted: "it is really true."

What horrendous criticisms these were for this proud doctor, age 30, to receive from a "mere woman," as she was probably viewed by this complacent male chauvinist. However, did Frau Bernays' scathing criticisms of Freud show that she was a mean-spirited, controlling "witch" when she characterized his behaviors over many months as those of a spoiled child, rather than a grown man? A quick reading of Jones's chapters seven and eight (the era of betrothal and early marriage years) should leave no doubt that she did not exaggerate her case against him at all. And when Frau Bernays made that shrewd analysis of Freud, noting that the sensible man in him was vying weakly with the spoiled child, she had pointed to a fundamental dangerous split in his personality. But she did not realize that this was the enraged, hypersexualized, spoiled child that was still secretly dominating his personality, dating from the era of "the Freiberg catastrophe," and that Martha had fully unleashed this demon by taking the place of nanny, in her jealousy-laden engagement with young doctor Freud.

Perhaps Zanuso missed the moral of Frau Bernays' letter as it pertained to hidden mind-splits in the master. When Freud verged upon emotional collapse concerning Martha in the early 1880s, probably this had causal relevance to the unleashing of demonic forces which provoked the cocaine deaths that stamped him a "public menace" (a partial acting-out of his revengeful feelings). If so, the collapse of his personal world and identity that he experienced in 1913-14 was actually a worse trauma for him probably, so we should not be surprised that the demonic child in Freud would again seek a vengeful release by arranging for a kind of dual death—the killing of Emanuel Freud, as a surrogate for the despised betrayer, Carl Jung.

To a modest degree, Ernest Jones's work (1955, p. 422) offers a discussion of dualistic aspects of Freud's thought and behaviors. Jones noted that: "Most students of Freud have been struck by his obstinate dualisms..." For example, the tendency to base theories on the interaction and clashing of two opposite powers is pervasive in Freud's writings. Here Jones cited the following basic pairings: "love-hunger; ego-sexuality; auto-erotism-hetero-erotism; Eros-Thanatos; life-death, and so on." Jones remarked that this "fondness for pairs" occurs repeatedly in Freud's work (conscious versus unconscious; love versus hate). Jones wrote that: "It is as if Freud had a difficulty in contemplating any topic unless he could divide it into two opposites, and never more than two. That there was a fundamental conflict between two opposing forces in the mind was for him a basic fact."

It's amusing that Jones dared to mention that all those dualisms in

Freud's work might tempt one "to correlate this tendency with its manifestations in Freud's own personality." Here he cited a few of the conflicts in Freud's personality, including: scientific discipline versus philosophical speculation; a passionate love urge versus great sexual repression; masculinity versus feminine needs; a desire to be the sole creator versus hope of obtaining stimulation from another person; love of independence versus clear dependency needs. Also, Jones suggested that there was "a deep ambivalence between the emotions of love and hate" in Freud, and cited his "pronounced mental bisexuality," as well. About this mental bisexuality Jones remarked that this "may well have influenced his theoretical views to some extent, a possibility to be borne in mind when assessing them." Unfortunately, Jones did not consider that these pervasive dualisms might relate to an underlying dual consciousness and aspects of split-mind in the master, nor did he pause to wonder whether Freud's deep ambivalences between love and hate would plausibly pertain to the oppositional forces found in a Jekyll/Hyde nature. (Later, we'll learn that Jones gave us some vibrant clues that point to the Jekyll/Hyde natures of both Freud and Jones *himself*, in connection with name magic and a bizarre episode involving Freud's disciple, Dr. L. *Jekels!*)

The psychoanalyst Laforgue (1973, p. 341) knew Freud personally and well over many years, and on the basis of his personal contacts with him wrote an article analyzing his personality. He was cognizant of numerous ambivalences in Freud that call to mind his Jekyll/Hyde nature. Laforgue wrote that: "One often mentions the contradictory aspects of his personality in speaking of the good and the bad Freud, but it is important to distinguish one from the other." He remarked that Freud was aware of his ambivalences "about men and their problems," and of his perverse need to find an enemy in each of his friends. Laforgue added that Freud did not realize "to what extent this ambivalence was conditioned by his own religious superego," which seems consonant with views expressed by Zilboorg (1967) and by Vitz (1988). However, Laforgue did not mention that ambivalences concerning Freud's "religious superego" probably were initiated by that cruel separation from his nanny in childhood, nor did he recognize that the "good" versus "bad" Freud seems to imply the issue of dual consciousness.

In *Brother Animal* (1969) Roazen made a grim psychological study of "the bad Freud" and the responsibility of his Hyde-self for the tragic suicide of his ailing disciple, Dr. Victor Tausk. In that volume, Roazen (p. 162) made this shrewd observation: "There were always at least two Freuds, one cool and rational, the other terribly furious and afraid." With that characterization, Roazen came close to specifying the Jekyll/Hyde structure of Freud's divided psyche.

Roazen's previous implication that there were always two men housed within Freud's breast (like Goethe and Faust) may be relevant to Ellenberger's discussion (1970, p. 462) of his personality, starting with this observation: "From the accounts we have of Freud, two very different pictures can be drawn." Ellenberger noted that many writers (including Jones and Joan Riviere) depicted the master as "an extremely kind and civil man, full of wit and humor and altogether charming." (Riviere was Freud's patient!) However, other persons who knew him well described Freud as an extremely revengeful man (including Wittels, Jung, Puner), and his friend Stefan Zweig stated that he had a fearful face in old age, ". . a face that oppresses and frightens rather than one that liberates and charms . ." (Puner, 1949, p. 292). Ellenberger added that various persons "were impressed by what they called Freud's coldness;" also that Jung insisted that Freud's primary characteristic was a corrosive bitterness, "every word being loaded with it." According to Jung, Freud always acted as though persons who disagreed with his views should be "stamped into hell." That last point is interesting, considering his strong identification with Satan, and my thesis that he may have been responsible for at least two murders.

Of course, there are several possible reasons why Freud might have been depicted in such strikingly divergent ways, including the tendentious effects of partisan "political" considerations involving pro-Freud versus anti-Freud factions, historically. However, one should not ignore the possibility that much of the reason for these starkly divergent views lies in the Jekyll/Hyde nature of the object of our inquiry, Freud's peculiar personality. It is interesting that Schur described Freud as acting like a chameleon in his interactions with different people, which reminds us of the time when Freud blithely compared himself with a quintuplet.

Helen Puner's biography (1949) of Freud offers many insights into malevolent aspects of his nature, and it is not surprising that this sensitive woman was aware of deep divisions in Freud's personality. For example, at one point (pp. 296-7) she discussed his belated concept that the formation of the superego (conscience) derives from the final stage of the child's Oedipus complex. Puner wrote that: "With the concept of the super-ego, Freud came at last to project as a scientific principle that inner voice of arbitrary authority which had plagued and divided him all his life." Notice that she was aware not only of a great division in his moral nature (redolent of the Jekyll/Hyde syndrome), but also that his private inner conflicts were apt to be projected into his scientific works—as even Jones recognized, to a limited extent. (See previous pages.)

While this hypothesis of Freud's Jekyll/Hyde nature is fresh in our thoughts, let's recall the extensive analysis of his personality by Anzieu

(1959) which emphasized numerous instances when Freud's fantasy identifications were in striking opposition to one another. Thus, in earlier chapters we've discussed that he made identifications with Satan versus Jesus, Hannibal versus Scipio Africanus, and several other pairs that were in serious conflict with one another. Some of these extraordinary examples point to inner currents of dual consciousness and to aspects of a Jekyll/Hyde nature that contrasts the "good" versus "bad" Freud, the latter apparently concealing destructive and murderous potentials.

As indicated in previous chapters, Paul Vitz (1988) can be regarded as the dean of current authors who make explicit claims about Freud's dual personality. Vitz wrote that Freud suffered from "moderate degrees of various psychological pathologies, such as splitting [of the ego] and aspects of borderline personality disorder," although he made the error of assuming that Freud's symptoms never reached psychotic proportions. In his review of Freud's multiple fantasy identifications (p. 145) Vitz interpreted these as a seeking of idealized identities that helped to focus various aspects of Freud's fractured (split) ego, and often these new identities also were expressions of "Freud's narcissistic grandiosity—for example, his comparing himself to Moses." According to Vitz, additional signs of ego splitting in Freud were his "involvement in the occult, his hearing of voices in Paris, the effects of cocaine, his belief in 'revenants,' and the like . ." Later, he noted (p. 195) the flagrant signs of Freud's splitting of his ego relating to the Acropolis episode in 1904. It's instructive that Vitz mentioned that the symptoms of Freud described above (including his uncertain sense of identity) "are similar to those of various character disorders" which often are related to one another and have hysterical elements as well.

Vitz provided additional arguments to support his idea that Freud was subject to ego splitting. He remarked (p. 143) that: "Freud's own early diagnosis of himself as an hysteric means that he suffered from a mild form of splitting or 'fracturing,' and that his understanding of splitting was in large part due to a sensitive observation of his own psychology." At that point, Vitz cited the psychoanalyst Gedo (1976, p. 289) as already having proposed the inference that Freud's awareness of splitting occurred first within his own personality. Vitz then pointed to some autobiographical aspects of Freud's writings on ego splitting and concluded (p. 144) that: "it is reasonable to assume that Freud suffered from occasional splitting of the ego . ."

Considerable attention was given by Vitz to Freud's explanation of the psychological origins of the Devil, which he claimed is the result of ego splitting. According to Freud (and Breuer) "the split-off mind is the devil" which, in earlier times, seemed to possess the minds of superstitious persons. Concerning the source of this ego splitting, Freud suggested that splitting gives rise to the Devil by dividing the father-image into two separate figures that possess opposite attributes (which reminds us of his own Jekyll/Hyde nature). On the basis of this analysis by Freud, Vitz concluded "that Freud's psyche was to some extent fractured into separate centers, and that at least one significant part of him was identified with the Devil." Moreover, Vitz suggested (p. 147) that this ego splitting in Freud was relevant to his sexual molestation by his nanny, stating the following: "Presumably that part of Freud that identified with the Devil was mostly unconscious, was associated with his early sexual abuse, and represented the frightening aspects of his father-image initiated by the threat of castration."

In recent years, Vitz noted, Freud's ideas on ego splitting have been supplemented by some different but related ideas in psychoanalysis based on object relations theory (O.R.T.), including the work of Mahler, Kernberg, and others. This approach assumes that splitting originates with the mother, not the father, in relation to inadequate or traumatic maternal factors in the pre-Oedipal period. In that era, if the mother traumatizes or abandons the child, then ego splitting often occurs (with negative effects on individuation and separation). According to O.R.T., the child's internal image of the mother is then split into "good mother" versus "bad mother" components, and since this image is crucial to ego formation the child's psyche suffers from splitting.

Vitz remarked that O.R.T. predicts that, in Freud's case, the negative aspects of his primary mother, the nanny, "would have split or partially split to form a separate part of his ego." Therefore, this "bad nanny" component of Freud's psyche would have constituted a kind of "witch image," and since the Freiberg nanny focused upon themes involving Hell and the Devil in her teachings of Sigi, "this internalized bad mother would be closely linked to demonic themes." Here Vitz noted that Freud described his old nanny as a witch-like woman, and that three of Swales' papers on Freud have powerfully indicated the witch theme in Freud's thought.

With shrewd insight, Vitz reminded us (p. 148) that the original split in Freud's ego might have been precipitated not only by nanny's sexual molestation, but also by her perceived abandoning of him when her services were terminated abruptly (thereby instilling rage about betrayal in him). Citing Kernberg's ideas deriving from O.R.T., Vitz noted that the presence of the internalized "bad mother" is related to the tendency to use projection (a major defense used by Freud); that megalomanic behaviors, like Freud's, are common characteristics of persons who suffer from splitting; and that internalized "bad affects" are often linked to uncanny feelings, with which he sometimes seemed to be obsessed. (See the next chapter, regarding number and name magic in his life.)

In an early paper (1894) Freud stated that it was then general knowledge that hysteria demonstrates the splitting of consciousness, which he described primarily as the result of trying to cope with an intolerable sexual idea—usually a sexual memory. It's not unlikely that he was secretly referring to his own dual consciousness which had resulted from shameful feelings concerning nanny's sexual molestation of him. As cited by Sulloway (1979, p. 287), in that same year of 1894 Jules Dallemagne (and Ribot in 1896) asserted that precocious sexual events in childhood, though forgotten, can persist in the unconscious mind and provide the hidden foundation for distorted adult sexuality. Writing about sexual pathology, Dallemagne insisted upon the existence of an unconscious subpersonality that, with an "undeniable clarity," reveals itself as the director of the conscious personality.

It's plausible that Freud read Dallemagne's article circa 1894 and recognized that it was applicable to the splittings of his own mind, which he so assiduously concealed from public awareness. However, in that same era, circa 1894, Josef Breuer finally coalesced his own diagnosis of Freud's mental illness—"moral insanity"—which seems suggestive of today's terminology regarding borderline personality disorders and even the neglected term "ambulatory psychosis." It would not be unexpected that Breuer put flesh on the bones of his diagnosis of Freud and gave clear reasons for believing that his younger colleague suffered from varying degrees of mind-splitting that could be dangerous to others and to himself, perhaps further recommending the need for intensive psychological treatment (which the fearful Freud could not bear to implement with a psychiatric colleague, instead leading to his vaunted self-analysis).

My strong agreement is given to the previously stated views of both Vitz and Gedo that Freud's early theoretical understanding of splitting was due largely to "a sensitive observation of his own psychology"—and here we find autobiographical factors, repeated endlessly. In fact, it is my belief that Freud's astonishing fixation on Breuer's treatment of Bertha Pappenheim (Anna O.) was mainly the result of the striking role of mind-splitting in her case, which Freud recognized was a major factor in his own psychopathology. Although this probably was the primary reason for Freud's obsession with this case, undoubtedly there were additional reasons for Freud's fixation on poor Bertha. For example, Bertha P. was a friend of Freud's fiancée Martha Bernays. There was also the influence of name magic, since Freud previously had been in love with another girl named Bertha, the daughter of his half-brother Emanuel (incest?). Also, the name of Bertha

Pappenheim's father was Seigmund, a close match with the name that Freud had adopted at age 19 (the same age as when he visited Bertha Freud in Manchester). Another possible link with name magic is hinted by Swales' recent report that Martha Bernays was adopted by Seigmund Pappenheim, upon the death of her father. By the way, considering that Freud was the editor of the *Studies on Hysteria*, it would be interesting to find out whether he, rather than Breuer, was the inventor of the pseudonym "Anna O.," since this would open up some fascinating possibilities in the realm of name magic (that are too complex to explicate here).

A complementary thesis of mine pertains to the reasons why Freud chose Carl Jung as his "son and heir" to lead the psychoanalytic movement, a decision that was viewed by his other disciples, especially his Viennese followers, as shocking, disloyal, and even absurd. The typical reasons given for Freud's decision were that Jung enjoyed high status in the clinical world, was valuable to the Cause because he was both a psychiatrist and a gentile, and had close connections with the eminent and influential Dr. Bleuler and other important clinicians. My suggestion is that those rational reasons might not have been as compelling for Freud as was one hidden, irrational reason. That is, Freud must have felt a powerful affinity for Jung, because this Swiss doctor so obviously suffered from a splitting of his consciousness, which Jung in later years acknowledged frankly on various pages of his autobiography. This also was likely to have been the reason for Freud's intense affinities for Wilhelm Fliess and Ernest Jones, the latter's duality receiving much discussion in *Secret SL*. Concerning Fliess's duality, his most knowledgeable biographer, Peter Swales, has described Freud and Fliess as psychological "twins," (in a television interview), which seems pertinent to the dual consciousness in both men which was implied by Strachey's sober judgment that they suffered from "folie à deux" (evidenced by countless bizarre interactions in their massive correspondence).

There were many partial instigators of Freud's dual consciousness and clues to the splittings of his ego. For example, the issue of duality in him is suggested by possibly uncanny effects of his dual birthdate, with subtle influences upon his sense of identity. Also, we've seen that Sigi had two mothers—his primal nanny versus his biological mother, Amalia—which reminds us of frequent public accusations in Vienna that Freud had two wives, Martha and Minna. Likewise, the boy had two fathers—his despised father Jacob (the incompetent) versus his fantasized father, the energetic and successful Emanuel. One can say that there were two conflicting images of the Freud family in Vienna: the socially acceptable family versus the shadow family that concealed egregious criminal activities. Then there was the image of Dr. Freud as a sexual "puritan" versus the recurrent public taunts that he was a sleazy libertine (similar to Dr. Starr's public accusation that he had led the life of a moral reprobate in the 1880s). Also, there was the claim that Jacob Freud's family lived in poverty despite clear indications that they enjoyed many elements of "the good life." In addition, we have reviewed claims that Sigmund held dual religious allegiances, being a reluctant Jew and a cryptic Christian—relating to nanny's religious influences. Of course, there are many other implied ambivalences that could be mentioned, the ultimate one in this volume contrasting the benevolent physician versus the cryptic murderer who sometimes incited persons to suicide or "arranged" other fatal outcomes.

Before leaving the general subject of Freud's dual consciousness some remarks need to be made about connections between his tendencies to create "doubles" (duplications of himself) in various ways and to create strange duplications of other persons—called "revenants," meaning replacements or surrogates. With regard to his tendency to create doubles of himself, there have been various articles on this topic including Kanzer's paper (1979) titled "Freud and His Literary Doubles" and Glenn's article (1979) called "Narcissistic Aspects of Freud and His Doubles." These papers, and others, reveal that Freud had a strange proclivity for making doubles of himself, among some of his friends and colleagues, along with various eminent novelists like Arthur Schnitzler, Romain Rolland, and others.

In Freud's letter to the Viennese writer Schnitzler dated May 14, 1922 (Jones, 1957, p. 443) he "confessed" why he had never tried to arrange a meeting with Schnitzler in Vienna, despite the uncanny similarities between their ideas and life experiences. Here, Freud acknowledged clearly that he regarded Schnitzler as "his double," stating that: "I think I have avoided you from a kind of awe of meeting my 'double.'" What Freud did not admit to Schnitzler, perhaps embarrassed about his own magical thinking, was that his fears about meeting his own doubles—men with characters, life styles, or physical appearances that were very similar to his own—was because he shared the magical beliefs of savage people that meeting one's double was a certain sign of impending death.

Accordingly, Freud's long-term physician Max Schur (1972, pp. 333-7) indicated that Freud's essay in 1919 titled "The Uncanny" described many uncanny factors pertaining to psychological or physical doubles that were projections of Freud's inner world. Schur noted that on two different occasions Freud had the frightening experience of encountering men whom he regarded as his doubles (in terms of their physical appearances). For example, on one of Freud's visits to Naples with his brother Alexander, they were riding on a train together when Sigmund met a man whom he "perceived" as his double. He then attempted to use irony and humor to conceal his great fear of death while asking Alexander whether seeing this uncanny duplicate of himself was a portent that he would die in Naples! Readers will be asked to remember that this strange fear of death in Naples occurred *on a train*, when we explore Emanuel's later death "by accident" on a train. We'll have to ask ourselves whether this man in Naples really looked like Freud very much, or whether factors relating to trains were apt to stimulate Freud's infantile fears and murderous feelings concerning trains, gas jets at Breslau, etc., prompting distortions of Freud's visual perceptions?

Apparently, Freud's unconscious creation of doubles was a way that his mind, using the magical thinking and perception of a pre-Oedipal child, attempted to protect his ego against massive fears of death. Some of these magical strategies can be described from studies of preliterate and mythic sources. Children and mentally unbalanced adults may create fictional doubles while employing the fantasy that the Angel of Death is stupid and can readily be tricked, in times of grave sickness or other dangers, into taking the life of the child's psychological or physical double in lieu of the sick child himself. One of the Hebrew myths describes a corresponding strategy by the mother of Josef, who became the master of dreams. When the lad was ailing, she simply dressed him in girls' clothing to ensure that his identity would be concealed from the demon of death, a ferocious figure but none too bright. The Hebrew practice of changing the name of a gravely sick child has a similar basis in magical thought (protection via deception), and also is a well-known practice among many preliterate people worldwide.

Another magical basis for Freud's creation of doubles is that the fantasied incorporation of the person who is one's double will increase the longevity of the initiator of this stratagem, which seems a counter-phobic way of denying that seeing one's double is a certain sign of one's death. Thus, when Freud transformed men into his doubles there was a hidden intent, in this incorporation, that he would be able to steal magically some of the years of life allotted to them. This strategy (reminiscent of his Satanic pacts) relies upon psychic mechanisms that are akin to "partial murder," so they must remain unconscious in most people. But if they are minimally exposed, at times when the initiator meets his own double, then a great dread of retribution is aroused, and he fears that he will lose his own life. Therefore, the creation of doubles is inextricably connected with the topics of protection from death and desire to murder, even when these issues are hidden from consciousness.

Closely related reasons why children and some mentally imbalanced persons may create doubles concerns their hidden desires to protect themselves magically from death by stealing years of life allotted to their doubles and by stealing their creative energies, talents, or products, i.e. by absorbing a double's energies the initiator of this strategy is in a better position magically to defend himself against death. The latter idea is similar to the widespread belief among preliterate people that when a man kills another person, either a tribal or personal enemy, he can incorporate the dead man's powers and enhance his own strength and capabilities. Therefore, this supports the thesis concerning Wilhelm Fliess, one of Freud's doubles or "twins," that Freud *did* plan to murder him in 1900 (see Swales) in connection with a clear, fervid desire to steal (plagiarize) Fliess's ideas about psychic bisexuality.

Concerning the previous paragraphs, it should be noted that in Glenn's article (1979, pp. 298-9) about Freud and his narcissistic doubles, the author claimed that Freud's supposedly "great achievements" derived from his infantile narcissism. According to Glenn, this force was operative in Freud's 1936 paper on the Acropolis episode which he offered as a birthday gift to Romain Rolland while competing with this great writer whom he apparently regarded as another of his doubles. In describing that act, Glenn indicated that Freud was identifying "with his double" (Rolland) and in doing so he did not only *absorb this double's creative ability* but "using his own innate talent . . he overshadows Rolland." Glenn's next remark was that: "The fantasied double forms a reassuring presence adding strength to the weak child." Sagely, Glenn added that doubles may protect a threatened child from various catastrophes. Indeed, the weak child does not need to fear castration, maternal deprivation, and other narcissistic losses and traumas, since the magical double "substitutes for that which may be lost . . ," as confirmed by Kanzer's writings.

In Kanzer's article (1979, pp. 292-3) he focused upon that same birthday gift—the paper on the Acropolis episode of 1904—which Freud offered to Romain Rolland in 1936. Kanzer analyzed Freud's paper and cited evidence in it showing that in 1936 Freud, nearing death at age 80, would have liked to switch identities with Rolland and with his own brother Alexander, both of whom were ten years younger than he was. According to Kanzer, what "comes to the fore" in this strange paper was Freud's: "desire to exchange identities with Rolland and Alexander . . . carrying with it the promise of ten years more of life for Sigmund while the younger . . . brothers, are sent to their death in his place." In a revealing additional remark, Kanzer wrote that: "Such an exchange of death wishes with Wilhelm Fliess had prevailed in 1904."

The preceding comments by Kanzer indicated his awareness that Freud's paper about the Acropolis episode uncovers his covert desires to steal years of life allotted to his doubles and competitors, consonant with powerful desires to enhance longevity that were involved in his Satanic pacts, as discussed later. However, it did not occur to Kanzer that Freud actually had arranged the deaths of various persons, including Emanuel and John Freud, partly with the motive of magically enhancing his own life span.

An additional perverse motive of Sigmund's in dispatching his elder brother Emanuel was to provide a triumph of the younger son over the older one (the theme of the Biblical Josef's story), allowing for replacement of the older son. In 1914 this presumed "murder strategy" unconsciously provided Freud with a magical reversal of his immense fears that he'd become the primal father of *Totem and Taboo*, whom his younger "sons" were plotting to destroy. Apparently, in arranging for Emanuel's murder in 1914, he killed his own primal father and thereby enhanced his threatened powers by becoming the new, indisputable leader of the Freud clan, at last fulfilling narcissistic goals of his early childhood years.

It is significant that, right after noting Freud's wish to switch identities with Romain Rolland and Alexander Freud in his Acropolis paper of 1936, Kanzer discussed elements in this paper relating to Freud's desire to triumph over both his father and his older brother, while alluding to Freud's impression that Napoleon (another double) bore a murderous hatred and rivalry towards his older brother, Josef. Subsequently, Kanzer discussed Freud's magical reconstruction of the story of Moses (a double) and his bizarre denial that Aaron, the younger brother of Moses, could ever have existed. Of course, this crude denial of Aaron's existence symbolized a reversal by Freud, constituting a raw act of denial that Sigmund, the younger brother, had wished for the elimination of his own older brother Emanuel and had achieved that lethal goal in 1914. Therefore, there is great significance in Kanzer's (p. 293) awareness that within *Moses and Monotheism* one can detect echoes of "legends and fairy tales both of the expulsion of the elder sons and of the favoring of the younger sons." No doubt these same echoes were aspects of Freud's covert confession in the Moses book relating to his elimination of Emanuel Freud. Likewise, the Acropolis paper written in that same era contains covert confessions about the murders of both Emanuel and John Freud, along with strong hints of Freud's desires to kill Fliess and Princess Marie Bonaparte, in my view of the 1936 article.

Before making a few comments about Freud's persistent coalescence of "revenants" throughout his lifetime, fusing together persons who were duplications and replacements of previous figures in his life, I'd like to mention briefly some of my ideas about why Freud chose Romain Rolland in 1936 as the specific double to whom his Acropolis paper made its covert confessions of murder. My thesis is that the choice of Romain Rolland was a symptomatic act partially based upon name magic and a disguised, symbolic instance of Freud's tendency to create revenants. With regard to name magic, my first emphasis is upon the French writer's given name and the fact that its first four letters constitute the name of Italy's capital city, Roma. As observed by many writers, that city was symbolic of Freud's intense lifelong desire to recapture his nanny, so one may assume that Romain Rolland had become a revenant of Freud's loving nursemaid. A study of Freud's earlier letters shows that he acknowledged the generous, maternal qualities of Rolland which prompted his readers to lavish affectionate feelings upon this kind, sensitive author. Ergo, when Freud made a secret confession of his crimes to this writer, that was tantamount to confessing to his beloved nanny (the originator of his primal crimes) from whom he hoped for deep understanding and psychic absolution. Also, in making this writer a double, he attempted once again to meld his spirit with that of his ancient nanny.

Freud's fixation upon this double, Romain Rolland, also relates to his preoccupation with mythical heroes and his promiscuous tendency to identify with them. This relates to the fact that the writer's surname evokes memories of the French hero (the song of Rolland) who has captivated the hearts of many generations of French school children. Among this warrior-hero's varied achievements, perhaps the greatest and most touching story of them all concerns the incredibly courageous spirit which he displayed in meeting his own death. It is no coincidence that in 1936, at age 80, Freud knew that soon he would face his own death. Evidently, he transformed the writer Rolland into a double to protect himself from the final humiliation of dying via his cancerous jaw, with all its grotesque aspects. By the magical incorporation of this author's great surname, Freud must have hoped that this would provide him with the courage required to achieve a truly noble death. Readers will decide themselves whether he attained that goal. In 1939, after decades of expressing contempt for "cowards" who killed themselves during painful illnesses, Freud arranged for his own suicide via a lethal dose of morphine administered by Dr. Schur.

This brings me to some final brief comments about Freud's extensive uses of revenants, noted by many sources including Schur's biography (1972) of Freud, which gives considerable attention to these symptomatic acts by the master. Various writers have expressed their own ideas about the specific progression of a particular series of Freud's revenants; here I will not attempt to sort out their ideas and merely will mention a few of my own thoughts. As an example, let's start with Freud's famous nanny. Included in her later series of revenants (replacements) in Freud's mind were Gisela Fluss, Martha Freud, Minna Bernays, Emma Eckstein, Josef Breuer (perhaps), Wilhelm Fliess, Anna Freud (his daughter), Marie von Ferstel (perhaps), Romain Rolland, and other persons.

To indicate the complexity of these phenomena, all of the preceding figures had a capacity to serve as a revenant for several persons who had preceded them, and to have several subsequent figures serve as revenants for them! Thus, Wilhelm Fliess served as a revenant for nanny, Julius and John Freud, Gisela Fluss, and perhaps was a composite of the father-figures Jacob and Emanuel Freud. In turn, the persons who served as revenants for the "lost image" of Wilhelm Fliess included Wilhelm Stekel, Alfred Adler, Carl Jung, Max Schur, and a mythical Greek figure associated with Jason and the Argonauts (discussed in the next chapter).

As was true of Freud's coalescence of scores of fantasy identifications (with heroes, savants, murderers, etc.) and with a number of doubles or "twins," his proliferation of many series of revenants was based upon his desire to maintain a "magical" control of death, and likewise to enable him to indulge in murder to assuage his ferocious death-wishes. In his associations to the *Non vixit* dream, he explained to his readers how this dream showed that many revenants were active in his dreamlife, revenants which he could destroy with impunity and without worry, since he could readily create new surrogates of this sort whenever he desired. What he did not admit to his readers was that many series of such revenants also were active in his waking life. Indeed, he was consciously aware of them to some extent (for he specified once that Adler and Stekel had been revenants of Fliess). Moreover, his murderous impulses posed great danger to some flesh-and-blood revenants due to that previous irrational notion, i.e. they were expendable, since new revenants could be "created" whenever he pleased.

Chapter Six

Name Magic, Death, and the Revenants

Freud's Magical Defenses Against Death

In this volume I have proposed that Freud suffered from a number of interrelated complexes connected to death, and that most of his biographers have chosen to ignore or downplay this. Overall, we can speak of a primary death complex dominating his psyche, intimately connected with several other dangerous psychic systems, including a murder complex (incorporating his Cain complex), and a suicide complex.

The preceding framework is more specific and extended than Choisy's orientation (1963) and Schur's (1972), both of whom recognized intense death anxieties in Freud but greatly neglected the issues of murder and problems with suicide. Schur did give some thought to Freud's death wishes, however, and was also aware of Freud's repeated anxieties about special death years in his life, and obsessive uses of revenants to protect himself from losses due to death or separation from important figures in his life. Choisy emphasized his repeated employment of four defenses against death (sex, drugs, extreme rationalism, and aggression), and claimed that Freud used all of them lavishly without, however, providing full descriptions that would support those assertions adequately.

Unfortunately, Choisy's discussion of Freud's defenses, while both reasonable and accurate, failed to recognize many factors involving *magical thinking* that he used to protect himself against massive death fears. Here is a partial list of magical strategies that were used by his unconscious mind to maintain control over the Angel of Death: 1. repeatedly, he created scores of fantasy identifications with mythic heroes, deities, murderers, and other powerful and famous persons; 2. he created various doubles ("twins" and alter-egos); 3. he produced numerous and complex series of revenants; 4. he used a profusion of name magic, in diverse ways, often using it as a vehicle for creating revenants; 5. in uncanny ways, he employed number magic for diverse reasons, but especially as a defense against death; 6. related to the previous item, he strongly endorsed Fliess's magical "periodicity theory;" 7. he entered into two or more Satanic pacts to prolong his life, using number magic as part of this strategy; 8. he manipulated a series of special death years, and their related anxieties, to control the unpredictability of death and to compensate for his murderous wishes; 9. he endured the Steinach operation on his gonads, hoping to effect a magical rejuvenating of himself, and to pay for death wishes; 10. he made repetitious assertions about his impending death to colleagues and friends, as a strategy to control death's unpredictability; 11. to control death, and for other irrational reasons, he committed various "accidental" homicides, provoked a number of suicides, and murdered two kinsmen; 12. he embedded the identities of lost persons, especially his Freiberg nanny, into various physical locations and into his writings, symbolically (by word play or via name magic); 13. he made magical infusions of his own identity into various physical locations and objects, and symbolically into his writings; 14. he developed a corps of adoring disciples who treated him like an omnipotent deity; 15. obsessively, he became the foremost champion of Eros and then abruptly switched his allegiance to Thanatos; 16. he used cocaine excessively, as if it were a magical substance, probably with homicidal motives, at times; 17. he developed Psychoanalysis as a worldwide empire with himself as emperor and founding father.

Blum is one of the few authors showing awareness that Freud had an obsession with death throughout his lifetime, and that he tried to control death by various remarkable strategies. According to Blum (1979, p. 154) "Freud suffered from the dread of death," and "he repeatedly tried to time his death," because he feared an untimely end (death's unpredictability).

I'm in agreement with Blum that Freud repeatedly tried to time his own death, unconsciously trying to accomplish this by specifying that he would die during special death years, such as age 51, 62, etc., and by entering into two or more Satanic pacts, which also set the limits for his years of life. Blum theorized that Freud's obsession with death had its roots in the traumatic loss of his infant brother Julius—whom young Sigi earnestly wished would die, stimulating uncanny guilt feelings—and in his mother's mourning for the infant, which coincided with her new pregnancy. (No mention was made of the crucial significance of the loss of Sigi's nanny.)

It was noted by Blum, however, that in Freud's letter to Fliess of April 16, 1896 he reported that he had just experienced "attacks of fears of dying," which he linked inexplicably to the recent cardiac death of the eminent

Viennese sculptor named Victor Tilgner, who was not even an acquaintance of Freud, as discussed by Schur. Blum emphasized that Tilgner died on April 15, the same day as Julius Freud, hinting that Freud's attacks of death anxiety after he'd read Tilgner's obituary in the newspapers was probably an "anniversary reaction" relating to baby Julius's death. There are also indications that Freud made an abrupt fantasy identification with Tilgner soon after his death, based on some remarkable similarities in their life situations.

Naturally, Jones's three-volume biography of Freud offers only brief comments about Freud's lifelong dread of death, since Jones did not wish to let himself consider whether this was actually a death complex burdening the master's psyche, one that perhaps was tied to murder and suicide complexes. Basically, Jones tried to downplay Freud's horrendous, lifelong death anxieties by largely confining his comments to *less than two pages* (pp. 279-280) of his third volume. Concerning Freud's fantasies about death, Jones remarked that Freud was preoccupied "by thoughts about death, more so than any other great man I can think of" (except perhaps for Montaigne and Sir Thomas Browne).

Jones mentioned that Freud said he thought about death every day of his life, which Jones sagely remarked "is certainly unusual." Moreover, starting from the early days of their relationship, when these colleagues parted from one another, it was Freud's habit to say: "Goodbye, you may never see me again." (This strategy for controlling death is listed as #10, on the previous list of magical defenses.) Also, Jones reported that Freud, throughout his life, suffered repeated attacks of *Todesangst*, (dread of death) and that his thoughts about death grew "increasingly clamorous" as he became older. Not surprisingly: "He hated growing old, even as early as his forties . ."

Near the end of his rather simplistic discussion of Freud's death concerns, Jones hinted that there was a dualistic aspect to Freud's preoccupation with death, an immense dread of death versus a "curious longing for death"! For example, in 1912 when Freud regained consciousness from a peculiar fainting spell in Munich, his first comment was: "How sweet it must be to die." In summarizing his ideas, Jones ignored the issue of "dual consciousness" but theorized that Freud continually harbored a double fantasy about death involving "dread of a terrible father alternating with desire for reunion with a loved mother." (Unfortunately, Jones ignored the critical loss of Sigi's nanny, just as Blum failed to cite her role as the lost primal mother.) Although Jones was aware of Freud's longing for death, this did not prompt him to consider the existence of a suicide complex in Freud, nor that this often has a natural psychical relationship to a hidden murder complex. If it is true, however, that Jones was the evil genius who inspired the "administrative murder" of Dr. Sadger in the 1930s, should we have expected him to provide any serious discussion of a murder complex in his beloved master?

Freud's loyal followers like to say that he was subject to a bit of superstitious thinking occasionally, but that otherwise he was always the most rational of men. That is perfect nonsense, of course. Especially where the subjects of death, birth, sex, and money were concerned, Freud's mind had an astonishing vulnerability to magical thinking (which had its roots in fixations of the pre-Oedipal era). In the remainder of this chapter we'll take a closer look at Freud's uses of number magic and name magic, particularly the latter. Our exploration of the astonishing varieties of name magic employed by Freud will help us to understand the complexity of his magical ideation and how it could lead to the sudden deaths of some people with whom he was associated. In turn, this will serve as a backdrop for our consideration of the eerie deaths of Emanuel and John Freud.

Freud's Number Magic and Name Magic

Over the past 25 years, I have been making extensive clinical and naturalistic studies of name magic, and I have almost completed a book by that title (*Name Magic*) that explores the complex workings of the magical manipulations of personal names by some famous murderers, mentally imbalanced persons, and some normal children and adults. Let me says at the outset that I have never encountered any individual who has utilized name magic to such a great extent as Sigmund Freud, both at unconscious and conscious levels of behavior. Before discussing his complicated uses of name magic, however, let's take a brief look at the ways that he used number magic—particularly the ways that number magic were related in his mind to the topics of death, revenge, and power.

In Schur's biography (1972, p. 25) he noted that Freud attributed positive *magical* significances to the number 17. For example, in childhood he chose the number 17 in a lottery that was intended to reveal a person's character, showing that he regarded it as his lucky number. Furthermore, he chose the 17th day of a month for his engagement to Martha, provoking Schur's strong suspicion that Jewish beliefs about magical numbers were "behind the fact that Freud chose the number in the first place." Jones also reported (III, p. 379) Freud's "superstitious" beliefs about the number 17, but seemed unsure as to whether Freud took such number magic seriously, or not.

In a later chapter of mine* titled "Freud Falsifies the Data," I have provided a great deal of additional data revealing Freud's fixations on the numbers 19 and 17, and that he regarded them basically as positive magical

---

*It appears in *The Fatal Freud*.

numbers that could help him to attain his life goals. Although I cannot take time to explain many details about these matters, my research in that chapter shows that probably Freud regarded the number 19 as his primary lucky number. Parenthetically, the number seven was also regarded as lucky by him, for he confided to Ferenczi that his periods of peak creativity occurred in cycles of seven years—which he may have correlated with the great significance of that number in the Josef myth, which brought Josef fame and fortune.

Allow me to explain reasons for believing that the number 19 was very highly regarded by Freud, as a magical number. First, I agree with Schur's intimation that probably in boyhood he'd absorbed some book about magic numbers in the writings of Hebrew mystics, and from such sources he accepted uncanny reasons for believing that 19 and 17 were lucky magical numbers. However, there is good reason to suspect that he decided that 19 was, *par excellence*, the number of triumph, revenge, and power in his life. This needs further discussion here.

That 19 was regarded unconsciously by Freud as the magic number that would enable him to defeat (to kill, eliminate, or dispossess) his key rivals will be shown by various data. To understand this point, we must first acknowledge the views of several writers that his repeated attacks of fainting spells were reaction-formations that stifled his murderous wishes (against Jung, Breuer, Emanuel, John, Julius, etc.). Furthermore, concerning Freud's murderous wishes towards his brother Julius, who died in infancy, Jones wrote (II, p. 433) that Sigi experienced repetitive guilt due to the belief that his murderous desires "were responsible for the intruder's early death." And according to Jones (p. 146), Freud admitted that all his fainting attacks "could be traced to the effect on him of his young brother's death when he was a year and seven months old" (*19* months old). Notice that here we have arrived at the connection between the number 19 and murderous desires in Freud's psyche.

It should be emphasized that Freud made a remarkably meaningful error (which was copied erroneously by Jones I, p. 7) in stating that he was age 19 months when Julius died, for it is a fact that Sigi was really 23 months old at Julius's death. Why did Freud make this particular error? No doubt that was because he regarded 19 as his magical, triumphant number and thus decided that Julius must have died (and been dispossessed) when his older brother's age had reached that victorious, lethal number of months (19). Notice that this involved the same primitive concept, albeit with a focus upon months, as was the case with Freud's pervasive belief that various magical death years (numbers) had the power to kill *him*. (My suggestion is that the fears about death years were grounded in Freud's fantasy that the number 19, in months, had given him the power to "eliminate" baby Julius.)

The idea that 19 was a triumphant magical number for Freud, with the power to eliminate rivals, is relevant to a variety of uncanny issues in his life involving that number. It relates to his eerie choice of the gloomy apartment building where he lived for more than 45 years, called Berggasse 19. Also, it pertains to his trip at age 19 to rejoin his wished-for "father," Emanuel. Likewise, it concerns his changing of the dream book's publication date to 1900. However, concealed in this victorious number was the threat of madness, since Freud was haunted by the fact that a male cousin of his had become insane at age 19—hinting that the number's positive valence involved a reaction-formation which was counter-phobic. Concerning, this underlying factor of madness, it is my additional thesis that the year 1919 had a magical, almost hypnotic effect on Freud, and that he chose that special year to "eliminate" his greatest rival, John Freud.

At this juncture, I'd like to offer some brief comments about Freud's strange choice of his residence at Berggasse 19 (which is covered in detail in *Dark Side*). Before discussing Berggasse 19, however, let's note that he had exhibited bizarre behaviors while choosing his prior residences in Vienna: 1. after his wedding, he was the first occupant of the dreaded House of Atonement apartment building on the site where 600 souls had been burned to death in a raging fire; 2. after the suicide of his "friend," Nathan Weiss, he had moved into the deceased's apartments saying that he was not afraid of the man's ghost, and then followed Weiss into a neurological career, as if "taking his place." Later, we'll see how this last item pertains to a perverse kind of revenge involving name magic, since Nathan Weiss had the same surname as the man (Simon Weiss) who ruined the reputation of the Freud family in Vienna in the 1860s, regarding the counterfeiting scandal. In effect, that expropriation of Nathan Weiss's apartment was a magical act of triumph and revenge for Freud. Probably, that was also true of his choice of the House of Atonement, which allowed him to triumph over those 600 charred citizens of Vienna whom he hated and despised as part of the populace that had ridiculed his family in the 1860s due to their connections with criminality.

The following anecdote about his choice of Berggasse 19 is quite remarkable, because it conjoins number magic and name magic in Freud's fantasy life. During his student days in Vienna, he was involved in revolutionary politics and attended a rally where the speaker was the socialist leader, Dr. Viktor Adler, a psychiatrist. During the heat of debate, young Freud had spoken very rudely to Adler, almost provoking a duel, but the older man calmed the waters by stating that this young fellow some day would change his views by returning to the safety of his father's tested beliefs—comparing Freud to the prodigal son in the Bible who returned to his father's home. Strange to say, months later Freud was in the company of his dearest friend Heinrich Braun, a kinsman of Viktor Adler, who took him to Adler's apartment *at Berggasse 19* for a family visit. Many years later, when Freud was married and seeking a larger apartment for his growing family, this was the very same apartment that he chose. Since Adler and his family had departed and his former home was vacant, Freud made a quick decision and moved his family immediately—despite Martha's consternation. She felt the locale was gloomy, was in an "unsuitable" section of town, etc. But she stifled her objections, perhaps sensing that her husband had to have this special place, for his own peculiar motives. (See McGrath, 1986)

Indeed, Freud needed to take this apartment for various uncanny reasons. Viktor Adler did not realize that by comparing Freud publicly with the prodigal son who was greatly blessed when he returned to his father's home and thereby triumphed over his stolid brother, he had instigated Freud's identification with that Biblical character—consonant with his many other Biblical identifications. Thereafter, the magical number 19 associated with Adler's apartment assured Freud that occupancy of this residence would enable him to return magically (simply by living there) to that Freiberg home and time when he had dispossessed his brother Julius. This number magic supported his fantasy that, by occupying the eminent psychiatrist's home, he had dispossessed another great rival (in spite of his powerful name, Viktor). Consider that the name Adler, in German, means "eagle," which was the great imperial symbol of ancient Rome and of Julius Caesar, which correlates Adler's identity with that of Freud's baby brother Julius. Thus, both number magic and name magic helped Freud to believe that, in dispossessing Adler, he had again triumphed over his earliest rival, his brother Julius.

In *Dark Side*, I've discussed the structural elements of "Berggasse" ("Berg" and "gasse") and how name magic enabled those elements—considering that *berg* means mountain, symbolizing the breast—to stoke Freud's fantasy that living in Berggasse 19 was tantamount to returning to his Freiberg home, and to his lost nanny's breast. In this way, he re-enacted his childhood scene in Freiberg (free berg) by becoming the king of this fantasy "berg" in Vienna, with Martha taking the role of his adoring mother and Minna, governess to his children, taking the seductive role of his former nursemaid, Monica. From the safety of this magical kingdom, Berggasse 19, Freud felt free to explore the powers of the nether world within himself, which he then used to promote his worldwide fame and to vanquish all his rivals and enemies, some real and many more who were imaginary and even ghosts (revenants).

Now let's look briefly at another of Freud's uses of the magical numbers 19 and 17 to achieve triumph and revenge. In the fall of 1873 he entered the medical school of Vienna University at *age 17*, which in itself was a personal victory for this Jewish lad from a family that had been viewed contemptuously by Viennese society in the 1860s, due to the counterfeiting scandal. Then at *age 19* Freud in 1875 made his first, eagerly desired visit to the home of his eldest brother Emanuel in Manchester. Since he'd often wished that Emanuel had been his actual father (and maybe he was), this was like the Bible's prodigal son returning in triumph to his father's home and lording it over his (fantasied) brother, John. For Emanuel did glorify Sigmund for his victorious entry into medical school, and even wished to interest him in marrying his daughter Pauline, who had been Sigmund's playmate in Freiberg. This material indicates that the magical, triumphant numbers 19 and 17 were both operative in Sigmund's victory over his ancient rival John, during that earliest visit to England in 1875.

Then there is the matter of Freud's avidly desired triumph over his enemies which he expected would occur, in terms of world wide fame, upon his completion of *The Interpretation of Dreams*. The book, in fact, was published in 1899, but Freud arranged to change the publication date to 1900. This change of the book's "birth year," hinting at Freud's concerns about the timing of his own birth, was again reflective of his pursuit of number magic, since 19 appears unaccompanied in the year 1900. By associating that magical number 19 with his alleged "masterpiece," Freud hoped that this would ensure his triumph over various rivals—Fliess, John Freud, *Julius* Wagner-Juaregg, and Breuer, whom he especially hoped would be made to "eat crow."

Although more extensive data about the numbers 19 and 17 is given in my chapter on Freud's falsifications of data (in a later volume), I'll break off this discussion now with my final example of Freud's presumed use of the magical number 19 to achieve a conquest of an ancient rival. This refers to my thesis that his compulsive fixation on 19 made him unable to resist using 1919 as the lucky year when he would be able to arrange for John Freud's disappearance and defeat, with impunity. More will be said about this issue in the ninth chapter, which is devoted to a full discussion of John's strange disappearance.

It should be emphasized that Freud's apparent belief that 19 was a magical number that could assist him in killing or otherwise defeating rivals is consistent with his terrified concerns in Trieste and Athens in 1904 that various dangerous, lethal numbers were "pursuing" him, wherever he went. Recall that Freud confessed this delusional thinking about lethal number magic directed against him in a letter to Jung, but was careful to suppress this information from his 1936 paper on the Acropolis episode that he directed to Romain Rolland and a wider public. Freud did not want us to know that in 1904, after having treated Fliess disgracefully, he feared that Fliess might destroy his reputation and professional identity. That fear became transformed into a delusion that Fliess, the master of numerical magic, had unleashed a series of lethal numbers against him in Trieste and Athens that were intended magically to destroy him.

This was similar to Freud's great fear that, in earlier years, Fliess had unleashed the number 51 to kill him. That is, Fliess had used his numerical magic relating to "periodicity theory" to predict that Freud would die at age 51 (in 1907), and for many years Freud felt great fear and anguish that he would die at age 51. In fact, that was perhaps the magical death year that was most threatening to Freud, along with age 62, in a series of these death ages (numbers). Schur's biography (1972) discussed that Freud was quite fearful that he would die at the death ages from 40 to 43, then at 51, 62, 67, and finally 81½ (the age at death of Jacob and Emanuel Freud). All of these death years provoked great anxiety in Freud, but paradoxically this was his way of controlling the uncertainty of death and providing compensatory payments for his own rabid death wishes, homicidal acts, provocations of others to commit suicide, and other grotesque "sins."

Some of these death ages had special magical significances for Freud. For examples there was additional number magic for him within the number 51, since it is the sum of 23 and 28. Those are the numbers which Fliess specified theoretically as the total days which reflect male and female cycles underlying all of human biology, in his notion of the basic bisexuality of all persons. Thus, it's likely that Freud was particularly fearful of the death age 51, because it secretly reflected anxieties about his own bisexual urges and due to his recurrent desires to plagiarize Fliess's various "discoveries" about bisexual functioning.

Many other instances could be cited of Freud's serious involvements with magical numbers, and my two chapters on his identifications with Satan and his falsifications of data have emphasized these great preoccupations of his. For example, we'll see that he seriously regarded his new telephone number in 1900 as if it had magical properties capable of predicting and extending his time to die, as he admitted to Jung. Also, we'll see that he manipulated the number 24 as if it were magical, and capable of extending his life. Thus, his famous clinical analysis of the spontaneous number 2467 (in his book on slips) is quite misleading, since he did not fully admit to his readers that he regarded the number 24 as being magical, with the capacity to extend his life by 24 years. This ideation is similar to his amazingly obsessive thinking about Satanic pacts, which also involved magical numbers (like 24) which he believed were capable of prolonging his lifetime.

All of this number magic pertaining to death makes connections with Freud's strong endorsements of Fliess's bizarre "periodicity theory," which Fliess claimed could unerringly predict the times of death and birth, the onsets of illness and wellness, and other notable events. At one point, Freud indicated that his friend had concocted this number magic as an unconscious reaction to the untimely death of his younger sister Pauline—after whom he named his daughter—intimating that Fliess's periodicity theory was designed secretly as a magical way of controlling the unpredictability of death. That is probably true. But it is equally true that Freud's endorsements of this theory (to which he devoted many pages of complicated numbers in their correspondence) had similar magical motives, despite that he sometimes seemed to be skeptical of Fliess's incessant juggling of numbers in pursuit of this balmy theory. One may even suspect that the child in Freud was primarily attracted to the Berlin numerologist, because he hoped that Fliess someday would concoct number magic that would allow Freud to greatly extend his life.

Introduction to Name Magic

Readers who wish to obtain a quick grasp of the historical and cultural origins of the concept I've called "name magic" are advised to read a small book by Edward Clodd titled *Magic in Names and in Other Things* (1920), and to review selected portions of Frazer's work *The Golden Bough*. Those anthropological sources, and many others, will reveal that in all the earlier epochs of mankind the central explanation of personality dynamics for men and gods involved beliefs about the magical powers of personal names to *determine* behavior and one's fate. Thus, the Bible makes it seem obvious that a man named Nabal should act like a fool, since that is the meaning of his name! Likewise, Plato's work called *Cratylus* gives a series of examples of men (real and mythical) whose unusual behaviors were apparently determined by the meanings of their names, a concept endorsed by that Greek philosopher and by most of the savants of his day, along with average Greek citizens.

Until the year 1911, modern men with scientific, rational outlooks had every reason to feel certain that the preceding ideas about the determining powers of personal names held by ancient and preliterate men could not explain any of the behaviors of current, civilized persons, i.e. such ideas must be regarded as balmy and unscientific, totally without merit, without further discussion. But in that year 1911, the psychoanalyst and colleague of Freud named Wilhelm Stekel published an article about name-compulsions titled "The Obligation of the Name." Artfully disguising the personal names of a long series of his obsessive-compulsive patients (to ensure confidentiality), Stekel demonstrated simply and persuasively that these patients unconsciously were acting-out the meanings and connotations of their names, sometimes in quite peculiar ways. For example, he noted that a man called Mr. Breir (Mr. Porridge) could not eat anything except that food; a man called Mr. Reich (rich) had a severe money-complex and often dreamed of bank books and safes; another man, Mr. Reiner (cleaner), suffered an intense phobia concerning cleanliness and dirt. And sometimes *opposite* meanings were magically and compulsively enforced, so that a man whose designated surname was Sicher, which conveys meaning of *certainty* in German, suffered dreadfully from morbid doubts about everything and was so paralyzed by uncertainties that he could hardly perform his clerical work. Stekel concluded that most of these obsessive-compulsive patients vaguely felt some "connection" with their names and acted unconsciously to materialize this connection or meaning. (In *Dark Side* I've explained that Stekel was acting-out some connotations of his own surname without being aware of this.)

Near the end of his career, Stekel provided additional clinical data about name-compulsions in the first volume of his work on compulsive neuroses titled *Compulsion and Doubt*. He tried to explain these compulsive behaviors pertaining to personal names as deriving partly from what he observed about the inner life of the compulsive patient, i.e. his mind is suffused with infantile magical ideation, mysticism, and fixations on the supernatural. Stekel claimed that the compulsive secretly regards every event as a metaphor, symbol, or omen and that all his compulsive acts constitute magical symbolism. Thus, any of said patient's behaviors may involve a "secret magic" and everything has secret meanings for him, cloaked in the supernatural. So it's not surprising that he regards his personal names as also having magical meanings, ones that often *command* obligatory behaviors, since our names are a central focus of the child's earliest sense of identity.

Stekel noted that the meanings and connotations of his compulsive patients' names often interacted "magically" with their unconscious fantasies of wrongdoing and guilt, and that urges towards criminal behaviors usually existed and were covered over in such persons. Concerning their vulnerability to magical formulae, he observed that frequently they used their personal names in compulsive rituals. Thus, a patient might feel compelled to speak his name repeatedly, ten times or more. Or he might be impelled to "mutilate" his name, i.e. to distort it in writing or in pronunciation. Some patients wanted to change their names, due to magical ideation. Others couldn't pronounce their names at all (a kind of name phobia), and others could only pronounce their names backwards, phonetically (which seems relevant to the mechanism called Withershins, in the worlds of magic and Satanism).

Stekel traced these name rituals to his patients' intense doubts and anxieties about their origins (the topic of birth), insisting upon this connection partly because the name is given at or near the time of birth. In addition, he claimed to have discovered that many name-compulsions are connected with the birth certificate. If so, perhaps factors involving the birth certificate and names thereon were fostering doubts about the authenticity of the patient's name and identity, even promoting compensatory identifications (calling to mind the case of Sigmund Freud's questionable birth certificate).

In his concluding thoughts about name-compulsions, Stekel remarked that they were not very important in many instances of neurosis, but in some cases they seemed to be *at the core* of a neurosis. He posited that a patient's "dominant idea," with name-compulsions at or near its core, might at first occupy only a small portion of the psyche and do little harm. However, he believed that sometimes these factors could continue to grow, then develop autonomous aspects, eventually taking possession of most of the personality. In some patients, name-compulsions might become very powerful and pervasive, indeed, and Stekel provided lengthy case materials to illustrate and support that contention.

Soon after Stekel's 1911 article appeared in print, his basic thesis concerning name-compulsion was affirmed in a brief article by the analyst Karl Abraham (1911). In the years following, there was a relatively small number of papers published about the clinical significances of personal names, including ones by Oberndorf (1918); Nunn (1929); Flugel (1930); Fodor (1956); and Murphy (1957). A paper by Düss (1948) deserves special comments, since she described the case study of a schizophrenic woman who made a rather quick "reconstruction" of her personality by strange repetitions of the phonetic elements of her personal (given) name. In Andersen's book *The Name Game* (1977) are found summaries of a number of clinical and experimental papers on personal names, and one of these offers experimental evidence which seems supportive of Stekel's concept of name-compulsion, in a modern African setting (Jahoda, 1954).

Before proceeding, I'd like to draw attention to the aforementioned papers by Flugel and Nunn. Their articles incorporate important materials illustrating the existence of a particular phenomenon in which personal names are subject to entire *series* of repetition-compulsions, sometimes over a lifetime. Flugel's paper showed that various poets and novelists, men of creative genius, might be subject to this phenomenon in its benign form, relating to love relationships. Thus, the poet Schiller fell in love successively with three women named Charlotte. Likewise, Lord Byron at age eight was fixated affectionately on a Mary Duff, and later had countless attachments to women named Mary, Marian, Marie, etc. (These similar names recur throughout a number of his poems.) In the second half of this chapter, we'll see that Freud was subject to these magical name-series, involving repetitions of given names or surnames, to a truly amazing extent. Moreover, we'll learn that Freud did not utilize such name-series only to maintain affectional connections with earlier loved ones; for sometimes he would use a name-series to effect uncanny kinds of *revenge*, substituting an innocent victim late in a name-series to receive punishment for an early transgressor in that same series.

The present author has used the term "name magic" to cover a diverse and complex set of phenomena involving *personal* names. The expanded concept that I call name magic incorporates all of the name phenomena included in the writings of Stekel, Düss, Nunn, Flugel, Murphy, and the other clinicians cited above, particularly all varieties of name-compulsions, name rituals, and name-series—along with the remarkable kinds of name data that are covered in anthropological literature, such as Clodd's book (1920). In effect, I have included under the rubric, name magic, all the peculiar behaviors regarding personal names that are assumed to result from the influences of magical ideation that originate in the precausal thought of children, and its sometimes powerful but hidden residues in the minds of adults. Also included in my concept of name magic are special kinds of "magical" name data that I have accumulated from my studies of the lives of famous murderers, which are covered extensively in my manuscript titled *Name Magic*.

Now, without further delay, let's begin to explore the rather amazing evidences of name magic in the life of Sigmund Freud. Readers need to keep in mind that, as extensive as these materials are, they include only a portion of the data about name magic in Freud's life that appear in several long chapters in *Dark Side*.

Freud's General Uses of Name Magic

Previous chapters already have produced various instances of name magic in Freud's life. It should prove informative to review a few of those earlier examples here.

Recall that name magic sometimes played an important role in Freud's coalescing of fantasy identifications with mythical and literary figures. For example, we saw that his Josef-identification with the Biblical master of dreams was abetted by the simple fact that the name of Freud's father was Jacob, as was true of Josef's father. Similarly, Freud's identification with the Biblical Jacob was fostered by the coincidence that Freud's father bore that name. (Of course, there were other factors that helped solidify both of those identifications—the name of the Biblical Jacob's father was Isaac whose meaning is "joy," which is the same as the meaning of "Freud.")

Also, we saw that one of Freud's childhood nicknames, the Moor, helped to coalesce his fantasy identifications with three literary murderers, and another historical killer with royal credentials. Freud's pet name

"Moor" (which he bore at the time of his early desires to kill baby Julius) was seen to correlate with Schiller's three killers: the Moor of Tunis, Franz Moor and Karl Moor. As noted, the fourth lethal Moor appeared in Freud's paper on the Acropolis episode, concerning his reference to the Moorish king named Boabdil, who killed that hapless messenger (whom I correlated with Freud's unconscious wish to kill Princess Marie Bonaparte). Probably, there was more name magic here, in Freud's mind, for we see that the first three letters of this king's name is "boa," the deadly snake, which carries forward the serpent theme embedded in the Acropolis paper. Also, we see that the first four letters of this princess's surname incorporates the same word "boa," if the letter "n" is ignored. Perhaps it was Freud's fantasy that it would be appropriate if this royal personage, Princess Bonaparte could be dispatched by a member of royalty like himself (his kingly fantasies), in the guise of King Boabdil.

Why did Freud's nickname, the Moor, have such lethal connotations in his mind? Jones tells us that his mother gave him that pet name in infancy, because he was born with "such an abundance of black ruffled hair." Evidently, the abundance and blackness of his hair reminded her of those swarthy men whom fair Europeans often stereotype as dangerous thieves and cutthroats, a bias reflected in Schiller's nasty characterization of *his* Moor, called Muley Hassan. Also, the concept of hairiness implies a primitive, savage quality, so one suspects that Freud's nickname was laden with connotations of dark, savage, murderous qualities in his unconscious mind, representing his lethal Mr. Hyde-self.

There was further name magic in Freud's fantasy identifications with Franz and Karl Moor in Schiller's play *The Robbers*. Recall that the play's main female character had a name that was a slight variation of the name of Freud's mother, Amalia (also called Amalie). Another significant character in the play was Fra Moser (the voice of conscience) whose name can be correlated with that of Frau Fanny Moser. Remember that Frau Moser, one of Freud's most important early patients, was the richest woman in Europe, and an accused murderess of her wealthy husband whose advanced age made him an obvious father-figure. Not coincidentally, Schiller's gory play is permeated by patricidal and fratricidal themes, and this helps explain why Freud used name magic so lavishly to cement his identifications with that play's characters.

It should be re-emphasized that Freud imitated (acted-out) a prominent segment of *The Robbers*, and that this involved both name magic and his murderous impulses. In their teen years, Sigi and his nephew John took the roles of Brutus and Julius Caesar respectively while acting-out, before a group of children, a duologue in the play that concerns the ghosts of Caesar and his assassin, Brutus. The reenactment indicated that young Freud was using name magic to express murderous feelings towards the ghost of Julius (his deceased brother), while simultaneously acting-out lethal impulses towards his great rival, John Freud. This was one of many instances when Freud used personal names "magically," as if they were "revenants" of former significant persons in his life, i.e. the name of Julius Caesar was used momentarily to resurrect the image of Julius Freud.

Before proceeding, it will be useful to explore how much Freud knew and acknowledged about the general topic of name magic, including Stekel's discovery of name-compulsions, the subject of magical name-series, etc. In Stekel's autobiography, he mentioned that he and Freud engaged in heated arguments about Stekel's desire in 1911 to publish his landmark paper on name-compulsion in their psychoanalytic journal.

According to Stekel, Freud was strongly opposed to the publication of this paper, asserting that critics might be skeptical about Stekel's clinical data on name-compulsions and could use this as a strawman for denigrating psychoanalysis. Despite the fact that Stekel was then its editor, Freud forbade the publication of Stekel's paper in their journal. However, Stekel went ahead and published the article in an alternate journal despite Freud's persistent objections, and Stekel claimed in his autobiography that this dispute about name-compulsions was the "final straw" that led to the eventual breakup of their relationship. Thereafter, it's likely that Freud's objections to this topic cast a pall over it, discouraging his analytic colleagues from exploring and writing about it, except for Abraham's very brief paper in 1911. In Jones's second volume, (p. 136) the Welsh analyst made a probably unfair disparaging remark about Stekel's name paper, while evading a real explanation of this topic called name-compulsion.

Sometimes I have wondered whether Freud harbored secret motives for vigorously opposing Stekel's article on name-compulsion. Was he jealous that Stekel was exploring a new clinical domain that demonstrated his outstanding creativity, a creative bent that Freud grudgingly acknowledged on several occasions when discussing Stekel's brilliant contributions on dream symbolism? Was Freud opposed to this clinical research on name-compulsions, because it puzzled him and did not readily fit together with his fanatic preoccupation with sexuality? It did not seem likely that one could explain the uncanny powers of personal names to compel neurotic behaviors in terms of the powers of Eros. Or was Freud personally afraid of this new clinical research on name-compulsions, dimly sensing that it might be used to unravel and expose many of his own perverse symptoms? Repeatedly he wrote that his entire life had been devoted to exposing uncomfortable hidden truths to the light of scientific scrutiny. But was there something about this topic of name-compulsions that caused him to pursue the opposite of that high-minded intention?

Considering that Freud wished to suppress Stekel's work on name-compulsions, would it surprise readers to learn that Freud's writings reveal that he *believed* in the reality of name-compulsions, and that he had an inordinate interest in psychological factors pertaining to personal names? In due time, all of this will receive further discussion, but presently let's remind ourselves that in his book on "slips" he showed considerable interest in the psychology of the forgetting of personal names—as occurred with his forgettings of "Signorelli," "Julius Mosen," etc. In subsequent pages we'll see that his interest in psychological factors pertaining to personal names was deeply rooted in him, for rather unusual reasons.

Emphasis should be given to two separate segments in Freud's dream book where he divulged some of his private ideas and feelings about personal names, for I will suggest that these two separate segments may have been connected by a common thread: his feelings of shame in adolescence that his family name had been ridiculed by Viennese society (due to the counterfeiting affair involving his uncle Josef Freud, and for its invidious sexual connotations). The first segment requiring our attention involves his comments concerning the dream he had titled the dream of three fates, which incorporates themes of madness and murder. Freud's associations to that dream included various hostile misuses or distortions of the surnames of persons known to him (Brücke, Fleischl, etc.). which he described as acts of retribution since "my own name had been the victim of feeble witticisms like these on countless occasions." The second segment in which he injected some of his private thoughts on personal names occurred during his extended commentary on the *Non vixit* dream (p. 522), when he noted that the name Josef played a great part in his dreams—citing the dream about his uncle Josef with the yellow beard and elongated face whom he described, in quite vague terms, as a criminal. Freud added that his own ego found it very easy to hide itself behind people with the name Josef, since that was the name of the Biblical interpreter of dreams.

In Freud's commentary on the dream about his uncle Josef, he took great pains to convince readers that he had not loved nor made an identification with this Viennese uncle whom we learned only recently was sentenced to ten years in prison in 1866, when Sigi was age ten. Indeed, Freud had protested too much about this matter, leading us to suspect that he had strongly identified (though ambivalently) with this very uncle who'd been highly publicized as a criminal in Vienna's newspapers. I'm in agreement with Renée Gicklhorn's (1976) descriptions of how Sigi must have been taunted unmercifully by his schoolmates about uncle Josef's imprisonment. And at that point the name Freud became so sullied that it must have taken on connotations for him of shame, criminality, and defeat that became mixed together in his mind with shameful connotations of sexuality from additional teasing to which he was subjected, as will soon be discussed further.

My guess is that young Sigmund used name magic to make a defiant, unconscious identification with the name of his uncle Josef, in order to compensate for the negative connotations that had accrued to the name Freud. Perhaps he noticed that the sentence that his uncle spent in the Emperor's prison was not much different from the 13 years that the Biblical Josef had spent in the Egyptian emperor's prison, helping him to equate his uncle with the ancient hero who had risen from a shameful imprisonment to a final, immense victory. In secretly identifying with the name of the Biblical Josef and his uncle Josef, young Sigmund prepared himself magically for a similar eventual triumph that was promised by this great name. Thereafter, he extended this magical name series by identifying with three additional men named Josef: Josef Breuer, Josef Paneth, and Josef Popper. From each of those Josefs he stole or expropriated something of great value. From Breuer he took, without due acknowledgment, the origins of psychoanalysis; from Paneth he took a valuable monetary gift *and* this friend's good name (by defaming him, after he had died); and from Josef Popper he stole the central, most significant hypothesis of the theory of dream functioning proposed in *The Interpretation of Dreams*. Thus, he used the name Josef three times, via name magic, to obtain revengeful victories, while giving his enemies "the finger" in a truly adolescent fashion that compensated for his own adolescent humiliations pertaining to the names Josef and Freud. (These assertions will be discussed again, later in this chapter.)

Now let's return to Freud's commentary about the dream of three fates. There he mentioned how he had dealt "naughtily" with various surnames including Popovic, Brücke and Fleischl. Freud was alluding to the fact that "Popovic" incorporates the childish word "popo," which signifies the buttocks. And the other two surnames have sexual connotations pertaining to the penis. In German the word *Brücke* means "bridge," whose arching qualities can symbolize an arched erection for psychoanalysts. Likewise, the German word *Fleisch* means "meat," which can connote the penis for schoolboys, as in the well-known American term "beat your meat," signifying masturbation.

While discussing his naughty (sexual) play with the preceding surnames in his dream commentary, Freud called this an act of retribution, stating that his own name had been subjected to similar "witticisms" *on countless occasions*. No doubt he was referring to his painful adolescent years when his own surname, Freud, was subjected to endless teasing in relation to shameful criminal acts by his uncle Josef Freud ('Hey, here comes our brilliant classmate, Freud the jailbird!'), and due to the invidious sexual connotations of "Freud." The latter point refers to the fact that in German the word *Freud* means "joy," and for devout Hebrews this often pertained to sexual joy. In the German language a connotation of profane, illicit sexuality accrues to the name Freud via the German word *Freudenmädchen* (joy maiden), which signifies a prostitute or whore. (In French, see "fille de joie.") Ergo, it's my contention that during adolescence Sigmund Freud was razzed repeatedly about negative sexual connotations of his surname, probably even being subjected to taunts that his sisters, aunts, and mother were no better than the common prostitutes who did a brisk trade in old Vienna.

Earlier, we saw that Freud's special incorporation of the name Josef caused him, via name magic and compensatory mechanisms, to pursue and master the interpretation of dreams. A similar view can be taken about his "adjustment" to his controversial surname. Since in adolescence he was subjected to nasty teasing about invidious sexual connotations of his surname, probably he adapted to this cruelty by defiant reaction-formations regarding "dirty sexuality," which then became connected with an intense name-compulsion. The unconscious name magic that he employed with enormous energy can be described, as follows: 'You claim that my name is contemptible because it connotes dirty sexuality, but I will prove to you that sexuality is positive and profoundly important, and that *my name*, therefore, should be honored throughout the world.' Thus, Freud became the champion of sexuality not only as a reaction-formation regarding nanny's sexual molestation of him, but also because of an intense name-compulsion pertaining to his surname.

With regard to name-compulsions and the topic of sexuality in Freud's life, it is quite significant that this factor may have pertained also to his names Sigismund, Solomon, and his early nickname, the Moor. Concerning his original given name, Sigismund, we've already seen in a previous chapter that its connection with the life story of St. Sigismund invested it with a powerful Oedipal connotation, connected with an implied incestuous theme (profane sexuality) and to the theme of patricide. With regard to Freud's Hebrew name Solomon, it is invested not only with a connotation of wisdom but also an exotic sexuality that derives from the well-known undercurrents of the Bible's erotic masterpiece, "The Song of Solomon."

A sexual connotation can even be discovered in connection with Freud's nickname, Moor, whose lethal significations already have been discussed. Let's take a playful stance in English and French with this nickname, since Freud was quite proficient in both of those languages. Using English, this nickname suggests that Freud was "a Moor," but those two words can be melded phonetically, as follows: "aMoor." Phonetically, this generates the French word *amour* (love, sexuality) which is also an English word signifying an illicit love affair. That latter connotation makes firm connections with "Sigismund's" and "Freud's" (surname) capacities to signify illicit sexuality, as described above. (In a later volume I've discussed how the nickname Sigi might have had a connotation of sexuality, in terms of Freud's possible identification with the Gnostic deity Sige, and the latter's relation to the figure called Hystera.)

It's unlikely that any famous man has borne personal names that were so likely to connote sexuality (Particularly illicit sexuality) as was the case with Sigmund Freud. Considering the power of name-compulsions to generate intensely fanatic behaviors relating to personal name connotations, one begins to comprehend one of the key reasons why Freud became so obsessed by sexuality, and made himself such a champion of this topic in general terms and concerning the neuroses that he might even have considered secretly that he deserved the appellation, "Dr. Sex." But really, is there any evidence suggesting that Freud could have been categorized with Stekel's obsessive-compulsive clients who suffered from uncanny name-compulsions? Indeed, Vitz (1988, p. 205) has listed many of Freud's behaviors which strongly indicate repetitive, obsessive qualities, and he cited Freud's self-diagnosis in a letter to Jung: ". . . I must claim for myself the class 'obsessive'. . ." Concerning Stekel's point that the minds of obsessive-compulsive clients are likely to be riddled with hidden magical ideation, we are reminded of Freud's persistent number magic, magical behaviors regarding Satanic pacts, death magic, and numerous other examples of his concealed magical ideation.

In *Dark Side* I've offered various discussions of Freud's compulsive acting-out of meanings and connotations of his own personal names, but also I emphasized his attraction to the personal names of many of his patients, colleagues, fantasy identifications, etc., as their name connotations were related to his own irrational complexes. Let's take a brief look now at how this worked with three of his early patients—Anna von Lieben, Fanny Moser, and Emma Eckstein—in relation to Freud's frenetic fixation upon the topic of sexuality.

In one of my future volumes, I'll present a long chapter, already completed, on Freud's strange relationship with Frau Anna von Lieben. She was the patient he disguised with the pseudonym Frau Cäcilie M. in his extensive comments about her case in *Studies on Hysteria*. In my review and interpretation of new data offered by Peter Swales concerning the fervid relationship between Freud and this extremely wealthy woman, Anna von Lieben, I have emphasized that she was driven by passionate feelings for various men, probably including her doctor; that her illness was probably the outcome of early "disturbances of passion," and that the intense infatuation between her and Freud might very well have resulted in illicit sexual activities between patient and doctor.

The patient's married surname was Lieben, which is the German word meaning "to love." It is my thesis that she may have chosen this new surname via marriage as an act of name-compulsion that expressed her great concerns about love and sexuality, as expressed in her poems and in other behaviors. Moreover, out of Freud's numerous early patients this woman was described by him as the patient who had been his "teacher" about the key symptoms and dynamics of hysteria. So it's my additional thesis that he unconsciously chose this woman whose surname signifies love and sexuality, as an act of projected name-compulsion by Freud. In effect, "Dr. Sex" became fixated upon the patient whose surname might secretly allow her to be called "Frau Sex." In describing this woman as his great "teacher," probably he equated her unconsciously with his earliest teacher about sexuality, his Freiberg nanny. (At the time that he treated Frau von Lieben, he knew almost nothing about transference and counter-transference factors.)

Concerning Freud's equally strange relationship with Fanny Moser (who outdid Anna's affluence by being the wealthiest woman in Europe), I've already noted his acts of name magic that correlated Fanny with Moses, Julius Mosen, brother Julius, and the cleric called Fra Moser who appears in Schiller's play *The Robbers*. In my long chapter for a later volume concerning Freud's therapy with Frau Moser, I have proposed a possible sexual relationship between Freud and this patient. In my view, he would have performed almost any unethical act to maintain his medical relationship with this wealthy woman, and I've described an instance of his unethical use of hypnosis for that purpose. But he did not succeed with this, and she finally became displeased and suspicious about him and abruptly terminated his services.

On at least two counts, Fanny Moser's name might have signified a sexual theme for Freud, via name magic. Her given name Fanny is a well-known term, in English, signifying the buttocks. That he might have desired to play with this patient's buttocks is hinted by the earlier instance (the dream of three fates) when he seemed to obtain perverse satisfaction by playing with the surname Popovic, which encoded children's primitive, naughty terminology signifying "the ass." In English slang, the term "piece of ass" pertains to a desire for intercourse, which may have indicated Freud's impulses towards this patient via name-compulsion, especially as a way of controlling her wealth.

The second way that Fanny Moser's name might have signified a sexual theme for Freud relates to the pseudonym which he invented for her—Emmy von N.—in the *Studies on Hysteria*. Freud's choices of pseudonyms for patients often involved name magic expressing his hidden, perverse motives, and we'll see this demonstrated with great force in the next chapter concerning his choice of the pseudonym Dora to represent the patient whose real name was Ida Bauer. My thesis is that he chose the pseudonym Emmy to unconsciously correlate with the given name of that highly significant patient Emma Eckstein, who helped him to lay the foundation, in theory and technique, for the essential factors underlying psychoanalysis. Ergo, he used name magic in creating the pseudonym Emmy N. to show that in some significant ways he equated Fanny Moser with Emma Eckstein. Momentarily, we'll see that the given name of Emma Eckstein had a decidedly sexual connotation for Freud—relating to the nanny who molested him. In turn, the names Emmy and Fanny were invested, therefore, with this same sexual connotation pertaining to the seductive nursemaid in Freiberg. By the way, the possibility that Freud was also involved sexually with Emma Eckstein is discussed frankly in *Dark Side*, which is germane to Masson's report of her possible conception of a son out of wedlock (1984).

In *Dark Side* I have offered a full discussion of Freud's magical fixation on both of the names of Emma Eckstein, so I will make only some brief comments here about this subject. In German, her surname means "cornerstone" signifying that unconsciously Freud wished to make her case the *cornerstone* of his development of psychoanalysis. (That meaning also pertained to his identifications with Jesus and his nanny, as explained in *Dark Side*.) The given name of the patient, Emma, had an Oedipal (sexual) connotation for Freud, since books that list name meanings show that it is an equivalent of the name Amalia, the name of Freud's mother. Furthermore, the name Emma also represented the figure of Sigmund's sexual abuser, his nanny, since a reversal of this name is *Amme*, the German word that means wet-nurse. (Freud had a penchant for name reversals, as is true with many compulsives.)

In general, one of the major meanings of the name Emma Eckstein for Freud is that unconsciously his infantile feelings about nanny and Amalia had provided the secret cornerstone for his erection of the complex structure of psychoanalysis. Each of the names of those three early patients (Anna Lieben, Fanny Moser, and Emma Eckstein) harbored connotations that pertained to Freud's infamous nanny whose repetitious images can be found pervasively throughout his thinking and his works.

Concerning that last point, I am one of several authors who insist that in the landmark dream of Irma's injection the patient whom Freud gave the pseudonym Irma is a composite figure representing Emma Eckstein, his nanny, and other women. In my view, Emma Eckstein provided one of the major images within the figure of the patient called Irma, as also seemed obvious to Max Schur. Authors who disagree with this idea should reflect upon Freud's repetitious uses of name magic and that the name Irma, in some name books, is directly equated with the name Emma! That Freud was aware of that equation is suggested by the fact that he was an inveterate peruser of name books, as will soon be discussed. (In *Dark Side* I've discussed that the reversal of Irma is Amri, which may have had great significance for Freud as the name of the Biblical king called Amri or Amre, considering that his identity for Freud may have been connected with issues relating to infanticide and patricide.)

So far I've explained how Freud's personal names and the names of some key patients were able to signify aspects of sexuality for him, but I will delay until the publication of *Dark Side* my explanations of how he was attracted to various key colleagues partly due to the sexual connotations of their personal names. Now an important question is this. To what extent was Freud aware that this name magic regarding his names, and those of his patients and colleagues, was operative in his psyche? My general viewpoint is that he was largely unconscious, but to a moderate extent was sometimes conscious, fully or partially, of this name magic that pervaded his psyche. To some readers that may seem to be a weakly equivocal position, but it's the best I can do at present on the basis of my diligent study of these matters.

Allow me to cite one instance when Freud seemed to be completely unaware that his psyche was involved in name magic. It concerns one of his own dreams in the dream book (1967, p. 302) called "Famous Speakers," which was quite brief. In the dream he was looking into the window of a bookshop and saw a new volume in a *series* of monographs that he was in the habit of buying which focused upon great artists, famous persons in world history, etc. His final dream thought was that: "The new series was called 'Famous Speakers' or 'Speeches' and its first volume bore the name of Dr. Lecher."

In Freud's short commentary on this dream he seemed puzzled that he had dreamed about Dr. Lecher, a member of the German Parliament who was famous as a non-stop speaker. Freud explained blandly that he'd taken on some new patients, causing him to talk for ten or more hours every day, giving this as his reason in the dream for identifying with Dr. Lecher. His final remark was: "So it was I myself who was a non-stop speaker." Here we see that Freud was completely unaware of his embarrassing use of name magic to ridicule the sexual connotations of his own surname, as had been done to him repeatedly in adolescence, for the dream asserts that *he* was the most famous "lecher" in Germany/Austria. Thus, he'd equated the names Dr. Lecher and Dr. Freud, not recognizing that in English the word lecher signifies a man who is lascivious and engages in ordinate, perhaps perverse, sexual activity. Notice that the term lecher originally referred to licking, so there is the possibility of infantile factors lurking here, as relates to Sigi's licking of the breasts of his wet-nurse, or other body parts.

Since he had inadvertently correlated his own lecherous impulses with the taking on of new patients, his dream hinted that he was having trouble controlling his unrelenting sexual urges towards patients. On the other hand, perhaps the dream also reflected his wish that he were more virile and could perform sexually in a non-stop manner, without slowing down. (Recall that nanny had criticized his sexual inadequacy, in some way.) Readers who are incredulous about my claim that Freud sometimes seduced patients (in *Secret SL*) should ponder that in this dream he equated his own endless "speeches" during therapy with behaviors that were sexually seductive (lecherous).

There are reasons to suspect, however, that sometimes Freud was at least minimally (vaguely) aware that name magic was operative in his life and psyche in various strange ways. Let me briefly begin to summarize some of these reasons for believing he was sometimes aware of his vulnerability to name magic. Already I've noted his remark that he tended to hide behind the name Josef repeatedly, and that he'd been teased endlessly about invidious connotation of his surname—probably most often in early adolescence. It's my view that those cruel teasings layed the foundation for Freud's great sensitivity towards personal names and his conscious and unconscious absorptions of the complex dynamics of name magic in his own life that was also fostered by his susceptibility to magical ideation, in general.

Furthermore, some evidence points to the probability that Freud sometimes consulted "name books" which supply the traditional meanings of given names. In two of his letters to Fliess at the turn of the century he congratulated his friend on the birth of his son Conrad and predicted that someday this lad would become "assistant and fellow worker" to his father, in Fliess's great work. The relevance of that prediction to name magic is that, in name books, the name Conrad signifies "courageous helper and adviser." Freud seemed to indicate here that he held a vague, positive belief in name-compulsion in Conrad's case, predicting that the lad would exhibit capable and reliable behaviors if he adopted his name's meanings "as a guiding principle for his future activities." In a similar fashion, Freud congratulated his son Ernst, during the dark days of the 1930s, for being "a tower of strength," which he felt was an indication that his son was living up to the meaning of his name, Ernst (earnestness).

The above examples can be used to illustrate the complexity and intermingling of conscious and unconscious factors that may be operative in various kinds of name magic, including name-compulsions. Let's say that a father gives his son the name Conrad and, early on, tells the lad what its meanings are in name books. Also, the father tells the boy that this given name was intended to honor the father's idol, the writer Joseph Conrad. If the son keeps this information largely at a conscious level and, in adulthood, exhibits various helping and advising behaviors (by counseling siblings and friends often), and becomes a writer somewhat in the heavy style of Joseph Conrad, it is still not clear that he has succumbed to name-compulsion, though it may be operative in him to a modest extent. However, if the lad largely represses that information about his given name's meanings and connotations and exhibits the correlated behaviors to an extreme degree, with a driven quality to those actions, it will seem much more likely that name-compulsion is operative here.

Also, there may be various complicating factors for a child who has obsessive-compulsive tendencies. Reaction-formation can become operative (reversal of meanings) with regard to the "helping" meaning of the name Conrad, as an aspect of name-compulsion, and the boy may strongly shun the dependency needs of others, irrationally. Or the boy may be given the playful nickname "Con" in his early years, with no clear definitions attached to it, yet his name-compulsion about this nickname might emerge later in life in terms of the compulsive deceitful behaviors of a con artist. Moreover, complicating factors may occur concerning the father's unconscious motives in naming his son, i.e. perhaps he was repressing the fact that he'd not only used Joseph Conrad as his template, but unconsciously also had named his son after a great rival and friend named Conrad who had died in early adulthood in a car crash. Thereafter, some of the father's unrecognized hostile feelings towards this deceased friend may be transferred to his son via name magic, and the son's dangerous exploits while driving cars may reflect name-compulsion relating to a very vague awareness of his father's ambivalent relationship with the earlier Conrad.

Other complications and accruals of meaning can occur with names (given, surname, nickname, pet name, pseudonym) that are similar to, or identical with, dictionary or slang words. Or names may accrue special connotations for rather strange reasons, as when a very significant adult provides some idiosyncratic connotation for a child's name. For example, in their later correspondence Freud and Fliess adopted the peculiar habit of referring to the human body as "the Conrad." I'm not sure of the reason for this, but I suspect that some kind of name magic was at work here that may have influenced Conrad Fliess's perceptions of his given name.

Since an earlier illustration has mentioned the subject of reaction-formations with respect to name-compulsion, this factor is worth considering with regard to Freud's surname. Let's assume that it's correct that powerful name-compulsion was operative concerning the joy-meaning of his surname, promoting his irrational emphases on sexuality. Since sexuality was such a taboo topic in his day, it's possible that his unconscious mind directed intense reaction-formations against the "joyful" and "sexual" significations of his surname, especially due to his molestation by nanny. This could help to explain the many periods of depression that Freud experienced throughout his lifetime, since one could argue that the opposite of joy is depression and sadness. Various authors have noted that Freud was often a very unhappy, depressed man but, of course, there were many reasons for this and name-compulsion was not necessarily a primary factor here, though perhaps it was an important one. It could have been a perpetually bitter, ironic fate for him to parade the name "Dr. Joy," if it's true that he usually felt quite miserable about his life. Also, one can wonder whether reactions-formations directed towards the sexual meanings of his surname caused him to suffer regular periods of impotency, since some writers have speculated about Freud having suffered from various sexual difficulties.

Returning to some additional factors suggesting that Freud exhibited a moderate awareness of name magic in his life, let's look at his views in the dream book (1967, p. 524) stressing his "magical" theory about revenants, i.e. that all people who have been lost to us (by death, breakup of relationships, etc.) are replaceable and can be "reincarnated" in new relationships, especially via the magic of names. Thus, he remarked that his friend Fliess had deeply mourned the death of his sister but recently had been blessed with the birth of a new daughter. Freud noted that he'd written to his friend "and told him I was sure he would transfer the love he felt for her on to the child, and that the baby girl would allow him to forget his irreparable loss." Apparently, Freud regarded the new baby as a magical revenant who could completely substitute for Fliess's dead sister. But Freud did not admit to his readers (perhaps because he was embarrassed about his magical ideation) why he felt so sure that the new baby could adequately replace the dead sister.

Freud did not inform his readers that his conscious belief in name magic was involved here, and did not disclose that Fliess's dead sister and his new baby daughter were both named Pauline. Apparently, Freud was relying upon the ancient magical theory that the essence of a person's soul resides entirely in the personal name, so that naming a child after a dead person serves magically to reanimate the dead person. (See Clodd; Frazer, etc.). Of course, it is ridiculous to think that a new baby can adequately substitute for the loss of a dead sister, or a previously deceased daughter, but this shaman named Freud did believe this because he seemed to acknowledge the awesome power of name magic to create actual revenants (reincarnations, in some real sense).

After providing the above material about Fliess's new daughter, Freud's thoughts ran ahead to the subject of the names of his own children. His reflection was that he'd named all of them "in memory of people I have been fond of." Probably, there was a magical significance underlying his next thought: "Their names made the children into *revenants*." He added that, children are our only path to immortality, so it's clear that unconsciously he felt that his capacity to create such revenants gave him the power to cheat death—as was also the case with his Satanic pacts.

In *Dark Side* I have discussed that Freud's accounts (via Jones) of his motives in naming his children probably were defective in important ways. Let's start with his claim that he named his first child, his daughter Mathilde, after the wife of Josef Breuer. I don't doubt that notion, but there's more to this story with regard to Freud's very ambivalent feelings towards Mathilde Breuer that are spelled out in *Dark Side*. One factor had to do with his feelings of sexual megalomania towards Mathilde Breuer, which he informed Karl Abraham were crucial feelings underlying the dream of Irma's injection. This raises a question of whether Freud's sexual feelings for Mathilde Breuer were transferred to his daughter Mathilde *via name magic*. In Freud's letter to Fliess of May 31, 1897 he cited a recent dream he'd had which expressed his incestuous urges towards his daughter Mathilde, although he euphemized these destructive impulses towards her by calling them "overaffectionate feelings." This reminds us that a man like Freud who had been sexually molested in childhood may become a sexual molester himself, even exhibiting incestuous behaviors towards his own children (also in imitation of his father Jacob's alleged incest).

Furthermore, there is good reason to suspect that Freud had named his daughter Mathilde unconsciously after another woman named Mathilde, about whom he may have had ambivalent and very destructive feelings. This was the young woman whom he "accidentally" killed by giving her an incautious dose of sulfonal (or perhaps cocaine), this death presumably occurring some months prior to his daughter's birth. If so, he unconsciously regarded his daughter Mathilde as a revenant for this woman (whose actual relationship with Freud is clouded by obfuscations). In *Dark Side* I have discussed the time when Freud's daughter was emerging from a severe illness, when he committed the bizarre act of breaking a small statue of Venus, and another time when he believed he saw the ghost of his patient Mathilde, as indications that unawares he may have made his daughter a revenant for the dead woman *via name magic*.

Concerning unconscious factors, a similar analysis can be made of Freud's naming of his first son, who was known to everyone as Martin, but whose full name was Jean Martin Freud. It is said truly that Freud named him after his famous mentor Jean Martin Charcot, but that neglects the suppressed name Jean, which is the equivalent of the names John and Johann. In terms of name magic, it is likely that Freud secretly had named his first son after that great rival named John Freud, fantasizing that this enabled him to subjugate his combative nephew, and that some of his murderous feelings towards John thereby were magically transferred to his son Martin. Probably, this is relevant to a number of Freud's dreams during World War I when Martin was serving in the army and was continually under heavy enemy fire, in the era just before John Freud mysteriously disappeared from his Manchester home. In several of those dreams Freud expressed obviously murderous wishes towards his son Jean Martin, which perhaps really belonged to John Freud, due to the transference powers of name magic.

The previous discussions of Freud's naming of his children Mathilde and Jean Martin have suggested that there were hidden destructive impulses towards the children that were expressed in those namings. The same can be said about Freud's naming of his daughter Anna whom it is said was named after a woman called Anna L., a close friend of the Freud family. With regard to name magic, let me suggest that Freud unconsciously also named his daughter Anna after his sister with that same name, who was next in line after Sigmund (due to Julius's death). At first this might seem implausible, since Jones advised us that Sigmund had a strong dislike for sister Anna, moreso than for any of his other siblings. But Jones did not clarify why this animosity had arisen. Was it merely rivalry for the next-oldest child, or were there some other reasons as well?

Recall that Freud charged that his father had sexually molested some of his siblings, without specifying which ones. Isn't it plausible that Anna had been the first of his siblings to be molested by Jacob, and that Sigmund developed intense jealousy and hostility towards her, feeling that she was receiving special attention from his father, because she provided these sexual "favors?" Considering that Jacob treated incest so lightly, it's possible that Sigmund punished his sister Anna by committing incest with her himself (following the pattern of nanny's sexual molestation of him). Thereafter, his hostility towards Anna might have been increased by his fear that someday she could enact retribution by exposing his incestuous abuses of her. This seems relevant to Kushner's (1967) claim that in some of Freud's writings he tried to manipulate readers into endorsing the legitimacy of incest as an acceptable kind of sexual behavior. By the way, sister Anna was the only offspring of Jacob Freud to make her home far outside of Europe—she and her husband lived way off in America—and one wonders whether early abuse by Jacob and/or her brother caused her to put such a long distance between her and them due to her hidden anger, resentment, and mortification.

Consider the young adulthood of these two Freuds, when Sigmund and Anna were engaged to Martha and Eli Bernays, both couples dating together at times. In itself, this love quadrangle hints at incestuous potentials, though Freudians are loathe to notice this. Prior to this arrangement, Sigmund had enjoyed a strong friendship with Eli and, considering Freud's homosexual urges, it's possible that Anna coalesced her relationship with Eli (stealing him away) as a partial punishment of her brother's earlier abuses of her, either sexual or mere bullying. This could help to explain the really bizarre, inexplicable anger that Sigmund developed towards Eli during this engagement era, which also could have been stoked by his fear that after his sister's marriage she might "spill the beans" to Eli. Thus, I have given two additional interpretations to Freud's forgetting of Signorelli, as follows: 1. Sig ignore(s) Eli, with the verb having a connotation of evasion; 2. Signor Eli, as a form of address requiring Freud to show deference to Eli as being a highly respected man, with bitter irony. That second interpretation might have been relevant to another of Anna's punishments of her brother. This one involves her possible manipulation of Eli into accepting the idea that they should settle in America (where he became a *millionaire*), recognizing dimly that Sigmund hated to lose love objects by such decisive emigration, dating back to that searingly painful exodus of Emanuel's family from Freiberg to Manchester.

With this behind us, I'm ready to suggest that Freud named his daughter Anna after his hated sister for invidious reasons. My first suggestion is that by this naming he hoped magically to ensure that his daughter Anna would become an incestuous object for him, but one who (unlike his sister) would never leave him and would give him all the attentions that a woman gives to the man for whom she bears a special love. Actually, Freud generated this incestuous bond between himself and daughter Anna via the utterly psychopathic act of providing psychoanalysis for Anna for at least four years, contrary to common decency and all the protective rules for analysis that he had stipulated for other analysts (not for himself). Today various authors have at least hinted that this was a blatant act of symbolic or perhaps actual incest by Freud and his daughter, but nobody has indicated the reasons why this correlates with his hidden motives in naming her.

Evidently, another reason why he named his daughter Anna was to reinstate the "incestuous" relationship that he'd had with his primal mother, his Freiberg nanny—following Martha's and Minna's reenactments of that same role. Having laid the groundwork during her psychoanalysis, Freud transformed this daughter into his nurturant nanny by manipulating Anna for decades into slavishly adopting the role of indulgent servant to him. This led eventually to the exhausting years of his endless cancer operations when she coddled him as if he were her lover, a child, or both. Probably, his transforming of her into his nanny was assisted by name magic that was accepted unconsciously by both of them. That is, in the Austrian context in which Freud and his daughter were raised the name Anna had a powerful connection with the term nanny (nursemaid). This was explained by Vitz (1988, p. 30) when he wrote that the customary Czech name for a nursemaid is "Nana," which is a frequent variation *of the name Anna*. In the Czech context where Freud was raised, "Nana" has been a popular equivalent for "Nanny," and also is a common nickname for "Anna." Vitz added that ". . 'Anna' and 'Nana' are in the case of a nanny inextricably connected." So it becomes clearer why Freud named his daughter "Anna," and then treated her like his indulgent nursemaid for decades.

A review of biographical writings about Freud's daughter Anna indicate that she never had a love relationship with any man, though a serious question exists about her having had an extended lesbian relationship in her later years. Apparently, there was a lot of gossip among European analysts in her earlier years that Anna would find it difficult to get involved with any man unless she could find one with strong similarities to her father. However, it is said that for a while she showed considerable interest in the analyst Siegfried Bernfeld. Is it possible, one wonders, that Ms. Freud had absorbed her father's vulnerability to name magic concerning her presumed infatuation with Dr. Bernfeld? Notice that his given name, when separated into the components "Sieg" and "Fried," offers a compelling approximation of the name Sig Freud. Moreover, the first syllable of this man's surname is "Bern," which is the same as the first four letters of Martha Bernays' surname. Accordingly, via name magic this analyst's names offered Anna Freud some strong connections with the names of both her father and her mother. Was this presumed name magic a clue to Ms. Freud's symbiotic relationships with her parents, her father in particular?

The preceding analysis seems to constitute a variation of some of Stekel's (1911) material on name-compulsion. He cited data suggesting that some persons may choose their partners in love relationships based partly upon name magic pertaining to the meanings and connotations of personal names. For example, an unmarried man mired in a mother-fixation might choose a woman to marry whose name contains elements like "ma" or "mar," signifying "mama." (This may have been an unconscious factor in Freud's choice of his wife *Martha*.) Stekel also noted cases in which an unconscious bond may be created between lovers when a portion of the woman's given name (or surname) is embedded within one of the man's names, or vice versa. For example, this bonding may occur "magically" with a couple named Mildred and Emile, who share the "mil" element in both names. Likewise, in the case of Anna Freud, an approximation of her surname appears in the given name of Siegfried Bernfeld, which may have helped to spark her interest in this analyst.

This brings us to a consideration of name magic connecting Josef Breuer and Freud. In *Dark Side* I've described their relationship as an ambivalent one suffused with homosexual undertones (which also was true of the Freud/Fliess relationship). The first aspect of name magic connecting Freud with Breuer was Breuer's given name Josef, as already noted. The second aspect of name magic connecting these men relates to material offered in the preceding paragraph that pertained to heterosexual couples. Notice that the element "reu" is the central element in the surnames of both men. In the German language that element is pronounced "roy" in both of their surnames—which in English sounds exactly like the given name Roy, whose meaning in name books is "King." (In French the word for "king" is "roi.")

In *Dark Side* I've discussed another of Freud's complexes, a basic factor in his persistent megalomania, which I have called his "king complex," an offshoot of what Wittels called his "Jehovah complex. There were a number of sources that helped to stoke Freud's kingly complex in childhood and in later years, and many golden threads were woven into this royal complex. For example, one aspect of it was his fantasy identifications with great kings, including: Sigismund, Oedipus, Alexander, Napoleon, Charlemagne, Solomon, Lear, Boabdil, etc. Probably, name-compulsion was one of the factors that instigated this king complex, since he bore the names of the famous kings called Sigismund and Solomon. Now there is the additional possibility that a hidden aspect of name magic was also provoking this king complex, in terms of the "roy" (royal) element that is a central portion of Freud's surname.

The preceding pages have offered several items indicating that Freud, to some extent, had a conscious awareness of the force of name magic in his life, but sometimes it was difficult to recognize that his behaviors regarding personal names had a connection with magical ideation. In Shengold's article (1979, p. 68) concerning Freud's connections with the Biblical Josef, master of dreams, he showed an awareness of Freud's preoccupation with personal names but did not notice that magical ideation was involved. Shengold wrote quite sagely that: "Similarity and identity of names always impressed Freud." For example, in the dream book (1967, p. 524) Freud mentioned that he had received "great satisfaction" when he learned that Fliess planned to name his baby daughter "Pauline," since that was the name of the niece with whom he had played during his childhood days in Freiberg, the daughter of Emanuel. Almost immediately thereafter, he remarked upon the fact that the surnames of his friends Fleischl and Fliess both began with the letters "Fl," which then provoked thoughts about how he had given his children the same names as certain honored persons, enabling his children to become revenants (or reincarnations). Actually, Freud often was seeking out such name equivalences in his life due to his frequent pursuit of "magical" name-series, which he expected would foster reincarnations of lost persons (as discussed later in this chapter).

At other times, Freud's behaviors made it clear that he consciously believed in various magical properties of personal names, consonant with his beliefs in number magic, magic pertaining to death and sexuality, etc. For example, there was the time when his daughter Anna complained to him that she did not like her given name (Young-Bruehl, 1988, p. 46). Her father replied that the name Anna is a great one, because it is a palindrome, reading the same backward or forward. What needs to be emphasized is that Freud was espousing a belief about the power of reversible names that was held for centuries by shamans who were adept at name magic. Moreover, this specific idea advocated by Freud pertaining to reversals of names and words seems to be consonant with his endorsements of some *Satanic doctrines*, including magic that depends upon such verbal reversals (called "Withershins"). Thus, the Black Mass of the Satanists is the regular Mass of Catholicism, but reversed and spoken backwards. In *Dark Side*, I have discussed my thesis that Freud secretly had adopted the reversible name Otto, representing his murderous Jekyll/Hyde nature, and that this baleful name of his was a factor in his destruction of the young schizophrenic "genius," Otto Weininger.

Alongside the conscious examples of name magic in Freud's own life were certain instances which, if valid, were probably unconscious. It's entirely possible that some aspects of substance abuse by Freud were connected with name magic that was unconscious. In introducing this topic, let me remind the reader of Stekel's (1911) example of an obsessive-compulsive patient named Herr Breir (signifying porridge) who was compelled to eat only that food. Considering that Freud was traumatized by the wet-nurse who suckled him, one would expect him to have severe problems in the oral phase of development, relevant to his weird adult complaints about food, and periodic irrational fears of starvation.

Therefore, it should not surprise us if Freud were vulnerable to name magic pertaining to substances that are ingested or held in the mouth. As an illustration, earlier I mentioned that he had made an unconscious fantasy identification with the Biblical figure of Cain (whose story is permeated by oral themes). In effect, as a factor in his intense Cain complex Freud had expropriated the name Cain. If so, this could have helped to generate, via name-compulsion, his egregious personal abuses of cocaine, his fanatic interest in it, and his killings of various persons with this substance whose spelling incorporates "cain" as its central element. (In *Dark Side* I've discussed why cocaine probably had a strong unconscious connection in Freud's mind with the given name of his Freiberg nanny, Monica Z.)

Now let's turn to Freud's longterm addiction to cigar smoking to learn whether this could have had a connection to name-compulsion. During 60 years of his adult life he was a ferocious smoker of large cigars, often smoking twenty of them daily. As early as his thirties, various physicians had asked him to stop smoking and warned him that cigars were injuring his health. His friend and doctor, Fliess, often demanded forcefully that he should stop smoking, and Freud tried to do so many times without permanent success. After his jaw cancer was diagnosed in 1923, his physicians became more and more demanding that he should stop smoking, but he was rather obstinate and uncooperative, because he dearly loved his daily cigars. Despite dozens of operations on his jaw and having an unwieldy oral prosthetic clamped into his mouth, he continued to smoke his cigars.

Was it simply that a severe addiction to nicotine kept him fixated on cigars, or was this addiction reinforced by some magical ideation? Consider that Clark (1980, p. 142) has written that "Freud himself always regarded the cigar as essential to his work . . " Evidently, Freud harbored the magical notion that a crucial factor in his creativity and productivity was his incessant smoking of cigars. Is it possible that name-compulsion had something to do with this self-destructive nonsense?

When we consider the English word *cigar* phonetically, we become aware that its first three letters comprise Freud's childhood nickname, Sig, and that this word can be rendered phonetically as follows: Sig gar. When we consult any English dictionary, we see that the word "gar" is a euphemistic term signifying "God." Ergo, the English word "cigar" can be regarded as generating this simple sentence: "Sig (is) God." That seems relevant to Wittels' charge that Freud suffered from a Jehovah complex, and to Freud's fantasy identifications with Zeus, Jupiter, Juno, Jesus, Satan, etc.– a series whose megalomanic theme correlates with the king complex noted previously. Notice that the simple sentence that is encoded phonetically in the word "cigar" provides one possible reason why Freud may have considered cigars as essential to his creativity, in a magical sense, which seems germane to the oral/ narcissistic era when he was called Sig by his nanny and Amalia. In that heyday of the names Sig and "golden Sigi," those indulgent women treated him like a little king, a golden deity, and continually predicted that he would become a great man, perhaps a genius.

In German the word "cigar" is spelled *Zigarre*, and it should be emphasized that "Z" is its first letter. In *Dark Side* I've discussed that Freud seemed to resonate, in dreams and waking life, with names and words beginning with "Z," as a reflection of his residual attachment to the surname of his nanny, which was Zajic. (Let's not forget the undue emphasis he placed on the coincidence that the names of his friends Fleischl and Fliess both commenced with the letters "Fl.") Concerning my thesis that Freud had a strong unconscious attachment to cigars partly because the initial letter of that word in German ("Z") is the same as the initial letter of his nursemaid's surname, this is similar to my idea in *Dark Side* that he was attached to cocaine partly because that substance had an unconscious connection in Freud's mind with the given name of that nursemaid (Monica). Presently, all that will be said about that latter idea is that Jones (I, pp. 81-2) revealed that in Freud's earliest writings about cocaine he treated this substance quite enthusiastically as "a magical drug," described cocaine "as if he were in love with the content itself . . ," and described how the cocaine deity called *Manco* (Capac) had sent the drug to mankind as a gift from the gods—as noted in tribal lore. Ergo, it's plausible that, unconsciously, he equated the names Manco and Monica due to their considerable structural similarity and his need to idolize this nurturant sex goddess of his Freiberg days.

Many of the preceding pages have demonstrated that Freud's thinking often was permeated by magical ideation about personal names. But we've also seen that he was vulnerable to magical ideation concerning a whole array of important topics, so one must wonder about the reasons for this holdover of "magic" in his psyche from the precausal era of early child development (see Piaget re precausal thought). Evidently, the primary reason lies in his fixations in that childhood era caused by the traumatizations relating to his nanny around his third year of life. However, it's conceivable that this holdover of "magic" in his psyche also relates to the power of name magic with regard to the nanny's surname, Zajic. Notice that this surname is similar structurally, in writing or phonetically, to the English word "magic"—English being a language that Freud knew very well by his fifth year. (In German the word for magic is *Zauber*, so there was also the coincidence that Zauber and Zajic both begin with the letter "Z.")

My suggestion is that Sigi's persistent yearning for his nanny and her "magical" surname Zajic promoted the diffusion of magical ideation throughout his unconscious mind, well into the adult years. In effect, he came to regard her as a numinous person equivalent to a powerful witch whose uncanny surname provided her with magical powers that he was able to share, as her consort. In a letter to Fliess (1/17/1897) we see that he adopted the peculiar idea that his patient Emma Eckstein could be regarded as the psychic equivalent of a witch, and that idea becomes more comprehensible when we understand that secretly he equated Emma with his seductive nanny. Considering that Freud harbored an intense identification with his nanny, it's very likely that he somehow regarded himself as a witch as well, and that this helped to cement his eventual identification with Satan.

There are numerous further examples that I could offer here to support the idea that Freud often regarded personal names in a magical way, but I will mention, only a few of them. As reported in Jones's third volume (p. 380), Freud wrote that during his Paris sojourn in 1886 he often heard *his name* being called aloud in the voice of his fiancée Martha (possibly a symptom of cocaine abuse).* That these auditory hallucinations indicate a vulnerability to psychosis should not be ignored, but they also hint at Freud's susceptibility to name magic. That is, he immediately ascribed a magical significance to these name phenomena, i.e. that Martha perhaps was trying to get in touch with him from Austria via a paranormal channel of some kind! Implicit in these experiences was the uncanny power that he attributed to the name "Sigi," which was the one he probably heard reverberating in the streets of Paris in Martha's ghostly voice, as a replay of the magical voice of his nanny.

It's quite likely that Freud regarded his given name as "magical" on other occasions. Already noted is the probability that he changed his name from Sigismund to Sigmund for reasons that were partly magical, particularly since this occurred at age 19, which was a magical number for him, a number ensuring a personal triumph. To some extent, this name magic may have been used by him to foster a magical healing process, since he was trying to cope with the fact that his cousin at Breslau had become psychotic at age 19. Surely Freud knew that for thousands of years the use of name magic for healing purposes was as common as its use by shamans to perpetrate destructive and even murderous acts (Clodd, 1920).

Indeed, he must have known about countless rituals among ancient people involving the nailing of names written on the walls of tombs with the intention of effecting murders, and other destructive acts of name magic. During his feuding with Carl Jung, when this Swiss shaman told him a story about a young king who effaced his father's chiseled name from all monuments and statues, Freud became very upset about Jung's intentions. Freud suspected that this represented Jung's desire to murder him via one magical means or another, ignoring his own desire to murder Jung via name magic with which the preceding tale was correlated by Freud, unconsciously. Thus, after the breakup of these two analysts Ernest Jones discovered that Freud was no longer able to utter the name of Jung, and instead repeatedly substituted Jones's surname for Jung's—an obvious symptomatic problem.

Undoubtedly, this represented Freud's desire to replace Jung, in his mind, with a follower whom he hoped would be more loyal. However, this inability even to speak Jung's name was similar to the kinds of symptoms that Stekel reported with some of his name-compulsive patients. To some extent, this symbolic effacing of Jung's name by Freud reflected his strong desire to obliterate Jung's identity—actually to murder him, as discussed in the eighth chapter in greater detail.

Recent paragraphs have returned us to instances of name magic that seemed to be quite unconscious for Freud, and I'd like to offer a few more of these examples reflecting unconscious processes. Later, when we review

---

*See *DSM III* (Third Edition, 1980, p. 146).

his frequent coalescences of magical name-series, emphasis will be placed upon his unconscious tendency to somehow interrelate persons having names (especially surnames) having structural similarities with one another. To illustrate, we'll see that two of these name-series included: 1. the names Fluss, Fleischl, Fliess (and perhaps Flechsig), which share the letters "Fls" 2. the names Brutus, Börne, Braun, Brücke, Breuer, Bleuler, Bernays, Bernheim, and Bauer—which share the letters "Br" and "e" or "u."

With these factors in mind we can regard as name magic Freud's tendency to make an unconscious equation of himself with some persons having surnames that were similar to his surname, or having surnames incorporating his nickname "Sig." In the first category, let's examine two cases involving Freud's peculiar equations of himself with men having the surname Freund, which has a close structural similarity to his own surname.

A letter by Freud to Fliess in November 1895 produced his angry accusation that a neurologist named C.S. Freund had just published an article on psychic paralyses in hysteria that Freud called "a piece of nonsense" and "almost a plagiarism" of ideas already published by Freud. His devoted disciple Jones has endorsed the master's idea that this was nearly a plagiarism of Freud's work, but Ellenberger (who demolished many of these legends) is a more reliable evaluator of Freud's claim. Ellenberger noted (1970, p. 448) that C.S. Freund's paper had "expressed a theory quite different from that of Freud, whom the author even mentions in that regard."

Therefore, one needs to ask why Freud made this seemingly absurd intimation that his work had been stolen by Dr. Freund? My answer again revolves around Freud's fixation on name magic, i.e. the great similarity (structurally) of these surnames caused him to identify with Dr. Freund and to fantasize that this eminent man's work belonged to him—to Freud. Of course, there was considerable projection by Freud in this incident, relating to the large number of times when he, over a lifetime, was accused of plagiarism, which coincided with his strong plagiaristic impulses in his breakup with Fliess, and with other instances. In that regard, we should note that structurally the name Freud is very similar to the English word "fraud," hinting that a name-compulsion involving fraudulent acts might have existed in him. As a more benign instance of possible name magic pertaining to the surname Freund, there was also Freud's identification with his patient and colleague named Anton von Freund who died of cancer near age 40, in January 1920. Freud's excessive grief at von Freund's death hints at identification based upon name magic, but there were also pecuniary factors, since the deceased was a millionaire who had greatly helped to finance the Cause. The name Freund means "friend" in German, and Freud had proved repeatedly that, for him, there was no friend so dear as a wealthy one.

Now let's turn to that second category, Freud's equation of himself magically with men having surnames incorporating his nickname, Sig. Earlier, I gave the famous case of his preoccupation with death, final judgment, and the name Signorelli, as an instance of this. In *Dark Side* I've discussed Freud's probable identification with the bumbling soldier he cited in his book on "slips called "Itzig" (rendered as "It's Sig!"), as another illustration of this same phenomenon.

Another example of this name magic was Freud's irrational identification with a rather famous physician and researcher named Dr. Paul Flechsig, of Leipzig. In Freud's letter to Martha dated November 4, 1885, he referred to this man as "my rival Flechsig" and passed on a description of him as being "an insignificant man" who was too incompetent to make proper use of his own discoveries. Previously, in a March letter to her he alleged that he was making excellent discoveries in brain anatomy which he hoped to unify in a large paper, but had discovered that someone from Leipzig (Flechsig) was frustrating him by publishing some of these gems "piecemeal every week."

Apparently, Freud's claim that he was a formidable rival of Flechsig was largely a fantasy, based on several factors including the "Sig" element at the end of this man's surname. Also, this fantasy was coalesced by the fact that this man was located at Leipzig, where Freud had lived painfully during the year following the "Freiberg catastrophe," in that same era when he was called Sig regularly. Another factor was that Flechsig was a great rival, in psychiatry and neurology, of Dr. Meynert—these men being regarded as two of the greatest European savants of that era, while Freud was still an utter nobody (except for his notoriety as a "public menace" in the initial cocaine fiasco).

In 1885 Freud was already regarded in a very disapproving manner by his former teacher, Meynert, which angered Freud greatly. Evidently, his fantasy that he was a true rival of Flechsig was partly a way that Freud employed to defend his ego, thereby regarding himself as the equal of his master, Dr. Meynert. One of the strange things that Freud had done to ruffle Meynert's feathers was to adopt some of Flechsig's ideas as a springboard for his (Freud's) research. Meynert was not aware that Freud probably had been compelled to do this symptomatically, due to the name magic involving his nickname "Sig" incorporated within Flechsig's surname. In a moment, I'll explain this point.

In 1883 and onward Freud's lab work had been devoted to attempts at discovering new techniques for examining nervous tissue. Two of these "discoveries" by Freud were hailed by Jones as triumphs (though actually they were rather unimportant and had fleeting scientific interest), and he noted that: "Both of them were elaborations of hints thrown out by Flechsig, Meynert's great rival, a fact that was perhaps the beginning of Meynert's estrangement from Freud." One of these new techniques by Freud exploited Flechsig's suggestion to use the fetal brain, in which only part of the neural pathways are myelinated. Freud's three published papers on this work were routine and plodding efforts concerned with roots and connections of the acoustic nerve; the inferior peduncle of the cerebellum; and several specific nerves. The second of Freud's new techniques involved his discovery of a method of impregnating nerve fibers with gold chloride.

Jones mentioned that when Freud created this new gold chloride technique for staining nervous tissue, he adopted an idea that Flechsig "had thrown out in 1876, but never followed up." Using Flechsig's idea, Freud experimented for several weeks with the help of a chemist friend, hit upon the special gold chloride solution, and then announced this in jubilant letters (very prematurely) as if sure that his discovery would quickly earn him fame and wealth. Actually, all of this was a magical enterprise relating to the "Sig" element of Flechsig's surname, which had compelled Freud to adopt this man's idea, because Freud's early nickname was inextricably linked with the magical substance, gold. The fact that Freud had been called "golden Sig" by his two mothers irrationally compelled him to adopt Flechsig's golden idea as a sure winner. Remember, this occurred in the same era of the 1880s when his hidden name, Cain, had propelled him into using cocaine in "research" which he felt certain would make him famous. That he was gripped by name magic in the gold chloride endeavor is also suggested by the surname of his chemist friend who worked with him on the project. This man's name was Lustgarten, which in German means "garden of *joy* or sensual desire".

Twenty-six years later Freud's rivalry with, and fixation upon, Dr. Flechsig surfaced again under strange circumstances pertaining to Freud's struggle with his own potentials for psychosis. In 1911 Freud published his essay analyzing the severe psychosis (paranoia or schizophrenia) of judge Daniel Schreber who had spent ten years in mental institutions due to severe mental illness. In 1903 Schreber published a long account of his countless delusions and other aspects of his illness which, however, neglected crucial data about his childhood and life history. Freud's analysis of this case was remarkable, since he had never seen the patient, and this was his first foray into explaining an area of psychosis using psychoanalytic ideas. The patient's symptoms were so florid and complex that a theorist could have "proved" almost any notion that he wished to endorse, which was always ideal for Freud's propogandistic purposes. Among Schreber's myriad delusions, Freud endorsed only two kinds as fundamental: the patient believed he was being changed from a man into a woman; he complained of having suffered homosexual attacks from his first doctor, and from God. According to Freud, repressed homosexuality was at the core of the patient's illness, whose love objects were his father, his psychiatrist, and God. (If projections were operative in Freud, we should recall his charge that Jacob Freud had molested his own children.)

Freud's theories about the Schreber case are sometimes interesting, but seldom convincing. Since he did not know about Schreber's childhood, he often missed the mark badly in trying to explain the patient's symptoms. Schatzman's book *Soul Murder* (1976) provides details about Schreber's agonizing childhood during which his probably psychotic (ambulatory) father "tortured" him repeatedly with weird mechanical devices, making Freud's ideas about the origins of his symptoms seem irrelevant or even nonsensical. But why did Freud jump head first into this muddy case? Well, Schreber's original psychiatrist in 1885 had been none other than Dr. Paul Flechsig of Leipzig! So it's probable that one of the reasons why Freud analyzed this case was as another act of rivalry with Flechsig, again prompted by name magic. Since Flechsig seemed to have missed the point in his treatment of Schreber, Freud decided to step in, decades later, to set his rival straight about the "real" underlying dynamics in this case.

But there may have been other reasons for Freud's foray into this case of psychosis *in 1911*. Freud claimed that his theories about the underlying condition were not based upon the case material, but came from ideas previously formulated by him from his earlier clinical experience. (He claimed he'd learned the secret of paranoia from Fliess, implying that he'd unraveled Fliess's paranoia!) This gave Freud great leeway to project his own psychopathology into his explanations about the Schreber case. Regarding the year 1911, there is good reason to believe that he was struggling mightily then to control his own psychotic impulses as his "empire" was beginning to crumble, with the start of dangerous dissensions from Adler, Stekel, Jung, and other disloyal disciples. Was Freud's version of the Schreber case an autobiographical endeavor? Vitz implied that this was so, and he remarked (1988, p. 246) that this case fits together well with Freud's own "homosexual" pattern, regarding his relationship with Fliess. Also, Vitz noted that Schreber's periods of maximum mental disturbance correspond with Freud's own eras of maximal mental imbalance. Significantly, Vitz concluded that probably Freud identified with Schreber "in his Flechsig relationship," thereby reenacting his early relationship with John Freud and later with Fleischl, Fliess, and Jung. My suggestion here is that in 1911 Freud wrote this monograph on Schreber as an effort to control his own fluctuating mental deterioration which, in 1914, led to lethal wishes against Jung and the murder of Emanuel Freud.

The preceding material hypothesized that Freud's childhood nicknames

"Sig" and "golden Sig (Sigi)" had cemented his strange, longterm connections with a rival named Flechsig, leading to Freud's concoction of the *gold* chloride method. A similar sort of argument will now be proposed about the coalescence of Freud's uncanny relationship with Wilhelm Fliess, in which these men propagated and shared astonishing amounts of magical ideation, perhaps including aspects of name magic. Specifically, my suggestion is that the nickname "golden Sig" helped to engender Freud's very loving but rivalrous relationship with Fliess, whose surname is pronounced identically with the English word "fleece," which is also the dictionary meaning of Fliess's name! In fantasy, Freud identified himself intensely with Wilhelm Fliess, so it's not surprising that the omnipotent child in Freud, called "golden Sig," should have assigned an equivalent mythological identity to his friend: namely, the "golden fleece." Further explanation will soon be offered for this viewpoint.

In itself, that wooly meaning of Fliess's surname was able to cast a magical spell over Freud's unconscious mind because of its powerful associations with Freud's family life in the lost golden realm of Freiberg. Great emphasis should be given to the fact that Fliess's surname means "fleece," since that meaning made a direct connection with the work pursued by Freud's father during the Freiberg days, namely the wool trade. Moreover, the large family with whom the Freuds were closely affiliated in Freiberg were also in the wool trade, and their surname was Fluss. (Sigmund was a dear friend of the three sons, and at age 16 he fell "madly" in love with their sister, Gisela Fluss.)

Notice that the surname Fluss, with its strong associations pertaining to wool in Freud's mind, has a striking structural similarity to the name Fliess, signifying wool. For Freud, this allowed Fliess's name to evoke compelling recollections of important persons who were with young Sigi in Freiberg, and even enabled Fliess to become a composite revenant of those lost figures (Julius, nanny, John, Emanuel, the Fluss children). With regard to Fliess's psychopathic tendencies, suggested by his being a dispenser of number magic and quackish cocaine remedies, there is even the possibility that the primary meaning of his surname (fleece), when used as an English verb, made a connection with the second "business" in which members of the Freud family were engaged—the counterfeiting trade. That meaning of "fleece" as an English verb is: to strip of money (gold) by fraud or deception.

Are there some readers who remain skeptical that the surname of Wilhelm Fliess provoked extremely compelling associations to wool and fleece in the unconscious mind of Freud? If so, let me offer a clear proof for that assertion. We need to consider that, for about ten years, Freud regarded Fliess as his dearest friend and his personal physician. Many writers have noted that Freud was gripped by powerful transference feelings which caused him to glorify Fliess as a medical genius and the ideal doctor, sometimes calling him "the Kepler of biology." Freud ended his friendship with Fliess in 1902 and was diagnosed with jaw cancer in 1923, and in that long interim did not invest any personal physician with the admiration and trust that he had given to Fliess. After his cancer appeared, he made various comments indicating that he yearned to have a physician like Fliess to care for him. Finally, in 1928 Freud chose a young analyst with a very special name to be his personal physician for the final twelve years of his life, none other than Dr. Max Schur.

Although it's true that Dr. Schur had been recommended to Freud by Princess Bonaparte, it's my contention that name magic operative in Freud's psyche was the primary, irrational factor which caused him to regard this young doctor as being extremely capable and trustworthy. For in German the surname Schur means "fleece," exactly the meaning of Fliess's surname, enabling Freud via name magic to transform Dr. Schur into a revenant of Wilhelm Fliess! Indeed, the wooly meaning of Schur's surname enabled him to become a revenant for all the important figures of the Freiberg years (nanny, John, etc.), as was true with Fliess. Perhaps, in terms of unconscious name play there was an additional reason why Freud invested this young physician with such great trust, considering that his name, Max Schur, sounds like the English words "makes sure." The first thing that Freud asked him to "make sure" of involved his promise to Freud that if the pain became too great, he would help his patient commit suicide.

If most readers now are convinced that Freud's mind was mystified by the fleecy meaning of Wilhelm Fliess's surnames let me return to my suggestion that unconsciously Freud regarded his beloved friend as "the golden fleece" of mythological fame. First, let me say that the bulk of Freud's letters to Fliess makes clear that Freud wished to use his friend's ideas and talents to assist in the erection of the grand conceptual structure of Psychoanalysis. Indeed, the historian Sulloway (1979) has argued persuasivley that Freud *did* obtain many of his seminal ideas from Fliess. That Freud hoped to use Fliess's "remarkable talents" as a healer to enhance his own skills and fame as a healer is seen in Freud's adoption of Fliess's nasal neurosis theory, including the dangerous surgery that Freud endorsed on the basis of that magical conception.

My point is that Freud attributed great healing powers to Fliess (fleece), which correlates with the idea that in a number of the Greek myths concerning the golden fleece, it was regarded as having magical healing powers. In Freud's dream book (1967, p. 67) he provided a footnote which gives an attenuated version of the healing legends concerning the golden fleece. He told how, in ancient Greece, a sick man would visit a temple and be stretched out on the skin of a sacrificial ram, whereupon he would sleep, and dream of the remedies for his sickness. This story hints that Freud was aware of the golden fleece legends in which supernatural healing played a part in the awesome powers of the fleece.

One of Freud's own dreams offers evidence that he had a special interest in the legends about the golden fleece. At the end of May in 1897, he wrote Fliess about his recent dream in which the name of his niece Hella appeared visually, printed in heavy type, after which he described his daughter Mathilde's utter fascination with ancient Greek mythology. That the name Hella appeared in bold print indicates that it referred to a name, written in a book about Greek mythology, which obviously pertains to the legend about a woman named Hella who rode through the air on the magical ram with *golden fleece*. Sadly, she fell off and was drowned in the strait which thereafter bore her name, the Hellespont. Her grieving brother then sacrificed the ram and hung up its fleece as an offering to Ares, the god of war. That is the start of the famous legend about the hero, Jason, who pursued this golden fleece in order to recover his lost kingdom. Recall that he built the swift ship Argo and then recruited a band of heroes (the Argonauts) to help him in his search for the golden fleece (including Heracles, Theseus, Orpheus, etc.). Eventually, he captured this magical fleece with the help of the sorceress Medea, but thereafter great tribulations befell the quest for his lost kingdom. (The legend about Hella perhaps fits together with the death of Fliess's sister, which may have prompted him to become a magical healer—the golden fleece.)

If I'm right that Freud unconsciously viewed his friend Fliess as "the golden fleece," then it is plausible that Freud had coalesced a fantasy identification with the Greek hero called Jason, consonant with many other of his identifications with figures deriving from ancient Greece. In fantasy, Fliess became the magical healer (golden fleece) who would help Freud to attain fame and fortune so that he could reclaim his lost kingdom: Freiberg and Queen Monica. (Notice that this is somewhat similar to Freud's identification with Oedipus who was, however, unaware that he was heading towards a confused reclaiming of *his* lost kingdom.) In Freud's fantasy identification with the heroic Jason, it's likely that his Argonauts eventually included those questionable heroes called Jung, Adler, Stekel, Gross, Sadger, Ferenczi, Jones, etc.

In conclusion, if Freud somehow regarded his friend Fliess as the mythological "golden fleece," this hints that he attributed an exalted status to his friend's healing powers, consonant with his identifications with both Fliess and with Jesus. Moreover, there is also the possibility that Freud was characterizing his beloved colleague as a sheep. If so, that may have symbolized his desire to maintain Fliess in the role of a perpetual follower, or disciple (reminding us that Jung's surname is connected with the German word Jünger, which signifies "a disciple"). Unfortunately for Freud, Fliess's megalomania matched his own, and eventually the Berliner refused to submit to that subservient role. Instead, he asserted suddenly that all of Freud's work and new conceptions could be subsumed under his own grand design, whereupon the friendship quickly ended. Sadly, the Kepler of biology discovered that his grandiose power motives were incompatible with those of the Newton of psychology.

Recent pages have offered only a few instances in which Freud's susceptibility to name magic prompted him to associate himself with colleagues whose name meanings or connotations were somehow connected with one or more of his irrational complexes. Readers will find many more of these examples in *Dark Side*, which offers a long section describing the many ways that name magic was involved in Freud's "Christ complex," and other strange instances of name magic in his life.

Freud's Magical Name-Series

Brief mention already has been made of Freud's unconscious tendency to invent magical name-series, such as Fluss, Fleischl, Fliess, etc. or Braun, Breuer, Brücke, etc. with emphasis upon his uses of structurally similar names (surnames or given names) to create revenants for "lost" figures who were important to him. In this section we'll explore how his tendency to invent magical name-series sometimes had quite destructive consequences. For example, at times a person whose name occurred late in a name-series, historically, was victimized by Freud due to some alleged offense perpetrated years earlier by a person whose name had occurred early in that series. These long-delayed and destructive aspects of name magic in Freud's mind will receive considerable emphasis by this author. For later they will be discussed as quite possibly having special pertinence to his long delays in killing Emanuel and John Freud (as delayed responses to their original "offenses" in Freud's childhood years).

Before exploring a few of Freud's destructive magical name-series, I'll offer evidence that he had partial awareness that somewhat more benign name-series also were operative in his mind. Let's go back to the year 1910 when Freud was experiencing great interpersonal difficulties with his younger colleagues, Alfred Adler and Wilhelm Stekel, in the era just before he ended his relations with both of those men. In those days he wrote to Ferenczi that he was having "an atrocious time with Adler and Stekel," felt "chronically exasperated" by these independent thinkers, and wished for a clean break from them. (Jones II, p. 130).

In turn, Ferenczi suggested that Freud was reenacting the painful "desertion" by Fliess, ten years earlier (ignoring that the "desertion" by nanny was the original template). Freud acknowledged that Ferenczi was right in his judgment, stating that: "I had quite got over the Fliess affair. Adler is a little Fliess come to life again. And his appendage Stekel is at least called Wilhelm." Notice that Freud's wording ("Fliess come to life again, etc.") indicates he believed that Adler had become a revenant of Fliess, and Stekel had also. Moreover, Freud's reference to the given name shared by Fliess and Stekel ("Wilhelm") hinted at Freud's dim awareness that he'd used a magical name-series involving the name Wilhelm to transform Stekel into a revenant of Fliess. (In *Dark Side*, I've discussed other men who belonged in the "Wilhelm" name-series.)

Similarly, Freud demonstrated partial awareness that he was involved in another magical name-series when he wrote in the dream book that his ego found it easy to conceal itself behind men named Josef, since the Biblical master of dreams had that name. What was implied by Freud in that message was that he had coalesced a magical name-series incorporating the given names of Josef Freud (his criminal uncle), the Biblical Josef, Josef Breuer, Josef Paneth, and—I will argue later—Josef Popper, from whom he plagiarized a critical dream theory.

Freud's magical name-series involving the name Josef, plus his fantasy identification with Napoleon, eventually prompted him to invent the questionable idea that the French emperor had likewise been emmeshed in a magical name-series regarding the name Josef. In Freud's letter to Thomas Mann of November 29, 1936 he proposed that Napoleon harbored a repressed and murderous hatred for his eldest brother Josef which he countered, via name magic, by forming a positive fantasy identification with Josef, the Biblical dream master (and *de facto* emperor of Egypt). Freud claimed that the emperor's marriage to Josephine B. was prompted decisively *by her name*, reflecting Freud's unstated theory that Napoleon must have been pursuing a magical name-series. Moreover, Freud implied strongly that name-compulsion was operative here (Stekel's concept), since he wrote that Napoleon's "love for Josephine B. was an obsessive one on account of the name . . " Freud seemed to give a further endorsement of the name-compulsion concept when he indicated that Napoleon's expedition to Egypt was also precipitated by the aforementioned name factors that were connected with the name of the Biblical Josef, prime minister of Egypt. That is, Napoleon became the master of Egypt in imitation of the Biblical Josef, according to Freud.

Focusing on the preceding paragraph, and the previous 30 pages, readers are now in a better position to evaluate Freud's fierce oppositon to Stekel's pioneering paper on name-compulsions in 1911, and his attempts to keep it from being published. Was it only in 1936, in his letter to Mann about Napoleon's uses of name magic, that Freud finally recognized the validity of Stekel's 1911 paper on name-compulsions? I doubt that. My own view is that in 1911, and in the decades thereafter, Freud hoped to prevent clinicians from studying and understanding the materials on name magic which he dimly sensed could be used to unravel many of his own personal symptoms, especially his compulsive urges regarding sexuality and murder.

The pages that follow will describe a complicated magical name-series by Freud that starts with his searingly intense love for Gisela Fluss, who rejected him painfully when he was age 16. This name-series extended over decades to ensnare a small network of other people, including a second woman with a similar name (Gizella), with lethal consequences for this woman's husband. Let me emphasize that this presentation is a condensed analysis of this name-series which appears at its full length in *Dark Side* (unfortunately, here omitting some materials that strengthen my arguments considerably).

In the summer of 1872, when he was age 16, Sigmund Freud returned to his beloved birthplace called Freiberg that he had left thirteen years earlier. He went on this pilgrimage as if it were a holiday, accompanied by two of his school chums, and was a guest at the home of the wealthy Fluss family (in the textile business). Their three sons (Emil, Alfred, Richard) had continued to be friends of his, and their two daughters were still friends of Sigmund's sisters. The Fluss family had maintained warm relations with the Freuds after they had moved to Vienna, so Sigmund was a welcome guest in their home that summer. In this idyllic small town, he was free to enjoy feelings of nostalgia in a setting that was suffused with memories of his first love, his dear nursemaid named Monica. As often happens at age 16, he soon fell passionately in love with the beautiful girl, Gisela Fluss, then age 15 and the younger of the two sisters.

In Freud's letters to his friend Eduard Silberstein, which quoted from the daily diary he kept about his Freiberg holiday with the Fluss family, he told about his passion for Gisela and described her exotic beauty which had stirred him deeply. He wrote his friend that: "Gisela's beauty is wild, I would say Thracian. Her aquiline nose, the long black hair, the tightlipped mouth she has from the mother, the dark-brown color of her face . ." But also he mentioned her "indifferent expressions," hinting that she was not too impressed with this studious friend of her brothers.

Evidently, Freud was too shy and immature at age 16 to approach this lovely girl as a potential suitor. He wrote that: "my shyness in thoughts prevented me from conversing with pleasure and delight with the half-näive, half-cultured girl." But there was some teasing and a few emotional sparks that flew between them, and Gisela reacted to this love-sick boy by playing some sort of joke on him, one that he later admitted had annoyed him for a long time. When she left for school at the end of the summer, he wrote: "I was very sad saying goodbye .. " With effort he tried to pull himself together and added: "I have now calmed all my surging thoughts and only flinch slightly if her mother mentions the name of Gisela .. " (One suspects that he had become fixated upon "the name of Gisela," whose first three letters encode a reversal of his childhood name, Sig.)

There is reason to believe that Gisela's appearance and unattainableness were very stimulating to young Sigmund, but quite maddening as well. The pain caused to his sensitive ego over feelings of rejection probably was responsible for a monumental alcoholic binge that summer during which he drank himself into oblivion, on the slim pretext that he was "curing an aching toothache." Freud wrote that during this drunken bender he was "raving the whole day." Then he "fell down unconscious" in a public place and Emil Fluss had to carry him upstairs to his bed where he vomited violently and later, when it was all over, suffered a severe hangover! One wonders how often he abused alcohol in this fashion (perhaps a precursor to his cocaine abuses), while still hardly more than a boy. Also, one wonders if his depressed feelings were intensified by a visit to the Town Council where an inspection of his birth certificate might have increased his doubts about his true birthdate, the identity of his *real* father, and uneasy feelings about his own identity.

In writing to his friend Silberstein about that drunken spree during his Freiberg holiday, Sigmund avoided mentioning that he was already trying desperately to blot out his feelings and memories relating to Gisela's rejection of him. Concerning the concealed depth of anguish that he experienced about the episode with Gisela, R.W. Clark wrote (1980) that it evoked: "Freud's lifelong determination to expunge it from his memory." Discussing this same topic, Jones seemed perplexed about "the quite extraordinary precautions [Freud] took to conceal a most innocent and momentary emotion of love in his adolescence," evading the fact that this was not a momentary or trifling fantasy, or Freud would not have expended so much energy to conceal it from his readers. That Sigmund's attempts to suppress his passionate feelings about Gisela were quite ineffective will be seen by the virulence of his response to later news of her marriage.

Another defense that Sigmund adopted concerning Gisela's rejection of him in 1872 was an attempt to transfer his amorous feelings to her mother, Frau Fluss! In erecting that defense, he wrote Silberstein that his other great "passion" (*Leidenschaft*) in Freiberg was Frau Fluss, and he expressed extremely warm feelings for her that combined admiration, gratitude for her maternal generosity, and elements of sexual feelings. He wrote that when he'd gotten drunk she "cared for me as for her own child." (Apparently, nanny's ghost was easily revived in Freiberg that summer.)

Freud wrote many pages to Silberstein praising Frau Fluss's kindness, intelligence, character, and extraordinary maternal qualities. Thus, the beautiful but rejecting Gisela was now exposed as a pale version of her awesome mother—so that Sigmund could claim defensively that it was the Fluss children's mother who was the true and original object of his affections, not Gisela. He wrote: "it seems that I have translated esteem for the mother into friendship for the daughter." In his outpouring of praise and affection for Frau Fluss he wrote that: "She obviously recognizes that I always need encouragement to speak or to help myself, and she never fails to give it."

At an unconscious level of mind, Sigmund was right in claiming that his love for Gisela had originated from a maternal source of immense power. But Frau Fluss was not the earliest template for this unattainable love. Rather, the return to Freiberg had stimulated Freud's deep longing for his first sexual partner, the near-mythic nursemaid called Monica, whose persistent residues in his psyche will be discussed extensively in my later works. She and Amalia Freud were participants in Sigmund's first love triangle involving two females and himself. This second triangle connecting Sigmund with the Fluss family's mother and daughter will later find its uncanny counterpart in Sandor Ferenczi's affair (promoted by Freud) with another "Gisela," again involving a mother and daughter. (Some persons have charged that another of Freud's triangles involved him with two sisters named Martha and Minna, as covered in detail in *Secret SL*.)

In late 1872 an additional defense by Sigmund against Gisela's painful rejection of him was the writing of a disparaging letter to her brother Emil in which he did some primitive name-calling. He referred to Gisela mockingly as "Ichthyoesaura," which refers to an extinct fishlike marine reptile. By using this term he was probably hinting that she was a cold, dead fish—an attempt to explain "her problem" in having rejected him, the dashing conquistador. R.W. Clark revealed a sensitivity to name magic by writing that the term Ichthyoesaura was "derived from the Greek for fluvial creatures and a natural enough name for a Fluss." Clark's comment refers to the fact that the German meaning of Gisela's surname Fluss is "river." So when Freud transformed her first name into that of a marine creature, he created an unconscious pun that connected her new "bad name" with the meaning of her surname. (His additional invidious motives in creating that pun are examined in *Dark Side*.)

In his letter to her brother Emil, Freud revealed another primitive verbal attack upon Gisela, hinting that his feelings of rejection were capable of eliciting lethal impulses towards his former darling. First, he told Emil that there was merely mockery, not seriousness, "in this whole flirtation" with his sister. Then he stated that in his correspondence with Silberstein about

Gisela "the poor creature was torn to shreds."

Was that simply a fanciful adolescent expression, or did it also reflect a homicidal desire to cut the beautiful girl to shreds for her rejection of him? Consider that during his anguished engagement to Martha, his feelings of rejection and depression caused him to express murderous impulses towards her along with self-destructive urges and lethal feelings towards the entire world. Also consider that only a few years after expressing those murderous feelings towards Gisela Fluss he was working in Prof. Claus's *marine* zoological station at Trieste (the city where his hero Winckelmann had been murdered, mysteriously). What was Freud's experimental task in Trieste? It was his job to slice up more that 400 lowly marine animals, reminding us that he'd mockingly given his beloved Gisela the name of a marine animal and then hinted broadly at a desire to cut her into pieces.

In Trieste Freud dissected hundreds of eels while seeking to locate and verify the existence of testes in this creature, which microscopic examinations allowed him to accomplish eventually. A suspicion arises that in this work he was discharging some of his great hostility towards Gisela (and we are also reminded of the bizarre surgery on Emma Eckstein that nearly killed her and disfigured her face). Unconsciously, he might also have been working-through some violent feelings about his own ambivalent sexuality, since Freudians regard the eel as an obvious phallic symbol and in this research Freud was trying to determine whether or not the eel possesses verifiable testes.

Let me emphasize that four years after his rejection by Gisela Fluss, Freud apparently was still obsessed by his feelings about her and was in Trieste displacing his rage onto hundreds of marine animals. There is also evidence that 23 years later, in 1899, he was still obsessed with Gisela Fluss's memory. In that year he published his paper on "Screen Memories" which gave his analysis of the screen memory of a supposed patient. Siegfried Bernfeld has offered convincing proof that this was a disguised autobiographical account about Freud himself (leading to ever-growing suspicions that he falsified many other "patient" stories and dreams that were really his own, and about himself).

In Freud's screen memory paper of 1899, the narrator related that when he was a young child he was forced to move from a happy country home to a harder life in the city. He recalled having played at age two in a field full of dandelions with a boy and girl his age and of snatching some dandelions from the hands of the girl, who was then given some black bread by a peasant woman. The narrator recalled that thereafter, *as a teenager, he visited his birthplace and fell in love with a girl of fifteen* in a yellow dress. At age 20, the narrator visited a well-to-do uncle who wished him to marry his daughter, but the young cousins failed to fall in love and marry as was expected of them.

Freud analyzed that screen memory in a way that related it to his theory about the nature of his patients' memories that occur in their dreams. For our purposes, however, we'll emphasize agreement with Bernfeld that the screen memory was about Freud himself—including his early childhood in Freiberg and forced departure from it, the visit to England at almost age 20 when a marriage with his niece was discussed, and his teenage visit to his birthplace where he fell in love with a girl who was 15 years old. Comparing those items with the data incorporated into the screen memory paper, there should be no question that in 1899 at age 44 Freud was still very preoccupied with Gisela Fluss and that summer of '72 when he'd fallen madly in love with her.

In the screen memories paper, the narrator (Freud) described his teenage love for the 15 year-old girl in the yellow dress as quite intense and claimed that he'd kept it a secret. Then he revealed that his beloved was now married and living in his own city. In the course of his musings he wrote: "A strange thing. For when I see her now from time to time—she happens to have married someone here—she is quite exceptionally indifferent to me. Yet I can remember quite well for what a long time afterward I was affected by the yellow color of the dress she was wearing when we first met, whenever I saw the same color anywhere else." That account indicates that in their later years, when their paths crossed on the streets of Vienna where Gisela and her husband were living, she still acted indifferently towards Freud. And we can assume that her coolness towards him must have inflicted repeated injuries to his massive but delicate ego. Probably, even when he was in his forties Freud had not gotten over the bitter feelings he experienced in 1875 when Gisela, at age 18, had gotten married—as will soon be made clear.

That Freud did suffer deep anguish when Gisela got married is evidenced by a caustic poem he composed "celebrating" the event, which he sent in a letter to Silberstein. R.W. Clark wrote that the poem was accurately characterized as ridiculing the style of Gisela's marriage by calling it "Antidiluvian." Its theme predicted that her husband would be a crass money-grubber and that she would be restricted to being a household drudge. Clark commented about the poem that: "Most of the attacks are obviously directed against the bride and dire envy fills the lines in which the snug appearance of the bride is described, and the groom's anticipations of its delights."

It's not hard to believe that Clark was accurate when he wrote that Freud responded with "virulence" to the news of Gisela's marriage. The unremitting power of her magical name in his psyche is emphasized by another point made by Clark. He wrote that: "More than a third of a century later, when the name 'Gisela' was mentioned during a psychoanalytic session with a patient, Freud felt it necessary to put three exclamation marks after the name written in his notes." That strong reaction to the mere mention of the name Gisela was at variance with the lie that Freud told Martha about his feelings for Gisela Fluss. He admitted that he had had a "crush" on her in adolescence, but insisted that she had been a momentary interest and was not of any lasting significance to him.

To the contrary, Freud had not recovered from the "madness" he felt for Gisela Fluss in 1876 when he was stabbing hundreds of sacrificial eels, nor had the madness disappeared in 1904-1905 when his protégé Sandor Ferenczi began to provide psychoanalysis for a young woman named Elma Pálos. At the same time Ferenczi was carrying on an affair with the married mother of the patient, whose name was *Gizella* Pálos. (Evidently, the affair was facilitated by the fact that sly Sandor had known the Pálos family for many years and was trusted by the husband of his mistress.)

Ferenczi fell in love with his young patient Elma and wished to marry her. Masson (1984), who had access to unpublished letters from Ferenczi to Freud, described that the letters reveal that Freud urged his disciple, who was slavishly obedient to him, to avoid marrying the young daughter Elma. Instead, in 1919* Ferenczi finally married the mother, Gizella, mainly because he had been *manipulated into doing so* by Freud and despite that she was eight years older than Sandor—who fervently wished that he could marry her daughter and have a child by her.

The man whom Ferenczi displaced, the ex-husband of Gizella, had not wanted the divorce that Freud helped to precipitate with his strong advice to pliable Sandor. He died on the very day that Ferenczi married Gizella, either of a heart attack or perhaps by suicide. Later, Ferenczi's letters to Georg Groddeck disclosed that he was very angry with Freud for destroying his chances for sexual fulfillment and happiness by convincing him to "trade" young Elma for the much older Gizella (who was closer to Freud's age). This union produced no children, of course, and Ferenczi complained bitterly to Groddeck about the fruits of Freud's meddling: "I want .. not an analytic interpretation, but something real, a young woman, a child."

As the scholar who had access to the unpublished Ferenczi/ Freud letters, Masson was able to give us a provocative glimpse into those deceitful, unethical actions by Ferenczi and Freud with regard to the Pálos family. On the basis of what Masson has written, apparently Ferenczi indulged in affairs with both mother and daughter (the patient!), perhaps simultaneously. If we are to take Masson's word for it, and he did read the unpublished letters, after all, it seems that Freud quietly condoned Ferenczi's unethical clinical behaviors. Masson indicated Freud's lack of a moral stance on these matters

---

*Notice that the year 1919, incorporating the magical number 19 twice, was a year of triumph for Freud— coinciding with the era when John Freud disappeared.

by writing: "The emotional complication of the two affairs seems not to have unduly bothered Freud." It should be stressed that Freud bore a special responsibility in these matters, because he had psychoanalyzed Ferenczi on *two* separate occasions and therefore was able to take advantage of powerful residual transference effects to manipulate his disciple. This helps us to comprehend why the latter was so strangely compliant with the master's urgings, allowing them to override his own strong needs and desires.

For readers who are now attuned to Freud's uses of name magic, it will seem obvious that it was not merely that Freud failed to become "unduly bothered" by his disciple's shattering of Gizella P.'s marriage. It should be clear that this was another instance of the irrational effects of a name-series in Freud's life, in which Gizella P. was magically substituted for her template, Gisela Fluss. Since he was not able to marry his Gisela, he manipulated Ferenczi into marrying the other Gizella, thereby transforming Sandor into his reluctant surrogate.

The parallel between Ferenczi's love affairs with mother/daughter and Freud's "passion" for Gisela Fluss and *her mother* during his Freiberg summer of 1872 seems rather astonishing. But it is less startling when perceived as an offshoot of Freud's propensity for compulsive kinds of name magic. For we can surmise that Freud, himself mystified by name-compulsion, played Svengali in all of this and cast a spell upon a gullible Ferenczi to stimulate his increasing interest in Gizella Pálos, despite that this hot-blooded fellow felt passion only for her daughter. One may wonder whether Freud had confided his lifelong obsession with Gisela Fluss to Ferenczi, thereby triggering some sort of imitative name magic towards *his* Gizella by the wild-eyed Hungarian analyst.

Many troubling questions about these matters might be clarified instantly if there were now full and unexpurgated publication of the correspondence between Freud and Ferenczi—perhaps 2,500 letters or more. But it's unlikely that the elite watchdogs of Freud's materials will allow this to occur even in the next century. The Pálos case, with all its deception and immorality by Ferenczi and Freud in collaboration with one another, gives only a hint of the sleaziness and irrationality that probably lie concealed in their suppressed correspondence. Surely those letters contain torrents of bizarre and/or near-psychotic ideation propogated by Ferenczi with Freud's encouragement, in the same fashion that he egged-on Fliess's flights of frenzy (all in the name of freedom to create and speculate). In *Secret SL* compelling evidence is offered that confirms Freud's condoning of, or failure to resist, his disciples' immoral sexual behaviors with their patients in the early years of psychoanalysis. As with the Pálos affair, it was not unusual for "Dr. Joy" to condone such immoral behaviors by the early analysts (Ferenczi, Jung, Jones, Gross, etc.) despite his exaggerated boasts that he was the most ethical of men.

It seems obvious that Freud gave his "moral support" for Ferenczi's breakup of the marriage of Gizella Pálos and her husband. In doing so, he must have enjoyed feelings of sadistic pleasure and revenge derived from his venomous anger concerning the marriage of Gisela Fluss in 1875. Furthermore, my suggestion is that Freud received a perverse triple satisfaction with regard to the Pálos divorce: 1. in fantasy he managed to win the heart of young Gisela, at last, using Ferenczi and Gizella as surrogates; 2. he managed to break up *Gisela's* marriage, at a fantasy level; 3. he was able to inflict incredible emotional anguish and death upon his ancient rival, *Gisela's* husband. The latter point refers to the death of Gizella Pálos's husband of a heart attack or suicide on the very day she wed Ferenczi, this unfortunate man having died in place of Gisela Fluss's husband whom Freud despised and wished that he could destroy. (Recall his virulent poem attacking this rival in contemptuous terms.)

Having previously demonstrated Freud's hostility towards Gisela Fluss's name (the mocking change of her given name to that of an extinct lower animal) and his later bitterness towards her marriage and her husband, my hypothesis now is that his hostile, competetive feelings towards her *married surname* provided a remarkably invidious inspiration for his creation of *The Interpretation of Dreams*. One could say that, to some extent, he created the book as a magical way of competing with her husband and his name. This involved a fantasy that he could steal his rival's original ideas about the nature of dreams, as a reflection of his desire to steal the man's wife.

My contentions about these matters are based upon extensive study of name magic, especially as it related to Freud's perverse personality traits, and to the fact that in 1875 Gisela Fluss married an acquaintance of Freud named Herr Popper. (His first name is not known to me.) In the next few pages, I hope to establish that Freud must have stolen a crucial aspect of his dream theory from another Herr Popper and then artfully concealed this theft by a clever deception. The latter individual was a renowned Viennese savant named Josef Popper whose dream theory was plagiarized by Freud in a tortuous manner in order to vanquish that other Popper—Gisela's husband. As already summarized, years later he vanquished her husband again in fantasy by arranging for the mental torture and demise of Gizella Pálos's husband. Concerning both of those instances, it must be emphasized that Freud's revenge was not inflicted directly upon Gisela Popper's husband but upon two surrogates or stand-ins, just as once he had chopped hundreds of eels to shreds as a displacement of his fury towards Gisela herself.

The two surrogates upon whom Freud inflicted his fury and revenge (as stand-ins for Gisela Popper's husband) were: 1. the husband of Gizella Pálos and; 2. the Viennese savant Josef Popper, whose given name (Josef) tempted Freud both to identify with him and to become his rival, also emphasizing that his surname (Popper) matched the surname of Gisela Popper's spouse. It seems clear that circa 1897 Freud stole a precious "baby," a brilliant creation, from Josef Popper, partly as a displacement of his fury towards the husband of Gisela Popper. (In *Dark Side* I've explained in detail my reasons for that claim.) However, as another of his clever manipulations, Freud wrote a self-serving article (1932) which he used to deny that he stole Josef Popper's remarkable dream theory that was published in a brief fictionalized work in 1899. In *Dark Side* I've exposed many falsehoods that Freud told in his 1932 article to absolve himself of having plagiarized Popper's dream theory, which he had slyly incorporated as one of the cornerstones of *The Interpretation of Dreams*.

My basic thesis about these issues will now be summarized briefly (see *Dark Side* for details). Probably in the years 1895 to 1897 the philosopher Josef Popper formulated his novel dream theory which explains various dream distortions and anomalies as reflections of the dreamer's psychic conflicts concerning hidden feelings about sexuality, murder, revenge, dishonesty, greed, etc. Popper was a renowned philosopher and cult leader who openly shared his ideas with his Viennese followers, and it's likely that Freud purloined Popper's conception via one of those disciples. The dream concept that Popper created proved to be essential to Freud's formulation of his own ideas about dreams, and Ellenberger (1970) is one of many authors who have been quite gullible in simply accepting Freud's word that he did not plagiarize this key concept from Josef Popper.

The sly article (1932) which Freud wrote to absolve himself of this theft protested his innocence to a ludicrous extent, thereby hinting at his considerable guilt. Freud's "proof" which supported his assertions of innocence was the bold claim that he had not yet read Popper's "essay" of 1899, incorporating the essential dream concept, at the time that he wrote his dream book—with the further allegation that he and Popper had created this same idea independently of one another. Moreover, Freud demolished his own credibility by insisting that he had *not even known of the existence* of this renowned Viennese philosopher, Josef Popper, until many years after 1900, when he finally stumbled upon this savant's numerous books which (acknowledging that they were the great works of a brilliant man) he then sat down and read in their entirety. Allegedly, that's when he finally read Popper's dream theory, published in 1899, and realized that they had created the same remarkable dream concept "independently" of one another, at about the same period of time! Also, Freud alleged that despite his enormous affinity for Popper, and that both men had been citizens of Vienna for decades, he'd never arranged to meet this hero, fearing that

Popper might disagree with him on some issues.

Freud's claim that he had not known of the existence of the Viennese savant Josef Popper until many years after 1900 is as absurd as Freud's claim that the writings of Nietzsche could not have influenced his psychoanalytic ideas, allegedly because he had not read nor otherwise absorbed any of Nietzsche's work or ideas until his own essential theorizing had been completed. Like a child telling a flagrant lie, Freud added that his "proof" for this assertion was that he had *deliberately avoided* reading all of Nietzsche's work, in the early years of psychoanalysis, to ensure that he would not be influenced by any of Nietzsche's concepts. However, in a letter by Freud to A. Zweig of May 11, 1934 he finally admitted that circa 1885 his friend Josef Paneth had become attracted to Nietzsche's writings "and he used to write to me a lot about him." (Jones III, p. 460).

The lie that Freud concocted about his not having absorbed the concepts of Nietzsche is a staggering untruth, which shows his contempt for the intelligence of his readers. However, his modern followers have endorsed that lie repeatedly. They have insisted that Freud was a genius with encyclopedic knowledge, possessed of a nearly photographic memory, yet this great Austrian thinker had known almost nothing about Nietzschean concepts that Viennese schoolboys of average intelligence (prior to 1900) had absorbed in their adolescent years. Just as staggering a lie was Freud's assertion in 1932 that, prior to formulation of his dream book, he'd known nothing about Josef Popper's existence. In *Dark Side* I've explained why Freud must have known a great deal about Josef Popper and his writings *prior* to 1900. The basis for this assertion will become clearer in later paragraphs, as we make a brief review of the life and works of this Viennese sage.

Josef Popper (1838-1921) was born in Czechoslovakia, like Freud, and both men were Jews who spent almost all of their lives in Vienna and became leaders of small cults of loyal followers. As early as the late 1800s, Popper was quite famous in Vienna, especially among Jews, as a daring political philosopher and social reformer, inventor, a physicist who studied the flight of birds in the mold of Leonardo, a poet, and also a theorist concerning the nature of dreams. Fritz Wittels was one of the disciples of this Renaissance figure, and Wittels later became a follower of Freud, as well. Wittels wrote (1947) that because of the power of Popper's ideas, especially his social and political philosophies, and due to the attractiveness of his deeply humane personality, a growing circle or cult of disciples came to surround Josef Popper. As one of those admiring followers, Wittels wrote: "He was our father and our oracle."

Although Popper was born a Jew, like Freud, he did not exhibit Freud's messianic urges, and was not motivated to propogate his ideas and fame beyond the Vienna woods. Nevertheless, he was a remarkable man who became quite renowned within Vienna itself. Some of that public attention was due to his extensive writings on human rights and the absolute sanctity of the individual. Contrary to Freud's bitter viewpoints about humanity, Popper insisted upon the innate goodness of people. His social reform ideas emphasized the need for a "double economy" (modified socialism alongside a totally free economy!), which was designed to bring a complete end to poverty. He believed that thereafter "all other desirable qualifications of the individual would bloom automatically." Popper's great emphasis upon human rights and the incomparable value of each individual life was *not* narcissistic (Freud's accusation against him), but was an expression of Popper's heartfelt love for all God's creatures. In many respects, he was an unheralded forerunner of psychological theorists like Adler, Allport, Rogers, and Maslow who have championed the dignity of the individual, personal growth, and self-actualization. (It would be surprising if the Viennese personality theorist, Alfred Adler, had not been directly influenced by Popper.)

Numerous reasons have been cited in *Dark Side* to support my claim that Freud was lying when he said that, prior to 1900, he had not known of the existence of Josef Popper and his remarkable works, including his formulation of that critical dream concept (that Freud plagiarized). Allow me to mention just a few of my reasons for that claim. First, let's consider the relative fame of Freud and Popper in Vienna in 1897, the year when Popper probably was formulating his novel dream concept. In that year, at age 41, Freud had attained only a modicum of eminence in Vienna for his co-authorship of *Studies on Hysteria* with Breuer, and for a few minor efforts that included his short-lived seduction theory of hysteria. In comparison, in that year Popper was age 59 and his diverse political and philosophical writings already had made him famous in Vienna, and sometimes infamous because of his utterly frank work *about incest and about Oedipal themes*.

Wittels wrote that, during the days of "the old Austria," Popper had produced a controversial work of fiction titled *The Fomenting Force of a Secret*, which emphasized the power of the incest motive. The story was set in Florence during the 1400s and told about a woman who had incestuous relations with her adolescent son, causing them to be burned at the stake. Wittels stated that Popper described these sexual matters in a direct reportorial style "veiling nothing, leaving no room for ambiguity, one of the most daring attempts in world literature." The result was that Popper's book eventually was banned and "indignant members of parliament in old Austria demanded jail for the author." It seems obvious now that Freud in the 1890s did not have to look to ancient Greece for the inspiration leading to his theory of the Oedipus complex, since similar thoughts and feelings already lay close at hand, ripe for picking, in the intellectual and artistic life of old Vienna—particularly in the work of Josef Popper.

One could easily argue that in 1897 Josef Popper was the most famous Jewish figure in Vienna, as the Viennese would have judged such matters. Belatedly, Freud described him as a man of overwhelming wisdom, and called him "a great man, who was a thinker and a critic and at the same time a kindly humanitarian and reformer." Now we have just learned from Wittels that in his early years Popper was also a daring writer on sexual matters, a man who would risk imprisonment and public condemnation (like Freud, himself) in order to depict the power of the incest motive in a shocking oedipal relationship. Yet Freud knew nothing about Josef Popper? At one time, all of Vienna must have been buzzing about the banning of Popper's sexually outrageous book, with special concern about this in the Jewish community. Yet Freud knew nothing of him?

Grollman has reported (1965) that in 1886 Josef Popper published anonymously a treatise titled *First Bismarck and AntiSemitism*, attacking the anti-Jewish policies of the German chancellor and the anti-Semitic writings of Richard Wagner and other German notables. That Popper published his work anonymously does not diminish his great courage, since the political climate in that era could have provided a terrible penalty if he had published it openly, under his name. In any case, one can be sure that intellectual Viennese Jews in 1886, among themselves, had rather accurate ideas as to the probable authorship of this tract defending Jewry so daringly, and that they "knew" the name of their hero.

Isn't is fascinating to learn that Popper was such an eloquent and courageous opponent of Bismarck, since Jones has written that Bismarck was the only public figure against whom Freud had expressed death wishes? (Jones reported that in 1892 Freud expended great energy waiting in a street crowd to get a glimplse of this chancellor whom he hated so passionately— but whom Jacob Freud had identified with by changing his birthdate to coincide with Bismarck's!) So here we find another important issue, besides dreams and incest, providing an obvious connection between the minds of Freud and Popper—their vehement opposition to Bismarck. Probably every educated Jew in Vienna in the 1890s knew of Popper's anti-Bismarck efforts and arguments. But now it is claimed by Freud's supporters that he did not know anything about those efforts and knew *nothing* then about this courageous Jewish intellectual and humanitarian, Josef Popper.

Staunch supporters of Freud might dispute my assertion that he plagiarized Popper's dream theory by emphasizing that Popper never charged that said plagiarism had been committed. But that's not a very effective defense of Freud, since it ignores that not all creative persons are as rivalrous and ambitious as Freud was. According to Wittels' description of Popper's mentality, this loving philosopher had no personal or selfish interest in establishing himself as the originator of the dream-distortion theory. Wittels has characterized him as a self-effacing humanitarian who was "above" such a priority dispute, as follows: "Popper-Lynkeus was so far away from claiming any priority that he did not even mention his contribution in his autobiography of 1916. He did not consider it important." In this instance, Freud had chosen a victim of plagiarism who did not care to defend his literary rights, whereas a few years later when he assisted the plagiarism of Fliess's work, he encountered a fierce rebuttal from this former friend who was well-aware of Freud's capacity for such deceit.

There are additional reasons for believing that Freud plagiarized the dream theory of Josef Popper that are rooted in Freud's repeated uses of unconscious name magic. Many pages earlier, it was noted that Freud experienced feelings of deep anguish when his first sweetheart Gisela was married in 1875 to a Herr Popper. His obsession with Gisela was still reverberating in 1899 when he wrote about his early love for her in disguised fashion in "Screen Memories." That same obsession was reflected in the 1900s when name magic impelled him to engineer the breakup of Gizella Pálos's marriage (another Gisela P.), causing the death of her husband.

It seems obvious that in the 1890s Freud was still brooding about Gisela Popper, a woman who stimulated painful feelings by greeting him with cool indifference whenever they met on the streets of Vienna. Earlier, evidence was offered indicating that he maintained a strong irrational fixation on her first name, so one can expect that he had a similar intense sensitivity (and considerable hostility) towards her married name, Popper. Given that simple and logical expectation, we can surmise that in the 1890s Freud's antennae were attuned to any mention of the name Popper, more than to any other surname in Vienna belonging to a Jewish male.

Given that Josef Popper was a famous man in Vienna in 1897 whose name sometimes appeared in newspaper and magazine articles, and that Freud was acutely sensitized to the name Popper, it is unthinkable that he did not know about Josef Popper and his ideas in that year, as he later professed. To the contrary, one can readily assume that, because of his irrational feelings about Gisela's husband, Freud was powerfully motivated in the 1890s to "follow" closely the career of Josef Popper and to seek out information about this "rival's" latest ideas from mutual acquaintances (persons similar to Wittels). My thesis here is that Josef Popper had become a "surrogate rival" of Freud because of the inexorable name-connection relating him to Gisela's husband, and also because of rivalrous factors pertaining to his given name, Josef (the Biblical dream master).

By now it should be recognized that florid kinds of name magic were bubbling within Freud's psyche in the 1890s, perhaps fostered by his habitual ingestions of heavy doses of cocaine. And it's likely that he sought-out and stole Josef Popper's dream theory partly because of a displacement of his revengeful feelings towards Gisela Popper and her husband. In effect, the formula was: this Popper for *that* Popper, just as years earlier it had been—this Mathilde for *that* Mathilde—relating to his not-quite-accidental killing of the sulfonal patient. Later, with Ferenczi's help the formula allowed for a similar substitution of Gizella P. for Gisela P. (just as Freud admitted substituting Wilhelm S. for Wilhelm F.).

As was evidenced by the bizarre breakup of Gizella Pálos's marriage, it's clear that Freud wished urgently that he could somehow steal Gisela Popper away from her husband. He was not able to do that. But in the 1890s he worked out a temporary displacement of that kind of revenge. Instead, he located another Jew named Popper and stole a prized possession, a "baby" so to speak, from him. This was the theft of Popper's momentous creation: a theoretical/literary explanation of dream-distortion. (The next chapter will show that the year 1900 was amazing in terms of Freud's hunger for revenge towards many people, including his famous patient called Dora.)

Allow me to embellish some of the preceding ideas. It's my thesis that Freud filched the dream-distortion theory originated by Josef Popper, because this philosopher was a stand-in for Gisela's husband. Moreover, it seems plausible to me that Freud obtained the purloined dream theory prior to May 1897, when apparently he began the formal writing of his dream book. (He claimed that he spent four or five years laboring on the book, but probably that included a couple of early years when he was merely collecting dreams from those patients who were the pioneers of psychoanalysis.)

If I'm correct that Popper's dream theory was obtained prior to the formal writing of Freud's dream book, it's likely that this theft served to markedly clarify Freud's thinking about dream dynamics and greatly encouraged him to embark upon the writing of his book. In that case, one could hypothesize that a major inspiration for the dream book was derived from Freud's perverse desire to defeat Gisela's husband—as represented by his surrogate named Josef Popper. And all of this indicates that a great deal of dishonesty and irrationality were infused into the genesis of this "masterpiece," which resonates with my later thesis (and Puner's) that the dream book largely represented a veiled confession of sins by Freud.

Much more needs to be said about Freud's irrational fixations on Josef Popper's names. It's encouraging, by the way, that I'm not the only clinician who has been aware of those name-fixations. In Dr. Wittels' article correlating Freud with Josef Popper, his last paragraph tried to explain Freud's prolonged "dodging" of Popper in terms of fear of a father-figure, making reference to Freud's admission that he'd avoided making Popper's acquaintance in Vienna for decades despite his intense attraction to

Popper's written works. Moreover, in his final footnote Wittels indicated that there was an additional reason for Freud's fear of Popper. In that footnote, Wittels suggested that Freud might also have avoided Popper for decades *because of his fear of his first name Josef*, thereby pointing to name magic as a partial basis for Freud's motivation. To support this ideal Wittels cited the dream book where Freud emphasized "that he always stood in awe of the name Joseph, beginning with his own uncle Joseph and several other Josephs including the biblical interpreter of dreams." (Probably, another reason why Freud "dodged" Popper for decades was due to his fear that the old man might rebuke him for his plagiarism.)

The use that Wittels made of his observation about name magic needs further discussion. Earlier, I cited reasons for believing that Freud was enmeshed irrationally in a strong rivalry with Josef Popper, in connection with name magic pertaining to Gisela Popper and her spouse. Now we have an additional reason, with regard to name magic, for Freud's irrational rivalry with Josef Popper: the fact that Popper was a master of dream theory, as had been promised "magically" by his Biblical given name, Josef! It's possible that Popper himself was involved in an aspect of name-compulsion concerning his given name, as evidenced by his brief entry into the arena of dream theory. In any case, the correlation of his given name Josef with the creation of a pioneering dream theory would have generated monumentally rivalrous feelings in Freud and great temptations to plagiarize, since this profound narcissist insisted on being the foremost Josef in the asylum.

Wittels was not enough attuned to name magic to consider that Freud was irrationally fixated upon both of Josef Popper's names. Already we've seen that Freud was fixated on "Popper" because that was also the married surname of his beloved Gisela. But there was another compelling reason why he was fixated on that surname, a strong oedipal reason. The name Popper has an obvious connotation of "father," because of its strong phonetic and written similarities with the term "papa." So, in wishing to steal Herr Popper's wife (Gisela), Freud was enmeshed in an intense oedipal rivalry (this reasoning now allowing us to confirm Wittels' general notion that Freud was oedipally involved with Josef Popper). These rivalrous aspects of name magic also were carried forward into his rivalries with Josef Popper and with the husband of Gizella Pálos, which culminated in the latter's death.

It seems likely that by 1897 Josef Popper, a revered cult leader and charismatic father-figure, was a man whose writings, ideas, and personality were quite well-known to Sigmund Freud. Since Popper had written about incest and oedipal themes in daring ways, and thereby had stirred great public controversy in Vienna, he was exactly the kind of rebellious figure, willing and able to challenge middle-class morality, whom Freud held in highest esteem. But Popper's achievements and his fame in Vienna were bound to have unleashed Freud's rivalrous feelings, as well. In the preceding decade, the same thing had happened regarding his rivalrous feelings for the eminent socialist physician, Dr. Viktor Adler. Freud's peculiar way of defeating this rival (whom he once denounced in a public meeting) was to occupy the man's former apartment and to live there for 45 years—a capturing of his castle. With the rival named Josef Popper, the means that Freud used to satisfy his rivalry was more infamous: a clever theft of the man's dream-distortion theory probably obtained by word-of-mouth from mutual acquaintances of his and Popper's. (Consider that Freud's fantasized rivalry with the renowned psychiatrist and neurologist named Flechsig was also based on quite irrational factors, perhaps including aspects of name magic, and that Freud expropriated some of this man's ideas, though not to the extent of plagiarizing them.)

And there is another strong reason why in 1897 Freud would have experienced intense oedipal rivalry towards Popper, as well as desires to steal his prized possession. That relates to the fact that in October 1896 Freud had experienced the death of his own father, Jacob, who had been the target of Sigmund's lifelong death wishes, per Dr. Schur's biography (1972). Earlier, I suggested that compulsive name magic had caused Freud to identify his father unconsciously with the biblical Jacob (allowing Sigmund to identify with Josef, the interpreter of dreams). And when his father died, Freud's irrational fears of retribution from his father were eased, and he was then stimulated by oedipal rivalry to steal and embellish the ancient Jacob's dream thesis which had indicated generally that dreams are produced by wishes. In this same time-period, soon after his father's death, he was again impelled by the interaction of name magic and oedipal rivalry to purloin a second important dream theory from another great father-figure: the dream-distortion theory originated by Josef Popper.

One final look should be taken at my hypothesis that Freud was directed unconsciously by oedipal motives to create his dream book because of the recency of his father's death. In the preface to its second edition, he wrote that only after completing the book did he learn that it had a subjective significance for him: "It was, I found, a portion of my own self-analysis, my reaction to my father's death . . . " He called this a "poignant loss," thereby denying the existence of insistent death wishes that he harbored for this man whom he had regarded as a failure and a coward unwilling to defend himself against a gentile's shameful insults. Actually, Freud was correct that the dream book was created partly as a reaction to his father's death. But most likely it was germinated by the invidious oedipal motives that have already been suggested, mixed with irrational *and* justified feelings of guilt. (Perhaps his oedipal guilt and identification with Oedipus was stronger than is true of most other men, because in childhood he had assumed that Jacob and nanny were married, in effect were his parents, and then had had a sexual encounter with her—the equivalent of having sex with his mother.)

Another reason exists for believing that Freud's murderous oedipal feelings towards his father constituted a primary stimulus for the creation both of the dream book and the early stages of psychoanalytic therapy. Those early developments in psychoanalysis were most closely associated with Freud's work involving his first analytic patient Emma Eckstein and the unnecessary nasal surgery that almost killed her. In the period 1895-1896 when Emma was suffering the brunt of Freud's deepest irrationalities, that brutal episode overlapped with the increasing decline in Jacob Freud's health leading to his death.

My emphasis here is that Freud's destructiveness towards Emma Eckstein was correlated in time with his feelings about his father's physical decline and death, and that there was probably a causal connection in Freud's psyche between Jacob's death and Emma's near-death. Recall that some previous material suggested that Freud chose Emma to become the foundation of his innovative therapy, psychoanalysis, largely because of name magic pertaining to her surname, whose meaning is cornerstone. As a corollary, it's likely that powerful death wishes *towards the father* underlay his creation of psychoanalysis, as was also the case soon thereafter with his theft of Popper's dream-distortion concept which served as a stolen foundation for Freud's dream theory.

Having made an exhaustive historical survey of dream research in the 1800s indicating that almost all of Freud's dream notions had already been discovered prior to the birth of his dream book, Ellenberger (1970) then left Freud with only a few items of dream innovation that would entitle him to some claim of originality on this topic. Perhaps foremost among them was the dream-distortion theory which Ellenberger believed had been discovered independently by Freud and Josef Popper. Ellenberger quite trustingly proclaimed that: " . . . Freud certainly did not draw his theory from him"— referring to Popper. However, Ellenberger did not offer any evidence at all to support his contention that Freud had not "borrowed" from the dream-distortion theory of Josef Popper. Why then should either he or Freud be believed, since neither has offered any kind of supporting evidence, in comparison with the previously cited evidence indicating, quite massively, that Freud did plagiarize the work of Josef Popper on dreams. Concerning the dream book's worldwide fame, are there some readers who will now begin to wonder what is the genuine basis for the catchy label: "Freud's great masterpiece?"

In all fairness, let's take one final look at Ellenberger's and Freud's claims that the dream-distortion theory was produced *independently* by

Popper and Freud in Vienna, sometime prior to the end of the century. To begin, an emphasis will be placed upon the period 1897-1898, since that can be regarded roughly as the gestation period for Freud's dream book (evidently he began the formal writing of the book in May 1897, per his letter to Fliess of 5/16/'97), and for Popper's short story that capsulized his dream-distortion theory. Census figures for that era given by Ellenberger indicate that the Jewish population of Vienna was then about 138,000 souls. In *Dark Side* I've estimated that there were around 50,000 Jewish males in Vienna of adult age, and that the Jewish intelligentsia (professors, physicians, poets, philosophers, etc.) probably numbered no more than 5,000 Jewish men in the professional and intellectual life of Vienna.

Of those 5000 outstanding Jewish males in the Vienna of 1897, we can estimate that there was an intellectual elite of perhaps 50 or fewer who were men of highly creative ideas and accomplishments. In this elite group, one would include the names not only of Josef Popper, who had already written remarkable and controversial works, but also the names of Sigmund Freud, Josef Breuer, Sigmund Exner, Arthur Schnitzler, and a few other eminent men.

What is now seen as utterly astounding is that two of those 50 Jewish males, in that Viennese intellectual elite, created the same complex dream-distortion theory *independently* of one another in or about the year 1897. Do you believe in that sheer coincidence, considering the nearly familial closeness of that Jewish community? Well, neither do I. But hundreds of psychoanalysts throughout the world claim that they do believe it, or at least remain silent about their skepticism.

Perhaps they can maintain their faith in Freud's integrity by citing the mere *possibility* that the two dream-distortion theories of Popper and Freud could have been produced independently and almost simultaneously. They may argue that historically such a co-occurrence of major scientific discoveries is not that unusual. An obvious rebuttal is that this has occurred in the physical sciences, when scientists with common credentials who pursue similar efforts and goals have shared a pool of scientific data that has made the time ripe for the emergence of a particular discovery. Then it becomes understandable that, within weeks or months of one another, two similar labs at opposite ends of the world sometimes have reported an identical scientific breakthrough. But surely that would not explain how an "independent co-occurrence" materialized in the same locale (Vienna), at about the same time, with two members of the same small ethnic community, concerning a complex dream theory that was supposedly discovered "independently" by a maverick neurologist and a philosophic writer of short stories and poetry. A far better explanation for this particular co-occurrence is plagiarism, in my opinion.

As stated earlier, my contention is that Freud probably obtained information about Josef Popper's new dream theory in 1897, or near that time, from mutual acquaintances of theirs. Some analytic readers can object that perhaps it was the other-way-around, and perhaps Popper received his dream theory from Freud's friends, with Freud being the true originator, and a victim of plagiarism. But Popper did not try to "dodge" Freud for decades in Vienna, and it was Popper who published the idea first. Moreover, anyone who makes a thoughtful study of Josef Popper's essay "Dreaming Like Waking" (1899) will find it almost impossible to believe that he expropriated the dream-distortion theory contained therein, from Freud or from anyone else. The simple story that he composed strikes one as an utterly unique and honest expression of Popper's own glowing personality, and the description of the hero's unusual dream processes seems an authentic autobiographical account of the author's own defenseless style of dreaming.

Besides, Josef Popper has not acquired a reputation as a plagiarist, whereas Freud has richly earned an indelible label of "plagiarist" concerning persuasive claims that he filched the ideas of Fliess, Janet, Moll, Neitzsche, Schopenhauer, Stekel, Groddeck, Spielrein—and others. That Freud plagiarized Popper's dream-distortion theory will seem quite plausible and probable to anyone who carefully reads his final letters to Fliess, in which he tried desperately to plagiarize his friend's bisexuality theory and then, when he was caught red-handed, tried to excuse his intended theft by alleging that he'd been an innocent victim of amnesia. Likewise, readers should review my companion volumes for accounts of Freud's nefarious assistance of Otto Weininger's plagiarism of Fliess's bisexuality theory, which probably was a key causative factor in the suicide of that unstable young man. Similarly, readers will recognize the relevance of Ernest Jones's surprisingly frank claim (Jones, III, p. 191) that Freud perversely assisted a patient of his (Dr. Jekels) to plagiarize a major work-in-progress by *Jones himself*—causing Jones to entirely drop this project on which he'd invested two years of his time.

Previous pages have suggested that some of Freud's magical name-series were capable of producing destructive or even lethal effects for persons whose names are found in such name-series. For example, we've explored the uncanny connections between the given names of Gisela Fluss and Gizella Pálos and learned how this name magic probably provoked Freud to punish the latter's innocent husband, causing him to suffer great anguish and death (as the surrogate for Gisela's husband, Herr Popper, in Freud's mind).

There is also the strong possibility that Gisela Fluss's surname had generated a name-series that included, among others, the names of Fleischl and Fliess. In *Fatal Freud* I've provided much material about Freud's very ambivalent relationship with his "friend" Fleischl, whom he professed to love and admire intensely, but whom he helped to "cure" of his painful illness by provoking this man's death by an overdose of cocaine. Concerning Fliess, we've already noted the great ambivalence that Freud held for this man, and we reviewed Swales' data suggesting that Freud planned to murder this friend during their final meeting, at Achensee, in that year of madness and revenge, 1900.

Likewise, in *Dark Side* I've discussed extensively that the given name of Mathilde Breuer, having absorbed the secret hatred that Freud felt for this woman and her husband, was probably transferred in a name-series to Freud's sulfonal patient named Mathilde, whom he killed via an "incautious" dose of that drug. Similarly, in the present volume I've noted that the given name of Margarethe Breuer probably was involved in a lethal name-series that helped provoke Freud's mishandling of the case of Margit Kremzir in 1900, leading suddenly to her suicide by hanging. Also, there is the possibility that the given name of Dr. Viktor Adler, whom Freud attacked verbally and quite viciously in his youth, was the template for a lethal name-series which helped promote Freud's gross mistreatment of Dr. Victor Tausk, soon precipitating his suicide, as told by Roazen's book (1969).

Furthermore, we've seen that the given name of Emma Eckstein (as a reversal pertaining to the word *Amme*, or wet-nurse), and the meaning of her surname ("cornerstone"), pointed to the name and identity of his Freiberg nanny—indicating that Emma and the nanny who "betrayed" Freud were connected by a subtle name-series, in the childish regions of his mind. This suggests that a lethal name-series was implicated in Freud's destructive acts towards Emma that almost killed her, and permanently disfigured her lovely face. Perhaps there was also a lethal element in the identical meaning ("fleece") connecting the surnames of Drs. Fliess and Schur, considering that Freud made a clear arrangement ensuring that the latter would become his "executioner."

In the next chapter there are some other fascinating name-series in Freud's life that I will be explaining. At the present time, however, I'd like to discuss another remarkable name-series that requires us first to recall what was presented in the first chapter concerning criminality in the Freud family and the well-publicized imprisonment of Sigmund's uncle Josef. Surely, he was subjected to vicious teasing over months and years from schoolmates who razzed him about that uncle—the "jailbird" serving ten years in prison who shared his surname. In his dream book (p. 240), he explained that his repeated distortion of surnames (the names of Brücke, Fleischl, etc.) in his own dreams were like acts of retribution by him for the "countless occasions" when his own name (Freud) had been "the victim of feeble witticisms." Though he did not clarify that remark, no doubt he was referring to repeated teasings about his own surname in childhood, partly the sexual connotations of his name but also teasing that related to the criminal implications that accrued to his surname due to its associations with the name of the infamous Josef Freud.

To a sensitive boy like Sigmund, who had been led to believe from an early age that he was destined for greatness and the world's admiration, the disgrace and ridicule that accompanied his uncle's notoriety in Vienna must have produced an extremely painful shock to the boy's proud ego. Krüll suggested (1986) that his "militaristic phase" seems to have begun in that same era, generating his identifications with famous conquerors like Napoleon, Alexander the Great, Hannibal, and many others. She made this provocative point: "It was as if he had set out to capture the bourgeois world ..." I would alter that remark to indicate that he'd set out to *defeat and punish* that straight-laced, bourgeois world that had condemned him moralistically for his uncle's offense. Henceforth, he would secretly identify with his uncle's "disregard for conventional morality", and use his daring intellectual powers to subvert and defeat bourgeois traditions and thought, exemplified finally in his creation of the revolutionary creed and movement called Psychoanalysis.

Young Sigmund's resentful reaction to his uncle's notoriety, and the cruel teasings relating thereto, probably helped to initiate and perpetuate his lifelong hatred of Vienna. His countless remarks denigrating Vienna and its citizens have usually been explained as his response to anti-Semitic currents or to his dislike of certain parochial attitudes among the Viennese. It's just as likely, however, that his hostility to the city and its people arose with great strength and persistence during that early gymnasium period when he was subjected to humiliating taunts about the criminality in his family— emphasizing that Josef's sentencing and imprisonment occurred in Vienna, accompanied by much newspaper publicity about his crime. Despite Freud's ill-concealed contempt for Vienna, he remained tenaciously in that city for 78 years, creating many works there and fighting many battles with the world and with countless adversaries. It was as if he were determined to achieve a glorious fame in that place, thereby forcing a grudging acknowledgment from the city that had mocked his name in childhood and in later years as well.

Besides generating his lifelong hostility towards Vienna, Freud's reactions to childhood teasing about his uncle's criminality probably had much to do with his general hatred and contempt for his fellow man. One author characterized him as one of the great haters in history, a view that receives general confirmation from the fact that Freud took the time to maintain a "hate list" of his enemies. In a work of 1925, Carl Jung noted that every word of Freud's speech was "loaded" with bitterness, and later (1963, p. 152) he hinted that bitterness was Freud's primary characteristic in life. (Think of his bitter and vicious expression when Paneth made him a large gift of money.) Jung added that Freud's bitterness reflected the attitudes of a person who felt "entirely misunderstood," and who retaliated with a manner that said: "If they do not understand, they must be stamped into hell." (Consider his identification with Satan.)

The present author's extensive research into Freud's personality has stimulated strong agreement with both of the above characterizations of Freud, as seen in an entire chapter of a companion volume that is weighted with remarkable evidences of his bitter feelings of hostility towards mankind generally, and against many specific individuals as well. Indeed, that virulent hostility of Freud's had such a primitive force that one readily suspects that it had childhood sources, including bitter feelings deriving from the great humiliation he had suffered due to uncle Josef's crime and notoriety.

The fact that Jacob Freud was greatly disturbed by the arrest and imprisonment of his brother Josef is confirmed by Sigmund's account of his father's hair turning grey overnight. Undoubtedly, Jacob's anxiety about the matter could not be prevented from being absorbed by the sensitive child, particularly since it's believed that father and son were often in close contact till the boy's ninth year, owing to the fact that Jacob was frequently his tutor prior to the advent of formal schooling. The anxiety which young Sigmund absorbed in response to uncle Josef's trauma must have been quite troubling and persistent, for it seems to have had the capacity to generate his uneasy dream about uncle Josef and his yellow beard, sometime in Freud's forties. And perhaps his susceptibility to generating magical name-series will provide further evidence that his strong emotions concerning uncle Josef's incarceration were carried forward into much later years of his life.

A very dramatic name-series will now be introduced by reminding the reader about my earlier summary of a Vienna newspaper's account of the February 21, 1866 trial of Josef Freud for attempting to pass counterfeit rubles. Recall that the newspaper reported that Josef Freud's trouble with the law began when he sought help from a commission agent in finding a buyer for some forged rubles, this man seeming to cooperate by accepting the tainted bills and later "betraying" Josef by taking the bills to the police and by then arranging to have him caught red-handed in the act of transferring additional counterfeit bills. It is highly significant that this man who betrayed Josef Freud and cost him a ten-year prison sentence was named Simon *Weiss*, since it is quite likely that young Sigmund read this hated and despised name Weiss in that newspaper report, and never forgot that this was the name of his uncle's betrayer.

The thesis being posited here is that the accumulated bitter resentment towards the surname of Simon Weiss in the mind of young Sigmund Freud generated a largely malevolent name-series. Moreover, it's likely that the second person in this name-series of Freud's was his "friend" Dr. Nathan Weiss who hanged himself (on 9/13/'83) in a public bath only ten days after returning from his honeymoon. On September 16, 1883 Freud wrote an extremely long letter to his fiancée Martha in which he made a complex analysis of Weiss's very undesirable personality. He described the dead man's character as having so many grave conflicts and flaws—being subject to "serious emotional upheavals," pathological self-love, feelings of gigantic self-importance, ruthlessness, great difficulty in forming friendships, incessant restlessness and the high energy output of "a raving maniac"—that it had seemed highly predictable to Freud, and as inevitable as the plots of many weak novels, that he should come to some sort of self-destructive end.

It's advisable to read carefully the analysis of Nathan Weiss's very pathological personality that Freud described in his letter to Martha and then to learn about the abominable conditions that had existed in Weiss's family situation, including lack of love and bitter poverty along with the incessant demands of a brilliant father whom Freud characterized as "a very hard, bad, brutal man" and whom Weiss called "a monster." After reading this material, it becomes clearer that probably Freud *was* able to predict long before the event (as he told Martha) the inevitable "downfall" of Nathan Weiss. Apparently, this predictability was strengthened when Freud assessed the typically undesirable outcomes of Nathan's many brothers. For as Freud phrased it, most of them "went to the dogs." In the final months of his life, an even clearer indication of Nathan's self-destructive potential surfaced in the six months prior to his death when one of his brothers shot himself.

In my view, Freud's relationship with Nathna Weiss was a strangely pathological one. In Freud's long letter to Martha, he remarked that he'd been the only friend that Nathan Weiss had made and that the man had even "grown fond" of him. So we must ask ourselves why this man, whose personality was allegedly so repugnant that Freud described him as being "incapable of friendship," nevertheless managed to become the friend of Sigmund Freud—telling Freud that he was permanently at his disposal and, in the event of his death, would make Freud *his heir?* My answer to that question is that probably Freud unconsciously was motivated to manipulate the relationship between Weiss and himself in ways that ensured Weiss's "fond" feelings for him and the consolidation of their friendship (not ignoring possible homosexual factors). And what was it that caused Freud to be attracted to this man whom he described as having an insufferable personality that repelled almost all other persons, and a character that had hardly any redeeming qualities? Apparently Freud was attracted to this man due to a powerful unconscious sense of *retribution*, stoked by a dim awareness of his urgent potentials for self-destruction and the fact that his surname, Weiss, was the same as that of the man who had betrayed his uncle Josef and brought public shame to the Freud family—Simon Weiss.

Jones wrote euphemistically (I, p. 166) that Nathan Weiss's character was "eccentric" and stated that "Freud was perhaps the only one drawn to him," without giving a clue as to *why* Freud was the only man attracted to this repulsive fellow whose primary characteristic he described as pathological self-love, bordering on self-adulation. An equally unpsychological and unperceptive stance was assumed by Jones when he merely hinted that Freud had formed a peculiar identification with his "friend" Weiss. For Jones wrote in his bland fashion that: "It was the death of Weiss, a promising neurologist, that emboldened Fraud to decide on a neurological career *in his place*." (Emphasis added.) Unfortunately, Jones did not add to that preceding information, which gave only a quiet intimation of Freud's uncanny identification with this dead neurologist, that he'd also put himself "in his place" in another way. This refers to Freud's weird insistence on moving into and occupying the former apartment of the dead man. Moreover, while writing his fiancée Martha about that decision, he mentioned his lack of fear of Weiss's ghost in a manner which suggested that much denial was operative in this counterphobic bravado of his.

Since it was Freud who conjured up the issue of Nathan Weiss's ghost, it's time to remind ourselves of his claim that persons who express concerns about a ghost are likely to harbor strong feelings of guilt towards the deceased. My explanation for Freud's presumed guilty feelings regarding Weiss's death is based on the assumption that he had harbored intense unconscious death-wishes towards this "friend" that were generated largely by hostile feelings which were triggered by his surname, in relation to the name of that despised betrayer Simon Weiss. Freud's death-wishes towards Nathan Weiss are evidenced by the extremely repulsive characterization of his personality that he painted for Martha, going on for pages without giving any positive statements about Weiss, despite that the man had hanged himself only three days earlier and that a real friend would be expected tearfully to find at least a few positive, perhaps loving, remarks to make about the deceased. Indeed, Freud's picture of Weiss's character was so bleak and ugly that he may have been exaggerating the man's faults to convince her, and himself, that his suicide had resulted inevitably from his tragic flaws and could not be blamed on others, particularly Sigmund Freud.

That last thought is related to my view that perhaps Freud was responsible, in some ways, for helping to precipitate Weiss's suicide (consonant with the emphasis in my companion volume that he helped provoke the suicides of various other persons, also). If his initial, irrational attraction to Weiss stemmed from hostile factors connected with his surname along with sensitivity to the man's self-destructive potentials, we can surmise that Freud's earnest digging into and analyzing of Weiss's pathological personality structure was not intended to benefit this "friend," but to harm him—in this era prior to Freud's analytic work.

In his letter to Martha, he indicated that the crux of Weiss's problems leading to his suicide was that his new wife had shown even before the wedding that she did not really love him. According to Freud, this showed that it was foolish and dangerous for Weiss's mental equilibrium that he should insist that the marriage must take place. Here, Freud portrayed himself as the wise and helpful counselor of the older man who, just before the wedding "implored him to accept the fact that she did not love him," and had suggested that Weiss should take a trip by himself to attain a more detached composure. In my opinion, however, we can definitely not accept Freud's implication that his counseling of Weiss was intended to benefit him. It's more likely that a transference of his irrational hatred for *Simon Weiss* came to the fore and generated questionable advice by Freud that greatly upset and confused Weiss's mind, thereby helping to provoke suicide in the same manner that his perverse "assistance" to Victor Tausk helped to precipitate his suicide, just after WWI. (Notice that 1883 was the heyday of Freud's indiscriminate prescribing of huge doses of cocaine to colleagues and friends, provoking the deaths of various persons, so one wonders whether Freud likewise prescribed awesome doses of cocaine for Weiss that stimulated irrational thoughts, depression, and suicide.)

When I suggested earlier that Freud had made an identification with Nathan Weiss, I was intimating a rather perverse aspect of identification in this case. It appears that Freud's lengthy characterization of Weiss was of a quite grotesque, if not monstrous, personality—but many of us will recognize that these were also descriptions of some of Freud's worst personality traits. It appears that he exaggerated the man's faults (partly impelled by his hatred of *Simon* Weiss) to the extent of creating Mr. Hyde in his repugnant friend, which then enabled the Hyde-aspect of Freud to identify itself with the "dark side" of this troubled man. In helping to precipitate Weiss's suicide (or at least in strongly wishing to do so), Freud helped to take his friend's life as a substitution for his tortured desire to take his own life—Freud's suicidal impulses being stressed in a companion volume. In that way, he took revenge on Simon Weiss by supplanting both him and the "friend" who was magically melded with him, Nathan Weiss. In effect, he supplanted the deceased Nathan Weiss by taking his place as a neurologist and, more primitively, by occupying the man's quarters (just as later he fulfilled hostile impulses by occupying the quarters of Dr. Viktor Adler at Berggasse 19). Perhaps Freud's identification with the Biblical hero Jacob was connected with these peculiar supplanting behaviors, for this was the meaning of Jacob's name ("supplanter") and was also reflected in his rivalrous actions towards his twin brother Esau and his kinsman Laban.

Remember that we have pursued the name-series involving the name Weiss, because it helps confirm that Sigmund Freud's childhood animosity towards Simon Weiss, his uncle Josef's betrayer, was carried forward into much later years of Freud's life when that murderous hostility was presumably transferred to some other persons named Weiss. Therefore, it seems to be relevant to the suicide-by-hanging of Nathan Weiss in 1883. A similar observation is that it also seems relevant to the suicide-by-hanging of Freud's patient named Margit Kremzir whose maiden surname was *Weiss de Szurda*. My previous discussion of invidious name factors in her case had suggested Freud's probable venom towards her given name, as a variant of the name Margarethe, since at that time he was furious that the marriage of Margarethe Breuer was promoting a schism between him and his beloved friend Fliess. Now we see why the maiden name of this extremely vulnerable patient (who was treated for two weeks by Freud and then hanged herself in a Vienna hotel room soon after he "dismissed" her) was far more potent than her given name in eliciting Freud's unconscious animosity towards her—in those months of his extreme mental instability when he acknowledged to Fliess that he was on the brink of madness and felt that his patients were his torturers.*

Another name in the same name-series might have been that of Dr. Edoardo Weiss, who was for decades the leading psychoanalyst in Italy and, for that reason, had a close relationship with Freud. Despite Dr. Weiss's writings which show him to be a strong admirer of Freud's ideas and character, Eissler has written (1983, pp. 75-6) about Weiss's ambivalence towards Freud. He referred to Weiss's claim that when Victor Tausk (whom Weiss knew very well) had fallen into deep depression upon returning from military service after WW I, Freud's abandonment of this close colleague had led directly to his suicide.

Eissler then cited the claim that Dr. Edoardo Weiss even had called Freud the "murderer" of Tausk, but Eissler tried to dismiss this accusation in a facile manner as reflecting the Italian's ambivalence towards the master, "as happened not infrequently to aging analysts who had been in personal contact with Freud and owed him a great debt." (Eissler is a leading advocate of the cunning idea that serious criticism of Freud is very likely to be reflective

---

*Recall that he also called these patients his "victims," which may have had special applicability to Margit Kremzir.

of the critic's pathologies, not Freud's—following the pattern laid down by Freud himself.) My own suggestion here is that Freud made Dr. Weiss a link in this name-series due to an unconscious sensing that this supporter would have the courage and honesty to criticize him severely, if warranted. In effect, this Italian analyst was positioned by Freud to "betray" him just as Simon Weiss, who had seemed to be uncle Josef's supporter but then turned out to be an honest man, had "betrayed" that psychopathic uncle of Sigmund's. Ergo, for one of the later names in this remarkable name-series Freud may have arranged unconsciously to find a man called Weiss who would imitate the earliest one (Simon) by incriminating him, in a murder—an offense even more vile than uncle Josef's crime (repeating the theme of needing covertly to confess his crimes).

That Freud was not willing to end this name-series with a "Weiss" who would condemn him is suggested by his choice of a woman to be his secretary in the 1930s, in the era when his declining health required that she act towards him almost as if she were his benevolent nanny. This was the woman named Julia Weiss. From this symbolic nanny, Freud could be assured of receiving the total love and absolution for his crimes that he desperately needed as he approached the Day of Final Judgment.

The above material concerning Dr. Weiss's alleged claim that Freud had been, in effect, the murderer of Victor Tausk prompts me to summarize accusations of this general nature. All of the persons who have made claims about Freud's lethal behaviors or intentions already have been cited in previous chapters, so I will just mention them or their ideas briefly.

First, there have been four persons who have made quite direct accusations about Freud's murderous behaviors or intentions. These persons include Fliess, Peter Swales (regarding the Achensee episode), Eric Miller, and the present author. Three persons have made less direct accusations of this sort, including Puner, Roazen, and Dr. Weiss. Recall that Puner, in discussing Freud's identification with Hamlet, suggested that Freud possessed the mind of a murderer. According to Eissler's writings, Roazen gave a rather clear indication in *Brother Animal* that he regarded Freud as the equivalent of Victor Tausk's murderer. Likewise, we now have Eissler's suggestion that Dr. Edoardo Weiss, who was close to Victor Tausk, regarded Freud as the equivalent of Tausk's murderer.

Three persons can be regarded as having hinted at Freud's murderous potentials, including Dr. Schur, Dr. Eissler, and Freud himself. Dr. Schur indicated that Freud suffered from a "Cain complex" (strong fratricidal impulses) and emphasized his extensive death-wishes towards family members and others, but with no suggestion that Freud had actualized his homicidal urges. Dr. Eissler expressed an astonished awareness that Freud had identified with the murderer Macbeth, but offered no further thoughts about the master's lethal potentials. Finally, Freud hinted at his own homicidal urges in his discussion of the Hollthurn dream when he acknowledged his firm identification with a patient who harbored intense concerns that he might be committing multiple murders during amnesic states.

The above list of names helps to establish that the present writer is not the only person who has pointed to strong homicidal potentials in Freud. Admittedly, my proposals about his suicide/ murder complex and claims that Emanuel and John Freud were murdered go considerably beyond the claims of other authors—except, perhaps, for Eric Miller.

Chapter Seven

1900: Freud's Madness, Revenge, and Dora's Case

Freud's Revenge

Several additional name complexes now require our consideration. They concern Freud's strange uses of magical name-series to foster his longterm needs for revenge that culminated in the suicides of two persons, and might easily have cost the life of a third person by suicide. In these analyses of additional name-series, I hope to show some remarkable connections interrelating the suicide of Freud's patient Margit Kremzir in 1900, the suicide of the young man named Otto Weininger (whom Freud used as a pawn to punish Wilhelm Fliess's infidelity), and the near-suicide of Freud's patient called Dora whom he treated for alleged hysteria in the last few months of 1900.

Since I will argue that Freud's prolonged and bitter feelings of revenge were crucially involved with all three of those persons—Mrs. Kremzir, Weininger, and Dora—I will first have to provide some background information about Freud's extremely revengeful urges, in subsequent paragraphs. All of this material about Freud's persistent desires for revenge, over long periods of time, is worth reviewing, since it will help us to understand data found in later chapters concerning his longterm revenge motives that eventually led to the presumed murders of Emanuel and John Freud.

It's reasonable to suggest that the destructive cornerstone for all of Freud's complicated revenge motives was layed in "the Freiberg catastrophe." The strange circumstances of the loss of his nanny, which he originally perceived as her murder by the males in his family, materialized undying feelings of revenge towards his kinsmen, and probably even towards nanny for faithlessly "abandoning" him. In his earliest years, the story about his urinating in his parents' bed—which provoked Jacob to verbally assault him with the prediction that he'd never amount to anything in life, was another factor in Sigi's revengeful feelings towards father-figures who "betrayed" him—intensified by his belief that his father was a coward, in that incident when his father's hat was knocked off by a Christian bully. In late childhood another major source of Sigmund's revengeful motives was the occasion of his uncle Josef's prison sentence, which was highly publicized in Vienna's newspapers. The catcalls by peers at school must have led to unbearable feelings of shame and anger in this sensitive boy, precipitating diffuse desires for revenge towards the self-righteous citizens of Vienna, and the world in general.

One can imagine that the vicious legacy of anti-Semitism in Vienna, which seemed to be suffered silently and without much complaint by Freud, was another source of very revengeful feelings in him that his self-analysis never really uncovered nor helped to alleviate. Relevant to the last point were his suppressed feelings of revenge towards Christians as revealed by his analysis of the "aliquis"-forgetting, which has been discussed by Swales (1982), and by his identification with Hannibal's destructiveness towards Rome, the citadel of ancient Christian values. Some writers have suggested that the motto of Freud's dream book, which hints at the raising of demonic forces from hell to punish humanity, reflects his generalized feelings of revenge; but when it is related to Juno's bitter vengefulness against Aeneas *and Rome*, it again encodes Freud's vengeful feelings towards Christianity and the Catholic nanny who betrayed him.

Previous pages have shown the intensity of Freud's revenge motives towards Gisela (Fluss) Popper and her husband, and towards Emma Eckstein whom he nearly managed to kill. Since those women were revenants of his nanny, we see that he bore murderous feelings of revenge, as well as love, for that maternal figure. Likewise, he harbored strong revengeful feelings towards his mother-in-law, Emmaline Bernays. Jones wrote (I, pp. 119-123) that during Freud's engagement period he developed extremely hostile emotions for Martha's mother and her brother Eli and insisted that his fiancée should "withdraw all affection from them—this on the ground that they were his enemies, so that she should share his hatred of them." At one point, Sigmund wrote Martha a letter stating that he would temporarily withdraw his vengeance towards her mother, saying that: "I have put a good deal more of my wrath in cold storage which will be dished up some day. I am young, tenacious, and active: I shall pay all my debts, including this one." His wording informs us that he had the capacity to wait many years to fulfill his murderously vengeful motives, which is probably relevant to the grim fates of Emanuel and John Freud.

In a companion volume I have discussed at length some truly horrific examples of Freud's acting-out of his revengeful motives that were connected with his murder/suicide complexes. In particular, my materials include the factor of revenge that provoked Freud to help trigger the suicides of his colleagues Victor Tausk and Herbert Silberer, and that of Otto Weininger. Similarly, I have gone into considerable detail to support my strong suspicions about the suicide of Freud's strange friend Nathan Weiss, and Freud's possible complicity in that event. Likewise, I've explained how Freud's vengeful motives played a covert role in the "help" he gave to his friend and colleague, Fleischl von Marxow, eventually provoking his death via an overdose of cocaine—which might have had psychological relevance to Freud's attempt to destroy the reputation of his deceased friend, Josef Paneth. Also, I've elaborated upon the strange deaths of Freud's friends Abraham, Ferenczi, and Rank and the quite subtle roles that Freud's vengeful motives played in the endings of their lives.

A considerable number of Freud's letters to Fliess from 1894 to 1900 reveal his increasing hatred, fear, and revengeful feelings towards his mentor and collaborator, Josef Breuer. The growing estrangement between Freud and Breuer was well-advanced in March 1896 when Freud cited his mentor's accusatory diagnosis of Freud's mental condition—"moral insanity or paranoia scientifica." Then Freud stated that their precarious relationship "casts a deep shadow over my existence here," and subsequent letters revealed his fears that Breuer's withdrawal of professional support would force him to relocate in another city or country, or even to leave the practice of medicine. In early 1898, Freud's letters (1985, p. 296) castigated Breuer for "his neurotic dishonesty," attacked him for "underhandedness" (p. 304), and demonstrated Freud's vicious desires for revenge when he wrote (p. 364) of his slim hope that someday a title would be bestowed on him, thereby forcing Breuer to "crawl on his stomach" in envy. In August 1901 he was still venting his hatred of Breuer to Fliess, while deceitfully alleging that: "I no longer despise him and have not for some time."

The Year of Madness and Revenge

Eventually, our coverage of Freud's revenge motives will bring us to an evaluation of his treatment, in the final months of 1900, of an adolescent patient called Dora. It has become one of his most famous cases, but has been badly misunderstood by almost all of the many authors who have written about it, because they have neglected to assess it in light of a full understanding of the horrendous, macabre stresses that were afflicting Freud throughout the year 1900. At this point, readers might like to review materials in chapter five that provide a brief and incomplete picture of the inordinate mental stresses that were distressing Freud in that fateful year (which now will be supplemented in the paragraphs that follow).

The year 1900 deserves to be called Freud's "year of madness and revenge," although some other years of his life could compete with it for that title. As already noted, the lucky number 19 within that year had greatly increased Freud's expectations that this year would deliver him from anonymity and professional insecurities. He hoped that his new dream book would provide instant fame, wealth, and a cherished professorship, allowing him to defeat all his detractors and "enemies," particularly Breuer and Fliess (who seemed to be entering a coalition in 1899 and early 1900 that was a threat to him, in Freud's view).

There were several factors that helped to drive Freud into feelings of depression, madness, and revenge in the early months of 1900. In those days the new dream book was receiving only a lukewarm reception, keeping his professional ambitions unfulfilled, and preventing him from lording it over Breuer and Fliess. To the contrary, he must have felt that Breuer and Fliess were able to crow about their defeat of him, in connection with his bitter complaints that Breuer had made a successful invasion of Fliess's household, in what Freud described as a "Breuerization" of the Fliess family. That is, Breuer began to treat Fliess's mother-in-law for her ailments, and on May 27, 1900 one of Breuer's daughters named Margarethe married Arthur Schiff, who was Fliess's intimate colleague and protégé. Concerning this Breuerization, Freud's feelings of hatred and revenge were increased greatly towards both men due to angry suspicions that they had conspired to betray him. And he also became enraged towards Fliess's wife named Ida whom he felt was a prime mover in the growing split between Fliess and himself—seeming to believe that Breuer had poisoned her mind (*Complete*, 1985, p. 447) with hints about Freud's homosexual yearnings for her husband. (We'll see later that Freud's desire for revenge against Ida Fliess had much to do with his dangerous desires for revenge against his patient Dora, with regard to another of Freud's magical transferences.)

The previous paragraphs provide a backdrop for understanding why there was a great escalation of Freud's desires for revenge against Breuer, Fliess, and Mrs. Fliess in 1900. No wonder that Freud's letters to Fliess in the early months of the year repeatedly revealed his feelings of depression, that he feared he was slipping into madness, and that he felt so inadequate in his work with patients that "every single one of my patients is my tormentor." That was written on March 11, when he also admitted that "I do not really know what I am doing," and that "I give myself over to my fantasies . . . " (Various clinicians have asserted that psychosis begins with immersion in fantasies.) Referring to his patients, Freud used a great deal of denial in insisting that he still felt capable of handling his "eight victims and tormentors." Here, we need to place emphasis on that word "victims," since it seems prophetic of a patient's suicide that was soon to occur in April, 1900. In that same letter of March 11th, Freud expressed bitter feelings that "the impending Breuerization" (Margarethe's marriage) was pushing him farther away from Fliess, hinting that their correspondence would dwindle and their meetings would stop entirely.

Possibly, Margarethe Breuer's marriage in the spring of 1900 was a harbinger of catastrophe, for in his letter of April 25, 1900 Freud informed Fliess that the patient—Mrs. Margit Kremzir—whom he'd treated for fourteen days and then dismissed for being paranoid, had hanged herself in a hotel room in Vienna.* The previous chapter has given some of my ideas about how an understanding of name magic (the name-series regarding Margarethe/Margit and the surname Weiss) indicates that enormously revengeful feelings in Freud might have made this woman a "victim" of his suicide/murder complex. In later pages I'll return to a discussion of additional elements of this patient's name to suggest how Freud's hostile and vengeful feelings towards her might readily have been transferred, at the end of 1900, to his *suicidal* patient called Dora and to another possibly suicidal person who appears in Dora's case history.

During the succeeding month, May of 1900, Freud's letters to Fliess hinted that he was still chafing at the prospect that, at the end of that month, Breuer's daughter would be marrying indirectly into the Fliess "family." In his letter of May 20th he admitted his continuing preoccupation with his mentor by stating: "I have asked myself why it is that I cannot finish with Breuer . . . " Just prior to that letter, he told Fliess about a female patient that Breuer had sent him four years earlier, whom Freud called his most difficult case. Freud claimed that after many setbacks the woman had just been cured by him and that the patient told Breuer about her great improvement, causing him allegedly to acknowledge Freud's superior wisdom. Freud then ridiculed Breuer's supposed admission of defeat and smugly proclaimed to Fliess that his "little triumph" had inflicted a measure of delectable revenge upon his mentor. Similarly, in his letter of July 1 Freud again exposed his intense need for revenge during that year of 1900. While expressing a hope that Fliess's widely condemned works would soon receive public approval, he hinted that his friend could then express his revengeful feelings. And Freud acknowledged his own great desire for revenge by writing that: "Such spiteful glee, such satisfied thirst for revenge plays an important role in my case; so far I have savored too little of this delicious fare."

One month later, at the beginning of August, apparently Freud's smoldering desire for revenge burst into an explosion that he directed at his friend Fliess. In their final meeting, at an Alpine resort in Achensee, the two

---

*Was there an invidious equating of this patient with Fliess, whom Freud later accused of being paranoid?

men engaged in acrimonious debate, apparently about Fliess's "priority" concerning the idea that bisexuality was a basic factor underlying human behavior and all the neuroses. According to Fliess, Freud became enraged at him about this issue at Achensee, and he characterized Freud's behaviors as exhibiting "violence" and "personal animosity," allegedly resulting from intense envy. As noted in chapter four, Fliess charged that Freud had a plan to murder him at Achensee by luring him to a mountainous area and pushing him over a precipice. That claim by Fliess has received considerable support from persuasive details found in an article by Swales (Spurling, 1989), and from my previous analysis of the "Acropolis episode" concerning Freud's identification with Daedalus whose envy caused him to push his rival from a great height to his death. (All of this suggests that in August of 1900, a few months before he began the *treatment of Dora*, Freud was hardly able to contain seething feelings of envy and revenge that had reached murderous proportions.)

In the summer of 1900, only a few weeks after his bitter quarrel with Fliess at Achensee, Freud committed an outrageous act of a sexual nature. He traveled with his wife's sister, Minna Bernays, in what can be described as a belated "honeymoon trip" throughout Italy, and later in a mid-September letter to Fliess he described in sensuous detail this unchaperoned journey with Minna. Surely, this letter was an act of revenge towards his former "love object" (Fliess), since it announced that henceforth he would be able to obtain emotional and sexual gratification from Minna and no longer would need Fliess's company.

Swales has argued (1982) that Freud's sexual journey in Italy with Minna, in the summer of 1900, offers a psychological "proof" that Freud did intend to murder Fliess at Achensee just prior to "taking" Minna sexually. Concerning those bizarre events, Swales's thesis is that: " . . . only a few weeks after their big quarrel, Freud sought to re-enact the mythical role of Oedipus by committing the crime of incest with the MOTHER—in Freud's case with a mother-substitute in the form of his wife's sister, Minna Bernays." Swales noted that the other side of this "oedipal coin" required "the murder of the FATHER—in Freud's case, necessarily of a father-figure." And Fliess was more of a father symbol than a brother-figure for Freud in the eyes of most analysts, Swales noted. (In *Dark Side* I've discussed that Minna was a revenant of Freud's primal mother, his Freiberg nanny, which was why he made Minna a governess in his household and relied heavily on emotional support from her.)

In my opinion, there is another uncanny way that Freud sought to obtain revenge against Fliess after the Achensee debacle in August 1900. I believe Fliess's assertion that these colleagues argued vehemently at Achensee about "priority" concerning the issue of bisexuality, since the final letters between the men makes rather obvious that Freud tried to steal for himself Fliess's bisexuality conception and, failing to do so, then viciously assisted Otto Weininger and Hermann Swoboda (Freud's patient) in their plagiarism of Fliess's ideas. In a companion volume, I've given a detailed chapter on the Weininger affair (that culminated in his suicide, largely due to Freud's machinations), and I've offered my reasons for specifying that Freud began his manipulation of Weininger—assisting his theft of Fliess's bisexuality theory—in October of 1900. If I'm right about that time period, it indicates that Freud's desire for revenge against Fliess at Achensee was so rabid that he was impelled quickly to locate this "pawn," Weininger, whom he used to punish and defeat Fliess via the young man's publication of Fliess's ideas (in a book that made Weininger famous titled *Sex and Character*).

Concerning my view that Freud began his revengeful relationship with Weininger sometime in October 1900 (while "advising" the pliable Otto about a draft of his doctoral dissertation and pumping him full of Fliess's theories of bisexuality), it should be stressed that Freud began his treatment of Dora in that same month. In a significant footnote, Swales has argued (1982) that "the direction taken by Freud in his treatment of the patient 'Dora' during the months following the Achensee meeting was profoundly influenced by a wish to assert his own independent claim to the principle of bisexuality . ."

Also, Swales stated his conviction that the Dora case history, in an early version, "must have featured substantially more of a discussion of bisexuality than it did when, in a partially revised form, Freud eventually saw fit to publish it in 1905 . ." I agree with that thesis, and point to Freud's hasty writing of his Dora case study during the first three weeks of 1901, right after she rejected his further treatment of her. Thus, I suspect that he hurried to write this "clinical gem," because he was so eager to take his revenge on her and on Fliess, by incorporating fanciful (and unconvincing) claims about her alleged bisexuality that would help establish his "priority" as discoverer of bisexuality in the neuroses.

Having shown that during the first ten months of 1900 Freud's psyche was permeated and inundated by urgent desires for revenge, it's time now to discuss his handling of the Dora case in the last eleven weeks of 1900. We'll see that he treated this adolescent girl with considerable sadism; regularly imputed motives of revenge to her that usually belonged to him; tried to pressure her into accepting and performing highly questionable sexual behaviors with an older man; badgered her and questioned her repeatedly in an inquisitorial fashion; tried to break down her sense of reality and her keen awareness of a campaign to accomplish her sexual seduction; tried to make her believe (falsely) that she wished to suck her father's penis, etc. Despite that he had lost another vulnerable female patient to suicide only six months earlier (Mrs. Kremzir), Freud's behaviors towards Dora were replete with roughshod destructive elements that could easily have precipitated her suicide, and I contend that a major portion of his unconscious mind desired that fatal outcome, due to his suicide/murder complex.

Name-series in the Dora Case

For the moment, I will postpone giving a brief summary of the Dora case, so that we may move ahead directly to assessing the role played by several magical name-series in unleashing Freud's destructive impulses onto this patient. First, we note that the patient's actual name was Ida Bauer, and that both of those names could have provoked his unconscious desires to injure the young woman. Thus, her name was Ida B. and the maiden name of Fliess's wife also was Ida. B. (her surname being Bondy). Furthermore, there is no question that Freud bore extremely hostile and revengeful feelings towards Fliess's wife, Ida. Swales remarked (1982) that Freud ultimately blamed Ida Fliess for breaking up his friendship with her husband (since she feared that Freud would disrupt her marriage).

Decker revealed some sensitivity to how Freud might be susceptible to name magic in her book on the Dora case. For example, she noted (1991, p. 238) that some of Freud's hostile feelings towards Dora could have been prompted by his bitter feelings for Mrs. Fliess whose "name was Ida Bondy, which the name 'Ida Bauer' was bound to evoke, and Freud did not like Ida Bondy Fliess, believing her to be jealous of his close relationship with her husband." Here we see that Decker had implicated a small name-series in explaining some of Freud's hostility for his patient Dora (Ida Bauer). What Decker did not specify is that Dora's actual surname, Bauer, also could have evoked hostility in Freud, due to its printed structural similarity to the name Breuer—not forgetting that Ida Bondy Fliess and Dr. Breuer seemed to have formed an alliance against Freud in 1900. Eventually, in a letter to Fliess in August 1901 Freud complained about the alliance between Ida Fliess and Breuer, claiming that his old mentor had planted a dark thought in her mind by hinting that Freud might "interfere" with her marriage (with homosexual implications being rather evident).

There is no doubt that Freud came to hate Mrs. Fliess. In a letter to Abraham dated February 13, 1911 he described her as a "clever-stupid, malicious, positive, hysteric," but this criticism was censored-out of the published letters. (See Gay, 1988, p. 182). It is plausible that the identical given name of Ida Fliess and Ida Bauer was apt to provoke name magic in Freud's mind when we consider how he played with it, in a childlike fashion, in his letter to Fliess dated December 4, 1896. There he flattered Fliess and his wife by speculating that her name "Ida" perhaps might be derived from the word "idea," hinting at her creative nature. Finally, it should be noted that Dora's actual name, Ida Bauer, suggests a hidden connection between two names (Ida and Breuer) that Freud hated, reminding him of the presumed alliance between those two "enemies" of his.

With regard to the Dora case study, Hannah Decker has uncovered a magical name-series involving the name Dora (though she did not use that terminology to describe her discovery). She discussed this in her chapter titled: "Who Else Was There Called Dora?" Decker noted that in his book on "slips" Freud remarked that unconscious determinism was responsible for his choice of the name Dora, the pseudonym given to his famous patient of 1900. He stated that, when he chose this pseudonym, only the name Dora came to his mind, and he'd felt that it was "a perfect fit." But then he began to analyze his choice by asking himself: "who else was there called Dora?" He then recalled that his sister Rosa had a *nursemaid* in her household named Rosa who chose to use the name Dora, to avoid being confused with her mistress. Freud concluded that, in searching for a name for his young patient (whose real name for practical purposes had to be suppressed), he must have been influenced by the choice of that nursemaid who could not use her own name. In addition, he wrote that a governess (nursemaid) within the patient Dora's family had "exercised a decisive influence" on the patient. All of this was used by Freud to support his thesis that the seemingly arbitrary choice of the name Dora was an example of unconscious determinism.

Although Decker did not make this observation, it seems clear now that Freud's preceding exposition was an unconscious "confession" that the patient Dora, whom he'd already treated, had provided a major counter-transference of his feelings for the crucial nursemaid in Freud's life—his Freiberg nanny. First, notice that the nursemaid in his sister's home who chose the name Dora thereby recaptured much of her true name Rosa, since that pseudonym has the identical length and vowel structure. Second, Freud's explanation of his choice of a pseudonym suggests that unconsciously it derived from two of his own nursemaids, relating to the thesis that he'd had two nursemaids named Monica and Resi. Third, notice that the name of Freud's nursemaid "Resi" has the same length and consonantal structure (R-s-) as the name Rosa. Concerning Freud's remark that his sister's nursemaid was trying to hide her true name (while still revealing it, I claim), we see now that Freud's choice of a pseudonym indirectly managed to reveal the name of one of his nursemaids, while still concealing it! That the name Monica remained fully concealed indicates that his repressed feelings concerning her were far more "dangerous" to his mental stability than those pertaining to Resi. And in the above analysis we see that for Freud the name Rosa stood as a link between the name Dora (nursemaid) and Resi (nursemaid).

The preceding analysis suggests that Freud had transferred onto his patient Dora many of the lustful, hostile, and revengeful feelings that he still harbored for his Freiberg nanny who had seduced and "abandoned" him, and that this produced destructive and revengeful consequences for his patient in numerous ways. That he displayed inappropriate behaviors showing that he wished to have sexual contacts with this young patient now becomes more understandable. That in 1900 he still suffered from feelings that his nanny had abandoned and betrayed him suggests that he felt compelled to produce destructive behaviors that eventually would ensure that Dora would reject his treatment and "abandon" him—as she did. In any case, Freud's nanny was only the first of many destructive countertransference figures that can be uncovered in this case, and our understanding of name magic will help us to detect their identities.

Chapter seven of Decker's book (1991) emphasized that Freud's answer to his own question ("who else was there called Dora?") fell far short of uncovering a full list of names. Insightfully, Decker provided her own answer to his query: "The answer is, quite an array of young women, none of whom have traditionally had positive images. That there was more than one Dora in Freud's mind should come as no surprise." Decker then supplied a list of fictional women whose names were Dora (or variants of that name) who played important roles in Freud's thinking, and in each case she showed that his feelings about these Doras were *quite negative*. This list of fictional women included Dora (Spenlow) Copperfield, the wife of Dickens's famous character David Copperfield. Next, Decker cited Freud's attendance in the early 1880s at the play called *Théodora* by the French playwright, Victorien Sardou—with Sarah Bernhardt in the leading role. Finally, Decker presented compelling arguments (using case material) to suggest that Freud unconsciously thought of his patient as the mythical Pandora who, "like Eve, stood for dangerous female sexuality." (Nanny again?)

I don't have time or space to give an adequate summary of all the cogent remarks that Decker made about Freud's probable "involvements" with those three fictional Doras, but it's clear that he had quite hostile feelings for them that he probably passed on to his patient called Dora. Accordingly, Decker remarked that: "Dora as Pandora helps explain Freud's antipathy toward his patient." She noted that this case study is permeated by comments about boxes (symbolizing the vagina), which hinted at Freud's fear of the evils of female sexuality. This correlated with Decker's point that they "were the very same evils Pandora had loosed on the world when she opened the box given by Zeus." (She failed to notice that underlying all of this was his persistent fear of his nanny's "evil" vagina.)

Hannah Decker discussed that Freud named his patient unconsciously after two real persons called Dora, the first being the nursemaid in his sister's household, and the second being one of Josef Breuer's daughters named Dora. It was noted by Decker that the patient and the latter Dora had been born in 1882, and that there were other similarities connecting the two women. Referring to the real name of the patient called Dora, she wrote that: "There is a great deal of evidence to suggest that Freud also named Ida Bauer after Dora Breuer and that Dora's psychoanalysis in 1900 came to signify the tempestuous feelings that still raged in Freud about Josef Breuer . . ." Next, Decker expressed surprise that the naming of Dora could signify so much, including "Freud's anger and erotic impulses toward his patient, his more general distrust of women, his ambivalence about . .Dora's treatment," and his painful emotions about Breuer.

Clearly, Decker recognized that Freud's unconscious naming of his patient after Dora Breuer had derived from complex motives, including his hostility and need for revenge against Breuer in 1900, and that Freud was unable to confront the sexual "attachment that had existed between him and Dora, an attachment like the one he believed had existed between Breuer and Anna O." Strong arguments were offered by Decker to support her thesis that Freud's patient called Dora was also an unconscious representation of his feelings about Anna O.'s relationship with Breuer, and she cited many remarkable similarities between those two "classic" patients. Likewise, she saw some impressive similarities between that patient Dora and Freud's patient called "Irma," stating that: "There is a direct line from Irma to Dora based on Freud's anger at Breuer, his acknowledgment of Breuer's experience with Anna O . ." (etc.).

Decker wrote that the patient called Dora shared with Irma (Emma Eckstein) "what Freud saw as negativism, and he was annoyed at them both." However, the term "annoyed" is an extreme euphemism, for in *Dark Side* I've explained that Freud harbored a murderous rage towards Emma Eckstein (based on counter-transference concerning his nanny's "betrayal" of him), and that a major portion of his psyche wished to destroy this patient, which he and Fliess almost accomplished. That same murderous hatred that Freud had felt toward Irma (Emma) was also beginning to be unleashed against her counterpart Dora, when she suddenly terminated her treatment, without giving notice to Freud. In my opinion, Ida Bauer (Dora) may have saved her own life when she terminated from analysis so abruptly.

At this point, we've seen that Decker had uncovered another magical name-series in Freud's life, this one involving the name Dora. In this name-series, Decker's list of names included Dora Copperfield, Théodora, Pandora, his sister Rosa's servant called Dora, the patient he called Dora, and Dora Breuer. Also, Decker had cited a smaller name-series involving the name Ida: Ida Bondy and Ida Bauer. Let me say that I thoroughly agree with these discoveries of Decker, and most of her interpretations about those name-series. Although I have no interest in challenging her "priority" about these matters, since she has published them first, let me say that I had figured out those two name-series many years before reading Decker's book in late 1991—though I had not incorporated the name of Dora Copperfield. In any case, I'm delighted with Decker's perspicacity and can endorse her discoveries by stating that I had made them independently of her, as part of my extensive writings on name magic, particularly in the life of Freud.

Now let me state that there were two additional "Doras" that Decker could have included in her list, and that both of these provide a major increment of hatred and revenge that was transferred to the patient's pseudonym by Freud's psyche. The first of these real women was Dora Meynert, the daughter of Freud's old mentor, Dr. Theodor Meynert, the eminent psychiatrist. Freud's hatred and desires for revenge against Meynert developed much as it did with Breuer, i.e. because both of these mentors had not continued to give him the credit and emotional support which he felt he deserved. Freud's "deathbed story" about Meynert, in which the dying sage allegedly admitted that he was a raging male hysteric, amounted to another childish lie concocted by Freud to take revenge on this man—taking advantage of a lack of other witnesses to this "confession." Likewise, he told another outrageous lie about a dead man who could not defend himself by inserting it casually in his dream book, for the delectation of gossips in old Vienna. In that instance he intimated that his deceased "friend" Josef Paneth had expressed deadly wishes towards a sick colleague, Fleischl, who had blocked his path to career advancement—a projection of Freud's own lethal wishes. (See *Dark Side* for my explanation of why Freud desired to take revenge on Paneth by staining his reputation, despite that this wealthy man had given Freud a very generous monetary gift during his engagement period.)

Apparently, Freud's hatred for Dora Breuer and Dora Meynert, and their given names, had a common basis in name magic that was operative in his unconscious mind. That he transferred this hatred to the pseudonym of his patient called Dora should not seem unusual, in his case. This seems germane to information offered previously about his hatred for the given name of another of Breuer's daughters, Margarethe, and how this probably was transferred lethally to the given name of his patient, Margit Kremzir, who killed herself in April 1900. That name-transference is discussed fully in *Dark Side*, along with many details concerning Freud's venomous hatred for his old benefactor, Josef Breuer.

One final "Dora" in Freud's life needs to be added to the previous name-series. This was Dora Teleky whom Freud mentioned in his letter to Fliess dated May 16, 1900 when she was one of only three students then attending his clinical lectures. Later, after Dora Teleky had obtained her medical degree, she became involved in a dispute with Freud that enraged him. In Masson's book (1984) he cited an unpublished autobiography by Albert Hirst, the nephew of Emma Eckstein—the patient that Freud called Irma. According to Hirst's account, Dr. Dora Teleky was a friend of Ms. Eckstein and her family who, while making a friendly visit to their home during a later stage of Freud's psychoanalysis of Emma, discovered "an abscess near Emma's navel and drained it." Hirst wrote that Dr. Dora T. then: "claimed that she had found the source of Emma's illness and had cured it. She thus confirmed Emma in her rejection of Freud's diagnosis of a recurrence of her old neurosis."

When Hirst told this to Freud the next day he became "furious" and dismissed Dora Teleky's diagnosis "as a fake." He called this a highly unprofessional interference with a patient under his care and immediately withdrew from the case, predicting that: "That is Emma's end. Now she will never get well." He was right, for Hirst related that she remained a hopeless invalid for the last ten years of her life. Hirst himself was an adoring patient of Freud, yet he expressed the suspicion that Freud was "not unhappy to be rid of a burdensome charity case." Masson questioned Freud's "fury" about this matter, asking whether this was largely a projection of his repressed anger onto Dora Teleky and Emma because he was unable to admit the great damage that he and Fliess had done to Emma Eckstein—nearly taking her life on several occasions and disfiguring her pretty face.

Masson did not provide a date for the preceding dispute between Freud and Dr. Teleky, but it's likely that it occurred some years following Freud's treatment of young Dora in late 1900. So I will not suggest that this heated dispute with Dora Teleky influenced Freud's choice of the pseudonym Dora for his adolescent patient, Ida Bauer. However, it's clear that he and Dora Teleky were already acquainted in May 1900 when she attended his lectures. Given that in later years she was an independent-minded woman physician who became quite skeptical concerning his treatment of Emma Eckstein, isn't it possible that in May 1900 she was already annoying Freud greatly by giving him signs of her skepticism about his theories and treatment approaches, in her responses to his lectures? If so, that would have provided an additional basis for Freud's decision to create the pseudonym Dora, since Ida Bauer likewise annoyed Freud repeatedly by expressing *her* skepticism and disrespect for his ideas while he was treating her.

Are there some readers who still harbor strong doubts that Freud was involved in a magical name-series pertaining to the pseudonym Dora? If so, let me suggest that Freud was unconsciously imitating an eminent man who already had produced such a magical name-series utilizing repetitions of "Dora." Recall that Decker (1991) specified that one of the links in Freud's name-series was *Théodora*, the play by Victorien Sardou that Freud saw in Paris and wrote about to his fiancée Martha. Decker wrote that: "Sardou seems to have been captivated by the syllable 'dor' and wrote three plays whose titles incorporated it: *Fédora*, *Théodora*, and *Thermidor*." In writing to Martha, Freud joked about Sardou's repetitive titles and suggested vaguely that a name-series pertaining to the name Dora was operative. Thus, in a jocular manner he claimed that Sardou "has written a *Dora* and a *Feodor* and is said to be busy on a *Thermidora*, *Ecuadora*, and *Torredora!*" It's quite provocative that Freud "invented" the aforementioned play he called *Dora*, and the others that ended in "-dora." Evidently, he made this joke because his unconscious mind was dimly aware that Sardou and other literary men, including Byron and Schiller, were compelled to produce various magical name-series, this one by Sardou involving "dor" and perhaps the name "Dora," behind it.

My suggestion is that 15 years later Freud unconsciously imitated Sardou's behavior by creating the pseudonym Dora, a name which he vaguely realized was part of his own magical name-series, correlating with that nursemaid named Dora in his sister Rosa's home. If so, this suggests that Freud might have made a fantasy identification with the playwright Sardou, after viewing his play *Théodora* during his Paris sojourn with Charcot. That play might have made a great unconscious impact on Freud's mind, because the empress Théodora had married a man (emperor Justinian) who was twice her age (similar to Amalia Freud), and then became unfaithful by taking a young lover (perhaps like Phillipp or Emanuel Freud?). Decker offered additional reasons why the empress Théodora might have represented Freud's mother Amalia to him, but I'll not provide her reasoning here. In any case, if Decker is correct about this, it could have helped greatly to fixate the name Dora in Freud's mind, thereby helping to consolidate the Dora name-series in 1900. In effect, the name Dora could have represented feelings about the infidelity of Freud's mother that he transferred to the patient he called Dora, his vicious actions towards her implying: 'You deserve to be mistreated just like my whorish mother deserved it!'

Notice that the central element of Sardou's surname is "ardo," an anagram of the name Dora. This uncanny detail might have caused Freud to focus on the playwright's last name, which ends with the letters "ardou." That element can be regarded as a truncation of the English word "ardour" (British spelling) which signifies sexual passion. Freud was so sensitive to personal names and their meanings that he might have noticed this factor, especially since the German meaning of his own surname (joy) readily generates a connotation indicating sexual passion. Perhaps this helped him to identify with Sardou and unconsciously to imitate the playwright's name-series involving "dor" and "Dora."

The Dora Case Study

Starting with the next paragraph, a brief summary of prominent aspects of the Dora case study will be offered, so that we can understand another destructive name-series created by Freud (the "K" series) and the possible role of Gisela Fluss's "image" in this case. Some readers may prefer to review the full case study by Freud (1952), or Decker's (1991) extensive synopsis.

Early in October 1900 Dora's father, a wealthy Jewish man at age 47 who lived with his family in Vienna near Freud's home, brought his daughter to Freud's office for treatment of allegedly hysterical symptoms—rather minor ones. She had been born in Vienna on November 1, 1882, so she was 17 (though Freud mis-represented this age, and her previous significant ages, as one year older than was factual!). In earlier years she had suffered from shortness of breath, cough and periodic loss of her voice, migraine, gastric pains, constipation, a vaginal discharge, and an attack of appendicitis. Over the years she'd been seen by many doctors, who typically did not know what was wrong with her, but at least one had recourse to the label "hysteria" despite that she did not exhibit any of the dramatic symptoms of that ailment (no paralyses, blindness or deafness, amnesias, dual selves, hypersensitivities, acute persistent pain, etc.).

In years prior to 1900 Freud had treated Dora's father for a syphilitic condition, and in 1898 he had brought her (at age 15) to see Freud once concerning the cough, severe hoarseness and intermittent loss of voice. But Dora was tired of seeing doctors, all of whose efforts seemed futile, so she adamantly refused treatment by Freud. Then on a second visit to Freud, at 17, she accepted his treatment reluctantly, since her father was deeply concerned about her depressed feelings (sometimes suicidal), and her increasingly "oppositional" attitudes. Dora's father told Freud that she had recently accused a dear friend of the family, Herr K., of making an immoral proposition to her. However, Dora's father felt sure that this was only a sexual fantasy of hers, but one that had induced depression, irritability, and suicidal ideation in her. Indeed, *a suicide note* by Dora had been found by her parents, and her father was very upset that for months she had repeatedly insisted that her family should break off all relations with the K. family, with whom they had been friends for many years. In recent years, Frau K. had been sympathetic concerning the poor state of health of Dora's father and had become a consistent friendly nurse to him, and a dear friend to Dora. He assured Freud that his relationship with Frau K. was an honorable one and that Dora's claim about Herr K. was a fantasy; therefore, he could not understand her hatred of the K.s and her efforts to have him break off with them. His final plea to Freud was: "Please try to bring her to reason."

The preceding paragraphs have provided a brief introduction to this case study, and now we will look at some salient factors concerning Freud's treatment of Dora. Without much trouble she convinced Freud that over many years her father and Frau K. had been involved in regular sexual relations, both in Vienna and in the resort town of Merano where both families had resided together, at times. Indeed, Dora's father and Frau K. had done little to conceal their affair from others, and Freud readily agreed with the girl's frequent bitter complaints "that she had been handed over to Herr K. as the price of his tolerating the relations between her father and his wife; and her rage at her father's making such a use of her was visible behind her affection for him." (Freud, 1952, p. 44) Thus, Freud agreed that Dora had been used by the adults as a sexual "pawn," and he recognized that the slow seduction of this girl had been going on since her earlier years. This must be emphasized, for we'll discuss later the reprehensible, immoral manner in which Freud manipulated this information during analysis when he encouraged the seduction of this vulnerable adolescent—probably as a kind of re-enactment of his own sexual molestation during childhood.

Freud spelled out that Herr K., acting like a friendly uncle to disguise his sleazy intentions, had been "courting" Dora for at least five years. For a whole year he sent her flowers every day, often gave her valuable presents, spent "all his spare time in her company"—yet her father pretended not to notice this romancing of his child. When Dora was *age 13*, Herr K. tried to seduce her in a quite serious effort. Very cleverly he arranged to be alone with her in his office to watch a passing church festival, enticed her into a quiet attic for a better view of this parade, then pounced upon her and kissed her fully "upon her lips." Dora experienced a "violent feeling of disgust," luckily escaped from his grasp to safety, and never mentioned this scene to anyone (until her treatment with Freud)—thereafter avoiding being alone with Herr K. for a prolonged period of time.

Then when Dora was age 15 (the age when she first saw Freud regarding symptoms), she and her father visited the K. family at a lake resort in the Alps. After a trip on the lake she walked briefly with Herr K. who "had the audacity to make her a proposal" (an indecent proposition), so she insisted immediately that her father should take her away from this ugly scene. She then ensured that her father learned about this seduction attempt, and he later questioned Herr K. about the matter. This lying rascal then denied everything and "proceeded to throw suspicion upon the girl," claiming that Dora had read books about sex and indicating that this had provoked sexual fantasies in her—particularly the fantasy that he'd tried to seduce her at the lake. All too willingly her father bought K.'s deceitful story. Thereafter,

Dora's bitter complaints about the K. family increased over many months, leading to the time in October 1900 when she became very depressed, wrote the aforementioned suicide note, and was brought to Freud for treatment.

Freud knew that just prior to K.'s attempt to seduce Dora at the lake, this Don Juan was successful in seducing a young governess in his employ whom he then "dropped" abruptly—which the love-struck girl immediately told to Dora. Nevertheless, Freud continually made excuses to Dora for Herr K.'s sexual harassments of her, and concocted the lie (or fantasy?) that K. probably had honorable intentions towards her in the lake incident, perhaps wishing to propose marriage to her (though Freud had no evidence to support this sexist fairy tale). Freud's absurd view of K.'s intention at the lake, presented to Dora in a very authoritative manner, was one of numerous attempts to "gaslight" (referring to the film with Boyer and Bergman) the young woman, i.e. to erode her sense of reality and self-confidence. In many ways, Freud tried to get her to adopt much more "advanced" sexual attitudes and behaviors, in effect to accept K.'s seduction in order to reflect her "mature" sexuality—thereby admitting that unconsciously she had lustful desires for him anyway, as Freud contended. However, to her credit, Dora did not agree with this charade and eventually she obtained K.'s confession that he had wished to seduce her at the lake (which she told to Freud months after treatment had ended, as explained later).

Freud patted himself on the back that he'd not become the lackey of Dora's father, paid to convince her to accept being a sexual pawn regarding his affair with Mrs. K., but a careful review of Freud's behaviors reveals that he did become a confederate of Dora's father and Herr K. In every way possible, his analytic interpretations were intended to intimidate Dora and make her conform to that invidious sexual charade. For example, early in his written case study Freud proclaimed (as the alleged "master" of hysteria) that Dora's feeling of disgust at Herr K.'s brutal kiss was an infallible proof that, at age thirteen, she "was already entirely and completely hysterical." At length, Freud insisted that any healthy, normal girl of that age should have experienced great lustful desires concerning that kiss (versus "sexual harassment," I say), Thus, he hinted that Dora was already a weird person at thirteen and totally ignored her reasonable feelings of disgust about that abrupt, unexpected betrayal by her "uncle" K., whom she had regarded as a *protector*. Surely, it was Freud who was the weird person here, in his probable reenacting and excusing of his own sexual molestation by his Freiberg nanny.

Probably, Freud tried to convince Dora that her feelings of disgust at age thirteen, about that kiss, revealed that she was mentally ill at that age, and still was sick, manifested by her continuing "unreasonable" feelings of anger about the lake incident. With pride he described the technique he employed repeatedly to undermine her sense of reality and morality about the manipulations by Herr K. and her father that were intended to obtain her sexual compliance. For whenever she complained angrily to Freud about their sexual gamesmanship, Freud immediately turned the tables on her and, using material pertaining to her alleged unconscious motivations, each time he showed that she was really the lustful "bad girl" who was to blame for her own sexual harassments. Using his clever psychologizing, he persistently browbeat her with claims that she harbored erotic desires for Herr K. and for her father; that she had been a naughty girl who became a hysteric by masturbating in childhood; that she had great interest in reading books about sexual matters, and the like. This was Freud playing the Grand Inquisitor who always knew how to twist Dora's words, or to use dream material selectively to punish and gain an advantage over his adolescent adversary. But this intelligent girl was no pushover, sexually or intellectually, and it angered Freud that she was not cowed by him—increasing his desires to take revenge on her, one way or another.

With his desire to punish her and break her will being apparent, and totally ignoring the dangers of her depressed and suicidal feelings, Freud eventually stooped to very low levels of behavior. Using tortuous logic, he dreamed-up the accusation that Dora was sometimes imagining that Frau K. was providing oral sex for her father, and then topped this crudity by claiming that Dora harbored a secret belief that she could do the job even better and wished that she could suck her father's penis. Many readers will suspect that this was a gross projection of Freud's own oral desires, relating to his fantasies in the 1890s that all of his neurotic patients had become ill because in infancy they were forced to suck their fathers' penises—coupled with Freud's allegation that his own father had employed this perversion with his own children. Also, it is germane that some writers (including Eissler) have recognized signs of Freud's strong desire to obtain gratification from oral sex in 1896, when Martha was confined with the pregnancy of Anna.

Near the end of the treatment, Freud tried to ram down Dora's throat another punitive sexual theory, in order to punish and take revenge on her. Out of whole cloth, he concocted the notion that Dora's alleged hysteria was based partly upon her deeply repressed lesbian lust for Frau K.! (At various times he theorized that her problems included lustful feelings for her father, Herr K., Frau K., and her doctor—and she was lucky that he didn't think to inquire about whether she owned a dog.) With this claim about her repressed lesbianism, Freud hoped to take revenge upon Wilhelm Fliess by laying a basis for challenging Fliess's priority concerning the idea that bisexuality was a primary factor in all neurotic problems. However, Freud's claim also served to shame and discredit Dora in the minds of his readers, and in the eyes of the Viennese public that he had good reason to expect would learn about the juicy details of his bawdy script for this Viennese soap opera—and would readily identify the true names of Dora, her family members, and the Ks.

In *Dark Side* I've discussed how much Freud loved to stir up notoriety in Vienna concerning his sexual ideas, as a stepping-stone to worldwide fame and fortune. In his extensive case study on "Emmy von N." (Fanny Moser) in *Studies on Hysteria* he provided countless obvious clues to the true identity of this well-known, alleged murderess, the richest woman in Europe (along with her identifying bizarre behaviors) to ensure that the reading public would readily fathom her true name and identity—while slyly insisting that he had maintained a rigorous medical confidentiality. Freud used this same scam in his case study of Dora (probably explaining why it was turned down by publishers between 1901 and 1905, when I suspect he finally toned-down an earlier "steaming" version).

Freud's case study on Dora dropped numerous clues to allow his Viennese readers to identify Dora and her family, and the K. family, and he probably relied on the two disgruntled governesses in this case to "spill the beans," as unhappy servants are known to do. (Consider the one who was seduced and "dumped" by K.). Furthermore, he ensured that the patient's friends and extended family, along with many members of the Viennese citizenry, would deduce Dora's true identity, thereby allowing him to have his final revenge on this victimized adolescent. It should be noted that Freud claimed (p. 13) that Dora's family life was not laid in Vienna, so her personal life would "therefore be practically unknown" to the citizens of that city, yet Decker revealed (p. 4) that in 1900 Dora's family was living in an apartment house in the Ninth District, the same general area where Freud's home was located.

Over the years I have read Freud's case study of Dora several times, and each time I've come away with positive feelings about her personality and character. Despite Freud's numerous attempts to depict her as an angry, complaining, mean-spirited, revengeful girl, I've gained a much more positive impression of her than he had. To me she has seemed like a basically decent, honest, long-suffering girl with affectionate feelings for her father and brother, for Frau K. and her children, and for Herr K. until he betrayed her trust—and even her critical, conflicted feelings towards her mother were tinged with concern. Moreover, it seems to me that Freud harbored angry, lustful, and revengeful feelings for this patient (feelings that he did not understand), and that he did not truly sympathize with her anger and fear about the horrendous sexual web in which Herr K. and her father were ensnaring her. Although Freud quickly acknowledged to her his recognition that she was being used as a sexual pawn, his behaviors showed that this was not done out of genuine sympathy but as a practical matter. That is, he knew that she had quickly dismissed many doctors before him, and he surmised that she would do the same to him if he showed the indecency and dishonesty of refusing to acknowledge the basic truth of her repulsive life situation.

Emphasis should be given to Freud's repeated unconvincing attempts to portray Dora as a revengeful person, which at times he tried to establish as the very core of her "neurosis." Indeed, he claimed that he found evidences of her vengeful nature almost everywhere, including in her dreams. In his quest to depict her as a vengeful witch, he even returned to his absurd idea that she could have been cured quickly by accepting Herr K. as her husband (!), but suggested that her desire for revenge against K. and her father prevented her from accepting this solution to her problems. He then cited this as the hallmark of neurotics' behavior, i.e. that they wanted to hold onto their desires for revenge far more than desiring solutions that would cure them. (This was a basic problem of Freud's, of course.)

My opinion about this issue of Dora's alleged vengefulness is quite opposed to Freud's position. I'd be foolish to write that there were no hints of revenge in any of her behaviors, but I'm convinced that Freud greatly exaggerated his claims, again due to projections of his own feelings and problems about revenge that permeated his behaviors in the first nine months of 1900 and in other eras of his life. It's my view that, on a scale of one to ten, Dora's vengeful behaviors might warrant a rating of three or less, while Freud's warranted the highest rating of ten.

Freud discussed Dora's allegedly vengeful nature on 17 pages of his case study, scattered throughout pages 109 through 150. Most of his discussion concerned his claims that she desired revenge against Herr K. and her father, but Freud also claimed that she desired revenge against him (pp. 148 ff.) as a way of maintaining her symptoms and to cruelly demonstrate the ineffectiveness of his treatment. Apparently, what particularly angered Freud and caused him to impute feelings of revenge towards him by Dora was the fact that she suddenly rejected him by terminating her therapy on December 31, 1900, about eleven weeks after it began. While mildly noting his possible errors in this therapy (which really were numerous and flagrant), he laid the blame for this "failure" on her; indicated that this was her vicious mode of revenge against him; and concocted the fantasy that her revenge was especially destructive, since he'd been within a hairsbreadth of curing her. (All of this added to his desires for revenge, of course.)

Freud also remarked (p. 146) that Dora had sought revenge against him due to a transference effect that he had not recognized, i.e. she had identified him with that deceitful seducer, Herr K., and then had transferred her vengeful feelings from K. to the doctor. Freud's comments made it seem that Dora was utterly irrational in transferring her angry feelings from K. onto the doctor, and he said that he should have dissipated her illusion by asking her frankly: "Have you noticed anything that leads you to suspect me of evil intentions similar .. to Herr K.'s?" But he was toying with us and knew that he was smart not to ask that dangerous question of her. Actually, she could have cited many clear evidences that Freud had identified (perhaps unconsciously) with Herr K., including the frequent occasions when Freud made lame excuses for K.'s seductive and sexually harassing behaviors towards her and his concoction of a pipe dream that K.'s behaviors at the lake reflected an honorable intention to marry her eventually.

Moreover, while grossly exaggerating possibly vengeful needs in Dora, Freud never mentioned one word about Herr K.'s possible needs for revenge. That is, K. had suffered public humiliation for years pertaining to the sexual domination of his wife by Dora's father, making revenge a quite plausible motive in his recurrent desires to seduce this "friend's" young daughter. How obvious a motive—yet the master of psychological dynamics never noticed it, because he was so intensely but unconsciously identified with Herr K.! We know that Freud had made a lasting identification with the nanny who "seduced" him and, since Herr K. was likewise a child molester (the kiss at age thirteen), this perverse similarity between nanny and K. could have helped to facilitate Freud's identification with this sly pervert, Herr K. (Freud altered Dora's ages upward, probably to prevent his readers from realizing that she was a mere child of thirteen when K. first began his perverted assault on her virginity.)

My assertion that Freud had made a compelling identification with Herr K. suggests that the doctor himself had strong lustful and vengeful feelings towards Dora (as K. had). There is further material that supports that claim, relating to my thesis that in Freud's psyche Dora was a revenant not only of his Freiberg nanny but also of nanny's counterpart, Gisela Fluss. Let me explain what I mean. Freud saw this intelligent, very pretty patient for the first time in the summer of 1898 when she was age fifteen and was suffering from a cough and hoarseness. One analogy here is that it was also in summer when he first met and fell madly in love with that intelligent, pretty girl named Gisela Fluss in Freiberg, and she also was then age fifteen. Another important similarity is that Dora's father was a wealthy owner of two textile factories, and Gisela's father was likewise an affluent owner of a textile mill in the same geographical region. (The textile businesses of both girls' families were relevant to the more plebeian work of Freud's father, who was a wool trader.)

To pursue these similarities further, we recall that Gisela Fluss at age fifteen laughed at Freud teasingly and rejected his timid advances. Likewise,

Freud wrote that by age fifteen Dora was "accustomed to laugh at the efforts of doctors," like himself. Indeed, when he initially proposed giving her psychological treatment she rebuffed his proposal, although he gave as the excuse that her discomfort had gone into a period of temporary remission. Ergo, at age fifteen both of these pretty Jewish girls had rejected Freud and thereby provoked his melded feelings of lust and revenge which he also felt towards his nanny (whom he felt had seduced and later rejected him). One can surmise that those feelings in him towards Dora helped to promote his strong identification with Herr K., who obviously harbored similar mixed feelings towards this young girl who had rejected his advances twice. But there were other reasons why Freud probably identified with Herr K., as we shall see later, including a possibly shared vulnerability to name magic and powerful suicidal tendencies in both of these deceitful, macho Viennese males.

There is another reason to assert that Freud harbored an intense identification with Herr K., pertaining to a bizarre mythological reference to Frau K. (p. 75) that Freud allowed to "slip" out while writing about the period of years when Frau K. and young Dora had shared a very friendly and close relationship. In those days, while Frau K. was carrying on an affair with Dora's father, the girl was a confidante to the older woman and at times was a caretaker for her two children. While Freud was writing about their intimate friendship, suddenly he described Frau K. as a "Medea," one who did not mind that her rival (Dora) was friendly with her two children. (p. 75).

Now, Freud's abrupt equation of Frau K. with the murderous sorceress Medea (wife of Jason who pursued the "golden fleece") reveals that Freud bore awesomely hostile feelings towards Frau K., which he did not expose nor explain elsewhere in his case study. Recall that Medea was the most viciously vengeful female character in all of literature who took revenge upon her husband Jason by gruesomely murdering their children. In effect, Freud had exposed his hidden belief that Frau K. had engaged in extremely sadistic behaviors towards her husband in her almost public affair with Dora's father. And we can be sure that Freud had bridled against her sadism, and could not help revealing his chagrin in this subtle fashion, because he had formed a powerful identification with Herr K. In fact, Freud took his public revenge against Mrs. K. by implying that she was a cruelly sadistic and vengeful female who was publicly punishing her husband's Don Juanism (knowing that the intelligentsia of Vienna eventually would deduce her true identity).

In a previous chapter, I expressed my certainty that Freud had formed a fantasy identification with the mythic hero Jason, relating to Freud's desire to use the golden "fleece" (Fliess, his comrade) as a magical instrument of his healing aspirations. Since he labeled Frau K. as Medea, this indicates that in his fantasies the role of her "victimized" husband was shared by Herr K. and Freud (as Jason), thereby cementing his identification with the "abused" figure of K., not ignoring that these men shared proclivities for "sexual megalomania." In effect, Freud's sudden labeling of Frau K. as Medea reflected his vengeful feelings towards all women (including Dora), and was also a vengeful "outburst" against Frau K. that reflected the fantasy identification with her husband—one that fostered an egregious pollution of his pathetic "treatment" of young Dora.

Of course, Freud was aware subliminally that Dora's father, Herr K., and Frau K. all were involved in sexually sadistic games that were intended to punish one another, Dora's mentally fragile mother, and the suicidal adolescent herself. But Freud had to remain totally silent about all this covert sadism, because he needed to fulfill his lucrative role as the lackey of all these "sophisticated" adults. Surely, he did not want to criticize their sexual philandering, since they were acting like enlightened disciples of the "advanced" sexual doctrines which he was then espousing. Also, it's likely that Freud himself was partaking of similar kinds of sexual sadism in triangular games that he was playing with his wife Martha and her sister Minna (see *Secret SL*), and there were modest limits to the hypocrisy he would indulge in styling himself as a model of morality (in a deceitful letter to James Putnam).

Now it's time consider my view that perhaps both Freud and Herr K. were susceptible to name magic regarding Dora's surname and that Freud's subliminal awareness that he and K. were vulnerable to this name magic might have helped precipitate Freud's identification with this child molester. In his case study (pp. 129-30) Freud remarked that Dora's true surname—which he did not reveal to his readers, of course—was able to denote various kinds of "objects," one of which he regarded as "improper" (sexually). Now we know that Dora's actual surname was Bauer, and Decker has explained (p. 116) that this surname "is part of the vulgar phrase *kalter Bauer*," which refers to semen, especially the semen released from a "wet dream" or from masturbation. Here again we see that Freud had chosen a patient to memorialize whose surname, like his own, had a decidedly sexual connotation (recall Anna von Lieben, also). Perhaps Freud was attracted to that sexual connotation of Dora's surname—semen—because it seemed to confirm (magically) his own childish fixation on the notion that masturbation was a primary causative factor in neurosis?

In considering Freud's hint that Dora's surname referred to "more than one kind of object," we should note that the major dictionary meanings of Bauer are: peasant or farmer; a pawn in chess; a bird cage. Those last two meanings indicate the two other objects to which Freud must have been referring in his oblique citation of Dora's surname. In my opinion, considering Herr K.'s crudely opportunistic behaviors towards Dora that took advantage of a silent contract allowing him to seduce her (as a mere sexual object) in payment for her father's affair with his wife, it's not unlikely that K. had a susceptibility to name magic that caused him to perceive and treat the girl as if she were a sexual pawn. Of course, even the chess meaning of "pawn" may correlate with its interpersonal meaning in English, i.e. one who is used or manipulated to further another person's selfish ends. Even the meaning "a bird's cage" could have had a perverse relevance to Dora in K.'s imagination, for it is likely that his overall perception of her plight caused him to regard her as a helpless bird trapped in its cage. That also might have been the way he perceived the young governess whom he seduced and then coldly betrayed, however. (The use of "bird" to refer to a female sexual object is now well-known in English slang.)

Perhaps Freud also was responding unconsciously and compulsively to those latter meanings of Dora's surname. If so, that could have precipitated feelings of inevitability in him that she was destined to be used as a sexual pawn, fostering his behavior which subtly excused K.'s sexual harassments, as well as Freud's hints that the girl would prove herself a mature woman by submitting to K.'s advances.

Dora's Illness, or Freud's?

In recent years, various writers have begun to ask why Freud bothered to create this weak case study about Dora (except for loyal Freudians who insist doggedly that it's a clinical masterpiece). For example, Stadden's article (in Spurling II, 1989) presented convincing data which established that Freud was grossly deficient in supporting his basic claims about this case. He argued convincingly that Freud was unable to show that Dora was "ill" or even irrational, nor that her alleged illness was "hysteria," and failed to show that his ideas about pathogenesis were proved by this case.

So a basic question remains. Why did Freud bother to produce and publish this weak, rather inconsequential case study, and then pretend that it was an important clinical work? He made this pretence despite that he called this study a "fragment" of an analysis, admitting that it did not reveal basic analytic techniques or transference factors, nor did it provide coherent ideas about the structure of the hysterias. Perhaps an underlying motivation was exposed by the fact that he wrote this case study rapidly, immediately following Dora's abrupt departure, in the first three weeks of 1901. At that point, he was under the pressure of "demonic" and irrational stresses that were similar to those which, in 1895, had compelled him to hurriedly compose his "mad masterpiece" called the *Project for a Scientific Psychology*. However, in 1895 he eventually came to his senses and disowned the *Project*, whereas the distorted mental pressures that caused him in 1900 and 1901 to become immersed in the Dora case and its written case study were just too powerful for him to ameliorate.

Already we've cited, or alluded to, some of the incredible pressures in 1900 that caused Freud to regard the Dora case study as a minor masterpiece, or as a buttress for *The Interpretation of Dreams* and its serious defects. Those pressures included his schisms with Fliess and Breuer; his conflicts with Fliess concerning priority regarding the topic of bisexuality; his growing desires for revenge against Breuer and Fliess and his plan to murder Fliess at Achensee; his presumably depressed and irrational reactions to the suicide of his patient, Margit Kremzir, and threats he felt from patients who were "torturing" him into feelings of madness; his distortions of libido relating to his "honeymoon" trip with Minna Bernays in Italy; and, especially, his rage at the lukewarm response to his dream book.

Concerning that last item, Freud began the treatment of Dora in October 1900 apparently bemused by the magical belief that God had sent him this young girl as a precious gift (Decker, 1991), and that his clinical work with her would enable him to establish his supremacy over all rivals, and critics of his new book. He was perturbed by knowing that even friendly critics of his dream book had assailed its glaring defect. That is, the "specimen" dream about Irma's injection was perceived (accurately) by some critics as a hodgepodge of interpretations without a central, unifying point. Furthermore, his analysis of the Irma dream did not reveal how a Freudian dream analysis could elucidate a patient's basic neurosis, nor how dream interpretations could be used to clarify and foster the progress of a patient's psychoanalysis. So, when Freud began his work with Dora he hoped that the data obtained from her case would allow him to write a full case study which would overcome those major deficits of the dream book.

Any clinician not subject to megalomania would have recognized upon Dora's termination that the scanty eleven-week period of her analysis could not have generated sufficient data to fulfill the aforementioned goal. But in January of 1901 Freud was gripped by his demons and ignored that simple fact in his embarrassingly overblown writeup of the Dora case study. The centerpiece of that study is his lengthy, detailed analysis of two "big dreams" provided by Dora. Now, what can I say? Some of Freud's interpretations of those dreams seem cogent, but most of them are unconvincing. Too often, in his imperious manner, Freud injected his own associations to those dreams rather than sticking with the client's associations. Again, as with the Irma dream, I was left with impressions of the clinician's self-serving and tortuous interpretations designed to support his preconceived ideas. And not infrequently, Freud's dream interpretations seemed to emerge from his own pathological depths rather than from the patient's psyche, as when (p.

148) he interpreted some of Dora's dream material as reflecting her "remorseless craving for revenge."

It's obvious that my preceding review of the Dora case study is predicated upon my belief that it reveals far more about Freud's deep psychopathology than any minor mental problems that might have afflicted the patient. Especially in the context of his own mind-boggling symptoms throughout 1900, his tendentious presentation of this case study can be perceived as fatally flawed by numerous counter-transference factors. It is sometimes claimed that this study is useful, because in it Freud presented new and valuable ideas about transference phenomena, but that also is an exaggeration, since he'd already discussed transference effects in prior works. In this study he merely glanced at difficulties that can arise when transference factors are ignored—his failure to recognize that Dora was perceiving him as the evil Herr K.—but he offered no new ideas here about constructive uses of transference factors to enhance the progress of analysis towards a final "cure." Moreover, the devastating deficiency of this case study was Freud's total ignoring of counter-transference factors, regarding his own blatant distortions that interfered with the healing process.

More Name Magic

On previous pages our understanding of name magic facilitated the uncovering of Freud's numerous counter-transferences, and we'll see that these factors have not been exhausted if we consider the actual names of Dora's father and Herr K. Let's start with the given name of Dora's father, which was Philip. That name was part of an important magical name-series in Freud's life that started with his older step-brother and with a boyhood friend named Philipp whom Freud described as giving him early instruction in sexual matters (without saying whether bisexual acts were included in this early education). It also included Freud's fantasy identification with Philipp of Macedon, the father of Alexander the Great, both of these being heroic figures with whom Freud identified.

Now we begin to understand that Philipp Bauer, due to name magic, must have had a greater salience for Freud's unconscious mind than we could have guessed. Consider that Dora's father was a reprehensible fellow who was regularly cheating with the wife of one of his dearest friends, Herr K., sometimes right under K.'s nose. Undoubtedly, this would have strongly reminded Freud of another immoral Philipp from his early years, none other than his stepbrother Philipp Freud. For Sigmund's boyhood dream about the bird-beaked figures, and his memory of himself as a child crying in front of a large cabinet, offered clues that his brothers Philipp and/or Emanuel were having sexual relations with the beautiful Amalia, right under the nose of Jacob Freud. This material suggests a tight correlation, in Freud's mind, between the names of Philipp Bauer and his brother Philipp Freud.

The plot thickens when we learn that the true name of Herr K. was Hans Zellenka, a handsome Jewish man who worked as a commercial agent. The given name of that man, Hans, is the equivalent of the name Johann, whose English form is John. These were items in another important name-series of Freud's that started with his nephew John (his greatest rival) and included Johann Zajic, Jean (John) Charcot, and Freud's oldest son Jean Martin. It also included his fantasy identifications with Johann Goethe and Johann Faust, as well as the young patient whom Freud called "little Hans," and others with similar names.

Because of Freud's proclivity for name magic, the names of Herr Zallenka (K.) would have made special correlations in Freud's mind with several important figures from his Freiberg years, particularly Johann Zajic, Monica Zajic (the infamous nanny), and John Freud. Notice that the name of Hans Zellenka is the equivalent of Johann Z., which coordinates with the name of the kinsman of Freud's nanny, also a Johann Z. In my previous name research concerning Freud, I've concluded that any surname beginning with the letter "Z" (like Zola) could have intense relevance for him, since that is the first letter of Monica's surname. Therefore, the true surname of Herr K. (Zellenka) provided automatic, magical correlations with the names and identities of both Johann Zajic and Monica Zajic. (Already it's clear that Herr K.'s real given name correlates with the given name of John Freud.)

What we now can understand is that, in terms of Freud's susceptibility to name magic, the names of Phillip Bauer and Hans Zellenka (Herr K.) had remarkable capacities to evoke in Freud's mind the names of Phillip and John Freud, Johann Zajic, and Monica Zajic—as well as the entire sexual maelstrom of those early years when young Sigi and John Freud were being "seduced" (molested) by their nanny and, in all probability, the adults in the Freud household were involved in immoral sexual games with one another. (Recall that Freud identified with important figures in the play *The Robbers* partly because names of key characters matched those of persons in his family life, and fantasies.)

On previous pages I've explained my reasons for believing that Dora was able to represent to Freud two figures connected with Freiberg, his nanny and Gisela Fluss. Now, the most recent material on name magic has shown how Phillip Bauer and Hans Zellenka could easily have represented additional figures connected with Freiberg including Phillip and John Freud, Johann Zajic, and the infamous nanny. Furthermore, it has become clearer now that Freud's unconscious mind might have dimly perceived that the adult figures in the Dora case study were involved in similar immoral sexual activities with one another, comparable to what was happening among the adults in his Freiberg family. In addition, the attempted seductions of Dora by an assumedly protective person were able to be correlated with the presumed seductions of young Sigi and John Freud by their "protective" nanny. Since Dora and Freud were similar kinds of victims in childhood, the despised feminine side of Freud's psyche probably made a punitive identification with the "evil" Dora, his patient, as another counter-transference factor that caused him to denigrate her.

All of this provides further significant reasons why Freud might have become so powerfully fixated upon the Dora case study, despite its obvious clinical weaknesses. That explanation emphasizes his lifelong cravings for revenge, rooted originally in "the Freiberg catastrophe," with all its sexual and existential complexities. A brief statement of my thesis is that Freud had maintained an undying need to revenge himself on all the sexually immoral adults in his family who had sadistically "killed" nanny by providing a public disclosure of their prior sexual degradation. Since he unconsciously correlated the key adults in Dora's life with the perverse adults of his Freiberg years, when he wrote that case study and dropped numerous clues that allowed for public exposure and ridicule of the perverse adults in Dora's case study, Freud was thereby (by analogy) taking his revenge upon his own corrupt kinsmen of the Freiberg era. In general, this was another of the many counter-transference factors that probably led to "distortions" in his brief analysis of Dora.

Revenge and Suicide

In my opinion, Freud's immense craving for revenge towards Dora, Fliess, Breuer, Ida Fliess (and many other persons) was the crucial counter-transference factor that contaminated the treatment of this girl in late 1900. Although revenge was the key contaminant, linked to it were factors of lust, power, grandiosity, and Freud's suicide/murder complex which, in my view, posed a genuine threat to Dora's personal safety, as also was true with Emma Eckstein, Margit Kremzir, and other patients.

Readers who evaluate the Dora case in light of the immense pressures on Freud in 1900, and for the rest of his life history, should not find it difficult to recognize that his personal problems with REVENGE were central in this case (though I have not cited various other revenge-factors, including his cold refusal to take Dora back into analysis when she allegedly requested this). Another crucial issue in this case concerned the theme of suicide, which was cloaked by Freud so that readers might find it difficult to recognize how very important it really was. So I'd like to say a little bit more about this now.

As already noted, the issue of suicide should have been compelling to Freud when he began treating Dora in early October 1900, since he had lost

Margit Kremzir to suicide less than six months earlier, near the time when he admitted to Fliess that he was struggling with madness and felt that his patients (called "victims") were *torturing* him. However, in spite of the suicide note that Dora had written just before starting analysis, and. the enormous stresses she's been experiencing for several years, *and* the fact that depressed adolescents pose special risks regarding suicide due to the volatility of their emotions—Freud had little to say about the suicide factor in her case! In fact, his neglect of this issue made it seem that he regarded it as unimportant. Or perhaps he was repressing its importance, if something more insidious were not reflected by his seeming neglect of this crucial and dangerous factor. Of course, it's likely that he downplayed the suicide factor in his case study, because it was in serious conflict with the ways that he ran roughshod over Dora's feelings while repeatedly accusing her of hypocrisies and gross sexual desires, in his role of the Grand Inquisitor (who was famous historically for his skill as a verbal torturer).

Actually, the theme of suicide ran throughout the Dora case study, although Freud managed to keep it under wraps. Not only was Dora suicidal, but also her father had been seriously suicidal at some point prior to her analysis with Freud. He mentioned this only briefly, the neglect of this topic again implying that it was an insignificant matter. However, he did report that Frau K. had provided emotional support for Phillip Bauer during his time of suicidal intentions. Evidently, he'd walked into a wood to kill himself privately, though Freud did not elaborate on the matter. Freud did indicate that Dora's father had not been too worried that she might kill herself, after reading her suicide note and taking her to Freud for help, but that is very doubtful since Phillip Bauer had experienced the ravages of suicidal ideation personally and knew how dangerous it could be. Freud himself should have reflected that the voicing of a suicide threat by a depressed adolescent ought to be a matter of serious concern to any parent or clinician, and that the decision to write a suicide note can accelerate the danger of an actual suicide attempt quite considerably.

Additionally, Freud hinted at the end of his study that Herr K. could also have been a suicidal person, considering that he'd been involved in a suspicious "accident," one that might have killed him in what could be regarded as a "cryptic" suicide. Months after Dora's treatment was concluded, one of K.'s two children had died, probably his daughter Klara, who'd been a fragile girl. Dora visited the family to express her condolences, and she also then confronted Herr K. about his behavior at the lake, and he admitted to her that he was hoping to seduce her then. Some months later she was walking on the street one day and unexpectedly came across K. "in a place where there was a great deal of traffic." When he saw Dora, suddenly he stopped in his tracks "as though in bewilderment, and in his abstraction he had allowed himself to be knocked down by a cart," but he was not injured badly. Freud added a note here, stating that this was "an interesting contribution to the problem of indirect suicide . ." One can guess that the death of his child had provoked guilty feelings in Herr K. concerning his destructive behaviors towards young Dora, and when suddenly he saw her on the street this triggered a cryptic suicide attempt by this man—who obviously had deep emotional problems, considering his attempt to seduce a child of thirteen and his strange tolerance of his wife's illicit behaviors.

Suicide and the K. Initial-Series

The above data has been offered as background for my final suggestion: that Freud chose the pseudonyms "Herr K." and "Frau K." to represent Hans Zellenka and his wife, as items in another magical name-series (really, an initial-series), perhaps created by Freud's psyche to reflect his irrational concerns about suicide and revenge. In comparison with Freud's firm declaration that he'd expropriated the name Dora from the name of a governess in his sister's home, he gave no explanation as to why he decided to give Hans Zellenka the pseudonym "K." But my own research indicates that this was tied to a magical initial-series (in *Name Magic* an extensive discussion of initial-series is found).

Freud's first use of the pseudonym Herr K. occurred in his letters to Fliess dated August 18 and August 23, 1894. He used it to describe a 24 year-old patient who developed an anxiety neurosis after falling in love with an unattainable (engaged) young woman who excited him sexually by being a flirt. This man suffered a series of dreadfully frightening "panic attacks," as well as attacks of deep depression lasting only a few minutes. Freud described the man's unpleasurable sex life as contributing to the patient's psychic enfeeblement, and compared his problem with the neuroses of men who suffer from prolonged engagement periods. Concerning the latter issue, one suspects that Freud identified with this patient K., since Freud himself had suffered numerous depressive symptoms during his prolonged engagement to Martha. He did not reveal the outcome of this case, but ended his comments by taking special note of the short attacks of deep depression suffered by this Herr K., hinting that Freud may have sensed an underlying problem with suicidal potentials in this man, which is always a possible factor with patients who suffer either depression or severe panic attacks. That the patient was age 24 also could have prompted Freud to identify with him unconsciously, when we consider his strange behaviors at age 24 which caused him to spend some time in a military jail, presumably as a reflection of his lustful yearning for his jailed nanny (that unattainable mother-image), which was at the core of his *suicide*/murder complex.

The next item in this K-series occurred in a short paper that Freud dated

November 10, 1899, which was six days after the publication of *The Interpretation of Dreams*, when his anxiety was high about the critical reception of the book he hoped would bring fame and fortune. This brief work is titled "A Premonitory Dream Fulfilled," and it appears as Appendix A of the Discus-Avon paperback edition of the dream book (1967, pp. 661-4).

Freud began this piece by relating that an estimable woman called Frau B. had told him some years previously that she'd had a prophetic dream. First, she had dreamed that she met Dr. K., "a friend and former family doctor of hers" in front of Hiess's shop on the principal avenue for shopping in the center of Vienna (the *Kärtnerstrasse*). Then the next morning, as she walked along that same street, she met that doctor "at the very spot she had dreamt of." (According to Freud's viewpoint, it must have been when she saw this doctor in front of Hiess's shop that she remembered her "prophetic" dream of the previous night, and he used that assumption of his to weaken any credibility by his readers that this was an actual paranormal dream.)

Freud then mentioned that when this woman was young she was cajoled into marrying an elderly but wealthy merchant. A few years later he lost his fortune, contracted tuberculosis, and eventually died. During their years of poverty, the young wife supported herself and her tubercular husband by giving music lessons, with emotional support from their family physician, Dr. K., who helped her find students and also treated her husband. Another friend was a lawyer, also a Dr. K., who handled the tangled legal affairs of her husband "while at the same time he made love to the young woman and—for the first time—set her passion aflame." At that time in her life she experienced what she felt was a "remarkable coincidence," which hints at her credulousness about telepathy. This love affair brought her no real happiness, but one day she was in her room "sobbing in passionate longing for her friend and helper," the lawyer, when he opened the door to visit her, at that very moment. (Freud noted that he probably visited her fairly often, making this "coincidence" not at all remarkable, actually.)

After that previous scene, 25 years elapsed during which she became the widow of a second wealthy man "who left her with a child and a fortune." But the old woman had remained in love with the lawyer, Dr. K., who now (in the era of her "prophetic" dream) saw her frequently as the administrator of her estate, but not as her lover.

At this point in his narrative, Freud used some complicated psychologizing to explain-away the woman's belief that she'd had a prophetic dream. He used several tortuous suppositions (which I'll not bother to describe) to support his view that she was the victim of mental distortions, one of which assumed that she had experienced mental confusion by equating the two men who shared the same pseudonym, the two doctors called "K." In effect, her dream concealed a wish that she might meet with her lover again, but that wish had been censored by the illusion that she'd had a prophetic dream about his counterpart, her family physician.

My assumption is that Freud unconsciously called the two "doctors" in the above paper by the pseudonym "K." due to some similarities that he dimly perceived with the earlier case of his 24 year-old patient whom he also called "K." In the case of that young K. in 1894, there was the strong theme of unattainable love and hints of infidelity (the flirt), along with Freud's comment about couples who wait for one another for very long periods of time. Concerning his paper about the pitiful Frau B., again we find the themes of unattainable love and waiting a very long time in hope of possessing the desired love object. (One can guess that in November 1899 when Freud wrote that paper about Frau B., he felt that he had waited a long time to attain his desired worldly success and, thereby, to repossess the lost love object, his nanny.) It would not have been unreasonable for Freud to imagine that Frau B.'s sobbing and depression during her first marriage hinted at suicidal feelings in her, which he might have connected with the melancholic attacks and presumed suicidal potentials of Herr K. in 1894, helping to knit the two narratives together in Freud's mind.

Also there were sexual themes that connected the two narratives of 1894 and 1899. In the first one we find a young engaged woman who was flirting and perhaps having sexual dalliances with other men, reminding us that Freud had suffered during his engagement period with grave fears that Martha was "involved" with another man (perhaps a replay of his fears and jealousies about nanny and John Freud). That engaged woman in the first narrative who possibly was unfaithful finds a correlation in the second narrative with the young wife who was engaged in sexual activity with her husband's friend and lawyer, Dr. K. One can imagine why Freud unconsciously identified with this lawyer called K., if it is true that Freud had a sexual relationship with his wife's dearest friend, her sister Minna, indicating somewhat analogous cheating behaviors by Freud. (Also recall that his first preference for a vocation was the law.)

Actually, Freud also would have identified readily with the second K. within the 1899 paper, since Freud and this man both played the roles of caring physician. That there were two men who played somewhat complementary roles towards Frau B., one a benevolent helper and the other a devious seducer, both of these men sharing the same "name" (Dr. K.), reminds us of the literary technique that splits one personality into two figures like Dr. Jekyll and Mr. Hyde. Therefore, the two men called Dr. K. could easily have raised the issue of dual personality in Freud's imagination. Unconsciously, being marginally aware of his own dual personality, Freud would thereby have had another reason for forming an identification with both of those men called Dr. K., just as he presumably had identified with the young man he called K. in his 1894 letter to Fliess.

Now we are ready to consider the fourth person who can be called "K." in this magical initial-series. About five months after Freud had finished writing his short article about Frau B.'s "prophetic" dream involving the two Dr. Ks, Freud completed his two weeks of work with the Hungarian woman named Mrs. Margit Kremzir. In his letter to Fliess dated April 25, 1900 he reported that he'd treated this woman for fourteen days and then had dismissed her as being an (untreatable) case of paranoia, whereupon she soon hanged herself in a Vienna hotel room. In his letters to Fliess he did not mention any of her ideation or behaviors that were uncovered during his brief work with her. Masson (1985, p. 412) has cited a short notice in one of Vienna's newspapers on April 20, 1900 which disclosed that she had hanged herself after consulting various professors about a severe stomach ailment, "out of desperation about her hopeless state." This newspaper account did not mention that she was a patient of Dr. Freud, and I don't know whether any other Vienna newspapers mentioned that fact. If a newspaper did mention Freud's name as her doctor, perhaps out of prejudice against psychoanalysis, a public disclosure of that kind could have put a great additional stress on Freud in 1900, further stoking his vengeful feelings. (It seems unlikely to me that a newspaper would have ignored medical confidentiality in that fashion, unless there were "yellow journals" in Vienna that disregarded such conventions.)

At the end of the previous chapter, I discussed that Freud probably had acted-out a great deal of name magic concerning the several names of Margit Kremzir, including her maiden name of Weiss de Szurda. If so, that would have caused her married surname, Kremzir, to take on a special salience for Freud, particularly its initial letter "K," facilitating his incorporation of this patient "K" into the magical initial-series we've just been examining. Further reasons for his incorporation of "Kremzir's" initial letter "K" into this series pertain to the factors of suicide and probably depression in this case in April 1900, as were also deduced in the previous cases that focused on various persons called "K." by Freud.

Now let's move on to the Dora case study and some of the probable reasons why Freud made Mr. and Mrs. Zellenka additional figures in his initial-series involving the letter "K." Conceptually and emotionally, there are a number of factors that could link the two adult Ks in the Dora case with the narrative about Frau B. and her two Dr. Ks. For example, like Frau B., the infamous Frau K. in Dora's story was sexually enmeshed with her husband's friend over many years. Recall that Frau B.'s story of 1899 incorporated the themes of unattainable love, and the desire over many years to possess the love object, while those same themes also occur with regard to Mr. Zellenka's longterm pursuit of young Ida Bauer. (The reader will notice that those same themes occur in both Dora's story and the case about K. in 1894.)

Previously, I mentioned my view that the themes of revenge and suicide were the two most powerful themes that Freud incorporated in the Dora case study. Those themes provided Freud with particularly compelling reasons for connecting the Dora case with the case of Mrs. Kremzir, thereby prompting him to carry her surname's initial letter "K." into the Dora case, as it then applied to Herr K. and his wife (the Zellenkas). Concerning the second of those themes, it's quite obvious that the suicide issue was prominent in the case of Mrs. Kremzir, as in Dora's story. With regard to the issue of revenge, near the end of the previous chapter I emphasized its probably powerful role in connection with Mrs. Kremzir's maiden name, Weiss de Szurda—concerning Freud's hatred of the man who who disgraced the Freud family in the 1860s, also named Weiss. Similarly, the issue of revenge was very prominent in the Dora case study, emphasizing Freud's projection of his own intensely vengeful feelings onto the patient he called Dora and, secondarily, the desires for revenge against Herr K. that did exist in her.

Concerning the above material, there is a related factor that pertains both to the Dora case and that of Mrs. Kremzir, providing another connection between those cases. This factor can be called: "waiting a long time to obtain satisfaction." In Dora's case, she had to wait from childhood, when Herr K. first tried to molest her, until her adult years when she confronted him at his child's funeral, to obtain revenge and satisfaction regarding his early betrayal of her trust. Concerning the case of Mrs. Kremzir's suicide, if one assumes that Freud used her as a bizarre surrogate to punish Simon Weiss's betrayal of his uncle Josef in the 1860s, one sees that Sigmund waited a very long time to obtain his vengeful satisfaction against Herr Weiss by provoking his patient's suicide in 1900. (Notice that this issue of "waiting a long time for satisfaction" also can be found regarding the earlier instances of this K-series.)

Now I will encourage the reader to think about the letter "Z" in the names de Szurda, Kremzir, and Zellenka and what connections might have existed in Freud's mind with the surname of his nanny, Monica Zajic, pertaining to my suggestion that he identified Dora with his nanny and with Gisela Fluss. Finally, there may have been another way that the Kremzir case was connected in Freud's mind with the case of Dora. Within a span of eight months in 1900 both of those cases represented painful clinical failures for Freud which, successively, should have been quite damaging to his ego and to his sense of competence as a therapist. However, he utilized his skills as a novelist in writing up the Dora case, in his usual tendentious fashion, and provided his followers with an exciting script which they used to demonstrate his "genius," transforming an abysmal failure into an alleged clinical triumph. If the initial letter K provided a magical link in Freud's mind between the Kremzir and Dora cases, his fantasized triumph regarding Dora might have enabled him to transform the Kremzir disaster into some semblance of a clinical success, at least in *his* fevered imagination.

Chapter Eight

The Murder of Emanuel Freud

An Introduction to Parricide

This chapter will focus upon my thesis that in October of 1914, soon after WWI had begun, the train mishap that took Emanuel Freud's life was not a mere accident. My claim is that he was pushed from that train by someone whose identity remains unknown—that an assassin committed this murder at the direction of Sigmund Freud, who probably paid a tidy sum for this killing. In great detail, the following pages will explore this thesis of familial assassination with such a wealth of supporting evidence that some readers may feel deluged by it.

But first, allow me to make a simple restatement of the major reason why Freud was driven to arrange for the murder of his eldest half-brother Emanuel. The core factors have to do with young Sigmund's "seduction" by his nanny, Monica Zajic, which generated the boy's guilty bond with this primal mother-figure and fixated his Oedipal death-wishes towards the particular father-figure, his brother Emanuel, whom he blamed for the "disappearance" of Monica. Those death-wishes towards Emanuel (and other kinsmen including Jacob, Phillip, John) were further intensified in 1859 when Sigmund experienced a horrendous uprooting of his family life by the Freuds' sudden departure by train for Leipzig, leaving behind the beloved nanny as a painful and irrevocable loss. This entire traumatic scenario has been characterized by me, and by other writers, as "the Freiberg catastrophe." With considerable certainty, I regard this as the primary wound underlying Freud's complex psychopathology and his desires to murder Emanuel and John Freud. However, eventually we'll see that there were other strange motives and fantasies that entered the picture, causing Freud to kill Emanuel with that strange weapon (a passenger train) and in the specific time-period that he chose, late 1914.

At the outset, some readers may doubt my claim that a severe emotional trauma that happened to Freud during his third and fourth years of life could have festered underground for 55 years before it finally provoked the murder of his eldest brother. If so, these skeptics should review materials in previous chapters which show that Freud sometimes waited many years before he took conscious or unconscious revenge upon persons (or surrogates) whom he believed had victimized him. Consider the case of Gisela Fluss Popper and her husband, whose marriage made him feel terribly rejected in his teen years, and the retribution which he delivered (as a displacement) to the husband of Gizella Pálos, many decades later. And wasn't Freud the man who announced after an argument with his mother-in-law, that he was capable of waiting a long while before taking revenge upon this woman who had criticized his willful, infantile behaviors?

Analysts may object to my claim that Sigmund waited 55 years before taking a fatal revenge upon Emanuel by insisting that, circa 1900, Freud had cured all essential aspects of his psychopathology via a "heroic" self-analysis. Contrary to their position, previous chapters have described his deeply pathological behaviors throughout the year 1900, also during 1904 (the Acropolis episode), and in later eras of his life. Furthermore, much evidence will become available in my future works which leads to the conclusion that Freud suffered deep mental imbalances periodically, *during his entire lifetime*.

Without further delay, let's examine my position that Freud's covert madness caused him to require compulsively that a speeding passenger train had to be chosen as the vehicle of retribution when he decided to arrange the murder of his brother Emanuel. This was a special instance of the Law of Talion (example: if a man is stabbed in the leg with a knife, then his assailant must receive the same punishment with a knife). Freud himself had described the workings of Talion in the lives of neurotics, as a holdover of unconscious infantile functioning. So it's not surprising that a trauma in his early childhood would have prompted his use of this same primitive mechanism. This refers to the dramatic climax of "the Freiberg catastrophe," when Sigmund was forced to leave his nanny and childhood home via a train ride that was enormously painful for him, leading him to fantasize that gas jets at the Breslau station were souls burning in hell. In effect, this vehicle represented a horrendous "hell train" for young Sigi. Thereafter, it infused many of his murderous impulses towards Emanuel, and the other male members of his family, into other trains and railway stations—and, more diffusely, into journeys of all kinds.

It seems clear that Freud's prolonged "railway phobia" originated in the previous childhood trauma, which became the cornerstone of his well-known "train and travel neurosis." So it will be useful for us now to examine this area of Freud's psychopathology.

Freud's Train/Travel Neurosis

Various authors have written about Freud's train and travel neurosis including Ernest Jones, who made scattered references to this topic in his three-volume biography of Freud. Also, Jones (1954) wrote a brief journal article with reflections upon this subject titled "Freud's Early Travels." He noted that the master had a great love of travelling, yet suffered from what Freud called a bad "travelling phobia." Jones resisted the use of that term phobia emphasizing that a true phobia has the function of inhibiting some activity, though "never for a moment did Freud hesitate to carry out any journey he had a chance of."

With that misleading disclaimer, Jones simply ignored Freud's early inhibitions about travelling to Rome, and his probably greater resistances to making a trip to Athens (until 1904). Also, Jones underplayed the significance of Freud's travel concerns by citing his allegedly mild anxiety about being late for trains and by delimiting his problem "to attacks of acute anxiety at the moment of embarking on the journey." Jones neglected to emphasize that this "acute anxiety" amounted to severe panic attacks in which the fear of death (and murder) were present covertly, and that Freud's persistent fear that loved ones would die in train accidents was one of numerous signs of his death and murder concerns (as will be explained). Innocuously, Jones stated that Freud's travel anxieties existed "because of the wish to escape from something unpleasant," something "forbidden," but Jones remarked that he had no interest in pursuing this matter. This is another example of Jones's dainty censorship ploys, which should convince us that this topic is filled with horrendous significances that he did not wish to explore with us.

A more informative article relating to Freud's train and travel neurosis is Shengold's work titled "The Metaphor of the Journey in *The Interpretation of Dreams*" (1979). Initially, it was noted by Shengold that Freud made "consistent use of the metaphor of a journey" in his dream book, and one can even say that the primary structure of the book is based upon the idea of a journey—reminding us that Dante's *Divine Comedy*, with its descent into Hell, is also "constructed around a journey." Shengold remarked that Freud's self-analysis can be viewed as "a truly heroic journey" of discovery, and that: "One of the main symptoms of Freud's neurosis, as he revealed to Fliess, was a 'travelling phobia' . . and this was the subject of much work in his self-analysis." (I would agree that Freud's train and travel complex was near the core of his pathology, for it related to his intention eventually to murder Emanuel Freud.)

Shengold endorsed Freud's assertion that his "travelling phobia" had originated with the train ride, at age four, that took him from Freiberg to Leipzig, leaving behind the nurse who was his "first instructress in sexual matters." Unlike Jones, Shengold did not shy away from endorsing an Oedipal interpretation of these matters, emphasizing that concerns about death must have been a major factor in Freud's travel neurosis. Shengold mentioned Freud's belief that "a journey symbolizes death, the last journey," representing the traumatic separations pertaining to "a going away from the mother and to castration . ." But, for Shengold, voyages also symbolize sexual intercourse and condense "both halves of the Oedipus complex"— sexual relations with one parent and "getting rid of" (killing) the other parent.

In that language, Shengold showed awareness that Freud's train and travel neurosis involved deep anxieties about sex and death, specifically his concealed desires to "get rid of"—to murder—his various father-figures, including Jacob and Emanuel Freud. It's too bad that Shengold did not go one step farther and express bemused wonderment that Sigmund Freud's preferred father-figure, Emanuel, was killed in an uncanny railway "accident"—then tying that item to the bizarre death of Wilhelm Fliess's father. (I'll discuss Herr Fliess's railway death later.) Shengold even managed to compare Freud's compulsive voyaging to his "re-tracing the path of Oedipus," the hero who killed his own father, though it did not occur to Shengold that Freud perhaps had "arranged" to kill some father-figures of his own: Fleischl, Emanuel, and maybe a near-miss with Fliess at Achensee.

In Anzieu's book (1986) about Freud's self-analysis he discussed Freud's dream about the death of his father Jacob (the "Close the eyes" dream), and remarked (p. 173) that it connoted Freud's dawning awareness that death can be symbolized as a journey. Briefly, this dream took place the night before Jacob's funeral, and in the dream Sigmund saw a poster, like those which forbid people to smoke in railway waiting rooms, with lettering that said: "You are requested to close the eyes." (etc.) Sagely, Anzieu remarked that the dream's citing of a railway waiting room referred covertly to Freud's railway phobia.

Also, Anzieu seemed to endorse (pp. 172-3) Conrad Stein's view that the preceding dream, and others in which Freud's father appeared, exhibited Sigmund's "still strong infantile wish to kill his father." Stein believed that, after Jacob's death, Freud still had a powerful need "to be the author of his father's death," i.e. Stein noted that the dream reveals Sigmund's need to undo his father's death, so that he himself could murder Jacob! (The relevance of Stein's viewpoint to Emanuel's death seems quite obvious to me, for Stein pointed to the connection between Freud's railway phobia in this dream and his intense patricidal urges, which cannot fail to include a primal father-figure like Emanuel.)

Articles by Mark Kanzer (1979, pp. 15-16, 262 ff.) suggest connections between Freud's travel neurosis, agoraphobic tendencies, and death-wishes towards various brother-figures.* Kanzer noted that agoraphobics "often can venture forth" in their journeying only when accompanied by persons whom they give special trust, but analysis shows that these trusted ones are covertly the recipients of their death-wishes. Commenting upon the years when Alexander Freud was his brother's travelling companion, Kanzer claimed that Sigmund's apparent affection towards the younger brother concealed his desires to destroy him (as was felt unconsciously towards Julius) "at the end of the journey (a death symbol)." While analyzing Freud's paper on "the Acropolis episode," Kanzer posited that Sigmund desired magically to obtain an exchange of identities with Alexander in order to gain a "decade of renewed powers while the younger brother is advanced that much closer to the end" of life's journey. Kanzer called this "A Faustian pact with the demons!"—which has great relevance to my later chapter on Freud's Satanic pacts and his identifications with the devil. (Kanzer's views seem applicable to the journey which Freud and Fliess made to Achensee in 1900, and to the latter's claim that Freud planned to murder him there.)

In different ways, the preceding viewpoints by Shengold, Stein, Anzieu, and Kanzer all contribute to the idea that Freud's train and travel neurosis was intimately connected to powerful urges to murder his kinsmen (and surrogates for them, like Fliess). A brief review of selected items from the Freud/Fliess letters should provide additional support for the idea that there were strong connections between Freud's travel neurosis and his murderous wishes.

Probably, Freud suffered from his train and travel neurosis in all the years prior to 1890, starting with age four at the Breslau station. Evidently, it was in 1890 that he first displayed his train phobia to Wilhelm Fliess (see *Complete*, p. 358). For in a letter to Fliess in July 1899 Freud reminded his friend about their first "congress," which took place in Salzburg in 1890. At the end of that meeting, together they made a brief journey, a walking tour to Berchtesgaden, so that Freud could catch a train there, back to Vienna. At the Berchtesgaden railway station Freud displayed to Fliess an intense panic attack relating to his train departure, which he later described as "one of my finest attacks of travel anxiety." That this was a florid attack of anxiety, comparable to a panic attack, is suggested by Freud's comment (p. 268): "You yourself have seen my travel anxiety at its height."

In Freud's letter to Fliess dated August 18, 1897 he mentioned an imminent and extensive train trip that he and Martha were about to take together. He wrote that Martha was greatly looking forward to the trip "though the daily reports of train accidents are not exactly apt to put the

---

Emanuel was both a brother-figure and father-figure for Sigmund.

father and mother of a family in the mood for it." Here, Freud implied his underlying fears that he and Martha would be injured or killed in a train accident, and he noted that though Fliess might laugh at him, he'd experienced episodic anxieties that "last for half a day." He added that: "Half an hour ago I was pulled out of my fear of the next train accident ... " Some positive thoughts about travelling had helped to "put a stop to the tomfoolery." His confession about this train anxiety was ended when he wrote to Fliess: "But this must remain strictly between us." (That final caveat indicates the veil of censorship that he placed on this sensitive subject of his train phobia.)

About three months later, in his letter of December 5, 1897 he wrote Fliess of his inhibitions about visiting Rome, and stated that: "My longing for Rome is .. deeply neurotic." Then he revealed that his self-analysis had shown that his childhood train ride from Freiberg to Leipzig, and the gas flames (spirits burning in hell) at the Breslau railway station, were connected with his train and travel neurosis. His words were that his "travel anxiety, now overcome, also is bound up with this . ."—and then he gave a farewell to Fliess, by asking for a quick answer to this *"meschuggene letter"* (Yiddish for "crazy").

In the preceding sentences, Freud made a vague but accurate connecting of his train and travel neurosis with that primal train ride from Freiberg to Leipzig, which was the immediate aftermath of "the Freiberg catastrophe." His sudden claim that his travel anxiety already had been "overcome" by his self-analysis was patently false.* The less-than-four months since his previous intense anxieties (concerning the train ride with Martha) testifies to this falsehood, as does his admission of still suffering then from his "deeply neurotic" phobia concerning Rome, which was one aspect of his travel anxiety. In ending the previous message with the notion that his letter (and he, himself) were *meschuggene* or "crazy," Freud revealed unconsciously that his train and travel neurosis, and the powerful murderous wishes underlying them, were major aspects of his ambulatory psychosis. (Recall Breuer's diagnosis of Freud's "moral insanity" and Freud's acknowledgment of his own madness in some of his letters to Fliess in 1900.)

Let's return to Freud's letter of August 18, 1897 in which he revealed intense fears that he and Martha might be injured or killed in a train ride they were about to take. This was one recurrent aspect of Freud's train phobia, and again it should be assessed in light of the Law of Talion operating in his unconscious mind. That is, Freud harbored very specific desires that some of his kinsmen and friends (like Fliess) would be killed intrain accidents, so his warped psyche provided retribution by plaguing

---

In his letter of December 21, 1899 he made another claim-that a new "solution" to his former railroad phobia had just been found pertaining to "infantile greediness." The word "former" reeks of falsity.

him with fears that he, Martha, and beloved friends (like Fliess) would actually be killed by passenger trains. (Later, we'll note his magical stratagem in 1925 to protect his daughter Anna from a train wreck.)

The preceding remarks are given some support by Jones's analysis (I, p. 312) of Freud's "constant excessive anxiety" over Fliess's "minor disturbances of health," and his persistent anxiety that Fliess might succumb to a train accident. Jones referred to these as familiar manifestations "of ill-disposed wishes in the unconscious"—which is euphemistic language indicating that Freud harbored murderous desires towards Fliess (which Jones, of course, had no interest in correlating with the murderous Achensee "congress" of 1900). But Jones was candid enough to remark that when Fliess was involved in railway journeys: "Freud's anxiety about railway accidents in general got personally applied to an unnecessary extent he was evidently ashamed of." Now why did Freud become so ashamed of this behavior, one might have asked the shrewd Dr. Jones, as we again point heirs of the great Welsh analyst towards the topics of murder and Achensee.

It's amusing that Jones (I, p. 305) cited Freud's occasional attacks of the "dread of dying" in the same context as his "anxiety about traveling by rail." Jones then deplored that Freud made no connection "between the two types of anxiety attack." His opinion was that most analysts "would now at once suspect" such a connection, so that one could not help feeling that Freud's "analysis of them was never quite complete." Of course, if Jones himself had been more honest he'd have correlated Freud's "dread of dying" and the railway phobia with his intense murder-wishes against his kinsmen and other persons, including Fliess.

At this point, I'd like to provide some additional items indicating that Freud's train and travel neurosis was connected with the subject of death, including Freud's wishes to murder and fears of being murdered. Let's start with a letter he wrote to Martha Bernays in the fall of 1883 describing a railway trip he'd just taken to Leipzig. He remarked that, especially on trains, he had a need for fresh air, and when he opened a window on the train (in winter) this caused a furor among the passengers who yelled that he should shut it, and muttered anti-Semitic remarks. When one man threatened him, Freud showed that he was "very ready for a fight" and invited this adversary "to step up and take what was coming to him." Freud added: "I was quite prepared to kill him, but he did not step up . . ."

So here we find that Freud was quite ready to kill a man, while riding aboard a train, on the slim pretext that he needed fresh air from a window. As I remarked in an earlier chapter, one could guess that train rides had a peculiar capacity to evoke murderous feelings and behaviors in this pedantic fellow, Dr. Freud. But there is more to the story.

His reason for travelling to Leipzig (above) was to meet his half-brothers,

Emanuel and Philipp, to discuss some family business. When Sigmund arrived in Leipzig, before his brothers did, he left the railway station and chose a hotel for their meeting place called the Hotel Stadt *Freiberg*, commenting to Martha that "by a strange coincidence" it's name incorporated the name of his birthplace. We can guess that this journey in 1883 was a magical reversal of the primal railroad trip that had taken him away from his nanny, from Freiberg to Leipzig, at age four—for which he still harbored murderous rage towards his brother Emanuel in 1883. One can imagine, therefore, that the fellow on the train whom he wished to murder—specifically aboard a train—was a convenient surrogate for his "beloved" Emanuel. (Remember that 1883 marked the era when Freud had begun to engorge himself regularly with cocaine, and to kill various people with it, which might help explain why he was so "courageous" with that train adversary.)

The above fracas on the train to Leipzig in 1883 was not an isolated case. In his engagement letters to Martha, Freud mentioned other instances when he got into quarrels on trains about his need to get fresh air by opening windows. My guess is that he suffered from an irrational fear of being suffocated on trains, and that these vehicles had a special capacity to evoke the old death fears he'd experienced as a child while riding that "hell train" from Freiberg to Leipzig, away from nanny. Perhaps this was connected to his early identification with this primal mother, and his childhood fantasy that nanny/Amalia had been murdered by being stuffed into a large wooden chest (*Kasten*).

Since the above material suggests that Sigmund's loss of his nanny was a crucial factor underlying his train phobia, it seems relevant to cite his letter to Fliess dated December 21, 1899. In that letter, he stated that a patient's case had provided him with a new "solution" or explanation for the riddle of his "former railroad phobia." He stated that: "My phobia, then, was a fantasy of impoverishment, or rather a hunger phobia, determined by my infantile greediness and evoked by my wife's lack of a dowry . . " By implicating "infantile greediness" as the core of his train phobia, Freud (unawares) clarified for us that the loss of his wet-nurse's succulent breasts was a key factor in this phobia, which signified starvation and death to the terrified child (Sigi) who was forced to leave Freiberg. His mention of Martha, in this context, reinforces the view that his wife was a pallid substitute for his seductive but supportive nanny.

The above paragraph suggests that Freud's nanny and the correlated topics of fantasized starvation and death, were important factors underlying his train phobia. And, if so, the flagrant sexual aspects of his relationship with her point to Oedipal issues that were related to his train phobia, including his desires to kill his father-figures, Jacob and Emanuel. In one of his books Freud hinted that covert sexual factors were present in his railway phobia, but he continued to suppress the fact that patricidal urges were also important in his train fears.

My reference is to the *Three Essays on the Theory of Sexuality* (1905) which provides material indicating that railway trips by children are potent sources of sexual excitation. Freud emphasized the rhythmic movements on trains, also that boys take extraordinary interest in railways, and interrelated these ideas with his observation about pleasurable sexual sensations experienced on trains. Noting that repression can turn childish preferences into their opposite, he remarked that these boys in adolescence and adulthood will react to train movements with feelings of nausea, may become "terribly exhausted" by railway journeys, or will experience attacks of anxiety on rail trips and will protect themselves by developing a dread of railway-travel. Krüll (1986, p. 142) commented wisely that here Freud was describing his personal experiences that were subjective impressions pertaining to train rides and his railway phobia. But it's my view that he cited only one portion of his dread of train trips, repressing awareness of the patricidal urges that were the most horrendous aspects of his train and travel neurosis. Thereby he prevented his self-analysis from exploring this deadly topic in ways that might have saved the life of Emanuel Freud.

That Freud's mind associated train travel with his underlying patricidal urges is suggested by a favorite joke he liked to tell, which will now be summarized. —A poor Jewish fellow boarded a train to Karlsbad, but had no ticket. So repeatedly he was caught by the conductor and kicked off the train. But each time he stubbornly reboarded it, and was met with increasing violence on each successive occasion. At one station he met a friend who asked him where he was headed, and he replied: "To Karlsbad, if my constitution can stand it." (This joke is given on pages 227-8 of the dream book.)

One wonders whether for Freud, unconsciously, the poor Jew who was kicked off the train so violently, was a representative of his secretly hated brother Emanuel. This relates to my claim that Emanuel was pushed off that train in 1914 that was probably taking him to a resort city on the English coast (where he owned a vacation cottage). Part of the humor in the preceding joke is that the poor Jew was heading towards the well-known resort city of Karlsbad (in Czechoslovakia, the land of Freud's birth), which was famous for the healing powers of its mineral springs. Thus, the core of the joke is that this Jewish fellow bewails that he is going to Karlsbad, presumably to be healed of his ailments: 'If the damned train ride doesn't kill me first!'

To my mind, the parallels with Emanuel Freud's final train ride towards a resort on the coast are uncanny, especially when one considers that

Karlsbad is also located on a body of water, the Ohre river, a tributary of the Elbe. Did Freud's tortured psyche consider it funny that Emanuel, like the pitiful Jew in his joke, would be kicked off a (moving) passenger train? If so, consider that some areas of criminological research have shown that bizarre killers sometimes regard their murderous acts as being both creative and humorous.

Compare the previous item with this next one, a "slip" of Freud's which he described in *The Psychopathology of Everyday Life*, one that connects train travel with Emanuel, and with Freud's covert hostility towards his eldest brother (during the year 1908). Freud noted that one summer he'd promised his strict eldest brother (Emanuel) that he would visit him at an English seaside resort. Sigmund asked Emanuel if he might get off the train in Holland (at Rotterdam), so that he could spend one day viewing Rembrandt's paintings, on his way to England. But the autocratic Emanuel refused this request and insisted that Sigmund should travel directly by train to their resort rendezvous on the English coast, with no delays. However, while Freud was travelling on this long journey, he got off the train at Cologne "to change into the Rotterdam express, but it was nowhere to be found."

Not finding the needed train he fell into "exaggerated despair," but then decided to take advantage of this missed connection by travelling to Rotterdam, enabling him to spend one day viewing Rembrandt's great paintings in the Hague. The next morning he was travelling in a train across England towards Emanuel when he realized the "slip" that had occurred. A clear memory emerged of himself in the railway station at Cologne where he'd seen a large printed notice. This poster had pointed him towards a waiting train, in fact the very train he'd needed to continue his journey without interrupting his direct train travel towards his brother in England. He called this slip an incomprehensible "blindness" which had enabled him to disobey "my brother's instructions," so that he could see the desired paintings. He ended by writing that this "was merely a contrivance to keep my resolution hidden from myself till it had been completely carried out."

Were there other acts of "blindness" involving Freud, trains, and his brother Emanuel, also connected to his secret hatred for this brother? Allow me to offer one of my interpretations of the preceding "slip" by giving expression to a complaint that Sigmund's unconscious mind might have been making in 1908 to his strict elder brother, as follows: 'When I was making the long, uncomfortable train ride towards that seaside resort to join you, and wished to get off that train to visit Holland, you refused to acknowledge my needs. At a later time (1914) I will take perverse satisfaction in doing just the opposite with you. While you are on a train ride wishing to go directly to your comfortable seaside resort, I will refuse to permit this and will force *you* to leave the train—by being pushed off it, to your death!'

The idea that train rides could stimulate Freud's fears of death, presumably as retribution for his own murderous desires and acts against others, can be illustrated by the three incidents which follow, the first of which was mentioned earlier. In his third volume (p. 382) Jones remarked that there were times when Freud might meet someone who resembled him greatly, evoking the impression that he'd seen his "double," which immediately made him think "that it might be an omen of his death." Jones referred to the time in August 1902 (II, p. 21) when Freud met his brother Alexander in Bolzano (Bozen) on the way to visiting Naples.

Freud had just made an overnight journey by train, and Jones wrote that "Breuer and Fleischl were on the same train." (This was an uncanny error by Jones, since Fleischl had died eleven years earlier.) When Freud met Alexander, he related having met his "double," evidently on the preceding train ride, and asked: "Does this signify *Vedere Napole e poi morire?*" He was referring, perhaps partly in jest, to the saying "See Naples and die," and Jones added that: "Death was seldom far from his thoughts." When Freud told Alexander about this double he'd seen, he added that this was not the man named Horch, whom Jones assumed was another of Freud's doubles— "Evidently someone who closely resembled Freud." That was name magic, as well, for the German word *Horcher* means both listener and eavesdropper, and being an analyst made Freud a famous eavesdropper on the secrets of others. Perhaps this signified that a portion of his death anxiety related to his being an "eavesdropper," considering that he became infamous for not being able to maintain confidences regarding secrets that his friends told him. For example, there is the instance of Fliess's theories of bisexuality which Freud passed on to Weininger, leading to this young man's death.

Those thoughts of mine lead to another incident involving Freud's fear of death, as it pertained to trains and his probable concerns about retribution for his own evil and/or murderous acts against others. Jones wrote about (III, p. 391) a discussion Freud had with Jung concerning his visit to Athens in 1904 (which is the subject of the "Acropolis episode," already described).

Regarding that trip to Greece, Freud told Jung quite guardedly, and tendentiously, about a mysterious experience he'd had when certain numbers seemed to be pursuing him by showing up frequently on various objects, like "railway tickets"! Of course, Freud did not explain to Jung that he'd been terrified and depressed that these events might be omens of his impending death, since those railway tickets signified the death fears latent in his train phobia.

Nor did he explain to Jung that the numbers he feared—61 and 62—were two of his "death years" that provoked fears of the crucial death year, age 51, which Wilhelm Fliess had assigned to him (in 1904 Freud was 48 and nearing that deadly age 51). If I'm correct that Freud's astonishing betrayal of Fliess (via Weininger) took place in 1900, now we can discern a connection between Freud's death fears in the previous Naples incident of 1902 and his Athens death fears of 1904. Probably, the key connection was his fear of lethal retribution for his betrayal of Fliess and death-wishes towards this friend, who stood as a surrogate for several of Freud's kinsmen, including Emanuel.

The third of these similar incidents, concerning trains and death, is given in Jones's third volume (p. 382), where he wrote that Freud had recorded "several instances of magical actions unconsciously carried out with the aim of averting disaster." (Jones claimed that Freud was only a bit superstitious, but here he admits to the master's magical thinking which "persisted through his life.") After noting a magical "sacrificial offering" that Freud once made to preserve the life of his ailing child (Mathilde), Jones described another of these sacrificial offerings by Freud which occurred in 1925 (indicating that aspects of Freud's train phobia continued into old age despite his claim that it had been cured in 1897).

Jones wrote that in 1925 Freud lost his spectacles and case in the woods, and this was another magical sacrifice to avert death. This occurred when he was expecting the arrival of his daughter Anna from a train journey. Jones's words are that: "There had just been a train accident, and by that sacrifice he was insuring against a repetition during her journey." Evidently, Freud acknowledged that he'd "lost" his glasses as a sacrificial offering, to prevent Anna's death in a train accident. (But a sacrifice to whom? Was it Satan, perhaps, as suggested by material in chapter ten?)

Allow me to propose that the above incident again involves Freud's fears of lethal retribution pertaining to his train phobia, which seemed to be redirected partially towards Anna, but also might punish himself, since she'd become his favorite daughter. Since the year was 1925, this opens up the possibility that Freud had severe concerns about retribution via a passenger train, if we consider the thesis that he'd arranged Emanuel's murder-by-train in 1914. Is it possible that Anna was involved in his 1925 sacrificial offering to avert her railway death, because she had played some special role in the train assassination of her uncle Emanuel? Later, I'll discuss that Anna, indeed, might have played a significant but perhaps unwitting role in the murder of Emanuel Freud.

As we come near to the end of this section, some general comments are needed about Freud's train and travel neurosis. Suzanne Bernfeld wrote (1951, p. 118) that this was not a phobia and that most analysts would regard it merely "as a remnant of the panic he experienced" on his train trip at age four from Freiberg to Leipzig, "which continued to make him uncomfortable on trains until he had worked through his self-analysis." These views by Bernfeld are far too pallid and protective of Freud's reputation as a mentally healthy man, though I agree with her and others that Freud's train and travel neurosis originated in that early Leipzig journey. However, I must emphasize the loss of his nanny which preceded it, the sexual acts with her, his hatred of his kinsmen for that seemingly lethal estrangement, and his undying need for revenge (murder).

Surely, there were several factors underlying this train and travel neurosis. Some authors have focused upon separation anxiety and sexual factors, and I would agree with both of these, particularly as they applied to nanny. Regarding the sexual factor, some writers have thought it pertained to Freud's mother whom he observed in the nude on the train ride from Leipzig to Vienna. When he wrote to Fliess that his sexual urge towards Amalia was awakened by seeing her nude on that trip, he used in place of the words "mother" and "nude" the Latin words *matrem* and *nudam*. Here, his seeming reference to Amalia was a mere screen for sexual and oral longings for the Catholic nanny, for his unconscious mind recalled her strong associations with the Latin language of her church.

So I have no doubt that the train and travel phobia had sexual factors underlying it, especially with regard to nanny, and with all the hidden terrors and desires pertaining to her grotesque sexual molestation of Sigi. Nevertheless, the *major* factors underlying this train neurosis (or complex) seem to be interrelated fears of death, desires of Freud to murder his kinsmen, and particularly the patricidal urge. The patricidal urge was so immensely powerful and pervasive in Freud's life, writings, and fantasy identifications that I could write an entire book about that single topic. However, most writers seem to have ignored or greatly downplayed the role of patricidal wishes in Freud's life and train phobia, so they have overlooked the grisly connection with the fatal train accident of Emanuel in 1914. Even Conrad Stein's assertion that the desire to kill Jacob Freud was connected to the railway phobia has a somewhat hollow ring to it, as if Stein thought this was merely a patricidal fantasy—which blocked Stein from countenancing the possibility that Freud harbored actual intentions someday to kill a father-figure like Emanuel.

In closing this section, let me say that Freud's circumscribed Rome phobia can be regarded as one part of his train and travel neurosis. Various writers have noted that concern about the nanny was a key factor in the Rome phobia, and on that basis alone one should recognize that fears of death and parricidal urges were present in the fears about visiting Rome. In commenting about the fourteen years that Freud was prohibited neurotically from going to Rome, Bernfeld added that: "He did not even dare to plan a visit to Athens." Her implied thesis that he also suffered from an "Athens phobia" (which ended in 1904), one that was even more powerful than the prohibition concerning Rome, is an idea to which I give full assent. My previous discussion about the "Acropolis episode" of 1904, and his 1936 paper about it submitted to R. Rolland, offers some of my reasons for believing that enormous fratricidal and patricidal intentions were submerged in that presumed "Athens phobia."

Predictions of Emanuel's Murder

This section, and another to follow, will focus upon impressive "happenings" in Freud's life which can be regarded as predictions that he intended to murder his brother Emanuel. The first topic that will fit this category is a long series of Freud's dreams about trains and death, dreams that point to his intense need to kill Emanuel and other relatives, while they were on board trains or somehow involved with railways.

In his short monograph *On Dreams*, published soon after the major dream book, Freud contrasted the medical view of dreams and popular opinions about them, the latter persisting in the belief that dreams have meanings which relate "to the prediction of the future and which can be discovered by some process of interpretation . . " Freud added that, to his great astonishment, he discovered that the popular opinions about dreams (not the medical view) "came nearest to the truth." Surely he did not wish to endorse the popular superstition that dreams can foretell the future, clairvoyantly via precognition. But it is interesting that he did not rule out a second possibility that in some cases—particularly when intense, perverse needs of one sort are represented in a series of dreams—they can be predictive and give strong clues to some limited aspect of the dreamer's future behavior. The point made here is that dreams may not only provide fulfillments of forbidden wishes (within the dream), but may also point to the actualization of some forbidden and/or acceptable behaviors, in future. (We'll return to this subject near the end of this chapter when we consider Freud's ideas about an emperor who arranged for the killing of a subject who had dreamed of murdering his ruler.)

In abbreviated form, let's return to key elements of Freud's Hollthurn dream (1967, pp. 492 ff.), the product of an actual train trip of Freud's which helped to evoke this dream. In the dream, Freud was in a stopped railway car looking out at women on the platform who crouched and then held up baskets of fruit, invitingly. Suddenly, he was "switched" to another compartment inexplicably, one so narrow that his back was compressed "against the back of the carriage," and wondered how this abrupt switch had occurred. In the new compartment there was an English brother and sister, and various books including one by Schiller. Freud felt the books were sometimes theirs and sometimes belonged to him. Freud wanted to intervene in their conversation; and later recalled that he spoke English to this couple, but corrected his own English usage, prompting agreement by the Englishman.

It's likely that this dream was a reworking of Freud's angry feelings about the primal train ride, at age four, that carried him away from his nurturant nanny, who appeared in the dream as one of the women who stood on the train platform and invited him to partake of her fruit (breasts). The compression of his body in the train carriage pertains to his helpless infantile state, with hints of a narrow baby "carriage." The English brother and sister represented his nephew John and niece Pauline who "abandoned" him by their train ride away from Freiberg (before his journey) and who then became longterm citizens of England. Sigmund's murderous hatred towards them and other kinsmen, for their betrayals, was signified by the Schiller volume, which pertains to the time when John and Sigmund acted-out the scene from Schiller's *The Robbers*—Sigmund as Brutus and John playing Julius Caesar—expressing Freud's murderous desires towards his nephew and others. Freud awakened from this dream drenched in perspiration "because all the windows were shut," hinting at his inner rage and suffocation fantasy pertaining to parricidal aspects of his train phobia (the *Kasten*/coffin connection).

Freud correlated his baffling "switch" of compartments in the dream to a fugue or amnesic state of mind, pertaining to a patient of his with whom he strongly identified, a man who believed he had committed many murders in amnesic states. While telling about his identification with this man, so obsessed with murderous wishes, Freud pointed to the man's Cain fantasy or complex! A comparison of Freud with this patient is imperative, since Freud revealed (p. 294) "that the basis of this distressing obsession was an impulse to murder his somewhat over-severe father," in fact a desire "to push his own father over a precipice from the top of a mountain . . " (The nexus with Fliess's accusation about Freud's murder plan at Achensee in 1900 seems obvious—or will the Freudian elite insist that this was only Fliess's "paranoia?")

It seems clear that the Hollthurn dream reeks with Freud's murderous wishes towards his English kinsmen, and one may even interpret that he wished to kill them aboard a train—considering the key juxtaposition of the Schiller volume which symbolized his patricidal and fratricidal urges. Concerning this dream and its associations, his wish to kill John and Pauline readily suggests his similar desire to murder their father Emanuel, likewise aboard a passenger train. The issue of pushing a father from a precipice, in the dream associations, seems to make a firm connection with the desire to push a father-figure from the platform of a speeding train in 1914. Also, consider my analysis of the "Acropolis episode" and the desire of Daedalus to murder his rivalrous nephew by pushing him from a precipice, emphasizing that John was Freud's nephew.

In *Dark Side* considerable information is given to support my contention that the dream book contains many dreams that Freud attributed to others, which were really his own dreams. For example, in that book (1967, p. 442) he noted that a man dreamed of his brother being in a box (*Kasten*), but while making interpretations the *Kasten* was replaced by a *Schrank* (cupboard). It seems assured that this was a dream by Freud in which he reversed that traumatic event described in his book on "slips" (1960, pp. 50-52), when at age three he was terrified that his nanny had been entombed in a cupboard by his brother, an anecdote in which the words *Kasten* and *Schrank* were paramount. Notice that in the falsified dream just mentioned, Freud's childhood situation was reversed, and the dream provided for his revenge by placing his evil brother in the *Kasten* (in place of the nanny).

Those prefatory comments will prepare us for another dream that probably Freud attributed falsely to a male patient, but which I believe was a dream of his own, appearing on page 461 of the dream book. In this dream the alleged patient's father "had met with a grave calamity." He'd been travelling on the night train when it was derailed, and the carriage seats were forced together so that "his head was compressed from side to side." The dreamer then saw his father lying in bed, with a vertical cut over his left eyebrow. He was surprised that his father had met with this calamity, *since he was already dead*. Finally, he noticed how clear his eyes were.

Assuming that I'm correct that the above dream is one dreamt by Freud, it's message is rather clear concerning his pressing desire that his father-figures should be killed specifically while riding aboard trains. Notice that in this dream, the lethal *compression* of the father's head, correlates with the compression of Freud's body in the Hollthurn dream, which is only one similarity that convinces me that this latest dream was dreamt by Freud. Also, this latest dream contains the presence of a dead, but seemingly revived father, which is similar to Freud's "absurd" dream about the years 1851 and 1856 (p. 471) in which the dreamer's (Freud's) father talked to him casually but "was already dead" (the identical wording in both dreams). This current dream gives a peculiar emphasis, at the end, to how clear the dead father's eyes were, which connects with the emphasis given to the dead father's open eyes in Freud's dream (p. 352) about his dead father Jacob ("close the eyes"). Notice that both of those dreams are about dead fathers, in the context of railway imagery, and that Stein asserted that the dream about Jacob's death incorporated Sigmund's burning desire to kill his father. The imagery of the latest dream, with the father's head being crushed in a train accident, likewise exhibits the dreamer's patricidal wishes in a quite clear manner. One wonders whether the dramatic crushing of the father's head in this dream was a portent that in 1914 Emanuel Freud would be hit on the head on the platform of a speeding train, before being pushed off, followed by a second injury to his head as he hit the ground with bone-breaking force.

The next dream was spoken by Freud in his university lectures on dreams in 1915 (published in 1916 and 1917 as the *Introductory Lectures on Psycho-Analysis* and appearing in Lecture 12 on Pp. 197-98, S.E.). Freud did not deny nor confirm that this was a dream of his own, merely stating that "a neurotic state in the dreamer was one of its preconditions," but it seems very likely to me that it *was* Freud's dream. The dream starts with the dreamer travelling in a railroad train, when the train stopped in open country. Then he thought there was going to be an accident "and that he must think of getting away." Then comes the final sentence of the dream, noting that the dreamer "went through all the coaches in the train and killed everyone he met," including the guard, engine-driver, etc.

It's my opinion that this is a dream relating to the murder of Emanuel Freud in 1914, but no information disclosed whether it was dreamt before or after Emanuel's death. My guess is that Freud dreamt this dream in the middle months of 1914 and that it was quite predictive of his intention to arrange Emanuel's railway murder, imminently. The intense pressure of death-wishes, to which Freud was responding, is suggested by the very brief dream that preceded this one in the lectures, which he gave *no* interpretation and simply called "another representation of death." That eleven-word dream is as follows: "An unknown gentleman left a black-edged visiting-card on him." My suggestion is that this was Freud, identified with Death, laying his calling-card on his "marked" eldest brother, i.e. marked for murder.

Concerning the prior dream in which the dreamer killed everyone he met on a train, that feature suggests Freud's unconscious desire to kill all his Freiberg relatives on a train. In his associations the dreamer recalled a story about a "lunatic" who killed a person sharing a train compartment with him. Freud interpreted that the dreamer "was identifying himself with the madman," due to a tormenting obsession that he needed to get rid of all "accessory witnesses." This seems quite relevant to Freud's clear admission in the associations to his Hollthurn (railway) dream that he strongly identified with a patient who had an obsession that he "would kill everyone he met" (1967, p. 293) while in amnesic states. The close similarity between the Hollthurn dream materials, and the present dream's lethal associations, make it obvious that Freud probably was the dreamer of both these dreams.

In his book *On Dreams* (1952, p. 48) Freud recited another of his train dreams. In this dream he was sitting in a railway carriage, holding on his lap a top hat ("cylinder hat") made of transparent glass. This made him think of the proverb: "If you go hat in hand, you can cross the whole land." The glass cylinder hat, a "discovery" of his, made him think of discoveries that might make him rich, and he also thought about "an incandescent gas mantle."

Freud gave no real interpretation of this dream, so I will do that now. This is another dream about his murderous rage towards father-figures, for the top hat pertains to that hat of Jacob Freud's that a Christian bully once knocked off his head, inspiring Sigmund's lifelong despising of his father. The above proverb relates to Jacob's hated submissiveness (or cowardice, in Sigi's eyes), and also pertains to the anecdote about the poor Jew entrained towards Karlsbad who used submissiveness to *cross the country* by rail, repeatedly encountering violence. ("Go hat in hand" signifies submissiveness.) We noted previously that this anecdote also signified Sigmund's desire to murder another father-figure, Emanuel, on a train.

Ergo, this dream about the glass hat likewise encodes Freud's rabid desires to kill his eldest brother. The glass hat is also a magical childhood symbol of the desire to make heads transparent, allowing one to "read minds" and dominate others (be an uncanny analyst), rather than submit to medical authority or civilized conventions. The incandescent gas mantle symbolizes the "gas jets" that Sigi, at age four, saw at Breslau representing souls burning in hell, indicating his lifelong vengeful rage to pay back Emanuel on a train.

The above dream regarding Freud's murderous wishes towards father-figures reminds me of another one, not a train dream, that also signified his similar death-wishes. This latest dream occurred, probably in 1913, while he was on a summer vacation at a mountain resort in the Tyrol (1967, p. 266). Simply, Freud had a dream that the Pope was dead, which he interpreted in innocuous terms as a dream of revenge against neighbors (Catholic Tyrolese) who made noise that disturbed his sleep.

My interpretation of this dream is that it signified Freud's vengeful desires to kill father-figures (the Pope symbol), including his brother Emanuel; for he inserted this dream in the dream book in 1914, the year Emanuel was killed. This dream also hints at Freud's death-wishes towards Carl Jung, a Christian, circa 1913. Since this dream occurred at a resort in the Tyrol mountains, one also wonders about a persistence of murderous desires toward Wilhelm Fliess, relating to Freud's alleged plan to kill Fliess at a summer resort in the Tyrol mountains (Achensee) in 1900.

Freud cited another train dream by a patient (1967, p. 443) that I suspect was dreamt by Freud himself. The man dreamed he was on a platform of a railway station just as a train arrived, and that a strange reversal occurred. He saw "that the platform moved towards the train, while the train stopped still." Freud made no real interpretation of this dream, except to make a bland comment upon dream reversals, referring to material on page 361.

In turn, page 361 refers to the "Up and Down'" dream (pp. 319 ff.)

which discusses on page 322 the succulent breasts of the dreamer's wet-nurse. Then, it is noted that the dreamer's *elder* brother appeared *up above* and the dreamer, *down below*, in relation to their respective social positions (as a reversal of reality). All of this hints that in the absurd dream of the moving train platform is encoded Freud's desire to rise above Emanuel and to cast his brother down from his high perch—to push him from a train, perhaps. It should be emphasized that the content of this dream does seem quite absurd, and that it precedes a section devoted to absurd dreams that I have characterized generally (in an earlier chapter) as secretly encoding Freud's strong patricidal wishes. The same conclusion can be drawn about this "moving platform" dream.

Freud's rambling dream about Count Thun (1967, pp. 241 ff.) incorporates a great deal of material, in its content and associations, about railway travel. In its long preamble, Freud told about an actual event on a railway platform when he'd observed the well-known figure of Count Thun hurrying past a ticket inspector in a great rush to board a train to Ischl, for an audience with the Emperor. Later, Freud boarded his own train, fell asleep in his compartment, and had a four-part dream starting when Count Thun was speaking before a meeting of students, in a contemptuous manner, causing Freud to make a fiery response. In the second part of the dream, Freud moved through a cordoned-off building from which he had to escape, and avoided being inspected by a stout woman, on his way downstairs. In the third part of the dream, his task was to get out of town. He got in a cab and ordered the cab driver to drive him to a *railway* station, saying: "I can't drive with you along the railway-line itself." (It felt like he'd already ridden along part of the train journey.) Freud decided to go to Graz, and soon sat on a train with a flower in his buttonhole. In the fourth segment of the dream he was again on the rail station platform accompanied by an old gentleman and thinking of a plan to remain unrecognized. The old man seemed to be blind, with one eye, and Freud became his sick-nurse. He handed the old fellow a glass urinal, and watched his penis as he urinated, as the dream ended.

My core interpretation of this entire dream is that it deals with Freud's murderous intentions towards various authority figures, particularly Jacob and Emanuel Freud, and with his desires to kill them and then escape unnoticed, out of town. The key role of his bitter feelings towards Emanuel were seen early in his associations when he wrote: "My associations then led me to England and to my brother's house there." In his analysis of this dream, Freud was right to focus upon the final segment on the station platform, showing clear recognition that the old blind man was his father who was dying (which I interpret as a patricidal wish). I'm in agreement with Schorske's view (1973, p. 342) that in that last scene on the train platform

Freud's father replaced Count Thun, showing that "patricide replaces politics." In effect, the blind dying father (a composite of Jacob and Emanuel) reflected Freud's vengeful desire that his father-figures would die on *railway platforms*, which probably was a "prediction" of Emanuel's train death in 1914. (This also connects with the railway platform at Breslau where little Sigi saw gas jets representing souls burning in hell, not forgetting that Breslau also symbolized madness regarding his insane cousin there.)

At this point, we've reviewed all of Freud's railway dreams that might have been connected with an unconscious intention on his part to murder his brother Emanuel on a train (thereby suggesting the "predictiveness" of these dreams concerning that grim railway death in 1914). Now, I'd like to present some data indicating that Freud probably fantasized a railway accident that led to the revolting sight of a dead body, as early as 1896, causing me to wonder whether this railroad victim was predictive of Emanuel's death in 1914.

In 1896 Freud produced a paper titled "The Aetiology of Hysteria" which is given as Appendix B of an important book on his theoretical equivocations written by Masson (1984). In that article Freud proposed to explain how a case of hysterical vomiting had originated from a great fright, due to a *railway* accident. Soon Freud asserted that his analysis of this male patient showed that the railway accident had aroused in this man "the memory of another, earlier accident" which caused him to be confronted by "a ghastly and revolting sight of a dead body."

But was any of this case material actually true? No, not at all! For eventually Freud admitted to his readers that he'd made up these examples out of thin air. (We can say that they represented his fantasy.) Concerning these examples, he slyly informed his readers: "I have to confess that they are not derived from any case in my experience but are inventions of mine." He called them "fictitious examples," acknowledging that they probably were even "bad inventions." My own theory is that these "bad inventions" were prompted by his desire and intention someday to arrange that Emanuel would be the victim of a train accident, with the effect that his dead body beside a train track would appear as "a ghastly and revolting sight." When Freud discussed these "inventions" as being "linked together in association," it's quite provocative that he compared them with "the genealogical tree of a family whose members have also intermarried." Did that metaphor hint at his lifelong confusion and rage about his paternity, and whether Emanuel was his true father who had abandoned him at age four?

My interpretations of many of the preceding dreams have suggested that Freud harbored powerful death-wishes against his brother Emanuel. At this point, I'd like to mention briefly one more of Freud's dreams that seems relevant, this one involving Emanuel's wife Marie. In Jones's third volume

(p. 403), he cited Freud's vivid dream "premonition" that Marie Freud had died, easily interpreted as a death-wish against both her and Emanuel. Freud's susceptibility to magical thinking, and the great power of his murderous desires towards his brother's wife, are evidenced by his behavior after having this dream. Jones tells us that this dream cost Freud "weeks of anxious waiting" before news arrived that his dream victim, Marie, had not died.

———————————

Now that we've explored the thesis that Freud's preceding dreams about railway deaths were connected with his desire to kill his brother Emanuel on a train, we need to consider whether the death of another man *on a train* had contributed, in a strange manner, to the lethal finality of Emanuel's train ride. The man in question was Jacob Fliess, the father of Wilhelm Fliess. In considering this factor involving Fliess's father, first we should note that during Freud's active relationship with his Berlin colleague he believed Fliess's story that his father had died of natural causes—that he was weakened by a chronic nasal condition and finally succumbed from a medical condition called erysipelas. As late as Freud's letter to Ferenczi dated January 10, 1910 (see Jones II, p. 446) he still believed that Jacob Fliess had died of those natural causes, which caused Freud to insist (inaccurately) that Fliess's conviction that his father "could have been saved was what made him into a doctor, and indeed into a rhinologist" (nose doctor).

We're fortunate that Peter Swales has studied Fliess's life and career and wrote various articles about him, including one (1982) about the issue of fratricide in the Freud/Fliess relationship (in Spurling II, pp. 302-330). In that article, Swales cited his research which indicates (p. 310) that Fliess lied to Freud about the cause of his father's death. Concerning the true cause of Jacob Fliess's death, Swales wrote that: "in 1878, faced with insurmountable debts *he had committed suicide* on the railway line between Leipzig and Berlin." It was Swales's view that Fliess was very sensitive about his father's death and had lied to Freud about this due to "the shame attached to such matters in those times." Indeed, an entire family was subject to years of disgrace in the event of the suicide of any of its members, particularly a father.

Although I can't offer my full reasons for this thesis, my study of Freud's dream about the Villa Secerno, found in the dream book, and in *Complete* (pp. 236-8), convinces me that this dream encodes Freud's latent awareness that Fliess was lying to him about the Fliess's family secret—father Fliess died by suicide, not natural causes. In the dream book, the brief Villa Secerno dream (about a telegraph message) practically overlaps with Freud's dream about the death of his father Jacob, whom name magic coordinates with the name of Jacob Fliess. Freud's interpretation of this dream emphasized his anger with Fliess for having kept a secret from him "for so long," i.e. the concealment of Fliess's vacation address, as a screen for the deeper secret regarding Jacob Fliess's death.

Discussing this dream in *Complete*, Freud emphasized his annoyance at Fliess's secretiveness, and correlated this with "my persistent reaction to your dream of defense, which tried to substitute the grandfather for the otherwise customary father." Here, Freud almost exposed his latent hunch that Fliess's dream was concealing a dark secret about his father, by substituting the grandfather. Finally, Freud mentioned a female patient who was trying to keep dangerous secrets from him (obviously relevant to his feelings about Fliess), including the criminal significances of her father's earlier behaviors (sexual). This compares with the point that there was criminal significance to the behavior of Fliess's father, namely suicide. In effect, the Villa Secerno dream hints that Fliess was maintaining secrecy about the criminal significance of his father's lethal behavior; and similarly Freud's dream about *his* own father's death ("close the eyes") hinted that he was being secretive about criminal behaviors of his father (sexual and financial).

Acknowledging that Freud did not know about the train suicide of Fliess's father before January 1910 (see his letter to Ferenczi), I think it would not be surprising that Freud finally learned the true suicidal cause of Jacob Fliess's death during the nearly five years between then and October 1914, when Emanuel died. Perhaps Freud learned this information from Karl Abraham, who could have obtained it from Fliess after starting a relationship with him in 1911—or Freud might have obtained it from his close friend Dr. Oscar Rie, who had become a relative of the Fliess family. If I'm correct in my strong suspicion that Freud did learn, prior to October 1914, that Jacob Fliess died by suicide, on a train, there could have been an uncanny significance to this, considering Freud's tendency to act-out the life stories of persons with whom he'd formed intense identifications.

In Swales's analysis of this mutually dependent duo, Freud and Fliess, he characterized them psychologically as "twins," which seems relevant to Strachey's surprised response to their complementary bizarre behaviors, when he stated that they suffered from *folie à deux* (madness for two). It's my hypothesis, therefore, that Freud did learn the true facts about the railway death of Fliess's father and that this helped to provoke his railway murder of Emanuel in 1914. In effect, this was an uncanny act pertaining to identification and imitation, in a period when Freud was highly stressed and again was suffering a severely unbalanced state of mind. For Freud, the perverse formula perhaps was also an act of rivalry, as follows: 'Your father died on a train via suicide, but I will go you one better by arranging for *my* father (figure) to be *murdered* on a train.'

More Predictions of Emanuel's Murder

Throughout Freud's life he exhibited various unusual behaviors that may be regarded as predictive of his desire and intention someday to murder Emanuel Freud on a train. One example, already mentioned, was his strong desire to kill a man on a train in 1883, regarding an argument they'd had about opening the window of a train, as Freud reported to his fiancée Martha. A recurrent example relates to his persistent extreme concerns about the possible injuring or death of Wilhelm Fliess, whenever Fliess traveled by railway. This was a reaction-formation concerning Freud's powerful death-wishes towards Fliess (who served as a substitute for some of Freud's family members, including Emanuel and John). Also, there is the question of Freud's desire to push Fliess off a precipice at Achensee in 1900, which perhaps was predictive of Emanuel's being pushed from his high perch, on a passenger train.

Now it's time to consider other remarkable behaviors by Freud that seem to have been predictive of Emanuel's murder. Initially, we'll focus upon a crucial number—2467—which is relevant to Freud's persistent number magic and to his desire to kill his brother/father Emanuel.

The number 2467 has become famous, because of the emphasis that Freud placed upon it in *The Psychopathology of Everyday Life* (1960, pp. 242-3). That number first appeared in Freud's letter to Fliess dated August 27, 1899 at the time when his dream book was nearing publication. At that time he wrote that there would be no further changes in his manuscript 'even if it contains 2467 errors.' He wrote a postscript to the letter giving an analysis of that number, and inserted it into his book on "slips." Freud argued that the number 2467 had not emerged into consciousness arbitrarily, but that it was determined by unconscious motivations.

He explained that the first half of this number "24" was generated by a recent discussion he'd had about the retirement of a military man called "E.M." or "M." who had been important to Freud at age 24, emphasizing that Sigmund spent his 24th birthday in jail, under military arrest during a brief period of army service. Having discussed events when he was 24, he noted that his current age then, in 1899, was 43, so he thought it logical to add these numbers together (24 plus 43) to produce the second half of 2467, which is "67." This satisfied Freud that 2467 had been generated by unconscious determinants. He explained that it was prompted mainly by his wish not to retire like "M." but to have another 24 years of work—which he regarded as a triumph over this man, whose years were at an end "while I still have everything in front of me."

Now I'll explain that Freud's analysis was simplistic and guarded, since it repressed the high probability that 2467 was generated by an intense desire to murder his brother Emanuel. That is, the numbers 24 and 67 have powerful connections with Emanuel, not ignoring Freud's clue that age-factors are prominent here. First, it must by emphasized that by the end of 1899 the age of Emanuel Freud was 67 (the second half of 2467), relating to the point that some authors give his birth year as 1832 (while others cite 1833). The number 24 was crucially related to Emanuel's age of 67, since 24 was the number of years separating Sigmund's and Emanuel's ages. Surely, that rivalrous child, Sigi, had always been rankled by those 24 years that prevented him from being the oldest and dominant son in Jacob's family. Ergo, the number 24 (in 2467) represented his secret wish to "eliminate" Emanuel in 1899, at age 67, so that he could expropriate 24 years from his brother's possible lifespan. All of this was relevant to Freud's magical wish to steal years of life from his brothers* (Emanuel and Alexander), to add onto his own lifespan—an unconscious Satanic pact that is explained more fully in chapter ten. (Chapter ten discusses that 24 years were crucial to Freud's Satanic pact as the number of years he asked Satan to add to his life, imitating the number chosen by Faust.)

An understanding of name and initial magic is also useful in helping us to recognize that Emanuel was closely connected with 2467. Thus, the man whom Freud wished to "retire" (permanently) was called "E.M.," but we can guess that this man was a "screen" for Emanuel, since the first two letters of his name are "EM." Also, this retiree's surname-initial was "M.," and this correlates with the doctor named "M." in Freud's Irma dream, a man whom he told us represented both Breuer and his brother Emanuel. For all these reasons, it becomes a tenable hypothesis that Freud's "creation" of 2467 in 1899, just preceding that fateful year of madness and revenge (1900), was a number predictive of his eventual murder of his eldest brother. That the number 24 pertained also to the 24th birthday that Freud spent in jail** concerns his vengeful feelings regarding his questionable date of birth (a rebuke against Emanuel) and the jailing of his nanny, which he also blamed largely on his eldest, dominant brother.

On September 24, 1900 Freud wrote a letter to Fliess referring to his earlier remark about the number 2467, which he'd mentioned as the possible number of "errors" (or mistakes) in his dream book. Just preceding this new reference to those 2467 "errors," Freud wrote: "to be in error—madness." The editor of *Complete* explained this cryptic notation by stating that Freud meant "that the sound of the German *Irren* (to err) reminds him of *Irre* (madmen)." With this tiny note Freud's psyche confessed that the number 2467 was closely connected with his own murderous madness,

---

*See Kanzer's comments about this perverse wish, discussed later.
**Elsewhere, I noted that this was his acting-out of nanny's jailing.

with regard to the presumed killing of Emanuel Freud.

Another remarkable behavior by Freud which can be considered predictive of his presumed arranging of Emanuel's murder takes us back to the summer of 1900 when presumably he planned the murder of Fliess at Achensee, this planning of Fliess's murder in a cold-blooded fashion correlating with the general manner in which he must have planned for Emanuel's demise in 1914. It's true that we have only Fliess's account of the matter, in what he reported to family members, to support the idea that Freud planned a murder in 1900 (as a prologue to the presumed murder in 1914). However, Freud's vengeful madness throughout 1900 tends to support Fliess's claim, and this entire volume's data concerning Freud's parricidal urges also support Fliess, especially because the Berliner was always a ready substitute for various family members towards whom Freud harbored bitter death-wishes.

But there was another man, a dear friend and ardent supporter of Freud's, whose written analysis tends to support Fliess's claim about Freud's plan to murder him at Achensee. That was Freud's beloved physician Max Schur (whose surname's meaning correlates with the meaning of "Fliess"). In Schur's biography (1972, pp. 168-71) he analyzed some of Freud's own dreams that he sent to Fliess in the years just prior to publication of the dream book, dreams whose meanings pointed to Freud's desire to "eliminate" his Berlin colleague, which Freud even "confessed" to Fliess in his letters. (These included the *Non vixit* dream, and the Irma dream.) Schur asked these questions: "Why did Freud have to 'do away with' Fliess at this time? Why did he have to confess it all to Fliess . . ?" Schur partly answered the latter query by noting that Freud managed to mute his guilt feelings by making dream interpretations that enabled him "to deny the importance of his death wishes regarding Fliess . . " Later Schur added that in 1899 "when Freud was finishing *The Interpretation of Dreams*, he could gloss over his wish to survive Fliess which necessitated 'killing him off' in fantasy." (p. 171)

Then Schur mentioned that: "Nevertheless, such fantasies, especially if followed eventually by the rupture of a friendship, leave their traces in our mental life." What Schur refused to acknowledge was that perhaps such "traces" in Freud's mental life reflected his actual intent to kill Fliess in 1900 (at Achensee), when the final rupture in their friendship had become quite obvious. Here we see that it was Schur who tried to "gloss over" Freud's plan to murder Fliess—dismissing this possibility as "fantasy"—though he'd already exposed Freud's burning desire to kill Fliess, in some of his critical dreams. Of course, we are now able to supplement Schur's citation of two murderous dreams by our list of lethal railway dreams pertaining to Emanuel, again emphasizing that Fliess was a ready substitute for Emanuel in Freud's mind.

In his book on "slips" (pp. 217-20) Freud cited two examples of his having made symptomatic errors in his dream book that I will interpret as predictive of his desire and intention to murder Emanuel. The first example of such an error occurred in chapter V B of the dream book (1967, p. 230) where it's noted that Hannibal, as a boy, swore an oath of vengeance against his mortal enemies, the Romans. At that point, the "error" that Freud made was in referring to Hannibal's father as Hasdrubal (the name of Hannibal's brother) instead of the father's actual name, Hamilcar. While discussing this error in the book on "slips" (p. 219), Freud connected it with his boyhood fantasy of having a preference that Emanuel should have been his father (not acknowledging that Emanuel might have been his true father, while suppressing his feelings of abandonment, rage, and revenge about that issue).

Concerning the above symptomatic error, we see that Freud unconsciously eliminated the name of a powerful father-figure, Hamilcar—which can be interpreted as signifying his desire and intention to murder his own father-figures Jacob and Emanuel, particularly the latter whose strict authoritarianism was consonant with Hamilcar's. We should remember Jacob's softness and piety, and that Hamilcar was a strong authority who made his son swear that brutal oath; also not forgetting Freud's close identification with Hannibal. Also, recall that Hannibal's task was to conquer Rome, which several writers have seen as a symbol for Freud's nanny and his wish magically to "capture" her (which related to his murderous feelings about Emanuel).

Immediately following Freud's initial discussion of the preceding error, he offered another example of a symptomatic error that he'd made in his dream book—making this same error twice, in fact (1967, pp. 290, 657). In this case, Freud had written that the god Zeus emasculated his father Kronos "and made himself ruler in his place." In his book on "slips" Freud expounded on this error by noting that Greek mythology (except for Orphic sources) asserts that it was Kronos who emasculated his father, not Zeus who did so. Again, we note that Freud had a fantasy identification with Zeus, indicating that the source of this error—the emasculation or killing of the father—can be found in Freud's desire to murder his fantasized father, Emanuel.

The eternal image of the nanny can be found in this scenario if one credits my thesis that for Freud the initial letter "Z" represented his nanny in various instances. In this case, the formula is that Zeus correlates with Zajic, her family name. All of the above material is relevant to an anecdote in Puner's book (1947, p. 215), who noted that Freud once remarked about one of his followers: "I cannot stand the parricidal look in his eye."

Obviously that was a projection, and a despising in others what one hates and fears in oneself.

In completing this section, I'll mention one final uncanny event in Freud's life that perhaps can be regarded as predictive of his murder of Emanuel Freud. In the third volume of the Freud biography, Jones wrote a chapter titled "Occultism" which describes Freud's attitudes and involvements concerning the area of paranormal happenings, especially telepathy. On page 389 Jones wrote that soon after the death of Emanuel Freud in late 1914: "Ferenczi expressed the opinion that it confirmed a prediction of Jung's that a great misfortune would happen to Freud in 1914." This view was expressed in Ferenczi's letter of November 25, 1914, and in Freud's written reply he stated that Ferenczi's idea about the prediction of Emanuel's death was "nonsensical" (this word suggesting that Freud was quite annoyed). Freud added: "You seem to be more caught up in occultism than I supposed." Then Freud asked Ferenczi whether the war itself wasn't "enough of a misfortune," implying that Jung's prediction might have been aimed at a larger misfortune than Emanuel's death, i.e. the start of WWI in mid-1914 which caused two of Freud's sons to be put at great risk in military service.

One might wonder why Freud got so annoyed and defensive about Ferenczi's "opinion" that Jung had *predicted* Emanuel's death in 1914. Was Ferenczi really indicating that Jung had used precognition, a foretelling of the future paranormally, to make a quite accurate prediction about Emanuel's strange death? That seems doubtful, since Jones's chapter offers no real evidence that Ferenczi or Freud were accepting of the reality of precognition, while it does give a great deal of evidence that both men were strong believers in the reality of telepathy (though Freud sometimes seemed to waver). Ergo, my suggestion is that perhaps Freud was very annoyed and defensive about Ferenczi's opinion, because that sensitive Hungarian analyst was implying that Jung's accurate prediction (presumably concerning Emanuel) had been based upon a powerful telepathic connection between Jung and Freud. The further implication was that Freud had planned and arranged to murder Emanuel and that Jung had sensed this telepathically.

But what else was Ferenczi communicating when he gave Freud his opinion that Jung had predicted the death of Emanuel in 1914 (although Jung had not specified Emanuel's name)? Well, it seems plausible that, at least, Ferenczi was implying strongly that the death of Emanuel in 1914 was predictable beforehand, without recourse to telepathy. What I suspect is that when Ferenczi, in November 1914, learned about Emanuel's peculiar manner of dying—falling from a speeding railway train—something clicked in the Hungarian analyst's head, particularly when he thought about Freud's bizarre fears that friends and family might be killed in railway accidents.

Moreover, Ferenczi's intense intimacy with Freud, in the years from 1908 to 1914, probably gave him many reasons to recognize Freud's parricidal urges towards Emanuel and to become aware of periods of severe mental imbalance in Freud's life, the mid-year of 1914 being one of the worst of these for Freud. Indeed, we'll learn later that Ferenczi was with Freud in the period just prior to Emanuel's death and observed strange symptomatic behaviors in Freud that caused the Hungarian analyst to decide that Freud was suffering from a bout of moderate psychosis, in that stressful time.

Putting "two and two together," Ferenczi must have been able to come to a vague hypothesis that Freud had somehow arranged Emanuel's train accident. However, he could not, of course, express that idea directly to Freud. Eventually, he made his veiled reference to this notion by asserting an opinion that Jung had predicted Emanuel's death, implying that this particular railroad death was a quite predictable event, for ominous reasons. Of special importance is that Ferenczi spent three weeks in analysis with Freud in Vienna just before Emanuel's death, giving him an excellent opportunity to notice any of Freud's peculiar behaviors or "slips" that might have revealed guilty or murderous feelings that might have seemed pertinent to Emanuel's "accident." In subsequent discussion we'll see that Freud's excessive "slips" in that period caused Ferenczi to decide that a general paralysis of insanity (G.P.I.) was lurking in Freud during that era immediately after the onset of the Great War.

In evaluating the above material, readers might like to assess for themselves the degree of intimacy between Freud and Ferenczi in 1914, to decide whether Ferenczi knew his mentor well enough to have such suspicions about Freud's lethal potentials regarding Emanuel. In Jones's second biographical volume (pp. 155-6) he noted that Freud's letters to Ferenczi "were by far the most personal" and that Freud's affection for the Hungarian was so great that he sometimes addressed him as "My dear Son." At times Freud wished that Ferenczi would marry one of his daughters, worked hard to help him overcome his neurotic problems, and tried "to train him to deal with life to an extent he never felt impelled to do with his own sons." In two separate periods, including 1914, Freud provided analytic therapy for Ferenczi, who became very dependent upon the master. Jones noted that their talks were often of a "highly speculative character" and that Ferenczi's "soaring phantasies, made a great appeal to Freud." Various writers have observed that their early relationship was so close and intense that Ferenczi, in many ways, became a substitute for Wilhelm Fliess in Freud's life.

Jones wrote (p. 158) that Ferenczi's: "Daring and unrestrained imagination always stirred Freud. It had captured him with Fliess years before . . ." Like Fliess, Ferenczi became the close friend who accompanied Freud on various trips throughout Europe, and even to America in 1909 along with Jung (to Clark University). Writing about Freud's life in mid-1914, Jones noted that for the previous six years Ferenczi had spent his holidays with Freud. Many of their trips together were aboard trains, so Ferenczi had opportunities, at first-hand, to experience Freud's residues of railway phobia. His contacts and correspondence with Freud continued at high frequency in 1913 and 1914, so Ferenczi had ample opportunities to witness the decline of Freud's mental health in 1914, which apparently became unbalanced even more severely than in 1900. Accordingly, Ferenczi's awareness of Freud's mental fragility in 1914 must have helped him to produce his vague hypothesis about the true cause of Emanuel Freud's railway death, as discussed earlier. In the next section, we'll focus upon the year 1914, the years just preceding it, and the ravages of that era that helped to create dangerous instabilities in the mind of Sigmund Freud.

The Stressful Era Circa 1914

The year 1900 was a time of murder and madness for Freud because of his feelings of betrayal by Fliess and Breuer, and his despair that his dream book had not made him famous and prosperous. But soon afterwards he obtained his professorship (via a bribe) and his prospects began to rise. With the publication of his popular books on "slips" and jokes, his celebrity increased. In the ensuing years he obtained a circle of followers in Vienna, including Stekel and Adler, who helped to make Psychoanalysis an influential movement in various cities of Europe. With the addition of Jung, Jones, Abraham, Gross, Ferenczi, and Brill as disciples the Cause spread to Zurich, London, Berlin, Munich, Budapest, and several cities in America and Canada. In 1909 Freud's well-publicized trip to Clark University's anniversary celebrations offered considerable positive publicity for Psychoanalysis in the New World. By the year 1910 Freud had reason to expect that Psychoanalysis would continue its growth and would become a powerful clinical empire throughout the civilized world.

But in the years from 1911 to 1914 this momentum was curtailed, for many reasons, and Freud's small empire began a precipitous decline, giving the appearance of being nearly extinguished in mid-1914 by the onset of World War I. During several years just preceding 1914 various key disciples had defected from Freud's cause, so that when 1914 presented its bitter news of war and deprivation Freud already had many reasons to feel that (as in 1900) he had been betrayed by his dearest supporters. Indeed, he had ample justification for fearing that he would lose the fortune and fame he'd garnered during the previous thirteen years. The stresses that had accumulated for him in 1914 were as enormous as those he suffered in 1900, providing a basis for understanding why 1914 became another year of madness and murder for the founder of Psychoanalysis. All of this is germane to the thesis that, as a factor in this madness, Freud arranged for the murder of Emanuel Freud in that year.

Let's take a closer look now at the pressures that plagued Freud in the years from 1911 to 1914. One of Freud's earliest disciples was Alfred Adler who became president of the Vienna Psychoanalytical Society and a coeditor of the analyst's first official journal. A man with great talents and independent thought, Adler developed his own clinical and theoretical approach (called Individual Psychology) which differed from Freud's on various essential points: organ inferiority and the inferiority complex, sibling rivalry, power and superiority strivings, masculine protest, social and ego factors as opposed to unconscious ones—and differences concerning repression, dreams, the Oedipus complex, infantile sexuality, etc. When Adler broke away from Freud in October 1911 he took a sizable group of disciples with him, and these clinicians helped Adler to form his own worldwide movement that still competes with Freud's today.

In the fall of 1912 Wilhelm Stekel was the next Viennese disciple to break away from Freud. Prior to joining Freud, this physician had studied infant sexuality and, while doing psychotherapy, had found connections between childhood factors and later neurotic illness. When he joined Freud, he became co-editor of the first analytic journal with his friend Adler and wrote many articles on psychoanalysis that helped spread Freud's fame in Vienna and beyond. Stekel was a brilliant thinker concerning dream symbolism, compulsive neuroses, name-compulsions, life and death instincts, etc. and Freud admired him greatly in the early years and then turned against him when Stekel showed too much originality and independence (like Adler).

In 1908 Stekel published a volume offering a theory of anxiety that was very different from Freud's, in which he downplayed sexual etiology and emphasized that all neuroses stem from a variety of psychic conflicts with roots in infantile experiences, not just sexual ones. To make matters worse, he was the only man among Freud's disciples to revive the seduction theory which Freud abandoned in 1897, though Stekel did not emphasize sexual seductions to the exclusion of many other conflicts that he believed could stimulate neuroses. Freud was incensed by these ideas of Stekel and made strong emotional rejections of them, while also slandering Stekel's character in analytic circles, with the sly assistance of Ernest Jones. The same emotional rejection and character assassination was applied to Adler, as an indication of the deep wounding of Freud that was caused by Adler's and Stekel's rejections of many of his ideas and his leadership. When Stekel left Freud, he took a number of disciples with him which further weakened Freud's Vienna group and added to the stresses caused by the losses of Adler and Stekel. However, Freud was an artful politician who repeatedly thundered that he was glad to be rid of all of these heretics.

The worst blow to Freud's ego came in 1913 when he finally lost Carl Jung as a disciple. This story will take a bit longer to tell (and many of the truly sordid details are covered in *Secret SL*). Historically, Jung became interested in Freud soon after he read Freud's dream book, near the turn of the century, and began using psychoanalytic ideas in the Zurich psychiatric hospital where he was senior physician, supervised by Dr. Eugen Bleuler. In the spring of 1907 Jung visited Freud's home and they had a very long talk which cemented their future collaboration. Soon after this meeting Freud decided to adopt Jung as his "Crown Prince," the man who would take over the political reins of his brainchild, Psychoanalysis, by becoming president of the international organization (despite bitter objections from the Viennese analysts). In his megalomanic manner, Freud once wrote to Jung: "If I am Moses, then you are Joshua and will take possession of the Promised Land of psychiatry, which I shall only be able to glimpse from afar . . " (Though Freud hinted here at his identification with Moses, surely he did not inform the somewhat mystical Jung about his identifications with Cain, Satan, and more than twenty murderers.)

Why did Freud wish to bypass his devoted Viennese followers to make this newcomer, Jung, the head of the psychoanalytic movement? The first reason often cited was that Jung was an eminent gentile clinician, whereas all of Freud's previous followers were Jews, and Freud believed it was important to enlist Christian sympathies if his Cause was to become widely accepted in the dominant world of the gentiles. Also, it was important that Jung was a psychiatrist (not a neurologist like Freud and Jones), since that would help to obtain friends in the psychiatric world. Moreover, Jung seemed to be able to "deliver" his boss Dr. Bleuler to the analytic fold, and this was a great coup, since Bleuler was one of the most famous and respected psychiatrists in Europe. Initially, by enlisting Jung and some of his Zurich colleagues Freud felt that his Cause had begun to spread to Christian psychiatrists in European centers of learning beyond Vienna, which was a hopeful sign of progress towards a larger empire.

But by suddenly thrusting Jung into the international presidency of the analytic movement, Freud had to betray the interests and ambitions of his Viennese followers, whose years of loyalty and intense effort made them feel that Freud's heir should have been chosen from one of them. Freud accomplished this betrayal of his original followers at a crucial international Congress at Nuremberg in March 1910 when he manipulated his trusted lackey Sandor Ferenczi into putting before this Congress the outrageous proposition that Jung should be elected as lifetime president of the International Analytic Society. Brome has noted (1968, p. 41) that Ferenczi's speech emphasized that "the Viennese analysts were of a definitely inferior order to those of Zurich and concluded that the future administration should be left in the hands of the men of Zurich." Brome added that some analysts at the Congress believed that Freud had deliberately used Ferenczi as a "stooge" to offer that revolutionary proposal that he knew was so inflammatory, anticipating the "storm of protest" and dissension which followed it. However, eventually Jung was elected president (not on a perpetual basis) and, as Brome remarked about Freud: "He remained the power behind the scenes."

In Stekel's autobiography he described how Freud had addressed a sullen meeting of the Viennese analysts to persuade them to adopt Ferenczi's demeaning motion to make Jung the president. The master predicted hard times ahead, intense opposition from official medicine, and increased anti-Semitism, and soon tears streamed down his cheeks. Grasping his coat dramatically, Freud wailed: "They begrudge me the coat I am wearing: I don't know whether in the future I will earn my daily bread." (The starvation theme, again.) He ended by insisting that: "An official psychiatrist and a gentile must be the leader of the movement."

The preceding events typify Freud's strange manipulative behaviors towards his followers in the critical period 1911 to 1914 (and later). These exemplified numerous occasions when he played the autocratic father demanding unreasonable compliance, while also helping to stir up dissension among his followers towards one another, and often towards himself. Thereby, he experienced great stress in trying to cope with all this dissatisfaction and dissension that he helped to create (almost deliberately) by his dogmatism, willfulness, and the peculiar Machiavellian twists of his nature. So this endless "pot stirring" helped to precipitate painful defections from his ranks, all of these factors contributing to a landslide of psychic pressures that began falling onto Freud's head in 1913, and finally buried him in 1914 with the advent of the Great War, as he sank more and more into depression and madness.

Before we begin to review some of the details of the breakup of Freud's relationship with Jung—which produced monumental, maddening pressures in the minds of both of these men during 1913/1914—we should take a brief look at some other factors that generated great stress on Freud in that era. A prime example involved Freud's repeated efforts to ensnare Dr. Eugen Bleuler into the analytic camp, since Bleuler sometimes showed signs of succumbing, but then exhibited "ambivalences" (he coined that term) and retreated despite Freud's persistent flattery. Finally, Bleuler made up his mind and withdrew his valuable support from the Cause, and then attacked Freud and Psychoanalysis by describing it as an "intolerant sect." In those years Freud was also under heavy attack from another famous clinician,

Pierre Janet, whose writings and speeches pointed out Freud's theoretical errors, megalomania, and his plagiarizing of Janet's own works—which kept alive the pervasive belief among clinicians that Freud had plagiarized the works of Nietzsche, Schopenhauer, and many lesser figures like Josef Popper.

During 1910-1914, another persistent source of attacks on Freud and Psychoanalysis came from many esteemed men in the ranks of official psychiatry and neurology. In the extensive literature about Freud's life and career (Jones, Schur, Brome, etc.) the discussion of this issue is often slanted heavily in Freud's favor. Typically, he is made to look like a hero and martyr who was unfairly persecuted by establishment clinicians who were fearful of sexuality and had no real basis for imputing sexual offenses or extravagances to Freud and his followers. A possible example of this slanting is found in Brome's (1968) third chapter titled "Resistance to Psycho-Analysis," and in other portions (p. 19 ff.) of his book. Jones and Brome have "ignored" extensive incriminating materials that I have included in *Secret SL*, damaging evidence which surely placed great burdens and stresses upon Freud's vulnerable psyche in 1911 to 1914.

For example, my later volume describes how Freud was stressed by knowing that Jung had sexually molested (probably anally) one of his severely unbalanced female patients while she was a hospital inpatient, under his care. (This should not have been too surprising to Freud, if he also knew that Jung had been sexually molested as a child by one of his male authority figures, perhaps a teacher or minister.) After recovering from her illness and victimization by Jung, this former patient carried on an extensive correspondence with Freud, apparently seeking some form of acknowledgment of Jung's crime, but Freud managed to "stonewall" the situation and then helped to silence this woman by helping her to become a psychoanalyst! Freud was also stressed by his contacts with the mad psychoanalyst Dr. Otto Gross of Munich, who not only sexually molested some of his female patients but also arranged to murder at least one of these women, and induced others to commit suicide. Gross's case became famous in Europe, for he was a well-known and brilliant madman who advocated Free Love (along with his personal friend, Ernest Jones), anarchism, and cocaine abuse. Unfortunately, brief periods of treatment by Jung and Freud did not help Gross to overcome his fluctuating bouts of dangerous insanity. Today, his grotesque life story and analytic career is largely suppressed by biographers of Freud and Jung. (See my companion volume re Freud's sex life.)

Undoubtedly, Freud was subject to heavy stress at times by his awareness of sexual excesses by Ferenczi and by Ernest Jones, the latter analyst involving himself in Free Love advocacy in an obsessive manner, sexual molestations of patients (leading to Jones's jailing and adverse newspaper publicity in London of the most notorious kind), compulsive lying, and strong signs of sexual psychopathy. Many of the detailed charges against Jones will be found in the final chapter of this book, which summarizes extensive materials in Secret SL. That volume also provides considerable data pertaining to Freud's sexual excesses, including questionable sexual behaviors with females patients (a probable affair with one very wealthy patient who apparently gave him a villa, before he "dumped" her). The triangular relationship among Minna, Martha, and Freud receives special attention in Secret SL, as this connects with the triangular relationships favored by Otto Gross, Jung, Ferenczi, and other analysts.

Brome has cited (1968, p. 32) the occasion when Professor Weygandt, speaking before a congress of German psychiatrists and neurologists in 1910, angrily denounced the activities of psychoanalysts as "a matter for the police." Similarly, Ferenczi wrote a letter to Freud in early 1911 reporting about a paper he had read before the Medical Society of Budapest. A member of the audience stood up and denounced psychoanalysis as pornography and insisted that Freud "should have been in the hands of the police, if not in prison." In America, in early 1912 the New York Times reported (April 5) that the eminent neurologist, Dr. Moses Starr, while addressing a medical group, had denounced Freud's lack of moral behavior while they were students together in Vienna—a charge that was "seconded" by another American neurologist of considerable repute. Freud's simple defense that he did not recall knowing any person named Starr, in his student days, was belied by the fact that Starr had introduced Freud's earliest articles in neurology into American journals.

In light of the damaging items described in the preceding paragraphs about sexual excesses in psychoanalysis from 1910 to 1914, it's understandable that many medical authorities "knew the score" about the erotic activities of some leading analysts, and were right to raise the issues of malpractice and criminality. Undoubtedly, Freud was severely stressed by these attacks against him and his Cause, though he always feigned an air of bravado and dismissed these charges as sheer nonsense. (However, recall that he almost fell apart mentally in 1904, under much milder public attacks by Wilhelm Fliess, which led to the brief bout of madness called the "Acropolis episode.")

It's time to take a closer look at the heaviest stress on Freud in that bygone era, the breakup of his relationship with Carl Jung, which in significant ways repeated the accumulation of murderous rage that Freud had built up towards Fliess when their friendship deteriorated and then ended in 1900. When one considers that Freud had instructed Jung in the art of betrayal by making him his "heir" and president of the analysts' international body, at the expense of Viennese followers who'd laid the groundwork for Freud's success, it was ironic justice that Jung eventually betrayed Freud by turning against the core ideas championed by the master. According to Jones (II, p. 144), the first clear sign of Jung's betrayal occurred in September 1912 during a series of lectures given by Jung in New York, where he expressed "his antagonistic attitude there to Freud's theories and even to Freud personally, who was being represented as an out-of-date person whose errors Jung was now able to expose." Evidently, Jung tried to make analytic ideas more palatable to the Americans by eliminating any emphasis on sexuality, and by greatly revising Freud's conception of the incest motive—which angered Freud when he learned of Jung's disloyal revisionism.

In subsequent months, the relationship continued to deteriorate and then an even greater act of betrayal by Jung occurred in August 1913 at the International Congress of Medicine in London. Ellenberger has reported (1970, pp. 817-18) that, at that congress, Pierre Janet read his report on psychoanalysis which gave numerous damaging criticisms of Freud's concepts. This was followed by Jung's "defense" of psychoanalysis, a speech which began with a jibe directed at Janet, followed by Jung's broad discussion of psychoanalysis, one that surprisingly offered "criticisms even more severe than those of Janet." Thereafter, Jung offered an outline of his new brand of Jungian psychology, quite at variance with Freud's ideas, emphasizing his intention "to liberate the psychoanalytic theory from the purely sexual standpoint." Jung's speech then described his revised version of libido theory, and a general explanation for neurosis that challenged Freud's and slyly endorsed the clinical concepts of Janet, who had been Jung's old mentor in 1902. (If this account of Jung's speech is accurate, Freud had every right to regard Jung's behaviors as a flagrant betrayal of him, and of Psychoanalysis.)

A few weeks later, in August 1913, Jung's presidency placed him in charge of the analysts' International Congress in Munich, where Freud and his followers met anxiously in private meetings to discuss what should be done to counter the disastrous new course that Jung and his Zurich colleagues were setting for Psychoanalysis. In describing Jung's chairmanship of that congress in her diary, Lou Andreas Salomé observed that Jung's behavior towards Freud was combative, dogmatic, and "brutal," and that the master stayed on the defensive but managed with difficulty to contain strong emotions while facing this schism with the "son" that he "had loved so much." Brome's book (1968) described the hectic political activity that Freud and his followers undertook to thwart the possibility that Jung might maintain his control over the international body, and to get rid of Jung and some of his Swiss circle. Freud's fears of losing dominance over his prized possession (Psychoanalysis/nanny) caused him intense anguish in the early months of 1914, along with waves of hatred and anger towards Jung, until the latter finally decided to resign his presidency in April 1914 when the schism between them became irrevocable.

Describing the imminent breakup between Freud and Jung in 1913, Ellenberger (p. 817) characterized that bitter event for Freud in the following terms: "In Vienna the psychoanalytic movement was undergoing the most severe crisis it had ever known." But Ellenberger recognized that the first few months of 1914—when Jung resigned his presidency, after which the Swiss analytic group was dissolved and Bleuler published his criticisms of Freud's theories—were more stressful than ever for Freud. Ellenberger noted that the early months of 1914 were "months of acute crisis in the psychoanalytic movement." But none of these brief descriptions can do justice to the enormous personal anguish, bitterness, and hatred that welled-up in Freud towards the traitor Jung in 1913/1914 when their relationship suffered its final rapid deterioration.

Another Year of Madness—1914

It's my contention that the breakup of Freud's relationship with Jung, which ended conclusively in March 1914, was a "replay" of Freud's relationship with Fliess which ended essentially in mid-1900, when Freud's rage about Fliess's disloyalty and betrayal impelled Sigmund to plan the murder of his erstwhile friend at Achensee. In previous chapters, that plan-to-murder was made rather plausible by data emphasizing Freud's need for murderous vengeance against Fliess in the year 1900, in the context of Sigmund's recurrent episodes of severe mental instability throughout that year. Now, in the pages that follow, we will explore evidences that by mid-1914 similar vengeful pressures had accumulated towards Jung, in the context of Freud's serious psychic imbalances, those factors precipitating a comparable need to murder Jung that was displaced onto Emanuel Freud in October 1914.

To begin this exploration, let's recall that by mid-1900 Freud had suffered many months of anguish about Fliess's betrayal and disloyalty, relating to the "Breuerization" factor and to Fliess's sudden disparagement of psychoanalytic concepts in favor of Fliess's new theories. Similarly, by mid-1914 Freud had suffered more than a year of bitter thoughts about Jung's betrayal, relating to the Swiss savant's fairly abrupt jettisoning of core analytic ideas in favor of the new Jungian theories emphasizing anti-sexual factors. These overall similarities between setbacks in 1900 and 1914 gave Freud every reason to develop as murderous a hatred against Jung as he had manifested against his former supporter, Fliess. Indeed, Freud had even greater reason to develop a lethally revengeful hatred towards Jung. His letters to Jung indicate that Freud felt he'd given this man an extremely precious gift by making him his son and heir, the Crown Prince of a worldwide psychoanalytic empire. Therefore, to Freud it was an unpardonable crime that Jung had repaid him by seeming to spit contemptuously upon him and Psychoanalysis in a series of grossly disloyal acts. If Fliess deserved to die at Achensee, how much moreso did Jung deserve a similar fate at the hands of Sigmund Freud?

It would be difficult for me to describe the full extent of Freud's revengeful bitterness towards Jung in 1913/1914, and readers can assess this for themselves by careful readings about the breakdown of this relationship in Brome (1968), Krüll (1986), and other sources. A patient study of the massive correspondence between these men (McGuire, 1974) is essential to an understanding of intense revengeful feelings that developed slowly on both sides of this relationship, one that was as "sick" and dysfunctional as the Freud/Fliess friendship. In reviewing the initial 80 percent of those letters, one finds Jung currying Freud's favor by repeatedly adopting, and being pressured into, the role of a servile lackey and yes-man to the Great Man. Considering this ill-treatment, it's no wonder that the dog finally bit its master's hand. Inevitably, the Swiss "sage" began to awaken from his transference sleep, and then realized that the great Viennese doctor was as mentally disturbed as his patients. In fact, in the final few letters written by Jung he stated that conclusion to Freud, angrily accusing him of being severely imbalanced (just as Breuer had done) and recommending that he should seek a genuine two-person analysis himself.

Naturally, those bitter accusations against him in Jung's final letters must have aroused feelings of deep humiliation and anger in Freud. However, in his letters responding to Jung's open attack upon his character and sanity, Freud managed to control his own anger and merely called for a cessation of their correspondence and relationship. Evidently he had to squelch his overt hostility towards Jung at the end of the correspondence out of fear that he would further antagonize Jung, whom he considered capable of inflicting great damage upon the Cause so long as he remained president of the international body of Psychoanalysis. Therefore, in the early months of 1914 Freud was forced to restrain his immensely hostile feelings towards Jung, because he feared Jung's potential for revenge, making this an excellent situation for the unconscious displacement of Freud's murderous anger onto an alternative power-figure in his life. That figure was Freud's ancient betrayer and enemy, his half-brother Emanuel.

At this juncture, a review is needed of some of Freud's most irrational behaviors in the period 1913/1914, actions that help clarify the imbalanced and lethal state of his mind in that era just preceding the "accidental" train death of his brother Emanuel. As already noted, in the early months of 1914 the dangerous state of Freud's mind was signaled by an anonymous contribution he made to the analytic journal *Imago* which was titled "On the Moses of Michelangelo." In that article, Freud imagined that he could read the sculptor's mind and true intentions, and offered the weird conclusion that his famous statue of Moses did not reveal the prophet's murderous anger as he was close to breaking the stone tablets, but showed instead Moses's immense efforts to control and defuse his righteous anger. Many years later (1924), when enough time had passed so that critics would not connect that murderous rage of Moses/Freud with the strange death of Emanuel Freud, it was revealed publicly that the author of that balmy article had been Sigmund Freud. Concerning the aftermath of that revelation, Ellenberger (1970, p. 821) remarked: "The consensus was that Freud had been projecting his own feelings."

Recall that in the Bible's frank discussion about Moses's murderous rage, he ordered the slaying of thousands of his disloyal disciples. In 1914, why did Freud try to rewrite this story by claiming that the bodily and facial expression of this statue of Moses revealed that the prophet was able to control and defuse his monumentally murderous intentions towards his own kinsmen? It seems clear that this fantasy involved Freud's fragile attempt to curb his own murderous desires towards a series of disloyal disciples who had abandoned him, including Adler, Stekel, Jung (and many other disciples in Zurich and Vienna). My thesis is that this weak, irrational stratagem did not succeed, and in the later months of 1914 Freud displaced his rage by ordering the killing of that earliest kinsman and "disciple" (supporter) who had abandoned him in childhood—none other than brother Emanuel. Like many other famous murderers, Freud published the Moses article as a covert "confession" of his lethal intentions in 1914, indicating that his impulses were about to overwhelm his defenses, and it should be obvious now why he insisted upon anonymity of publication.

In the period 1912/1913 there was another balmy publication by Freud that reveals the murderous state of his mind in that era. The fourth section of *Totem and Taboo* was finished in May 1913, soon after the emotional breakup with Jung, containing that ridiculous notion that patricide in the primeval horde has been passed on to each generation via genetic factors. Freud's discussion of the primal horde focussed upon a violent and jealous father who kept all females for himself, and drove away his sons as they matured. But the brothers formed an alliance, and later killed and ate their father, ending this patriarchal horde. This brutal father had been the model for the sons, and while eating him they completed their guilty identification with him, thereafter obeying his dictates due to their guilt—implying that the dead father still ruled their minds. Freud noted that this murder of the primal father had originated the "father gods" (to whom the sons atoned for their guilt), along with the modern patriarchal family, as a kind of covert reviving of the former patriarchal horde.

Paramount in Freud's theories in *Totem and Taboo* was the subject of murder, the killing of the primal father. Strangely, Freud pursued his Lamarckian bent by asserting that the murder of the primal father has influenced the mentality of every male child throughout history, because "psychical dispositions" concerning that murder are passed along genetically, i.e. the ancient patricide by the primal horde is somehow preserved indefinitely in the unconscious minds of all males. Various writers including Krüll (1986, p. 193) seem to have recognized that all of this astonishing gibberish about the primal sons' murder of their violent father was another of Freud's unconscious projections of his own situation in 1912/1913. Krüll wrote that: "At that time, with so many of his followers in open rebellion, Freud felt that he himself was a primal father whom the horde of envious sons wished to overthrow"—by murdering him. In this context, Krüll remarked that Freud "could not bear Jung's destructive ambitions." Thereby, she recognized Freud's dark suspicions that Jung wished to overthrow and kill him, though Krüll noted that Freud did not have a victim's mentality and was not prepared "to let himself be 'slain by his sons'."

Now we can see why Freud concocted that absurd fantasy in 1912/1913, soon after the break with Jung, regarding the primal father who had been killed and cannibalized* by his sons. As with the Moses article, this was another effort by Freud's fragile ego to cope with his feelings of murderous rage towards his disciples by reversing them. Thus, Freud's totem fantasy indicated that his disciples (the sons) wished to murder him (the primal father), to deny and hide the true state of affairs, i.e. that he was hardly able to control his own desires to kill Jung and other "disloyal" disciples. These intense desires to murder probably stimulated irrational counter-measures in Freud's psyche, provoking conscious and unconscious fears that Jung and others really wished to kill him.

Ergo, the irrational state of Freud's mind in 1914 (discussed later in some detail) forced him to cope with the fantasy that his disciples wished to murder him; and apparently his perverse solution was actually to murder someone else in order to preserve his own life. This "solution" corresponds with behaviors of numerous mentally unbalanced killers whose psychic processes disclose this insane formula: 'I killed only to prevent myself from *being killed*.' Likewise, Freud believed he was saving his own life by identifying with the envious sons who murdered their primal father, and then by acting-out this identification (in addition to his role of the primal father). My thesis is that this caused him, in 1914, to arrange for the murder of his own wished-for "primal father," his stern, and authoritative eldest

---

**The cannibalization theme hints at psychotic processes in Freud's mind that were quite powerful.*

brother named Emanuel. In this regard, Krüll (p. 194) wisely commented that when Freud stood before Moses's statue he harbored a twofold emotional ambivalence as "both a son and father," each role demanding that he subdue murderous passions.

The above discussion emphasizes Freud's acting-out of a defensive fantasy identification with the "primal sons" as one of several possible explanations for his uncanny murder of Emanuel Freud. Reminding the reader that previous chapters have provided numerous instances of such acting-out of fantasy identifications by Freud, including ones that seriously harmed other persons, it's time to consider whether in 1913/1914 Freud's breakup with Jung was partly a repetition and acting-out of his break with Fliess in 1900. Some pertinent information is found in Brome's book (1968, p. 41) regarding Freud's breakups with Adler and Stekel, which just preceded his break with Jung. Brome quoted correspondence between Ferenczi and Freud that is not available publicly, in which Ferenczi suggested that the master's "atrocious" difficulty in separating from Adler and Stekel was "even more highly charged than Freud suspected because it recalled the whole Fliess episode and Freud might be living over again the Fliess desertion of ten years before." Brome reported that Freud "unhesitatingly agreed" with Ferenczi's suggestion that, with Adler and Stekel, he was acting-out the painful issues involved in his estrangement from Fliess. Later, in a 1913 letter to Binswanger, Freud acknowledged that some of his repressed feelings towards Fliess were being displaced onto Jung. (Sulloway, 1979, p. 427).

Therefore, why shouldn't we assume that in his break with Jung (who was far more important to him than Adler and Stekel were) Freud in 1913/1914 had much more intense reasons for acting-out crucial aspects of his prior break with Fliess? If so, we need to focus upon Fliess's accusation that Freud's mental instability had caused him to plan Fliess's murder at Achensee in the summer of 1900. This leads to my thesis that after Freud's break with Jung his propensity for acting-out compelled him to devise a partial imitation of his earlier murder-plan by concocting another vengeful murder-plan in 1914 to punish that "disloyal supporter," his brother Emanuel (as a displacement of murderous feelings towards Jung, Fliess, and other betrayers).

My suggestion that Freud's breakup with Jung imitated some perverse elements of his break with Fliess is supported by another small detail. The final break between Freud and Fliess occurred at their contentious Achensee meeting in 1900, and immediately thereafter Freud sought solace by taking his sister-in-law Minna Bernays on a romantic unchaperoned trip through Italy. Likewise, the final break between Freud and Jung occurred in September 1913 at the last Congress of the International Psycho-Analytical

Association at Munich—featuring vitriolic battles between Jung's followers and Freud's—after which Freud "immediately went off to his beloved Rome, where his sister-in-law, Minna Bernays, joined him." (Brome, p. 135) Was it merely coincidence that the breakups with Fliess and then Jung were immediately followed by consolation by Minna in Italy, not forgetting that Rome symbolized nanny to Sigi? (And was Brome too polite when he wrote about the 1913 trip: "It was interesting that his sister-in-law not his wife went to Bologna to meet him.")

Perhaps some readers need further convincing about my claim that Freud earnestly desired to kill Carl Jung in 1913/1914 (with regard to my displacement theory relating to Emanuel's death). As a preface, it should be said that Freud's psyche sometimes tried to mitigate his incessant death-wishes towards others by provoking fantasies that they harbored desires to kill him—which in his 50s elicited his fears that many of his disciples wished to "eliminate" him. So, it's not surprising that in his very first meeting with Jung in 1907 Freud interpreted one of Jung's dreams as harboring murderous wishes towards him. Later, during their trip to America together Jung disclosed his dream about burrowing into the earth where the skulls of two ancient skeletons were discovered, but he deliberately falsified his associations to those figures, relating them falsely to his wife and sister-in-law, since he knew that Freud was nervously intending to interpret them as proof of Jung's death-wishes against the master.

At various times Freud made direct accusations that Jung desired his death, implying the Swiss disciple's wish to murder him, which Jung denied vehemently. Apparently, Jung did not feel secure enough to defend himself by saying: 'No, it is the reverse—you wish unconsciously to kill *me*, because part of your psyche is envious that I am your appointed heir who will take full possession of your creation, Psychoanalysis, in future years.' With regard to these matters, the subject of Freud's fainting spells is relevant, since they are closely connected to Freud's lethal wishes towards Jung.

One of these fainting spells occurred in August 1909 when Freud, Jung, and Ferenczi met at a luncheon in Bremen, just before their departure together to America (the Clark University trip). At that meeting Jung expressed interest in the peat-bog corpses of northern Germany (apparently the bodies of prehistoric men) and several times Freud burst out anxiously: "Why are you so concerned about these corpses?" Suddenly, Freud fainted. According to Jung, when Freud had revived he claimed that Jung's talk about corpses meant that he harbored a death-wish towards the master. Jung was greatly surprised by Freud's peculiar interpretation and moreso "was alarmed by the intensity of his fantasies—so strong that obviously they could cause him to faint."

It seems obvious to me that Freud's fainting spell was caused by his own powerful death-wishes towards Jung and other persons. Indeed, he pointed obliquely to his own death-wishes when he analyzed this fainting spell later, relating it to his persistent death-wishes in early childhood towards his baby brother Julius, which left him with a horrendous sense of guilt. However, Freud's rigid defenses did not allow him to draw the obvious conclusion that his lifelong death-wishes towards Julius and other rivals were revived in lethal feelings towards Jung, which had provoked his fainting spell at Bremen. Instead, he used slippery arguments to connect a small personal victory over Jung with his "defeating" of Julius, thereby evading the recognition that his fainting fit at Bremen had been provoked by his own deadly wishes towards Jung. (Of course, Jones and other disciples have endorsed Freud's little con game.)

Another of Freud's fainting spells with Jung occurred in Munich in November 1912, at a time when the relationship was almost dead and bitter recriminations were close to expression by both men. At Munich there was a luncheon meeting at the Park Hotel attended by Freud, Jones, Jung, a Swiss analyst named Riklin (and others). According to Jung's account, during lunch there was a discussion about an Egyptian pharaoh who allegedly had defaced chiselings of his father's name on shrines, an idea that Jung's literary research caused him to challenge and "correct." According to Jones (I, p. 317), Freud then reproached Jung and Riklin for writing articles on psychoanalysis without mentioning his name. Jung replied that this had seemed unnecessary, since Freud's name was so well known as the originator of psychoanalysis, but Freud persisted in his reproaches. Suddenly, he fell onto the floor, having fainted once again! The tall, powerfully-built Jung picked up the diminutive Freud, and carried him onto a sofa in the lounge, where he soon revived. Jones claimed that Freud's first words were strange ones—"How sweet it must be to die"—as an additional clue "that the idea of dying had some esoteric meaning for him."

Jung remarked that while he carried Freud in his arms he began to revive: "and I shall never forget the look he cast at me. In his weakness he looked at me as if I were his father. Whatever other causes may have contributed to this faint . . . the fantasy of father-murder was common to both cases." I'm confident that great emphasis should be placed upon these observations by Jung. The first one indicates that Freud regarded him not only as a supportive son, but also as a powerful, authoritative father-figure (like Moses)—which hints that Freud's psyche was able to make a compelling correlation between Jung and another desired father-figure, his brother Emanuel. This helps to support my thesis that Freud's unbalanced mind in 1914 made it possible for him to equate those men, allowing him to displace his murderous intentions against Jung onto Emanuel. Jung's second observation was that both of Freud's fainting spells involved an unconscious fantasy of father-murder. That remark provides further support for my belief that Freud's fainting spells involved murderous fantasies towards Jung that eventually were actualized in the murder of Emanuel Freud.

Concerning the preceding fainting spell, Jones (I, p. 317) added some valuable information. Soon after the incident occurred, Freud wrote a letter to Jones confiding that it had been a "repetition," i.e. an imitation of a previous fainting spell that Freud had suffered many years earlier (with less intense symptoms), "in the *same* room of the Park Hotel." Then Freud connected those two fainting spells, years apart, by relating the earlier fainting spell to his ambivalent feelings towards Wilhelm Fliess (which included both murderous and homosexual feelings). About that previous fainting incident Freud wrote: "I saw Munich first when I visited Fliess during his illness and this town seems to have acquired a strong connection with my relation to that man." He then cited the role of "unruly homosexual feeling" but ignored his death-wishes towards Fliess. It seems clear that Freud's two fainting spells at the Park Hotel in Munich (the *same* room) reflect his murderous wishes towards Fliess, near the end of their relationship; which then were transferred to Freud's lethal feelings towards Jung at Munich in 1912* (via fainting at the Park Hotel again); and finally were transferred to lethal intentions towards Emanuel in 1914. (Freud's letter to Jones is a bit ambiguous, and hints that he might have had three fainting spells in that same room of the Park Hotel in Munich, "six and four years" apart.)

Clark has written a fine chapter on "The Break with Jung" (1980) whose final pages summarize the deadly intensity of Freud's anger towards Jung in 1913/1914. As shown by Clark's research, in the months before Jung resigned the presidency of the international body, while Freud still greatly feared that Jung might find a way to expropriate the leadership of Psychoanalysis from him, Freud's hostility towards the Swiss leader increased dramatically. In November 1913 Freud wrote to Jones that Jung's position was very strong, but "our hope is still he will ruin himself." The underlying death-wish towards Jung is unmistakable, and Freud urged his Welsh ally to fight Jung in England and America even if the struggle were long and hard. Describing his feelings towards Jung in that era, Freud wrote to another disciple (Putnam) about Jung's alleged "lies, brutality, and antisemitic condescension towards me," which elicited Freud's "disgust with saintly converts."

Besides writing vicious statements against Jung in personal correspondence, Freud tried to find some relief for his murderous rage by publishing a series of writings that were intended to "defeat" Jung. For example, Krüll has noted (1986, p. 191) that in the last section of *Totem and Taboo*: "written

---

*The final break with Jung occurred <u>in Munich</u> at the International Congress of September 1913.

after Jung's defection, Freud tried to get even with his former disciple." Clark noted that, in the last weeks of 1913, Freud began writing his "polemic" titled *On the History of the Psychoanalytic Movement* which set forth the essential ideas of psychoanalysis and showed that the theories of Jung and Adler were completely incompatible with them, which Freud viewed as a public rejection of Jung which he hoped would provoke "the desired rupture" between them. In March of 1914, when a draft of the "History" was completed, Freud wrote to a friend that he'd used it to give "a good clobbering" to Jung (and other enemies). He sent the draft to Abraham, who responded by calling it a strong "weapon." Another draft was sent to Jones who objected that some of the language was too vitriolic, though in principle he was not in favor of showing mercy "in such an important war." It's obvious that this initial draft was not a simple clinical history, but was a bitter excuse to make war on Jung—just as war clouds were gathering in Europe with the advent of World War I.

Clark remarked (p. 336) that the "History" was not Freud's "only weapon for attacking Jung . . " Another literary "weapon" used to clobber Jung was Freud's essay "On Narcissism: An Introduction," which Freud began writing in Rome in September 1913 (after the explosive Munich Congress) and finished in Vienna early in 1914. This article was used to castigate and "correct" Jung's writings that had attempted to modify the libido theory. Before the end of 1914 Freud began working on his case history of the Wolf Man, which Freud admitted (per Clark) was written as an attack against reinterpretations by Jung and Adler of psychoanalytic theory.

Did those written attempts to defeat and punish Jung in 1913/1914 give Freud an adequate emotional release of his lethal rage towards Jung? Apparently not, for we recall that in 1914 he tried to cope with his deadly feelings towards Jung by denying that he wished to murder Jung and other disloyal disciples, using that "peculiar" essay he wrote about Michelangelo's statue of Moses. That anonymous essay, whose authorship was concealed until 1924, was Freud's unconscious way of trying to fool the public by saying: 'I am not the man who in 1914 wished to murder those disloyal men who betrayed me, Carl Jung and Emanuel Freud.'

On April 20, 1914 Jung resigned the presidency of the international analytic organization, for reasons that remain unknown to me. One might guess that this resignation relieved Freud of some stresses pertaining to his fears that Jung hoped to steal the psychoanalytic movement from him. But Jung was still an official member of the analytic Association, with many Zurich analysts in his camp, and that fact continued to plague Freud who feared that Jung could cause untold mischief against the Cause by public speeches and by his writings. In a letter to Jones of May 17, 1914 Freud revealed his ongoing intense anxieties about Jung when he wrote: "I expect no immediate success but incessant struggling." He exposed additional fears about Jung by remarking that: "Anyone who promises mankind liberation from the hardship of sex will be hailed as a hero, let him talk whatever nonsense he chooses."

Freud exposed his great fear of Jung's influence by gruffly pretending he was not at all afraid of the Swiss savant. In June of 1914 he wrote to Jones: "I am not in the least afraid of whatever he does but I affirm that no one can foretell what he will do." Freud then referred to public speeches that Jung was about to make on psychoanalytic topics in England, that summer of 1914, and encouraged Jones to attend at least one of those events. He advised Jones to: "Let him talk, and defy him afterward in print drily and mercilessly." It was obvious that Freud regarded the coming "incessant struggling" with Jung as a war to the death—at least a public-relations war, with many salvos of vicious words and accusations. Ironically, war clouds were growing thicker over Europe and Britain in that same era, for during July and August of 1914 the Great War began to explode across the continent.

But just before that catastrophe arrived, the early weeks of the summer found Freud under greater stress than ever before, because Jung had not yet resigned his regular membership in the analytic Association and Freud was undoubtedly fearful about the outcome. That summer in Aberdeen Jung addressed the annual meeting of the British Medical Association on "The Importance of the Unconscious in Psychopathology" and seemed to set himself at odds with the master. Also, it was depressing to Freud that Jung lectured in London that summer and had great success in presenting his anti-Freudian ideas, as he learned in a long letter from Jones. Clark summarized (p. 338) Freud's painful situation by noting that: "By the summer of 1914 there were thus three competing schools in operation: Freud's, Adler's and Jung's." Moreover, Freud had reason to fear that henceforth Jung might elevate Adler's ideas to an equal status with his own, for at the Munich Congress in September 1913 Jung had analyzed psychoanalysis, and proposed that Freudian and Adlerian theories were complementary. About that conclusion, Steele (1982, p. 258) remarked that Jung "had completely relativized psychoanalysis by putting Freud's work on the same plane as Adler's." It was that kind of heresy and betrayal by Jung that was most likely to enrage Freud, and to provoke deeply irrational processes in him.

Throughout the first half of 1914, Freud was under great emotional pressures as he struggled to devise complex political machinations that were intended to prevent Jung from maintaining power within the psychoanalytic organization. (See Brome, 1968, Ch. 10.) Freud wanted Jung to resign from the presidency, and then removed as a regular member, but he must have had much ambivalence about succeeding in his schemes to attain those ends. For example, Freud had to be worried that the large Zurich contingent of analysts might remain loyal to Jung, and would resign with him. Also, the American analysts in several cities had had more contacts with Jung than any other analytic leader, so there was a danger that many of them might leave along with Jung. Indeed, with Jung's resignation there was a danger of losing a third to one half of the total membership worldwide, which was extremely painful for Freud to contemplate in the summer of 1914. After much anxious waiting to hear the outcome, at last Freud learned in mid-July that finally Jung had resigned as a general member, and he put on a brave face about the secessions of "the brutal, sanctimonious Jung and his disciples." Thus, Freud pretended that it was not a blow to his megalomanic dreams of empire that the Zurich group voted, by fifteen votes to one, to withdraw from the International Association.

The months of June and early July 1914 must have been enormously stressful and maddening for Freud, as he waited anxiously to hear about Jung's resignation, and whether a dreadful number of analysts would decide to defect with Jung. Indeed, it's my thesis that Freud's mental imbalances in early 1914 (soon to be discussed) had combined with the vicissitudes of the early summer months to provoke a brief psychotic break that was similar to the Achensee psychosis of 1900 (which apparently caused Freud to plan Fliess's murder). My assumption here is that sometime in June 1914, or even during the first days of July, Freud's mind "snapped" again, and that his murderous rage towards Jung became displaced in a bizarre plan to murder Emanuel Freud. Therefore, it seems credible to me that the strange July 7th departure of Freud's young daughter Anna, on a trip to visit her uncle Emanuel in England, was somehow causally connected with that uncle's death in October 1914.

Although this is not an accusation of complicity by Anna, a few pages later I'll discuss her possible role as an unwitting helper of Freud's presumed murder plan. But first, let me discuss some details about the pathological state of Freud's mind in the year 1914 (and with regard to 1915, in later pages).

Freud's Mental Turmoil in 1914

An earlier chapter revealed that the year 1900, when Freud feared the defeat of his dream book, that Fliess had betrayed him, and that his psychoanalytic empire could not get started, was a horrific year of depression, revenge, and madness for him. Soon we'll see that those same negative factors pertained to the year 1914, while he struggled mightily with Jung's betrayals and possible expropriation of his brainchild, and with fears that his new psychoanalytic empire was about to disintegrate.

Freud's key biographers (Jones and Schur) protected his heroic reputation by not acknowledging that he sometimes suffered prolonged periods of depression with psychotic undercurrents. They did not clarify this point regarding the years 1913/1914, also because they did not want the public to recognize how badly their hero suffered emotionally in his break with Jung. For the analysts have promoted the fiction that it was only the weak and "crazy" betrayer, Jung, who became vulnerable to psychotic processes in the era of the Freud/Jung schism and thereafter. However, there is good reason to believe that Freud himself suffered a prolonged depression in the years 1913/1914 under the pressures of his break with Jung, including the extended battle to control Psychoanalysis and save it from total disintegration.

Jones was willing to hint at only a small part of this story. In his second volume (p. 99), he remarked that Freud's daughter Anna told him that the summer of 1913 "was the only time she ever remembers her father being depressed," which seemed relevant to the point that "he no longer felt up to analytic work . . " Anna's memory must have been quite unreliable and porous if she remembered only one time when her father showed symptoms of depression, but her acknowledgment about that despondency in the summer of 1913 indicates that it must have been a particularly depressing period for Freud. Her biographer Young-Bruehl noted (1988, p. 63) that Freud's depression in the summer of 1913 was provoked because he felt himself mired in a "tragedy of ingratitude" with his recalcitrant heir, Carl Jung. And another of Freud's children gave us a clue that the master's depression of 1913 might well have extended into the first half of 1914, and later. For in Martin Freud's biography of his father he mentioned (1958, p. 179) that his father was deeply depressed during the year 1914.

Accepting Anna's evaluation, let's assume that Freud was quite depressed during the summer of 1913. That this depression (and underlying psychotic ideation) persisted from September 1913 into the first half of 1914 is suggested by Freud's work on his pathetic essay about the Moses statue of Michelangelo. In 1937 Freud finally admitted that he layed the background for that essay by spending three *lonely* weeks in Rome (symbolizing nanny) during September of 1913, standing every day in front of the statue—sketching and "analyzing" its hidden meanings. Emphasis has been placed on the word "lonely" above (his term), as an obvious reflection of his depressed state in that era. Jones remarked that (II, p. 366) the winter of 1913-1914 "was the worst time in the conflict with Jung," when Freud was "feeling bitterly disappointed at Jung's defection" and was engaged in "an inward struggle to control his emotions." Then on Christmas day of 1913

(Emanuel's birthday) Freud made the decision to write the Moses essay, finished it on January 1, 1914, and in later weeks of 1914 argued about its anonymous publication with Jones and other colleagues (who feared that his authorship of that weird essay would become known publicly). Regarding that essay, Jones seemed aware (p. 367) that it showed Freud was struggling mightily to control his lethal feelings (just as Moses struggled to preserve the Tables of Law), in order "to save something of his life's work, psychoanalysis" from that traitor, Carl Jung.

It is interesting that in a brief letter which Freud wrote to Abraham on June 1, 1913 he asserted that Carl Jung had become "crazy," and that he would have liked to see Jung "wreck himself" before separating from him. That allegation that Jung had become psychotic was perhaps an indication that Freud was defending against recognition of his own murderously psychotic impulses towards his former "heir." By September 1913 Freud's three-week vigil in front of the Moses statue, and his later balmy essay about the statue, were quite clear indications that he was struggling with murderous psychotic impulses towards Jung and others, given his denial of Moses's mass slayings of his disciples. Moreover, we'll soon review additional evidence of Freud's psychotic tendencies that emerged in the years 1913/1914. In the fall of 1913 there were further signs of Freud's depressed feelings when he wrote Abraham on October 26th that: "These are gloomy times . . or perhaps only a time when gloomy moods predominate." The implication was that despondent feelings then were dominating his fragile psyche.

My claim that in early 1914 Freud experienced a dangerous upsurge of murderous psychotic impulses towards Jung can be supported by some of the letters to Abraham. In mid-March of 1914 Freud's impatience regarding Jung had escalated dramatically and dangerously, for Jung did not resign from the International body's presidency until the following month, on April 20th. Nevertheless, it is astonishing that in Freud's letter to Abraham dated March 16, 1914 he mentioned the possibility that "aggressive action against Jung" might be effected somehow, and that this would soon be discussed with Rank, and Sachs, and probably London (Jones).

There is a compelling reason to believe that the "aggressive action" against Jung mentioned in the March 16th letter involved Freud's discussion of his plan to murder Jung, with the cooperation or approval of Freud's closest disciples, in order to wrest the presidency from the traitor. This thesis about a plan to murder Jung (like the plan to kill Fliess at Achensee in 1900) is supported by Freud's next letter to Abraham just nine days later, dated March 25, 1914. The first brief sentence of this letter noted that a letter from Jones was enclosed. Then, Freud's next statements are as follows: "It is quite remarkable how each one of us in turn is seized with the impulse to kill, so that the others have to restrain him. I suspect that Jones himself will produce the next plan." This wording suggests that Jung was fortunate that he resigned the presidency voluntarily, less than four weeks later, since he might have fallen victim instead to some bizarre murder plot concocted by Freud, and/or by Jones. Readers who remain skeptical that Freud was considering an actual plan to kill Jung in March 1914, as the preceding letters strongly suggest, should review chapter eleven's account of the plotting by Jones (and probably Freud) to effect the "administrative murder" of the fallen analyst Sadger in the 1930s, to prevent the publication of his explosive manuscript about Freud. (It is obvious to me that many letters in the Freud/Abraham correspondence are "missing," so there is no further information there to corroborate the start of a plot to kill Jung, and almost all correspondence with Ferenczi is still being suppressed.)

In Freud's previous remark about killing someone (surely Jung), notice his hint about a need to be restrained from committing the murder impulsively. This matches the same covert theme in his recently finished Moses essay about the need to be restrained from savagely killing disciples who had betrayed his dogma. This should help convince us that in March 1914 Freud was concocting a plan to murder Jung, imitating the Achensee debacle with Fliess, and that this signifies that Freud's lethal psychotic impulses were quite active and dangerous in 1914. If so, we should not be surprised that in June 1914 he displaced his fury by devising a long-distance plan to arrange the murder of Emanuel Freud, thereby slyly reducing the risk that he would be suspected of being the perpetrator of a killing.

The letters to Abraham in April and May of 1914 provide evidences that Freud's depression and unwellness continued into those months. On April 24th he wrote that he was struggling with "an indisposition I could not account for," which soon showed itself to be a severe tracheitis-laryngitis. He added that he was not well at all, and particularly was "quite inactive intellectually." This difficulty with his throat and speaking reminds me that in the era of his break with Jung he developed a very peculiar, restricted problem with speaking Jung's name. In fact, he became totally incapable of uttering Jung's name and automatically substituted Jones's name each time, in its place! One imagines that this was Freud's primitive version of the obliteration of Jung's name and identity, hinting at death-wishes towards the Swiss analyst. This symptom reminds me of Freud's fainting spell that was preceded by the story about the Egyptian prince who allegedly erased his father's chiseled name on numerous monuments, which Freud interpreted in terms of murderous wishes towards the father.

On May 7, 1914 Freud wrote to his Berlin ally that he was "still unwell and without energy for work," noting that he'd just passed his 58th birthday. Then he began his letter of May 13th by complaining that he'd been ill again and was having a bad time in general, "as if worry and work were at last wearing me down." The theme of depression appeared again in this letter when he wrote: "What really upsets me is my lack of desire or incapacity for work, which has persisted since Easter." (But he had done some work on the "History of the Psychoanalytic Movement," which he was using to "clobber" poor Jung—in lieu of killing him, apparently.) He ended this letter by apologizing for its "low level of morale."

In the early weeks of June 1914 Freud was still under considerable stress while waiting for news about whether Jung would resign as a regular member and, if so, whether a large portion of the analytic membership would resign with him. Although Freud did not receive that news until mid-July, in that month allowing him some relief from uncertainty and waiting, during middle June's accelerated pressures he made a surprising announcement that his depressed feelings had lifted quite suddenly, just when one might have expected their more precipitous decline. In his letter to Abraham dated June 14, 1914 he announced, out of the blue, that: "I have to report that I feel quite well again."

My suggestion is that Freud's sudden relief from depression resulted from his initial contemplation of a fateful decision that enabled him, at last, to express his murderous rage towards Carl Jung and Emanuel Freud. The thesis here is that Freud's depression lifted suddenly in middle June of 1914, because that was the most likely time when he began considering a bizarre plan to direct the assassination of his eldest brother (in October 1914) by having a professional killer push him off the train that he regularly rode to his vacation home at a seaside resort. In effect, Freud's internal pressures during early June had built up to an alarming degree, so that flagrant psychosis was imminent; but that was avoided by a substantial release of his murderous tensions, provided by his plan to arrange Emanuel's killing.

The idea that Freud devised a serious murder plan by late June 1914 (discussed in the next section) assumes that in the aftermath of that planning, in July and August, he would have continued to exhibit evidences of irrational behaviors and thought. That will receive support from three factors that testify to his irrational state of mind: 1. his decision in early July to send his young daughter Anna to England, despite great danger to her welfare caused by the arrival of the Great War; 2. his strangely manic ardor for the war, in the months of July and August; and 3. symptoms during August which Ferenczi regarded as the onset of insanity in Freud. The first of those factors will be discussed fully in the next section, so now I'll cover the last two items pertaining to Freud's irrational behaviors in that summer of 1914.

A thumbnail sketch of the war situation is needed here. In World War I the Central Powers included Germany and Austria (also Turkey, Hungary and Bulgaria) versus the Allied Powers of Britain, France, and Russia (also Italy, Belgium, Rumania, and America). In the middle of the summer of 1914 events unfolded swiftly. On July 23rd Austria gave an ultimatum to Serbia and then declared war against Serbia on July 28th, whereupon Russia mobilized on July 30th. Next, Germany declared war upon Russia on August 1st, then crossed into France the next day. Also, Germany invaded Belgium and, in response, Britain declared war on Germany on August 4th. By August 1914 the main combatants were aligned against each other, and the long and savage war had begun.

In the early weeks of the war, Freud's response to it was quite peculiar. Despite that his sons served with the Austro-Germanic forces in this bloody conflict, in the initial weeks Freud seemed delighted with the war, as if it were an exciting picnic. Jones noted that the master did not greet the war "with simple horror, as so many did." Instead, his initial response was of youthful enthusiasm, showing "a re-awakening of the military ardors of his boyhood." In writing a friend, he praised the rage of the Germans and the Austrian rebirth, stating that: "All my libido is given to Austro-Hungary." Though Jones failed to say so, Freud was obviously a bloody militarist and imperialist, as befitted his conquistador self-image. Jones pretended that Freud's manic militarism lasted only a few weeks, when allegedly he came to his senses, but even in September he "expressed the hope of sharing the jubilation over the expected fall of Paris . . " He talked of "our" battles and "our" victories, and his letters to Abraham much later in the war—when things were not going well for Austro-Germany—sometimes showed glimpses of his old ferocious militarism, though considerably chastened.

Just prior to the outbreak of war, the Austrian Foreign Minister, Count Berchtold, layed the groundwork for catastrophe by making his ultimatum to Serbia, in what was a dangerous bluff that Jones characterized rightly as a "reckless playing with fire." More than any world leader, Berchtold was responsible for making war inevitable and for many millions of lost lives and untold destruction. But on July 26, 1914 Freud's murderous psychotic impulses were close to the surface, causing him to refer approvingly about Count Berchtold's irresponsible action as being "a release of tension through a boldspirited deed." (Jones II, p. 171) Why did Freud feel that way? My guess is that the immense stresses in his life that summer caused *him* to require "a release of tension through a boldspirited deed"—namely, the deranged act of planning Emanuel's murder.

During August of 1914 Freud's intense ardor for the war was accompanied by some disturbing symptoms that Jones described (II, p. 171) vividly. Jones wrote that: "He was quite carried away, could not think of any work, and spent his time discussing the events of the day with his brother Alexander." Also, he noted that Freud: "was excitable, irritable, and made slips of the tongue all day long." Evidently, the latter symptoms continued into late September and early October, for in those weeks they were observed by Ferenczi who came to Vienna for an analysis by Freud that lasted less than a month (due to his military call-up). Concerning Freud's last symptom, the making of excessive slips of the tongue (which Ferenczi also was prone to make), the Hungarian analyst decided that this was a sign in Freud of the onset of general paralysis of the *insane*, (G.P.I.) With that diagnosis of his master's condition, Ferenczi became the second close colleague to fix a label of insanity on Freud, recalling Breuer's diagnosis of "moral insanity," and Strachey's later diagnosis of Freud's and Fliess's dual insanity—folie à deux. (Also, we should not dismiss Jung's belated claim that Freud was quite mentally imbalanced.)

Let's assume that Ferenczi was correct in diagnosing Freud as entering a psychotic state in October 1914. Can this moderately psychotic condition of Freud's be explained simply as his reaction to the emotional pressures accompanying commencement of a general state of war? That explanation seems to be inadequate, considering that millions of middle-aged men and women in Europe experienced the same stresses in early October of 1914 without "going to pieces." However, a further explanation is at hand in Freud's case: the additional psychic pressures deriving from a grotesque murder plan that he had concocted to obtain revenge upon his betrayers, Emanuel and Jung (as well as Fliess and Breuer, in fantasy). For any clever murder plan can go awry and bring about a terrible retribution for the perpetrator and his loved ones, a thought that might have troubled even a confident, megalomanic manipulator like Freud.

Anna's Trip to England

This section will focus upon my claim that young Anna Freud was sent to England by her father in the summer of 1914 primarily as a manipulation by him that furthered his plan to arrange the killing of Emanuel Freud. It's my hunch that Anna acted as an unwitting courier for her father, while she enjoyed (at age 18) her first visit to her Manchester relatives and a sightseeing trip to southeast Britain. My version of this manipulation is that it maneuvered her into providing three crucial services for her father.

First, during July and August her frequent letters from England to her father (which surely he must have insisted on) would have kept him informed about any fluctuations in Emanuel's plans for train travel in September or October 1914. Thereby, Freud was able to learn quite early the date of his brother's fateful train trip from Manchester to his resort home on the coast (on October 17th), so that this information was able to be mailed by Freud beforehand to a chosen assassin living in England. Second, Anna probably carried with her regular suitcase an additional small satchel, with instructions from her father that a designated person would contact her and accept the satchel from her (in London, or elsewhere), giving her some plausible pretext for this transfer. She would not know that the satchel had a false bottom or side in which a "payoff" (currency or jewels) was hidden to recompense the assassin for killing Emanuel. Third, Anna may have carried in her purse a sealed envelope, addressed to someone who used an alias. The envelope was given to her by her father, and she would be required to mail it when she set foot in England. The enclosed letter would have carried Freud's earliest general instructions to an assassin, perhaps someone well-known to Sigmund, advising that Emanuel Freud was to be pushed from a train on a certain date (with information about the train route and departure date to be provided in a later coded letter). The assassin also would have been advised to contact Anna Freud upon her arrival in England, to receive a satchel enclosing the assassination "fee." (Some of these items will be mentioned again, momentarily.)

In the previous section I've explained my reasons for believing that Freud's mind became somewhat unstable in June of 1914, and that during that month his psychotic impulses impelled him to formulate a murder plan involving his brother Emanuel. It's my view that in that month he strongly surmised that the outbreak of continental war was perhaps only days or weeks away and that he needed to act quickly to set up his plan with an assassin in England, due to the possibility that the lines of communication between Austria and England would soon be curtailed or disconnected by war. What Freud needed in late June of 1914 was a trustworthy and obedient courier to effect his plan, but one who could be "kept in the dark" in case the plan somehow went awry during or after the murder, helping ensure that Emanuel's death would not readily cast suspicion onto himself. He took advantage of the fact that his daughter Anna was trustworthy and completely obedient to his every wish, and that for months she had been wishing that she could make a summer visit to her relatives in England. In early July Freud actualized her wish by sending her on that visit to Manchester, with his own murderous agenda in mind.

Some readers might be skeptical about the previous scenario, because it makes two unusual assumptions: 1. that Freud would have had knowledge of a shady character in England who was willing to act as a paid assassin; and 2., that Freud would have known how to smuggle contraband into England, in the way I've suggested. My reply concerning both of these possible objections is to remind readers of material in the first chapter indicating that the Freud family, historically, had strong connections with counterfeiters of currency, and probably other sorts of criminals as well. Moreover, the business of counterfeiting currency, especially in Europe, could quite naturally involve acts of smuggling. The eleventh chapter describes a dangerous smuggling escapade by Ernest Jones involving currency, circa 1919, one that Freud might easily have been involved with along with Jones (as will be discussed later). In the modern age, it is not difficult for even genteel persons to contact paid assassins via adventurist magazine advertisements, to "eliminate" unwanted enemies or relatives, and we should not be surprised that Freud could have made a similar underworld "contract" in 1914.

Further details concerning the previous scenario need to be mentioned here. When Anna was dispatched to England on July 7th, Freud would have instructed her on some artful way to learn from Emanuel what his planned departure date would be, in late September or October, for his vacation trip to the English coast. Perhaps Freud told her to obtain the information artfully, because he might visit his brother on the coast if the dates were convenient, but didn't want Emanuel to know about this possible "surprise," so that this rigid man would not be able to regard this as a firm promise that Sigmund would visit him. Emanuel was a creature of habit, and probably the Vienna Freuds knew that he made that trip from Manchester to his coastal vacation cottage regularly each year, but Anna would have needed to ascertain the precise departure date he had in mind for that year. She needed to mail that information quickly back to her father in Vienna, so that he could immediately mail back that information (perhaps encoded) to the designated assassin in England, to ensure that he was on board the death train. Time was of the essence, considering that Anna arrived in England on July 18th, and Freud probably sensed that his plot was being hatched perilously close to the declaration of war between Austria and England (which was the case), after which communication with the assassin could be subject to long delays and official censorship.

Even in June and early July, Freud might have feared that mail from Austria was already being "monitored" by English officials. This prompted my suggestion that he relied upon Anna to hand-carry his initial letter giving the assassin general information about the impending train murder, and about the satchel bearing a substantial payment. Also, one can imagine Freud's deception with Anna about this satchel: 'The letter you mail for me is to my colleague named Smith, who loaned it to me at a conference in Munich; so I've advised him to get it back from you in London, and it will enclose some recent clinical papers of mine that might interest him.' A simple encoding of the final letter to the assassin was assumed by me, as a protection for Freud in case the letter was monitored by English officials, followed by a bungling of the killing with police finding it on the killer's person or in his home.

Apologists for Freud will object strenuously to the previous scenario, arguing that he dearly loved his youngest daughter Anna and never would have embroiled her, unwittingly or otherwise, in a murder plan that could have gone askew, exposing her to being regarded as an accomplice to murder. My first reply to that objection is that, in the summer of 1914, Freud was gripped by psychotic impulses that disregarded Anna's welfare, along with increases of megalomania that probably made him feel certain that his plan was "perfect" and, since he was omnipotent and a genius, no harm could befall Anna or himself. Moreover, the objection that he would never place Anna in harm's way is belied by two incredibly irrational behaviors by Freud in the summer of 1914. The first of these was his decision to send Anna to England just as the war was about to commence; and the second was his decision to place this innocent virgin, Anna, into the hands of a notorious sexual psychopath and seducer of young women. Let's examine these issues, one at a time.

Clark reported (1980, p. 338) that on July 7, 1914 Freud wrote a letter to his nephew Samuel Freud in Manchester stating: "Today my youngest daughter, Anna, now a girl of 18 1/2 years, has set [out] for a journey to Berlin, Hamburg, and England, where she will arrive the 15th or 16th with the 'Amerika.'" Freud informed Samuel that money was being sent from Vienna to Manchester, and this nephew was asked "to play the role of her banker until the end of Sept., when we are to meet in Holland." Notice that Anna's visit to her English relatives that summer, including a tour of the southeast coast, was expected to last 2 1/2 months; and she was to be escorted by a family friend named Anna Lichtheim. (Young-Bruehl, 1988, p. 65) However, the vacation trip of Anna Freud had to be altered drastically by the outbreak of the Great War, which put her in danger of being interned in England for the war years, with all the emotional stress of being separated from her family in Vienna.

Freud's apologists try to defend his strange sanctioning of Anna's trip to England in 1914 by implying that he was merely short-sighted about dangerous political happenings, including various obvious signs of the war's imminence that appeared in June. Jones wrote: "In his judgment of political events Freud was neither more nor less perspicacious than another man." My claim, to the contrary, is that Freud in June already was aware of the great dangers that were crystallizing in Europe, but was forced to ignore them out of a need to pursue his murder plan. Indeed, Jones remarked that as early as December 8, 1912 Freud wrote that the political situation in Austria was quite stormy, indicating "that they must be prepared for bad times ahead." Jones realized that the master was referring to Austria's relations with Serbia and Russia, which in fact most Austrians suspected were teetering on the brink of disaster in the spring of 1914.

Consider this remarkable sequencing of events. Already we've noted that on July 7, 1914 Freud's letter to his nephew in Manchester announced that young Anna would soon be visiting England, despite that the world had been shocked *about one week earlier* by the news of a catastrophic assassination. (Did this assassination help to provoke Freud's assassination plan, one wonders?) On June 28, the heir to the Austrian crown, Archduke Franz Ferdinand, had been murdered at Sarajevo by a Bosnian man—an Austrian subject who allegedly had been inspired by conspirators in Serbia. As Jones noted (II, p. 169), this was the opportunity which the Austrian militarists were awaiting to foment war with the Serbs. On that same day, the 28th, Freud wrote this fearful comment to Ferenczi: "I am writing while still under the impact of the astonishing murder in Sarajevo, the consequences of which cannot be foreseen." Freud's comments about unforeseen consequences hinted at his fears that a disastrous war might be imminent. Jones added that when Franz Ferdinand's corpse was passed through Vienna late at night, without fanfare, Freud "sagely" remarked: "There is something dirty going on behind this." Like many other people, Freud seemed to suspect that a war was being plotted by the militarists, followed only three weeks later (July 30) by Austria's declaration of war against its much weaker neighbor, Serbia—signalling the start of the Great War that most savvy Austrians had been expecting.

The above material indicates that in late June, and during July of 1914, Freud had strong suspicions that a programmed war probably was imminent—one involving Austria and other great powers, perhaps including England. Indeed, Jones commented (II, p. 170) that he wrote a warning letter about the impending war to Freud. But always eager to protect Freud's reputation, Jones pretended that Freud had simply misjudged "the gravity of the international situation," and was deceived by unclear events in June "otherwise he would hardly have allowed his youngest daughter to leave for Hamburg on July 7, and certainly not to continue her journey to England . . . on July 18." Of course, Jones's implication was correct, i.e. it made no sense at all for that authoritarian father, Freud, to approve Anna's very dangerous trip to England in July. Then why did he do so? My reply points to the compulsive effects of his bizarre murder plan, with perhaps the further element of his incessant imitative tendency—one great assassination helping to provoke a lesser one.

It should be said that Anna spent a number of enjoyable weeks in England before the war finally curtailed her visit. She was touring southeast England with her cousin Rosi Winternitz when Austria and England became official enemies. Thereafter, communication became difficult and the letters to and from her parents had to be routed through the analyst van Emden in Holland. On August 25th Freud wrote to Abraham that Anna had become a prisoner-of-war in England, and was behaving bravely. Eventually, she was fortunate that arrangements were made for her to join the departing Austrian ambassador, requiring her first to make visits to the police for travel permits and visas. Before she left England she joined "a group of soldiers at their mess in Southampton," and found this to be an exciting event. Jones wrote (II, p. 173) that: "Freud's daughter Anna, who it had seemed might be marooned in England, got home safely in the third week of August, having traveled via Gibraltar and Genoa in the care of the Austrian Ambassador."

When Jones took note of the danger that Anna might be "marooned," that term clarified the great risk that she could have been interned for four years of the war as an enemy alien. Once again, this emphasizes the serious risks that Freud took with his daughter's welfare by sending her to England in July 1914, especially when one considers her vulnerability to emotional disorder that would have made internment a "living hell" for Anna. Young-Bruehl has revealed (pp. 57-60) that in the years just preceding her trip to England she had exhibited repeated neurotic symptoms, i.e. psychasthenia, including a kind of intellectual retardation (a mental slowing down, out of fear of growing up) along with restlessness, hypersensitivity, and "adolescent turmoil." Also, it was reported (p. 66) that during her trip to England her father "was worried by his daughter's unresolved, though muted, symptoms." Apparently, these problems still were not resolved in 1919 when she began several years of analysis with her own father. (One wonders whether one of his motives in analyzing her himself was a fear of what another analyst might learn about him, particularly about his strange behaviors in 1914 that could have "spilled the beans" about Emanuel's death?)

Keeping in mind that Anna's underlying emotional vulnerabilities persisted into 1914, this makes even more astonishing that Freud found a second way to endanger her welfare in mid-July of that year. This refers to the fact that he delivered this shy, virginal young woman (age 18) into the hands of a notorious seducer of young women, when he sent her to England in July 1914. With Freud's blessing the bachelor Ernest Jones (age 35) met her boat from France. He brought a bouquet of flowers for Anna, and this was the beginning of his "courting" (attempts to seduce) the impressionable and inexperienced adolescent, with great energy and attention applied to that amorous task in succeeding weeks. For Ernest Jones was a sexual psychopath whose history eventually included numerous sexual conquests of young women, including children and analytic patients, using his exploitive Free Love doctrines—as described in detail in chapter eleven. (YoungBruehl's biography gives many of the details of Jones's courting behaviors with Anna Freud in the summer of 1914.)

When Freud sent Anna to England in July 1914 and arranged for Ernest Jones to meet her boat from France, he should have surmised that this was like placing Red Riding Hood into the jaws of the big, bad wolf. Freud had every reason to recognize that Jones was a compulsive seducer of young women, since he must have received a bitter account of the Welshman's sexual escapades when he analyzed Loe Kann in Vienna during 1912. For seven years, this beautiful, wealthy, and neurotic woman had been one of Jones's mistresses, and he had subjected Loe to various cruel manipulations. As discussed in *Secret SL*, her anger and resentment towards him probably increased after she learned about his sexual molestation of one of his female analytic patients (in Canada), which Jones tried to blame on the patient after attempting unsuccessfully to bribe her into remaining silent. It's likely that Loe Kann's choice of Freud as her analyst was a way of retaliating against Jones for his infidelities. In turn, the sadist Jones tried mightily to interfere with Loe's analysis with Freud. He did that by having Loe discover that during her analysis Jones had openly seduced a young woman named Lina who'd been the trusted maid and confidante of Loe Kann! (Lina became his mistress for several years thereafter, but he repeatedly showed his contempt for this working-class woman and finally "dumped" her in a brutal manner.)

In June of 1914 Loe took her revenge on Ernest Jones by marrying another man named, Jones (a kind of wounded, infantile name magic), and by having their father-figure, Freud, present at the wedding. Ernest Jones recognized the cruel significance of this name magic, and immediately conferred the name "Jones II" on Loe's husband, to indicate that he'd "had" her first and would always remain "Jones I" in her secret heart. In June and July of 1914, Ernest Jones was at the peak of furious anger towards Freud (though he denied this, naturally), blaming his manipulative master for Loe's decision to leave him and marry the man with that painful surname.

All of this should convince us that Ernest Jones had an additional powerful reason (besides compulsive sexuality) for wanting to seduce the shy and pretty Anna Freud in July and August of 1914: the desire to inflict his revenge on Freud for taking Loe away from him. Indeed, Freud possessed many clues enabling him to foresee the dangers that Jones posed to his daughter, sexually and in terms of her mental health. Yet he *still* allowed Anna to stumble into Jones's seductive snares in July 1914, so great was his need to send her to England to be used as a foil in his murder plot against Emanuel (if my thesis is correct about the nature of that lethal plan).

According to Anna's biographer (Young-Bruehl, pp. 66-69), she was fortunate that in 1912 she had befriended Loe during her analysis with Freud. For Loe was in England when Anna arrived there and was able to recognize Jones's seductive intentions towards Anna. Apparently, Loe sent a letter to Freud warning him about this danger and Freud, who already was very "suspicious of Jones's motives," immediately "sent a letter to Jones suggesting that the courtship was inappropriate because Anna was too young . . " Freud also wrote quickly to Anna and warned her that he'd learned "that Doctor Jones has serious intentions of wooing you." Artfully, Freud pretended that Jones's intention might be marriage rather than sexual seduction strongly laced with the motive of revenge. Young-Bruehl has indicated that also he feared that Anna, so susceptible to "mysterious psychosomatic complaints," might become a candidate for hysteria "if too abruptly courted" (i.e. seduced by the Welsh wolf).

But Freud "knew the score" about Jones's perverse seductive intentions regarding Anna. For Young-Bruehl revealed that he wrote Ferenczi a letter expressing open annoyance with Jones's behaviors towards Anna, commenting that the Welshman was pursuing "an obvious act of revenge" against him. Concerning this letter to Ferenczi, Young-Bruehl indicated some of Freud's language which specified Jones's "desire to wreak revenge on Freud for Loe Kann's decision in favor of Jones the Second." This wording suggests that Freud already had adopted Ernest Jones's contemptuous manner of speaking about Loe's new husband. If so, this hinted at Freud's recognition that Loe had largely married him, with her special emphasis on name magic, as an act of revenge towards that sexual psychopath, Ernest Jones. (This is what Freud would have called a "well-analyzed patient"?)

―――――――――――――――――――

Let's go back to my previous scenario suggesting that Freud probably arranged for an assassin to murder Emanuel Freud. I'd like to explain how my interpretation of Freud's famous dream called *Non vixit* helps to support my view that he wished to murder many persons closely affiliated with him, with impunity. In this dream there were three main characters, besides Freud. It included his friend Fliess (whom Freud later planned to murder at Achensee, some months after the dream book with its *Non vixit* dream was published). Also, the dream included his dead friend Fleischl, whom Freud had introduced to huge doses of cocaine, eventually resulting in a lethal overdose. Finally, the dream incorporated Freud's dead friend P. (Josef Paneth), towards whom Freud had harbored secret death-wishes and whose reputation he tried to defame and destroy in Vienna (leading Paneth's widow to become enraged towards her former friend, Freud).

Freud acknowledged that the central feature of the *Non vixit* dream occurred when he gave P. a piercing look. Under his gaze this former friend turned pale, his form grew indistinct while his eyes became a sickly blue "and finally he melted away." In the dream this delighted Freud, for he realized about Fleischl and P. "that people of that kind only existed as long as one liked and could be got rid of if someone else wished it." My interpretation of this dream content is that Freud wished to have some rather easy ways of murdering rivalrous persons who were affiliated with him, for example using drug overdoses or simply by killing them with a lethal gaze. My interpretation of the latter detail relates to Freud's megalomania and to his "king complex," noting that in factual history and in dramatic works pernicious and powerful kings have been able to kill their enemies at court with a "knowing" gaze, or a wink, at some henchmen who would carry out their lethal wishes. Thus, the *Non vixit* dream points to Freud's wish to be able to commit murders merely by arranging them via assassinations, as I have suggested that he did with his brother Emanuel.

This correlates with my suggestion concerning his "Acropolis episode" paper that he had identified with the ancient king Boabdil who frivolously arranged for the murder of a messenger who brought him bad news—which I related to Emanuel Freud, who had brought Sigi the bad news about his nanny's "death." Also, I point here to Freud's identification with the murderous nobleman Fiesco (in Schiller's play) who *arranged* for murders using the assassin called "The Moor" (Freud's nickname as a child). Furthermore, let me mention that Freud's prolific tendency towards murder in the *Non vixit* dream reminds me of one of the train dreams he cited—in which the dreamer walked through the carriages of a train, killing everyone he met.

Of course, Freud provided facile interpretations of the *Non vixit* dream that directed his readers' attention away from his lethal desires that are strongly encoded in that dream. Nevertheless, that dream is one of the most obvious examples of dreams which reflect his death-wishes towards others, and it can even be regarded as predictive of his later murderous behaviors, such as the Achensee debacle with Fliess in 1900, and arranging for Emanuel's murder in 1914. The three other "big dreams" dreamt by Freud that should be studied in terms of his murderous desires towards Emanuel and others are the Irma dream, the Hollthurn dream, and the dream about Count Thun—although some other of Freud's own dreams reflect his murderous desires less directly.

Apparently, I am not the only student of Freud's life and work who reflected upon his capacity to arrange for murder (including arranging Emanuel's murder). Let's consider a surprising statement made by Dr. K. R. Eissler, who is probably Freud's most avid apologist in modern times. While discussing the possibility that Freud had some responsibility for the bizarre suicide of his rivalrous colleague Dr. Victor Tausk in July 1919, Eissler (1983, p.2) asserted that "Freud did not kill Tausk or hire anybody to do so . . " Concerning this strange remark about the non-hiring of a killer, why did Eissler choose to invent and then deny this gratuitous notion that nobody yet had offered, i.e. that Freud might have hired someone to murder Tausk (and presumably made it look like a suicide, with a phony suicide note)? Was Dr. Eissler's unconscious mind trying to make an indirect accusation about Freud that the conscious mind of Eissler did not wish to acknowledge and consider carefully, regarding Freud's capacity to arrange assassinations?

The Months and Years After Emanuel's Death

Previous pages have reviewed the idea that early June of 1914 was a period of extremely high stress for Freud as the culmination of his struggle with Jung. Furthermore, his sudden announcement to Abraham in mid-June that his depressed feelings had lifted abruptly was seen as a sign that he'd begun to formulate his murder plan involving Emanuel Freud, as his way of avoiding a florid psychotic break with reality. But there are many signs that Freud's deep mental instability continued into the months from July to October, and even later. During early July his mental fragility was evidenced by his weird decisions concerning his daughter Anna: sending her to England in the face of ominous war clouds, and putting her into the grasp of that arch seducer of young women, Jones, whose revengeful motives he surely had sensed. And by early October 1914, in the same month that Emanuel was killed, Ferenczi was with Freud in Vienna observing some obvious rumblings of psychotic processes in the master: inability to work, excessive discussion of the war, excitable and irritable behaviors, and repeated slips of the tongue "all day long."

Getting back to that fateful July, Jones wrote (II, p. 172) that: "In the July of 1914 Freud was feeling worn out after a year of very hard work and of distressing complications." Surely those "distressing complications" referred to the vicious battle with Jung for control of the psychoanalytic empire. Then, after Freud learned about Jung's resignation in mid-July, one might have expected that Freud's distress and bitterness might have abated somewhat. However, in a letter to Abraham dated July 29th he referred to the "showdown" with Jung and congratulated his own honesty, saying that his writing was becoming "bolder and more ruthless." Perhaps that increasing ruthlessness in Freud was relevant to the presumed murder plan involving Emanuel and was another sign of mental instability and inappropriate release of aggressive impulses.

One suspects that the increase of Freud's admitted ruthless feelings in July 1914 was related to a likely upsurge of dangerously ruthless feelings towards his own patients, as occurred in early 1900 during the break with Fliess. Perhaps a parallel exists between the years 1900 and 1914, in terms of a partial deterioration of patient care in both years? It seems that one factor involving the murder plan against Fliess at Achensee in the summer of 1900 bears comparison with the presumed murder plan against Emanuel in the summer of 1914. Recall that only a few months before the Achensee incident in 1900 Freud terminated a seriously disturbed foreign patient,

Mrs. Kremzir, who then committed suicide in a Vienna hotel. This compares with Freud's surprising termination of another foreign patient in July 1914, only a few months before Emanuel's fatal "accident" took place.

The latter patient was the famous "Wolf Man" (whose case history Freud began to write in that fatal October of 1914, completing it in November, but delaying its publication till 1918). Freud began this man's treatment in 1910. The patient was a Russian nobleman and son of a lawyer in Odessa who was a very wealthy landowner. The man was treated by Freud for an obsessional neurosis, but recent evidence (Obholzer, 1982) seriously questions that this was the real problem. Jones wrote (II, p. 275) that: "For more than four years Freud struggled without making any progress." Ever the apologist for Freud, Jones made it seem a virtue that Freud announced suddenly to the patient "that he intended to break off the treatment in whatever stage it was in at the time of his summer holiday in July (1914).." Jones acknowledged that this was a "risky procedure," and one that often has been abused by analysts. However, he made no criticism of Freud, instead alleging that this risky termination procedure was effective and enabled the analysis to be completed successfully early in July. Jones stated that the patient then returned to Russia, and implied that his mental health had improved considerably.

But it is highly improbable that this man's analysis was completed successfully in July 1914, as Jones pretended it was, nor that his mental health had improved considerably. For Jones knew that Freud needed to analyze the Wolf Man again in early 1919. This time he was analyzed by Freud for four months, and the diagnosis was conveniently changed to "an obstinate hysterical constipation" (which Freud suffered himself for decades), and then Freud passed the unfortunate fellow on to a long line of analysts. In later years, the diagnosis became "paranoic psychosis," as an indication of how little Freud's treatment had helped this man. According to the eminent Harvard psychiatrist Hobson (1987, p. 88), this famous patient "continued in treatment in Vienna for some 60 years after Freud left off. In fact, it appears that the Wolf Man's successor analysts went to great lengths to keep him quiet about Freud's failings." Hobson indicated that the Wolf Man's case was one of Freud's striking failures, not the great success advertised by Jones.

Let's go back now to what were probably the real reasons why Freud terminated the Wolf Man in July 1914, after four years of unsuccessful treatment. I agree with Jones's remark that this termination was "risky" (even quite dangerous), and I'd add that the man might easily have committed suicide due to this abandonment, as Mrs. Kremzir had done in 1900 after Freud abandoned her. Why did Freud take this dangerous step in July 1914? First, let me point again to the likelihood that Freud's mind was severely unbalanced that summer and on the brink of a florid psychosis. Actually, Jones underplayed the danger of psychosis by noting that Freud was "worn out" that same July, while only weeks later Ferenczi was noticing more disturbing symptoms described earlier (inability to work, repetitious "slips," irritability, etc.) that he attributed to underlying psychotic processes in Freud.

Second, if I'm correct that in July of 1914 Freud's mind was actively involved in pursuing a murder plan against his brother Emanuel, one can find a corollary explanation for his destructive termination of the Wolf Man in July 1914. In that month Freud's ancient hatred towards Emanuel was able to become unleashed, partly because Freud sensed that this brother was about to become his mortal "enemy," with regard to a clash of empires* that Freud identified with irrationally. Thus, Freud dimly recognized in July that England was about to become his (and Austria's) enemy, provoking hostile feelings that he displaced onto that feared brother Emanuel, whom Martin Freud described as the epitome of an English gentleman. In the letters to Abraham in late 1914, Freud gave various indications (citing "British perfidy") that he'd readily transformed England into his enemy, and on September 3, 1914 he even conferred that status onto his disciple Ernest Jones, writing that: "Jones is of course our 'enemy.'"

And what does all of this have to do with my claim that Freud made a destructive termination of the Wolf Man in July of 1914? That point should be fairly obvious by now, since this patient was a member of the Russian aristocracy which had become the warlike enemy of Austria and of that ardent militarist, Sigmund Freud. Furthermore, this patient had become one of Freud's mental "tormentors" (a term he applied to his patients in 1900), since for more than four arduous years Freud had struggled without making any progress with this man's case, as Jones admitted. What further reason would Freud's unstable mind require, in July 1914, to make him propel this "enemy" off a precipice of depression by cruelly terminating the man (reminiscent of Mrs. Kremzir)?

The remainder of this section will explore evidences in Freud's letters and written works that in the months after October 17, 1914—the date of Emanuel's presumed murder—the younger brother, Sigmund, struggled irrationally with guilty and fearful feelings pertaining to that killing. Various writers have suggested that the progressive hardships of the Great War had profound effects that influenced Freud's increasingly depressed mood and thinking, and strongly infiltrated his works of that period. That is no doubt true. But I will argue that perhaps another large factor in this was the guilt and fear which he suffered relating to Emanuel's murder, as we shall see.

---

*Likewise, Jung was involved in a clash of empires in trying to expropriate Psychoanalysis, enabling Freud to equate Jung with Emanuel.

A careful review of the Freud/Abraham letters from July through December 1914 shows that both men exhibited confidence and optimism about the war until December, when Freud's armor began to show numerous cracks while Abraham remained steadfast and brave. My suggestion is that Freud's fears increased greatly in the month of December not because of any bad news about the war, but particularly due to guilty fantasies stimulated by the advent of Emanuel's birthday of December 25th (which was also a reminder of Freud's nanny and her savior, Jesus). Jones reported (II, pp. 179-80) that at the beginning of 1915 "Freud's mood was fairly hopeful," and at the start of that year he expressed the optimistic view that the war might end in October 1915, with his side victorious. Therefore, one can conclude that December of 1914 was an island of depression and pessimism in a series of optimistic months for Freud, which I have attributed to the baleful effects of Emanuel's birthday falling in December. This relates to the magical effects which birthdays had in Freud's mind, deriving from childhood concerns about his own disputed birthday.

In Abraham's letter of December 6, 1914 the Berlin analyst displayed courage by offering his belief that the war was "more in our favor than we know," and he expressed concern about the "present pessimism" Freud had just begun to express. Freud's next letter (December 11, 1914) stated that the political situation was "one of continual crumbling," that his nerves were fraying, and that his work had "plunged into deep darkness." In contrast, he noted that Lou Salomé's letters continued to express great optimism about the war. On December 21st, as Emanuel's birthday came closer, Freud wrote that he needed someone to give him courage and had little left, while fearing that his working energy would "finally succumb to my depressed mood." His primitive oral anxieties were expressed when he stated: "Sometimes I have a horror of the meal to come." (Perhaps this related to fears of punishment associated with Emanuel and with Christ's "Last Supper?")

What additional reasons are there for suspecting that the above fears were connected with guilt about Emanuel's murder? Consider Jones's comment (II, p. 177) that "in this depressing autumn" of 1914 Freud wrote a postcard to Lou Salomé asking: "Do you still believe that all the big brothers are so good? A word of cheer for me?" In a footnote, Jones commented that this was an allusion to her six brothers who were all so supportive of her "and also to the Great Powers" (Germany, Austria, England, Russia, France, Belgium). With that cynical remark questioning the supportiveness of the "big brothers," Freud hinted at his fears that the Great Powers might destroy him and his sons (all soldiers), and also that the ghost of his own "big brother," Emanuel, would wreak vengeance upon him for that railway murder. Notice that Freud's strange remark aligning "big brothers" with the Great Powers of the continent hints at his fantasy equating his English brother, Emanuel, with the dangerous adversary, England. (This is consonant with his unconscious equating of his nanny with several European places including Rome.)

Freud's postcard to Salomé alluding to the "big brothers," and to his own biggest brother Emanuel, was written in early December 1914. This indicates that Freud's irrational fears that permeated the month of December were closely related to his guilty feelings about Emanuel's death, which came to the fore at the time of his "magical" birthday, December 25th. (The theme of "big brothers" who can be supportive or punishing was also noted by Freud in his December 11th letter to Abraham when he referred to Salomé's "six big brothers, all of whom were kind to her.")

Some other letters by Freud, near the time of Emanuel's birthday in 1914, should also be given close attention. Freud showed his despair in a December 15th letter to Ferenczi when he wrote: "Now I am more isolated from the world than ever, and expect to be so later too as the result of the war." Another of Freud's letters near that time (Jones II, p. 177) stated that, though mankind would surmount the war, he knew for certain that he would "never again see a joyous world. It is all too hideous." He concluded that mankind was unfit for civilization, would have to "abdicate," and that Fate would need to repeat the experiment with another race of beings. Freud's mention of mankind's need to "abdicate," hinted that his covert death-wishes towards family members and colleagues had escalated towards all living men. In his letter to Abraham dated December 21st he hinted that his working energy might finally succumb "to my depressed mood," though he asserted that his work was going well.

On Emanuel's birthday, December 25th, Freud wrote a letter to Jones (II, pp. 178-9) that revealed his continuing despair, and perhaps his expectation of retribution regarding Emanuel's death. He wrote that the "flowering time" of Psychoanalysis was being disrupted violently by the war, with bad times ahead and only slim hope of a rebirth of their science. Dejectedly he remarked: "What Jung and Adler have left of the movement is being ruined by the strife of nations." He added that everything they had cultivated was running wild, that the near future seemed hopelessly clouded over, and that it was reasonable for some rats to leave the sinking ship—concluding with a request for Jones's loyalty: "Hold fast till we meet again."

Freud's letter of December 28, 1914 to the Dutch clinician Dr. van Eeden seems particularly informative about his guilty, murderous feelings near Emanuel's birthday. While trying to impress van Eeden that psychoanalytic theories fully explained the cruel mental impulses of human beings that provoked the war, Freud gave a summary of his negative beliefs about human nature—and, coincidentally, about himself. He stated that psychoanalytic research had shown that man's intellect is feeble and that we are ruled by our impulses and emotions. Also, this research showed that "the primitive, savage and evil impulses of mankind have not vanished in any individual, but continue their existence" while repressed in the unconscious mind awaiting "opportunities to display their activity." Of course, the savage and evil impulses mentioned by Freud pointed indirectly to his own murderous feelings and behaviors, so we can take this as a "covert confession" of his murder plan against Emanuel during the previous summer. Citing analytic evidence for man's evil impulses, he mentioned the study of "mental slips," reminding us of his own excessive mental slips observed by Ferenczi in the preceding October, just prior to Emanuel's "accident."

Why is it, finally, that in December 1914 Freud was exhibiting anxiety, fear, depression, and considerable pessimism about the war while his colleagues (Abraham, Ferenczi, Salomé) were able to maintain their high morale, and considering that only weeks earlier Freud had shown high spirits and imperialistic ardor favoring the war? My suggestion is that the "ghost" of Freud's great father-figure, Emanuel, had begun to haunt Sigmund during December, the month of his birthday, as a reaction to Freud's murderous activities during the preceding July that arranged for his brother's death. Consider that the month of July was a baleful one for Freud, since it's name pertained to the name Julius, the brother who persistently haunted him due to Sigmund's death-wishes towards the deceased infant. Also, consider that on July 17, 1914 Freud had written to Ferenczi (Jones II, p. 372) that he had just begun to make a special study of the play *Macbeth*. He wrote that *Macbeth* "has long tormented me without my having been able to find a solution. How curious it is that I passed the theme over to Jones years ago, and now here I am . . taking it back."

Why, indeed, did Freud take back the study of *Macbeth* from Jones precisely in the month of July 1914? Various writers, including this one, now recognize that Freud had made a fantasy identification with the murderer Macbeth who vilely made a plan to kill the king who was his great father-figure (as Emanuel was to Sigi). Therefore, I claim that Freud took back the study of *Macbeth* in early July 1914, as a strong indication that his unstable mind had begun to concoct a murder plan against his own "English" father-figure in Manchester. Jones wrote (p. 372) that Freud decided that the remorseless Lady Macbeth and her faint-hearted husband "were psychologically one and the same person," which helps expose the lethal duality of Freud's nature. Surely, he hinted at his own "dark side" when he wrote quizzically that: "There are dark forces at work in the play."

It is instructive that in 1925 Freud inserted a footnote into his dream book (1967, p. 555) concerning events that may interfere with a patient's analysis whose responsibility cannot be attributed to the patient's intentions. As examples of such interferences, Freud wrote: "His father may die without his having murdered him; or a war may break out . . " What astonishing examples Freud gave here! All he had to write was that the man's father might have died, as an interference with analysis, but his guilty unconscious mind compelled him to add the second gratuitous factor as a confession: "without his having murdered him." In effect, Freud confessed to the murder of a father-figure and even specified the time period—near the outbreak of the war (thereby pointing to Emanuel's murder in October 1914, soon after the war started). Moreover, the preceding example suggests that Freud refused to accept responsibility for taking Emanuel's life in October 1914, implying that his mind had been so unbalanced that he should not be blamed for that murderous act. We'll soon see that some of his writings in 1915 can be interpreted in the same way—reflecting his belief that he should not be blamed for killing Emanuel.

Now it's time to study the amazing turn towards aggression, death, and murder which Freud's works took in 1915. In this brief review, I will give my reasons for stating that his abrupt shifting from sexuality to man's darkest actions (including murder) was the result of his inward, disguised preoccupation with the killing of Emanuel Freud rather than simply the effect of the war's brutality upon his "sensitive" mind, as some writers have claimed.

Only a relatively short time after Emanuel's death, in March of 1915 Freud began a huge project which he announced to all his colleagues, a plan to write twelve essays (to be incorporated into one book) constituting a new, comprehensive description of *all* mental processes. This ambitious synthesis of mental functioning is called his "metapsychology," and one of the tentative titles for the essays was *Introductory Essays on Metapsychology*. At a breakneck pace Freud wrote all twelve essays in early 1915, but only five have been published—the other seven being mysteriously "lost." At this point, I'll discuss two of those five essays, plus another one that also was written early in 1915.

In one of those five essays titled "Instincts and their Vicissitudes" Freud decided to explore "instinct theory" to confront the issue of aggression (Adler's topic) in mental life. In his circuitous manner, Freud posited that aggression is not an instinct but can be viewed as an independent nonlibidinal "trend," which he ascribed to the ego instinct. He discussed conflicts between sexual and ego (aggressive) instincts, but also pointed to states of fusion between sexuality and aggression. In a revision of his previous ideas, he claimed that sadism arises from the aggressiveness of the ego instincts, which were now seen as generating "hatred." Also, he presented some vague ideas about the transformation of love into hate (as a vicissitude of the sexual instinct).

This essay tried to explain the development of love (not just sexuality) in childhood, and thereby made a discovery of the ego's independent disposition to "hate." Initially, Freud noted that "hate" is not present at birth. However, narcissism and the pleasure/unpleasure principles repeatedly make contacts with "objects" and two factors result. A. Pleasurable objects are internalized as ego-positive, and B. non-pleasurable and painful objects are discarded as being ego-alien. Freud noted that from this affective split "hate" develops in the child, as an ego function, and there is an aggressive disavowal of certain objects and events. From this reasoning, Freud concluded that the ego learns to feel repulsion against certain objects, events, and persons and to "hate" them, stating that: "this hate can afterwards be intensified to the point of an aggressive inclination against the object—an intention to destroy it . . "

Notice that Freud made a giant and totally unwarranted leap from those early classifying functions of the ego to the idea that hatred thereby arises naturally with intentions to destroy objects and persons, i.e. to murder them. Indeed, Freud's troubled mind—under the guilty pressure of having destroyed Emanuel Freud—was seeking a rationalization, a "reasonable" explanation rooted in early ego development for having committed that murder. (Really, his own pressures in childhood with nanny were at issue.) Then he went on to argue that "The ego hates, abhors and pursues with intent to destroy all objects which are a source of unpleasurable feelings for it," indicating that this derives from a normal goal of survival and "from the ego's struggle to preserve and maintain itself." (Why ignore simple avoidance?)

In a critique of "Instincts and Their Vicissitudes" Stepansky (Mono. 39, p. 149) remarked that when Freud ascribed aggressive trends to ego instincts this was "the product of accident," and that in tracing the child's development of love Freud "stumbled across" the origin of what might be called the aggressively "hateful" ego. Also, Stepansky noted that Freud had changed the usual picture of early aggression, previously correlated with childish egoism, for in his new scheme "it is now ascribed a large dose of positive survival value." Stepansky seemed to recognize that Freud was making a subtle endorsement of hatred, even murderous hatred, as a natural expression of the instincts of self-preservation. Moreover, he noted that, for the first time, Freud was tentatively approaching the equating of "aggression" with health! What Stepansky did not recognize was that, with this mumbo-jumbo, Freud was asserting that his murderous act regarding Emanuel was not insane, and was really healthy and adaptive (considering the pain that Emanuel had caused him). Actually, Sigmund Freud did not "stumble" upon the adaptive hating (murderous) ego, whose glorification was the basic reason why he composed this essay, i.e. to excuse his killing of Emanuel Freud.

In "Mourning and Melancholia" Freud admitted that the "hating ego" sometimes could be directed to pathogenic ends in melancholia, with self-contempt and "delusional expectation of punishment," yet he continued to assert a healthy role for the hating ego. He argued that the melancholic person's self-revilings result from incorporation of the lost "object" (Emanuel?), via identification, to prolong its existence irrationally. However, self-reproach also involved aggression directed against the lost/introjected person due to the conflict of ambivalence (love versus hate). Partly, this reflects the ego's prerogative to hate (taking enjoyment from hating), but it also indicates a healthy function—the ego's slow killing of the introjected lost person, to loosen his hold. Ergo, Freud again posited that aggression and hatred could constitute therapeutic functions of the ego, arguing that the ego "hates" so that it may reinstate health. If we recall that Freud was one of the most prolific haters in history, who regularly maintained hate-lists of his "enemies," we will begin to see that the above folderol provided a disguised excuse for having killed Emanuel. In effect, he implied that aggression, hatred, and murder were beneficent ego-assisting functions which helped him to adjust his mental imbalances in 1914 and to regain full mental health!

It was noted by Stepansky (p. 153) that only in Freud's metapsychology essays of early 1915 did he assert that "hate" is a "purposeful ego-syntonic necessity." Stepansky added that: "Clearly, a fundamental shift in his conceptualization of the potential for 'healthy' aggression had occurred." What caused this fundamental shift in early 1915? Stepansky attributed this to the effects that the aggression of World War I had on Freud, but my reply is that in early 1915 the grinding brutality of the war had not yet had time to influence Freud that deeply. A better explanation, I believe, is his troubled response to the killing of brother Emanuel in October 1914.

Besides the essays on metapsychology, Freud wrote several other papers in 1915. One of these was "Thoughts for the Times on War and Death," which Jones (II, p. 187) tells us also was written early in 1915. A few of Freud's comments in that essay are worth reviewing, since they deal with the subject of murder. At one point he wrote that: ". . we spring from an endless series of generations of murderers, who had the lust for killing in their blood, as, perhaps, we ourselves have today." At another place he wrote that: ". . we ourselves are, like primeval man, a gang of murderers." For those who remember the persistent death-wishes in Freud towards many persons, it's interesting that he noted how war overcomes the humdrum quality of everyday life and that massive killings in war make life "interesting" and "invigorating." Assertions of that sort, and his rabid militaristic ardor in

1914, help us to recognize the lust for killing that existed within Freud, which seems quite relevant to the killing of Emanuel near the war's onset.

The preceding allegations by Freud that we are all murderers were statements that helped him cloak and excuse his own lethal actions. He implied that, after all, if all of us are killers unconsciously, then how can we blame him for relieving his inner pain by committing one "justifiable murder"? Correspondingly, in this essay Freud rationalized man's inability to avoid these "pathogenic relapses," since they derived from a phylogenetic inevitability. It is informative that Stepansky, regarding Freud as "guilt-ridden and conflicted about his own aggressive propensities" (murderous wishes towards Julius, John, and many others), saw him now as taking a somewhat counterphobic "functional pleasure" by endorsing "the developmental primacy of the 'hating' ego." He indicated that this was Freud's belated attempt "to master his own infantile anxiety about the expression of aggressive tendencies." Although I agree that Freud created the concept of the adaptively "hating" ego due to his personal problems with aggressive impulses, the hateful issue he was trying to cope with was not the war but his own lethal behaviors from July to October 1914 in arranging his brother's murder.

There are various lines of evidence supporting my view that Freud was still quite mentally unstable in early 1915, and that his concealed preoccupation with Emanuel's murder was the essential reason why he composed the twelve essays on metapsychology, in such a frenetic state of mind. The first piece of evidence concerns a letter he wrote to Ferenczi on February 22, 1915 (Grotjahn, 1973, p. 444) just before he began writing the metapsychology series in mid-March. In that letter he wrote about the status of his self-analysis, allowing a brief exposure of "that *murderous* firebrand and ever-active *devil* in me (who has now become visible)." (Emphasis added.) Concerning this murderous demon within his breast, he wrote that he intended to "bury him so deeply even from myself that I could regard myself as a peace loving man of science." His wording suggests that a Jekyll/Hyde struggle was bubbling over, that his murderous impulses were still quite active in him, that he was battling to suppress them, and that his new monumental project (the twelve essays) would be used to drain off those lethal impulses. Thus, it appears that he embarked upon the metapsychology papers in an effort to stifle his anxieties about the killing of Emanuel, which helps to clarify that these 1915 essays already reviewed are permeated by his semi-psychotic ideation concerning the adaptively "hating" ego. (Notice that he cited the "devil" in himself, which pertains to his Satan identification, and will soon be interpreted as an indication that his murderous impulses had been directed towards Emanuel, as a Christ-figure.)

Another line of evidence for unraveling this puzzle concerns Jones's remark (II, p. 185) that Freud began writing his series of twelve essays on March 15, 1915. Having studied Freud's penchant for number and name magic and key anniversary dates, my suggestion is that this date was quite portentous, since it is "the ides of March," the anniversary of the assassination of Julius Caesar. In this manner, Freud's febrile mind informs us that his twelve essays were secretly relevant to several notable assassinations—the murder of Julius Caesar; the fantasized murder of that other Julius (Freud's brother); and the recent murders of another brother, Emanuel, and Archduke Franz Ferdinand. Perhaps that date also was connected with the intended murder of Freud's nephew and fantasized brother, John Freud, recalling that he had once played the role of Julius Caesar in a playlet which featured Sigmund as the assassin, Brutus.

One wonders if there was also number and name magic in Freud's choice of twelve essays to comprise his "masterpiece" on metapsychology. My suggestion is that the choice of twelve essays (ones that would support his claim to fame and adulation) was the same number as Christ's twelve disciples. This relates to the probability that Freud fantasized that his brother Emanuel was a figure equated with Jesus Christ. The key factors were his brother's birthday of December 25th and various aspects of name magic. The name Emanuel was used in scripture to signify the coming figure of Christ. Also, Emanuel Freud had acted-out the fantasy by marrying a woman named Marie (Mary), and by suggestively naming two of his early offspring John (cousin of Jesus) and Pauline (a veiled reference to St. Paul). It's possible, therefore, that Freud's deranged murder of his brother not only enabled him to fulfill his Cain complex but also the killing of Christ, permitting Sigmund to take the role of the new and more powerful Christ, in terms of his own ambivalent identifications with both Jesus and Satan. Symbolically, the twelve essays on metapsychology could have represented Freud's twelve "disciples" who would spread his new message to a world hungering for enlightenment.

One final line of evidence indicates that a murky pool of madness was submerged beneath the twelve essays on metapsychology in Freud's mind. This relates to my thesis that he undertook this incredible project in 1915, the twelve magnificent essays, as a sort of replay of the balmy monograph titled *The Project for a Scientific Psychology*, which I've labeled "the Project" in earlier chapters. Recall my assertion that Freud created this megalomanic "Project" in an accelerated fit of "cocaine madness" in 1895 (acknowledging the psychosis underlying this work in a November 1895 letter to Fliess) as a revengeful way of coping with the loss of Breuer's support, and his diagnosis that Freud suffered from "moral insanity." It's relevant that Freud, on March 1, 1896, revealed to Fliess this issue of "moral insanity" while hinting that Breuer's diagnosis was connected with the creation of "the Project."

In a brief discussion of Freud's twelve metapsychology essays of early 1915, Jones unwittingly offered various clues which indicate significant parallels between the composition of the "Project" and the twelve essays of 1915. First, he noted (II, p. 185) that Freud invented the term "metapsychology" and used it initially in a letter to Fliess of February 13, 1896 during the same period when he was still reeling from the aftereffects of writing the "Project." Second, Jones used very dramatic language when he wrote that Freud composed the twelve essays in an incredibly brief period of time, in a burst of creative activity that "would be hard to equal in the history of scientific production." Jones forgot to mention that Freud composed the "Project" in a quite similar barrage of creative activity, with near-sleepless nights that pointed to weeks of cocaine frenzy. (This should make us wonder whether Freud had resumed cocaine intake while composing the 1915 essays.)

Third, Jones told his readers "a sad story" about the fate of the twelve essays. He commented that the last seven essays were never published, "nor have their manuscripts survived," asking: "And why did he destroy them?" Their "loss" seems quite similar to the fate of the "Project," whose manuscript Freud sent to Fliess for review, but which he never requested should be returned to him after realizing that it had been concocted during a prolonged fit of madness. (Almost by accident, it surfaced again in the 1930s when Mrs. Fliess revealed its existence.) My suggestion is that actually Freud had intended that the "Project" would forever remain "lost" (suppressed), and that his same intention applied to the seven lost essays of 1915, for the same reason—his eventual recognition that these were "mad" essays, perhaps incorporating even more deranged ideation than the "adaptive hating/murderous ego" that he endorsed within some of the published five essays.

Further parallels should be noted between the metapsychology essays and the "Project," without an implication that their contents were similar, only the grandiose motives underlying them. In 1915 the twelve essays were composed soon after the "loss" of Emanuel, apparently to help Freud cope with an upsurge of his vengeful feelings towards Emanuel, with emphasis on the psychic equation of Breuer and Emanuel in the Irma dream's figure called "Dr. M." Finally, we should note that the "Project" was composed soon after the near-killing (by Freud and Fliess) of Emma Eckstein, who represented the image of his "murdered" nanny. Similarly, the twelve essays in 1915 were composed soon after the killing of Emanuel, whom Sigmund held responsible for nanny's "death" in Freiberg. The exposure of all these parallels makes one suspect that the seven lost essays of 1915 were riddled with more of Freud's balmy ideas rationalizing various acts of mayhem and murder to an absurd extent, pointing backward a few months to that peculiar railroad death in October 1914.

In the preceding pages I have emphasized that Freud suffered a serious mental breakdown in the months of September and October 1914, showing how this might have correlated with the killing of Emanuel Freud in October 1914, and that intimations of murderous psychotic processes can be found in letters and works produced in late 1914 and in 1915. It is interesting that Jones gave credibility to the idea that Freud suffered a severe mental breakdown in early October 1914, near the start of the war, by seeming to accept Ferenczi's observations on that point (though Jones "politely" avoided a real discussion of this psychotic behavior). Similarly, Stepansky's historical research on Freud's aggressive impulses in 1914 caused him to conclude (p. 160) that Freud, on December 28, 1914 was "still laboring under the onus of his own emotional relapse at the outbreak of war." However, Stepansky did not attempt to provide a convincing explanation as to why Freud experienced that sudden mental disintegration soon after the outbreak of the war, and Jones had not attempted to do so, nor to offer any explanation by Ferenczi.

In earlier pages, however, I've suggested that Ferenczi perhaps sensed that Freud's breakdown was "predictive" of Emanuel's death, even hinting to Freud that he might have murdered Emanuel (which might have seemed plausible to Ferenczi if he'd been privy to the presumed aborted murder plot against Jung, and was sensitive to Freud's capacity for displacement of aggressive feelings). However, this horrific connection did not occur to Stepansky in his exploration of the master's aggressive urges and theories, for he neglected to ask himself the following question. Since Freud allegedly possessed the healthiest of minds imaginable, after years of brilliant self-analysis, why was he the only one of countless European analysts who quickly succumbed to a severe emotional breakdown only a few weeks following the onset of war? Perhaps this question was too troubling for Stepansky to consider, in the context of its time, for that might have caused him to de-repress a plausible connection with the bizarre train death which had occurred almost simultaneously, only several weeks after the symptoms of Freud's peculiar breakdown (witnessed by Ferenczi).

During the years beyond 1915 Freud's unconscious mind provided various "clues" which, taken together, offer provocative evidence that Sigmund was involved in foul play in the "accidental" death of his brother Emanuel in late 1914. The first item in this series is the mysterious disappearance in 1919 of John Freud, eldest offspring of Emanuel and

Sigmund's greatest rival. The next chapter covers John's disappearance in detail (presumed to be another arranged murder by Sigmund), and we'll see that these two events in 1914 and 1919 deserve to be paired psychologically, enabling John's disappearance to serve as a clue to Sigmund's culpability regarding the previous train murder, and vice versa.

Another clue regarding Sigmund's presumed role in the murder of Emanuel occurred in late 1922, as noted in an earlier chapter. Jones reported in his third volume (p. 88) that after the son of an old servant of Freud's had shot his father, allegedly while the old man was attempting to molest the youth's half-sister, Freud paid all the legal expenses for the defendant. (Was it necessary to shoot an "old man," one wonders?) Most interesting are Jones's remarks that Freud "did not know the youth personally," and that he wrote a protective memo to the court—which apparently intended to divert attention from the full truth. By Jones's account, Freud's memo stated "that any attempt to seek for deeper motives would only obscure the plain facts." Can one imagine the father of psychoanalysis arguing against a search for deeper motives? The suspicion arises that Freud's peculiar desire to defend this defendant from his attempted patricide was an unconscious clue to Freud's murder of his own great father-figure, Emanuel. (It is interesting that molestation was an issue in this case, since young Sigmund probably had suspected that his eldest brother had "killed" nanny because of her molestation of Sigi himself.)

Another clue was dropped by Freud in 1925 when he inserted a peculiar footnote in his dream book (1967, p.555). This "slip" concerning murder was cited previously in this chapter, referring to Freud's discussion of events that may interfere with analysis "which cannot be laid upon the patient's intentions." Then he offered this example: "His father may die without his having murdered him; or a war may break out.." Earlier, I correlated these weird remarks with Freud's murder of Emanuel, near the outbreak of the Great War. In the annals of crime and homicide, this is an excellent example of the dictum that: "Murder will out."

Additional clues were provided by two peculiar letters that Freud wrote during the 1930s. One of these was Freud's letter to Thomas Mann about Napoleon's compulsive name magic which included Freud's concoction of the fragile notion that Napoleon bore a lethal hatred towards his eldest brother. Considering Freud's fantasy identification with this emperor, the fiction about Napoleon's fratricidal feelings that Freud "invented" can be regarded as a projection of his murderous hatred towards his own eldest brother, Emanuel. Also in the 1930s, Freud's letter to Romain Rolland about the "Acropolis episode" incorporated Freud's comment about the Moorish king who arranged for the killing of a messenger who brought "bad news" to him. Since Freud's nickname was The Moor and he identified with many kings, this item indicates his desire to arrange for the murder of a man who brought bad news to Sigi—pointing to the time when Emanuel brought him bad news about the "downfall" of his nursemaid.

Finally, some compelling clues about the presumed murder of Emanuel Freud can be found in Freud's strange book of the 1930s titled *Moses and Monotheism*. In my view, this was one of Freud's balmiest books, wherein his madness lurked beneath the surface of numerous pages, placing it in a special category of "extreme weirdness" with such writings as his Moses essay of 1914, *Totem and Taboo*, the "Project," some of the metapsychology essays, and many portions of the published letters to Fliess. In a previous chapter, I have endorsed Puner's view that Freud's dream book encodes a secret "confession" concerning various criminal-type activities for which he harbored guilty feelings. It's my opinion that Freud's final "masterpiece," his book about Moses, incorporates covert confessions regarding the murder of his brother Emanuel. That claim will require considerable explanation, and initially I'll need to discuss my thesis that Emanuel Freud represented two religious heroes in Sigmund's fantasy life.

Previously, I explained why Emanuel probably became a surrogate for Jesus Christ in Sigmund's fantasy life. Likewise, there is reason to believe that Emanuel became a surrogate for a condemning image of Moses in the young boy's fantasies. One senses a childhood basis for equating Emanuel and Moses deriving from Sigi's belief that Emanuel was a superior man, a savior of the Freud family who led the larger group out of a savage wilderness (anti-Semitic Austria) into the "promised land" called England, where prosperity and fair treatment for Jews beckoned. This is consonant with the fact that many times Sigmund referred to England as the "promised land," whereas he regularly frowned upon Austria, and expressed hatred for Vienna. Another reason why he probably invested Emanuel with Mosaic qualities was because he was a much-older brother with a rigid, authoritarian personality who expected others in the family to give strict obedience to his wishes and dictates. Even in Sigmund's 30s, and much later, this strong father-figure, Emanuel, still commanded him to obey his "orders," and the younger man regularly showed deference to the older man's wishes.

If I'm correct that various "magical" factors caused Emanuel to become a surrogate for Jesus in Sigi's fantasy life, that could help explain why Emanuel became a surrogate for Moses, as well. Considering that Freud had become confused about his own religious orientation—in effect, becoming half Jew and half Christian due to the powerful proselytizing influences of his Christian nanny—it is not surprising that he incorporated images of both Jesus and Moses into his primal father-figure, Emanuel. For both of those heroes are found at the pinnacle of religious thought, and in many ways are equatable messianic figures, each of whom brought a "new vision" to the

Jewish people.

As stated, it is plausible that young Sigmund incorporated into his fantasies about Emanuel aspects of the harsh, punitive side of Moses's image, considering the rigid authoritarian personality which characterized this older brother. Since the boy absorbed the major Bible stories in childhood, he would have known about Moses's slaughtering of the sinful disciples, correlating that harshness with Emanuel's rigid and dour personality. Furthermore, in light of Sigi's probable fantasy that Emanuel had dealt a lethal punishment* to nanny as retribution for her molestation of him, thereafter the boy must have harbored the fear that someday this Mosaic figure would mete out a similar punishment to him (for those sexual indulgences with his "primal" mother).

Emphasis now must be placed upon Suzanne Bernfeld's (1951) essay concerning Freud's preoccupation with archeology and its artifacts, and her plausible view that unconsciously he countered his pervasive death-wishes by fantasizing that "lost" persons were incorporated within various places (cities) and objects (statues, vases) and that such persons could be magically resurrected. Thus, we've discussed that his lost primal mother (nanny) was infused into Rome and other places, but it is also likely that Freud incorporated nanny magically into his great lifework, Psychoanalysis—which would bring him the immense recognition (fame, wealth) that she had prophesied for him. (That Psychoanalysis became an unconscious substitute for nanny does not preclude other irrational and rational reasons for its invention, of course.)

Eventually, in the summer of 1914 when Freud's unstable mind was reeling from his intense fears that Psychoanalysis (nanny) was about to be destroyed by Jung's betrayals and by the certain onset of world war, this provoked an upsurge of feelings that once again he might lose nanny (his masterwork), due to that long-delayed punishment by Moses/Emanuel. To counter that primitive fear, evidently he decided that he would act first and would kill Moses (Emanuel) before Moses could destroy him or his creation. That was another strange reason for arranging Emanuel's train murder, and it might have included an equally weird corollary reminiscent of the beliefs of primitive men that they can magically introject the strengths of persons whom they kill. An additional fantasy by Freud in July 1914 probably was that in killing Moses/Jesus he would magically expropriate their awesome powers, enabling him to revise psychoanalysis successfully and become the new messiah.

Having reviewed the above preface to prepare for my thesis that the

---

*The Bernfelds' research (Ruitenbeek, 1973, p. 194) reveals that nanny was "put into jail by the resolute Emanuel" (also asserted by Puner). The Bernfelds claim Emanuel informed Sigi humorously about nanny's disappearance by saying "She is cased in," implying she was killed and entombed, or put in a coffin.

murder of Emanuel Freud is a primary encoding in *Moses and Monotheism*, we're ready to absorb a brief synopsis of its peculiar contents to serve as a basis for further discussion of the killing of father-figures. One can say that the subject of patricide was secretly as much of an obsession of Freud's as sexuality was, and this point will become clearer in my subsequent commentary on the Moses book. A synopsis of the work follows.

In Freud's version of Moses's origin he simply dismissed the Bible's statements that he was the infant son of Hebrew slaves who countered Pharaoh's edict that their newborn males should be killed when they floated him in a basket in the Nile, where he was found by an Egyptian princess who adopted him. On the basis of flimsy evidence, Freud contended that Moses was not a Hebrew but was an Egyptian of high rank (thereby depriving the Jews of their greatest hero). As an adult, the aristocratic Moses refused to convert from monotheism when a revolution occurred and pagan cults returned to power. Instead, Moses chose the Hebrew slaves as his people (an extremely fragile notion), taught monotheism to them, and led them out of Egypt to Sinai where they united with the Midianites (who worshipped a petty, vengeful god called Jahwah).

Eventually, a rebellion occurred against the strict and irascible Moses and he was murdered by the Jews. But sixty years later, the two tribes were reunited by a new leader whose name again was Moses. (Exposing his affinity for name magic, Freud asserted that in later eras these two men with the same name were confused with one another and treated as one man.) A compromise of monotheism and Jahweh-worship occurred, providing the basis for a dual structure of the Hebrew nation and religion. The teachings of later prophets revived the memory of the first Moses, and the guilty wish for the return of this murdered leader stimulated a longterm belief in the "return of the Messiah." The final pages of the book emphasized Freud's accusation that the Jews had murdered their ancient father-God but would not admit their guilt, thereby bringing untold suffering upon themselves down through the ages.

During the years of the 1930s while Freud was writing this book he was visited by various eminent Hebrew scholars and leaders who begged him not to have it published, fearing that the book might subject the Jewish people to ridicule. But Freud adamantly insisted upon publication, though he acknowledged the book's weaknesses and throughout its pages apologized for its fragile evidence and weird assumptions. Numerous historians of religion criticized the strange volume for its repeated errors and absurd impossibilities, and some castigated Freud for injecting himself into a field for which he was not qualified. Jones noted (III, p.373) that when a great scholar visited Freud and advised him that one of his crucial sources of data had been discredited, Freud simply shrugged his shoulders and replied: "It might be true all the same." Apparently, therefore, Freud acted quite irrationally about his final "masterwork," as if he were obsessed by it. Again, my thesis is that he was actually obsessed by the father-murder that was the keystone of this volume, and by his need to make a subtle confession that he had once committed such an act himself, as he approached his death in 1939.

There is one author whose commentary about *Moses and Monotheism* I have given my partial endorsement. This is Marianne Krüll whose book (1986) about Freud and his father provides a long section on the Moses book. She described the volume as having "a chaotic structure," and as if it had been dictated by Freud's unconscious mind, hinting at its obsessive qualities. (I would add that it is a hodgepodge of crackpot religious and personal ideas with a rippling undercurrent of psychotic ideation.) Krüll seemed to view the Moses book as if it were a patient's long dream, whose manifest and latent contents needed to be clarified and interpreted carefully. She cited it as the only work by Freud on a specifically Jewish subject, and said that it can be regarded as covertly autobiographical and "a resumé of his own life and work." She added that: "It is also his final confrontation with his father." (She thought that confrontation was with Jacob Freud, whereas I think it was with Emanuel, his murdered brother/father.)

Krüll maintained (and I agree with her) that a typical reader of the Moses book is apt to be deceived by taking its statements at face value. Instead, she asserted that there is a great deal of "coded" autobiographical material that is disguised via symbolic language. She cited approvingly the explanatory comment by Marthe Robert (1975, p. 145) that this was Freud's "historical novel" about Moses which was actually "the novel of his own life," which had to be completed "before he could die." (Originally, he'd conceived of the book as a novel.)

It was Krüll's view that the Moses book is permeated by "coded autobiographical confessions." By hiding the meanings which pertained to his own life, he generated "the confused style, the many repetitions, incongruencies, and open contradictions" which constitute the work's chaotic structure. She added that: "These inconsistencies now appear as forms of the code he used to hide the actual meaning." (Generally, I agree with Krüll's position but claim that, understandably, she missed the central horrific point—that the key covert "confession" pertained to the murder of Emanuel Freud in 1914.)

A valuable contribution by Krüll was that she specified five "encoding planes" in the Moses volume. The first two planes include a reinterpretation of the historical events relating to Moses's life, and accounts of the childhood development of neurotic and normal personalities. The third plane indicates Freud's feelings about his approaching death. The fourth plane is preconscious and presents Freud's life story and relationship with his father, partly depicted as a general description of psychic development, and also conveys Freud's identification with Moses and the Israelites. Finally, the fifth plane is unconscious and includes fantasies about Freiberg and "events that had puzzled him" there, i.e. "the disappearance of his nursemaid . . ," the questionable behaviors of his mother, brother, and father, etc. Krüll subsumed all these mysteries under a provocative heading: "the murder of the primal father." This material stimulated Freud's new ideas about the Moses myth, and about his own development and his father's, which he fantasized under the rubric: "the patricide of yore" became "the inheritance of man." (The latter reflects his Lamarckian idea about the transmission of inherited guilt, through the ages.)

After specifying those five "encoding planes," Krüll examined various parts of the Moses book, to show how those planes were interwoven with eight of Freud's central arguments or theses, thereby exposing the predominance of preconscious and unconscious dimensions throughout the text. I will not summarize her major efforts here, which were interesting but not particularly relevant to my own primary thesis. Where Krüll and I part company concerns her failure to recognize that the central covert focus of the Moses book was Freud's great concern about murder, particularly the killing of father-figures—although she sometimes came close to recognizing this.

Perhaps Krüll would have realized that father-murder was the secret focus of this book if she had asked herself this question: What prompted Freud to write it? It is Jones who gave us the answer (III, p. 373) when he noted the great influence that Ernst Sellin's murder-hypothesis had exerted upon Freud. In the twenties Sellin was a Hebrew-scholar who wrote that he'd found "some evidence" (later apparently repudiating it) which pointed to the murder of Moses. Eagerly, Freud endorsed this murder-hypothesis of Sellin's and in the thirties it provoked the creation of his Moses book. Jones added that: "It was Sellin's suggestion that made Freud decide to write his book; it fitted so well with his views on the importance of parricide." If Jones was right, it seems clear that Freud's intense concern about father-murder was the very nucleus of his quixotic book about Moses.

David Bakan has given considerable support for my idea that the murder of Moses/Emanuel was the central factor underlying the bewildering complexities of the Moses book. Bakan wrote (1958, p. 164) that "Freud's book is itself *about* a murder, the murder of Moses . . . What is really of moment, however, is that the murder of Moses is Freud's own doing!" Drawing upon his wide knowledge of Biblical matters, Bakan cited the Moses book as "one of the grossest distortions of the Biblical text committed in modern times," implying that the thesis about Moses's murder was the worst of these falsifications. He noted that any evidence for Moses's murder was "very tenuous," but this assassination was something that Freud needed to "assert as a fact." Why? Because this was a personal fantasy of Freud's, Bakan noted, one that was dominant "at the very moment of writing" the book.

Then Bakan remarked (p. 164) with italicized wording that: "*It is Freud who wishes that Moses were murdered . .* " But this was explained as Freud's wish to kill "repressive and oppressive forces associated with the Mosaic image." Thus, Bakan assumed that Freud's murderous wishes were directed only against societally repressive forces, since Bakan (like Krüll) could not countenance the horrible possibility that Freud's death-wishes had been directed successfully against a real man I've called Moses/Emanuel. A few sentences later Bakan remarked that in the Moses book Freud had referred to the murder of Moses as "the murder of the Father." However, Bakan did not recognize that this was partly a confession by Freud that in 1914 he had killed his own great father-figure, for many perverse reasons including retribution for Emanuel's presumed murder of Sigi's primal mother, his nanny.

There are various lines of evidence indicating that in the Moses book Freud's secret goal was a fantasized reenactment of his killing of Moses/Emanuel. At the very outset his task was to destroy Moses's identity, the essential core of the hero, by stealing his Hebrew heritage and transforming him into a despised gentile via the weak fabrication that he was really an Egyptian. To accomplish this destructive act Freud used a deadly little "name game," consonant with his longterm fixation on name magic,

He concocted the absurd "proof" that Moses must have been an Egyptian, because his name was an Egyptian name. In his account of the matter, Freud overlooked the Bible's statement that the Egyptian princess who became his adoptive mother gave him the name Moses, saying: "Because I drew him out of the water." It's true that this "Moses" was an Egyptian name, but Freud ignored that she probably gave it to him hoping to deceive Pharaoh into accepting that this was an Egyptian orphan, since she'd taken a grave risk in disobeying his edict that all Hebrew male newborns should be killed. However, she must have known that the special meaning of his name—being drawn out of water—was derived from an analogous Hebrew expression meaning "to draw out." Ergo, she had tricked Pharaoh twice, since this apparently Egyptian name Moses can be said to have this special connotation when correlated with the Hebrew tongue, by which she slyly implied that the deeper essence of this child pertained to his hidden Hebrew identity. Of course, Freud ignored all of this, since it was his intent to "prove" that Moses was an Egyptian, and a gentile, by making destructive attacks on his name. Again, this reminds us of Freud's fainting spell, disguising murderous feelings, after hearing Jung's story at Munich about an Egyptian prince who seemed to make destructive assaults on his father's identity via name-attacks.

Although the Bible does not say this, one can imagine that Moses's Hebrew mother, a servant of the princess, helped persuade the latter to choose "Moses" as the baby's name. Again, the reason could have been to deceive Pharaoh into believing that this name showed that the babe was of Egyptian blood. However, another subtle reason why this could have been the Hebrew mother's choice has to do with the motive called "identification with the aggressor," which Freudians know well. Thus, a mother who is a member of a despised minority (slaves) might give her son a name belonging to the culture of her oppressors to provide "protective affiliation" and higher status for her child. It is interesting that Freud had a personal concern with this same naming issue, since he had changed his name from the despised "Sigismund" to the popular "Sigmund." In Austria and Germany the former name had become a laughing-stock, and was used as a derisive generic name for a Hebrew male (as the name Rufus was once used contemptuously to signify all black males, in America).

Still smarting from the venomous attacks on his own given name, Sigismund, and from vicious attacks on the name Freud, the author used his Moses book to make a destructive assault on the name (and identity) of Moses. This name-attack was a veiled form of murderous behavior that derives from the precausal infantile period. The research of Wolfenstein and others regarding children's destructive name-related behaviors shows that their attacks on personal names, including provocative changes of others' names and cruel name distortions (sometimes implying excremental functions), can disguise quite murderous feelings and intentions via subversions of identity. In effect, by attacking Moses's name, Freud was employing the precausal child's (age three) strategy of the destruction of personal identity of an adversary. This was an expression of his primitive lethal feelings towards Emanuel/Moses that had originated in the precausal era of Sigi's Freiberg rage against the males in his family.

Of course, the more direct evidence that Freud used the Moses book as a fantasized reenactment and covert confession of his actual murder of Emanuel/Moses is the strange invention he added to the life story of Moses—that he became too demanding and irascible, so his followers killed him. Bakan was quite right in saying that Freud wished that Moses had been murdered, that this murder was of "Freud's doing," and that he needed to "assert as a fact" the killing of Moses. In making these points, the astute Bakan was only a hairsbreadth from recognizing the reality of Freud's murderous behavior (in 1914). And Marthe Robert (1975) was also correct in stating that the Moses book was actually a novel about Freud's life, one that he had to finish before he could allow himself to die. My suggestion is that this tortured, obsessive man needed to make a cryptic confession of murder in 1939 to permit himself to be at peace and arrange for his own suicide/murder, with the help of Dr. Schur (a surrogate for Freud's old confessor, Fliess).

The final piece of evidence for my above thesis occurs near the end of the book when Freud made his outrageous and destructive claim about the Jewish people. He stated that their suffering over centuries had occurred, because they (in a state of denial) had refused to admit their ancient crime of having murdered the father-God. In this manner, he projected onto his people blame and guilt for having killed their great father-figure, as a screen for his own murder of Emanuel Freud. In effect, he told his fellow Jews that they needed to make a confession of their ancient patricide, hinting that he had obtained "peace" by making his own veiled confession of patricide in the Moses book.

With that bizarre language he implied that all Jews were no better than he was, that they all shared the actual crime of father-murder (inherited genetically!), but he suggested that finally he'd become superior morally to his fellow Jews (despite early criminality of the Freuds) by having admitted his crime. In the end, this was a destructive accusation which Freud made against all Jews, expressing murderous hatred against them, since this was equivalent to old accusations made by fanatic Christians that they were brutal Christ-killers. His hatred of the Jews is also shown by his attempts to destroy the identity of their magnificent leader Moses, at the very time of greatest peril for the Jews in the late 1930s when they were subject to widespread murderous attacks by the Nazis.

If one treats the Moses book as a bad dream, a chaotic one with many inter-locking planes and theses, it would not be amiss to treat Moses as a composite figure—since Freud taught us that many figures in dreams are composites. In doing this I'll suggest that there are at least seven "faces" of Moses that are encoded in Freud's last book: the Biblical Moses; the Jews who have identified with Moses; Jung; Emanuel; Julius Freud; Jesus Christ; and Sigmund Freud himself. Moreover, Freud harbored murderous feelings towards all seven of those aspects of Moses, as we'll see.

The first of those aspects of Moses, the Biblical one, is obvious and overt. Freud's murderous hatred towards the Biblical figure was seen in his attempts to destroy the hero's name and identity, and by inventing the superfluous story that he was murdered by his faithless disciples. The second aspect of Moses pertains to countless orthodox Jews, through the ages, who have identified with Moses and with essential elements of Mosaic law. Freud's lethal hatred towards those Jews, representing Moses, was discussed two paragraphs earlier.

That Carl Jung became an aspect of Moses, in Freud's fantasy life, is suggested by the fact that he elevated Jung to the crucial role of leader of the new religion called Psychoanalysis, and expected Jung to be the powerful gentile (re the "Egyptian symbol") who would lead downtrodden analysts into the promised land of worldwide approbation and affluence. The notion that Jung represented an aspect of the Biblical Moses in Freud's unconscious mind is not my original idea. It was discussed explicitly by Roazen (1968, pp. 178-80) on several pages following this question: "How can one be so sure of the image of Jung behind the man Moses?" That Freud bore murderous hatred towards Jung in 1913/1914 (and later) has been discussed in previous pages, so nobody should be surprised that Freud's lethal hatred towards Jung was still simmering in the 1930s during the Moses book's creation.

The fourth aspect of Moses listed above was Emanuel Freud, as already noted. If it is correct that Jung and Emanuel both were aspects of the composite Moses in Freud's fantasies, this helps explain why Freud was able to shift his murderous intent from Jung onto Emanuel in the summer of 1914, resulting in the killing of Emanuel. Of course, Freud was not flagrantly psychotic in that era, and it made perverse sense for him to displace his lethal rage onto Emanuel. That is, if a murder attempt had been made on Jung that went awry, or somehow looked less-than-accidental, suspicion might have fallen quickly upon Freud due to the immense animosity between the two men in 1913/1914. And it might not have been difficult to establish Freud's complicity in Jung's murder. So it made sense to substitute Moses/Emanuel for Moses/Jung when Freud concocted his murder plan in the summer of 1914.

The fifth aspect of Moses in Freud's fantasy life was his deceased brother Julius, as suggested by his famous "forgetting" regarding Julius Mosen in *Complete*. That baby Julius became a hidden aspect of the composite Moses might have been due to Freud's lifelong death-wishes towards his little brother, which probably evoked self-punitive accusations that were aligned with a relentless Mosaic authority in Sigmund's mind (enforced by the threat of Emanuel's punitiveness during childhood). That the guilty and murderous feelings towards Julius persisted for more than 80 years makes one wonder whether Sigi had ever attempted to commit some lethal act against his infant brother, like pushing him off a table top or stuffing a pillow against his face. If so, and if Freud arranged for John's "disappearance" in 1919, there would have been three murderous acts against brothers, considering that nephew John Freud was equivalent to an older brother-figure during Sigmund's childhood years.

The sixth aspect of Moses in Freud's unconscious mind was Jesus Christ. Various writers have noted that Moses and Jesus are equivalent figures religiously, and some argue that the messianic Moses was a prefiguration of the Christian messiah. Freud had made a rather overt identification with Moses, and a more covert but intensely irrational identification with Jesus. I've argued that, in Freud's mind, Jesus was partially equated with his brother Emanuel, so the covert murderous hatred towards Emanuel would have been directed simultaneously against the figure of Jesus (consonant with Freud's allegiance with Satan, discussed in chapter ten.)

The seventh aspect of Moses in Freud's mind was Sigmund Freud himself, due to his intense fantasy identification with the Jews' greatest of religious heroes. Does this mean that the Moses book encoded Freud's murderous intentions towards himself? I think it does, and that the book was almost a deathbed confession of murder and of Freud's intention to "murder" himself by ordering the overdose of morphine which Dr. Schur administered to him in September of 1939. One is reminded that the analyst Zilboorg contended that Freud had a great fear of the Day of Judgment. Also, we recall the quotation which Freud used as the motto for his dream book, indicating that if he could not arouse the "higher powers" of the mind, he would call forth the fires of hell.

That quotation from a classic work referred to the calling forth of the murderously revengeful Furies of Roman mythology. However, in the myths of the ancient Greeks the calling forth of those demons, the Furies, was reserved as a horrible retribution to be inflicted upon anyone guilty of parricide. This hints at the specific reason why Freud was fearful of Judgment Day: his parricidal desires and behaviors that were relevant to the murder of Emanuel Freud.

Indeed, the very beginning of the dream book was reflective of Freud's parricidal intentions, in terms of its motto's lethal meaning, while some compelling material near the very end of that "masterpiece" on dreams is also secretly reflective of his parricidal concerns. Since Freud often advised that both first things and last things are crucial to understanding major psychic events, special emphasis should be placed on the last few pages of his dream book (1967, pp. 658-660). On page 658 he discussed again (as on page 99) the story of the Roman emperor* who executed one of his subjects who had dreamed about murdering his ruler. Freud expressed opposition to the emperor's punitive act that had been based upon an endorsement of the presumed accuracy of the predictive functions of dreams in relation to future behaviors of the dreamer. Freud's first objection was that the preceding dream's true meaning had not been assessed, noting that probably its meaning was different from what it appeared to be (not murderous). A more important objection by Freud was summed up by

---

*Did this encode Julius Caesar and Freud's brother Julius, whom he earnestly wished to kill in childhood?

Plato's dictum that virtuous men are content to dream what an evil man actually does in reality. Thus, in general Freud seemed to deny that wishes in dreams (including lethal wishes) can be predictive regarding future behaviors (including murders relevant to said wishes). In any case, it's extremely important that the issue of murdering an emperor is an obvious symbolization about the killing of a great father-figure, and that Freud placed this issue at the very end of his dream book, pointing to his unending concern about the burning topic of patricide.

Furthermore, it is fascinating to note that there is a "catch" in Freud's use of Plato's dictum, above. For it may be true that a virtuous man will be content to express his lethal wishes only in dreams, but this does not imply that a man with a strongly evil nature will do the same. Freud simply ignored the possibility that an evil man might express murderous wishes in his dreams and then fulfill them in actual killings, particularly in the case of men (like Freud) who had many dreams revealing murderous wishes, some with repetitive contents, i.e. his dreams concerning trains and killing. (It's provocative that on page 99 he inserted his use of Plato's dictum into the dream book in the year 1914, the year of Emanuel's presumed murder.) Readers will decide for themselves whether Freud—with his repetitive vengeful feelings and persistent death-wishes towards numerous persons—exhibited a variety of personal characteristics that deserve to be called "evil," not forgetting his lethal behaviors. The later chapter describing his Satanic pacts and identifications with the devil might help some readers to make their final decision on that point.

Chapter Nine

The Disappearance of John Freud

Historical Discrepancies, Revisited
At the outset, let me acknowledge that my grim hypothesis concerning the fate of John Freud suffers from an obvious weakness, in comparison with what I posited about the demise of his father Emanuel in 1914. Admittedly, my "case" regarding John is flawed by the absence of a *corpus delicti*. After reading this chapter, however, many readers may deduce that circa 1919 John probably *was* abducted from his home in Manchester, England and then was murdered (and perhaps buried) by an unknown assassin employed by his uncle, Sigmund Freud.

My assumption is that Freud arranged for the sudden disappearance of his older nephew in early 1919 when John was age 63. If readers are convinced that Freud was responsible for Emanuel's train death in October 1914, they will not find it difficult to entertain the idea that four years later, again in a semi-psychotic state of mind, he planned the abduction and killing of John. As mentioned previously, the key motive behind John's vanishing may have been Sigmund's revenge for all those horrendous disappearances of nanny, Emanuel, John (et al.) that constituted the "Freiberg catastrophe" of 1860, although later I'll suggest additional strange motives that could have helped to seal John's fate.

In the first chapter we learned that there is a mystifying time discrepancy which separates two groups of writers concerning the disappearance of John Freud. Recall that the first author who accused Freud of murdering John was Eric Miller, by asserting that Freud arranged his nephew's disappearance in the 1870s. To support his thesis that John had vanished at that time, Miller (1984, pp. 83-4, 285) cited a published statement to that effect by Dr. Max Schur (1969) and a private communication from Schur's widow which confirmed that John had disappeared in the 1870s.

In contrast, there have been writers who indicated that John Freud did not disappear in the 1870s, but was still alive in Manchester during subsequent decades, including Sigmund Freud and Ronald Clark. Various writings by Freud discussed John's continuing existence in Manchester in the 1890s and thereafter. For example, his dream book in 1900 mentioned this point and, several years earlier, Freud had written a letter to Fliess specifying that John was then living in Manchester. Finally, Clark's biography revealed (1980, p. 394) that in May of 1919 Freud received news, presumably from Samuel Freud, that his older brother John "had left his parents' home and was not to be heard of again."

Nothing further was reported by Clark concerning John's apparently abrupt departure in 1919, a presumed "disappearance," providing no indication whether Samuel or Sigmund were perplexed or distressed about John's circumstances. As an afterthought, some readers might find it odd that Clark did not follow his typical procedure by citing Samuel's letter and its precise date in his endnotes. In any case, his style of writing did indicate that this final news about John was given in a letter from Samuel to his uncle Sigmund which presumably was read by Clark carefully. By Clark's account, Samuel's letter noted that his older sisters ("the old ladies," Pauline and Bertha) were doing well and that he was successfully carrying on his father Emanuel's business. (We have no way of knowing whether this business contained a secret component of counterfeiting currency, as pertains to data in chapter one concerning possible criminal activities of Emanuel in the 1860s.)

Previously, I stated my view that the letter of Samuel Freud cited by Clark is authentic, reflecting my belief that John Freud vanished suddenly in early 1919 (or late 1918), not in the 1870s. But we must consider that Krüll's volume (1986, pp. 234-5) replicates a document called the "Jacob Freud Family Tree" which includes John's name and Freiberg birthdate of 8/13/55 and a notation stating: "vanished after 1875 *or in 1918.*" Apparently, this notation helped stimulate Krüll's euphemistic remark that: "In any case, John's disappearance remains unexplained."

Considering the above material, one must now explain why Dr. Max Schur wrote in his 1969 essay that: "John came to Vienna for a visit in 1870 when he was 15 and Freud 14, and mysteriously disappeared in 1872." How could Dr. Schur, the physician and close friend of Freud and his family for many years, have made such a grotesque error in this assertion that John vanished in 1872 (either at age 16 or 17)? Immediately, we can see that Schur did not obtain his information from the above "Family Tree," since its initial specification is that John might have "vanished" after 1875—when he was age 20 or older.

Then from whom did Schur obtain his firm conviction that John had "mysteriously disappeared in 1872"? It's most likely that he obtained that mis-information from Anna Freud when, during the formulation of his deeply psychological biography of her father (1972) he became curious about the later life and fate of Freud's nephew, who'd had such a strikingly ambivalent effect (love/hostility) on his development, as admitted by the master himself. Similarly, it is conceivable that in the late 1960s, when Schur was collecting materials for his biography of Freud, he stumbled across a vague rumor that, at some unspecified time in his life, John Freud had disappeared from his father's home forever. Schur would have wanted to pin down this strange historical item by contacting his good friend, Anna Freud, since surely he'd noted that Jones's second volume provides considerable data about Anna's trip to Manchester in 1914, where John Freud had lived with his kinsmen.

Why do I suspect that Anna gave totally erroneous information about John to Max Schur (which he must have passed on to his wife, according to Miller's statement)? My reason pertains to extensive data offered in the preceding chapter concerning Anna's ill-fated sojourn in England during the summer of 1914, when she visited her relatives in Manchester. It's likely that she then met John Freud or, if he was away on a holiday, was given a full description of his life and activities by his siblings and father, to take back to her own inquisitive father. (Freud's persistent feelings of rivalry would have required him to ask for full details about John, to determine whether his older nephew was as successful in life as he was.) Surely Anna knew that John Freud was alive in Manchester in 1914 and beyond; and it is extremely improbable that Dr. Schur did not contact her to make an inquiry about John's fate before publishing that amazing item about his strange disappearance in 1872.

Young-Bruehl's biography (1988) of Anna Freud reveals the countless "fictions" she concocted during her childhood and adolescent years, and I'm suggesting that this was another fiction that she foisted on Dr. Schur when he inquired of her what the fate of John Freud had been. Indeed, she might have embellished her tale by saying that Sigmund told her that young John had argued with his autocratic father in the 1870s and abruptly emigrated to Australia or Canada where, at an early age, he died of a heart problem or other illness. Then, perhaps she added that Emanuel was so grief-stricken that he and his family pretended thereafter that John was still living on the outskirts of Manchester and someday, like the prodigal son, would return to his father's home to ask for his forgiveness and blessing.

Also, Anna might have told Schur that her father "honored" this pretense by mentioning in the dream book (and in some letters) John's continuing presence in Manchester, and she would have advised Schur not to discuss this topic with any of the Manchester relatives, saying that it was still a painful topic for them. In such fashion, and by claiming that John *was* absent during her 1914 visit to Manchester, Anna could feel secure that Schur would not investigate this subject with any of the Freuds of Manchester while composing his biography of Freud circa 1969-1971, and would not give John's disappearance any coverage in that volume. This could help explain an astonishing anomaly: that Schur cited John's "mysterious" disappearance of 1872 in his 1969 essay, but did not mention it at all three years later in his huge biography of Freud.

The above scenario suggests one possible way that Anna Freud could have kept Schur ignorant of the fact that John Freud did not disappear from Manchester *until early 1919*, convincing him instead that John had vanished abruptly in the early 1870s. If later Schur had contacted a Manchester relative who disclosed John's sudden disappearance in early 1919 and that Anna had met him during her 1914 visit, she could then reply to Schur's further questions that for unknown reasons (perhaps rivalry) her father had blotted out her memories of John during her analysis by claiming that he'd vanished in the 1870s. And she would have added that the Manchester informant was mistaken, i.e. she had not met John in 1914, or perhaps "forgot" that she had.

Why do I assume that Anna misled Schur into believing that John had vanished in 1872, not in 1919? My intuition is that she recognized that Schur was a basically honest man who might tell the truth about Freud (if he knew it). For Max Schur understood that his subject's mind, over a lifetime, was dominated by parricidal death-wishes and a "Cain complex" that were potentially very pertinent to the disappearance of his "brother figure," John Freud. It's plausible that Anna had some grave suspicions herself about her father's semi-psychotic episodes and their possible connections with Emanuel's train death, as well as with John's disappearance in 1919. Therefore, she probably decided to keep Schur "off the track" by pushing John's disappearance into the far distant past, so that Schur would not recognize that Emanuel's strange death in 1914 was uncomfortably close to John's probable demise (by foul play?) in 1919. For that could have raised the specter of assassination in Schur's mind, with Freud as a likely suspect.

In the preceding material, I've made the frank accusation that Anna Freud probably used her authority and cleverness, in one instance, to influence the formulation of Schur's biography of her father in a tendentious and dishonest manner. If I'm wrong about this issue, then why didn't Ms. Freud immediately write Dr. Schur in 1969 to correct him concerning his published remark that John Freud had disappeared mysteriously in 1872, forcefully advising him that John was still alive in Manchester during her summer visit in 1914? Indeed, in that case we can assume that she did read Schur's 1969 article, or certainly was informed by colleagues concerning Schur's citation of that mystery about John's alleged disappearance in 1872, but then did nothing to inform Schur of his grievous error. For if she had done so, that essentially honest author would have corrected this error in his 1972 biography of Freud, and then would have provided materials (as Clark did) concerning John's disappearance in 1919, derived from Schur's additional investigation of this issue with living Freud relatives that he would have questioned very carefully. (And his widow would not have persisted in this error by passing it on to Eric Miller.)

Readers who are loyal to Ms. Freud's pristine image will be less offended by my preceding claim that she probably deceived Dr. Schur about the fate of John Freud when they read my chapter in *Dark Side* titled "Freud's Watergate Scandal." In that chapter I offer my strong reasons for claiming that Ms. Freud probably managed to deceive J. Masson, editor of the volume ironically titled *The Complete Letters of Sigmund Freud to Wilhelm Fliess* (1985), by preventing Masson from obtaining crucial letters pertaining to the bizarre surgery that Freud arranged to be performed on Emma Eckstein's nose, nearly killing her. If I'm convincing in my analysis which indicates that Ms. Freud deceived Masson, then it will seem more plausible that she also deceived Dr. Schur. (In deceiving Masson, she was protecting her father from public awareness of his semi-psychotic ideation that nearly cost the life of Ms. Eckstein, who was a revenant of his Freiberg nanny—similar to her reason for deceiving Dr. Schur.)

Likewise, in my other works I've reviewed evidence indicating that Ms. Freud was the "gray eminence" controlling many essential aspects of Jones's three biographical volumes. I'm convinced that she was a powerful influence in Jones's distortions of key areas, and especially his omissions of many crucial subjects: the true and full story of Freud's involvement with Emma Eckstein; considerable data about the breakup of Breuer and Freud's relationship, which permit an entirely different understanding of this issue; many bizarre elements in the Freud/Fliess relationship and in their breakup; the connection of Freud with Weininger, and his suicide; damaging aspects of the relationship between Freud and the psychoanalytic murderer, Dr. Gross; Freud's connections with the sexually psychopathic behaviors of Jung, Jones, and Ferenczi; Freud's responsibility for the suicide of Dr. Victor Tausk, and many other persons as part of his suicide-murder complex; the full extent of Freud's severe psychopathology over decades; his destructive behaviors towards patients, besides Emma E.; the counterfeiting affair involving uncle Josef of Vienna, and perhaps the Freuds of Manchester; etc.

My next proposal is that Anna Freud probably influenced Jones to omit from his three biographical volumes all information about John Freud's disappearance in 1919. Rather than cleverly deceiving Jones about this matter, as I've assumed she did with Dr. Schur, she could have relied on Jones's pressing psychopathic potentials (described in chapter eleven) to tell him openly that he should not include any material about John's "mysterious disappearance," whether in 1872 or in 1919. In whatever fashion she conveyed this prohibition to Jones, it was quite effective. For readers can study Jones's three volumes for themselves to determine that his first volume offers only six brief references to John Freud, with the latest time-period involving John's summer visit to the Freuds of Vienna in 1870 (Jones I, p. 23). Volumes two and three make no mention at all of John's later years, nor of his year-long visit to Jacob's home circa John's seventh year as discussed by Swales (see below). Of course, Jones's work does not even hint at John's strange disappearance in 1919, this being an outrageous "lapse" in what pretends to be an all-encompassing, official biography of the master's life. (Again, Freud's repeated assertion that all biographies are filled with deliberate distortions and lies was amply confirmed by his own official biography.)

The Magical Year 1919

In chapter eight we saw that one of the factors that might have triggered Freud's plan to murder Emanuel Freud was the baleful year 1914 itself, in terms of that year's special military significances for Sigmund. Accumulated stresses in the prolonged "battle" with Jung over who would capture the Psychoanalytic empire were combined, in Freud's mind, with the dangerous military maneuverings of conflicting empires as the Great War began in the summer of 1914. His ideation and feelings became possessed by an irrational militaristic ardor which hinted at a regression to the militant obsessions of his boyhood when there had been countless battles using toy soldiers, great conquests on the floor of his room, and passionate identifications with famous battlefield heroes. Underlying those military skirmishes and victories of childhood, however, were murderous rivalries with key idealized figures in his life, particularly Emanuel and John, and his immense need for revenge against them.

My contention is that in the period 1914 to 1919 those dominating figures of childhood, Emanuel and John, once again became hateful and dangerous battlefield enemies in the deranged thinking of Sigmund Freud. At a conscious level, he wrote openly to some colleagues that his disciple Jones had become an English "enemy," and of the treachery of the English foe. During the era of the Great War, Freud's mind was regressed to the battle-mode of childhood when he felt the need to destroy those who had murdered nanny and might also kill him. Consequently, the urges to kill and take revenge upon, his English enemies, Emanuel and John, were revived and acted-out while he and his family suffered the terrible emotional stresses and physical deprivations of the war—two of his sons being combatants who repeatedly came close to death on the battlefield.

In my view, there were several peculiar reasons why 1919 was the year chosen by Freud for arranging the disappearance and presumed murder of John Freud. Within his mind, it was connected with the sequence of first- and-last events. Thus, his deranged response to the commencement of the war had been the murder of his English "betrayer," Emanuel. So it then became appropriate for him, soon after the armistice of November 11, 1918 when the war officially ended, to arrange for the destruction of his second English "betrayer," John Freud in early 1919. In Freud's unbalanced thinking the armistice had represented a personal defeat for him (see below, his "battle" with President Wilson, whom he felt had betrayed him), and it became necessary to reverse this defeat by obtaining a personal "victory" right after the war's official ending, represented by this triumph over his most ancient foe, his nephew John.

Also, the choice of 1919 for John's capture and demise was partly a reflection of Freud's persistent number magic, relating to material in previous chapters which showed that number 19 was his lucky number which magically ensured triumph for him. For example, we reviewed that his street address Berggasse 19 magically provided him with victory over his enemies Viktor Adler and his baby brother, Julius. Now we see that the year 1919 had a capacity for doubly signifying "triumph over enemies" in Freud's mind, since it is composed of a doubling of the number 19. Therefore, it was an extremely auspicious year for obtaining an ultimate victory over Freud's most bitter rival, his nettlesome nephew, making him unable to resist the magical power of 1919 for ridding himself of his ancient tormenter.

Having discussed why Freud could regard 1919 as both a triumphant year for himself and a lethal year for his enemies, let me suggest that he might have decided to use its magical powers to remove a deadly curse from himself and transfer it onto his nephew John. My reference here is to Freud's belief that he definitely was fated to die near the start of 1918 at age 61, or later in 1918 (or early 1919) at age 62—which he told to various disciples including Ferenczi and Jung. For example, in Jones's second volume (p. 392) he noted that Freud informed Ferenczi in 1910 about a belief he'd obsessed about "for a long time," i.e. that he was doomed to die in February 1918 (at age 61).

In Jones's third volume (pp. 390-1) he discussed Freud's strong conviction that he'd die at age 61 or 62, which he cited "over and over again in his correspondence." Jones remarked that this weird belief had originated in 1900 and that Freud's "numerological friend Fliess" was somehow connected with its origination in Freud's mind. But the Welsh analyst covered up artfully, censoring the point that the plan to murder Fliess at Achensee in 1900 was the actual stimulus for this "superstitious belief." Although Jones *did* remark that the dreaded death-ages 61 and 62 "suddenly came together and acquired significance" at the time of the breakup with Fliess (in mid-1900), no mention was made of the plan to murder Fliess at Achensee and that the guilty payback was Freud's fear that he would die, probably at age 62. Cleverly, Jones diverted attention from this by noting that in 1900 Freud's new telephone number, 14362, contained the number 62, which helped convince Freud that he'd die at age 62. Then Jones mentioned that during Freud's visit to Greece in 1904 (the Acropolis episode), the numbers 60, 61, and 62 "pursued him with all objects that bore a number," including *railway* tickets. In chapter eight I've stated that Freud's brief episode of psychosis in 1904 at Trieste and Athens was causally related to the murder plan at Achensee, so the hallucinated pursuit by those numbers (including 62) was a symptomatic factor reflecting intense guilt, and fear of retribution, concerning the intention to murder Fliess.

From 1904 through early 1918 Freud was plagued by the fear that he'd die at age 61, provoking greatest anxiety for that number in February 1918 (as he neared his actual birthday on March 6th). After his 62nd "official" birthday in May of 1918, the feelings of doom pertaining to the number 62 increased progressively in late 1918 up until his next official birthday on May 6, 1919. Probably, the feelings of fear increased for Freud to a near panic level in the spring of 1919, which leads to my next suggestion. Consider the idea that it was no mere coincidence that in May 1919 Freud received his nephew Samuel's letter disclosing that John Freud had disappeared, most likely in the days just prior to the letter's arrival in Vienna. The timing here indicates that Freud's heightened anxiety about his own impending death in the early months of 1919 caused him to institute a magical strategem to avert his own doom. (He had "dodged the bullet" once, in February 1918, making the danger of death progressively much worse in the early months of 1919.)

Using the magical power of the year 1919, Freud may have tried to avert the curse of death upon himself by transferring it to John Freud, arranging for his nephew to be kidnapped and killed in the early part of 1919 (or perhaps in late 1918). This deflection of death by sacrificing John's life is consonant with the proposal by Kanzer (1979) that some of Freud's behavior during the Acropolis episode represented his desire to deflect his own death by magically expropriating a portion of the life-span of his brother Alexander—similar to his desire to extend life via various devils' pacts, as reviewed in chapter ten.

It makes sense that Freud's fear of dying in 1918, or in early 1919 at age

62, originated in his murder plan against Fliess at Achensee, and that this fear of death was countered in 1919 via a plan to kidnap and murder John Freud. The perverse logic connecting those seemingly disparate plans to murder Fliess and then to kill John derives from the fact that Fliess served for many years as a revenant or substitute for John (which helps to explain why Freud often deferred to Fliess and over-valued his thinking). It's reasonable to suspect, therefore, that the failed intention to kill Fliess in 1900 was finally actualized in fantasy by the disappearance of John Freud in 1919.

Having already considered the possibility that the magically destructive powers which Freud attributed to the year 1919 might have helped to provoke the abduction and murder of John Freud, it's time to discuss whether 1919 helped stimulate Freud's lethal behaviors towards some other persons, as well. Briefly, it should be noted that on November 4, 1918 Dr. Victor Tausk returned from military service to Vienna and resumed his psychoanalytic practice. Roazen (1969) has described the peculiar rivalry that had developed in preceding years between Freud and this charming, younger man which became intensified when they competed for the attention and affection of that seductive woman, Lou Salomé, who became Tausk's lover. Upon returning from the privations of military service, Tausk seemed to exhibit a broken spirit and considerable depression, exacerbated by a tenuous analytic practice and severe poverty. He sought analysis from Freud, who refused him for rather insubstantial reasons, adding to his feelings of humiliation and despair. In January 1919 Tausk entered psychoanalysis with Dr. Helene Deutsch, then an inexperienced analyst who was herself in analysis with Freud. (The fatal suggestion that she should treat Tausk was made by Freud, hinting at his rather destructive manipulation of both Tausk and Deutsch.)

Tausk used his sessions with Dr. Deutsch to express many complaints about Freud, which she dutifully reported to the master. Freud's old animosities and rivalry towards Tausk became reinvigorated and in March 1919 Freud took the initiative to require Deutsch to terminate her analysis with Tausk, claiming that it was interfering with her own analysis. When she complied with Freud's manipulative "request," Tausk's depression and sense of desperation increased greatly. As a consequence, on July 3, 1919 he committed suicide by hanging himself. Though he left a note absolving Freud of responsibility, it seems obvious that Freud's callous and manipulative behaviors were largely responsible for his colleague's death. My suggestion is that Freud obtained his ultimate revenge on Tausk by triggering his suicide, and that part of his perverse motivation for destroying this rival was connected with the promise of "triumph over enemies" that was provided by the magical year 1919. (Besides number magic, there was also name magic in Freud's victory, since his victim's given name was Victor.)

There was another very destructive event, engineered by Freud, that occurred in the first half of 1919. As noted in chapter six, Freud badgered Sandor Ferenczi (whom he had analyzed twice) into marrying an older woman named Gizella Pálos. Actually, Ferenczi did not wish to marry her, and desired instead to take her young daughter in marriage. Perhaps, he also balked at marrying Gizella due to guilty feelings, since Gizella's husband had been a friend of his whom he betrayed, with Freud's encouragement. Due to Freud's outrageous manipulations, Ferenczi finally married Gizella *on March 1, 1919.* Her former husband became Freud's victim immediately. He died on the very same day of a heart attack (or perhaps suicide). Previously, I explained that Freud's manipulations, via name magic, enabled him to triumph over his childhood "sweetheart" named Gisela P. and her husband, using this painful triumph over Gizella Pálos and her former husband. My suggestion now is that it was not mere coincidence that this cruel triumph of Freud's occurred in March of 1919, under the auspices of that magical year.

Notice that the high-handed manipulation of Dr. Deutsch to cancel Tausk's treatment, and the destructively engineered marriage of Ferenczi to Gizella P., both occurred in March of 1919 while Freud's anxiety was extremely high for many reasons, including the "curse" that he would die during those final few months of his 62nd year. Is it difficult to believe, therefore, that near this same month of March 1919 he would engage in additional bizarre ideation by arranging the kidnapping and murder of John Freud, in an attempt to transfer that curse to John?

1919: Stress and Latent Psychosis

Previous chapters suggested that evidences of Freud's psychotic thinking in 1900 and 1914 enhanced the plausibility that murderous behaviors occurred at Achensee towards Fliess and in relation to Emanuel's train death in England. Now we need to inquire whether there are evidences of psychotic thinking by Freud in the period 1918/1919 that increase the probability that he arranged the disappearance and murder of his nephew John.

To begin with, let's review the enormous stresses that were placed on Freud's mind and body near the end of the war years, reminding ourselves that he did not manage stress very well despite his disciples' tales about his heroic nature. Relying upon numerous excerpts from Freud's letters to his colleagues, Jones's materials about the Great War (II, chapter seven) present an incredibly bleak picture of Freud's life in Vienna from 1916 to 1919. Like many Viennese families the Freuds were subject to lack of heat in winter (making their apartment almost an ice locker), and severe restrictions of their natural diet on many days. By 1918 there was a great scarcity of meat, sometimes months passing by with hardly any being served. The family's diet of weak vegetable soup was inadequate for good health, and hunger pangs were common. Jones wrote (III, p. 3) that the winters of 1918-19 and 1919-20 were the worst of these terrible periods, with life becoming almost unbearable in Vienna. The times were especially difficult for Freud who often treated patients for hours in a "deadly cold" room, protected by an overcoat and thick gloves, followed by evening hours when he answered correspondence using "half-frozen fingers" to grip his pen.

There were many sources of anxiety for Freud as the war years progressed. Inflation was rampant in Austria and his income was unable to keep pace with numerous increases in prices, so he was forced to live on savings intended for use as a private pension for his old age. Eventually, he lost all his savings, and a life insurance policy for his wife's benefit became worthless. Even greater anxiety was provoked by constant fearful thoughts about his three sons, all of whom were in military service and two of whom were involved in heavy fighting. The most intense concerns involved his eldest son Martin who, in late 1918, became a prisoner of war in Italy, particularly because many months passed by without any word being received about him. In July 1917 Freud had written to Abraham that his sister Rosa's son, age twenty, had just been killed on the battlefield and that her grief "surpassed description." Worriedly, he added that "There is no news about my warriors," reflecting increased fear about his own sons.

A careful reading of the Freud/Abraham correspondence during the war years reveals that Freud often did not refrain from expressing to this friend his depressed and pessimistic feelings as the war progressed, while Abraham usually maintained a brave, optimistic outlook. During 1917 Freud's great hope for a German victory declined, and he became increasingly pessimistic about the war's outcome. By fall 1917 he felt the Germans were about to lose the war and seemed to expect a complete collapse of the Central Powers following the failure of submarine warfare, remarking that the future seemed "pretty dark for us." In December he began to express great hostility towards Germany, and poutingly expressed the idea that both sides of the conflict were "stinkers." Undoubtedly, his hostility towards Germany was partially provoked by its failure to provide him with the great military triumph that his insufferable egotism and militaristic fantasies demanded.

It is informative concerning Freud's mental fragility to review the course of his depressed and pessimistic comments from 1917 onward. On May 20, 1917 he wrote Abraham that the war seemed to have become a "disaster" that had overtaken everyone. He then said that he'd grown old, frail, and tired and had given up work, noting that: "Life bears too heavily on me." Unconvincingly, he denied being gripped by depression, saying he was "not more depressed than usual . . "

Writing to Abraham on November 11, 1917, Freud claimed that hard work kept him from brooding and worrying, but said he was aging rapidly and doubted that he would live to see the end of the war, or ever see Abraham again. He then made a bleak reference to the "end of the world," and noted that the future seemed dim. Then he mentioned a new Lamarckian project he had begun, one so bizarre that it exposed the latent psychosis that was fermenting in Freud's mind—as discussed in a later section. (Abraham's reply in early December expressed distress that Freud's thoughts were so "gloomy.")

Intimations of severe depression and latent psychosis were also suggested by Freud's letter of November 20, 1917 to Ferenczi. Freud wrote that: "I have been working very hard, feel worn out and am beginning to find the world repellently loathesome." He even hinted at self-destructive feelings by claiming that now his superstitious idea that he would die in February of 1918 often seemed like a pleasant idea. He added this grim remark: "Sometimes I have to fight hard to regain ascendancy over myself." Evidently, this meant that he was on the brink of another mental breakdown, perhaps a touch of psychosis similar to what Ferenczi had witnessed in Vienna during October 1914—G.P.I. or "general paralysis of the insane," according to Ferenczi's diagnosis.

In Freud's letter to Abraham dated January 18, 1918 he described some good news about his analytic practice, but again expressed bitter feelings about the war. He wrote that: "If the war lasts long enough, it will kill off everybody any way." A month later he noted that "The world is surely in a chaotic state." Then a few months later, after his birthday, he expressed some surprise that he had really reached age 62. (This was another horrendous death age for him, as retribution for the plan to murder Fliess at Achensee.) He soon added these depressed comments: "My prevailing mood is powerless embitterment or embitterment at my powerlessness." A few months thereafter Freud wrote that he did not answer Abraham's previous letter because: "I was then too angry and too hungry." Hunger and other deprivations continued to wear down his spirit, and in late October 1918 Abraham expressed the hope that he was not suffering too badly from the "general deprivations in Vienna about which we now constantly read."

In due time, I will focus upon the increased deprivations and concomitant depressed feelings that Freud experienced during the six months encompassing November 1918 through April 1919. That was a terribly stressful period for Freud, which will need emphasis due to my hypothesis that sometime within the first few months of 1919 his mind, unable to bear the pressures, "snapped" once again, provoking the murder plot against John Freud as a perverse way of relieving his internal stresses. So far as "timing" is concerned, this hypothesis would seem to make a reasonable correlation with his receiving, in early May, the news from his nephew Samuel in Manchester about John's mysterious "disappearance." Although Clark did not specify the exact date that John vanished—was abducted and killed, in my view—one could guess that it was late March or early April when Freud contacted an assassin in England to arrange for John's abduction. This meshes with Clark's comment (1980, p. 394) that direct, uncensored communication between Austria and Britain was renewed in April 1919—although throughout the war Freud had used various indirect ways for getting mail through to persons in England.

The above hypothesis is similar to my view in chapter eight that unbearable stresses on Freud in July 1914, near the start of the war, caused a similar "mind-snapping" (a term lay readers will understand) which provoked his contact with an assassin in England who then effected Emanuel's train death. My guess is that the same assassin was employed by Freud in both cases, but I have no support for this assumption except parsimony and my guess that Freud would place reliance upon demonstrated expertise and success.

Now let's return to the enormous pressures on Freud's mind from November 1918 through April 1919. Psychologically, perhaps the greatest stress for Freud in November 1918 was the armistice that was signed in that month. This meant that the forces of the great conquistador, Freud, had been defeated officially, despite the prophecies in his boyhood that he would become a victorious hero. (Did he always fear this would be the case in his identification with Hannibal and Napoleon, both of them "losers?")

At the end of the war, more concrete deprivations occurred for Freud. Jones reported (II, p. 199) that his clinical practice "virtually disappeared for a while." In a letter to Ferenczi of November 27, 1918 Freud wrote that the general privations had increased so greatly that they were "scarcely to be borne." This was at the start of a long period when many people began to starve in Germany and things were not much better in Vienna. The general misery and starvation became so widespread that it led to the heyday of the murderer Fritz Haarmann who kidnapped and killed many young boys and sold their body parts for meat to the unsuspecting populace, until he was caught and executed.

Near the end of December 1918 Freud's letter to Jones ended with this comment: "Life is harsh you know already." That was an understatement. Misery flourished and on the last day of the year, Jones's mournful task was to advise Freud of the death of his old friend and supporter, Prof. J.J. Putnam, and Freud "felt his death as a great loss." The true extent of how much worse conditions had become in Vienna were expressed in Freud's letter to Ferenczi of January 24, 1919. He complained that "all the four years of war were a joke compared with the bitter grimness of these months and doubtless also of the ones to come." Near that time he wrote to Jones that the last months were "becoming the worst we have had to endure while this war lasted." He added that everyone was "slowly failing in health and bulk . ." and gave the grim assessment that "Prospects are dark." Jones noted (II, p. 202) that conditions had gotten so bad in Austria that Freud was advised to emigrate to another country, and disciples in Hungary, Switzerland, and England offered him sanctuary, which he refused.

When Freud wrote to Jones (above) that he and his family were slowly failing in health, that complaint soon had special relevance to his wife Martha. Jones reported (III, p. 8) that in March 1919 she "was struck down with a severe influenzal pneumonia from which she took some months to recover." Martha's disease must have instilled great anxiety in Freud since many people were dying with it, and nearly a year later he lost his daughter Sophie from this same illness. The Freud apartment was a bad place for Martha's recuperation, for in a February 1919 letter to Abraham he began by saying that "it is bitterly cold here in this room . . " Jones wrote (II, p. 206) that as time went by the only change in the Freuds' situation was for the worse. It's no wonder that in late May 1919 Freud wrote to Jones (III, p. 6) that: "I can't remember a time of my life when my horizon was so dark . ."

Stepansky's research convinced him that by May of 1919 Freud was experiencing clinical depression. In his monograph about aggression in Freud's life and thought (p. 171) he wrote that: "By May, 1919, economic misery, social isolation from his protégés, and the serious illness of his wife coalesced in another episode of depression." In general, I agree with this view but believe that severe depression with psychotic concomitants was present even earlier in 1919, perhaps beginning in March. It should be noted that Stepansky's view that Freud was experiencing depression in May 1919 is in conflict with Jones's claim (II, p. 206) that in March Freud had "rallied from the pessimism induced by the war," giving no convincing evidence (in terms of actual behaviors) that this alleged relief from depression had occurred. What Jones failed to consider adequately was Martha's serious illness in March (lasting several months) and Freud's ongoing deep anxieties about the fate of his imprisoned son, Martin, who had been taken captive in Italy and was not released until sometime beyond May.

Perhaps the most gnawing stress on Freud's mind during the first half of 1919 was the dangerous situation involving his eldest son Martin, which

I believe so unsettled his mind in March 1919 that it helped provoke his decision to kidnap John Freud. Let me give some brief comments about Martin's military service and imprisonment, and Freud's reactions to this. Starting early in the war when he volunteered for service, Martin had been fighting continuously at the front in either Galicia or Russia, and narrowly escaped death several times. He fought in a unit of the Field Artillery and in 1915, after being wounded, was cited for gallantry in the field. Understandably, his parents were particularly worried about this brave son who seemed almost to court danger. On December 2, 1918 Freud wrote to Abraham that Martin had not returned home from the front as expected, although some vague news had been received indicating that he and his entire unit had been taken prisoner. What was worse, Freud noted, was that he had not had any news about Martin's "personal fate" for many weeks—since October 25th. On Christmas day of 1918 (Emanuel's birthday), he wrote to Abraham worriedly that no news had yet been received about Martin, and he still did not know where he was located (if alive). Gloomily, he remarked: "That contributes to the depression of these times."

Writing to Abraham on February 5, 1919, Freud remarked that he still had no news about Martin's condition, but had learned that he was imprisoned at Genoa, Italy. Two weeks later he wrote to Jones (II, p. 253) that he was becoming an old man, and was prepared to die a poor man. (He was age 62 and was plagued by the longterm magical belief that he would die at that age.) In expressing his anxieties about his son, whom undoubtedly he felt he would not live to see again, he complained that: "Martin's captivity is pressing hard on my spirits. Don't you know anyone who is traveling to Genoa where he is detained?"

Freud's grave concerns about Martin continued for at least several more months. On May 22, 1919 Freud's letter to his nephew Samuel in Manchester related that his son was still a prisoner near Genoa, and that he had received letters from him indicating he was in good condition. (Probably, he was not released and permitted to return to Vienna until late summer of 1919.)

The depressed and anxious tone of Freud's letters about his son suggests to me that, in March of 1919, he greatly feared that he might not see Martin alive again—partly stoked by that uncanny fear that he would die before his 63rd birthday in May 1919, after having "dodged the bullet" regarding the February 1918 curse. To these fears was added the great anxiety in March 1919 that Martha might die of her dangerous illness.

Ergo, in March of 1919 Freud greatly feared that his son would die, that his wife might die, and that he would die via that magical curse involving age 62. My thesis is that the strain of these death fears and the awesome privations of his life were too much for his mind to bear, and that it "snapped" again, as it did in July 1914 with Emanuel and in mid-1900 at Achensee with Fliess. In March 1919 his mind sought protection using the great powers of the mystical year 1919, and employed this number magic to arrange for the abduction and killing of John Freud, as a way of relieving increasing psychic pressures that were heading towards flagrant psychosis.

My additional thinking is that in March of 1919 Freud's deranged decision to arrange the kidnapping of John Freud was provoked not only by a triumphant number magic involving "19-19," but also by an upsure of name magic in his mind. This refers to his severe anxieties in March 1919 concerning his son Martin who had been, in one sense, "kidnapped" and imprisoned. Concerning name magic, consider my remarks in a previous chapter that unconsciously Freud had named this eldest son, Jean Martin Freud, not only after the famous French neurologist, Jean Charcot, but also after his dominating nephew, John Freud. (That is, John=Jean=Johann.)

My further suggestion is that name magic might have compelled Freud to arrange the kidnapping of John Freud as a tit-for-tat that imitated the "kidnapping" and imprisoning of his namesake, Jean Freud of Vienna. Emphasis is placed upon my idea that Freud's mind had regressed considerably during the war and sometimes was immersed in the battle-mode of his play with toy soldiers in childhood. Thus, he may have arranged the capture of the English "enemy," John Freud, as a fantasized bargaining ploy that would ensure the safety of his imprisoned counterpart, Jean Freud. Perhaps Freud's instruction to his English henchman was to capture John Freud in Manchester and hold him incommunicado until after his son's release, but that criminal might have decided that the more prudent course of action was to kill and bury John Freud without delay.

Despite the plausibility of the above proposition, which relies upon Freud's strong susceptibility to name magic and an upsurge of his psychotic ideation, I tend to doubt one of its corollaries. It seems dubious that Freud would have instructed his English henchman to take John Freud captive but later to free him, if at some later point Martin were freed from his prison at Genoa. More likely, Freud would have called for the abduction of John Freud followed quickly by his murder, for various reasons. This would have been the safer course for the assassin and for Freud, since "dead men tell no tales." Also, with regard to magical thinking, this would have allowed Freud to obtain the additional years of life belonging to John, as noted in a previous section. Finally, there was the simple matter of revenge and Freud's longterm desire to kill his nephew John that derived from the exigencies of the "Freiberg catastrophe," and his bitter rivalry with John.

Allow me to emphasize that there are various factors and pressures that converge upon the month of March 1919 as the probable time when Freud would have felt compelled to arrange the kidnapping and murder of his nephew. For example, we have noted Freud's increased anxiety, which needed a perverse alleviation, deriving from Martha's dangerous illness that began in March 1919. Also, we have discussed Freud's presumably intensified fears of death relating to the end of his 62nd year, as his 63rd birthday drew nearer—which might have been focused more fearfully upon March 6, 1919, since he surely knew that this was his alternative birthday and probably the correct one. Moreover, we saw that in March 1919 his sadism was directed towards the abrupt interference with Victor Tausk's analytic treatment (leading to his suicide that summer), and towards the culmination of Freud's longterm manipulations that ensured the marriage of Ferenczi to Gizella Pálos. That occurred on March 1st, the day her bereaved husband died of a heart attack (or perhaps suicide).

The above material suggests latent psychotic ideation in March 1919, particularly Freud's brutal behaviors towards Tausk; his destructive manipulations in the Pálos case; and the fears of death at age 62 deriving from his plan to murder Fliess at Achensee. Moreover, that unbalanced thinking in early 1919 was preceded by recurrent hints of madness that were manifested during the later years of the war, as Freud revealed in his letter to Abraham of November 11, 1917. That was the letter in which he expressed great pessimism about the course of the war, mentioned doubts that he'd live to see its conclusion or ever see Abraham again, and referred to the end of the world. In the same letter he hinted that submarine warfare had failed and that Germany had lost the war, followed by mention of a new book by Fliess, which perhaps stimulated ancient fears of retribution. For an upsurge of psychotic ideation then caused him to describe a new Lamarckian project that *he* had just begun, and thereafter spent months "cultivating." (His anxious awareness that the war already was lost may have provoked this deranged thinking, along with jealousy about Fliess's book.)

Freud explained this new project as an attempt to place Lamarck's ideas entirely on the same grounds as psychoanalytic theory. He would do this, he informed Abraham, by showing that Lamarck's concept called "necessity," which he claimed creates and transforms bodily organs, "is nothing but the power of unconscious ideas over one's body . . ," analagous to the claims for "omnipotence of thoughts" found in some mental disorders. Freud then asserted that his new work would supply a psychoanalytic explanation for biological adaptation, and this would become the crowning achievement of psychoanalysis.

In this peculiar wedding of Lamarckian and psychoanalytic theory, Freud offered a hope of providing clinical proof that the unconscious mind has the capacity to alter the growth and development of bodily organs. This is as absurd an idea as any of Fliess's most farfetched biological fantasies, and deserves to be categorized as an instance of psychotic ideation that is perhaps in a class with Freud's endorsements of Fliess's "nasal neurosis" theory. Concerning this new Lamarckian project, Freud hinted that he would demonstrate a sound basis for the "omnipotence of thoughts," which suggests the ability of unconscious ideas to alter bodily processes or even environmental ones. But notice that the "omnipotence of thoughts" constitutes the magical thinking observed in severe mental disorders, such as schizophrenia. By using this language, Freud was inadvertently diagnosing his own state of mind during the late war years, i.e. was disclosing his susceptibility to latent psychosis. Probably, this psychotic ideation had increased markedly by March 1919, given the additional pressures on Freud that month, reflecting a grave mental instability that helped stimulate the plan to abduct and murder John Freud.

John and the Death Instinct

This section will emphasize that in the fateful month of March 1919, designated as the probable month when the abduction of John was arranged, Freud began to draft his weird death instinct theory. In my view, its timing and content, and especially its sudden and radical departure from his previous psychoanalytic theories, can all be seen as relevant to the notion that in March 1919 his thinking became deranged and was directed towards the murder of John Freud. Before attempting to support this argument, I will need to give a brief summary of Freud's death instinct theory, and provide some discussion about its primary features.

Stepansky has specified (Mono. 39, p. 172) that precisely in March of 1919 Freud began to write down his ideas about his new death instinct theory which later appeared in his book *Beyond the Pleasure Principle* (1920). His new theory was a striking departure from his previous theory of the neuroses which had depicted sexuality (Eros) as dominant in human affairs, and had emphasized that two contrasting groups of instincts (sex and self-preservation) were eternally in conflict. The new theory tentatively proposed another dualistic scheme. This time the Life Instinct (Eros) was in conflict with the Death Instinct (later called Thanatos). And now Eros included both the sexual and self-preservative instincts, while the death instinct included powerful drives to return to the inanimate state.

The older theory had emphasized that mechanisms involving the pleasure-unpleasure principle were regulators of stimulation. However, the death instinct theory claimed that new findings had gone "beyond the pleasure principle." In his newer work Freud focused upon the "compulsion to repetition," now used to explain certain clinical and everyday events. He stressed that unpleasurable events repeated themselves in some kinds of children's play, in hysterical symptoms, and in the repetitive dreams of traumatic neuroses. Also, during psychoanalysis there were unconscious revivals of childhood events, as found in transference situations; and in everyday life some individuals will continually repeat negative or destructive actions. In his theorizing Freud concluded that drives do not have a progressive nature, enhancing the development of individuals and the species. Surprisingly, he decided that, in the conflict between Eros and the death instinct, the latter was more basic. Finally, he endorsed Schopenhauer's peculiar teleological notion that "the goal of life is death."

At first Freud proposed these unusual concepts quite tentatively, describing his ideas as "often far-fetched speculation," but over the years he closed his mind and insisted that his new theory was correct. He claimed that the death instinct definitely exists, pointing towards an inexorable tendency involving the decay of all life and an eventual return to the inanimate state. He announced that though Eros and Thanatos are inseparable, life is a temporary compromise with the death instinct which finally must achieve a total, worldwide victory.

Many writers had visited the concept of a death instinct prior to Freud, though none had carried this idea to such extremes. In his autobiography Stekel raised the issue of plagiarism, indicating that Freud had adopted some of his ideas without giving him credit. In one of Stekel's works he had stated that basic anxiety arises from a conflict between the life instinct and the death instinct, but Freud failed to acknowledge this precedent. In 1912 the analyst Sabina Spielrein had absorbed some of Stekel's ideas when she wrote an essay on "Destruction as the cause of becoming," which Freud perused thoughtfully, as her mentor, during her early days in Vienna. There were other precursors of Freud including Von Schubert, who described the wish to die during the later years of human life. Novalis had emphasized teleology by stating that "life is for the sake of death," and claimed that "the characteristic of illness is the instinct of self-destruction." The concepts of destructive and self-destructive instincts were common in the nineteenth century, incorporating the ideas of Hobbes, Darwin, Lombroso, and Nietzsche. Freud might have borrowed some ideas from Fechner who wrote a strange essay which proclaimed that destruction was a more fundamental principle than creation. Also, Freud's new theory seemed to make concessions to Adler's idea of an autonomous aggressive drive, which he had rejected in 1908.

Freud's metapsychology papers of 1915, in which he found the origin of hatred in nonlibidinal ego instincts, were the forerunners of his death instinct theory. As noted by Ellenberger (1970, p. 513), Freud ascribed increasingly greater importance to aggressive and destructive instincts, reformulating many of his clincal conceptions to incorporate them, and "put as much emphasis on these as he had formerly placed on the libido." Considering that no really scientific support existed for the death instinct theory, it was a question of replacing one mad obsession with another, and rather suddenly at that.

Freud hoped that biological advances would someday permit a formulation of his death instinct theory in scientific terms, but even at birth this was a lost cause. Eminent biologists soon proclaimed that there was no biological support for a death instinct, and that it was useless and unscientific to postulate that death was the telos (final aim) of life. Even psychoanalysts had a hard time in finding any merit in Freud's death instinct notion. Jones commented (III, p. 266) that at first there was some acceptance by Freud's most loyal disciples, but three decades later among analysts there was no support at all for this theory. Nevertheless, as with his peculiar endorsements of Lamarckianism, Freud continued for many years to champion his death instinct theory and felt compelled to reinterpret his thinking about various clinical conditions, such as melancholia, in line with the force of the mythical death instinct.

In recent years, apologists for Freud still have not been able to offer sound reasons to support the content of his death instinct theory. It provokes great embarrassment in them (as with Lamarckianism, endorsement of nasal neurosis theory, the writings on Moses and Woodrow Wilson, etc.), so they have struggled to find something nice to say about the death instinct theory. What they have hit upon is the fiction that it shows how flexible and open to new ideas were the channels of Freud's unconscious when at age 63 he quickly demolished his old theory of the mind and suddenly, in 1919, replaced it with the death instinct framework of conceptualization. But nothing could be farther from the truth than the claim that this abrupt reversing of gears demonstrated Freud's flexibility of mind. Instead, this needs to be categorized, more accurately, as a bizarre switch which sometimes accompanies a "snapped mind," i.e. as a reflection of pathological mental processes.

One can imagine how flabbergasted Freud's adoring disciples must have been in 1920 when they first read his ideas about the primacy of the death instinct. Ellenberger wrote that his followers were "greatly surprised;" Clark noted that "it was something of a shock" to them; and Bernfeld wrote that the disciple Fritz Wittels "was amazed at the sudden change in Freud's interests." What these disciples were so astonished by was that the death instinct theory was a revolution without a cause—at least a cause that was observable and convincing. And as stated by Clark, it "called for considerable restructuring of the basis on which psychoanalysis rested." However, Freud had offered very insufficient reasons for that restructuring, and it all had happened so abruptly. Wittels tried to explain this on the basis of a traumatic subjective factor, suggesting that the new theory was provoked by Freud's reaction to the death of his daughter Sophie (on January 25, 1920).

However, Bernfeld noted (1951, p. 124) that Freud had countered Wittels' suggestion in a letter which emphasized that Sophie had died after he had written *Beyond the Pleasure Principle*. Curiously, as noticed by Bernfeld, Freud wrote about this as if he had partly endorsed Wittels' viewpoint, implying that he might have reacted intensely to the death of someone else in 1919. Sagely, Bernfeld inquired: "one may ask whose death is actually responsible for the return of Freud's thinking to his earliest intellectual problem?" She then pondered the death of his nephew Herman Graf, much earlier in the war, and judged that his death "had no influence on Freud's thoughts, and no other relative or close friend died in those four years."

Bernfeld probably was quite wrong in her final remarks, if one accepts my thesis that another of Freud's nephews besides Herman Graf had died during the wartime era. My claim is that one of the cornerstones of Freud's personality structure—his nephew John Freud—not only vanished permanently (equivalent to death), but was actually murdered in 1919. That John was acknowledged by Freud as the cornerstone for key elements of his personality seems quite relevant to his sudden impulse to restructure the entire edifice of Psychoanalysis in 1919. It was as if a mad architect had decided suddenly to present his completed plan for restructuring the Eiffel Tower, in a manner that would abruptly transform it into a full, identical copy of the Empire State building, a megalomanic project that nobody in the world would endorse except himself (and perhaps a few adoring disciples).

Previously, I suggested that Psychoanalysis provided a symbolic representation of Freud's nanny. That is still my belief, but I should emphasize here that his memories of John Freud were closely intertwined with her images deriving from the Freiberg era. Therefore, when John died, presumably in the spring of 1919, that event could have provoked a sudden restructuring of Psychoanalysis in Freud's mind—a restructuring that was imbued with the themes of death and murder. (In a moment, I will explain my belief that the death instinct theory was a coverup and rationalization for the crime of murder, in Freud's unconscious mind.)

Let me put this another way, introducing the factor of Freud's guilty feelings and the irrational ideas they evoked in his attempt to cope with fears about flagrant psychosis in the spring of 1919. The older theory of psychoanalysis had been strongly symbolic of the nanny's sexual and nurturant dominance over Sigi, so the theme of sexuality and love in many guises became dominant in that theory. But perhaps after Freud had arranged for the murders of Emanuel in 1914, and John later, a great problem confronted him, one that first influenced him in 1915 when he brought forth the concept of the murderously hating ego. This problem of guilty feelings regarding murder became greatly exacerbated in March of

1919, when the disappearance of John was arranged, prompting the initial drafting of the death instinct ideas during that same March.

That March of 1919, after having arranged for John's kidnapping and death presumably, Freud's unconscious mind was left with considerable guilt, fear, and a major conceptual conflict. He must have felt suddenly that he could no longer champion a theory in which sexuality and love (libido) were said to determine mankind's affairs when, in his personal life, he had demonstrated twice that his behaviors were dominated by a murderously destructive drive. Partly as an act of atonement, a painful public admission that his previous theory was woefully inadequate, he abruptly concocted his death instinct theory. This was somewhat similar to the sudden departure from his older theories in 1915, after Emanuel's death, when he created the notion of a murderously hating ego—which he endowed with adaptive capacities for men and society as a rationalization that "excused" his own lethal behaviors. Similarly, the death instinct theory was inspired by complex motives that included desires to atone for murder and to rationalize his murderous acts. That is, this new theory could readily be used to excuse the viciously destructive actions of mankind (and Freud), since these behaviors were alleged to be inborn and inevitable.

Since he was frightened and gripped by deranged ideation when he began writing his death instinct theory in the spring of 1919, Freud used it to seek atonement, to calm anxieties by punishing himself, and also to provide himself with subtle excuses for his murderous behaviors in 1914 and 1919. But we can surmise that, as with many other mentally imbalanced persons, there was a strong element of "insincerity" in his effort to punish himself by suddenly proposing a new theory that seemed to demolish his previous decades of theorizing. Both Jekyll and Hyde were at work in the formulation of this new work, but the efforts of the devious Mr. Hyde were dominant. For it was Hyde who manipulated the text so that the new theory turned out to be quite absurd, ultimately posing no real threat to Freud's earlier work.

My proposal is that this new theorizing was an unconscious scam that Freud was not aware of himself, that probably unfolded somewhat as follows. After arranging the murder of John Freud in March 1919, Freud was left with great fear that Fate would mete out some terrible retribution. That could have come in many ways: the death of wife Martha via her dangerous illness; the injury or death of son Martin in his prison camp; the death of Freud in some manner related to the curse concerning his 62nd year, etc. My research shows that he had a history of making magical atonements when faced with the possibility of some awesome punishment by Fate—which he called "Ananke." Since his crime of double murder (Emanuel and John) was extremely grave, it required a rather dramatic act of atonement, in this case the sudden destruction of his own beloved conceptualizations (symbolic of nanny). Indeed, for many years his greatest fear was that one of his unfaithful disciples would betray him by formulating a theory of the mind that would destroy his own great work.

Therefore, in early 1919 Freud's self-destructive urges compelled him suddenly to identify with his betrayers. In effect, he took the roles of Adler, Stekel, and Jung in fantasy and used them, to concoct his death instinct theory. One can say that unconsciously he expropriated some of their ideas about aggression and death, which he wove into a parody of an authentic theory by adopting extreme conceptual positions and absurdly unscientific thinking. With this unconscious strategy he mocked their ideas and demonstrated the superiority of his original theory concerning the libido. Even Jung was drawn into this charade when Freud allowed himself to be influenced by Sabina Spielrein's ideas about death and destruction. For he was aware that she had been Jung's adoring mistress and that the formulation of her essay (reflective of her stormy encounters with Jung) had been "guided" by the Swiss seducer and contained many of Jung's ideas on this grim subject.

Various writers have suggested that Freud's horrified reactions to the widespread carnage and brutalities of the Great War impelled him to conceive the death instinct theory. Although that idea seems plausible, there is no convincing data to support it. Accordingly, Jones's discussion (III, pp. 266-80) failed to emphasize that notion. Like most other analysts Jones was not favorably impressed by the death instinct theory, and he admitted that there was no real scientific evidence for it. His conclusion was that: "If so little objective support is to be found for Freud's .. theory of a death instinct, one is bound to consider the possibility of subjective contributions to its inception, doubtless in connection with the theme of death itself." With regard to subjective factors, Jones described a number of Freud's peculiar ideas and feelings about death which indicated that "his attitude was a rich and complex one with many aspects." For example, he noted that throughout Freud's life he was preoccupied with daily thoughts about death, and also suffered repeated attacks of "dread of death." Jones concluded that Freud's strange and complex attitude towards death, as the master admitted himself, had been derived from "the lasting influence of his death wishes in infancy."

In this manner, Jones implied that the key subjective factors underlying Freud's conception of the death instinct theory were those powerful death wishes toward family members that had arisen during the Freiberg era. For once I agree with Jones. However, much more specifically, my thesis has been that Freud's creation of the death instinct theory was provoked by deranged ideation connected with his ancient death wishes towards his greatest rival in life, his nephew John Freud—and as a reaction to arranging for John's disappearance and murder in the early months of 1919.

The Assassins of Berggasse 19

The preceding section on the death instinct theory seemed somewhat bleak and mournful to me. So I will ask my readers' indulgence in the present section, while I entertain myself by taking a playful stance towards the topic at hand.

First, I will address myself to readers who are still skeptical about my two major theses: that Freud arranged for an assassin to murder his kinsmen, Emanuel and John Freud. Let me add that if I am correct that Freud employed an assassin to eliminate both those men, it is not unreasonable to classify Freud as an assassin himself, albeit an indirect and sly murderer.

Having plausibly labeled Freud as a dangerous assassin, there is an important question that I must raise with my most skeptical readers. If, for argument's sake, they will concede temporarily that Freud might have been an assassin, would their minds be boggled by learning that he was not the only famous male assassin to reside in that same building where he lived for more than 45 years, at Berggasse 19? Perhaps our skeptics' hearts will beat a little faster when I now insist that a famous assassin did reside in that same building.

My next question will seem even more controversial. What if I were to insist that a male assassin, quite famous as a killer in the eyes of Viennese citizens, lived in the very same apartment that Freud occupied for all those years? The minds of some readers might be racing now, if they remember materials in previous chapters indicating that Freud had some very peculiar attachments to that particular apartment having to do with desires for victory over his enemies—in relation to number magic focused upon the number "19" (which appears in his street address).

When I claimed, above, that a famous assassin lived in the very same apartment occupied by Freud, some readers might have wondered whether one of his male servants had been a famous killer. But that was not the case. With tongue in cheek, and for the sake of entertaining my less-skeptical readers, I used language that disguised an important time-factor. That is, the assassin at Berggasse 19 who was famous with the Viennese citizenry had lived in Freud's apartment as a child, just prior to the time when Freud and his family began to live there.

Some readers who are very knowledgeable about Freud's life have realized that I am referring to Friedrich Adler (son of the Socialist leader Victor Adler), who during the war years shot and killed the Austrian Prime Minister whose name was Stürgh. There was a noteworthy "meeting" between this famous assassin and Freud which occurred when Sigmund was a young man and Friedrich was a young child. After having publicly debated and insulted his father, Viktor Adler, Freud later was taken for a visit to Adler's apartment at Berggasse 19 by Heinrich Braun, a kinsman of Adler's who was a dear friend of Sigmund's. On that visit the infant son of Adler, the later famous assassin named Friedrich, was observed by Freud as a member of this Socialist psychiatrist's household.

I hope that my skeptical readers have not suffered annoyance because of my introduction of this material in a lighthearted manner. Understandably, they might say that all of this is poppycock and rubbish. For even if one concedes that Freud saw the assassin Friedrich Adler one time when he was an infant, living at Berggasse 19, surely this could in no way support my thesis that Freud probably was an assassin himself. Of course, if I could prove that Freud had had an ongoing relationship with this assassin, Friedrich Adler, up to the time that he shot and killed the Prime Minister of Austria, that hypothetical relationship with a dangerous killer would generate suspicions that Freud himself was vulnerable to indulging in assassination—requiring further investigation of this entire subject.

However, I must admit to having no evidence at all that Freud had an adult relationship with Friedrich Adler, and I seriously doubt that he ever saw him after that time when Friedrich was age two. Nevertheless, I believe that Friedrich may have had a quite powerful influence on Freud which helped provoke his arranging the disappearance and murder of John Freud in early 1919. There is some plausible evidence, involving psychological and other factors, which supports that belief of mine, as will now be explained.

First, I will suggest that Freud probably had formed a strong fantasy identification with Friedrich Adler in 1917. His letter to Abraham of May 20, 1917 hinted at his depressed feelings (though he denied them) when he wrote that: "Life bears too heavily on me." In this context, he mentioned the current murder trial of Friedrich Adler, noting that he had "been born in the rooms in which we live" and had been seen in this apartment by Freud "when he was a boy of two." Freud introduced this subject by commenting that: "Our inner turmoil here is perhaps nowhere so plainly revealed as it is by the extremely notable trial of F. Adler."

The previous remark indicates that in May of 1917 Freud's mind was experiencing "inner turmoil" with regard to Adler's trial for assassinating the Prime Minister. Indeed, there is a hint here that Freud was following closely the daily newspaper reports of this trial, and one should ask why this was so. It's likely that this was not simple curiosity but was impelled by considerable magical ideation in Freud. Recall Freud's vulnerability to "birth magic," here connected with the fact that this famous killer had been born in Freud's apartment, which itself (along with its number 19)* was immersed in a magical network within Freud's unconscious mind. All of

---

*Concerning number magic, Freud might have believed that the number 19 on this apartment building had ensured Friedrich A. that he would be victorious over the Prime Minister, encouraging Freud to achieve a similar lethal victory over John Freud.

this suggests that Freud must have made an intense fantasy identification with Friedrich Adler, whose father Viktor once had treated Freud patronizingly as if he were a wayward son (equating Sigmund with the Bible's "prodigal son")—which implied that Sigmund and Friedrich both were "sons" of this Socialist leader. This fantasy identification also would have been cemented by the patricidal urges shared by these two men, shown by Friedrich's murder of an obvious father-figure represented by the Prime Minister of his native land.

My suggestion is that in May 1917 Freud coalesced a deranged identification with the famous assassin, F. Adler, and that this helped to provoke his lethal impulses towards John Freud in early 1919—a famous assassination inspiring a lesser one. That is similar to wording I used in the previous chapter when I proposed that the presumed assassination of Emanuel Freud in October 1914 was partly provoked, during the previous summer, by Freud's fascination with the famous assassination of Austria's Franz Ferdinand, which had sparked the Great War. My above suggestion that Freud's identification with F. Adler was a deranged symptom receives some general support from his vulnerability to psychotic ideation in that year, including his letters to Abraham in October and November introducing his Lamarckian project to establish the "omnipotence of thoughts" as a reality. (See prior section.)

The previous paragraph hints that a subtle reinforcement effect might have stimulated Freud's lethal impulses in early 1919. Once the famous assassination of Franz Ferdinand in mid-1914 had helped provoke the killing of Emanuel Freud, that made it all the more likely that Friedrich Adler's assassination of the Austrian Prime Minister in 1917 would reverberate madly in Freud's mind, prompting his murder of John Freud.*
And it's likely that Freud was mystified and fascinated by his realization that two famous assassins had resided in the same apartment at Berggasse 19. Certainly, that amazing coincidence would have appealed greatly both to his dualistic nature and to his pervasive magical ideation.

Finally, our thoughts return to an important question raised in chapter four: did Freud's tendency to act-out the behaviors of figures with whom he had formed fantasy identifications include some famous murderers? Recall that this question had been answered affirmatively by Peter Swales who suggested that Freud was imitating the patricidal behavior of Oedipus when he attempted to kill his father-figure, Wilhelm Fliess, at Achensee in 1900. Now we may have uncovered a second instance of this phenomenon with regard to Freud's imitation of a political assassination by Friedrich Adler, later directed towards a man who had become Freud's "political enemy," his

---

**Chapter four revealed Freud's identification with the professional assassin, Muley Hassan, one of Schiller's characters. Also, he identified with Brutus, in adolescence and in old age.*

English nephew John Freud.

Predictions of John's Murder

The previous chapter cited various behaviors by Freud that occurred in the years and months prior to Emanuel's train death, actions that can be regarded as being predictive of the elder brother's presumed murder in late 1914. Now it is time to review behaviors by Freud that were manifested prior to John Freud's disappearance in 1919 which may reflect Sigmund's desire and intention to murder his nephew and can be viewed as being predictive of that event.

To begin, we need to go back to an item already covered for a closer look. Recall that John Freud made a visit to the Freuds' home in Vienna when Sigmund was age fourteen and John was fifteen. During that visit the two boys put on a playlet for some of Sigmund's school chums by acting out a scene from Schiller's play *The Robbers*. Since this was one of Sigmund's favorite plays and considering his identifications with the two brothers who are its main characters (McGrath, 1986, pp. 25, 80), it is reasonable to believe that it was Sigmund who assigned the two roles from this play that he and John Freud acted out. In a brief duologue involving two denizens of the spirit world, Sigmund took the role of the assassin Brutus and John became his victim, Julius Caesar.

Since Brutus was one of Caesar's murderers, in itself this item may have been predictive of Sigmund's intention someday to murder his nephew John. This event becomes even more lethal when we notice that the name assigned to John in this playlet was Julius, the name of the baby brother for whom Sigmund had borne intense death wishes ever since the Freiberg era. In effect, John's assumption of the name Julius reflected Sigmund's homicidal hatred for John. That lethal animosity derived from their rivalries concerning the nanny who probably seduced both boys during the Freiberg years, when baby Julius was their contemporary.

Sigmund's lethal motives in re-enacting a portion of *The Robbers* with his nephew John were multi-determined. One factor in this play is its patricidal theme, but its greatest emphasis is upon the fratricidal conflict between the brothers Franz and Karl Moor. In a very complex manner, Sigmund identified with both of those murderous Moor brothers (his childhood nickname being "the Moor"), and probably also he identified his nephew with both of them, facilitated by his regarding this nephew as a brother-figure. As a strange replay of Sigmund's and John's rivalry concerning their nanny, the two brothers in Schiller's play are likewise involved in a rivalry over a woman with nurturant, maternal characteristics. An additional aspect of name magic is that this woman's name, in the play, is Amelia—which is the equivalent of the name of Freud's mother, Amalia.

The above material should make us wonder whether Sigmund enmeshed himself and John Freud in that murderous playlet because the boys were involved in intense rivalries over nanny and over Amalia Freud. The latter possibility concerning Amalia Freud may be relevant to data reported by Peter Swales (in McGrath, 1986, p. 67) who cited a letter to Bernfeld by Oliver Freud in the 1940s. This letter revealed that "when John was very young he lived for a year with his grandparents after they moved to Vienna, and .. when he was fifteen or sixteen he visited for a winter in order to learn German."

Since the above letter refers to John's being "very young" during his lengthy visit to Vienna, one can imagine that this occurred when John was about age seven and Sigmund was age six. if so, the timing was during Sigmund's oedipal period, and one can imagine a murderous intensification of his rivalry with John from having to share Amalia's affection with his nephew for an entire year, the mother then being a quite beautiful woman still in her late twenties. It should be obvious that this new information is likely to be relevant to Sigmund's identification with the fratricidal Moor brothers in Schiller's play who vied over their Amalia. All of this enhances the probability that Sigmund's manipulation of that playlet at age fourteen not ohly expressed death wishes against his nephew but the intention someday to kill John Freud.

Before we leave Freud's grim fascination with *The Robbers*, and the strange way in adolescence that he connected himself and John Freud with that play, let's give special attention to an insightful point (p. 69) made by McGrath. It was McGrath who emphasized that Schiller's play has some striking similarities to the Bible's story about Josef, master of dreams, in "many of its themes, particularly the central theme of brother rivalry for the father's inheritance."* Indeed, the play makes some direct references to the story of the Biblical Josef. For example, at one point Schiller's lovable patriarch (called "Old Moor") is mourning the presumed death of his prodigal son, Karl, and he asks Amelia to read from the Bible the story of Josef to console him. But when she arrives in the story at Jacob's mournful response to the report of Josef's death, the Old Moor suddenly feels overwhelmed and falls into a deathlike coma.

Since we know about Freud's intense identification with the dreammaster, Josef, it seems reasonable that he would have identified himself with the references to Josef that appear in Schiller's play, particularly with the hints about Josef's *sudden disappearance* from his father's home due to the machinations of his rivalrous older brothers, who intended to murder him. Probably, Sigmund identified with this hero because he had suffered from sudden disappearances at the hands of his rivalrous "brothers" (Emanuel,

---

This connects with Freud's fantasy that he and John both were Emanuel's sons.

Philipp, and John). First, there had been the sudden disappearance of his nanny, and then the disappearance of himself from the home of his idealized father (Emanuel) who had left for England without him. Thus, in connecting John Freud with a murder victim in *The Robbers*, Sigmund at age fourteen perhaps was signing a retributive promissory note. That is, he promised himself that someday he would arrange for John Freud to disappear from his family's home just as the hero, Josef, and he, Sigmund, had been made to disappear suddenly from their family homes.

An earlier chapter discussed "the Acropolis episode" of 1904 when Freud stood upon that famous precipice in Athens and had a brief psychotic breakdown in which he experienced himself being split into two selves. I explained my view that the precursor and cause of the 1904 event was Freud's guilt and fear about planning and having attempted to kill Fliess by pushing him from a precipice at Achensee in mid-1900. Having failed to kill Fliess at Achensee, Freud immediately took his revenge by assisting the plagiarism of his friend's bisexuality research. His 1904 trip to Trieste and Athens were preceded by intense fear of retribution by Fliess regarding the plagiarism issue. Freud's mental breakdown started in Trieste with depression and delusions that certain baleful numbers were pursuing him, reflecting symptomatic guilt and fear that Fliess's number magic soon would take his life. The experience of depersonalization on the Acropolis was accompanied by a magical defense against flagrant psychosis via a sudden feeling of triumph. Freud explained this triumphant feeling in terms of rivalry with his father, Jacob, noting that merely standing on this famous precipice showed that he had "outdone" his father in life.

My thesis is that this explanation masked deeper rivalries and triumphant feelings that Freud did not wish to acknowledge, particularly his rivalry with Fliess who was a substitute for the greatest rival of all, John Freud. Thus, Freud's victorious stand upon that Athenian precipice reflected his fantasy identification with the Greek hero, Daedalus, who had murdered Talos on that very spot by pushing him off. In effect, Daedalus's murder of his rivalrous nephew was connected with Freud's secret fantasy that someday he would defeat his own contentious nephew by killing him—and probably that he would try to protect himself from Fliess's destructive number magic by doing the same to Fliess. One can say that Freud's triumphant feeling on the Acropolis reflected his promise to himself that eventually he would find a way to relieve persistent inner stresses by murdering John Freud, which he accomplished finally in early 1919.

Mark Kanzer has emphasized (in Kanzer and Glen, 1979, pp. 16, 274, 281, 292) that Freud's brother Alexander, ten years his junior, accompanied him to Athens in 1904. Mentioning scattered references to Alexander in Freud's work, Kanzer claimed that they were suggestive of Freud's death wishes towards Alexander and of desires to kill him "as he had once done in his unconscious with Julius." In his analysis of "the Acropolis episode," Kanzer pointed to Sigmund's wishes to magically exchange identities with Alexander, thereby expropriating ten years of the younger brother's life in order to extend Sigmund's life by a decade, even though this would place Alexander much closer to death. Referring to an historical precedent, Kanzer remarked that: "Such an exchange of death wishes with Wilhelm Fliess had prevailed in 1904." This kind of deadly ideation in Freud was described by Kanzer as: "A Faustian pact with the demons!"

Was Kanzer's previous statement a bit exaggerated and melodramatic? Not at all, as we shall see in the next chapter which reports Freud's identification with Satan and his uses of devils' pacts in the hope of extending his life. Kanzer's above comments, and much data in chapter ten concerning Freud's satanic pacts, are supportive of my prior suggestion about one of Freud's quixotic motives in arranging John Freud's death in early 1919. That suggestion was that Freud's intense fears of dying in February 1918, or in early 1919 at age 62, caused him to arrange John's murder in order to transfer this "curse" to John. The transmitting of this curse to John will seem particularly appropriate when we recall that it had originated with Fliess's lethal number magic against Freud, and that Fliess was a man who had substituted magically for John, in Freud's unconscious mind. In effect, the curse was nullified by placing it back upon its originator, Fliess.

Chapter eight revealed that there were many of Freud's dreams whose homicidal contents were found to be predictive of his intention to murder Emanuel Freud in 1914, particularly his lethal train dreams. Now we must examine which of Freud's dreams were predictive of his intention to murder John Freud.

The two dreams by Freud that were most heavily laden with his desires to slaughter his kinsmen and colleagues were the *Non vixit* dream and the Hollthurn dream. Both of those dreams were cited briefly in the previous chapter as containing elements that were predictive of his intention to murder Emanuel Freud and will now be re-examined concerning his presumed intention to kill John Freud. We will start with the *Non vixit* dream.

The *Non vixit* dream is astonishing in the boldness and rawness with which it exposes Freud's desires to "eliminate" (kill) kinsmen and colleagues, particularly competitors who blocked the satisfying of his pathological ambitiousness. The dream's content and associations parade a series of these figures whom Freud wished to victimize, best exemplified by the moment when Freud turned his lethal gaze (like the basilisk, or even Medusa) upon a "friend" and competitor called P. (Paneth). Under this murderous glance, Josef Paneth's form became indistinct and then "he melted away," i.e. he disappeared. This marked the dream's ending, accompanied by Freud's delighted realization that such persons were merely substitutes or "revenants" (literally, ghosts) who could be made to disappear whenever he wished them to be gone.

Early in his analysis of the dream, Freud noted that it exhibited a "sacrificing to my ambition people whom I greatly value" and that: "The central feature of the dream was a scene in which I annihilated P. with a look." But later he employed nimble and clever footwork to mislead readers into accepting the view that his murderous urges were not significant in this dream and that its key wish was a benign desire that persons who were substitutes could always be found for lost or deceased friends. Not everyone was fooled by that self-serving interpretation, for Shengold (in Kanzer and Glenn, 1979, p. 73) remarked that this destructive dream "deals mainly with death wishes and reproaches for death wishes."

In his discussion of the *Non vixit* dream, and its associations, Freud gave numerous indications that its hidden central character was his nephew John Freud and that its other figures were merely "revenants" of John. For example, he remarked that there was no realistic basis for the dream's hostility towards his friend P., which "must therefore certainly have gone back to my complicated childhood relations to John." Much of Freud's discussion of the dream focuses upon lengthy descriptions of his boyhood rivalries and fights with his nephew John, and remarks about their play-acting during adolescence when they took the roles of Brutus and Julius Caesar in a duologue derived from Schiller's *The Robbers*. Previously, we saw that Sigmund's manipulation of that playlet at age fourteen was loaded with his homicidal feelings towards John, so it carried that same lethal significance within the *Non vixit* dream's associations via the prominent role given to this playlet, within the dream and Freud's discussion of it.

It is my conviction that the core meanings of the *Non vixit* dream concern deadly feelings towards John Freud, particularly involving Sigmund's intention someday to make his rivalrous nephew disappear (die), just as he had made Paneth disappear in the dream by casting that fatal glance at his friend. In effect, this was a prediction that was fulfilled in 1919 with John's mysterious disappearance. The dream association's long discussion of the boys' vicious fighting in childhood encoded Sigmund's murderously vengeful feelings towards John, as was also true of the emphasis placed upon Schiller's playlet concerning Brutus and Caesar, which they reenacted in their adolescent years.

The title of the *Non vixit* dream encodes another crucial person from childhood, an image intertwined with John's, whose painful hidden presence helps explain Sigi's impulses to kill his nephew. Per my previous comments, any use of Latin by Freud signified the secret presence of his seductive nanny, so it is likely that her ghost is concealed within the Latin term *Non vixit*, particularly because the latter word sounds like the English word "vixin." Freud explained that the term *Non vixit* in his dream pertained to his hitting of John, and that in childhood the German verb *Wichsen* was commonly used to signify "hitting." This German verb sounds quite like the English word "vixin," as Freud pointed out. Thereby, he exposed the old woman's ghostly presence, since a Webster's definition of "vixin" includes: "a shrewish, ill-tempered woman." (That is how he had characterized his nanny to Fliess regarding the petulant demands she often made upon Sigi.)

Undoubtedly, therefore, the ancient history about hitting John was tightly connected in Sigmund's mind with the lost nanny. But it was more than that. Her loss was connected with Sigmund's desire to annihilate John and other kinsmen whom he had blamed for her "murder" at Freiberg. Her sudden disappearance, so painfully experienced by the vulnerable child she had seduced, left him with an unquenchable desire someday to retaliate by arranging the disappearance of nephew John. When Sigmund caused Joseph Paneth to disappear suddenly (melt away) in the dream, that was merely a "warmup" for what he intended to do to John and eventually accomplished in 1919.

Readers should not be distracted by the series of Josefs who appear in the *Non vixit* dream and its associations, including Josef Breuer, Josef Paneth, etc. Freud's conflicts with those men named Josef were merely replays of his childhood battles with John Freud. Shengold was correct when he wrote about Breuer's role in the dream that: "This Joseph, Breuer, had become a revenant of John as the enemy, and the closeness between the two men [Breuer and Freud] became 'violent antipathy' . . " In his discussion of the dream Freud gave a hint that all persons in it named Josef could be equated with John Freud, on the basis of name-play. In his childishly magical way Freud noted that persons whose names begin with the same two letters "Fl" were equivalents (like Fliess and Fleischl). Thereby, he implied that men named Josef were substitutes for John, since all their given names begin with the two letters "Jo." Likewise, his discussion of misunderstandings and conflicts with Fliess reflected replays of childhood disputes with John, since previously we noted that Fliess, in his role of a brother-figure, was a substitute for John Freud. (Fliess was also a father-figure at times.) My concluding thought is that, with regard to the *Non vixit* dream, all roads lead to Sigmund's beloved nanny and to the murders of John and

Emanuel Freud.

The second dream by Freud that deserves consideration is the Hollthurn train dream. This dream's manifest content does not expose Freud's murderous wishes towards kinsmen and colleagues in the obvious way that the *Non vixit* dream does. However, an understanding of its complex associations reveals that the Hollthurn dream is perhaps even more reflective of Freud's lethal impulses than the *Non vixit* dream is, particularly against John Freud.

In the first segment of the Hollthurn dream Freud was in a train resting at a station, looking out the window at women on the platform who held up their baskets of fruit, invitingly. Suddenly, he was surprised to learn that his body had been somehow instantly "transferred" into another compartment that included "an English brother and sister" and a shelf of books on the wall, books that sometimes were theirs and sometimes his. This Englishman asked his sister whether she had forgotten a book by Schiller. In an almost forgotten final segment of the dream, Sigmund spoke in English about one of the books, making a simple grammatical error which was self-corrected within the dream, eliciting the Englishman's endorsement of this correction.

Various writers have asserted that the English couple in this dream represented John Freud and his sister Pauline, Sigmund's constant companions in Freiberg. However, these authors failed to emphasize Freud's intense hostility to them in the associations, and that he "ignored" (repressed) that this English couple obviously represented his Manchester relatives, John and his sister. In the dream, this English couple shunned Sigmund, thereby eliciting his "fearful vengeance" upon them, although he concealed from readers the full extent of this revenge. (He did not say whether it included his thoughts or fantasies about murdering them.)

Actually, he must have suppressed murderous anger towards this English couple within the dream, for his associations disclose that he was "longing for some fresh air" yet they blocked him from opening any windows. This was the replay of a conflict he had had on a train in the 1880s, when a male passenger prevented him from opening a window. As Sigmund wrote to his fiancée Martha, he became so enraged that he was quite ready to kill this adversary! This helps us understand that his suppressed feelings towards John Freud in the Hollthurn dream were quite murderous ones.

Immediately after mentioning his desire for fearful vengeance upon his English companion on the train, Freud focused on his instantaneous transfer in the dream from one train compartment to another, and connected this detail to his admitted identification with a patient of his who fearfully believed he had murdered many people during amnesic states. His citation of this lethal identification offers another obvious clue that the core of the Hollthurn dream concerns Freud's immense death wishes towards John Freud, since he noted that this severely imbalanced patient had suffered from a "Cain phantasy." This term was pertinent to Freud's lethal urges towards his brother-figure, John, who is prominently encoded in the dream as the stuffy English gentleman.

In his associations, Freud remarked that his fearful patient had such rabid homicidal inclinations that he felt a compulsion to watch carefully every man who passed him in the street, fearing he might suddenly have killed someone during a brief amnesic episode. So he was compelled, while walking down any street, "to make certain where every single person he met disappeared to," to make sure he had not killed any passerby without knowing it! We need to emphasize Freud's clear identification with this patient who worried enormously about the *disappearances* of numerous persons, fearing that he might have killed them, for it is my claim that this signified Freud's unconscious desire and intention to arrange the disappearance and murder of John Freud.

Concerning the issue of "lethal disappearances," one can argue that this concept also applies to the most striking element in the manifest dream, i.e. Freud's being transferred abruptly from one compartment to another without knowing how this had happened. We don't have to fully accept his explanation that this might have signified an amnesic gap in memory. Just as readily this could have occurred due to the "magical" vanishings and re-appearances that dreams allow to many dreamers. If so, we can take the perspective of a traveler who might have occupied the first compartment with Sigmund, who would have observed his sudden *disappearance*. Ergo, the issue of his abrupt disappearance on the train was encoded in that peculiar detail about his instantaneous transfer between compartments. And that can be related to his boyhood feelings that *he* had disappeared abruptly from his "father" Emanuel's home when the family of this eldest brother had boarded a train headed ultimately for Manchester, "abandoning" him. Undoubtedly, Sigi became murderously enraged that they had disappeared, and in the magical ideation of childhood he must have felt that he also had disappeared, just as Julius and his nanny had disappeared previously. All of this pertained to his vengeful desires that someday he would arrange Emanuel's disappearance from a train, and the disappearance of John Freud as well. So it was appropriate that Freud connected this strange dream detail to feelings of compulsion to murder, in relation to his mentally disturbed patient and to himself.

The previous chapter explained how Freud's desire to murder Emanuel was encoded in the Hollthurn dream, and now we have seen that it likewise incorporates his wish to annihilate John Freud. Death wishes towards the latter individual also were encoded via mention of that Schiller volume on the train, which seemed to belong to both Freud and the Englishman. This sharing of a work by Schiller seems obviously related to the time in adolescence when Sigmund and John shared a duologue written by Schiller, taking the roles of Brutus and Julius Caesar, and thereby provided an outlet for Sigmund's lethal feelings towards his nephew.

Sigmund's death wishes towards John were likewise indicated by a somewhat remote association (1967, pp. 293-4) to the Hollthurn dream in which Freud again discussed the amnesic patient who feared he might kill anyone who passed him in the street. Freud's analysis revealed that the basis for this obsession was the man's impulse to murder his father, which had originated very early in childhood. To protect potential victims of his death impulses he had walled himself up in his room. For he believed that a man like himself "who was capable of wanting to push his own father over a precipice from the top of a mountain was not to be trusted to respect the lives of those less closely related to him . . "

In my view, the above material pertaining to Freud's death wishes that are encoded in the Hollthurn dream reflects his own desires to kill men who were father-figures and/or brother-figures by pushing them over precipices from the tops of mountains. That perverse desire—symbolizing attainment of a paramount position—nearly became actualized in 1900 at Achensee when he tried to push Fliess off a precipice; and in 1904 it occurred again in "the Acropolis episode" in his fantasized imitation of the hero Daedalus, who murdered his nephew Talos, by pushing this very creative rival from a precipice. Since both Fliess and Talos were substitutes for John Freud, it becomes clear that the deadly pushing-from-a-precipice concept found in the Hollthurn associations signifies homocidal feelings towards John that are really quite pervasive in the Hollthurn dream.

Probabably, the lethal "pushing" impulses towards John that are encoded in the Hollthurn dream originated in fights and pushing that occupied Sigi and John in the Freiberg years. In the *Non vixit* associations, Sigi's childhood anger was expressed when he complained to John: "Why did you try to push *me* out of the way?" One wonders if they often played that vicious pushing game called King of the Mountain, and whether Sigi felt humiliated and enraged by regularly being the loser? Or did he feel that John was always pushing him away from his relations with Emanuel and nanny? In any case, it is my assumption that Sigmund's complex infantile feelings and motives that derived from "the Freiberg catastrophe" were the true stimulants for the Hollthurn dream.

In my view, the first segment of that dream depicts the enraged Sigi on the Hell Train that took him away from his beloved nanny, who appears on the platform as a nurturant woman holding up her fruit (or breasts), who is being left behind. Then, it is Sigi's wish to overcome the "disappearance" factor, and he magically joins John and Pauline on their train that was taking them to The Promised Land (England) circa 1859. But in the dream they shun him, showing that he can no longer regard himself as a member of their family, and his retaliation is to transform them into an elderly couple, signifying that he has advanced them much closer to death. This was an indication of Sigmund's desire to steal years from the life of John Freud, magically expropriating them to extend his own life, and of his intention someday to annihilate his nephew.

One final point needs to be made about the Hollthurn dream. Freud indicated that the most important part of the dream was the last portion, the segment under greatest repression, since it was recalled by him only as an afterthought. That was the portion whose meaning would seem to be most mystifying and resistant to interpretation when one realizes that it merely encodes his recognition within the dream that he had made a simple grammatical error, confirmed by the English gentleman (John Freud). My explanation is that this "error" signified his intention to murder John Freud, as this pertains to the 2467 "errors" which he had informed Fliess might still be embedded in the dream book. (Previously, I explained how Freud once slipped and revealed to Fliess that these "errors" were reflections of his homicidal madness.) Furthermore, this grammatical error at the end of the Hollthurn dream makes a firm cross-reference with Freud's recognition within the *Non vixit* dream that he had made a grammatical error regarding the Latin terms *Non vixit* versus *Non vivit* (both symbolic of his rage regarding nanny's loss). This cross-referencing phenomenon shows that the powerful indications of Sigmund's intentions to kill John Freud contained in the *Non vixit* dream are fully applicable to the Hollthurn dream as well. The final promise was that the deadly meanings of those similar Latin terms ('he did not live'; 'he is not alive') would someday be applied to his nephew with deadly force.

According to Jones (II, p. 180), Freud had several dreams "about calamities to his sons, which he interpreted as envy of their youth." By that interpretation, Freud seemed to indicate frankly that this series of dreams about his sons reflected his unconscious wishes that grave harm, or even death, should befall them, giving as the rather simplistic motive that he envied their youth. However, considering that we are fully aware now of his rabid death wishes towards the male members of his family (Julius, Emanuel, John, etc.) we are justified in seeking alternative explanations for Freud's destructive impulses towards his sons in some of his dreams. Concerning dreams involving death wishes towards his eldest son, Jean Martin, it will be my thesis that, at least in part, these represented his desires and intentions to murder John Freud. The primary basis for this thesis is the name magic (discussed previously) which enabled Freud to make a covert equation between his son "Jean" M. and his nephew John, whose given names are equivalents.

Jones wrote about (II, p. 180; III, pp. 389, 403) an especially remarkable dream on July 8, 1915 that Freud had about the death of his son, Jean Martin, noting that it "was one of many" dreams about this son's death that Freud dreamt during the war. However, this dream of July 8th was extremely disturbing to Freud, for it "was so vivid that he awaited news from the Russian front with anxiety." In fact, this dream of his son's death was so vivid that (II, p. 180) it "made Freud wonder if it were not an example of clairvoyance, so he wrote to make inquiries." That is, Freud wrote a letter to his son to learn if he had been seriously wounded near the time of this vivid dream, but there was no clear confirmation of that notion.

The intense vividness of this dream caused Freud to suspect that it was a clairvoyant event—a harbinger of his son's actual death. Alternatively, all of this suggests how very powerful were Freud's death wishes in this dream towards his first-born son, and rival for Martha's affection. If we recognize that this was a replay of the Freiberg rivalry for nanny's affection by two boys who were "seduced" by this woman, it becomes clearer that the covert murderous wishes in this dream were really directed against John Freud. Indeed, it was to perpetuate this rivalry that Freud unconsciously named his first-born son after his hated competitor, John, knowing that he could always defeat the new rival by having exclusive sexual rights to Martha.

Jones wrote that this dream of July 8th was one of only two dreams by Freud which the master regarded as being possibly clairvoyant (III, p. 403). The second dream was also very vivid, involving the premonition that his sister-in-law in England had died, this being Emanuel's wife named Marie. Jones wrote that this dream, like the other one, cost Freud "weeks of anxious waiting before news arrived that both dream victims were safe." By his use of the term "dream victims," Jones indicated his recognition that Freud's son and Marie Freud were "victims" of intense death wishes that produced each of these "clairvoyant" dreams. In the previous chapter I suggested that the death wishes towards Marie were substitutes for Freud's strong desire to murder her husband, Emanuel. Similarly, I regard this other "clairvoyant" dream about Jean Martin as a reflection of Freud's powerful intention to kill his nephew John Freud, the son of Emanuel and Marie.

In 1919 Freud inserted into the dream book one of his dreams about calamities that could have happened to his son Jean Martin during his wartime service, this probably being the dream of July 8, 1915. A shortened version of this dream follows.

The dream started when Freud told his wife that he had some special news for her. This alarmed her and she refused to listen. He began to tell her that their son's officer's mess had sent a sum of money, something pertaining to "distinction" and "distribution." Suddenly, Freud saw his son Jean Martin appear and he was not in uniform but in sports clothes. This son stood beside a cupboard, as though he wanted to climb onto the cupboard, to put something on top of it. Freud called out to him but got no reply. It seemed that his face or forehead was bandaged, that he was adjusting something in his mouth, and that his hair was flecked with grey. Freud wondered whether his son was very exhausted and had false teeth? At this point Freud awakened, without anxiety, but with his heart beating rapidly.

Early in his associations Freud mentioned that for more than a week he had been without news of Jean Martin, his son, who was fighting at the battle front. He wrote that: "It was easy to see that the content of the dream expressed a conviction that he had been wounded or killed." As noted by Freud, the dream's mention of a "distinction" referred to honors awarded to an officer who had fallen in battle, and also there would have been a "distribution" of Jean Martin's belongings upon his death.

The element of climbing in the dream (re the cupboard), and Jean Martin's sports clothes, were connected by Freud to his son's being an avid mountain climber and skier, once having had a serious fall in which he broke his thigh. His position in the dream next to a cupboard reminded Freud of an accident of his own when he was between two and three years old. Sigi had climbed upward to reach something on top of a cupboard, then had slipped and fallen, badly injuring his jaw. Freud admitted that all this pointed to a "hostile impulse aimed at the gallant soldier" (constituting his vicious death wishes towards his son) but ultimately he softened this by claiming it merely involved "envy which is felt for the young by those who have grown old."

There are various clues in the above material that the murderous feelings which Freud directed towards his son by arranging for his symbolic death in the manifest dream, were merely substitutions for his desire and intention to kill John Freud. For example, in this dream Freud converted his son into an old man by giving him grey hair and false teeth. Thereby, he moved him much closer to the time for dying, just as he had done to John Freud in the Hollthurn dream by converting him into an elderly English gentleman (towards whom he felt great hostility). To some extent, this indicates that John in the Hollthurn dream can be equated with Jean M. in the wartime dream.

Likewise, in the Hollthurn dream's associations Freud had expressed covert homicidal intentions towards Fliess and John Freud in connection with the topic of mountain climbing. That is, Freud had identified himself with the patient who felt urgent compulsions to murder many people, and also wished to kill his father by pushing him off a precipice on top of a mountain, which is what Freud wished to do to Fliess and John. This is why Freud unconsciously incorporated Jean Martin's mountain climbing accident into this wartime dream. Since this son was a substitute for Freud's nephew, his accident on a mountain was dredged out of Freud's memory and inserted into this wartime dream's associations as a reflection of his desire to kill Fliess and John in a similar manner.

In this dream about Jean Martin, the mention of a cupboard (*Kasten*) also had relevance to Freud's murderous wishes towards John Freud. This was connected to a horrendous childhood memory about Freiberg when Sigmund stood next to a *Kasten*, believing that Amalia/nanny had been locked up in this "coffin," thereafter reflecting his feelings of homicidal revenge against his dominant male kinsmen, including John. The recollection of the injury to Sigi's jaw, which took place beside a *Kasten*, signified self-punishment for those murderous desires towards John Freud and others. (Freud offered this wartime dream as an example of a self-punishment dream—one that punishes the dreamer for a forbidden impulse.)

Perhaps there is another aspect of this wartime dream that encodes Freud's desire to kill John Freud. In the dream, Freud suddenly saw his son appear, as if by magic, though actually he was hundreds of miles away at the fighting front. This again raises the question of a man's sudden appearance and disappearance, as was also seen in the Hollthurn dream when Freud instantly was transported from one train compartment to another. In interpreting that element, I posited that it pertained to Freud's intention someday to arrange the sudden disappearance of John Freud from his home. If so, it seems plausible that this interpretation is applicable to this sudden appearance/disappearance in the wartime dream that concerns a wish for Jean Martin's death, especially because Freud's son was a substitute for John Freud. There is ambivalence of motivation underlying the dream, since Jean Martin, or his ghost, is transported to the safety of his home, signifying his sudden disappearance from the fighting front. Thus, the dream wishes are ambivalent about this son, directing towards him both death impulses and magical transport to a safe home, although the element of "disappearance" also reflects the wish to murder John Freud (perhaps substituting his death for the son's).

Finally, one suspects that there was special significance in Freud's inserting this dream into the dream book in the ominous year, 1919. The notion that this was done in 1919 mainly because of his heightened anxiety about his son's imprisonment, during the first half of that year, seems very questionable. To the contrary, Freud should have experienced strong feelings of shame and guilt about exposing this dream publicly in 1919, since it reveals obvious lethal wishes towards his imprisoned son. Then why did he overcome that prohibition and publish this dream in 1919? My answer is that, in his unbalanced state of mind, he could not resist exposing the dream's covert message of death towards John Freud. Thereby, he showed that 1919 was his magical "year of triumph" in which he had accomplished the ultimate defeat of John Freud by arranging for his disappearance and murder.

The Destruction of Woodrow Wilson

One of the strangest and most self-revealing books that Freud ever wrote was the psychobiography titled *Thomas Woodrow Wilson: A Psychological Study* (1966) which he co-authored with the American diplomat William C. Bullitt. This work will be given considerable attention, because it helps confirm Freud's powerful identifications with Jesus and Satan, his recurrent periods of psychotic ideation, and that he probably made arrangements in March of 1919 to murder John Freud.

It was reported by Clark (1980, pp. 474-7) that while Freud was in Berlin in 1930 he was visited by the American diplomat William C. Bullitt, whose second wife had been a patient of Freud's. Bullitt found Freud to be "greatly depressed," but he perked up when he learned that Bullitt was preparing to write a book on the Paris Peace Conference of 1919, which Bullitt had attended as a minor assistant to President Wilson. According to Bullitt, Freud astonished him "by saying he would like to collaborate with me in writing the Wilson chapter of my book." At first, Bullitt resisted the idea, but Freud was very persistent and eventually the men decided to collaborate in writing a psychobiography of President Wilson. It was decided that Bullitt would provide the historical material on Wilson's life and career, and Freud would supply the psychological interpretations of his personality. Although there was a pretense that both men collaborated on each sentence of the book, Bullitt's historical segment on Wilson's early years was only 31 pages long, whereas Freud's portion (the psychological study) comprised most of the remaining 260 pages.

At the conscious level of Freud's mind, it is obvious that his well-known hatred towards Wilson motivated him to write this biography as a way of destroying the president's reputation, although we will see that Freud's unconscious again was telling his own story, as he also did in his Moses volume. In his introduction to the book (p. xiv) Freud vigorously denied a "misconception" that the Wilson book was written "with a secret purpose to prove that Wilson was a pathological character . . in order to undermine in this roundabout way esteem for his achievements. No! That is not our intention." As Freud liked to say about other dishonest authors: "the lady doth protest too much."

Roazen has written a long epilogue (1968) about the Wilson biography in which he stated that: "It was axiomatic among Freud's pupils that he hated Wilson." We will need to keep in mind that the reasons for Freud's hatred of Wilson went back to crucial actions of the president during the Paris Peace Conference in March and April of 1919, the very months previously emphasized as those in which high stress might have caused Freud's mind to snap, perhaps prompting him to arrange John Freud's disappearance.

In that same year, during the summer of 1919, Ernest Jones made his first trip after the war to visit Freud in Vienna. One of the topics that Jones and Freud discussed was Wilson's futile behaviors at the Peace Conference, those negotiations having reached a critical stage during the previous March and April. According to Jones, Freud "had hard things to say about President Wilson, whose vision of a friendly Europe based on justice was rapidly becoming illusory." (III, p. 16) When Jones tried to defend Wilson, noting that the situation was very complex and that the peace settlement could not be dictated by any one man, Freud replied: "Then he should not have made all those promises." Similarly, a later work by Freud referred with hostility to the "fantastic promises of the American President's Fourteen Points." In the Wilson biography Freud called Wilson a dangerous fanatic who thought he was God, compared him to the pathetic figure of the balmy Don Quixote, and admitted the "antipathy" he felt for Wilson.

A careful reading of the Wilson biography will convince most readers that Freud's exaggerated portrayals of Wilson's personality defects were barely able to conceal this analyst's venomous hatred for his subject. Apparently, he feared that his vicious intentions towards Wilson might be recognized by many sensitive readers. This prompted him to insert in the book's introduction that transparent disclaimer which vehemently denied that the volume's secret purpose was to prove that Wilson had been mentally imbalanced during crucial periods of his life, in order to undermine the public's esteem for his achievements. Moreover, there are reasons to believe that William Bullitt also harbored antipathy and resentful grudges against Wilson for personal reasons. Roazen cited (1968, p. 310) a remark made by a patient who was close to Freud and his family, as follows: "Bullitt and Freud fell in love at first sight on the basis of their hatred of Wilson." Also quoted by Roazen was the American diplomat Allen Dulles who stated that each of these authors "appears . . to be a man bitter towards Woodrow Wilson and, as over long years they worked together on this book . . undoubtedly the bitterness of the one played on that of the other . . "

Roazen has discussed (1968, p. 311) some of the political and economic factors pertaining to the ending of the Great War that helped generate Freud's hatred for Woodrow Wilson. During the waning days of the war,

Freud at first agreed with many other Austrian citizens who regarded Wilson as a "savior" who would fulfill his repeated promises to use the Fourteen Points in ways that would ensure "complete justice" for the defeated nations, particularly Germany and Austria. However, Wilson's good intentions were no match for the secret diplomacy of the major Allied powers, especially England and France, and eventually the Treaty of Versailles imposed a disastrous peace agreement that dismantled Germany's colonial empire and military complex, extracted very costly war reparations, etc. More painful for Freud and other Austrian citizens was the downfall of the Austro-Hungarian Empire, the wresting of lands from Austria's control, and other economic sanctions. Strangely, Freud placed the major blame for this catastrophe on the shoulders of Woodrow Wilson, including the tragedy of Vienna's being wrecked economically and that Freud lost most of his savings.

Obviously, Roazen was aware (p. 311) that there were psychological and "personal reasons" that were considerably more potent than the above socioeconomic factors in generating Freud's rabid hatred for President Wilson. Roazen's perceptiveness was demonstrated when he hinted that Freud initially had formed a strong positive identification, and then a negative one with Wilson, citing many ways in which the two men were alike. That this was largely a magical or fantasy identification was sensed by Roazen in his first comment on this matter. He remarked that a "crucial clue" concerning this identification was provided by Bullitt, who stated that Freud "had been interested in Wilson ever since he had discovered that they were both born in 1856."

In this fashion, Roazen exhibited awareness that Freud's fantasy identifications sometimes were prompted by variations of "birthday magic" (pertaining to deep concerns about his own questionable birthdate and paternity). Roazen commented that persons who had studied Freud's life carefully "would spot such an identification as characteristic," supporting this remark with the instance when young Sigmund had established an identification with one of Napoleon's generals largely on the basis of their shared birthdays (100 years apart).

Concerning Freud's presumed identification with Wilson, Roazen added that: "It need not be surprising that there was an identificatory tie between Freud and Wilson if we assume that there must be some explanation for the empathy which any psychological study presupposes." In the case of the Moses biography, Roazen remarked, Freud used him as "a projective screen" and seemed to recognize partly that the Moses book was autobiographical, incorporating key aspects of Freud's life story. On several pages of Roazen's critique he insisted that the Wilson biography also was autobiographical for Freud, but a telephone conversation (p. 312) with Bullitt convinced him that: "neither Bullitt nor Freud ever guessed that this study was in any way autobiographical on Freud's part." The present writer is in full agreement with Roazen that, in many ways, the Wilson book is autobiographical for Freud and that he projected numerous aspects of his own history and psychopathology into his descriptions of Wilson's life and personality. (In some instances, this probably was based upon shared pathology rather than merely distortions of reality by Freud.)

After emphasizing that Wilson and Freud were born in the same year, Roazen cited many other similarities between the two men that might have helped Freud to identify with the American president. Here is Roazen's list of similarities, with brief discussion of some items. 1. The Wilson book emphasized the president's "pleasures connected with his mouth, especially his talent for rhetoric." It is well known that Freud smoked constantly, and had impressive abilities as an orator. 2. Freud often kept women around him "as an audience for his ideas," and Wilson did likewise. 3. Freud had early ambitions to be a political leader, similar to Wilson. 4. "Freud was a man with a mission, like Wilson . . " (Erich Fromm wrote a small book about Freud's mission-oriented goals, and the book with Bullitt is filled with Wilson's messianic behaviors.) 5. Both Wilson and Freud were men with one-track minds. 6-7-8. Both men grew up surrounded by sisters; both worked without secretaries at times; and both became invalids. 9. Both men lived in relative isolation.

Roazen emphasized (p. 313) that "the whole treatment of the theme of betrayal and persecution" which Freud saw in Wilson "is most strikingly relevant to Freud himself . . " Both men were "among the world's great haters" of their adversaries and both men "were fighters who never forgave their opponents." When Wilson's and Freud's old opponents at times tried to effect reconciliations, neither of these two men would grasp the olive branch of forgiveness.

It was implied by Roazen (p. 314) that the repeated theme of betrayal-by-disciples in Freud's portrayal of Wilson's life was quite similar to Freud's problems in that area. A major thesis in the Wilson biography is that the president was ruled by a father-complex which made him stumble at many critical points in his career. Roazen noted that in Freud's life controversies often were focused upon the father-son theme (echoing the early biography by Maylan whose main thrust is that Freud suffered from a father-complex). According to Roazen: "Freud had to become a father, to escape being a son; to be bested always meant to be put back into the role of a son." Similarly, Roazen claimed that the underlying motivation which Freud discerned in Wilson's handling of "younger disciples fits Freud's own life perfectly." Not surprisingly, both of these authoritarian leaders were afflicted by repeated betrayals or defections of their most cherished disciples whom they had forced into the roles of sons.

In discussing the many ways that the Wilson book was autobiographical for Freud, enabling him to project his most vicious and destructive characteristics into his subject unwittingly, Roazen (p. 315) concluded that: "It seems to have been welcome to Freud to have such a projection of his worst self in Wilson, without being identified." Unfortunately, however, Roazen did not come close to revealing the very worst, most insane and dangerous aspects of Freud's personality that he projected into the image of Wilson in this biography. In subsequent paragraphs I will attempt to fill in the gaps, since eventually this untold story will help confirm that Freud arranged the murder of John Freud in 1919.

To begin my coverage of similarities between Wilson and Freud that were not mentioned by Roazen, I will emphasize Freud's repeated allegations that Wilson, over the course of his lifetime, suffered from fourteen or more episodes of severe mental breakdown due to his persistent inability to cope with heavy stresses in his life. Allegedly these "nervous breakdowns" were sometimes so disruptive that they forced Wilson to take calming trips abroad to restore his faculties to working order, and these breakdowns were said to occur even during his presidencies of Princeton University and of the United States. It is my judgment that Freud wished us to suspect that perhaps many of Wilson's periodic breakdowns were reflective of underlying psychotic processes. There is little doubt that this was his intention concerning his discussion of two alleged breakdowns that occurred in early 1919 during the Paris Peace Conference, and regarding his very questionable claim that Wilson descended into a paralyzing psychosis during the final years of his life.

About all of this, let me remind my readers of my persistent claims that throughout Freud's lifetime he suffered from numerous periodic episodes of borderline psychosis, and that probably he suffered one of them in the early months of 1919. Ergo, it is my suggestion that one of the essential factors that caused Freud to identify with Wilson was his assumption that there were similar periodic episodes of mental imbalance in the president's life. However, it is not unlikely that Freud exaggerated the severity of some of Wilson's episodes, particularly during 1919 and the alleged severe psychosis during the final years of Wilson's life (which reputable historians apparently have not endorsed).

There are various themes in the Wilson biography which Freud used to stimulate our suspicions that psychotic processes often bubbled dangerously close to the conscious level of Wilson's psyche. One of them was the repeated claim that Wilson thought he possessed Godlike qualities and apparently even identified himself with God-the-Father. This was an obvious hint about grandiose and megalomanic aspects of Wilson's personality, which Freud related to his father's having been an eminent

Christian minister with grand pretensions whom young Woodrow utterly adored and idolized. At one point, Freud asserted (1966, pp. 127-8) that compensation for a personal defeat caused Wilson to become unconsciously both "God the Father as well as God the Son. The extraordinary confidence in his own righteousness, the ability ruthlessly to push on to power . . leave no doubt as to what had happened in his unconscious." Freud claimed that thereafter a segment of his unconscious unfailingly told Wilson: "You are God. You are superior to all men. Whatever you do is right because you do it." He cited this as Wilson's "identification with God."

As I have discussed in various sections of the present book, Freud himself had made identifications with God—including Jehovah, Zeus, Jesus, etc.—as one aspect of his own grandiose and megalomanic functioning. His disciple Fritz Wittels made the earliest assertion that Freud suffered from a "Jehovah complex," which Freud denied quite firmly. Clark has discussed (1980, p. 476) Bullitt's comments about his combative collaboration with Freud on the Wilson book. With frankness, Bullitt admitted that both he and Freud were "extremely pig-headed" and "somewhat convinced that each one of us was God."

On more than one occasion Freud wrote letters to colleagues describing himself as the most righteous and moral of men, this absurd lie surely deriving partly from his own identification with Almighty God (probably as a reaction to intense self-hatred emanating from his "monstrous" sexual behavior with his primal mother). It was this identification with God that allowed Freud to push himself ruthlessly on to power, a characteristic which he saw in Wilson whom he alleged was a vicious double-crosser of friends and trusted allies. That this accusation was partly a projection by Freud is seen in various instances when he double-crossed his own friends and allies: the time when he robbed Fliess of his bisexuality research via Weininger; his similar action when he passed on Jones's research about Napoleon to Dr. L. Jekels; the time when he elevated Jung to the analytic presidency, betraying his Viennese disciples; his lethal manipulation of Tausk in 1919, etc.

It is astonishing to me that Roazen failed to mention Freud's repeated claims that Wilson had identified himself, in quite irrational ways, with Jesus Christ. Surely this was one of the major themes of the biography and a crucial aspect of Wilson's personality, according to Freud's analysis. Freud placed such great emphasis upon Wilson's alleged identification with Jesus Christ that he made references to this identification on more than 50 pages of his psychological study of Wilson. On many of those pages there were two or three separate items pertaining to Wilson's presumed identification with Jesus, so I would estimate that the total number of references to this topic reached 100 items or more. The book's Index, on page 306, lists only about

30 pages relating to Wilson's "identification with Christ" and twelve pages pertaining to his "identification with God." Similarly, page 305 lists ten pages relating to Wilson's belief that he was "chosen by God."

Certainly, Freud knew that millions of modern Christians have formulated positive identifications with Jesus that help them to develop benevolent, moral characteristics in their lives. But it is clear that he believed that Wilson's identification with Jesus sometimes went far beyond any rational limits. Freud indicated that Wilson at times acted-out his identification with Jesus, perhaps in somewhat balmy ways. In this regard, he pointed to unusual behaviors during Wilson's presidency which suggested that he was imitating Jesus in his role as "Savior of the World." Likewise, Freud pointed to Wilson's seemingly grandiose behaviors intended to achieve worldwide peace, which hinted that he was imitating Jesus's role as the "Prince of Peace." In doing so, Wilson often made public statements indicating the world's need to follow the moral principles of Jesus, prompting many citizens of war-torn nations to regard him fervently as a "savior." Finally, Freud asserted that Wilson's imitations of Jesus at times generated irrationally destructive behaviors that harmed millions of people. He cited Wilson's Christlike actions at the Paris Peace Conference that relied upon futile peaceful actions towards his adversaries instead of the aggressive and punitive behaviors that were necessary to achieve constructive results that would have benefitted all the world's people for decades.

As I have mentioned briefly in the present book, and extensively in *Dark Side*, Freud himself made intense identifications with Jesus Christ (the foremost hero of his nanny) which he acted-out in his grandiose role as a "great healer" and leader of the worldwide "religious" cult called Psychoanalysis. As noted previously, Freud's identifications with Jesus and Satan were connected with an intermingled Jekyll/Hyde theme in his personality structure. With Freud the Satan identification was largely conscious and the Jesus identification was almost entirely repressed, whereas just the opposite balance may have been true, to a lesser extent, with Wilson.

Freud indicated that the aggressive and Satanic side of Wilson was quite repressed, apparently connected with his inability to express murderously angry feelings towards his sainted father. Concerning Freud's claim that there were lethal consequences of Wilson's identification with Jesus, my suggestion is that this was largely a projection of Freud's irrational behaviors as a megalomanic healer whose "accidental" or unintentionally destructive behaviors sometimes inflicted death on patients like "Mathilde" and patient-surrogates like Fleischl and Tausk, as well as the near-deaths of others like Emma Eckstein.

One wonders whether Freud's obsessive interest in Wilson's identification with Jesus was prompted by Freud's secret rage towards the president for attempting to usurp his own messianic role on a worldwide stage. On this score, some readers will be reminded of the clinical study titled *The Three Christs of Ypsilanti*. This work discusses three mad inmates of the asylum at Ypsilanti, Michigan, each of whom believed that he was the genuine reborn Christ, causing each savior to become enraged towards his two insane rivals. This example, and others like it, teaches us that the most hated enemy of a mad Jesus is not a mad Satan, but another mad Christ who is a competitor. Perhaps this can help to explain why Freud harbored such a passionate hatred for Woodrow Wilson?

At this point, we have learned a great deal about Freud's hidden identification with this American president whom he obviously hated and despised, and about his tendency to project aspects of his own psychopathology onto Wilson (sometimes abetted by genuine similarities between the two men). Moreover, it is reasonable to assume that the characteristics that Freud hated most in Wilson were ones that he secretly despised in himself. Probably, that aspect of his own self which Freud had most reason to despise was that he was a cowardly murderer. Ergo, that point will soon bring us to the issue of whether he likewise regarded Wilson as an infamous murderer, which we will find to be strangely connected with a key question: Did Freud arrange the murder of John Freud in 1919?

Now we have arrived at that portion of the Wilson biography which Freud offered as the climax of the president's life and career. This involved a presentation of "evidence" that Wilson suffered an alleged borderline psychosis at the Paris Peace Conference of 1919, thereby generating confused behaviors that dashed the aspirations of the civilized world for longterm stability and peace.

It is my impression that Freud used much of the beginning three quarters of his psychological study of Wilson to provide tortuous analytic interpretations of the president's motives and inner dynamics, in ways intended to convince readers that Wilson harbored severe psychotic tendencies. For example, on page 160 Freud alleged that Wilson in 1915 not only had an unconscious identification with Jesus Christ that made him strive for world peace, but also nurtured a contradictory unconscious identification "with the Hebrew Jehovah who delighted in smiting his enemies, and his SuperEgo was constantly demanding that he should become the ruler of the world." However, Freud provided no convincing basis for the claim that Wilson had identified with a violent Jehovah nor that his psyche was split by a Jekyll/Hyde conflict between a peaceful Jesus image and an angry, destructive image of Jehovah. In my opinion, that was a projection of Freud's inner dynamics. In this manner, utilizing an unsupported accusation that Wilson concealed an extreme megalomanic desire to become the ruler of the world, Freud encouraged us to believe that Wilson was essentially a madman, so that we would later accept his central thesis that Wilson became overtly insane at the Paris Peace Conference, thereby ensuring the eventual destruction of the civilized world. (Particularly relevant is Wittels' claim in 1924 that Freud suffered from a "Jehovah complex," an accusation that he later withdrew.)

In the 26th chapter Freud focused upon the Paris Peace Conference whose negotiations in the early months of 1919 were expected to establish a lasting peace. At that meeting Wilson contended vigorously with two major adversaries, the famous British leader Lloyd George and Clemenceau of France. In the first paragraph of this chapter Freud "set up" his readers to accept his later thesis about Wilson's psychotic breakdown at the conference by the way he described the events of January and early February during Wilson's first five weeks in Paris (prior to his returning temporarily to America in February before resuming negotiations at Paris in March). It was alleged by Freud that during those initial five weeks Wilson "worked harder than he had ever worked in his life [and] . . was not used to hard work." Freud indicated that this hard work caused Wilson's physical and emotional defenses to break down, claiming that when he embarked for America "he was close to physical and nervous collapse." Slyly, Freud added that "his mental condition may be judged from his self-deception in the matter of the preliminary treaty." (Later, Freud alleged that Wilson's extreme mental confusion while negotiating this preliminary peace treaty caused him to utterly botch this crucial negotiation, leading to a final treaty that was a total negation of America's proclaimed position to achieve a just peace.)

On February 24, 1919 Wilson's ship landed in Boston and Freud claimed that immediately he attacked his domestic opponents "in an emotional address" that Freud hinted was filled with balmy notions that presaged the president's mental collapse upon his return to Paris. In describing this public address Freud stated that: "Many portions of his speech show that he had lost touch with reality." Coming from a famous analyst, those words surely were intended to signify that Wilson was starting to surrender to madness, but when Freud proceeded to offer quotations from this speech they were devoid of any convincing evidence that Wilson was becoming insane.

Likewise, in describing Wilson's behaviors after he returned to the Paris Peace Conference in mid-March, Freud's language tendentiously reinforced the unfounded idea that Wilson's mind quickly became submerged in near-madness—as evidenced by allegedly contradictory and quixotic actions of the president during the period from March 14th to March 17th. According to Freud, Wilson returned to the negotiating table on March 14th with the full intention to endorse his Fourteen Points and creation of a League of Nations without making any real compromises to Lloyd George or Clemenceau in these matters, nor about their fervent desires to impose a hard, punitive peace treaty on Germany, Austria, and other Central powers. However, in the 27th chapter Freud required only a few unconvincing pages to describe the American president's extreme mental confusion and eventual quixotic concessions that amounted to a total defeat of his position, which Wilson nonetheless regarded as a victory (as only a presumed madman would interpret the events depicted by Freud).

In evaluating the above ambivalent behaviors by Wilson—which more charitable historians might attribute to his strong fears of renewed hostilities that might destroy various European nations and eventually permit their takeover by Lenin's communist forces—instead Freud (p. 240) insisted that they were the products of Wilson's incipient madness. He claimed that the president's actions provided "evidence of the divorce from reality which was beginning to characterize Wilson's mental life." Furthermore, Freud indicated that it was Wilson's identification with Jesus Christ that generated his allegedly autistic thinking and actions.

Strongly insisting that in mid-March Wilson was succumbing to psychosis, Freud wrote that: "He was rapidly nearing the psychic land from which few travelers return, the land in which facts are the products of wishes, in which friends betray and in which an asylum chair may be the throne of God." To this picture of Wilson's accelerated mental disintegration, Freud added (p. 246) that on April 3rd the American president "collapsed in a complete nervous and physical breakdown," causing him to surrender unnecessarily to Lloyd George and Clemenceau in ways that (p. 255) "wrecked the economic life of Europe." In a few subsequent chapters Freud alleged that Wilson's psychic deterioration continued steadily after April, as he was forced to realize that he was not Jesus nor the savior of the world. By September 6, 1919 the dawning awareness by Wilson of his supposedly infamous behavior in Paris (p. 286) "had driven him close to psychosis." Thereafter, by Freud's account, on September 26, 1919 Wilson collapsed *on a train** and then retreated into psychosis where he vegetated for the next four years, until his death on February 3, 1924.

Now we are in a position to evaluate Freud's intense identification with Woodrow Wilson, his strong tendency to project his own psychopathology onto Wilson, and his unfounded claim (or personal fantasy) that Wilson became immersed in a near-psychotic state of mind on March 14, 1919 that eventually had lethal consequences for most of the world. Our first question

---

*Notice that Freud alleged that Wilson's final retreat into psychosis began on a train (p. 287).

is this: What did Freud's fantasy about Wilson's near-psychosis in March 1919 really signify? My answer is that Freud was projecting onto Wilson his own state of mind in March of 1919, as well as its lethal consequences for John Freud. This will receive some elaboration below.

In a previous section of this chapter, I pointed to Samuel Freud's letter to Sigmund of May 22, 1919 advising him of John Freud's disappearance, and I deduced that Sigmund probably initiated arrangements for that murder in March of 1919. That hypothesis made sense to me due to the time that might be needed (several months) to set-up such an assassination, and also because there were various indications that March of 1919 was a remarkably stressful time for Freud. It was my observation that by March those stresses were so intense that they probably caused Freud's mind to "snap" again, as presumably also occurred in the summer of 1914 as the harbinger of Emanuel's assassination several months later, in October 1914.

Concerning Emanuel's "accident" in 1914, I emphasized the probable significance of Freud's near-psychotic condition several months earlier, as testified by Ferenczi's description of Freud's near-psychosis during the Hungarian's visit to Vienna that summer. Concerning the case of John Freud's disappearance, when I posited that March 1919 was the most likely month that Freud would have arranged that assassination, many readers must have compared the second presumed assassination with the first one and asked themselves: Is there any evidence that Freud suffered a borderline psychosis in March 1919, similar to his mental crisis in the summer of 1914? Now, in due time, the Wilson biography has offered some fairly convincing evidence that Freud did suffer a near-psychotic episode in March of 1919, and that evidence comes from Freud's own pen. In concocting the fantasy that President Wilson was nearly psychotic in March 1919, Freud's unconscious mind proclaimed boldly that he, himself, was a hairsbreadth from flagrant psychosis in that same month. That is, he projected his presumed borderline madness of March 1919 into his famous alter ego, in that highly tendentious psychological study of Woodrow Wilson.

But there is more to be said about this matter, which requires me to return to Freud's suspect account of Wilson's state of mind just before he confronted Lloyd George and Clemenceau at the Paris Peace Conference on that fateful day of March 14, 1919. First, it is important to emphasize Freud's claim (or fantasy) that Wilson harbored an unconscious desire to be the wrathful Jehovah (p. 169) and that unconsciously he had identified himself (p. 160) with "the Hebrew Jehovah who delighted in smiting his enemies . . ," in contradiction to his identification with a loving Jesus. Thereafter, Freud became a mind-reader (pp. 235 ff.) who was able to plumb Wilson's private intentions as he rejoined the negotiations on March 14th. He asserted that Wilson met his two great adversaries "determined to lift the negotiations to the plane of the Sermon on the Mount, determined to make no compromises . . " However, if unable to convert his enemies to the path of righteousness, he was also just as determined "to wield the weapons of Jehovah" against them by using America's financial might to destroy them economically.

Freud asserted that initially Wilson was determined to wield the swords of Jehovah against Lloyd George and Clemenceau, if they did not submit to his righteous will. He wrote: "That Wilson, on March 14, 1919, was determined to use these masculine weapons rather than submit to an evil peace is certain." (p. 235) But according to Freud, when Wilson began his battle for peace on that date his identification with Jesus soon clouded his mind, and he became a pathetic, passive creature who "adopted the weapons of femininity" (p. 237), causing him quickly to descend into a cowardly submission "by making the most extraordinary concession he had ever made." In the course of Wilson's submission to his adversaries, Clemenceau blatantly insulted the president and, according to Freud (p. 243) Wilson's weak retaliation "was the product of unadulterated femininity . . " (Freud's equation of feminine characteristics with cowardice was the result of his own intense gender conflicts, some might argue.)

The above material should enable us to understand what Freud was really demanding from his "double," Woodrow Wilson, keeping in mind that Freud's psyche was permeated with death wishes towards any rival or "enemy." With an emphasis on the British negotiator, Lloyd George, who was Wilson's most powerful adversary, it is obvious that Freud expected the president to somehow destroy Lloyd George when he refused to accept a treaty that would have benefitted Germany and Austria. At a primitive level of Freud's mind, what he seemed really to desire was for Wilson to find a way to annihilate (or arrange for the assassination of) this unbending, sometimes deceitful British opponent.

What Freud was confessing unconsciously was that in March of 1919, unlike the submissive Wilson, *he* had not taken a cowardly "feminine" path in dealing with *his* British rival and enemy. Instead, he had acted in a masculine manner, grasping the sword of Jehovah with determination, and then using it to smite John Freud (by arranging for his murder). Thus, this psychological study of Wilson informs us of two major happenings in March of 1919: first, that Freud had entered a near-psychotic state of mind in that month and, second, it was probably in that same month that he arranged to kill John Freud as a final act of revenge.

In his account of Wilson's core "problem," Freud gave us a hint that his own unconscious identification with Jesus—relating to his unending rage about the loss of his nanny—was an important hidden motive in his decision to exterminate his nephew John. In many ways, Freud's complex study provided unintended revelations about his own inner dynamics. Freud's powerful identification with Jesus Christ was one of these revelations; another was his broad hint that he, like Wilson (allegedly), had experienced a great number of near-psychotic episodes throughout his lifetime; and that, similar to Wilson, he tended to act-out some of his fantasy identifications.

There were many other psychic traits that Freud attributed to Wilson that were also applicable to himself. On several pages he noted Wilson's strong tendency to transform colleagues into alter egos—the president having stated on several occasions that he always had the identical thoughts and feelings of his trusted ally, Colonel Edward House—this being a well-known trait of Freud's in relation to Fliess, Rank, and others. Likewise, Freud attributed to Wilson continual self-deception; the tendency towards lying and then justifying it; the persistent distortion of facts to conform to personal wishes; the tendency to be discontented and depressed after achieving numerous personal successes; etc. All of these were personal characteristics of Freud's.

There was another damning characteristic that Freud attributed to Wilson that was also quite applicable to Freud. It was Freud's belief that unconsciously Wilson was a horrendous criminal (which should be compared with his own murderous actions towards Emanuel and John Freud). According to Clark (1980, p. 476), on one occasion Freud told an American that Wilson was the silliest fool of the century, adding: "And he was also probably one of the biggest criminals—unconsciously, I am quite sure." There is good reason to suspect that Freud equated Wilson's alleged criminality with unconscious murderous tendencies, believing that he had exterminated thousands of American soldiers needlessly, as the result of megalomanic and sadistic motives. Freud told this same American that Wilson was to blame for putting his country into a war that America should not have entered at all, marking the president as both an incomparable fool and a great criminal. Hinting at his belief that Wilson harbored massive homicidal tendencies, Freud wrote (1966, p. 294) that at times Wilson realized that the treaty he negotiated at Paris "was in truth a sentence of death for European civilization."

By the above language Freud implied that Wilson's unconscious death wishes were so intense that they concealed his desires to be the greatest mass murderer of all time, secretly wishing to destroy all of European civilization. The seeds for this absurd idea were planted by Freud in the first half of the book when he alleged that in the early years of Wilson's career he bore considerable feelings of hostility to various European nations, but not England. Likewise, Freud planted the seeds for his readers to suspect that, even in childhood Wilson exhibited murderous tendencies, by telling the very same anecdote twice (pp. 11 and 57). This story involved Woodrow at age eleven playing "Indians" with a girl cousin whom he struck with an arrow. Then "with wild remorse" he carried her limp body into the house while crying out: "I am a murderer. It wasn't an accident. I killed her." But she had merely fainted and recovered quickly. (This tale reminds me of Sigmund's physical harassment of his niece Pauline during the Freiberg era—abetted by his nephew John—as described in his "Screen Memory" paper.)

Quite unwittingly, Freud revealed another striking similarity between Wilson and himself. On various pages of the biography (including pages 57, 69, 90-1, 143-4, and 205) he claimed that Wilson was vulnerable to name magic, although Freud did not use that precise term. For example, Freud stated (p. 57) that: "The extent to which like names produce identifications in the unconscious can scarcely be appreciated by one who has not made special study of the subject." Here, Freud claimed that it was almost certain that during childhood Wilson (while susceptible to name magic) had identified his cousin Jessie Woodrow Bones with his mother, whose name was Jessie Woodrow Wilson, and transferred a considerable portion of libido towards his mother onto this cousin.

So, in one of his final books Freud at last acknowledged that name magic can help produce powerful fantasy identifications in the unconscious mind, including instances when "like names" help to facilitate such identifications. Notice that he implied that he had made a "special study" of this topic, although he did not indicate how it might have applied to himself. For example, one readily suspects that his Hebrew name Solomon helped him to generate a fantasy identification with the Biblical king named Solomon, capitalizing on Freud's ambition to be recognized as a profoundly "wise man." And Freud's pet name in childhood, the Moor, helped him to identify powerfully with Schiller's rivalrous characters, the brothers called Karl and Franz Moor.

Freud's great preoccupation with the name Josef inspired him to detect one instance when Wilson might have been similarly preoccupied with that name. He remarked (pp. 69, 144) that "the most unjustified distrust of Wilson's life" was towards his young secretary named Joe Tumulty, who bore the same name as Wilson's younger brother, also named Joe. Freud believed that Wilson harbored a "paranoid sense of betrayal" towards his brother Joe which was partially transferred to Joe Tumulty, abetted by the shared given names of those younger males. He wrote that (p. 69): "Joe Tumulty, to Wilson's unconscious, may well have represented Joe Wilson. The actions of a human being are often determined by far more absurd identifications than this."*

Surely Freud's unconscious was telling us about his own absurd "fantasy identifications," and of his irrational hatred towards his younger deceased brother, Julius. On a later page (p. 144), he noted again that Wilson's "mixed feelings" towards Tumulty sprang "from the accident that Tumulty's name, like the name of Wilson's little brother, was Joe." He added that in Wilson's unconscious Joe Tumulty "represented the little brother whose birth had aroused in him the mingled feelings of affection, dislike, and a sense of betrayal," causing Tumulty to become "the recipient of those emotions." Apparently, in this analysis Freud was projecting his own lethal and tumultuous feelings towards baby Julius, while failing to notice that the surname Tumulty encodes the English word "tumult."

Freud also claimed that unconscious name magic was involved in the president's decision, at age 25, to change his name from Thomas Woodrow Wilson to Woodrow Wilson. He explained that in 1881 Wilson was in love with his cousin Hattie Woodrow, whose surname was the same as his mother's maiden name. Wilson proposed marriage to Hattie, but she refused him. He then (p.90) "for the first time began to call himself Woodrow Wilson, dropping Thomas." According to Freud, Wilson gave various reasons for this name change that were quite unconvincing, indicating that an unconscious factor had dominated his decision.

Freud asserted that: "The unconscious reason for Wilson's dropping his name Thomas is, in fact, clear." He then remarked that "the Ego normally replaces a lost love-object by identification of the self with the lost object." Thus, when Wilson was rejected by Hattie he "lost a mother representative whose name, like his mother's name, was Woodrow" so unconsciously "he replaced the lost mother representative by himself." Freud added that: "He dropped Thomas . . . and became unadulterated Woodrow. Thus he identified himself with his mother and satisfied his need for a mother representative by becoming himself his mother."

This explanation by Freud about Wilson's magical changing of his name, in effect eliminating his original given name Thomas, reminds us that at age 19 Freud dropped the name given to him at birth, Sigismund, and replaced it with the name Sigmund. It's likely that a similar dynamic can be applied to Freud regarding this change of name. His name Sigismund was widely regarded with contemptuous humor in Christian Vienna as being the quintessential name for a Hebrew male. So one can say that Freud eliminated his Hebrew-related name and replaced it with Sigmund—a proud Christian name. If effect, he dropped a considerable portion of his Jewish identity and secretly replaced it by an enhanced identification with his

---

*Recall Freud's fantasy that Napoleon was fixated on the name of the Biblical Josef due to the Corsican's alleged hatred of his eldest brother, named Josef. Freud ignored that Wilson's father also was named Joseph

Christian self which was connected with his lost love object, his Christian nanny. Adopting the name Sigmund helped him unconsciously to become the Christian primal mother for whom he yearned (covertly) throughout his lifetime—just as Wilson perhaps became *his* own mother via name magic. Unfortunately, the name Sigmund might have helped to perpetuate Freud's perverse desire for his lost nanny, along with his murderously angry feelings towards Emanuel and John Freud, whom his unconscious mind blamed for "killing" her, as the core of that old "Freiberg catastrophe."

Freud hinted at another instance of name magic in Wilson's life that perhaps had significant ramifications concerning the disappearance of Freud's nephew John Freud. It was noted by Freud that during the early years of Wilson's presidency of Princeton University he formed "an intense friendship" (p. 103) with Professor John Grier Hibben. About this relationship Freud wrote that Wilson "loved Hibben deeply and, as Hibben was devoted to him, he found great joy in this friendship." It was said that Wilson tried to see Hibben every day and made no plans without talking them over with his friend. Freud commented that (p. 113) when Wilson's father died "his love for Hibben became even more intense than it had been before. It is clear that by identifying Hibben with himself as a child he was contriving to receive from himself the love he wanted and could no longer get from his father." Then in 1907 Wilson originated a controversial policy proposal in which he invested great time and energy, believing that he had Hibben's support for getting the Trustees and faculty to approve his new plan. But at a crucial moment, Hibben revealed in a faculty meeting that he strongly opposed Wilson's pet project, which shattered their relationship. (There are some analogies here with the stormy Freud/Fliess relationship.)

Freud wrote that (p. 123): "The conversion of Hibben into a Judas was doubtless made easy for Wilson by his unconscious identification of himself with Christ." Freud indicated that Wilson's identification with Christ had been greatly increased by the death of his father, and within "the portion of Wilson's unconscious in which he was Christ his younger friends were certainly his disciples." At this point Freud claimed that: "John Grier Hibben was doubtless John, the Beloved Disciple." By that language, Freud was implying that Wilson had identified Hibben with Christ's disciple named John, because they both shared the same name—another instance of name magic in Wilson's life.

Freud indicated that it was quite easy for Wilson to employ "the mechanism used by paranoiacs" while converting Hibben into Judas Iscariot. But Freud did not offer any real evidence to support his assertion that Wilson had converted his "betrayer," John Hibben, into Judas Iscariot. In effect, this signified that Freud had projected onto Wilson a retaliatory desire to somehow arrange the death of his own former friend and ally, his nephew John. This pertained to the Bible's story about Christ's final days, for it was Judas who betrayed Jesus, soon followed by a talionic reprisal—the death of Judas by hanging.

Concerning Freud's intense identifications with Wilson and Jesus Christ, the above material suggests that Freud was projecting his own fantasy about converting a former ally (John Freud) who had "betrayed" him into the figure of Judas Iscariot, thereby exposing his desire for the death of John/Judas. Furthermore, we might consider that young Sigmund often had fantasized that his brother Emanuel was his father, and that both name and birthday magic indicated that Emanuel (born on December 25) was Jesus. Perhaps in Sigmund's fantasies this made him think of himself as "Jesus, Jr." relegating John Freud to the role of John the Baptist via name magic.

Emphasis needs to be placed upon Freud's theory that Woodrow Wilson had used his identification with Jesus and name magic to equate John Hibben with "John the Beloved Disciple." Accordingly, there is no reason to ignore the clear possibility that Freud used his own identification with Christ, along with name magic, to equate his kinsman John Freud with John the Baptist (the cousin of Jesus who announced to the world that Jesus was the Messiah). Young Sigmund would have enjoyed that idea immensely, since it reversed the childhood power-balance between John Freud and himself. That is, in his assigned role as the wild Baptist, John Freud would have become decidedly inferior to Sigmund/Jesus and a supporter of his glorified rank as the Christ. Also, this transforming of Sigmund's nephew into the Baptist would have allowed Freud to express his covert death wishes towards John Freud, since his role as the Baptist required him eventually to be killed via decapitation by King Herod. The parallel to this was the time in adolescence when Sigmund expressed the covert desire to assassinate John Freud by taking the role of Brutus, opposite his nephew's portrayal of Caesar.

Does it seem incredible that Freud identified himself with Jesus and his nephew John Freud with John the Baptist, partly as an unconscious way of expressing Sigmund's desire for his nephew's execution? If so, there is another aspect of Freud's use of name magic that helps to confirm this lethal fantasy. Consider that Freud's most famous female supporter for decades was an analyst named Lou Salomé, who was somewhat infamous due to her sexual liaisons with many "kings" of the cultural elite (Nietzsche, the poet Rilke, and others). Perhaps one of the factors that attracted Freud so intensely to this handsome woman was name magic since her name, Salomé, is identical to that of the seductive woman who obtained the head of John the Baptist by demanding that King Herod should arrange for his decapitation.

Is it plausible that Freud identified Lou Salomé with the Bible's murderous Salomé mainly on the basis of "like names?" Well, let's remember that Freud emphasized "like names" in explaining three of Wilson's instances of identification: Joe Tumulty and little Joe Wilson; cousin Jessie Woodrow and Wilson's mother, Jessie Woodrow Wilson; and John Hibben and the disciple of Jesus named John. So let's not be skeptical about Freud's equating the Biblical Salomé and her seductive counterpart, Lou Salomé, whose compulsive sexuality indicated that she had captured the heads and hearts of countless male partners.

Probably Freud's mind was playing unconsciously with other kinds of name magic as he pursued the destruction of Wilson's reputation by writing this tendentious biography. We should consider that his co-author, William C. Bullitt, claimed that Freud nearly twisted his arm to get him to agree to their joint work on this book (though Jones's account reverses this pressure, alleging that the diplomat sought out Freud). If it is correct that Freud pressured Bullitt to undertake this project, as seems more likely to me, what were Freud's motives in securing this particular individual as his co-author? Part of the answer lies in their joint hatred of Wilson; in the fact that Bullitt was known as an eminent diplomat (an Ambassador to France); and that Bullitt had an insider's knowledge of the Paris Peace Conference, making it seem that Freud's views were endorsed by a man with special expertise in this area in which Freud was a novice. Those are some of the rational reasons why Freud desired Bullitt's collaboration, but a consideration of name magic might provide us with some of the less-rational ones.

Was Freud attracted to the idea that he was using a Christian named Bullitt in his endeavor to ridicule and smear Wilson's sometimes excessive attachment to his Christian beliefs? Clark quoted Bullitt (1980, p. 476) as saying that he and Freud had a dissimilarity in their beliefs on most topics besides Wilson, and here Bullitt emphasized that Freud was an agnostic Jew, while: "I have always been a believing Christian." With regard to possible influences of name magic, we should underline that Bullitt's middle initial "C." stands for the name Christian. Nevertheless, he silently endorsed many sentences presumably written by Freud that mocked the force and effectiveness of Christian values and beliefs, implying that these beliefs, and Wilson's reliance upon them, were primarily to blame for the devastation he unleashed upon European civilization. One wonders whether Freud obtained perverse pleasure in using a man named Christian to assault Christian values, and to emphasize their futility.

Regarding another aspect of name magic that might have influenced Freud's psyche, notice that the name Bullitt, both as written and in its phonetic structure, bears a striking resemblance to the English word "bullet." The lethal significance of that word, and the aggressive—even murderous—significances of the American diplomat's surname might have been a special delight to Freud's unconscious mind. Unconsciously, did Freud hope to employ this angry, embittered "bullet" (Bullitt) to destroy Woodrow Wilson?

Perhaps Freud enjoyed the juxtaposition in the diplomat's name of the seemingly contradictory concepts: "Christian bullet." From Freud's perspective, this could have signified the hypocritical and contradictory aspects (loving/murderous) of the victorious Christian nations that viciously sealed the fate of Europe at the Paris Peace Conference. Moreover, Freud's characterization of that Prince of Peace, called Woodrow Wilson, could be summarized by the name "Christian bullet." To Freud, this might have signified Wilson's peaceful, loving intentions that were undermined by his unconscious desire to kill his enemies (smite them) and become the ruler of the world. In one of its meanings "Christian bullet" pertains to the Jekyll/Hyde syndrome, and thereby is particularly applicable to Freud and, to a lesser extent, to all mankind.

Roazen's lengthy critique (1968) of the Wilson book indicated that he was dismayed and somewhat disgusted by it, but that he could not help being fascinated by its egregious failings. He called the book (p. 300) "a disappointingly bad one," and complained that it is riddled with errors. Roazen also described it as (p. 320) "the Wilson fiasco" whose style is "appalling." (p. 303) At the outset, he remarked (p. 301) that: "one would like to think that this was so startlingly bad a book that critics would have to sit down and find out why it was such a mechanistic application of psychoanalytic concepts to the life of one of America's great men."

There were many specific criticisms that Roazen made of the Wilson book which will now be summarized briefly. Roazen called it a "psychoanalytic antique" and decried the "cheap quality" of the interpretations that Freud made about Wilson's behaviors. He also disliked "the brutal quality of the Wilson book, the monotonous and cold treatment of a human life" (p. 303) and said that Wilson was portrayed as a "robot." It was said that his psyche had been divided up into separate little boxes (p. 308) "with each of his complexes securely isolated," and with little consideration for the important "inbetweens" of his personality. It was noted that "the whole man" was not described, and that no real discussion was given of the president's strengths and his considerable achievements as "a great teacher, a legislative and administrative leader, or a molder of world opinion." (p. 309) Also, it was remarked that the book ignored the social context of Wilson's life and "relied on sources which are no longer considered trustworthy."

Roazen complained that the Wilson book ignored that the president's public failures were not simply due to his personal limitations, if one considers the worldwide political and economic factors that constrained him. Also, he criticized (p. 309) the book's audacity in alleging that it had revealed the neurosis controlling Wilson's life and its recklessness in describing him as "very close to psychosis" in September of 1919. Roazen commented (p. 306) that "Freud's aversion to Wilson had mainly emotional causes, and was not the conviction of a seasoned student of world affairs." Finally, he castigated the book's shoddy tendency (p. 319) towards "psychiatric name-calling," and described it (p. 318) as one of Freud's "worst" efforts.

According to Roazen (p. 300), the publication of the Wilson biography in 1967 created a literary sensation, but thereafter the book was "consigned to a limbo" (p. 301)—similar to the fate of the Moses book. Roazen mentioned that many analysts were greatly anguished by the Wilson book and decided to regard it as if it were a forgery—something like the fraudulent "Protocols of Zion." In this manner, "they feel justified in dismissing the Wilson book altogether by maintaining that Freud had very little hand in it at all." (p. 301) The scam that they invented was that the book was almost entirely the creation of Bullitt, with very little participation by Freud. This scam was abetted by the "disappearance" of the original manuscripts that were in Freud's handwriting, and by the claim that Bullitt "forgot" the name of the secretary in Vienna who translated the book from Freud's original draft. Roazen wrote that "it is a bit hard to believe that so much should have disappeared so completely." (Of course, the same can be said about John Freud.)

Unfortunately for the scam artists, when Ernest Jones first read the Wilson manuscript in 1956, "although he considered it a poor book he never contested the authenticity of Freud's collaboration with Bullitt." (P. 304) Later, Jones described the Wilson volume as a "joint work," and he remarked that "it is not hard to distinguish the analytic contributions of the one author from the political contributions of the other." The present writer holds to his own judgment that the Wilson book was almost entirely the creation of Freud, with little conceptual participation by Bullitt, whose major contributions might have been limited to the work of translating Freud's German into a somewhat breezy style of English and providing some of the historical data.

Roazen has provided some unconvincing reasons to explain why the Wilson book was completed sometime between 1930 and 1932, yet was not published until 1967, approximately 35 years later. It is my belief that this was another aspect of the aforementioned scam, but I will not dwell on this matter here. However, I will emphasize that Freud worked on his Wilson and Moses books in the same general era, and that both books can be regarded as extended unconscious fantasies that incorporate numerous hidden aspects of Freud's own life and psychopathology. In a prior chapter, I offered my reasons why Freud's 1914 paper on Moses was not published until many years later, and I will simply say that I suspect that some of that reasoning is applicable to the delayed publication of the Wilson book.

However, some new factors undoubtedly apply to the long delay of the Wilson book's publication. Roazen commented (p. 315) that part of Freud's hatred of Wilson came from his rabid hatred of the U.S.A. and its citizens. It is likely that the long delay in publication of the Wilson book derived, to some extent, from analytic concerns that this volume would bring into public focus Freud's intense hatred for America; and there is a legitimate question about whether his worst criticisms of this country and its people were censored from Freud's manuscript, considering that it "disappeared" so conveniently. Roazen remarked that it might take many years to learn Freud's most vicious criticisms of America and its citizens "since for the sake of the psychoanalytic movement in America some of his comments have been deliberately censored from his letters." (Here, he made an indirect reference to Anna Freud's unpublished letters to Jones that are concealed in the Jones Archives.)

In this context, Roazen attributed (p. 315) some of Freud's hatred towards Americans to his expectations that American psychoanalysts would someday repudiate his work. According to Roazen, Freud retaliated by directing devastating death wishes towards America and its people. Indeed, Freud was reported to have said about Americans that: "This race is sentenced to disappear from the face of the earth." Roazen indicated that this death wish towards Americans was then transformed into a vicious "curse" by which Freud predicted that someday all Americans would become unable to speak, or eat, and "they will die of starvation." Notice that this murderous curse began with Freud's wish that all Americans would *disappear* from the earth. Isn't it likely that his lethal wish for a disappearance was strongly applicable to his American enemy, Woodrow Wilson, whose surrogate in 1919 was Freud's greatest enemy, John Freud? One wonders whether he not only caused his nephew to disappear, but also to be starved to death (while John perhaps was held a prisoner like Freud's son, Jean M.).

This brings me back to my earlier thesis that during the Great War a major portion of Freud's psyche regressed to the murderous, militaristic phase of boyhood when he had used fantasy battles and identifications with military heros to retaliate lethally against Emanuel and John Freud regarding "the Freiberg catastrophe." It was my view that during the war this mental regression caused Freud to make the Allied leaders, particularly Lloyd George and Wilson, his personal enemies. Thereafter, he displaced his desires to kill them onto his English "enemies," Emanuel and John, helping to provoke his assassinations of both those kinsmen. It was Herman Melville who wrote that "All wars are boyish, and are fought by boys." However, the boyish segments of Freud's psyche that were re-activated during the war were filled with murderous, psychotic desires and enormous needs for revenge against presumed enemies who had "betrayed" him. In 1919 there was a great upsurge in his homicidal hatred for two of those betrayers, Woodrow Wilson and Lloyd George, who were probably coalesced in Freud's mind. In order to avoid a descent into total madness, he found a way to exterminate them, in fantasy, by arranging for the assassination of their template, John Freud.

Concerning my view that Freud in 1919 harbored a very personal, morbid, and autistic hatred for the Allied leaders that was partly displaced onto John Freud, we have now found some indirect evidence for this in his rabid hatred and often bizarre treatment of the American president's behaviors in the biography just examined. Freud's claim that Wilson almost became insane in March 1919, provoking various lethal consequences, was perceived to be a projection of Freud's near-psychosis in that month which led to the assassination of John Freud. Concerning Freud's highly personal treatment of Wilson's life and personality, the following point needs emphasis. As an aftermath of the Great War, surely there were hundreds of European analysts who were bitter about the war, the peace conference at Paris, and the relative failure of Wilson's policies. However, there was only one analyst, Sigmund Freud, who concocted a tendentious biography that was intended to destroy Wilson's reputation, as a reflection of the desire to annihilate the man himself.

In conclusion, let me respond to Roazen's remark that the Wilson book has been consigned to a limbo in cultural circles. In my opinion, it is very unfortunate that hardly anyone reads it anymore, and Roazen did not help by attacking the book so forcefully, leaving an impression that it is largely trash. To the contrary, this is a book that is very worth reading by scholars, clinicians, and lay persons. It is questionable how much accurate information it provides about Woodrow Wilson, but a careful reading will offer (like the Moses book) numerous unexpected insights into the quixotic and lethal personality of Sigmund Freud. If the analytic elite is taking the absurd risk of denying Freud's authorship of the Wilson book in the hope of banishing it into a limbo, then you know it must be a dangerous and valuable work, indeed.

After John's Disappearance

The previous chapter cited some peculiar behaviors of Freud's in the years following Emanuel's train death that suggested his possible complicity in his brother's "accident." Now we will do the same with the aftermath of John Freud's disappearance in 1919, mentioning strange behaviors of Freud's that indicate his possible complicity in the disappearance (and presumed assassination) of his nephew.

In his third volume about Freud's life, Ernest Jones described (III, p. 25) the time in 1920 when his disciple Eitingon commissioned a bronze bust of the master's head for posterity. The book by Eric Miller, which accused Freud of being a medical murderer, took special notice of this event (1984, p. 258). Miller reflected upon the time in adolescence when Sigmund used a school playlet to assume the role of Brutus opposite John's role of Caesar, and connected this with Freud's reaction to his new bronze bust in 1920. That is, Miller cited a letter by Freud dated August 3, 1920 in which he again made a striking identification with Brutus by remarking that the new bust "gives the impression of a head of Brutus, with a rather overwhelming effect." Surely, this overwhelming effect only existed in Freud's mind, causing Miller to emphasize that: "Even in the 1920s Freud was still identifying with Brutus."

Comparing Freud's identification with the assassin Brutus in adolescence and in 1920, Miller stated that: "Apparently this early youthful association of political murder and ambition had a lasting effect upon Freud." According to Miller, in 1921 Freud mentioned this bust of "Brutus" again, stating that it had entered his home as a "ghostly, threatening, bronze double" of himself. Miller's wise response was: "Thus Hannibal, the militarist, and Brutus, the assassin, were Freud's first and continuing political prototypes."

What is most important about the above material is that in August 1920, only a year or so after the disappearance of John Freud, Sigmund again exhibited his powerful identification with the assassin, Brutus. This is a strong clue that early in 1919 this lethal identification with Brutus already had been re-activated, indicating that it had helped provoke the arranging of John's disappearance. And in 1921, why did Freud call this bust of "Brutus" a ghostly and threatening presence, except that it prompted his fears of retaliation for having murdered John? In describing this bust of "Brutus" as a double of himself, he not only confessed to having murdered "Caesar" (John and Emanuel, melded), but also pointed to his lethally dualistic nature, regarding the Jekyll/Hyde syndrome.

If one concedes that the ghosts of Brutus and Caesar were haunting Freud in the early 1920s, it is understandable that likewise his fear and guilt caused him to be haunted by the ghost of John Freud, and by his strange disappearance in 1919. One wonders whether Freud's lasting guilt about John's disappearance compelled him in 1924 to become irrationally "involved" in the famous case of a young fellow who disappeared and later was found dead with a bullet in his head. My reference is to the mysterious disappearance of Philippe Daudet, which has been discussed by Ellenberger (1970, pp. 847-8).

Ellenberger noted that "Freud's intervention" in the case of Philippe Daudet was widely criticized and condemned in France, and in other nations of Europe. On November 20, 1923 this French lad disappeared from his home and several days later was found dead from a ball shot into his skull. He was the son of the renowned writer and royalist leader, Léon Daudet, and grandson of the famous author Alphonse Daudet, so this case created a public sensation in France and beyond. At first it was thought that the boy had committed suicide, but serious doubt was cast upon this idea when a judicial investigation revealed that Philippe had been in close contact with an anarchist group. His bereaved father was certain that his son had been assassinated by the French secret police. Therefore, he "conducted a violent press campaign against those whom he accused of having trapped and murdered his son."

Eventually, an anarchist who was a vehement foe of Léon Daudet released a questionable story intended to support the idea that Philippe's death had been a suicide. This anarchist, André Gaucher, claimed that just before Philippe's disappearance he had received a visit from an "unknown adolescent" who asked him whether it was true that Léon Daudet was a pornographic writer. Gaucher claimed that he showed this lad crucial excerpts from Daudet's novels that proved his reprehensible sleaziness. Ellenberger wrote that: "Gaucher implied that this boy was Philippe Daudet, who, upset by the revelations about his father, could have committed suicide." This flimsy idea did not explain why the boy would have selected his father's arch enemy for such "instruction," and many citizens must have seen how vicious this tale was in blaming Daudet indirectly for his son's probable murder while transforming it into a suicide.

Capitalizing upon the public furor caused by this case, Gaucher began to write a book about it that subjected Léon Daudet to public disgrace. He tried to enroll Pierre Janet, the famous psychologist, in this campaign but did not succeed. Also, he turned to Sigmund Freud to assist in his smear campaign and sent him a segment of the manuscript he was writing about Daudet. Freud cooperated by writing two letters to this infamous anarchist, commenting that he had met Léon Daudet on several occasions in Paris, in 1885 and 1886, but had not read his works. However, one of Freud's letters noted that his father Alphonse Daudet was a syphilitic (which many persons believed was hereditary), adding that syphilis was a major cause of the predisposition to neurosis.

Ellenberger paraphrased Freud's letters as having concluded that: "Philippe Daudet's case, as well as any other one, could be explained by psychoanalysis." With this outrageous and extravagant claim, Freud again was "tooting his own horn," as he often did throughout his career. Furthermore, having read Gaucher's abbreviated manuscript, Freud wrote in one letter that Léon Daudet "would perhaps have been choked by his neurosis if he had not possessed a talent great enough to enable him to discharge his perversions into his literary production." With that language he gave splendid assistance to Gaucher's campaign to disgrace Daudet publicly, since the implication was that Daudet was a mentally unbalanced pervert whose writings were pervaded by his sexual perversions.

Soon afterward, Gaucher published his book (1925) defaming Léon Daudet whose title was followed by this tantalizing notice: "With letters from Freud and from Pierre Janet." In a strikingly naive manner, Ellenberger commented that: "Obviously Freud had been unaware that André Gaucher was a notorious anarchist who would hasten to utilize these two letters for his own questionable purposes." However, at least Ellenberger did provide a more realistic evaluation of Freud's vicious and destructive letters, by quoting the German journalist Tucholsky who deplored that Freud could have "given his papal blessing to that evil action."

Now we must ask why Freud took the risk of provoking great public disapproval by intruding himself into the case of young Philippe Daudet in 1924—assuming, as I do, that Freud expected that his letters to Gaucher would be published. First, allow me to intuit some fairly rational motives of the master. One of these was that Freud often operated on the principle (as seen in his fervent "sexual campaigns") that receiving even contemptuous notoriety is better than just being ignored—if one hopes to attain worldwide fame. Next, there is the revenge factor, which is always important in understanding Freud's behaviors. Consider that over many years prior to 1924 Léon Daudet had earned a reputation as an anti-Semite, reactionary, and a royalist. Also, in 1919 his volume *Le Monde des Images* appeared. It is plausible to assume that someone had informed Freud that this book on psychology was extremely anti-Freudian, and that this annoyed Freud considerably. —So much for the "rational" reasons that might have prompted Freud to intrude himself into the case of Philippe Daudet.

My intuition suggests that the irrational reasons for Freud's intervention in this case were far more compelling than any rational motives. Emphasis is placed on the fact that this case involved the sudden disappearance of a male person from a famous family, which parallels the disappearance of another male member of a famous family, John Freud. My suggestion is that Freud was compelled unconsciously to intrude into the French case because of the "disappearance factor," and perhaps the issue of murder, that connected the cases of Philippe Daudet and John Freud.

It is interesting that Freud's letter to Gaucher indicated that psychoanalysis (Freud himself) was capable of "explaining" (solving) the case of

Philippe Daudet. My guess is that this was a displacement of Freud's recognition that he was capable of explaining (solving) the case of another sudden disappearance—the matter of John Freud's vanishing. If so, one might say that Freud's peculiar intrusion into the case of Philippe Daudet was an unconscious "public confession" that he bore responsibility for John Freud's disappearance. Perhaps another irrational reason for Freud's strange behavior pertains to the compelling effect of name magic on his psyche, relating to the point that young Daudet's given name is like the name of Freud's brother, Philipp. This might be relevant to Sigmund's ancient desires that his brother Philipp would disappear someday, as retribution for the part he played in effecting the disappearance of the seductive nanny at Freiberg.

Analytic Gamesmanship in Defending Freud

Over the years I have become increasingly aware of the sly tactics employed by various pro-Freudian writers in defending their hero against books which have posed serious threats to his personal reputation. For example, in recent pages it was shown that the Wilson biography by Freud and Bullitt has an obvious potential for damaging Freud's reputation with the American reading public. However, the book is hardly read any longer, and one of the factors in this neglect is that some analytic critics may have created strong doubts about the book's authenticity in the public's mind. By their unfair tactics, they have helped to banish the book into a kind of limbo, thereby curtailing a reasonable questioning of Freud's strange behaviors that were projected into the Wilson biography.

Another example involves a valuable book by the analyst Jeffrey Masson titled *The Assault on Truth* (1984) which provides a comprehensive discussion of Freud's peculiar suppression of his "seduction theory." Masson showed that Freud renounced this theory, which had endorsed the actuality of early sexual abuse of children, in order to introduce a questionable notion that his patients merely had fantasized their early memories of "seduction" and rape. Masson ignored the possible role in this reversal of Freud's own sexual molestation by his nanny, but he did emphasize that Freud's theoretical renunciation (paving the way for the structure of psychoanalysis) was a cowardly and unscientific act.

Naturally, the Freudian establishment was very displeased with Masson for his apostasy. Soon after the publication of his book, various attacks were made against Masson's reputation including charges which implied that he was a psychopath who had manipulated Anna Freud to gain access to crucial private documents and had betrayed her trust. In my opinion, the attacks on Masson probably succeeded in clouding his reputation with scholars and the public, diverting attention from the crucial issue—the credibility of

Freud's scientific image—thereby undermining the impact of Masson's book.

Another example of this kind is especially instructive. It has to do with Roazen's important volume titled *Brother Animal: The Story of Freud and Tausk* (1969). As already noted in a previous chapter, that book described Freud's brutal behaviors, in early 1919, towards his depressed analytic colleague Victor Tausk that were partly responsible for Tausk's suicide that summer. Many analysts were anguished by Roazen's book, but none opposed it so vehemently as the chief of the analytic elite, Kurt R. Eissler. He wrote a book expressing his outrage about Roazen's above volume titled *Talent and Genius* (1971) which denied that Freud had acted cruelly and manipulatively towards Tausk in 1919, also denying any responsibility by Freud for Tausk's suicide.

When I finished reading Dr. Eissler's book in the 1970s, it was my feeling that he had done a poor job in his attempt to show that Freud bore no responsibility for Tausk's suicide, and that few readers would be convinced by his arguments. Perhaps Eissler agreed with me, since he published a second book, even more strident in tone, on this same topic which he titled *Victor Tausk's Suicide* (1983), again hoping to convince the public of Freud's blamelessness regarding Tausk's death. In the second book, like a good gambler, Eissler "raised the stakes" by trying to show that Tausk was a moral monster, not deserving of our sympathy, and that Freud was not a vicious near-murderer. Indeed, Eissler tried to prove that in early 1919 Tausk had revealed his own substantial blame for his problems by seducing a young female patient *during the first analytic hour, making her pregnant*. Eissler attempted to "prove" Tausk's crime by publishing a letter (pp. 88-91) from a female analyst named Olga Knopf who claimed that in the spring of 1919 Tausk had brought this woman to her for an abortion, or to induce a miscarriage. This "convenient" letter was dated June 12, 1970 and Dr. Knopf's death was in 1976—so she could not be questioned about her charges. In a previous chapter, I have discussed some of my reasons for being highly skeptical about her story and her stated intention to show that her claims conflict with Roazen's "ideas about his hero and do not make Freud into the villain . . . "

The preceding material will serve as a background for my expectation that pro-Freudian critics (or their allies) might create a scam or two to quickly discredit my major thesis set forth in the present chapter. The fastest way to do that is to publish a book or articles "proving" that John Freud was not assassinated in 1919, by showing that he had lived for a number of years past that time, perhaps into his seventies. Of course, if uncontestable proof were offered of John's continuing existence after the spring of 1919, I would gracefully withdraw my current thesis while continuing to emphasize the materials provided in chapter eight and the thesis that Freud arranged the train death of Emanuel in 1914.

But now let me discuss, and warn readers about, what might constitute uncontestable proof of John's continuing existence after the spring of 1919. First, let's consider that the key period of time occurred more than 70 years ago, making all such "proofs" somewhat blurry at this time. Whatever proofs are offered of this sort, they will have to be interwoven with a very plausible account of why John left his family home at Manchester in early 1919. Will this story adequately explain why a well-established businessman, age 63, would have completely uprooted himself from the extended family life which he shared for 58 years, presumably to plant new roots as a stranger in some other locality—without letting his family know his whereabouts?

Will we be told that John's prosperity enabled him to take an early retirement by himself in some sunny region, like the Riviera in France? Even so, why did that familial letter to Sigmund in May 1919 mention John's "disappearance" then, although Dr. Schur, a close friend of the family, believed that John had disappeared permanently in the 1870s? Likewise, why had the "Jacob Freud Family Tree" (Krüll, 1986, pp. 234-5) included a notation that John had "vanished" sometime after 1875, "or in 1918?" And why did Ronald Clark's account of a family letter specify that John "had left his parents' home and was not to be heard of again." To my mind, that does not sound as if John had taken an early retirement in another locale, but more like the case of a man who had vanished inexplicably and permanently—making no further contacts with any of his family members in Manchester, Vienna, or America (where Anna and Eli Bernays resided).

However, I am anticipating the appearance of a new article or book (after mine is published) which will claim that John Freud was in contact with some of his family members, or old Manchester friends, after the spring of 1919. Perhaps, we will be treated to the publication of a newly discovered cache of letters, allegedly in John's handwriting, dated after 1919, and stories that will attempt to explain and nullify John's "disappearance," in a plausible manner. This expected material might be accompanied by photographs of John, alleged to be in his late 60s or older, showing children in the photographs who now are said to have written published letters claiming that they posed with John, more than 68 years earlier. Likewise, we may see the publication of testimonial letters from eminent elderly persons (judges, physicians, etc.) claiming that they, and/or their family members, had intimate contacts with John Freud when he resided in their locale in his late 60s or 70s. Further proof may be offered in the form of published court documents, including a death certificate, showing that John Freud was still alive in his late 60s and did not die until his 70s, etc.

I must ask scholars and lay readers to maintain an attitude of skepticism about the publication of any such "proofs," no matter how apparently genuine, until painstaking scientific examinations have been made of each of them, to rule out forgeries and other kinds of fraudulence. With regard to the issue of the forgery of letters and official documents, reconsider the material in the first chapter by Gicklhorn indicating that some of the Freud family members at Manchester might have been experienced in the counterfeiting trade (where forgeries abound), and were privy to contacts with the criminal underworld of Europe—which sometimes can convince even eminent men to participate in fraudulent schemes.

If the present volume receives favorable attention from scholars and clinicians, along with a widespread perception in the public mind that Freud probably was the deranged assassin of Emanuel and John Freud, this could place immense pressure on some analysts to protect their hero's reputation by false means, no matter what risks of exposure might be involved. A few of these persons might take the risk of concocting a fraudulent scenario involving falsified letters, photos, and documents, all intended to prove that John Freud's life had extended well beyond the spring of 1919. If a book of this sort is published within the next few years, my advice to readers is: Let the buyer beware. And what about readers who feel I have maligned analysts by intimating that even one of them would participate in such a dangerous and corrupt scheme? My reply is that they should pay special attention to that segment of the eleventh chapter which describes Ernest Jones's daring caper in which he smuggled a large amount of currency past border guards in 1919, and Jones's participation in the "administrative murder" of Isidor Sadger to prevent the public from reading Sadger's exposé of Sigmund Freud.

Chapter Ten

Freud Identifies with Satan

The Satanic Superman

One of the most intriguing volumes ever written about Freud's hidden motivations is David Bakan's book titled *Sigmund Freud and the Jewish Mystical Tradition* (1958). Over the past thirty-five years, numerous scholars who have written about Freud's life have made a point of discussing one of the major theses of Bakan's book. That thesis began with the notion that Freud's family had migrated from Galicia which "had been saturated with Jewish mysticism" of the Kabbalist variety. The ideas and practices of that mystical sect were shown by Bakan, in some detail, to provide remarkable anticipations of some of the critical features of psychoanalysis (free association, for example). A conclusion that can be drawn from Bakan's evidence is that Freud was probably influenced in the creation of psychoanalysis by the highly magical and somewhat sinister doctrines of Kabbalist mysticism.

Another major thesis of Bakan's book rarely has been mentioned by those same scholars who have shown an interest in the idea that Freud had been influenced by Jewish mysticism. This second thesis of Bakan's is that Freud, like many depressed persons in the Middle Ages, had developed a bizarre identification with the Devil. Bakan was quite serious about this contention and offered various kinds of evidence to support it (which will soon be reviewed). So one must wonder why most Freudian scholars have failed to acknowledge this second thesis of Bakan's. Perhaps the answer is found in various comments that the eminent behaviorist psychologist, O.H. Mowrer, once made in response to Bakan's thesis that Freud had formulated an identification with Satan.

Mowrer noted that often we are remarkably slow "to perceive realities which we do not expect, or wish to be true . . " In this connection, he cited Bakan's book (1958) which shocked him by providing evidence that Freud not only had repudiated Christian and Hebrew ideas about God, but actually "identified himself with the Devil." (Mowrer, 1961, p. 114)

Since Mowrer has alerted us to the probability that previous scholars have tended to sweep under the rug Bakan's evidence that Freud identified with the Devil, it behooves us to pay careful attention to Bakan's thesis in the following pages. At the outset, we will need to look at *The Interpretation of Dreams* from the standpoint of "demonic influences," just as earlier we examined its potential for encoding confessions of Freud's sins. All of this may suggest that Freud was involved in the acting-out of a peculiar morality play at the deepest, most repressed levels of his psyche.

In his book on Freud and the Jewish mystical tradition, Bakan argued the thesis that: "Freud's major work, *The Interpretation of Dreams*, was associated with the idea of a Satanic pact." More to the point, Bakan suggested that Freud entered into a Satanic pact, at least metaphorically, during the months when his famous dream book was being written.

To support this thesis Bakan began by pointing to the Latin motto appearing on the title page of Freud's dream book: *Flectere si neques superos, Acheronta movebo* ("if the gods above are no use to me, then I'll move all hell"). This quotation is taken from Virgil's *Aeneid*, and the passage from which it was extracted is even more suggestive of the theme of a Satanic pact: "Well, if my powers are not great enough, I shall not hesitate . . to ask help wherever help may be found. If the gods above are no use to me, then I'll move all hell."

Those words spoken by the goddess Juno were expressive of her brutally revengeful motives and her intention to punish her enemies by summoning murderous demons from the underworld to torture and destroy them. That Freud would identify himself with this revengeful motto was suggested by his intense boyhood hatreds and identification with Hannibal's vow of revenge, as that was associated with his father Jacob's humiliation at the hands of a rude Christian. And later, when Freud was writing his dream book he had accumulated many additional insults that needed redressing, for he believed that the medical world of Vienna had coldly rejected his sexual theories concerning the neuroses. With this revenge motive so strong in him, it is plausible that Freud allied himself with demonic powers either metaphorically or at an unconscious level, as Bakan suggested.

Bakan also emphasized that Freud cited the above Latin motto within his dream book in a manner that associated it with Bakan's notion that the Devil can be viewed as the suspended superego. His insightful ideas on this subject noted that when God is identified with the superego, then the antagonistic image is Satan. In the psychoanalytic hour the analyst represents both the superego and the tolerant, understanding father. And what is Satan, psychologically, according to Bakan? The answer is that Satan is "the suspended superego" or the "permissive superego." Bakan's idea is that: "The Devil is that part of the person which permits him to violate the precepts of the superego."

Bakan referred to Freud's idea that the mere production of dreams constitutes the beginning of man's rebellion against the superego. It was stressed by Bakan, however, that stripping a dream of its disguises (as in Freud's uses of dream-analysis) is an even more rebellious act. Bakan wrote that: "It is a *conscious* rebellion against the superego, which is perhaps the major reason for *resistance* against interpretation." The point here is that the Devil is the crucial figure in rebellion against the superego (God) and that the master of dream analysis, Freud, must have aligned himself with the Devil unconsciously in order to have learned the art of stripping dreams of their disguises. Put another way, Bakan argued that in "some way the hold of the superego must have been suspended"—in Freud.

To provide further evidence for his thesis that Freud had entered a Satanic Pact while writing his dream book, Bakan referred to Freud's paper "A Neurosis of Demoniacal Possession in the Seventeenth Century." The paper gives an analysis of an artist named Christoph Haizmann who apparently entered into a written contract with the Devil, offering his body and soul at the end of nine years in return for success in his painting and for an end to his depression. As the day approached for consummating the contract, Haizmann became increasingly disturbed in his behaviors and sought protection and relief through priestly intervention, eventually joining a monastery. (Freud, 1923)

In his paper on demoniacal possession, Freud began by stating that various modern neuroses would have masqueraded formerly in "demonological shape." What were once thought to be demons or evil spirits are regarded today by analysts as evil wishes that are repressed and projected into the outside world. Having offered these preliminary insights, Freud then discussed and analyzed the documents relating to Christoph Haizmann's case to search out the underlying psychological factors that were involved in the painter's decision to enter into a satanic contract.

Bakan noted that Freud's examination of the Haizmann case's documents caused him to conclude that the essential conditions that caused Haizmann to sign a Satanic pact were as follows: (1) the painter was quite depressed; (2) the depression had been caused by the death of his father; and (3) the painter was concerned about earning a living. With regard to these three items, Bakan then made the following point: "From the Fliess correspondence we know that these conditions actually coincide exactly with Freud's own state at the time that *The Interpretation of Dreams* was being written." Bakan's implication was that Freud was writing covertly about *his own* Satanic pact in the process of describing the conditions causing

Haizmann to conclude his devil's pact in the 1600s.

Similarly, at the beginning of his twenty-ninth chapter concerning the composing of *The Interpretation of Dreams*, Bakan remarked that he would present a series of quotations from Freud's letters to Wilhelm Fliess to reveal his state of mind while he was writing his dream book. Then he stated again: "We find confirmation that it was fashioned under conditions specified by Freud as leading to the Satanic Pact: the death of his father, depression and financial pressure." Soon thereafter Bakan cited passages from Freud's correspondence in 1897 showing that he had in that year immersed himself in the literature on satanism "and that the desired effects, the liberation from depression and ability to work, are achieved." Thus, Bakan indicated his belief that in 1897 Freud had achieved a metaphorical alliance with the Devil, via his immersion in demoniacal literature, to free himself from depression.

There is no question that Freud was writing the first draft of his dream book during 1897 and that he completed the first draft during the early months of 1898. But does solid evidence exist to support Bakan's contentions that during 1897 Freud was still suffering from the death of his father (deceased on October 24, 1896), that he was quite depressed, and also that he was anxious about the financial status of his medical practice? Having read Freud's letters to Fliess carefully, especially the letters written in 1897, the present writer is convinced that ample evidence exists to support Bakan's contentions.

In particular, Bakan cited a long passage from Freud's letter to Fliess dated October 27, 1897. Because of its length, this passage will not be quoted in its entirety here, but it clearly shows the fact of Freud's depression, his anxiety about money matters and that business was "hopelessly bad," and also incorporates a reference to the classical tale involving a Satanic pact, namely Goethe's Faust. In this letter Freud wrote that he was then experiencing in himself "all the things" he had witnessed in his patients, including "days when I slink about depressed . . ."

There's a bit more to be said about comparisons between the demon-possessed Christoph Haizmann and Sigmund Freud. In analyzing the documents on this case, Freud noted that the painter was not interested in obtaining the usual benefits from the Devil—wealth, immunity from dangers, power over mankind and the enjoyment of beautiful women. What *did* the painter want, then? Well, he had become depressed when his father died, and then was unable to paint properly, and became anxious about his livelihood. The Devil then appeared to him, asked about the reasons for his depression, and promised to help him in every possible way. Freud's emphasis was that this man sold himself to Satan "in order to be freed from a state of depression." He added that this was an excellent motive, to those who recognize the torment of depressed states of mind and understand "how little the art of medicine can do to alleviate the malady."

Bakan was shrewd in noting that Freud's allusion to the art of medicine was incongruous. That is, Freud's comment would have made greater sense if he were commenting about medicine in the nineteenth or twentieth centuries, especially in contrast with psychoanalysis. This helped to convince Bakan that Freud's paper about Haizmann really held a contemporaneous meaning for Freud. Again Bakan's implication was that in writing about a depressed man who was the subject of demoniacal possession, Freud was writing covertly about himself. Perhaps that helps explain why Freud felt Haizmann's depression had given the painter an "excellent motive" for selling himself to the Devil, as a rationalization for a pact that Freud himself had negotiated with Satan.

But let's also emphasize that the preceding quotation hints strongly at Freud's belief that the Devil can be regarded as a great healer, particularly as a master of the difficult art of curing depression. Here we have found another reason for Freud's unconscious pact with Satan. For one of his primary goals in life was to gain recognition as the world's foremost healer of the neuroses, and *depressive* neurosis is one of the most common forms of that disorder. In identifying himself with the Devil, therefore, Freud unconsciously tried to ensure that he would gain mastery over mental illness for the benefit of his patients, to cure his own disorders, and to achieve fame, wealth, and glory.

At this point, many readers may question whether Freud really believed in the Devil, and whether a failure to do so would have weakened the thesis that he entered into a devil's pact. Bakan confronted this issue by noting that Freud was a modern man who did not believe in supernatural beings. But he pointed out that Freud's paper on demoniacal possession questioned the seriousness even of Haizmann's belief in the Devil. Bakan concluded that: "what Freud is saying is, in effect, that the full acceptance of the supernatural reality of the Devil is not an essential feature of the motivation of the Satanic Pact."

Therefore, Bakan claimed that Freud's failure to accept the Devil as a historical reality did not prevent him from entering into a satanic pact metaphorically or at an unconscious level. Indeed, Bakan's position (1958) was that: "Perhaps precisely because Freud did not accept the supernatural reality of the Devil, he could permit himself the full exploitation of the metaphor." However, Bakan seemed to sense, or imagine, that "at times the sense of possession became quite strong" in Freud's thought and feelings. He noted that it was "this feeling of possession that Freud is analyzing in his paper."

Bakan's preceding point that there may have been times when Freud felt strongly that he was possessed by the Devil is not as far-fetched as it seems. For Bakan noted that Freud once insisted to his colleagues that he was the Devil, claiming to them that all his life he'd had "to play the Devil, in order that others would be able to build the most beautiful cathedral with the materials that I produced." (Bakan, 1958, p. 181)

There are several versions of that same story that have been written by Freud's followers, and all of them agree that Freud insisted rather vehemently that *he* was the Devil. For example, there was a version offered by Maryse Choisy (1963, p. 15) which told of an evening when the disciples had gathered at Freud's home to hear Nunberg read aloud his manuscript of the *Theory of Neuroses*. Freud interrupted the speaker by mentioning a famous painting at the Pinacothèque which portrayed Saint Jerome, with the devil behind him, the devil bringing huge stones to the saint so that he could build his cathedral. Freud asked his guests: "Who is the devil here? Nunberg or myself?" Freud's pupils replied that *he* represented Saint Jerome and Nunberg was the devil. Freud retorted that they understood nothing, saying: "The devil is me. Other people will build the cathedrals."

René Laforgue's version of this incident (in Ruitenbeek, 1973, p. 342) told about an occasion when Freud's pupils had gathered at his home to hear one of them give a lecture on the Ego. Then Freud mentioned a painting by Schwind portraying a saint who sold his soul to the devil to obtain materials required for constructing a cathedral. Referring to himself, Freud asked them who represented the saint and who was the devil, and all his disciples replied that he was the saint. But Freud asserted that *he* was the devil, exclaiming: "During my lifetime I have had to play the role of the devil in order that others might construct cathedrals with the materials I have brought."

One can see that Bakan's brief version of this story is almost identical with the last few lines of Laforgue's version and that Choisy's rendition coincides closely with Laforgue's, except for the satanic pact in Laforgue's. The basic similarities cause me to conclude that these stories constitute slightly different versions of the same real event involving Freud's dramatic insistence to his disciples that he was the Devil, perhaps more than metaphorically.

Scattered throughout the writings of Freud and his disciples are various indications and evidences that he harbored an identification with the Devil. For example, in a prior chapter we noted Freud's letter to Sandor Ferenczi dated February 22, 1915 in which he commented that his ongoing self-analysis had just exposed "that murderous firebrand and ever-active devil in me (who has now become visible) . . ." About this devil, Freud said he would "bury him so deeply even from myself that I could regard myself as a peace loving man of science." But that gives us a clear idea that powerful and murderous satanic impulses were operative in Freud's unconscious mind, some of which were very close to the conscious level.

One of Freud's early disciples, Fritz Wittels, published a highly uncomplimentary biography of the master in 1924, but later recanted some of his negative remarks under pressure from Freud. In chapter nine of his book titled "Freud's Personal Characteristics" Wittels mentioned the first time he listened to a public lecture of Freud's in 1905. Remarking on Freud's lecture style, Wittels wrote that: "Amiably, almost enticingly, he" . . . (chided the) "representatives of traditional psychology, reminding us of the way in which Hauff's Satan genially appeals to his victim Hasentreffer with the words: 'Come along over here; it doesn't hurt a bit!'" (Wittels, p.130)

But Freud was sometimes wary about letting other people know that, metaphorically or otherwise, he had become the Devil's disciple. For example, Wittels gave a quotation by the master (p. 257) in which Freud noted that an investigator like himself could, while following a divergent train of thought, act like a *devil's advocate*. Hurriedly, Freud added that this "does not mean that he has sold himself to the devil." In light of what Bakan has taught us about Freud's demonic affiliations, we can guess that the last quotation of Freud's words again represents evidence that "the lady doth protest too much."

The above example is not the only instance of Freud's denial of his intimate relationship with the Devil. Consider the paper he wrote analyzing Michelangelo's statue of Moses, which he did not sign with his name but published anonymously. Freud spent several weeks sitting in front of the statue enabling him to assess with exquisite patience every fine detail of its composition. After having taken those excruciating pains, he then composed his remarkable paper which analyzed the fine structural details of the statue in ways that enabled Freud to elucidate the deepest motivations of Michelangelo and of his Moses.

Only one thing is wrong with Freud's analysis. In denial, he failed to make a meaningful comment upon a striking feature of Moses's head, namely that there are two large horns protruding from the statue's forehead! Did it worry Freud perhaps that the sculptor might have attributed some satanic qualities to the pious Moses? But this should not have been too surprising since Moses in his early years was a volatile impulse-murderer, if one recalls his impulsive slaying of the Egyptian overseer. Or did Freud conveniently forget the commandment "Thou shalt not kill," causing him to overlook the demonic significance of Moses's crime?

If Bakan was correct in claiming that Freud had entered into a Satanic pact, perhaps he had reason to fear the final payment demanded by such a contract involving hellfire and brimstone. Actually, it seems that Freud was concerned that he would eventually end-up in hell even in his preschool years. For example, he wrote to Wilhelm Fliess in 1897: "At the age of three I passed through the station when we moved from Freiberg to Leipzig, and the gas jets, which were the first I had seen, reminded me of souls burning in hell."

Since we are entertaining evidence that Freud may have had special concerns about hell and hellfire, it would pay us to reconsider a dream of Freud's reported in an earlier chapter. It came from the sixth chapter of Freud's dream book and was a dream involving an examination that he was supposed to take, because he was suspected of having stolen a missing article. Near the end of the dream, Freud was taken into a large hall that resembled "an Inferno with its hellish instruments of punishment" and was not allowed to leave there. It seems obvious that the dream signified that Freud feared eternal punishment by hellfire for not having been an honest person, and probably for many other sins as well.

Hellfire was again on Freud's mind while he was conversing with his disciple Hanns Sachs about his hatred of waiting, which prompted him to remark that the most unnecessary expenditure he knew of was all the coal needed for hell-fire. Wistfully, he noted that it would be much better for a sinner to receive final judgment, be condemned to "hundreds of thousands of years of roasting," and instead be led into a room to wait. Freud stated that: "To have to wait would soon became a worse punishment than being actually burned." (Sachs, 1944).

Do the above comments indicate that Freud wished secretly that he could divert and lessen the sentence of hellfire that he believed he really deserved? An example can be given of Freud's fear of incineration, which could be a symbolic instance of his fear of hellfire. Puner has reported that Freud once remarked to one of his patients: "At least they have not burned me at the stake . . " (Puner, 1949) While this may simply have reflected his concerns that he would be punished by society for being an iconoclast, it might also suggest his fears of hellfire as punishment for his sins, or retribution for a satanic pact. (Being burned at the stake was the punishment typically received by a witch for entering into a satanic pact.)

Marie Balmary (1982) has given another possible example of Freud's preoccupation with punishment by hellfire in connection with his presumed identification with Don Juan, whose life was ended when he was dragged into hell. Balmary offered two reasons for her belief that Freud had formed an identification with the legendary Don Juan. Her first reason was that Freud displayed a great fascination for Mozart's opera *Don Giovanni*, almost to the exclusion of interest in other operas. (The names Juan, John, and Giovanni are equivalents.)

Balmary's second reason involved her contention that Freud had become fixated upon the opera's scene in which the malignant Don Giovanni invited a revengeful statue (the Commander) to have dinner with him. Balmary compared this with Freud's eccentric behavior at his dinner table. It was routine for Freud to sit quietly at his dinner table and to demand that his family members remain silent, so that he could concentrate his attention on the latest statuette that had been added to his collection.

This piece would be placed directly in front of Freud's dinner plate and he would rivet his gaze upon it, sometimes for hours. Thus, Balmary suggested that we can look at Freud's behavior in a symbolic way and say that regularly he was inviting statues to have dinner with him. Balmary's point was that Freud was imitating unconsciously Don Giovanni's dinner invitation to the Commander's statue. If so, Freud also would have been fixated upon the final moments of that dinner when the evil Don received his just desserts by having the statue drag him through the floor and *down into hellfire.** (This should be compared with the material, cited earlier, which concerns Freud's obsessive study of Michelangelo's statue of Moses over several weeks. In that effort, Freud tried to convince himself that the statue's expression did not any longer reflect Moses's murderous anger towards his kinsmen—suggesting that Freud was hoping the statue was not lethally angry at him.)

While we are on the subjects of Freud's fear of hellfire, of being burned to death (burned at the stake), and of his fixation on the opera Don Giovanni, it is interesting to consider that Freud and his wife barely avoided being burned to death in an opera house fire. Early in their engagement period, Sigmund and Martha were scheduled to attend the opera in Vienna in the, company of Freud's sister Anna and her fiancé. However, some difficulty arose and the couples were forced to cancel their plans to attend the opera together, thereby saving their lives.

At the performance that they had planned to attend, a fire occurred that burned down the opera house to the ground. The loss of life in the fire was staggering—more than six hundred persons. That Freud was very involved emotionally in this catastrophe was suggested by what happened after the fire.

On the site of the State theater which had been razed by the fire the authorities quickly built an apartment house. It was called the Suenhaus, The House of Atonement, and was dedicated to the souls lost in the fire. Because of dread relating to the fiery deaths at this site, superstitious Viennese in need of housing were quite reluctant to seek occupancy at the Suenhaus, so it was very slow at first in obtaining residents. However, after their marriage, Sigmund and Martha Freud were among the very first couples to rent an apartment at the Suenhaus, this being their residence

---

*Balmary's thesis was reviewed early in chapter four.

before they moved to Berggasse 19.

One can imagine that when Freud came so close to losing his life in that opera house fire, it could have had a powerful effect on his unconscious mind, in terms of intensifying his identification with the Devil. At the unconscious level, Freud would have viewed that senseless holocaust as Satan's punishment towards the persons who were destroyed, equating the dreadful fire at the opera house with hellfire. But Freud would have emphasized that *his* life had been spared, enabling the early prophecies of his future greatness the chance to be fulfilled. At that point, it would have been easy for Freud's unconscious to conclude that the Devil had been his protector, just as many depressed persons in the Middle Ages had similarly concluded. In turn, this would have fostered Freud's entry into the Satanic pacts which will be discussed later in this chapter.

Previous chapters indicated that Freud harbored an unconscious identification with the legendary figure of Faust. Supporting this idea is the evidence presented by Bakan that Freud had entered into a Satanic pact, which immediately suggests a parallel with the story of Faust. Also supporting the notion of a Faust-identification are the evidences already presented of Freud's concerns with hellfire and eternal damnation.

Freud's identification with Faust is further indicated by his use of scores of quotations from Goethe's *Faust* throughout his extensive writings. For example, the very first quotation appearing in Freud's autobiography presents words spoken by the Devil (Mephistopheles) in Goethe's *Faust*. James Strachey wrote that Freud's favorite lines from literature were: "After all, the best of what you know may not be told to boys." These words were spoken by the Devil in Part I of Goethe's *Faust*. Freud was so fond of this quotation that he inserted it twice into *The Interpretation of Dreams* and quoted it in letters to Fliess dated December 3, 1897 and February 9, 1898. When he received the Goethe prize in 1930, he used these lines from *Faust* again, applying them to Goethe himself.

If Marie Balmary is correct that Freud had identified with Don Juan, this suggests an interrelated identification with Faust. That is because the story of Don Juan seems to conceal that he was involved in a Satanic pact which provided him with the conquests of hundreds of desirable women. These promiscuous sexual conquests were among the most common reasons for a man to sell his soul to Satan. Ergo, it makes sense that Don Juan was finally dragged into hell, reflecting the final payment relating to his covert devil's contract.

One further piece of evidence suggests that Freud had identified with Faust and had entered into a Satanic Pact to ensure himself additional years of work and life. This new evidence has to do with Freud's famous remark that there might be 2467 errors in his dream book (prior to publication), yet he did not intend to make further changes in it. The following pages will give my reasons for believing that "2467 errors" was a term reflecting another Satanic pact of Freud's, but first some background material on this matter will need to be presented.*

Before we can understand the full significance of the number 2467 to Freud, we will need to explore the magical portent to him of his phone number, 14362, which in 1899 coincided with his remark about 2467 errors. In a letter to Jung dated April 16, 1909 Freud explained why he then believed that he would die at either age 61 or 62 (around the year 1918). He explained to Jung that in the year 1899, when that idea first struck him, he was assigned a new telephone number, 14362, and in that same year he published his famous dream book. The "logical" link between these events was quite obvious, Freud remarked. That is, the number 43 in the telephone number was the same as his age in 1899. Therefore, Freud insisted (in the magical style of Wilhelm Fliess): "What, then, was more natural than the other numbers should signify the end of my life, namely 61 or 62?"

The above account shows that the magical thought of Sigmund Freud produced a kind of devil's contract in 1899 which was designed to ensure that he would not die till another eighteen or *nineteen* **years had passed, enabling him to live till ages 61 or 62. But, in my view, Freud was not quite satisfied with the additional years that magically had been allotted to him. So in the same year 1899 he entered into another covert devil's contract that was designed to stretch his allotted additional time from nineteen years to twenty-four years, allowing him to live beyond age 62 to age 67. That second contract involved his play with the number 2467, analogous with his aforesaid magical play with the number 14362.

Of course, Freud's discussion of his play with 2467 did not mention that the number had involved him in a devil's contract, but in a while it will become clear that this was the case. Freud discussed this number in a letter to Fliess which he wrote in 1899 and later in *The Psychopathology of Everyday Life*. As noted earlier, the number was introduced when he stated to Fliess that he'd just finished reading the proof sheets of *The Interpretation of Dreams* and did not intend to make further changes in it "even if it contained 2,467 mistakes."

In *The Psychopathology of Everyday Life* Freud related that he had realized that even this humorous and apparently arbitrary number (2467) had somehow been formulated according to the laws of the unconscious. To explain how this might be so, he stated that he had just read in the news-

---
*Refer to data in chapter eight concerning "2467," as predictive of Emanuel's murder.
**Nineteen: his triumphant number!

paper (in 1899) that General E. M. had been *retired* as Inspector General of Ordnance.* Freud had followed this man's career since first meeting him in a military hospital in 1880, when Sigmund was 24 years old, and when reading about him in the newspaper was surprised that he had already reached retirement.

But what did all of this have to do with Freud's "arbitrary" choice of 2467 in the year 1899? Well, he pointed out that he had been age 24 when he first met the General, and remembered that well because his 24th birthday had been spent in a military prison as punishment for being absent without permission. And this same number 24 appears as the first two digits in 2467. Next, Freud took the number representing his age in 1899, which was 43, and added that to 24 to get 67, the final two digits of 2467. Freud added: "That is, to the question whether I wished to retire I had expressed the wish to work 24 years more."

My strong disagreement with Freud involves his view that 24 represented only the wish to *work* 24 years more. For this must be compared with the "contract" involving his phone number giving him, at most, nineteen years *to live*. Thus it seems obvious that his magical play with 2467 was intended to give him 24 years more of life, in order to extend the nineteen years of life previously contracted, thereby enabling him to live till age 67.**

Notice that Freud associated the number 24, relating to "the wish for additional time," with his earlier minor criminal activity, i.e. being locked in prison at age 24 for a token kind of criminal infraction. My suggestion is that, therefore, the wish for an additional 24 years was tainted by a covert criminal intention. That is, unconsciously it represented Freud's wish for a devil's contract that in 1899 would have ensured him an additional 24 years of life. (Freud knew that contracting with the Devil was a criminal offense in the middle Ages).

There is another major reason for believing that the 24 years of "additional time" (which related to Freud's "2467 mistakes") is reflective of a devil's contract intended to last for 24 years. My argument here returns to the previous evidence which suggested that Freud had formed an identification with the literary figure of Faust. This brings us to the point that the original German tales of Faust in the 16th and 17th centuries appeared in anonymous "Faust-books," which went through many editions and sequels. These books tell how Faust turned his back on God and sold his soul *for* 24 additional years of knowledge, power, and for obtaining the services of the Devil.

My position is that it is no arbitrary coincidence that Faust's Satanic pact

---

*This information about Gen. E.M. appears in Chapter 12 of *The Psychopathology of Everyday Life.*
**As noted earlier, he was contracting to live till age 67, his brother Emanuel's age in 1899, while cursing his brother to die at that age.

lasted *precisely* 24 *years* and that Freud in 1899 was seeking 24 years of additional life. That is, Freud unconsciously selected the number 24 (as a portion of 2467) as an expression of his identification with Faust and his desire to enter into a Satanic pact. So it is now becoming more and more obvious what a devil Sigmund Freud really was, and more will need to be said about that at the end of this chapter.

But now let's consider whether Freud was required to make some kind of dreadful payment at the conclusion of his devil's pact, as was always the case when such pacts were negotiated in the Middle Ages. Georg Groddeck was one of the rare European analysts who paid serious attention to Freud's comments in 1899 concerning "2467 mistakes" and his desire for 24 years more of work. It impressed Groddeck greatly that when 24 years were added to 1899, this generated the year 1923. To Groddeck it was no coincidence that Freud's jaw cancer was first diagnosed in 1923 (then followed by sixteen years of painful surgery and disfigurement).

Groddeck was the author of *The Book of the Id* (1928) and a radical thinker who believed that the unconscious mind is all-powerful, even capable of producing cancer as a neurotic self-punishment. Thus, he believed that in 1899 Freud in effect had unconsciously predicted that a dreadful calamity would befall him in 1923, which took the form of his jaw cancer. Groddeck knew Freud personally and received patient-referrals from him, including analysts in need of treatment. So after 1923 he dared to hope that Freud might go to him for treatment of the psychological factors which he presumed were at the root of the recurrent outbreaks of cancer. Of course, Freud never did seek treatment for his mental problems with anyone, so far as we know, relying instead on that frail reed called self-analysis.

If we take Groddeck's position seriously, that in 1899 Freud made a prediction that a tragedy would befall him in 1923, we could add to this our knowledge of his desire for a Satanic pact and could conclude that his cancer was the punitive payment for that pact. That position may seem a bit fragile to some readers, but the story has not yet been concluded. We still need to consider another remarkable "prediction" of his cancer by Freud *in 1899*, one that was not known to Georg Groddeck since it occurred in letters that for decades were suppressed from publication. This new prediction appears below.

Freud's physician for the final twelve years of his life was Dr. Max Schur who wrote about Freud's letter to Wilhelm Fliess of February 19, 1899 that it "contains some sentences that create an uncanny impression because of the particular choice of metaphor 24 years before that metaphor was to become a tragic reality." In the sentences by Freud to which Schur had referred, Freud first compared Fliess's huge work project to a kind of cancer (neoplastic tissue) that sucks up all faculties, then infiltrates and replaces healthy tissue. Next Freud wrote these very peculiar words: "I have turned completely into a cancer . . " He added that he was supposed to go to the theater on that day, but that idea was a ridiculous one, "like trying to graft on top of the cancer." He noted that: "Nothing can adhere to it, and so from now on the duration of my life is that of the neoplasm."

Dr. Schur then noted that Freud was using a metaphor above, by referring to his intense drive to work as if it were a cancer, or neoplasm. However, Schur remarked that Freud had never used this same metaphor previously or afterward, and wondered why he used it just at that moment in 1899—though Schur ignored those "2467 errors" or anxiety about the new phone number. To help unravel this puzzle, Schur observed that in the same letter Freud had revealed a new discovery. In that same letter to Fliess in February 1899 Freud had written of his discovery that: "A symptom arises where the repressed and the repressing thoughts come together in the fulfillment of a wish. The wish fulfillment of the repressing thoughts is seen in the symptom, e.g. in the form of punishment; self-punishment . . " (Here he referred to self-punishment for masturbation.)

Schur then asked himself whether Freud was thinking about self-punishment as payment for his heavy smoking, or retribution for having revealed the secrets of the mind. It did not occur to the loyal Dr. Schur that Freud might have committed sins that were far more serious. He did not consider that Freud's self-punishment could have taken the form of cancer as retribution for a Satanic pact, and for many malignant actions towards others over a lifetime.

Moreover, Dr. Schur took explicit pains to deny that Freud in 1899 could have made an accurate prediction of his own cancer that first appeared in 1923. He stated that, unlike some other people, he was disinclined to believe that the unconscious mind can "know" about "a future illness 24 years before it becomes manifest." Also, he expressed disbelief that "Freud's cancer was a *direct* consequence of guilt feelings . . " However, he did feel that Freud never forgot that metaphor about cancer in 1899 "so that some of the expressions he used in letters written during the last year of his life take on new and tragic meaning." Schur admitted that Freud did "punish" himself eventually, i.e. "while he did not develop his cancer out of guilt, he contributed to its recurrence by persisting in his heavy smoking." (Why punish himself, if guilt was absent?)

Schur merely asserted that Freud didn't develop his cancer out of guilt, contradicting Dr. Groddeck's belief that Freud did just that. Dr. Schur would have claimed naively that Freud had nothing serious to feel guilty about. But more likely he would have denied the medical plausibility of a thesis alleging that cancer can be caused by psychosomatic factors.

However, in 1993 a growing number of medical researchers will entertain the possibility that cancer sometimes can be crucially influenced by psychogenic factors. More and more in the medical literature we are learning about research data that tie cancer-proneness to variable personality characteristics. Is it plausible, then, that the remarkably powerful and distorted personality of Freud had some special capacity to produce psychogenic effects, including the triggering of a cancer within a specific time-frame of one year (1923)? If so, perhaps Dr. Schur has given us a partial clue to this mystery by noting that Freud contributed to recurrences of his cancer by persisting in his heavy smoking. This suggests that if Freud was programmed to produce his cancer precisely in the year 1923, perhaps he greatly assisted the attainment of that goal by a massive increase of smoking in 1921 and 1922, seriously irritating the tissues of his throat and jaw and perhaps producing pre-cancerous growths. And it seems relevant to remind ourselves that previously we learned about Dr. Felix Deutsch's claim that *in 1923* Freud had asked Deutsch's assistance in committing suicide. Taking Dr. Deutsch's claim into account, it seems likely that the seeds of self-destruction were thrusting upward in Freud's mind even in 1921 and 1922.

The previous paragraph suggested that Freud might have been involved in self-destructive behaviors in 1921 and 1922 in order to effectuate the lethal fulfillment of his devil's pact in 1923. But can one offer any hard evidence that he was trying to harm himself in 1921 or 1922? No, there is none that can be offered, but at least there is some indirect evidence that in late 1922 Freud was sensitized to the imminent arrival of 1923, as the year culminating his devil's pact.

That Freud was sensitive, at least on an unconscious level, to the fact that 1923 would be the dreaded year ending his devil's pact of 24 years was indicated by his activities during the last few months of 1922. According to Jones's biography, those months were spent by Freud in writing his paper on the devil's pact of Christoph Haizmann, which was first published in 1923! And remember David Bakan's assertion that when Freud wrote about Haizmann's Satanic pact he was secretly referring to his own pact with the Devil. Thus, it seems likely that Freud's decision to write about Haizmann in late 1922 was impelled by his growing concern that his own devil's pact would soon expire in 1923, perhaps with disastrous consequences.

And if Freud was so sensitized to the years 1922 and 1923 in relation to his devil's pact, it is not far-fetched to believe that his unconscious mind would have accelerated its self-destructive behaviors (extremely heavy smoking) in 1921 and 1922. (An earlier chapter informed us that Freud spent a huge sum of money for the legal defense of a man not close to him, during 1922, to defend him against the charge that he'd murdered his father. Perhaps the outlay of this money was partly self-punitive and also a magical good deed intended to "buy" mercy and leniency as the year approached culminating his devil's pact).

Now we've covered the essential materials pertaining to Freud's "2467 mistakes," as that relates to the ending of his Satanic pact in 1923. But there is a small postscript that needs to be mentioned relating to his emphasis on the number 24. Recall that he connected that number with his 24th birthday which he spent in a military jail for being absent without permission. By connecting the number 24 with his minor criminal activity, Freud gave us the hint that 24 could be classified as a "bad" number in his psychic system.

If that is so, then *why* is it so? Our first clue here is that Freud obtained this "bad" number by splitting 2467 into two halves. So let's do the same with 24. What we get are the numbers 2 and 4, and Freud has already given us the clue with 24 years that these smaller numbers should be regarded as ages, and that they likewise signify a time of "badness". In effect, Freud's psyche was referring to that *bad time* between ages 2 and 4 when he had sex with, and then lost, his nanny (see chapter two).

Freud constantly argued that unconscious events, such as dreams, made secret references to powerful childhood memories. That is now being claimed here, with regard to the hidden references relating to Freud's "2467 mistakes," particularly the claim that its first two digits (24) pertain to jailing for criminal activity. Here, ask yourself who was the most important person in Freud's formative years who spent time in jail, allegedly for a rather minor criminal offense. That was his feared and beloved nanny who was sent to jail by his family for ten months between the 2nd and 4th years of Sigmund's years at Freiberg.

Now we're in a position to explain the real reasons why Freud spent his 24th birthday in jail celebrating what he called his "coming of age." Unawares, he got himself *put* into that jail, I suggest, because of guilty feelings about his nanny, since his incarceration was an unconscious imitation of her jailing in his childhood. In getting himself jailed for being absent without permission, he was imitating her having been jailed and absent without permission, i.e. she had not received *his* permission to leave him. Also, his adult dream life told him that she had helped him to "come of age" by being his instructress in sexual matters, so it was fitting that he should spend that birthday which he related to "coming of age" in a place that symbolized her presence so powerfully—a jail cell. Given his great fascination with number magic, these imitations were triggered on his 24th birthday because it encodes the numbers 2 and 4 and the childhood ages to which these two numbers refer.

The above factors suggest that Freud harbored massive feelings of guilt relating to his nanny's jailing. And one can imagine the great intensity of this guilt by the evidence of his having gone to the extreme of getting himself jailed on his 24th birthday. But what were the true reasons for such strong guilt feeling about nanny, remembering that he called her the primary instigator of his neurosis? Was it just that they had stolen money together or had shared some sort of sexual play, as was mentioned in chapter two?

Perhaps Freud felt a more direct responsibility for nanny's jailing than he ever admitted. One can imagine the scene in childhood when his mother and brother first suspected that nanny was a thief. Very likely they would have gone first to young Sigmund to ask him whether he could confirm that nanny was stealing things from them. If so, he might have blurted out her guilt, as children often do at such times. If he had been fearful about disclosure of his own complicity in theft, he might have lied a good deal while putting all the blame on her. In either case, he would have ended up with a great deal of guilt about nanny, especially since she was sent to jail and he did not receive a similar punishment. So perhaps he gave himself a token jail sentence on his 24th birthday, as an expression of his persistent guilt about his governess's jailing and *his* role in that punishment and reprisal.

The preceding paragraphs have linked Freud's guilty feelings towards his nanny with his famous reference to "2467 mistakes." If this is correct, it should be recalled that the number 2467 has also now been connected with Freud's recurrent death anxieties, in this case involving the fantasy that he would have only 24 years more to live after 1899, sealing his death at age 67. Do these death anxieties pertaining to 2467 have anything to do with Freud's nanny? My answer goes back to what was stated in the second chapter. That is, it's likely that in his earliest years young Sigmund suspected that his missing nanny had been "boxed-up," placed in a coffin, as punishment by his family for her thievery. Perhaps in the later years of childhood he learned the truth, that she had been jailed, but the earlier mistaken idea (death) could have retained a powerful hold on his unconscious mind, even contributing to his formation of the idea: "2467 mistakes."

A Moralistic Devil

The earlier portions of this chapter were concerned with providing evidence that Freud's psychopathology was expressed partly by his identification with the Devil, as was shown by Bakan's data relating to Freud's Satanic pact. If it is correct that Freud had made this identification with the Devil, some readers might conclude that this was a unique type of pathology in a modern man. If so, I'd like to suggest that perhaps that is not true. Perhaps other deeply neurotic and/or psychotic individuals harbor their own metaphorical Satanic pacts which they manage to conceal from their therapists, and sometimes even from themselves. Maybe Freud's pact was just less metaphorical than most others, because it was tied to number magic and his death fears.

That the Satanic pact is a grim reality in the neurotic process was emphasized firmly by the eminent clinician Dr. Karen Horney (1885-1952). She stressed the role in neurosis of "the search for glory" involving pathological ambition, the need for vindictive triumph, and self-idealization (Freud as the little king). Horney claimed that the most pertinent and crucial symbol for the neurotic process, triggered by the search for glory, is the *ideational theme of the Satanic pact* as reflected by such classics as Goethe's *Faust*, Benet's *The Devil and Daniel Webster*, and Wilde's *The Picture of Dorian Gray*.

In each of the above stories, a troubled man struggles towards a godlike status, in the process giving up his own soul (his real self) and ending up in a kind of hell, the hell of his own bitterness and self-hatred. To Horney, the arrogant search for glory causes these neurotic individuals to become hated strangers to themselves. She emphasized, therefore, that the neurotic process parallels the legendary devil's pact in which a distressed individual arrogates awesome powers to himself, thereby losing his soul in the torment of self-alienation.

Both Karen Horney and David Bakan wrote about this issue of the Satanic pact as if it always remained at the level of a metaphor. My assertion is that, in the case of Sigmund Freud, that was not true. In terms of Freud's identification with the Devil there is good reason to believe that he acted-out that identification in numerous ways, especially in terms of actualizing his urgent death-wishes towards others (Emanuel and John Freud, Fleischl, Tausk, Silberer, Fliess, etc.) In this regard, remember that it was the Devil's primary task to slaughter countless individuals (and to consign them to a fiery eternity in hell).

In a moment, it will be shown how Freud acted-out his identification with the Devil in various ways while writing one long letter relating to the topic of "morality and religion." But first, let's consider the personality attributes of Satan that might have appealed to Freud's imitative tendencies, considering that he was so fond of quoting the wisdom of Mephistopheles as expressed in Goethe's *Faust*.

The personality attributes of Satan have been described in world literature over many centuries. The Devil is described as being very clever, witty, charming and an excellent speaker.* As the arch deceiver and falsifier, he is portrayed as the greatest and most talented LIAR imaginable. Thus, as part of his great deceit, he lies repeatedly about his moral standards and pretends to be elevated to the highest moral plane. (As part of his moral facade, he loves to quote holy scripture.)

The Devil is also portrayed as a great flatterer and seducer, as seen in his

---

*Freud was widely perceived as having all these characteristics.

uses of seductions regarding intellectual and moral issues. Of course, he is the great tempter who slowly corrodes our ethical restraints, inviting his victims to abandon themselves to sexual license and other indulgences. Finally, he is the great destroyer. In tempting a man to destruction, he might offer him—as with Jesus—power over the entire world (Horney's search-for-glory). However, his deepest hidden motive involves a burning hatred of man and the world, and the desire to destroy man and the world, utterly.

In subsequent paragraphs, a long letter of Freud's will be analyzed to reveal how he used it to act-out his identification with a whole spectrum of Satanic qualities. This was a letter dated July 8, 1915 which he wrote to Dr. James J. Putnam whom Freud had met about six years earlier while visiting Clark University in America. Putnam was Professor of Neurology at Harvard University and became important to Freud in 1906 when he wrote the first article in an American scientific journal explaining Freud's clinical and theoretical discoveries. Evidently, Freud's letter to Putnam in July 1915 was in response to the latter's suggestion that Freud should become more favorably disposed in his writings to moral and religious considerations in mental life.

Early in his letter to Dr. Putnam, Freud was assertive in stating that he considered himself to be an extremely moral human being. Indeed, his compulsive honesty forced him to admit that his sense of justice and consideration for his fellow man had elevated him to the ranks of the best people he had ever known! Moreover, he claimed that he had "never done anything mean or malicious," nor had he even felt any temptation to do so. With regard to sexual morality, Freud's wording was quite evasive, but he ended by implying that his record had been excellent concerning sexual conduct.

Near the end of this self-congratulatory letter, Freud pretended to modesty concerning his ability to understand the origins of his exceptionally pure morality. He stated that he had no idea why he *and his six adult children* were compelled to be "thoroughly decent human beings." At this point, notice that Freud attributed this compulsive goodness to himself and to his children, with no mention of his wife Martha, suggesting the hidden wish that only his genes would be perceived by Putnam as carrying the superbly moral traits that he had boasted about.

Patting himself on the back for having this immensely moral nature, Freud then proceeded to compare himself with the rest of mankind. He stated to Putnam that he had no idea why he had persisted in being honorable, noble, and kind at all times despite having learned that this caused him to suffer harm from his fellow man. For long ago, poor Freud had learned the terrible truth—that "other people are brutal and unreliable." This caused him to recognize, he added, that he was *much better* than other people. But this recognition of his moral superiority over others did not give him any "recognizable satisfaction," or so he claimed.

There are other portions of this letter to Dr. Putnam that will be mentioned later. But let's study what has already been summarized in this letter, in relation to the characteristics of Satan set forth in world literature for centuries. Like Satan, it seems clear, Freud qualifies as a great deceiver of mankind by palming himself off as a supreme moralist. And his faithful biographer, Ernest Jones has helped to perpetuate that deceit in myriad ways.

For example, Jones had the audacity to incorporate Freud's letter to Putnam into his long chapter "analyzing" Freud's personality and character, evidently presenting this letter as proof of Freud's sterling moral qualities. Needless to say, that entire chapter in which Jones pretended to analyze Freud's personality is itself a gross deception and a ludicrous sham. For it incorporated an entire printed *eulogy* by one of Freud's ardent followers, giving us an idea of the degree of objectivity that was obtained by Jones regarding Freud's warped personality.

The letter to Putnam revealed Freud's great narcissism in regarding himself as far better than other people. This is also the expression of a satanic quality. For the Hebrew myths about Satan described his great beauty and his extreme vanity, which caused him to become envious and enraged at the beauty of the newborn creature Adam whom he regarded as a rival for the attention of God and of the other angels. Immediately this reminds us of how greatly Freud was spoiled in his youth by his parents and other family members, to the detriment of his siblings.

Another satanic attribute involves the corrosion of ethical restraints and the tempting of victims to indulge in sexual license. In the 1915 letter to Putnam, Freud stated that he regarded society's view of sexual morality as "very contemptible." In contrast to society's position, he asserted: "I stand for an infinitely freer sexual life.."* One should note, however, that anyone who truly champions an *infinitely* greater expression of sexuality is secretly inviting others to indulge in sexual license.

And that charge was made against Freud by numerous critics in earlier decades, but was always quickly denied by expert apologists who cited the master's saintly qualities as proof that he would never undermine sexual morality. Perhaps some readers will ponder this issue anew and decide for themselves about Freud's incitements to sexual license after reading Kushner's (1967) small book. Kushner has sampled Freud's writings that incite us to the breakdown of incest taboos and other sexual restraints, finally concluding that some of Freud's writings are a menace to society's

---

*The next chapter will discuss numerous gross acts of sexual immorality by Ernest Jones, all under the cloak of "sexual freedom."

moral life.

There is another obvious satanic quality cited in world literature that we have not yet mentioned here: contempt for God and intense opposition towards Him. With regard to this quality, early in his letter to Dr. Putnam, Freud wrote: " . . I stand in no awe whatever of the Almighty." Then he asserted that if ever he were to meet God, he would have more reproaches to make of God than the Lord could make of him.

Thus, he expressed not only his opposition to and contempt for God but also hinted at his *moral superiority* over God, by way of deserving fewer reproaches than God deserves. But this does not do full justice to Freud's anger and hatred towards God. This evil flower blossomed fully in his lengthy attacks against God and religion in his books *The Future of an Illusion* and *Civilization and its Discontents*. Undoubtedly, these books have persuaded hundreds of thousands of intellectuals around the world to develop disbelief in God and contempt for religion, while emulating Freud's stance of intellectual and moral superiority.

Related to Satan's deceitfulness is his reputation as a masterful liar and con artist. Already Freud is revealed as a consummate liar in his outrageous assertions to Dr. Putnam about being one of the supreme moralists of his era. This is similar to the boastful lie that Freud penned in *The Psychopathology of Everyday Life*. There he claimed that his immersion in psychoanalysis was so therapeutic for him that it had made him incapable of telling a lie. That was truly a satanic lie, for only the demonic liar insists on his compulsive truthfulness, as Mark Twain understood very well. Contrary to his boast, Freud's writings are studded with scores of lies, half-truths, and deliberate distortions, although his apologists have refused to acknowledge Freud's deceitfulness.

Again it should be emphasized that the Devil is described as having the talents of an extremely clever and charming con artist. In the Putnam letter Freud expressed these talents by pouting prettily and complaining that God had not endowed him with sufficient intellect. Thereafter, his charm increased dramatically when he confided to Putnam that he had always been dissatisfied with his intellectual endowment, as if he felt that he possessed only average intelligence or slightly higher. In a very clever manner, Freud then implied that though he'd been given only modest intellectual endowments, his great achievements had been fostered by a gift that compensated for his average intellect, namely his incredibly elevated moral nature!

The preceding little con game was like countless others that Freud spread lavishly throughout his letters to persuade others of his greatness, lack of ambition, modesty, honesty, etc. In the above game, Freud decided to downgrade his superior intelligence expecting that this display of "modesty" would disarm Putnam and obtain his tolerance for Freud's compensatory claim to moral superiority. Of course, in this game Freud had reason to believe that in 1915 his noteworthy achievements had already made it difficult for Putnam to accept that Freud had anything but a brilliant intelligence.

Moreover, this con game was "very good for business" in dealing with the Christian world that Freud envied and feared so greatly. Surely, he was aware that Christians of his day constantly were worried about the high intelligence and cleverness of Jews, so here was a perfect opportunity to deceive one of these dullards by telling him what he wished were true— 'Freud isn't very smart, so you can relax and not fear him, especially since he's so honest and committed to the highest ethical standards.'

Finally, we should examine Satan's hatred of mankind and of the world, and his desire to destroy both, in order to consider how this correlates with Freud's destructive urges. Already in the Putnam letter Freud was found describing his fellow man as brutal and unreliable. Recall that his hatred for mankind was expressed more forcefully in *Civilization and its Discontents*. In that little book Freud spat out his venom towards people, claiming that we were deserving only of his hatred on the pretext that we would readily slander and insult *him* if given the chance. Along the way, he compared mankind with insects and savage beasts, thereby providing a hidden justification for his cruelty towards others throughout his lifetime.

Concerning Satan's desire to destroy mankind and the world, it's not hard to believe that Freud shared such a grotesque motive in his pathological identification with the Devil. For in an earlier chapter we noted that he once wrote to Martha in a fit of anger and depression, as follows: " . . . had I the power to destroy the whole world, ourselves included . . .I would do so without hesitation." But if Satan's disciple cannot destroy the world, there is still the chance that he will find a way to dominate and control it. No one should ignore Erich Fromm's thesis that Psychoanalysis is a worldwide political and religious movement created by Freud as a means for influencing and dominating the world's intellectual elite.

Having gone down the list of satanic attributes in comparison with qualities found in *one* letter written by Sigmund Freud, perhaps it seems more reasonable that Freud is deserving of the label "the evil genius," if he deserves to be called a genius at all. The Viennese journalist Karl Kraus was one of the most brilliant social critics of his era. At the turn of the century he had a ringside seat at the birth of Psychoanalysis, and soon became one of its most vehement critics. For Kraus came to know Freud and his penchant for character assassination very well, and was probably the first observer to label Freud as an "evil genius."

With all the accolades that Freud has received from admirers and apologists during the past eighty years, it's comforting to know that some people, like Kraus, have been able to see through Freud's saintly veneer. And especially in relation to Freud's own psychopathology, we can continue to ponder Kraus's famous aphorism: Psychoanalysis is a disease masquerading as a cure.

Devil's Pacts, Delusions and Murder

The beginning of this chapter focused on Bakan's book (1958) which emphasized various behaviors and statements by Freud that pointed to his identification with Satan. But Bakan is not the only thoughtful writer who has recognized Freud's demonic identifications. Paul Vitz's book (1988) offered copious data showing that Freud's unconscious mind was permeated by religious issues and identifications, and in an impressive chapter concerning Freud's connections with the Devil he wrote that a central and very important part "of Freud sided with Satan against God . ." Vitz mentioned Velikovsky (1941) as being the first author to be aware of Freud's ideological connections with Satan, and the first writer to assert that Freud probably had entered into a Satanic pact of some kind.

Both Velikovsky and Bakan endorsed the idea that Freud entered into only one Satanic pact during his lifetime. Vitz went further and gave arguments supporting his belief that Freud had devised two devil's pacts. However, all three of those writers claimed that Freud had taken a metaphorical stance towards Satan, not believing in the reality of the Devil's existence, and likewise that he viewed the Satanic pact(s) as being metaphorical. (Perhaps Vitz viewed this topic a bit more concretely, for he noted that Freud had early and deeply rooted ties to Satan, and that he might have entered into an actual blood pact.)

The present writer both agrees and disagrees with the previous authors' belief that Freud regarded Satan metaphorically, as I will explain. My view is that those authors have taken too simplistic a view of this matter, and that their conclusion is misinformed because it does not take into account that Freud was often very depressed and struggling with borderline psychosis. At such times, Satan became more real and non-metaphorical to him, in comparison with periods of better mental health and more lucid thinking. Furthermore, emphasis should be given to a decided *split* between Freud's conscious and unconscious functioning. Major portions of his unconscious mind were dominated by autistic, delusional thinking that sometimes clouded his conscious thought. Thus, his unconscious was permeated by delusions that he could use number magic in relation to Satanic pacts to control death; to counter deep insecurities and weaknesses, while attaining fame and power; and to receive help in destroying his enemies (including Emanuel and John). Since Velikovsky, Bakan, and Vitz failed to recognize that, at times, Freud's death wishes became quite real and patently murderous, they also failed to understand that there were time when Satan also was very real to him.

Concerning the above split in Freud's thinking, it should be said that he was not the only apparently rational psychologist to exhibit this problem. That most intellectual and rational of analysts, Karl Abrahan, exhibited this same split in the final months of his life, when his mind suddenly descended into dabbling with number magic and the balmy theories of Wilhelm Fliess, the Berlin magician who had shared a *folie à deux* with Freud. Also, many scholars have recognized the same split in Jung's thought, part rational and the rest clouded by countless magical ideas and tendencies. Likewise, the allegedly most rational of psychologists was Freud's hero named Gustav Fechner—the creator of psychophysics and grandfather of experimental psychology—who tried for years to conceal the split between his scientific ideas and his extremely mystical ones. His mystical side endorsed the notion that the physical world is a "system of souls," as well as an animistic theory endowing plants and animals with souls.

Having reminded my readers of the extreme split in Freud's personality between rational and irrational thinking, allow me to call attention to his flagrant uses of magical thinking in his symbiotic relationship with the near-madman Fliess during the period from 1890 to 1900—particularly their shared affinity for number magic, which was the basis for Fliess's balmy "periodicity theory." Regarding that era, it is my thesis that Freud used a covert form of number magic (involving his triumphant number, 19) to concoct another Satanic pact, his *third* and earliest of these pacts. In *The Fatal Freud* my chapter titled "Freud Falsifies the Data" offers numerous insights into his covert uses of number magic including many details about his devising of this earliest devil's pact, so I will now limit myself to giving only some general information about this subject.

First, I will remind readers of my claim that at age 43, in 1899, Freud concocted two covert Satanic pacts involving the number 2467 (extending his life for 24 years) and his new phone number 14362, which extended his life for 19 years) ending in 1918 at age 62. (Recall that for many years he suffered from repeated fears that he would die in February 1918 at age 61, and also that he might die at age 62.) My emphasis now is that *in the year 1899* Freud obviously was experiencing such massive death fears that he felt compelled to create two devil's pacts in that year to ensure his greater longevity via magical thinking. What explains that this bizarre behavior occurred in 1899, in my view, is that 1899 must have marked the ending of a previous devil's pact for Freud.

If so, my deduction is that Freud had devised an earlier devil's pact whose duration probably was for 19 years, since 19 was his triumphant magical number, and is consonant with his use of 19 for extending his life, in regard to his new phone number which he received in 1899. (Also, 19 connects with the death of John *in 1919*, and the triumphant lethal significances of Berggasse *19*.) This implies that his earliest pact was negotiated near the end of 1880, and that it specified 19 years of additional life, which then forced him, in dire fear of death, to negotiate in 1899 his new devil's pacts to extend his life again. One can guess that the pact negotiated in late 1880 did not only promise him 19 years of life but also a magnificent achievement of some kind, which perhaps is why his now-famous dream book was ready for publication precisely in 1899.

There are other reasons that cause one to suspect that late 1880 was when Freud negotiated his earliest Satanic pact. The year 1880 was when he became 24 years old. Concerning his covert pact involving the number 2467, he seemed to indicate that this pact (devised in 1899) was connected with his age of 24 years in 1880. That is, he related 2467 to the time in 1880 when he became fixated on General E.M. whose *time ran out* in 1899, due to retirement—and also to Sigmund's having spent his 24th birthday in a military jail. Sigmund's release from jail was consonant with the release of the Biblical Josef from prison, on a charge of wishing to sexually molest an older woman (the nanny theme), and also was relevant to Sigmund's concerns about the Freuds' jailing of his nanny and child Sigi's guilty feelings that he deserved the same punishment. Thus, Sigmund's release from jail at age 24 signified his rebirth, like Josef; that he would not be "murdered," like nanny; and that he was entitled to at least another 19 years (his magical number) of life, as provided by the strange pact which assured him life until 1899.

If I am correct that Freud formulated a Satanic pact which lasted from late 1880 to late 1899, this might help explain his solid endorsement of Fliess's weird periodicity theory, particularly during the years from 1894 through 1899. There are at least two strange reasons why Freud might have embraced Fliess's childish play with number magic pertaining to this periodicity theory, in omnipotent ways which asserted his ability to use various uncanny calculations to predict precisely the time of any person's death, many years in advance. First, he might have accepted Fliess's claims about predicting deaths accurately because he, Sigmund, believed that he could predict that his own death would occur in 1899, due to his unconscious Satanic pact negotiated in 1880. (If he had died in the early months of 1899 he would have been age 42, which explains why Schur relates that he feared death at age 42.) Second, Freud eventually may have accepted the awesome predictive power of Fliess's periodicity theory, because the Berlin magicians's arcane calculations foretold that age 51, in 1907, would be the time of Sigmund's death.

During the 1890s Freud might have been strongly motivated to accept

Fliess's periodicity theory and its prediction that he would die at age 51, because this gave him about eight more years of life than his first Satanic pact of 1880 had provided. However, in 1899 Freud took matters into his own hands and created those two additional devil's pacts, permitting him either 19 or 24 years of additional life. This carried him far beyond the time of life allotted by Fliess's theory, though until age 51 was passed it still maintained a fearful grip upon Freud's paranoid feelings and imagination.

The preceding material has demonstrated the shared delusional ideas of Freud and Fliess concerning relations among number magic and predictions about death, along with their concealed tendencies pertaining to murder. After his breakup with Fliess, Freud did not hesitate to accuse Fliess of harboring strong paranoid and delusional (psychotic) tendencies which Freud alleged had been eliminated in himself, presumably by his self-analysis. However, there is reason to believe that during his breakup with Fliess, in 1899 and 1900 (including the plan to kill Fliess in August 1900 at Achensee), Freud's lethal impulses became connected with his Satanic pact concerning his new phone number, which was to end his life at age 62. Thus, in 1904 he fantasized, during his trip to Trieste and Athens, that Fliess's number magic was pursuing him murderously in connection with his belief that the number 62 was "following" him on *railway* tickets—just preceding a brief psychotic episode that Freud suffered on the Acropolis at Athens. All of this lethal number magic in Freud's mind was part of a near-psychotic delusional system which showed that he was just as close to insanity, from time to time, as Fliess was.

At the start of the previous paragraph, I suggested that Freud's and Fliess's uses of number magic were connected with murderous tendencies in both men, and this requires explanation regarding Fliess. My assumption is that Fliess's use of periodicity theory to predict the deaths of countless people was a reflection of his hidden lethal tendencies. I would argue that he used these predictions not only to effect a magical control of death but also, in a concealed fashion, to express murderous tendencies. Thus, when he used his arcane calculations to predict that Freud would die at age 51, this was a reflection of his desire that magically he could *cause* Freud to die at that age. At an unconscious level, Freud must have sensed Fliess's death wish towards him and that is partly his reason for seeking Fliess's death at Achensee, and for trying to overcome Fliess's death wish regarding age 51 by replacing it with the Satanic pact of 1899 relating to the new telephone number. Surely, Freud regarded his rivalrous friend as a Faustian character, like himself, so in 1899 and 1900 this became a titanic struggle in Freud's mind whose outcome would show which man could have greater influence with Satan to destroy the other.

The final sentence above hints at another reason why Freud may have negotiated his devil's contracts, relating both to his persistent fears of death and his countless death wishes towards other persons. These Satanic pacts alleviated his own fears of death via fantasies that allegiance to the Devil enabled him to extend his life indefinitely. Likewise, they also satisfied his pressing death wishes towards others via the fantasy that Satan required him to cut short the lives of numerous persons, while stoking his feelings of omnipotence by believing that the Devil was his powerful ally in destroying his endless list of enemies. Freud's wish that he could assist Satan in destroying large numbers of people reminds us of the promiscuous cocaine deaths of the 1880s, and his letter to Martha in that era expressing his desire for immense power to destroy the entire world, which he stated he would use "without hesitation." Also, we are reminded of his letter to Ferenczi admitting that his self-analysis had revealed a "murderous . . and ever-active devil" in himself that he intended to hide from the sight of others, and even from himself.

In previous chapters I suggested some dark Satanic reasons why Freud might have arranged the murders of Emanuel and John Freud. Since the presumed murder of John occurred in 1919, near the conclusion of Freud's pact of 1899 concerning his phone number, this led me to suggest that this nephew might have become a sacrifice and substitute for Sigmund's death. This is consonant with Satanic lore in which a client of the Devil can be freed from a death-payment if he can persuade or trick someone into signing a devil's contract, forfeiting this new soul for the original victim's soul. However, the assassinations of Emanuel and John also might have been motivated by Sigmund's desire to propitiate his master, the Devil, for more general reasons. Thus, he was assisting the general work of destroying "evil" persons who deserved to have their souls consigned to hell. The latter motive can be subsumed under Sigi's desire to lethally repay his kinsmen for "murdering" his nanny, with regard to "the Freiberg catastrophe."

Even in the final months of Freud's life, we can find evidence that he was still trying to propitiate his vicious master, Satan, by uttering a curse that would consign a soul (an English soul) to everlasting hellfire. The occasion was Freud's letter of December 13, 1938 to the writer Arnold Zweig, whose son seems to have escaped injury in a serious car accident, which Freud apparently blamed on an English officer who was alleged to have been drinking. In this letter Freud expressed to Arnold Zweig his anger about the unreasonableness of fate, the uncertainty of life, and his concern about the welfare of Zweig's son. Freud said he was glad that this son was "blameless" regarding the car accident, and implied that the English officer had been the real culprit (evidently being the driver of a second car). (In Jones, III).

After referring to general information about this car accident, Freud gave the following curse against that unknown English officer: "May the devil not forget that drunken officer when he is choosing from the English." In effect, this was Freud's wish that this Englishman should be thrown into hellfire. Apparently, this was his manner of expressing his cruel and relentless obedience to the fiery will of his master, Satan, as well as his longterm desire to immolate his English enemies, as had also occurred with Emanuel and John Freud. (Regarding the name Zweig, recall my view that names starting with "Z" usually related to his anxious concerns about his nanny, Ms. Zajic.)

The preceding anecdote also calls to mind Freud's secret desire to immolate John Freud in a fiery death as a sacrifice to Satan. My reason for assuming that Freud wished to destroy John via hellfire is relevant to another act of name magic by Freud. This pertains to Marie Balmary's book (1982) in which she cited Freud's identification with Don Juan, also known as Don Giovanni, in relation to Sigmund's fantasy that he deserved Don Juan's fate—being dragged down into hellfire by an enraged statue (representing betrayed father-figures).

Why do I suggest that Freud's identification with Don Juan indicates his desire to send his nephew John to a fiery grave? Name magic tells us that Sigmund identified himself and John with the figure of the sexual criminal, Don Juan, since the given name of John Freud is the equivalent of "Juan." In Freud's mind, this reflected his evil identification with his nephew and that both men should have had identifications with Don Juan, since at Freiberg they were both perverse children who had enjoyed sexual relations with their primal mother, the nanny called Monica Zajic. In this fashion, they had betrayed their father-figures, just as Don Juan had betrayed his father-figure represented by the Commander's vengeful statue. Therefore, when Sigmund killed John in 1919, he was providing a magical substitute for himself, a substitute who had fully shared his primal crime and so deserved the same hellfire that Sigmund believed was awaiting him on Judgment Day.

Chapter Eleven

Dr. Ernest Jones: Eminent Psychopath

With Anna Freud in 1914

In chapter eight we saw that in August 1914 Ernest Jones's former mistress, Loe Kann, was in England when Freud's fragile and neurotic daughter Anna, age 18, arrived there on her way to visit her relatives in Manchester. Anna was greeted at the pier by Ernest Jones who gave her gifts and assumed the role of her protector and guide. Loe Kann was staying in London then and soon contacted Anna, with whom she had become friendly while Loe, in previous years, had been Freud's analytic patient in Vienna. To her dismay, Loe soon realized that Ernest Jones had begun a campaign to seduce this vulnerable girl, Anna Freud, because he wanted to take revenge on Freud whom he blamed for Loe's recent marriage to another man (also named Jones).

As discussed previously, Loe quickly wrote to Freud alerting him to Jones's vicious motives regarding Anna. Freud did not doubt Loe's claim that Jones intended to seduce Anna, and he wrote Jones a strong letter to forestall that event. My assumption is that Freud believed Loe's accusation readily, because her months of analysis must have given her ample opportunity to apprise Freud of Jones's remarkable record as a sexual psychopath during the seven years that she had been his mistress. The clear likelihood that Freud had known that Jones was a seducer of young women makes it seem astonishing that he would have delivered his inexperienced daughter into Jones's hands in August 1914, but that is what he did. (In earlier pages I have argued that this was evidence of Freud's extremely unstable thinking then, and of his compulsion to use Anna as a dupe in his presumed plan to assassinate Emanuel Freud in October 1914.)

While reviewing that material in the eighth chapter, readers might have asked themselves whether Loe Kann's accusation that Jones intended to seduce Anna was a falsehood spawned by Loe's lasting resentments towards Jones. That seems unlikely, since years later he bothered to deny that seductive intention while slyly informing Anna that he had been in love with her in the summer of 1914, despite the great difference between their ages. Readers will make up their own minds about Jones's denial that he intended to effect a manipulative seduction of Anna in 1914, presumably because his love for her then had been honest and true. Loe's accusation that he intended to deceive Anna in 1914 will seem quite plausible after the contents of this chapter have been absorbed, since this material will disclose numerous sexually psychopathic behaviors by Jones over decades.

As a preface to the forthcoming data, I should mention that these materials will summarize two long chapters about Jones's sexual escapades that appear in *Secret Sex Lives*. Most of this information involves my discussion and re-interpretation of data found in Jones's extremely defensive and dishonest autobiography (1959), and a somewhat less defensive biography of Jones by Vincent Brome (1982). Before writing his book, Brome had close, even friendly contacts with Jones and his family members, and some critics might regard him as an apologist for Jones to a modest extent, although he does cite various damning anecdotes that do not appear in Jones's romanticized book about himself. (My chapters in *SSL* compare Jones's autobiography with Brome's work so that readers will recognize the outrageous deceptions that Jones fostered about himself, a smokescreen that is relevant to his often deceitful methods in concocting the Freud biographies of the 1950s.)

Jones's Early Years

On January 1, 1879 Ernest Jones was born in a Welsh village later called Gower, and was the first child of his parents and their only son. His two sisters named Elizabeth and Sybil were about two and four years younger than Ernest. When he was born his father, Tom Jones, was 25 and his mother, Mary Ann, was 23. She was a dark, short woman who was excessively devoted to her son, while Tom was a tall, blond and handsome man with considerable intelligence. Apparently, Ernest was spoiled by his mother but felt that he was treated arrogantly by his father. Perhaps, in later years he was bothered by his father's height, since the adult Ernest reached a size of only five feet and five inches (two inches shorter than Freud). One suspects that this size factor helped provoke Jones's great preoccupation with the life of Napoleon Bonaparte, with whom Freud identified strongly.

In his autobiography (1959), Jones described his mother as being openly affectionate and his father as a man who placed strong restraints on his own emotions. Tom Jones was a successful businessman and engineer who rose to progressively more important positions in the coal and steel business, causing him to travel abroad frequently. In his later years he held eminent positions with several Boards of Directors in London and Cardiff. In his autobiography, Ernest admitted having feelings of hostility towards his father, a man who practiced a high level of integrity in business and preached a lofty code of ethics. Perhaps this impelled Ernest to take an opposite path in his life, regularly demonstrating unethical behaviors while pretending to be virtuous.

In Vincent Brome's biography titled *Ernest Jones: Freud's Alter-Ego*(1982) the first paragraph cited Jones's sexual precocity and that he engaged in sexual intercourse in early childhood. Brome wrote that "complicated sexual urges were disturbing him at the age of three. . " Jones noted that sexual intercourse was a common practice of young children in his village, that the boys often talked about sex in explicit terms, and that one lad expressed a wish to have intercourse with young Ernest's mother! This steamy sexual scene in childhood may have helped Jones to become a fervent advocate of the free love doctrine in his adult years.

Some clues exist that Ernest might have indulged in sexual acts with his younger sisters, particularly Sybil, the youngest child. Concerning possible incest, Brome seemed uneasy in reporting that young Ernest shared the same bed with his sisters. His relationship with Sybil was a love/hate affair and at times he treated her arrogantly (as his father treated him), but claimed that he was very fond of his sister. Ernest's feelings of sexual sadism towards her were suggested by a strange obsession with Sybil's name—a kind of name magic—that he evidenced from age twelve into his adult years.

He wrote a letter to Freud in 1910 describing his "obsession never to write anything, a letter, address an envelope, school task, etc. without undersigning it" with a mark like this, ∞ which seemed to be a reclining letter S (in a horizontal position). At first, he claimed that this symbol stood for Science, but later admitted that: "I know that it stands for Sybil, the name of my younger sister." His explanations reveal that Jones was obsessed by desires to place his sister's name horizontally under his own name—to place her under himself (sexually) using name magic. To Freud he admitted the sexual obsession involved here, remarking that: "In writing, which with me is very directly *sexually* symbolic, I therefore put her *below* me, in a double sense (a) as my child, (b) *erotically.*" (Emphasis added.)

Jones gave a strong intimation that he had been involved in sexual play with Sybil, perhaps starting in those childhood days when they shared the same bed. In his autobiography he gave no data about her childhood or adolescent years and failed to mention Sybil's uncanny death, probably in her early thirties. Brome's book reported that she had a malicious sense of humor and died from a fit of laughter, while eating. She had found a remark to be very funny, roared with laughter, and choked to death on her food! Some Freudians might wonder whether unconscious guilt in Sybil had provoked her bizarre death, the oral factor in her demise perhaps relating to some oral sex-play with her brother. (Perhaps guilty feelings in Jones caused him to censor any mention of Sybil's dramatic death?)

Jones obsession with that symbol resembling a reclining letter "S" suggests that his love of Science was permeated by very erotic feelings, ones that were relevant to his misuses of his scientific credentials as a psychoanalyst. This mixing of Science and eroticism was connected with another obsession during his childhood, involving Ernest's intense love for his family doctor. This man lived in the Jones's home until the boy was age three. In a letter to Freud in 1910, Jones noted that his early identification with this handsome physician had decisively influenced his choice of a medical career.

Apparently, young Ernest developed erotic feelings for this doctor, whom he suspected was having an affair with his mother. About this doctor, Jones's dreams convinced him: "I have no doubt that I was in love with him." When Sybil was born, Ernest fantasized that she was the child of the boy and his mother; but he also suspected that she was the child of the doctor and himself. Considering Brome's remark that sexual urges were *disturbing* Ernest at age threat one wonders whether some sort of sexual abuse was prompting Ernest's erotic feelings towards this doctor who lived with his family.

Evidently, young Ernest's identification with this handsome "daredevil" doctor was fostered by his belief that the physician had sexual access to all the women of the village, including Ernest's mother. For he remembered being impressed by another boy's remark that this doctor was loved by *all the women* of their village. Since Jones admitted having sexual intercourse by age six, that comment must have signified that all the village women were having sex with this physician. The doctor's promiscuity was confirmed for Ernest at the time of the man's early death when he observed "the enormous crowd of weeping women. . at his funeral." At this point in his letter, Jones stated: "Now I have always been conscious of sexual attractions to patients; my wife was a patient of mine." The implication is that Jones's recurrent sexual desires for his patients were merged with memories of this family doctor's alleged sexual voraciousness towards *his* patients. Here, we have found the seeds of Jones's free love doctrine concerning patients, which he totally censored from his autobiography—a doctrine that permitted him to have sexual relations with a number of women whom he "therapized," as we shall discover later.

Identifying with this beloved village doctor, at age 15 Jones decided to become a physician, probably with expectations that he would imitate his idol's propensity for enjoying the sexual favors of his patients. In 1895, at the age of 16, he entered Llandovery College and his modest achievements there may have been due to religious conflicts and profound guilty feelings. Finally, he set aside religious doubts by starting his lifelong commitment to atheism, later admitting that his religious struggles had pertained to painful sexual concerns. Turning 17, he became enrolled at the University College of South Wales as a medical student and became absorbed in the study of neurology. In that era, socialist ideas became attractive to him and he read many radical writers including Saint-Simon, Marx, Bakunin, and others.

In 1898 Jones was 19 when he entered University College Hospital in London to complete his medical studies. Twenty months were spent there before he obtained his medical qualifications at the early age of 21. During those years he became a friend of Dr. Wilfred Trotter, who later became his medical partner and eventually married his sister Elizabeth.

Now we are ready to consider the first of many outrageous acts by Jones that demonstrated the pressure of his sexually psychopathic impulses in relation to patients. While at University Hospital he engaged in behavior that he called a "prank," one of many instances in his career when he broke hospital rules. In his autobiography Jones described an instance when he smuggled his friend Bertie Ward into the surgical clinic, both of these pranksters being disguised as surgical dressers. Their intrusion into the operating arena was inspired by voyeuristic impulses relating to the presence of a pretty actress who was undergoing an operation that day.

This was not the end of Jones's childish peeking at this actress's "wound." The Sunday after her operation, he and his friend Bertie were dressed in silk hats and froak-coats when they "most improperly paid a professional visit" to the patient's room—and, quite outrageously, "dressed the wound." Thus, pursuing his sexual interest in this patient, Jones had the audacity to lay hands upon her body, subjecting her wound to an unauthorized change of dressing. Blandly, he ignored that this was another doctor's patient (as he did in another case, later). Perhaps Jones was acting-out his identification with that beloved family doctor who allegedly felt that *any* woman in the village should be accessible to his erotic "attentions." Some apologists will regard this as a harmless joke, but in my view it reflects psychopathic impulses in Jones towards female patients—impulses which in later years were exhibited clearly when he was charged with sexually abusing some patients.

Starting in 1903, at age 24, there was a downturn in Jones's new medical career when he began having conflicts with colleagues and to break hospital rules in ways that caused him to lose important jobs. This led to several years when he was forced to do a series of menial medical tasks that were outside his main interests. In 1906, those defeats were made worse by the first serious charge of sexual misconduct brought against him, relating to two retarded girls (soon to be discussed). It is likely that Jones was suffering some serious aspects of mental instability during this period that spanned a four-year decline in his work. In that era, some dangerous and foolish behaviors while he was doing amateur mountain climbing (alone) nearly cost his life, hinting at suicidal impulses and underlying guilt feelings. At age 79 he wrote about that early era and seemed aware that he had suffered from great mental vulnerability then, which he connected with an "omnipotence complex." In a chapter on "Failure." he cited that period in the early 1900s when he'd had "an unwarranted belief in the omnipotence of my wishes which lulled me with the fatal promise that I should get whatever I wanted." Having been spoiled in childhood like Freud, Jones suffered from similar problems with megalomania.

Just prior to the above "years of failure," Jones showed signs of having difficulty controlling his sexual impulses. For example, there was the time when he was expected to be the "best man" at the wedding of his colleague named Sidney Bree, who was marrying into a Catholic family in Belgium. When Jones accompanied Sidney to visit the family home of his fiancée in Brussels, it happened that the lady had a sister who was also engaged to be married. Somehow, this diminutive Don Juan (Jones) persuaded this sister to have a "quickie affair" with him, right under her parents' noses! This sexual outrage caused her fiancé to challenge Jones to a duel, a threat to life which the girl's mother managed to thwart with calming words.

Jones ended this narrative by telling that, when he departed the chaotic family scene in Brussels, the young woman whom he had seduced accompanied him as far as the historic city of Bruges. In that city Jones had sexual relations with her again "at the top of its famous belfry." Concerning his sexually psychopathic behaviors, it is obvious that Jones had no concern that he had dishonored his friend Dr. Bree, had dreadfully soiled Bree's new family situation, nor that he had dishonored the young sister and shamed her fiancé. This was merely a warmup for Jones, a preface to additional actings-out of sexual and hostile impulses in later months.

In the subsequent paragraph of his autobiography, Jones described his seduction of a *second* engaged girl, in the week following his sexual exploit in Belgium. This occurred when he spent a few days vacationing with his family in Gower, his birthplace. He claimed that this next girl, a friend of his sister's, was engaged unhappily—so Ernest was kind enough to make love to her, taking her fiancé's place. His defense about breaking up this engagement was that he himself became engaged to the girl "for a time," though this is suspect since he never bothered to cite her name.

I have an explanation for Jones's unconscious dynamics in seducing these two engaged women, successively. In the first case he seduced the woman in her own family setting, and in the second case he seduced the young woman, in a sense, within his own family setting at Gower. Thus, in both cases he was acting-out his identification with the handsome doctor of his childhood—a man he regarded as a Casanova who could gratify any sexual wish (omnipotence) with any of the village women, even *within their family settings*. Ernest had become sexually competitive with this doctor, and here he was showing that he could rival or even outdo his hero by seducing two engaged women only weeks apart, under the very noses of parental figures.

Jones claimed (1959) that he was engaged briefly to this lady in Gower in 1903 while he worked as a resident medical officer at the children's hospital in London. That summer he decided to begin a six hour's journey to Gower on a Friday so that he could visit his beloved over a full weekend. In doing this, he defied a firm hospital rule forbidding a resident to spend a night away from the hospital without first obtaining permission from the full surgical committee. Instead, Jones claimed that he received a vague clearance for his absence from the senior surgeon, who was not authorized to give it. After his weekend in Gower and return to his post, the committee demanded his resignation for breaking a serious hospital rule. Jones's writings characterized this dismissal, in a cavalier manner, as harping on "unessentials"—a typical psychopathic response to wrongdoing.

Jones offered some weak excuses to his readers concerning this episode, alleging that his enemies at the hospital had conspired to obtain his forced resignation. After examining hospital records, Brome (1982) contradicted Jones's version of the event and noted that Jones had gone A.W.O.L. on two previous occasions when he "had been forced to apologise for absenting himself from duty without permission." It was the repeated contempt for hospital rules that cost him his job, and Brome commented: "His omnipotence had revealed serious shortcomings." It should be emphasized that, in giving precedence to a weekend of pleasure with his girlfriend in Gower (whom he said was sick and needed him), Jones revealed lack of concern for his sick hospital patients whom he abandoned temporarily to satisfy his "omnipotent desires." All of this constituted grave irresponsibility by a physician towards the welfare of sick children under his care, in this "children's hospital fiasco." Perhaps the sick child in Jones rebelled at being required to meet the pressing demands of the sick children for whom he was responsible?

The years from 1904 to 1907 continued to be years of defeat and failure for Jones, a time when his own mental problems seemed to provoke his persistent difficulties. After losing his hospital position, he was forced to take a series of menial jobs in medicine that were beneath his level of training. In 1905 he tried to establish a private medical practice, with his friend Dr. Trotter as partner, but it was not very successful. Near the end of 1905 he was given a part-time post as assistant physician at a seaman's hospital, but he needed to continue doing various odd jobs to earn a living. He remarked that, as these bleak months went by his failures seemed to snowball, noting that: "Every application refused meant that I became more and more widely known as a person who was in some way undesirable, and thus to be avoided." He seemed to believe that "enemies" were working against him and spreading the word that he was a very difficult man to work with (making no mention that he refused to follow medical rules). About these shadowy colleagues, he concluded that "many of them were intellectually very inferior people, a fact that did nothing to mollify the rage in my heart."

Emphasizing that destructive rage in Jones and his persistent struggling with failure in late 1905, it is clear that he was undergoing enormous stresses as 1906 began, and those great pressures must have helped precipitate the next episode of sexual acting-out. He described this event of early 1906 as the most disagreeable experience of his entire lifetime. Although the specifics are not clear, apparently it involved a charge that he had sexually molested two mentally retarded children (for whose care he was briefly responsible).

Using very unclear terms, he discussed this incident (p. 145) in his autobiography. He started by noting that he had been doing research on aphasia for many months using normal and mentally defective children, testing each child individually for phonetic articulation (about five minutes per child) in a teacher's office. One morning Jones was asked by the director of a school for mental defectives, a Dr. Kerr, to meet in the director's office to confront charges by a woman teacher that he had behaved indecently with two children (probably girls) while giving them articulation tests. Jones failed to specify the children's accusations against him, which apparently involved sexual molestations. Considering that he tested the children individually, probably one child in the office at a time, the case against him may have been made worse by the fact that *two* children had accused him. Jones wrote that the teacher "appeared to believe them," but he did not specify their gender nor give any hint as to what indecent behaviors were mentioned by the children.

Despite Dr. Kerr's reluctance to act, the teacher insisted that the complaint should be reported to the Education Committee, which delayed matters for a full two weeks and then made "the panicky decision of placing the matter in the hands of the police." The police soon arrived to take Jones to jail, and he spent that night alone in a jail cell while the London newspapers "made the most of the sensation on their placards." The next morning the case was remanded and Jones was released from jail, on an unspecified amount of bail.

A lawyer was obtained by Jones, and he explained to this barrister that probably the children had been involved in some sexual activity between themselves and that: "I was being made the scapegoat for their sense of guilt." Brome's version of Jones's excuse, which he obtained from Mrs. Jones in 1977, was somewhat different, but at least specified the factor of sexual abuse. In this version, Jones claimed that children often created "false stories" of sexual abuse, partly because they fear such abuse and also due to their 'hidden desire to know what took place in sexual intercourse.' (This second version hints that Jones may have tried to engage them in sexual intercourse, or perhaps he had raped one or both of them.)

Jones then experienced legal delays that took many weeks, and he wrote that: "For two dreadful months I lived on the edge of an abyss." (Recall his mountain climbing episode.) During that time all his professional work was suspended, and the police told him they expected the magistrate to commit him to a criminal court for trial. Jones was convinced that this would leave an indelible stain on his record, even if he were tried and found not guilty. Without providing essential details that might convict him in the reading public's mind, he wrote that for two months he lived in a state of suspense "aware that evidence of one little girl corroborated by an ill-educated puritanical teacher was about to ruin" his career. (He did not explain why the two accusing children allegedly had been reduced to one child only; and notice his arrogant description of this courageous woman teacher as "ill-educated," reminding us that he characterized his other "enemies" as his intellectual inferiors.)

Suddenly, Jones's account of this episode leaped to its shocking conclusion, without further explanation. He simply wrote that: "At last the magistrate decided to dismiss the case, and he afterwards took the unusual step of sending me a friendly and sympathetic letter.'" My own guess is that a judge who was "friendly" to this socially approved doctor circumvented honest judicial processes by peremptorily deciding against a trial, thereby showing contempt for the human rights of two retarded children and their defenseless teacher. One senses that the prestige of the doctor's work and high social class prompted the magistrate in that outrageous step of sending a little "love letter" to Jones, after dismissing the case. A review of Masson's book (1984) reveals that near the end of the last century there was an epidemic of sexual assaults against children in Europe, often involving well-educated men. In many cases there was no chance that justice could be obtained because of court philosophies insisting that child sexual abuse was always a matter of children's vivid imaginations and/or lying in order to punish adult authority. In Austria, a man convicted of sexually abusing a female child (even from a wealthy family) would be punished by only one to three months in jail! The climate against children's rights was not much better in England during Dr. Jones's heyday.

Jones wrote that some medical colleagues in London gave credence to the children's accusations against him "under the doubtfully flattering pretext that clever people were apt to be queer." This was another verse of Jones's old ditty in which he complained that jealous and intellectually inferior colleagues were conspiring to destroy his reputation. (He seemed to be doing a good job of that without the help of those unnamed enemies.) Then he acknowledged that he would have to be very cautious about his actions in future to avoid further controversy, stating that: "Personal respectability would not be enough in future; only the most rigid medical orthodoxy would save me."

However, Brome wrote that: "Barely two years later he was once again in similar trouble." As we shall see, this amazing repetition of his previous sexual abuse of children should convince us that Jones's sexual molestations were obsessive, i.e. his mind was extremely disturbed regarding sexual psychopathy, making him unable to control his criminal sexual impulses. This leads me to suggest that his presumed sexual abuse of the two mentally retarded girls represented a replay of his sexual behaviors towards his own *two* sisters in childhood, reflecting sibling rivalry and his need to maintain superiority over his sisters by stressing intellectual and sexual dominance over them. (Recall his placement of Sybil's name-initial beneath his own name, with emphasis on intellectual and erotic dominance.)

Now it's time to consider the next sexual fiasco in which Jones became embroiled, again relating to a charge that he was involved in indecent sexual behaviors with a young girl. In this case the alleged object of Jones's sexual interest was a ten year-old hospital patient. This occurred at the beginning of 1908 while he was acting as medical registrar at the West End Hospital for Nervous Diseases. At that time Jones was just becoming interested in psychoanalysis and, by reading Freudian literature, was just learning "to practice it," i.e. to provide analytic treatment. He wrote that he was the assistant to Dr. Harry Campbell, with whom he sometimes discussed children's sexuality in terms of Freud's theories. At that time, there was a ten year-old girl in the hospital whose problems with her left arm, in Jones's view, were due to an hysterical paralysis related to some sexual source. According to Jones, whom many persons have called a compulsive liar, Dr. Campbell challenged him to demonstrate the sexual source for the girl's paralysis, as Freud's theory required—despite that she was the patient of another doctor and Jones had no right to interview or treat her.

In his clever style of writing, Jones claimed that he declined this challenge, having been made wary of the risks of interviewing children alone (referring to the previous fiasco). But then he succumbed to Campbell's alleged dare and added that "to my undoing . . I allowed him to over-persuade me." It is very doubtful that Campbell made this dangerous challenge, but by claiming that he did, Jones implied that his superior was to blame for what followed.

Jones stated that he responded to his boss's arm-twisting by proceeding to interview the girl about various sexual matters, ignoring the sexual charges involving young girls that nearly cost him his career in 1906. Unhappily, this girl in 1908 was a patient of Dr. Savill who was regarded as an expert on the neuroses and had written a book on the subject, which Jones dismissed contemptuously as "banal." Brome noted that the precautions Jones took to avoid another catastrophe "seemed totally inadequate." Thus, he neglected to obtain Dr. Savill's permission for the interviews about sexuality, ignoring that Savill regarded himself as an expert on this child's affliction. Also, Jones did not arrange for a nurse to be present during the interviews, as hospital rules required, merely claiming that he interviewed the child in a place "with the door open and nurses moving in and out."

Jones wrote that his interviews showed that there was a sexual source for the arm problems of this girl, relating to an episode concerning an older boy who had tried to seduce her, after which her arm went numb and remained paralyzed. Jones concluded that her paralysis revealed a compromise between her desire to be seduced and her moralistic resistances. Also, he wrote that after interviewing this child she boasted to other children on the ward that the doctor had talked about sex to her, and eventually the word got back to her infuriated parents.

Her father complained angrily to the hospital committee, which interviewed Jones and then demanded his resignation—as had happened four years earlier when he had broken hospital rules by an unauthorized absence from the care of sick children who were his responsibility. In this case in 1908, Jones found a scapegoat in Dr. Campbell whom he claimed was a weakling who failed to protect him from the committee's verdict that Jones should be ousted. (Perhaps the anger of this child's father was intensified by his having read, or been told about, newspaper accounts of Jones's child abuse case of 1906?)

After reviewing the longterm perspective of Jones's florid sexual history, it becomes difficult for me to believe that he did not have an illicit sexual intention towards this child in the hospital in 1908. Indeed, it is quite possible that his story about a "psychoanalytic research interview" was utterly fabricated by him, or greatly exaggerated—when he wrote his autobiography at age 79—as a cover-up for his having talked to the child with an illicit intention. My basis for this suspicion partially relates to Jones's fanatic devotion to the free love doctrine, which he was shrewd enough to censor from his autobiography but is revealed clearly in Brome's biography. Today, even laymen have realized, after viewing cable television programs about free love advocates, that many of these persons endorse strange beliefs that adults should indoctrinate young children in a variety of sexual acts, for the developmental welfare of the children! So it would not be surprising that this was part of Jones's mental baggage in 1906 and 1908, helping to precipitate his sexual acting-out towards the two retarded children and the young patient of Dr. Savill. (My suspicion is that most of Jones's devotion to the free love doctrine derived unconsciously from infantile factors pertaining to frenetic sexual activity and fantasies of his childhood years—and perhaps actual sexual abuse of Ernest in his early years.)

A Refuge in Canada

When Jones was forced to resign that second hospital post in February 1908, he decided that "all hope vanished of ever getting on to the staff of any neurological hospital in London. . " Apparently, he realized that his career in neurology had been ruined by his two forced resignations and his unsavory reputation in England regarding the sexual accusations made against him. It had become time for him to switch his orientation to the new field of psychoanalysis, and that is what he did—also changing his locale to Toronto, Canada.

Somehow Jones managed to wangle a position as a "demonstrator" in psychiatry at a new psychiatric clinic affiliated with the University of Toronto. Evidently, he used his recent immersion in psychoanalysis as the questionable basis which allowed him to qualify for this clinic position. For several years he used this position as a homebase while he made propagandizing trips in many American cities, spreading the gospel of psychoanalysis to countless physicians in the New World. During his years in Toronto he promoted his free love doctrine quietly, while living in a clandestine relationship with his mistress Loe Kann, falsely describing her to everyone as his wife. Jones worked in that clinic position, under the aegis of the University of Toronto, for more than three years before he stirred up a new scandal and eventually was forced to resign "under fire" for a third time.

This new sexual scandal was described by Jones in his selfserving letter of January 13, 1911 which he wrote to a naive supporter, Prof. James Putnam of Harvard,* a strict moralist who must not have known anything about Jones's previous sexual fiascos in London. Jones wrote that he was in serious trouble in Toronto, because a female patient whom he had treated in four sessions had accused him of having sexual intercourse with her. He added that the woman had denounced him to the university president, was

---

*In chapter ten, review Freud's falsely moralistic letter to this man.

threatening legal proceedings, and had attempted to shoot him. (He alleged that he was being guarded by an armed detective.)

Jones then described this woman in ways that would elicit Putnam's biased feelings against her. He called her an hysteric who had been divorced for adultery and had had a female lover (being "pronouncedly homosexual"), but who feared that she might satisfy sexual desires by appealing to some man on the street. Jones claimed that this lesbian patient had made "unmistakable overtures" towards him, and when he rebuffed her advances, she became furious at his rejection and broke off the treatment while in a fit of transference. But he noted that he had not treated her with psychoanalysis, merely getting her to talk and trying to calm her down. (Whether or not these were mostly lies by Jones, notice that he totally ignored confidentiality by disclosing this clinical information to this layman, Prof. Putnam.)

Also, Jones claimed that the woman then "got into the hands of some doctors of doubtful reputation," including a woman doctor of "very severely strict views" who *fell in love* with the lesbian patient "and it was reciprocated." (The implication was that the woman doctor's strictness about sex was a weak coverup for burning lesbian desires!) Jones added that this patient and the woman doctor then became enmeshed in "delusions," and "cooked up rumours" about his lax views and harmful treatment, i.e. "stupid stories about my prescribing adultery, illicit intercourse, etc." (It is clear that their accusations against Jones were consonant with his devotion to the free love doctrine, but Putnam surely did not know about Jones's free love beliefs, nor that "Mrs. Jones"—whom he had met—was actually his mistress.)

Jones admitted to Putnam, in that letter, that he had made one bad mistake. In response to this patient's claim that he had seduced her, and had sexual intercourse with her, he acknowledged: "I foolishly paid the woman $500 blackmail to prevent a scandal." Finally, he remarked that he was "very worried indeed" about this debacle.

In *Secret Sex Lives* I have written many pages about this scandal, so I will only make a few comments about it here. It is my firm opinion that this case reflected another instance when Jones had been unable to resist powerful urges to sexually molest or seduce a female patient. I would not insist that every ugly claim that Jones wrote about this patient was undeniably false. However, I will stress that these characterizations were offered by a man who was a practiced and accomplished liar. And each day for years he deceived dozens of respectable people in strait-laced Toronto concerning his own sexual life and beliefs (free love)—matters that would have outraged the medical community if not artfully concealed by him. Let me emphasize that he was called an inveterate liar by four of his eminent colleagues (Morton

Prince, Freud, Jung, and Anna Freud), the latter three persons being tolerant of him despite his lying habit. Isn't it likely, therefore, that he created a blizzard of lies and innuendos to denigrate this defenseless patient, so that he could protect his medical reputation from a final eclipse? (Readers will not be surprised that this case appears in Brome's book, but not at all in Jones's autobiography.)

Notice that Jones's letter to Putnam made this woman appear to be a sick and disgusting criminal type, a "moral monster" who was an adultress, lesbian, and a potential streetwalker. Can we guess that these were projections of some of Jones's own sexual impulses, recalling his seduction of the two engaged women and his intense love, in childhood, for that handsome family doctor? It does not seem implausible that this female patient in Toronto became furious when Jones seduced her in a therapy relationship and then "dumped" her, as prompted by his sadistic impulses towards women. Her rage makes it understandable that she might have demanded and received $500 for "damages," and the fact that he alleged giving her this large sum suggests that he was not blameless in this dispute. Indeed, that was a huge sum of money in those days, probably comparable in purchasing power with $15,000 or more in the 1990s.

Let me emphasize, however, that no proof exists that the patient demanded or received $500 from Jones. He was a very clever liar who might have invented this $500 payoff to convince Putnam that the patient was a crass, psychopathic manipulator who invented accusations against him and then tried to profit financially from her lies. What seems questionable about this was Jones's claim to Putnam that the woman had taken the $500 blackmail money, yet was still threatening to bring legal proceedings against him. One would expect that the huge payoff, if true, would have forestalled any additional threats of legal action that could have exposed her as a blackmailer. We'll review the outcome of this case momentarily, but first some related matters require discussion.

Concerning the above case, Jones wrote letters to Freud revealing the name of the female Canadian physician, a Dr. Gordon, who had tried to help his patient bring a legal suit against him. To Freud he alleged that this woman doctor was secretary of the local "Purity League," echoing his claim to Putnam that she had "severely strict views." Here, Jones ignored the paradox that this super-moralist supposedly was romantically involved with her female patient who was in great mental distress. Implying that new and fantastic (delusional) charges had beet concocted by Dr. Gordon, he told Freud that he had been accused by her of sending young men to prostitutes, and of recommending free love to young women. Then he confided that: "Two of the latter became pregnant—there were three last May—but one seems to have disappeared."

One wonders how he knew about these pregnancies, whether any of them involved infants that he had fathered, and if there was an ominous significance to the disappearance of the third young woman? (Did Jones provide an abortion that led to her death?) It seems likely that Dr. Gordon learned about Jones's free love activities by having young women patients come to her with their pregnancies, ones that resulted from their "involvements" with this analytic con artist.

Concerning the patient who said that Jones seduced her (whom he allegedly gave $500), and Dr. Gordon's desire to help the woman expose Jones's victimization of her, the final outcome was destructive for both women. Jones went to see the president of the university, whose daughter had been treated by Jones and who readily sided with Jones's version of this affair, probably hoping that this would protect the university's reputation. In Jones's final letter to Putnam about this incident he described the forceful intimidation of the patient and Dr. Gordon, which ended the matter. He wrote that Dr. Gordon had visited the president, Robert Falconer, and urged him to dismiss Jones to save the youth of Toronto from his sexual excesses. Jones remarked that Falconer told Dr. Gordon "he was convinced the whole story was nonsense and flatly advised her to keep her mouth shut otherwise she would find herself in a serious legal action."

Jones added that he was collecting information about the patient's past, and hoped to get her deported as an undesirable alien, referring to her as a psychopath. Thus, he had damaged this woman by seducing her during treatment, and ended by striving to find ways to sully her reputation in order to get her deported from Canada, If some readers wonder why I am willing to believe this Toronto patient's claim that Jones seduced her, rather than accepting his firm denial, I must point to a number of key factors that have influenced my thinking. Those factors include: his identification with the family doctor who reputedly seduced all his patients; Jones's fanatic devotion to the free love doctrine; his long record of complaints by females who charged him with sexual abuses; the clear evidence that he seduced his patient Joan Riviere, discussed later; his obvious intention to seduce the young girl, Anna Freud, in 1914, for sadistic reasons; and the fact that Jones was an inveterate liar and sexual psychopath.

Concerning the above Toronto patient, it is fascinating that Jones asserted to Prof. Putnam that she was threatening to create a scandal, because he had moralistically refused to have sexual intercourse with her. His story implied that her frenetic lust for his irresistible body had been kindled in only four sessions, despite his claim that she was a flagrant lesbian. Apparently, Jones thought he was some kind of "love god," and that women often became fatally attracted to his sexual magnetism. In fact, he hinted that women could have orgasms just by being near him! In August of 1911 Jones described, in a letter to Freud, a miraculous orgasm of this kind in a female patient of his. He wrote that: "The patient. . did not touch me, would close her eyes, get flushed cheeks, breathe rapidly, make movements of coitus. . and come to a climax just as in orgasm. She did not use her hands for masturbation. . " Therefore, among his myriad accomplishments Jones was the pioneer of free love and orgasm via telepathy, though his track record suggests that he advanced beyond telepathic coition with this patient to the more mundane, physical variety.

As with the psychopathic behaviors which caused two of Jones's forced resignations in London, requiring him to jettison his neurological career and escape to Canada, several scandals involving Jones eventually led to his pressured resignation from his university clinic position in 1913 and his return to England. These scandals included the ones already mentioned concerning the Toronto patient who accused him of seduction (whom he called a lesbian), later Dr. Gordon's claims about young women who had absorbed Jones's free love doctrine and then were made pregnant, and his encouragement that young men should visit prostitutes. The third scandal involved the public uproar caused by Jones's published case history that accused Jesus Christ of being a pervert, particularly an advocate of oral sex. That bizarre incident will now be discussed, starting with a brief introduction.

In 1910, two years after his arrival in Canada, Jones was co-editor of a hospital journal in Ontario, and he often filled its pages with his own articles. During that year, he inserted in this journal a controversial case study titled "Psycho-Analytic Notes on a Case of Hypomania." In this case study Jones described his unnamed female patient who was seduced at age 16 and later made pregnant by a man she married at age 19.

Jones wrote that she was seduced at age 16 by her music teacher, who often had sexual intercourse with her a dozen times per night. After marriage her sexual demands reached nymphomanic levels beyond her husband's sexual capacity, and in frustration she turned to the church for solace. Next, Jones alleged that a minister suggested to her in veiled language that true sexual relations involved inserting the penis into her mouth and Jones added these blasphemous remarks which implied that Jesus Christ was an advocate of oral sex: "The seed was in this way to enter into the body—had not Christ said 'Take and drink'—where it would perform its function of creating and nourishing a child."

Then Jones alleged in his article that his patient did a perfect pantomime of the Holy Communion ceremony, placing a glass of water on a Bible and sucking its rim slowly, while revolving the glass, until she had provoked "a complete and exhausting orgasm." The analyst then implied that the patient's remarks revealed that, in her mind, the Communion cup had symbolized a vagina—thereby confirming Freudian symbolism—and that Holy Communion was a veiled form of cunnilingus.

Notice that this lurid and offensive case study published by Jones pertained to the seduction of a 16 year-old girl who later revealed her nymphomania. This reminds me that Jones had been repeatedly accused of sexual improprieties with young girls. In reporting, or "inventing" this case, perhaps he offered the unconscious defense that it was *their* hidden lust that had ensnared him, i.e. they were really to blame and he was not.

The psychopathic element in the presumed "inventor" of this case study shows through most clearly in Jones's intention to portray Jesus as secretly being a pervert of some sort. This was a childish way that Jones expressed his atheistic feelings and also allowed him to vent his repressed hatred for Jesus, indicating his fear of a truly moral and great man who could judge him for his own perverse nature and actions. In addition, this expressed considerable envy of Jesus's beautiful, compassionate nature which a stunted character like Jones's was forced defensively to regard with great contempt.

According to Brome's account (1982), Jones's publication of the preceding case study provoked great public anger in that era when he was employed by the University of Toronto. When the preceding article came to the attention of the Provincial Minister, he called the Dean into his office to complain about the "filthy stuff" that Jones had published and demanded that he be removed as the co-editor of the hospital's journal. However, for a number of years, Jones was clever enough to manipulate the support of powerful officials of the university, including President Falconer, to help him maintain his clinic position despite the aforementioned scandals that jeopardized his employment.

Finally, Jones was pressured to resign his clinic position when the heat became too intense, this being the third instance of his pressured resignation in the early years of his career. Brome has written (1982) that "the precise reasons why Jones was eventually asked to resign" in 1913 from his clinic position with the University of Toronto "are still not quite clear." It seems reasonable to assume that the above scandals and the decline of Jones's reputation with the university's Board were influential factors in this forced resignation. Prof. Cyril Greenland, who has written articles on Jones's years in Toronto, wrote a letter to Brome stating: "I also have in my files letters from the Hon. Dr. Herbert A. Bruce, deceased, describing in a florid style why Jones resigned. This letter was written to me in strict confidence and I am unable to disclose its contents. . ." One can imagine that if Jones's resignation provoked that florid style of expression, and strict confidentiality, that the above scandals were prominent in Jones's pressured resignation and departure from Canada in 1913.

Sadism Towards Four Women

When Jones left Canada under a cloud in 1913, he returned to London and set up a private practice in psychoanalysis. In later pages we will review the rather sordid "training" in psychoanalysis that he received from Dr. Gross in Munich as the foundation for his new career in London, but first it will prove instructive to summarize Jones's sadistic behaviors towards four women in the period from 1910 to 1914, including some of the years in Canada and the first year of his return to England. (His sadism towards these four women is discussed extensively in *SSL*.)

The first of these four women on whom Jones vented his sadism has already been mentioned, namely the patient whom he seduced in 1910 in Toronto. This was the "lesbian" whom he allegedly bribed with $500, and whose reputation he tried to ruin in 1911 so that she would be deported. At times Jones became frustrated because his mistress Loe Kann was depriving him of sexual relations, and he may have "arranged" the preceding sexual debacle (not expecting it to get out-of-hand) to punish Loe for her sexual resistances. If so, this was only one aspect of his sadism towards Loe.

By the summer of 1911 there were intense strains in the relationship between Ernest and Loe, who probably had found out about the scandal involving the aforementioned patient. That summer Loe exhibited constant pain and her drug addiction worsened, causing her to ingest huge doses of morphine, and making him fear her suicide via an overdose. In mid-1911 she began pressuring him to arrange psychoanalysis for her with Freud, and in September at the Weimar Congress Jones obtained Freud's reluctant acceptance of her request. The day after Freud agreed to her analysis, Jones had a dream whose central wish was that Loe *would die* instead of getting better in analysis. This dream was the harbinger of his sadistic intentions concerning Loe's analysis with Freud, hinting that he feared her cure would enable Loe to break away from him and disclosing his sadistic preference that she should die instead.

Loe began her analysis with Freud in the summer of 1912 while Jones was still employed in Toronto. During most of her months of analysis with Freud, she stayed in a rented apartment in Vienna while Jones continued working in Toronto, though at least once he visited her in Vienna. Sometime in early 1913, at the very time when Freud thought that Loe was beginning to make great progress in analysis, Jones's sadistic impulses boiled over, and he found a way to sabotage Loe's analysis at its most crucial stage.

During Loe's long stay in Vienna she had employed a maid and companion named Lina in whom she placed a great deal of trust. Brome revealed (1982) that Jones found a way to sexually seduce Lina, probably in

Loe's apartment (if not in her bed). And then undoubtedly he made sure that Loe discovered this betrayal by both Jones and Lina. Loe was crushed by this betrayal and began to distrust not only Jones but also Freud, nearly ending the analysis with him at that point.

But Jones's sordid strategy did not succeed, for Loe later bounced back and continued her analysis with Freud, eventually managing to complete it satisfactorily. This paved the way for her marriage in 1914 to another man named Jones (Herbert). On his part, soon after returning to Toronto from Vienna where he had seduced Lina, Jones wrote a letter of apology to Freud concerning his attempt to sabotage Loe's analysis. Admitting his sexual escapade with Lina in Vienna, he explained that "some devil of desire" had made him yield to this temptation but admitted that this was "dictated by a repressed spirit of hostility against my dear wife, and you can imagine what heart-rending remorse that is causing me." He added that it was almost beyond endurance to bear the idea that he had done something to wound Loe, since he loved her and "would do anything to save her"—ignoring his dream revealing his sadistic desire that she should die rather than be healed by analysis!

So Loe was the second of four women towards whom Jones directed brutal sadism during the years in question. The third of these women was Lina, the maid, who loved Jones and whom he used as a mere pawn in his vicious strategy to punish Loe and interfere with her analysis. There is more to be said later about this woman, Lina, whose extended and unhappy relationship with Jones is discussed in Brome's book (1982). But first I would like to mention a strange triangular relationship that developed among Jones, Lina, and Loe after the latter's analysis with Freud had been suspended in early 1913.

By August of 1913 Jones was living in London again while setting up his new psychoanalytic practice. Brome has reported that at that time Jones's letters began to indicate that he was living with Lina and Loe *at the same time*. Brome wrote that: "he appears to have taken back into his home none other than Loe Kann, simultaneously remaining involved with Lina." On a later page he wrote that Jones was now involved with these women in an *"a trois* situation,*"* referring to a *menage á trois*. Obviously, Jones's adherence to the free love doctrine had provided the basis for this bizarre triangular relationship that enabled Jones to express his desire for dominance over both of these victimized women. (Was this another replay of young Ernest's erotic dominance over his sisters in childhood?)

Brome disclosed that this triangular affair lasted from August till November 1913, after which Loe returned to Vienna briefly to complete her analysis with Freud. But during her involvement in that triangle, Loe managed to ventilate a great deal of her hostility onto Ernest for having betrayed her with Lina, whom she now detested. Probably, Ernest repaid Loe's hostility towards him (which she also expressed in 1914 by marrying that other man named Jones) by continuing to keep Lina as his mistress for an additional three years. In doing so, he also managed to express his sadism towards this poor woman, Lina, in many manipulative ways. Obviously, he regarded her as being beneath his intellectual level and social status, finally "dumping" her in early 1917. His breaking off with Lina was marked by a cruel trick that he played on her, one that managed to shame her and his own father in the same sadistic manipulation.

At the end of that era, 1910 to 1914, the fourth woman against whom Jones directed his sadistic feelings was Anna Freud. Recall that in mid-1914 Loe Kann and Herbert Jones were married, with Freud in attendance at the wedding, and that this marriage secretly infuriated Ernest towards the master. That is, Jones blamed Freud's analysis of Loe as being the fulcrum for her breaking of their "marriage" relationship and for provoking her punitive wedding to Herbert Jones, whom he called "Jones II"–the man who had expropriated his name and his "wife." Thus, when Freud's neurotic young daughter, Anna, visited England in August 1914, Jones immediately began to romance her, with an obvious intention to seduce this vulnerable girl. His intention was to obtain a cruel revenge against her father, but in attempting to do so, he directed covert sadistic feelings against Anna, as well. Once can assume that he hoped to take Anna's virginity, and then expected to drop her cruelly following this conquest, thereby shaming and disappointing the girl–if he had succeeded.

Actually, the seduction of Anna Freud in 1914 would have enabled Jones to attain four sadistic goals simultaneously, an irresistible act of cruelty for this psychopath. The first two were the acts of sadism towards Freud and his daughter. But a sadistic "bonus" was operative in this seduction, since Anna and Loe Kann had become dear friends from 1912 to 1914, while Loe was in analysis with Freud. Thus, if Jones had managed to seduce Anna, he could expect that Loe would have felt that Anna had betrayed her friendship (as had been the case with Lina's betrayal of her). In seducing Anna, Jones would have been able to express an intense additional increment of his sadism towards his former mistress, Loe.

Finally, it should be recognized that when Jones set out to "court" young Anna in August 1914 he was then living with a new mistress. This was Loe's former maid named Lina who had been Jones's mistress then for less than a year, and retained that privileged status for more than two additional years. One can assume that it was the flexibility of the free love doctrine, always manipulated by Jones to his own advantage, that enabled him to enjoy sex with his newest mistress, Lina, while proceeding to attempt the seduction of the virgin, Anna Freud. (That he had seduced Lina for punitive, sadistic reasons makes it more plausible that he intended to seduce Anna for similar reasons, as Loe suggested to Freud, who readily believed her.) In any case, we can see that if Jones had been successful in seducing Anna, this also would have enabled him to express either overt or unconscious sadism towards his long-suffering mistress, Lina, who loved him for years despite his contemptuous treatment of her. Indeed, his very attempt to seduce Anna can be seen as an act of sadism towards the maid named Lina.

Not surprisingly, this was the same era when Jones had an uncanny encounter with a crocodile in the London zoo, not ignoring that the crocodile is an apt symbol of ferocity and sadism. While immersed in that weird encounter he worked energetically, tipping the beast over onto its back, to discover whether the male crocodile possesses an external genital organ! Will Freudians claim that this is not relevant to castration anxiety in this psychopath and to his recurrent acts of sadism towards women?

Back to London, After Munich

After leaving Canada in the summer of 1913, Jones returned to London to begin a longterm private practice in psychoanalysis, continuing to spread the Freudian gospel and presumably the free love doctrine as well. Brome commented that he was then still "partly ostracized by London society." Apparently, his sleazy reputation from the earlier London scandals still hung over his head and continued to offend some members of London's medical community in 1913. Jones regarded himself as intellectually superior to all his critics, so it is doubtful that he worried much about their negative opinions about him.

Before reviewing the next instance of Jones's seduction of an analytic patient, it should be useful to consider how he obtained his initial training in the art of psychoanalysis. Recall that in 1908 when he got into hot water by his unauthorized analytic interviews with a young female hospital patient of Dr. Savill's, Jones already had revealed his budding interest in performing psychoanalysis and his immersion in Freud's writings. Later, upon his arrival in Toronto he began treating patients with psychoanalysis. Naturally, we need to inquire how he received his initial training in performing psychoanalytic treatment, and how extensive that training had been.

Even in the early years of psychoanalysis there were some non-Austrians who traveled to Vienna to sit for weeks or months at Freud's feet, to learn the art of analytic treatment from the master. Sabina Speilrein and Lou Andreas Salomé were persons who took that reasonable course of action. In Jones's case, he went to great expense to arrange a long journey to Austria, but he did not obtain his initial training from Freud in Vienna. For some "peculiar" reason, Jones instead traveled to Munich (in 1908, and evidently in 1907) in order to become the student of Dr. Otto Gross who probably was the first psychiatrist to endorse Freud's teachings. (Analytic historians ignore Gross's priority.)

In *Secret Sex Lives* I have discussed in detail the murderous and disgusting career of this madman Gross who was an advocate of free love, sex between patients and analysts, drug abuses, anarchism, inducements of patients to commit suicide, etc. The allegedly brilliant Dr. Gross did not offer psychoanalytic treatment in an office or clinic situation, instead doing analysis until late hours of the night at a table in a notorious café frequented by thieves, drug addicts, anarchists, and Bohemian artists. That is where Jones sat with him for a number of days absorbing his pyrotechnic psychoanalytic interpretations with his various "patients," almost in the style of a charismatic faith healer.

No historian has clarified why Jones's initial psychoanalytic training occurred with that psychopathic analyst, Otto Gross. My suggestion is that Jones was strongly attracted to this man's seamy reputation throughout Europe and to Gross's immense psychopathic impulses—in particular, his open advocacy of the free love doctrine and the permissibility of sexual activities between analysts and their patients. There is evidence that Gross invited his disciples to "share" the favors of his wife, and that Jones probably indulged in that sexual offering, for it was said that Mrs. Gross fancied Ernest, as disclosed in letters between Jung and Freud. (Some readers will wonder whether Gross was immersed in name-compulsions concerning his surname's connotations in both English and German.)

This brings us to consider Jones's employment of the free love doctrine to seduce another of his analytic patients, namely Joan Riviere, who later became a well-known analyst herself and a forceful opponent of Jones. Evidently, his seduction of Ms. Riviere occurred during 1916 and 1917, the early years of her analysis with him. However, her full analysis with Jones probably lasted about five years, from 1916 to 1920. Apparently, the sexual relationship between Jones and Ms. Riviere ended in early 1917 when he married his first wife, Morfydd Owen, who was twelve years his junior and died suddenly of an illness in mid-1918.

A review of Ms. Riviere's background shows that she had been a brilliant Cambridge graduate who was very attractive, displaying a superb physique and strong personality. Her precise symptoms upon entering analysis are not known to me, though depression and low self-esteem were likely factors, since it is said that she felt people disliked or did not appreciate her. At the age of 23 she married a distinguished attorney and gave birth to Diana, her only child. The girl was eight when her mother became Jones's patient, suggesting that she then was in her mid-thirties. Her husband knew that she had begun analysis, but surely did not know about the analyst's free love ideas which paved the way for the seduction of his wife by Jones. In later years Jones described her case as "the worst failure I have ever had," and it is clear that his sexual sadism had a lot to do with that.

The hectic love relationship between Jones and his married patient, Ms. Riviere, is amply covered in six pages of Brome's book (pp. 114 ff.) which provides excerpts from her letters to Jones starting in October 1918, soon after the death of his wife Morfyyd. The patient expressed pity for his grief, but discounted that she would soon return to analysis with him, implying that she would not resume their affair, either. Obviously, she felt hurt by his marriage and subsequent rejection of her and wrote: "I have been through the hardest time of my life over all this—the final stage of the long tragedy of my relations with you. It nearly broke me. ." Ms. Riviere did express her love for Jones, but decried his hardness towards her. That is, she cited the withdrawal of his love for her (abandonment) after he had married Morfyyd, a loss which she refused to experience again. Stating that she never completely lost faith in him, she noted that he had failed her repeatedly. Also, she called him a "madman," remarking that she had thought about his potential madness a million times. Her references to his latent psychosis became a persistent theme in her letters to him.

Apparently at his request, on October 30th she wrote him a long letter giving a detailed analysis of his deficiencies of character and personality structure. In this letter she returned to the theme of his latent psychosis, remarking about his longterm susceptibility "to states of mind in which you see things temporarily in an unreal and totally subjective light." She commented that this had been confirmed by other persons who knew him well, and she claimed that his need for self-analysis "was urgent and extreme." (The allegations of latent psychosis in both Jones and Freud are very provocative for men who were described as mirror images of one another.) Mrs. Riviere cited Jones's extreme grief reaction at his wife's death as markedly irrational, and hinted at his covert satisfaction at Morfyyd's death that pointed to underlying sadistic and even murderous impulses.

During the fall of 1918 Ms. Riviere's letters to Jones repeatedly expressed desperate feelings relating to having been abandoned by Jones after he married Morfyyd. Also, she noted that following the marriage important changes had occurred in his sexual attitudes. For example, she cited a less liberal attitude towards homosexual men whom he now regarded with "a tone of contempt regrettable in an analyst." Similarly, she wrote that: "since your marriage I have noted changes in regard to your attitude to marriage and free love. ." (Decades later, when his daughter grew up, he reversed himself completely about the free love doctrine, since he did not want it to contaminate her, but it was too late to save dozens of women whom he had already infected with that doctrine.)

In one of Ms. Riviere's letters to Jones she wrote: "After you have taken away my belief in myself what can you give me now . .?" Obviously, his seduction of her during analysis had cost her a great deal in terms of feelings of self-worth. In a letter to Freud in January 1922, Jones revealed that this patient was still quite mentally disturbed and needed further analysis, this time by the master. Jones acknowledged that this was his "worst failure" but did not admit to Freud his sexual relationship with Ms. Riviere.

In early 1922 Ms. Riviere resided in Vienna while she was a patient of Dr. Freud (to some extent replaying the situation with Loe Kann, years earlier). That Ms. Riviere had this intense personal access to Freud became a serious problem for Jones, who had to cope with the expectation that she would expose his seduction of her, and his many other psychopathic manipulations. Of course, Freud should have known about such behaviors of Jones by his analysis of Loe Kann, enabling Jones to hope that his mentor again would simply ignore his transgressions.

On January 22, 1922 in the week preceding the start of Ms. Riviere's analysis with Freud, Jones wrote a letter to Freud summarizing his lengthy analysis of this patient. He used this letter as a con artist's strategy to prejudice Freud against this woman, implying that she suffered from deeply rooted characterological defects that his analysis could not cure or alleviate. Thus did he excuse his egregious clinical failure while also hoping to bias Freud against her honesty and truthfulness, since some character disorders are accompanied by habits of lying and dishonesty. In this way he hoped to undercut her claims about his own psychopathic manipulations.

Jones wrote that during the first year of his analysis he had made the error of lending her his country cottage for a week (ignoring that Freud would sniff out his plans for a tryst with her), and that this led to a "declaration of love" from the patient and a broken-hearted cry when he rejected her sexual advances. Thereafter, due to his rejection of her desire for sexual relations, she tortured him with great energy and ingenuity, without letup. Jones's story was that the patient was punishing him dreadfully for refusing his sexual favors, this being the same claim he had made to Prof. Putnam about the Toronto patient who allegedly accepted his $500 bribe! Finally, he claimed that his new marriage had greatly provoked Ms. Riviere's punitiveness, and that the treatment collapsed when he was unable to master the "negative transference."

As the months of Ms. Riviere's analysis with Freud proceeded in the spring of 1922, his letters to Jones became increasingly hostile as Freud absorbed the nature of her complaints against her former analyst-lover. Brome remarked (1982) that Freud's comments to Jones escalated from suspicion and coldness, to eventual expressions of anger. Finally, Freud wrote a humiliating denunciation of Jones, revealing his great disappointment in learning about Jones's transgressions. Freud wrote: "I had to find out that you had less control of your moods and passions, were less consistent, sincere and reliable" than he had expected on the basis of Jones's eminent status. Notice that Freud emphasized Jones's difficulty in controlling his impulses, pointing to powerful psychopathic tendencies that Freud could ill-afford to ignore in himself.

In his next letter Jones pretended that he was totally bewildered by Freud's insulting reference to "his passions," but finally it had dawned on him to associate this complaint with Ms. Riviere. Then he tried to sell a pathetic explanation to clear up Freud's "misunderstanding" of the issue. Jones claimed that she had made a forceful declaration of love to him, which a friend had misperceived as a declaration of love *by Jones*. Apparently, Jones was concerned that someone once had overheard him professing love to Ms. Riviere and had passed on this item to Freud, forcing Jones to make the absurd contention that this unnamed person mistakenly believed that Jones had been speaking of love instead of Ms. Riviere!

On April 1, 1922—April Fool's Day—Jones wrote a letter to Freud that was intended to clarify his previous relationship with Ms. Riviere. He mentioned to Freud his surprise "at your suspecting any sexual relations" between him and the patient, and said Freud's error may have occurred due to his misreading "of the expression 'declaration of love,' which was of course on her side only." Jones noted that Ms. Riviere "is not the type that attracts me erotically," acknowledging admiration for her intelligence, however. Generally, he assured Freud that there was no reason to fear that he might get involved amorously with patients, and added: "It is over twelve years since I experienced any temptations in such ways," and felt sure he could deal with them now. (Subtracting twelve years from 1922 would have placed Jones's memorable temptation in the year 1910, the same year he treated the Toronto patient whom he allegedly paid $500 after seducing her.)

A later volume of mine, *Secret Sex Lives*, will discuss more extensively Jones's destructive relationship with this patient, Joan Riviere, whom he obviously seduced and abandoned, with a review of his other sexual "problems" as well. Also in *SSL* readers will find my analysis of an astonishing case study in Freud's *Psychopathology of Everyday Life* concerning a man with disturbances in his sexual life, which I insist is a thinly disguised study of some aspects of Jones's life story, starting with his fixation on the family doctor whom he regarded as a Don Juan.

It is time now, however, to temporarily set aside our investigation of the sexually psychopathic behaviors of Ernest Jones. Ahead, the final section of this chapter will review striking examples of alternative psychopathic behaviors of this man who has rightly been called Freud's alter-ego.

Smuggling and Administrative Murder

The biography by Brome (1982) describes a remarkable "smuggling caper" by Jones that nicely displayed some of his hidden psychopathic potentials regarding money, and his contempt for the law. It was around 1916, during the war, that Jones first established a press (or publishing house) in London to promote psychoanalytic literature, employing a young man named Eric Hiller as his assistant. According to Brome, Jones informed him that he and Hiller later acted together to smuggle (from Vienna to London) a large sum of money to assist the work of their press. The probable timing of this smuggling caper was in the summer of 1919, soon after the Great War had ended, when Jones made his first postwar visit to Freud in Vienna, accompanied by Hiller.

The start of Jones's dangerous venture into currency smuggling began when a wealthy Hungarian named von Freund made a donation to Freud of a princely sum of money (100,000 pounds) towards the founding of a private psychoanalytic publishing house. The existing currency controls made it permissible to transfer only a quarter of that money to Vienna. Thereafter, Jones, and perhaps Freud, made a decision to transfer half of that amount, about 12,000 pounds (a small fortune in those days) from Vienna to England by smuggling it past the customs authorities. It seems inconceivable to me that Freud would not have been a key decision-maker in this criminal activity, as will soon be discussed.

Brome wrote (1982) that Jones conspired with Hiller to smuggle the money across the Austrian frontier, relying upon information that customs officials strip-searched anyone whom they suspected of smuggling, but only made random checks on persons who were not under suspicion. The stripping of a suspect occurred first, and then his suitcases were searched, one procedure being independent of the other. Brome did not know whether it was "by luck or cunning" that Jones's suitcase was searched first, before Hiller's suitcase. All that Jones told him was that: "I then calmly fetched the roll of notes from Hiller's case and placed it in my own which had now passed through customs." Brome remarked that the maneuver seemed so simplistic that it would not have deceived a child, and that Jones gave no further details.

So the first phase of the conspiracy to smuggle this small fortune past Austrian customs officials was successful, but immediately Jones and Hiller faced a second obstacle. For they expected a second customs search on the next day when their train was scheduled to leave for Switzerland. Instead, the following morning Jones hired a car and drove over the Rhine bridge separating the two countries. According to the account that Jones gave to Brome, when he and Hiller reached the farther boundary "they could justly claim that their luggage had already been examined." (Perhaps they had a receipt proving this.) In this way, Jones succeeded in smuggling the money past the Swiss customs officials, as well!

Upon its completion, this daring escapade not only provided Jones with an illegal fortune for developing the London publishing company, but must have afforded him great satisfaction from having made fools of the customs police—a personal satisfaction often observed in criminals who outwit the authorities. Notice Jones's statement that he *calmly* switched the illegal money from Hiller's suitcase to his own luggage, almost under the noses of the customs officials, such calmness and boldness being the hallmark of a true psychopath. Also, he exhibited pride in accomplishing that dangerous smuggling maneuver and needed to flaunt his criminal success in front of Brome and his readers. Jones's coolness and lack of concern that this criminal scheme might have gone awry, costing him years in prison and loss of his medical license, is symptomatic of a genuine psychopathic disorder— which perhaps he was usually able to mollify by periodic abuses of his analytic patients.

It seems probable that Freud helped to concoct this smuggling caper, since it is unimaginable that he handed over that 12,000 pounds to Jones without awareness that moving it to London would require a smuggling effort. Also, Freud was always regarded by analysts as the final authority about all matters occurring in Vienna, so Jones would not have made that decision to smuggle currency without first consulting the master and obtaining his approval. Consider that, especially in Europe, smuggling of currency often has a close connection with the counterfeiting of currency. Therefore, it is quite plausible that in 1919 Freud employed his family's previous expertise regarding the movement of counterfeit currency in assisting the conception of Jones's daring smuggling enterprise.

Joan Riviere, who eventually became an eminent analyst and diagnostician, often stated her belief in letters to Jones that he had suffered repeatedly from episodes of near-psychosis. Indeed, she referred to him repeatedly as a "madman," stating that there was a "mad side", to Jones (perhaps a Jekyll/Hyde personality structure), and noting that on countless occasions she had thought about his potential madness. Similarly, at times she hinted at her suspicion that a murderous personality might be lurking within Ernest Jones. For example, in one of her letters she called him "my darling loved one. . my terrible one," and rhetorically asked "how many times will you kill me Bluebeard. ." Was this merely a colorful use of language by Ms. Riviere, or did she actually suspect that there were homicidal impulses buried in Jones that could sometimes surface and become lethally dangerous to people whom he hated?

Evidences from many phases of Jones's career indicate that (like Freud) he could be a very angry, vengeful, and vicious person towards numerous persons whom he regarded as enemies or rivals. In my second long chapter about Jones in *Secret Sex Lives* I describe the episode in which he had a bizarre "confrontation" with a live crocodile at the London zoo. In my view, his weird interaction with that animal was symptomatic, and was a reflection of Jones's near-madness, revealing his identification with that "very short" but deadly creature. In effect, Jones was a crocodile himself, in terms of his murderous potentials towards various people—lethal tendencies that rippled just below the surface of observable behavior. It may be quite relevant that Jones's first mentor in the art of psychoanalysis was a madman who eventually acquired a widespread reputation as a murderer of women, Dr. Otto Gross (another Bluebeard).

Keeping in mind Jones's probable identification with the crocodile, we will now examine his role in the cruel death of his analytic colleague, Dr. Isidor Sadger. Both Vincent Brome and Paul Roazen have offered information about Jones's destructive inclinations towards Sadger in the 1930s. Roazen wrote (1975, p. 351) that Jones did his best to suppress the publication of any material that might prove unflattering to Freud's image. When one of Freud's Viennese followers, Sadger, completed a damaging book about Freud in the early 1930s, Jones became so enraged, according to Roazen, that "he recommended in a letter to Federn that Sadger (who was Jewish) be put in a concentration camp. . to make sure the book never appeared. (It was never published." Many readers will recall that Federn was the most obedient of Freud's followers in Vienna for decades.

Brome's account (1982, p. 156) of this matter is similar to the above. He wrote that in the twenties and thirties Jones busily attacked any book that criticized Freud or psychoanalysis. According to Brome, such a book had been prepared by Sadger, and this incensed Jones so ferociously "that he went beyond all normal limits in a letter to Federn." That is, he insisted that Sadger, a Jew, "should be put in a concentration camp to prevent the book from appearing."

It seems clear that Jones's anger was so intense that he was willing to demand that Sadger's life should be placed in the hands of the Nazis in order to forestall publication of a book that could have injured Freud. (One wonders if the book concerned Freud's homicidal behaviors relating to Fliess, Emanuel and John Freud?) There is reason to believe that Jones was successful with his brutal request that Sadger should be interned in a Nazi death camp. It was Roazen who offered a clarifying comment about Sadger's tragic demise. He wrote (p. 536) that "only one Viennese analyst, Sadger—who was already out of favor with Freud—perished at the hands of the Nazis.." This helps explain what was meant by Brome when he observed that Jones went "beyond all normal limits" in pursuing the destruction of his colleague, Isidor Sadger.

The preceding similar materials by Brome and Roazen, concerning Jones's hounding of Sadger into a Nazi death camp, made references to the same three letters, as follows: a letter by Jones to Federn on October 10, 1934; another from Jones to Eitingon on December 10, 1934; and a third letter from Anna Freud to Jones dated December 31, 1932. Evidently, all three of those letters were in the Jones Archives and all were relevant to the death-sentence which Jones placed upon Sadger. Hopefully, biographers will now be allowed to publish those letters fully, since the apparently "arranged death" of Sadger is such an important subject. Those three letters just cited might reveal the names of all parties in a cabal that arranged Sadger's death, and how the vicious deed was accomplished. (In SSL I have noted that there are date-discrepancies concerning these letters that need resolution, with regard to Brome's versus Roazen's citations of them.)

Readers might appreciate having some brief information about the career of this man, Dr. Sadger, whose life was sacrificed to protect Freud's reputation. Sadger was one of Freud's earliest followers, and in 1906 he became a regular member of the Wednesday analytic society's meetings that met weekly in Freud's home. In 1907 he introduced his nephew Dr. Fritz Wittels (whose mentor had been Josef Popper) into Freud's circle, and in that year Sadger produced some notable achievements. Jones wrote that in 1907: "Sadger began a series of valuable contributions by an exposition of Freud's methods." In January 1909 Jung wrote Freud about his male patient who was moving to Vienna and who asked that an analyst be found to treat him in that city. Freud responded by sending the addresses of several analysts, while noting that: "Sadger is the ablest practitioner; he is most in need of encouragement."

Little information is available about Sadger in Jones's biographies of Freud, or in other historical sources consulted by me. Probably, Jones paid scant attention to Sadger in his writings because of his anger that this colleague was disloyal and a traitor for writing that 1930s volume (unpublished) that was unflattering to Freud, and to suppress his role in getting Sadger interned in the Nazi death camp where he died. Probably, other analytic writers have followed suit by minimizing any attention to Sadger's life and work in historical writings, partly out of embarrassment about the murderous betrayal of this pioneer in psychoanalysis.

Sadger's personal conflicts with Freud did not start in the thirties but went back to the earliest years of their relationship. In early 1910 Freud wrote to Abraham that he no longer got any pleasure from his Viennese disciples and had "a heavy cross to bear" with the older generation of analysts, particularly Stekel, Adler, and Sadger. Actually, those were the only disciples who dared to question the master's dogmas, but Freud explained his problem differently. He wrote that: "They will soon be feeling that I am an obstacle and will treat me as such, but I can't believe that they have anyone better to substitute for me." Again in 1911 he listed Sadger, Stekel, and Victor Tausk (whom he induced to commit suicide in 1919) as the disciples who were then giving him the most trouble.

Inquiring minds will hope to learn the precise circumstances that caused Sadger to be delivered into a Nazi death camp, including the date and manner of his arrest, the specific charges made against him, the names of any accusers, etc. Obtaining that kind of information will be left, in future, to dedicated historical researchers like Peter Swales. However, I would like to mention a plausible thesis about the kinds of charges that might have been made to the Nazis about Sadger, assuming that he was cleverly betrayed by members of the Vienna analytic circle at Jones's request.

In SSL I have offered my reasons for believing that Sadger probably was denounced secretly to the Nazis on a charge of indulging in (alleged) sexual perversions. It was well-known that Sadger had written articles on various perversions, masturbation, homosexuality, and sado-masochism. That he wrote about such topics offers no real proof that he suffered from any severe sexual pathology, but many Nazis were homophobic and anxious about hints of perversion. Probably, it would not have been difficult to convince them that Sadger was some sort of pervert, assuming that Jones and his cohorts in Vienna were adept in the art of character assassination. This "administrative murder" of Sadger could have resulted after highly placed friends of psychoanalysis (particularly gentiles) had secretly used innuendos or somehow denounced Sadger's "perverse sexual tendencies" to Nazi officials, using rumors about his withdrawn personal life and the sexual themes of his published articles as "proofs" that he was a reclusive pervert.

Future research needs to answer many questions relating to Sadger's death. Is it factual that he was the only Viennese analyst to be interned in a Nazi death camp, and to die there? Are any copies or portions of his anti-Freud manuscript still extant, or did any of Sadger's allies report on the contents? Is there any evidence that Freud, or his daughter Anna, helped to propel Sadger into a death camp? Is there a cache of Sadger's letters and private papers being held in trust somewhere? (It is predictable that new "research" from pro-Freudian sources will soon hold Jones and his allies blameless for the internment and death of Dr. Sadger, but this will be readily discounted by Jones's and Freud's critics.)

As we conclude our discussion of Jones's murderous potentials, let's consider Freud's early judgments of this man who became his alter-ego. Many writers have decided that Freud was a poor judge of the characters of men he knew, including his disciples, yet his negative first impressions of

Jones were quite accurate, in his letter to Jung of May 1908. Freud was quickly aware (and so was Jung) that Jones was a repetitive liar. Moreover, Freud described him as a fanatic who didn't eat enough. At this point, he quoted Caesar's desire to have men around him who were fat, noting that Jones reminded him "of the lean and hungry Cassius." This instinctive comparison of Jones with a famous assassin suggests that Freud's own murderous tendencies (he identified strongly with Brutus) instantly had made contact with the sadistic and homicidal impulses that constantly stirred within this ever-hungry crocodile, Ernest Jones.

Readers are encouraged to invest time and energy in making careful comparisons between the present chapter's exposition of Jones's life and career and his discussions about himself in his autobiography, and in volumes II and III of his Freud biography. Such comparisons will make it obvious that Jones's portrayals of himself were suffused with deliberate lies and deceptions, half-truths, and omissions of crucial data, mainly to conceal his repeated unethical behaviors and his generally psychopathic nature.

The countless deceptions that Jones palmed off about himself were not unlike the repeated distortions and scams that he concocted in many portions of his three-volume biography of Freud, in order to lionize the master and protect his inflated reputation. Near the end of my second chapter about Jones in *Secret Sex Lives* I have listed 24 areas of major deception to clarify *some* of the deliberate distortions that Jones artfully wove into his Freud biographies. An energetic investigation of those scams by thoughtful readers will help them to realize that the public image of Sigmund Freud was constructed initially by an incessant liar and psychopath, his alter-ego named Dr. Ernest Jones.

Postscript

In this final section, two literary works will be discussed that came to my attention as this present book was at the typesetter—the Freud/Jones letters and an article by K. Eissler. Because these works were reviewed briefly by me, at the last minute, I have appended them to my bibliography. They require some discussion, since they can add significantly to our understanding of the Freud/Jones relationship and its possible connections with destructive aspects of Freud's personality.

The larger of these works is *The Complete Correspondence of Sigmund Freud and Ernest Jones 1908-1939* edited by Paskauskas (1993). Since I have had a chance to review only selected portions of this massive volume—though this brief search was a painstaking one—my negative comments will necessarily be tentative and subject to later revision.

My main concern about this work is whether it deserves the allegation of completeness that appears in its title. There are various caveats that come to mind. The editor's preface noted that he had obtained photocopies of Freud's letters to Jones and that "numerous passages had been obliterated by the Sigmund Freud Archives of New York." He claimed this had occurred due to concern with preserving patient confidentiality, but that he'd already had access to a British transcript which, except for "minor omissions" and mistakes "was basically intact." Having worked with Freud materials for many years, let me express my deep distrust about words like "basically intact" and "minor omissions." The editor then noted that "the passages blotted out by the appointees of the Archives" pertained to Loe Kann's analysis by Freud which already had been published in Vincent Brome's biography of Jones. Really? *Only* passages about Loe Kann were blotted out? What about the fiascos involving Joan Riviere, and others? And why should we feel secure that Brome's biography had done an adequate job of reporting dangerous materials? (In any case, we should remember that Jones defecated sadistically on Loe's analysis with Freud, hoping to destroy it and her.)

Later, in R. Steiner's long introduction to these letters, he wrote on page xxix (third paragraph) a vague and confusing statement about the physical size of the original letters, which were often quite lengthy. Here, he hinted that it was impossible to include in printed works various unsavory materials, which may have necessitated the exclusion of "certain judgments of colleagues or Freud's violent reprimands of Jones" and his actions, "while certain other matters had perforce to be omitted or ignored." (This fancy word "perforce" makes me feel distrustful of glib explanations.) My own inference is that an unknown number of embarrassing items may have been deleted from these letters, by someone unnamed, thereby preventing the public from learning about some vicious, if not *murderous*, judgments about colleagues and about brutally psychopathic behaviors by Jones that had provoked violent reprimands from Freud. One wonders whether comments were deleted about plans in 1914 to kill Jung, or plans in the early 1930s to subject Sadger to "administrative murder."

Concerning the possible censorship of Freud's severe accusations against Jones, let me return to the issue of the Welshman's sexual seduction and betrayal of his patient, Joan Riviere. About this topic, some crucial comparisons can be made between Brome's biography of Jones (1982) and the new volume of the Freud/Jones letters (1993). Let me return to my previous section which gave Brome's account of Freud's angry denunciation of Jones in 1922, when Freud's psychoanalysis of Ms. Riviere in that year seemed to convince him that she had been sexually betrayed by Jones, during the earlier analysis. Brome reported that Freud penned this bitter reproach to his colleague: "This last year brought a disappointment not easy to bear. I [learned] that you had less control of your moods and passions, were less consistent, sincere and reliable than I had a right to expect of you and than was required by your conspicuous position." (1982, p. 135)

A great problem with the new Freud/Jones letters is that my thorough search of its relevant pages failed to locate the above "bitter reproach" by Freud, nor any language that resembles it. One might argue that perhaps that letter was written in German by Freud, and that Paskauskas's translation was somewhat different from Brome's, but I doubt that this is an adequate explanation. To the contrary, I suspect that someone had totally censored that bitter denunciation by Freud from the newer work. And it is no small matter, since Freud's grave insults hinted that Jones probably was a sexually obsessive psychopath who dealt with patients insincerely, unreliably, and without control of his emotions.

It is interesting that the new volume of letters provides Jones's letter of January 14, 1923 in which he answered an unspecified reprimand, one that seems correlated with the above "bitter reproach" by Freud that has vanished. In this letter of early 1923 Jones stated: "when you say that I am insincere and not to be trusted, there I am sure, with all respect, that your judgment is at fault." Jones added that he would not reproach himself nor feel resentment about Freud's accusations, since he was certain that there was no truth in Freud's mistaken judgment of him! This suggests that Jones was making a highly defensive reply to Freud's "bitter reproach" which is now missing from the published letters, and probably was penned sometime during the latter half of 1922.

Most likely this missing item was written by Freud soon after his letter of June 25, 1922 in which he accused Jones of insincerity, saying that their friendship had "gone through a severe test." but had survived it. However, he angrily blasted Jones again, emphasizing "the fact that accuracy and plainness is not in the character of your dealings with people." He added that "distortions and evasions, lapses of memory, twisted denials" and "a predilection for sidetracks" were prevalent in Jones's behavior. Then he noted that in analyzing every single dispute between Ms. Riviere and Jones—whom the latter described as "a fiendish sadist" (p. 454)—he discovered that Jones's contentions were always doubtful while this maligned patient "was right and could not be refuted." (So then, who might the fiendish sadist have been—Riviere or Jones?)

There is another matter that will strain the credulity of readers about the alleged completeness of the new Freud/Jones letters (1993). In Brome's biography of Jones (1982, p. 135), he mentioned again the (missing) item in which Freud castigated Jones about "his passions." According to Brome, this "completely bewildered [Jones] until he associated it with Mrs. Joan

Riviere, his ex-patient." Then Jones explained this situation to Freud, alleging that she had made "a declaration of love [to him] and a friend had misunderstood this as a declaration of love by Jones." In this sly excuse by Jones he apparently referred to himself in the third person, and it must be emphasized that Brome cited this as a *direct quotation* of Jones's words in his letter to Freud. But these directly-quoted words by Jones do not appear anywhere in the new version of his letters to Freud, edited by Paskauskas. Apparently, this is another glitch reminiscent of the famous 18 minutes that were missing from Pres. Richard Nixon's tape.

I am not implying that the new letters are so suspect that they are worthless to scholars. Indeed, they seem to contain a few gold nuggets. For example, I advise a close reading of Jones's letter of January 30, 1913 in which he admitted his use of sexual seduction to destroy his mistress's psychoanalysis with Freud, yet had the brass to deny "any abnormality in myself." And note that in Freud's reply (p. 191), he almost made a grotesque joke, by assuring Jones that he was incapable of doing anything "mean and treacherous," simply denying that blatant act of sexual sadism by his valued henchman.

While I am on the subject of Jones's sexual sadism, let me recommend a close reading of his letter of June 28, 1910 in which he described his childhood love for the village doctor with whom he identified intensely, as a Don Juan. Not only does this letter discuss the boy's intense sexual feelings for this doctor, but it also suggests a competing core of hatred for this man. For it reveals that when Ernest was age three this doctor, who lived with his family, subjected him to a grotesque act of sadism. Ernest wrote that the man never liked him much, because he disturbed him with his crying. And then the child's world crumbled, unexpectedly. "One day in a rage he hung me in a high water-hutt, which with other traumata formed the later basis for a phobia of heights." No doubt, the man's *rage* must have been terrifying to this young boy.

Now we understand better why love and hatred were closely entwined in Jones's psyche, and a basis for his relentless sexual sadism. Also, we can guess why he may have wished to kill himself in that solitary mountain-climbing escapade during the stress of his early career. Considering the issues of heights/sexuality/ sadism, we can also guess why he stole another man's fianceé and had sex with her high atop a belfry at Bruges, Belgium— when he was a young man. Also, think again about his fetish, in writing his name at the ends of letters and documents, that forced him to place beneath his own name that strange design symbolizing his sister Sybil's identity. The editor of the Freud/Jones letters remarked that almost every one of Jones's letters had that symbol placed beneath his signature.

Another gold nugget can be found in Paskauskas's book, in the first footnote to Steiner's introduction to that work. This footnote referred to Freud's letter to Jung of May 1908 in which he described his very first meeting with Ernest Jones. It was obvious that Freud was distrustful of Jones immediately, for he cited his "racial strangeness" and fanaticism, comparing him with the lean Cassius who had incurred Caesar's grave suspicions. (In Jung's letter of July 1908, he replied that Jones was an intellectual liar, adulator, and opportunist.) Steiner's footnote noted that young Freud had played the role of Brutus on two occasions, hinting at his fantasy identification with this Roman assassin.

Steiner's final comment about this matter in the footnote was that Freud's first impressions of Jones connected him with Cassius, and by implication, with the figure of Brutus (who was Freud's model). Steiner's final innocuous comment was that: "Both participated in the assassination of Caesar." Sadly, repression was operative in Steiner and he did not add that this suggested that murderous father-complexes existed in both Jones and Freud, particularly in the latter man. This prevented Steiner from considering that his own father-figure, Freud, might have been greatly disposed to murder his own "preferred father," Emanuel Freud in 1914.

This brings me to a discussion of K. Eissler's article (in Garcia, 1992) titled "An Interpretation of Four of Freud's Letters." In this article Eissler gave repeated attention to a problem that had bemused him in an earlier work, namely that Freud had expressed strong identifications with literary murderers like Hamlet and Macbeth.

This recent paper by Eissler focused upon Freud's identification with the king-killer who was embodied in the figure of Macbeth.* He returned to Freud's letter of August 1878 to his friend Wilhelm Knöpfmacher, when Sigmund was age 22. (On page 130, Eissler noted that this fellow was an *intimate* friend of Sigmund's, and students of name magic will note that he had the same given name as Fliess.) In that letter Freud announced that he was sending along his "collected works," referring to his first two published papers on the nervous system. He added that these would soon be followed by a series of three more papers, which caused him to be *frightened* in the way that Macbeth was when he viewed (or hallucinated) the entire series of "the ghosts of the English kings." Here, Freud implied that his scholarly works someday would stretch out in a long line (or series) reaching to "the crack of doom," in the words of Shakespeare's Macbeth—alluding to the Last Judgment which Freud feared over his entire lifetime.

Despite the force of intense repression, Eissler did his best to understand why young Freud had identified himself with the intensely ambitious murderer, Macbeth. He wrote, "It is possible that unconsciously he had

---
*Brutus, Macbeth, and Hamlet all were symbolic father-killers, like Freud.

formed a megalomanic self-fantasy that may have resulted in a minor euphoria . . . " But then Eissler realized that this did not explain Sigmund's identification with a brutal killer, and that he would have to explore the matter in greater depth. Repression began to lift somewhat when Eissler noted that: "It is uncanny to ponder that the young student setting out on his scientific trek identified with a figure who killed a king and was a murderer of children. The ominous portent of that identification must by no means be underrated." How true. Unfortunately, Eissler did not correlate this with Freud's intense identification with Oedipus, the killer of a king who happened to be his own father.

Thus, Eissler failed to recognize how Sigmund's identification with Macbeth was tied to his longterm unconscious intention to murder Emanuel, and the feelings of guilt and terror pertaining to that "patricidal" urge. Largely, Eissler remained mystified, but he did generate some good thinking anyway. He noted that in 1878 Sigmund's quixotic remarks about his series of scientific papers showed his closeness to Macbeth who had viewed that line of ghostly kings and then realized that his murderous crimes had been fruitless, i.e. his wishes would be foiled and his adversaries' progeny would reign, *not* his own. Eissler remarked that Macbeth's murders had "loaded his conscience with devastating guilt," causing his plans to fail. Turning to young Sigmund, Eissler asked: "Why should a stigma of guilt—ostensibly of crushing intensity—be attached to the forthcoming papers. . ?" Unsuspecting of Freud's patricidal intentions, Eissler acknowledged that he felt somewhat bewildered and had a right "to lay down his arms."

However, he did not give up easily and for many pages thereafter tried to comprehend the basis for Freud's identification with the murderer, Macbeth. Citing the "dismal gloominess of the Macbeth imagery that followed Freud into his adult years," Eissler asked himself: "What was the probable unconscious meaning of Freud's general sense of culpability?" Finally, he decided that Sigmund's gloom in 1878 about that forthcoming series of papers reflected unconscious concerns that he might be accused of plagiarisms, which turned out to be a common occurrence in his later years. Thus, the guilty feelings associated with this Macbeth identification might have been related to Freud's fears that ownership of his public works might be taken away from him, somehow. Likewise, Eissler cited evidence that Freud sometimes feared that someday his rightful "ownership" of Psychoanalysis might be taken away from him, by unkind public sentiments and judgments. Indeed, near the end of his article, Eissler observed that in old age Freud seemed to foster this "unfrocking" by repeatedly making disparaging criticisms of his earlier works, perhaps irrationally.

In all this we see that Eissler had the same problem with repression that Steiner had, failing to consider that Freud *was* an assassin (like Macbeth,

Cassius, et al.) who harbored the intention to kill a father-figure, namely Emanuel Freud. Will Eissler now reconsider Sigmund's crushing sense of guilt, as well as his numerous forms of death-anxiety and his fears of Judgment Day?

But I think that Eissler had a sound idea in sensing that the guilt-ridden Freud, in old age, was unconsciously trying to punish himself by having Psychoanalysis (nanny) wrested from his ownership—an atonement for his lethal behaviors, I would argue. My speculation is that he fostered that process unconsciously in his final years by ordering his obedient daughter, Anna, to eventually turn over the formulation of his biographies to Ernest Jones. Repeatedly, Freud had said that all biographies are fraudulent works, filled with subtle lies and deceptions. Since he had known Jones intimately for decades and absorbed mountains of evidence that "the Welsh liar" (Anna's term) was a compulsive fraud and psychopath, his conscious mind expected that Jones's massive biographies would constitute a very clever, thoroughly deceitful epic glorifying his reputation and his works.

On the other hand, Freud's unconscious mind knew that Jones's charlatanry was so immense and flagrant that soon authors would begin to unmask him, causing the public to gravely doubt his objectivity as a biographer. Moreover, when Jones's outrageous crimes finally proceeded to full public awareness, Freud had reason to believe that his close relations with this biographer and alter ego would eventually bring a day of reckoning for Freud himself. In effect, Freud's strange alliance with Jones was unconsciously intended to defame the Viennese master—and it will certainly do that in the years just ahead.

Appendix A

Freud's Fantasy Identifications—Some Literary Sources

The following items repeat the long list of Freud's fantasy identifications shown in chapter three, along with the names of authors found in the Bibliography whose works incorporate these identifications. Some identifications have been cited by more than one author, but usually only one author's name will be offered for each fantasy identification listed.

Paul Vitz's work (1988) supplied the first 28 identifications, including: Alexander the Great, William the Conqueror, Napoleon, Gen. Masséna, Hannibal, Oliver Cromwell, Garibaldi, Ulrich von Hutten, Moses, Jacob, Josef (master of dreams), Jesus Christ, Scipio (Africanus), St. Paul, Franz Brentano, Romain Rolland, Satan, Oedipus, the anti-Christ, Faust, Frollo, Leonardo da Vinci, Goethe, Brücke, Charcot, Fleischl von Marxow, Fliess, and Schnitzler.—A volume by Anzieu (1986) duplicated some of Vitz's list, and offered an additional list of thirteen of Freud's identifications, including: Aeneas, Julian Boufflers, Leo Vincey, Gargantua, Gulliver, Hercules, Dante, Emile Zola, J.J. David, Eduard Lasker, Lassalle, Johann Winckelmann, and Ignatius Loyola.

The following is a list of sixteen identifications that Freud made with figures (real or fictional) who were murderers, or were strongly suspected of being murderers or potential killers. (Four more of these items appear in chapter four.)

1. Macbeth—Eissler (1971).
2. Hamlet—Holland and Trosman (1972).
3. Cain—Schur (1972) re Freud's "Cain complex."
4. Brutus—various authors, re Freud's duologue with John Freud.
5. Don Juan—Balmary (1982).
6. Fiesco—Grinstein (1968); Anzieu (1986).
7. The Moor (Muley Hassan)—McGrath (1986).
8. Karl Moor—McGrath (1986).
9. Franz Moor—McGrath (1986).
10. St. Sigismund—Vitz (1988).
11. Josef (Military Messiah)—Bakan (1958).
12. Jekyll and Hyde—Scagnelli (1993), and later works.
13. Hollthurn patient, who feared killing during amnesia—S. Freud (1967).
14. Man accused of attempted patricide—Scagnelli (1993).
15. Fanny Moser—Scagnelli (1993).
16. Dr. Otto Gross—Scagnelli (*Secret Sex Lives*).

What follows is an additional list of 41 fantasy identifications that Freud made with various figures (real or fictional).

1. Zeus—Roazen (1969).
2. Siegfried—Scagnelli (later work).
3. Pope Julius II—Roazen (1968); Scagnelli (later work).
4. Lessing—Puner (1949).
5. Friedrich Schiller—McGrath (1986).
6. Copernicus—Roazen (1969, p. 91); in *Introductory Lectures*, Freud compared himself with Copernicus and with Darwin.
7. Darwin—Same as above.
8. Galileo—(by implication), Ellenberger (1970, p. 798).
9. Kepler—(by implication), Ellenberger (1970, p. 802).
10. Newton—(by implication), Ellenberger (1970, p. 802); Jones (1955, p. 414).
11. Adam—Scagnelli (later work).
12. King Solomon—Krüll (1986, p. 127); Freud's admission, in *Psychopathology of Everyday Life*; Simon (1989, p. 78).
13. Homer—Schur (1972, pp. 343-4).
14. Horace—McGrath (1986).
15. Julius Freud—various authors (negative identification).
16. Charlemagne—Sulloway (1979).
17. Columbus—Roazen (1969, p, 159); Fromm (1959, p. 80).
18. Dr. Lecher— Freud (1967, pp. 302-3).
19. Monica Zajic—Scagnelli (*Dark Side*).
20. Resi Wittek—Krüll (1986, p. 119).
21. King Lear—Jones (1957, p. 457); Roazen (1975, p. 437).
22. Solomon Almoli—Bakan (1958).
23. God/Jahweh—Wittels (1924).
24. Victor Tilgner—Schur (1972).
25. Anton von Freund—Schur (1972).
26. Emanuel Freud—Scagnelli (1993); Krüll (1986, pp. 122-3).
27. Victor Adler—Scagnelli (1993); Fromm (1959, p. 70).
28. Alfred Adler—in 1910 letter to Ferenczi, Freud admitted that A. Adler and W. Stekel were "revenants" of Fliess (with whom he had identified intensely).
29. Wilhelm Stekel—Same as above.
30. G.T. Fechner—Sulloway (1979).
31. Robinson Crusoe—Sulloway (1979, p. 449).
32. Jupiter—see #1. Zeus, Greek god, equals Jupiter, Roman god.
33. Prometheus—Glenn (1979).
34. Shakespeare—Roazen (1968, p. 177); Jones (1957, pp. 428-30).
35. Socrates—Eissler (1971, p. 243), by implication.

36. Daniel Schreber—Vitz (1988, p. 246).
37. Karl L. Börne—Grollman (1965, p. 26).
38. Adolf Fischof—Schorske (1973).
39. General "M"—Scagnelli (1993).
40. Woodrow Wilson—Roazen (1968, p. 312); Scagnelli (1993); negative identification subsequent to positive identification.
41. Admiral Dewey—McGrath (1986, pp. 257-8).

In chapter three, an additional list of Freud's fantasy identifications is offered. It includes 34 items uncovered by the present author's research, and these will be discussed in his later books or journal articles.

Bibliography

Most of the works of Sigmund Freud are listed in accordance with the *Standard Edition of the Complete Psychological Works of Sigmund Freud* (cited as S.E.), translated under the general editorship of James Strachey (24 vols.). The Institute of Psycho-Analysis, The Hogarth Press, London, 1953-74.

Abraham, Karl (1911) "On the determining power of names." *Clinical Papers and Essays of Psychoanalysis.* N.Y. (Also, *Zentralbl fur Psa.*, II, 1912, p. 133.)

Abraham, Hilda and Ernst Freud, eds. (1965) *A Psychoanalytic Dialogue: The Letters of Sigmund Freud and Karl Abraham, 1907-1926.* N.Y.: Basic Books.

Adams, Leslie (1954) "Sigmund Freud's correct birthday: misunderstanding and solution." *Psychoanalytic Review*, 41.

Anderson, Christopher (1977) *The Name Game.* N.Y. Jove/HBJ Books.

Anzieu, Didier (1959) *L'Auto-Analyse. Son Rôle dans la Découverte de la Psychoanalyse par Freud.* Paris: Presses Universitaires de France. (Also see English edition titled *Freud's Self-Analysis.* London: Hogarth Press, 1986.)

Bailey, Percival (1965) *Sigmund the Unserene. A Tragedy in Three Acts.* Springfield, Ill.: Charles C. Thomas.

Bakan, David (1958) *Sigmund Freud and the Jewish Mystical Tradition.* Princeton: Van Nostrand.

Balmary, Marie (1979) *L'Homme aux Statues, Freud et la Faute Cachée du Père.* Paris. (English version, *Psychoanalyzing Psychoanalysis: Freud and the Hidden Fault of the Father.* Baltimore: Johns Hopkins University Press, 1982.)

Bernfeld, Siegfried (1946) "An unknown autobiographical fragment by Freud." *American Imago*, 4, 3-19.

Bernfeld, Siegfried and Suzanne Bernfeld (1973) "Freud's early childhood." In *Freud As We Knew Him*, edited by Hendrik Ruitenbeek. Detroit: Wayne State University Press.

Bernfeld, Suzanne (1951) "Freud and archaelogy." *American Imago*, 8.

Blum, Harold (1979) "The prototype of preoedipal reconstruction." In *Freud and His Self-Analysis*, edited by Mark Kanzer and Jules Glenn. N.Y.: Jason Aronson.

Brome, Vincent (1967) *Freud and His Early Circle: The Struggles of Psycho-Analysis*. London: Heinemann.
_____ (1982) *Ernest Jones: Freud's Alter Ego*. London: Caliban.

Bugliosi, Vincent (1974) *Helter Skelter*. N.Y.: Norton.

Choisy, Maryse (1963) *Sigmund Freud: A New Appraisal*. N.Y.: Philosophical Library.

Clark, Ronald (1980) *Freud: The Man and the Cause*. N.Y.: Random House.

Clodd, Edward (1920) *Magic in Names and in Other Things*. London: Chapman and Hall, Limited.

Decker, Hannah (1991) *Freud, Dora and Vienna 1900*. N.Y.: The Free Press.

Düss, Louisa (1948) "The psychological function of the proper name in the reconstruction of the personality of a schizophrenic." *Psychiatric Quarterly*, 22.

Eissler, Kurt (1971) *Talent and Genius: The Fictitious Case of Tausk Contra Freud*. N.Y.: Quadrangle

_____ (1983) *Victor Tausk's Suicide*. N.Y.: International Universities Press, Inc.

Ellenberger, Henri (1970) *The Discovery of the Unconscious*. N.Y.: Basic Books, Inc.

Flugel, Ingeborg (1930) "On the significance of names." *Brit. Journal of Med. Psychol.*, 10, II.

Fodor, Nandor (1956) "Nomen est omen." *Samiksa, Journal of the Indian Psycho-analytic Society*, 10.

Fraiberg, Selma (1959) *The Magic Years*. N.Y.: Charles Scribner's and Sons.

Freud, Martin (1958) *Sigmund Freud: Man and Father*. N.Y.: Vanguard Press

Freud, Sigmund (1894) "Abwehr-Neuropsychosen, Die." *Neurologisches Centralblatt*, 13.

_____ (1895) *Studies on Hysteria*, with Joseph Breuer. S.E.: 2.

_____ (1896) "The aetiology of hysteria." In Appendix B of *The Assault on Truth: Freud's Suppression of the Seduction Theory*. U.S.A.: Farrar, Strauss and Giroux, 1984.

_____ (1895) *The Project for a Scientific Psychology*. S.E. 1: 283-387.

_____ (1905) *Three Essays on the Theory of Sexuality*. S.E. 7: 125-245

_____ (1911) "Psycho-analytic notes on an autobiographical account of a case of paranoia (dementia paranoides)." S.E. 12: 9-82. (The case of Daniel P. Schreber).

_____ (1912-1913) *Totem and Taboo*. S.E. 13: 1-161.

_____ (1914) "The Moses of Michelangelo." S.E. 13: 211-236.

_____ (1914) "On narcissism: an introduction." S.E. 14: 73-102.

_____ (1914) "On the history of the psycho-analytic movement." S.E. 14: 7-66.

_____ (1915) "Instincts and their vicissitudes." S.E. 14: 117-40

_____ (1915) "Thoughts for the times on war and death." S.E. 14: 275-300.

_____ (1916-1917) *Introductory Lectures on Psycho-Analysis*. S.E. 15 & 16.

_____ (1917) "Mourning and melancholia." S.E. 14: 243-258.

_____ (1919) "The uncanny." S.E. 17: 217-252.

_____ (1920) *Beyond the Pleasure Principle.* S.E. 18: 7-64

_____ (1925) "A neurosis of demoniacal possession in the seventeenth century." *Collected Papers.* Vol. IV. London: Hogarth Press.

_____ (1927) *The Future of an Illusion.* S.E. 21: 3-56

_____ (1930) *Civilization and Its Discontents.* S.E. 21:59-145.

_____ (1932) "My contact with Joseph Popper-Lynkeus." S.E. 22: 218-224.

_____ (1936) "A disturbance of memory on the Acropolis." S.E. 22: 239-248.

_____ (1936) Letter to Thomas Mann about Napoleon dated November 29, 1936. (#287). In *Letters of Sigmund Freud,* edited by Ernst Freud. N.Y.: Basic Books, 1960.

_____ (1939) *Moses and Monotheism.* S.E. 23: 3-137.

_____ (1952) *The Case of Dora and Other Papers.* N.Y.: W.W. Norton.

_____ (1952) *On Dreams.* N.Y.: W.W. Norton.

_____ (1953-1974) *Standard Edition of the Complete Psychological Works of Sigmund Freud.* (24 Vols.) Edited by James Strachey. London: Hogarth Press.

_____ (1954) *Origins of Pscho-Analysis, The: Letters to Wilhelm Fliess, Drafts and Notes, 1887-1902.* Edited by Marie Bonaparte, Anna Freud, and Ernst Kris. N.Y.: Basic Books.

_____ (1966) *The Psychopathology of Everyday Life.* Edited by James Strachey. London: Ernest Benn, Limited.

_____ (1967) *The Interpretation of Dreams.* N.Y.: Avon/Discus. (First publication date, 1900.)

_____ (1967) *Thomas Woodrow Wilson, Twenty-eighth President of the United States. A Psychological Study,* with William C. Bullitt. London: Weidenfeld & Nicolson.

_____ (1985) *The Complete Letters of Sigmund Freud to Wilhelm Fliess, 1887-1904*. Edited by Jeffrey Masson. Cambridge, Massachusetts: Harvard University Press.

Fromm, Erich (1959) *Sigmund Freud's Mission. An Analysis of His Personality and Influence*. N.Y.: Harper and Brothers.

Gay, Peter (1988) *Freud. A Life for Our Time*. N.Y.: Norton.

Gedo, J. (1976) "Freud's self-analysis and his scientific ideas." In *Freud: The Fusion of Science and Humanism*. N.Y.: International Universities Press.

Gedo, J. and E. Wolff (1976) "The Ich. Letters." Gedo & Pollack, eds.. *Freud: The Fusion of Science and Humanism. Psychol. Issues*. N.Y.: International Universities Press.

Gicklhorn, Renée (1976) *Sigmund Freud und der Onkeltraum. Dichtung und Wahrheit*. Vienna.

Gilman, Sander (1988) "Constructing the image of the appropriate therapist." In *Freud in Exile*, edited by E. Timms and N. Segal, New Haven: Yale University Press.

Glenn, Jules (1979) "Narcissistic aspects of Freud and his doubles." In *Freud and His Self-Analysis*, edited by Mark Kanzer and Jules Glenn. N.Y.: Jason Aronson.

Gould, Rosalind (1972) *Child Studies Through Fantasy*. N.Y.: Quadrangle.

Graves, Robert (1982) *The Greek Myths*. Middlesex, England: Penguin Books.

Grinstein, Alexander (1968) *On Sigmund Freud's Dreams*. N.Y.: International Universities Press.

Groddeck, Georg (1928) *The Book of the Id*. N.Y.: Nervous and Mental Disease Publishing Company.

Grollman, Earl (1965) *Judaism in Sigmund Freud's World*. N.Y.: Appleton-Century.

Gross, Martin (1978) *The Psychological Society*. N.Y.: Simon and Schuster.

Grotjahn, Martin (1973) "Sigmund Freud and the art of letter writing." In *Freud As We Knew Him*, edited by Hendrik Ruitenbeek. Detriot: Wayne State University Press.

Hobson, Allan (1987) "Psychoanalysis on the couch." *Encylopedia Brittanica, Medical and Health Annual.*

Holland, Norman and Harry Trosman (1972) "Words and psychoanalysis: Hamlet again." Contemp. Psychol., 17.

Jahoda, G. (1954) "A note on Ashanti names and their relationship to personality." *British Journal of Psychology*, 45.

Jones, Ernest (1953; 1955; 1957) *The Life and Work of Sigmund Freud.* N.Y.: Basic Books.

_____ (1954) "Freud's early travels." *International Journ. of Psychoanlaysis*, 35.

_____ (1959) *Free Associations: Memories of a Psychoanalyst.* London: Hogarth Press.

Jung, Carl (1963) *Memories, Dreams, Reflections.* N.Y.: Vintage Books.

Kanzer, Mark (1979) "Freud and his literary doubles." In *Freud and His Self-Analysis*, edited by Mark Kanzer and Jules Glenn. N.Y.: Jason Aronson.

Kanzer, Mark (1979) "Sigmund and Alexander Freud on the Acropolis." In *Freud and Self-Analysis*, edited by Mark Kanzer and Jules Glenn. N.Y.: Jason Aronson.

Kanzer, Mark and Jules Glenn, eds. (1979) *Freud and His Self-Analysis.* N.Y.: Jason Aronson.

Krüll, Marianne (1986) *Freud and His Father.* N.Y.: W.W. Norton.

Kushner, Martin (1967) *Freud–A Man Obsessed.* Phil.: Dorrance and Company.

Laforgue, René (1973) "Personal memories of Freud." In *Freud As We Knew Him*, edited by Hendrik Ruitenbeek. Detroit: Wayne State University Press.

Masson, Jeffrey (1984) *The Assault on Truth: Freud's Suppression of the Seduction Theory*. Farrar, Straus and Giroux.

Masson, Jeffrey, ed. (1985) *The Complete Letters of Sigmund Freud to Wilhelm Fliess*. Cambridge, Mass: Harvard University Press.

Maylan, Charles (1929) *Freuds tragischer Komplex. Eine Analyse der Psychoanalyse*. Munich: Ernst Reinhardt.

McGrath, William (1986) *Freud's Discovery of Psychoanalysis: The Politics of Hysteria*. Ithaca: Cornell University Press.

McGuire, W., ed. (1974) *The Freud/Jung Letters*. Princeton, N.J.: Princeton University Press.

Miller, Eric (1984) *Passion for Murder: The Homicidal Deeds of Dr. Sigmund Freud*. San Diego, Cal.: Future Directions, Inc.

Mowrer, Orval (1961) *The Crisis in Psychiatry and Religion*. Princeton: D. Van Nostrand Company, Inc.

Murphy, William (1957) "A note on the significance of names." *Psychoanalytic Quarterly*, 26.

Natenberg, Maurice (1955) *The Case History of Sigmund Freud. A Psychobiography*. Chicago: Regent House.

Nunn, Percy (1929) "The fatal name." *Int. Journal of Psycho-analysis*, 10.

Oberndorf, Clarence (1918) "Reaction to personal names." *Psychoanalytic Review*, V.

Obholzer, Karin (1982) *The Wolf-Man: Sixty Years Later*. N.Y.: Continuum.

Popper-Lynkeus, Josef (1947) "Dreaming like waking." Translated by A.A. Brill, *The Psychoan. Review*, 34. (First publication in *Phantasien eines Realisten*, Vienna, 1899).

Puner, Helen (1947) *Freud, His Life and His Mind*. N.Y.: Dell, 1961.

Roazen, Paul (1968) *Freud, Political and Social Thought*. N.Y.: Alfred A. Knopf.

_____ (1969) *Brother Animal. The Story of Freud and Tausk.* N.Y.: Alfred A Knopf.

_____ (1975) *Freud and His Followers.* N.Y.: Alfred A Knopf.

_____ (1990) *Encountering Freud.* New Brunswick, U.S.A.: Transaction Publishers.

Robert, Marthe (1976) *From Oedipus to Moses: Freud's Jewish Identity.* London: Routledge and Kegan Paul.

Rokeach, Milton (1964) *The Three Christs of Ypsilanti.* N.Y.: Knopf.

Ruitenbeek, Hendrik, ed. (1973) *Freud As We Knew Him.* Detroit: Wayne State University Press.

Sachs, Hanns (1944) *Freud: Master and Friend.* Cambridge: Harvard University Press.

Sagan, Eli (1988) *Freud, Women and Morality.* N.Y.: Basic Books.

Scagnelli, Paul *The Fatal Freud: His Suicide Complex, and Falsifying of Data.* (Unpublished manuscript.)

_____ *The Dark Side of Freud.* (Unpublished manuscript.)

_____ *Secret Sex Lives: Freud, Jung, and Jones* (Unpublished manuscript.)

_____ *Name Magic: In Murder, Madness, and the Normal Mind.* (Unpublished manuscript.)

Schatzman, M. (1976) *Soul Murder: Persecution in the Family.* Harmondsworth, England: Penguin Books.

Schorske, Carl (1973) "Politics and patricide in Freud's *Interpretation of Dreams.*" *The American Historical Review,* 78.

Schur, Max (1969) "The background of Freud's disturbance on the Acropolis," *American Imago,* 26. Also in Kanzer, M.; Glenn, J.; eds. *Freud and His Self-Analysis.* N.Y.: Jason Aronson, 1979.

_____ (1972) *Freud: Living and Dying*. London: Hogarth Press and the Institute of Psycho-Analysis.

Shengold, Leonard (1966) "The metaphor of the journey in *The Interpretation of Dreams*." *American Imago*, 23.

_____ (1979) "Freud and Joseph." In *Freud and His Self-Analysis*, edited by Mark Kanzer and Jules Glenn. N.Y.: Jason Aronson.

_____ (1979) A parapraxis of Freud's in relation to Karl Abraham." In *Freud and His Self-Analysis*, edited by Mark Kanzer and Jules Glenn, N.Y.: Jaron Aronson.

Simon, Ernst (1989) "Sigmund Freud, the Jew." In Spurling, L., ed. *Sigmund Freud, Critical Assessments*. Vol. I. London: Routledge.

Spitz, René (1958) "On the genesis of superego components." *Psychoanalytic Study of the Child*, 13.

Spurling, Laurence, ed. (1989) *Sigmund Freud: Critical Assessments*, Vol. I & II. London: Routledge.

Stadden, Anthony (1989) "Was Dora ill?" In *Sigmund Freud: Critical Assessments*, II, edited by Laurence Spurling. London: Routledge.

Starr, Moses Allan (1912) Newspaper article attacking Freud's personal morality in the 1880s. *New York Times* of April 5, 1912.

Steele, Robert (1982) *Freud and Jung: Conflicts of Interpretation*. London: Routledge and Kegan Paul.

Stein, Conrad (1968) "Le père mortel et le père immortel." *L'Inconscient*, 7.

Stekel, Wilhelm (1911) "*Die Verpflichtung des Namens*." (The obligation of the name.) *Zeitschrift fur Pschotherapie v. Mediz. Psychol.*, III.

Stepansky, Paul (Monog. 39) *A History of Aggression in Freud*. In: *Psychological Issues*, X.

Sulloway, Frank (1979) *Freud, Biologist of the Mind: Beyond the Psychoanalytic Legend*. N.Y.: Basic Books.

Swales, Peter (1982) "Freud, Minna Bernays, and the conquest of Rome." *New American Review*, I, No. 2/3.

_____ (1984) "Ce que Freud n'a pas dit." In A. Verdiglione, ed. *La Sexualité d'ouvient L'Orient? Ou val' Occident?* Paris: Belfond.

_____ (1989) "Freud, Fliess, and fraticide: the role of Fliess in Freud's conception of paranoia." In Spurling, L. ed. *Sigmund Freud: Critical Assessments.*, I, London: Routledge.

_____ (1989) "Freud, cocaine, and sexual chemistry: the role of cocaine in Freud's conception of the libido." In Spurling, L., ed. *Sigmund Freud: Critical Assessments.*, I, London: Routledge.

Szasz, Thomas (1976) *Karl Kraus and the Soul-Doctors.* Baton Rouge: Louisiana State University Press.

Thornton, E.M. (1984) *The Freudian Fallacy: An Alternative View of Freudian Theory.* Garden City, N.Y.: Dial Press. (Previous title: *Freud and Cocaine*, 1983).

Tomkins, Silvan (1963) *Affect, Imagery, Consciousness.* II. N.Y.: Springer Company.

Torrey, E. Fuller (1992) *Freudian Fraud: The Malignant Effect of Freud's Theory on American Thought and Culture.* N.Y.: Harper and Collins, Publishers.

Velikovsky, Emanuel (1941) "The dreams Freud dreamed." *Psychoanalytic Review*, 30.

Vitz, Paul (1988) *Sigmund Freud's Christian Unconscious.* N.Y.: Guilford Press.

Weininger, Otto (1903) *Sex and Character.* Vienna, Wilhelm Braunmüller.

Weiss, Edoardo (1970) *Sigmund Freud as Consultant: Recollections of a Pioneer in Psychoanalysis.* N.Y.: Intercontinental Medical Book Corporation.

Wittels, Fritz (1924) *Sigmund Freud. Der Mann, die Lehre, die Schule.* Leipzig: E.P. Tal.

_____ (1931) *Freud and His Time*. N.Y.: Grosset and Dunlop.

_____ (1947) "Freud's correlation with Joseph Popper-Lynkeus." *The Psychoan. Review*, 34.

Young-Bruehl, Elizabeth (1988) *Anna Freud: A Biography*. N.Y.: Summit Books.

Zanuso, B. (1986) *The Young Freud*. Oxford: Basil Blackwell, Ltd.

Zilboorg, Gregory (1967) *Psychoanalysis and Religion*. London: George Allen and Unwin.

Addendum

Paskauskas, R. Andrew, ed. (1993) *The Complete Correspondence of Sigmund Freud and Ernest Jones*. Cambridge, Mass.: Harvard University Press.

Eissler, Kurt (1992) "An interperetation of four of Freud's letters." In *Understanding Freud: The Man and His Ideas*, edited by Emanuel E. Garcia. N.Y.: New York University Press.

Index

Abraham, Karl, 9, 96-7, 104, 171, 241, 289, 223, 343, 369-72, 377, 384-6, 417-18, 421, 423, 441, 498, 531

Acropolis episode (1904), 143, 154, 169, 184-95, 201, 213, 335-6, 355, 381, 435 ff., 500: and desire to push Fliess off cliff, 134, 154, 187 ff.; on Freud's confessions of murder135, 142, 213; on Freud's identification with Daedalus 188 ff.; and split in Freud's psyche, 186-7

Adams, Leslie: study of Freud's birthdate, 61-64

Adler, Alfred, 7, 8, 169, 257-8, 351, 359, 361, 386, 429, 531

Adler, Friedrich: murder trial, 431-2

Adler, Viktor, 221-2, 274, 278, 284, 413, 431

Ambition, pathological (Freud's), 36, 109, 115, 117, 121, 202

America, Freud's hatred of, 466

Amri, biblical king: as reversal of Irma, 237

Anzieu, Didier, 325: Freud's identifications, 72, 78 ff., 81, opposing identifications in Freud, 206

Assassins at Berggasse 19, 430-3

Bailey, Percival: Freud as crass manipulator, 180

Bakan, David, 54, 87-89, 197, 400, 402, 475-81, 484, 492, 497: and Freud's identification with military messiah 186 ff.; and on Freud's murderous impulses, 137 ff.,

Balmary, Marie, 111-12, 117, 197, 482-4

Bernays, Eli, 2, 242-3, 288

Bernays, Emmeline, 202-3, 288

Bernays, Minna, 57, 106, 166, 168, 292, 361-2: on Minna, and Monica Zajic, 57, 155

Bernfeld, Siegfried, 244

Bernfeld, Suzanne, 426-7

Birthdate falsification (Freud's), 61-70: and Schiller's birthplace, 130

Birthday magic, 95-96, 130, 448

Bizarre ideas by Freud, 172 ff.

Blum, Harold, 217-218

Bonaparte, Marie (Princess): on Freud's ucs. desire to kill her, 194 ff., 213

Bonaparte, Napoleon, 99, 100, 193 ff., 213, 504

Borderline Personality Disorder, of Freud, 28, 29, 78, 184, 200: with psychotic trends, 184

Breuer, Dora, 297-8

Breuer, Josef, 6, 7, 123, 167-8, 171, 179, 199, 232, 244-5, 289-91, 294-5, 297-8, 358, 392-3, 411, 438: diagnosed Freud's moral insanity, 109-11, 208, 373; joins Fliess and angers

Freud, 147 ff.

Breuer, Margarethe, 291

Breuer, Mathilde, 241, 278

Brome, Vincent, 21, 352-6, 358, 361-2, 366, 504-5, 509-11, 516, 519, 521, 525, 526, 528, 530-1

Bullitt, William, 446, 448, 451, 463-4

Cain complex (Freud's), 10, 88, 112-13, 131, 246, 252, 285, 392, 410, 440 (see Fratricidal urges)

Charcot, Jean M., 6, 198

Choisy, Maryse: on Freud's death fears, 182, 216; Freud as Satan, 480

Clark, Ronald, 15, 16, 91, 92, 103, 106, 164, 247, 260, 263, 364-6, 376, 408, 411, 419, 426, 446, 451, 458, 473

Cocaine excesses, 6, 81, 96, 166, 167, 182, 203: cocaine and nanny, 248

Conquistador Image, 137, 202, 370, 419

Criminality in Freud family, 1-4, 11, 17, 40, 41, 46, 51, 60, 81, 116, 122, 278-9, 374, 474

Daedalus, 144, 292, 337, 435, 441: and Acropolis episode, 188 ff,

Dark Side of Freud, The, 11, 17, 25, 27, 28, 31, 52, 56, 72, 75, 77, 84, 88, 95, 103, 107, 123-4, 126-7, 160-2, 166-7, 168, 178, 226, 234, 236-7, 241, 245-7, 258-9, 261, 267-9, 276, 278, 292, 297-8, 305, 337, 452,

Daudet, Philippe, 170, 127, 469-71

Death instinct theory, 170-1, 177, 424-29

Death - wishes towards sons, by Freud (see Freud, and death wishes), 139, 442 ff.: and name magic, 140

Death-year fears (Freud's), 89, 95, 181-2, 224, 413-15, 418, 421, 436

Decker, Hannah, 294-5, 296-8, 300-301, 311

Deutsch, Felix: on Freud's suicide request, 20, 170, 489

Disappearances of people, 131, 440-1, 445-6, 468-71, 473

Don Juan and Freud, 111-12, 116-17, 133

Dora case, 7, 169, 236, 272, 287, 289-300, 301 ff.: on Dora as replay of Gisela F. and nanny, 307-8; on name magic, 309-10; on name series re"Dora," 294-301; on revenge motives of Freud and Dora 305-9; and summary of case, 301 ff.

Doubles ("twins"), of Freud, 210 ff.

Dream of dishonesty, 116 ff., 134

Dream of self-dissection, 134

Duality, 120, 122, 140: on Freud's dual personality 195-8; on history of dual personality, 198-200, 218

Eckstein, Emma, 10, 11, 75, 118, 236-7, 275, 297, 299, 314, 452: equated with Fanny Moser, 236; equated with nanny 11, 236, 278; nose surgery, 11, 55, 159, 168, 171, 174, 183, 411

Eissler, Kurt, 102, 108-9, 139-40, 143-4, 284-6, 381, 472, 533 ff.

Eitingon, Max, 129, 468, 531

Ellenberger, Henri, 4, 100, 176, 182, 184, 198, 205, 250, 267, 275, 357, 359, 426, 469-70

Index   page 556

Fatal Freud, The, 11, 17, 26, 152, 171, 219 n., 278, 429

Faust, 86-89, 90, 197-8, 202, 205, 478, 484, 486-7, 492

Ferenczi, Sandor, 8, 9, 19, 171, 178, 196, 220, 264 ff., 272, 289, 342, 348-50, 353-5, 361, 370, 373, 377, 380, 384, 386-7, 391, 394, 412-13, 416, 418, 423, 456, 480, 501

Fiesco, 114 ff., 122, 130

Flechsig, Paul : fantasy of rivalry by Freud, 251-3, 274

Fleischl (von Marxow), 12, 75, 278, 289, 298, 438, 452

Fliess, Ida, 149, 168, 290, 294-5, 393

Fliess, Jacob : and suicide on train, 342-3

Fliess, Wilhelm, 7, 10, 12. 33-36, 38, 51, 63, 108, 110, 133 n., 134, 146 ff., 158-9, 162, 167-9, 171, 173-4, 212, 214-15, 223-25, 238-9, 240-1, 245, 253 ff., 258, 265, 278, 289-94, 297, 326-8, 344-6, 349, 357, 361-2, 364, 381, 408, 411, 413-15, 416, 422, 423, 432, 435-6, 438, 445, 458, 461, 485, 487, 498-9, 500: and Acropolis episode, 187 ff. ; on   Freud's plan to kill Fliess, 146 ff., 346; as "golden fleece," 156, 254-6, 308; on train suicide of Fliess' father 342-4

Fluss, Gisela, 5, 66, 165-6, 273, 277-8, 313, 323: on Gisela's name-series, 259 ff.

Folie à deux, 157

Fraiberg, Selma, 74, 75, 77

Fratricidal urges (Freud's, etc.), 10, 12, 111-13, 121-2, 126-7, 131, 342, 395, 433: and connection with

Julius Mosen - forgetting, 126 (see Cain Complex)

Free love doctrine (See E. Jones): on Freud's endorsement, to cure neurosis, 175

Freiberg catastrophe, 22, 38, 40, 98, 105, 164, 178, 183, 193, 197, 203, 287, 322-3, 327, 407, 422, 441, 461, 466, 501

Freud, Alexander, 185 ff., 212, 213, 345, 436

Freud, Amalia, 5, 30-32, 37, 38, 43, 45, 46, 55, 61, 65, 66, 69, 300, 433-4: and her possible mental instability, 51

Freud, Anna (analyst), 2, 9, 24, 29, 42, 243-4, 328, 367-8, 371, 409-12, 503-4, 522-23, 531-2: and ego psychology, 9; on name as palindrome, 246: on trip to England, 373-80, 409 ff.

Freud, Anna (S.F.'s sister) 2, 5, 242-3

Freud, Bertha 208

Freud, Emanuel, 1, 5, 11, 17-23, 30, 39, 40, 42, 43, 46, 61, 67-69, 78, 80, 96, 97, 100, 113, 145, 154-5, 169-70, 177, 183, 193, 194, 197, 203, 213, 287, Chap. 8: on Hollthurn dream and Emanuel's death, 131; and murder plan re Emanuel, 373 ff., 367, 370, 407, 410, 412-13, 416, 421-2, 428-30, 443, 456, 461, 466-7, 501-3: on predictions of Emanuel's murder, 335-344, 344-350; as Sigi's father (fantasy), 43, 48, 61, 63, 66-68, 97, 110, 130, 221, 347, 360, 363, 434n., 435, 462; and train neurosis of Freud, 324-335

Freud, Jacob, 1, 5, 30, 32, 41, 43, 45, 48, 51, 52, 55-56, 59, 61, 63, 66, 69, 100, 102, 274-5, 280, 288, 342-3, 347, 435, 476: as sexual pervert, 41,

44-5, 50-1, 84, 168, 242

Freud, John, 5, 8, 11-16, 18, 22-3, 30, 40, 46-50, 76, 78, 80, 113, 143-5, 170, 177, 202, 213, 223, 241-2, 395, Chap. 9, 501-2: and Acropolis episode, 188 ff.; and duologue with Sigi, 13, 76, 111, 120, 126, 229-30, 336, 433-4, 468; and forgetting of Julius Mosen, 125-6; maybe vanished in 1870's, 13-16, 408 ff.; name-series and John, 313; on predictions of John's murder, 433-4

Freud, Josef, 1-3, 17, 85, 96, 38, 118, 122, 164, 231-3, 279, 280, 285, 288, 412

Freud, Julius, 5, 22, 31, 32, 45, 51, 217, 220, 363, 387, 392, 405, 413

Freud, Marie, 30, 342, 443

Freud, Martha, 2, 18, 53, 166, 208, 248-9, 300, 326-7, 327-8, 420-1, 423, 428, 444, 496, 501: on adoption by Seig.. Pappenheim, 209; as replacement for nanny, 196, 203

Freud, Martin (Jean), 8, 169, 242, 368, 384, 417, 420-2, 428, 443-45, 466

Freud, Mathilde, 241

Freud, Philipp, 3, 5, 18, 22, 30, 37, 38, 39, 42, 43, 45-6, 170

Freud, Sigmund: on analysis of Joan Riviere, 526-7: on analysis of Loe Kann, 503, 520-2, 499; on anger towards Jones, 527; and birthday issues (see birthday magic; birthdate falsification); on borderline personality, Freud's, 29, (see separate item); on childhood years, 5, Chap. 2; and cocaine (see cocaine excesses); on death-wishes (see Cain; fratricide; patricide), 11, 12, 18, 20, 38, 360, 363, 365, 380 ff., 390, 397, 406, 429, 437, 439, 500-502; on double birthdate 60-69, 95; on duologue with John (see John Freud); on early sex abuse by nanny, 41 ff.; on his ego-splitting (duality), 28, 29, 33, 40, 43, 52 ff., 74, 78, 198 ff., 200 ff., 206 ff.; on fainting spells and murder, 362 ff.; on fantasy identifications (100+), 70 ff., 105, Chap. 4 (murderers), 460; on fantasy of healthy murder, 389-90; on fears of dying, 216-18; on fears of murder by kin and colleagues, 19, 38, 80, 81, 92, 110, 169, 176, 179, 184, 189, 249, 360, 362-4; on identifications, acting-out, 81 ff., 96 ff., 155 ff., 492 ff.; on identification with Jesus, 56-58, 70, 76-7, 96, 107, 121, 166, 404-5, 446, 452-3, 457, 462; on identification with Satan, 40, 53 ff., 58, 77-8, 87, 248, 391, 446, 479-81, 491 ff., 501-2; on insanity in family, 43 ff.; on many who claimed Freud murdered, 285-6; on medical school days, 6; on near-psychosis in 1914, 372-3; on near-psychotic episodes (14), 20, 28, Chap. 5; on patricidal man's legal fees, 128 ff.; as plagiarist 267 ff., 275 ff., 277, 425; on plan to kill Fliess 146 ff., 414; on plan to kill Jung (see Jung, C.), 369-70; on psychotic ideation, admitted by Freud, 161-2, 290; on revenge impulses, 38, 39, 40, 50, 83 ff., 85, 97, 112, 155, 373, 501-2; on rivalry with John, sexual, 50; on Screen Memory, 48 ff.; on splitting (Hebrew/Christian, etc.) 52 ff., 186, 200, 201 ff., 206 ff., 208, 497-8; as spoiled child, 202-3, 494, 507-8; on suicide complex, 28, 38, 75, 143; on symptoms and ailments (Freud's) 167; on train phobia (see train phobia); as unscrupulous liar, 119, 492; on wardrobe scene, 37

Freund, Anton, 250

Index

Freund, C.S. (name magic), 250

Fromm, Erich, 180, 496

Gicklhorn, Renée, 1-4, 11, 17, 46, 60, 164, 231, 474

Gilman, Sander, 159, 182

Glenn, Jules, 212

Golden fleece, and Jason, 255 ff.

Gould, Rosalind, 74

Grinstein, Alexander, 79, 80, 115-118

Groddeck, Georg, 170, 487-8

Gross, Martin; cites Freud's severe neurosis, 180

Gross, Otto, 140-2, 354-5, 412, 520, 523-4: as advocate of suicide, 141; on Freud's identification with Gross, 140 ff.; as murderer, 140 ff.

Haizmann, Christoph, 477-9, 489

Hamlet, 109-10

Hannibal, Winckelmann and Rome, 77, 79 ff., 82 ff., 87, 347, 468, 476: Freud confuses Hannibal's surname, 130

Herzl, Hans & Theodore, 145 ff.

Hollthurn dream, 131 ff., 286, 335 ff., 338, 381, 436, 439, 440-2, 444-5; as predictor of Emanuel's death, 131; as predictor of John's death, 440-1

"Homicidal" Hollthurn patient: as object of Freud's identification, 131 ff., 150

Horney, Karen, 492; on neurosis and satanic pacts, 492

Interpretation of Dreams, 7, 15, 16, 25, 35, 84 ff., 90 ff., 94, 99, 100, 101, 127, 267, 273, 274, 298, 311, 317, 342, 346-7, 367, 381, 395, 405-6, 408, 476, 478, 482, 484-5: on Latin motto and revenge, 85-6, 288, 405, 476; as secret confession of sins, 119; written to compete with Gisela's spouse, 266

Irma's injection (dream), 118, 134, 168, 180, 236-7, 297, 311, 346

Jocob (Biblical), 100 ff., 113, 274, 284; and wish-fulfilment theory, 100 ff., 103

Janet, Pierre, 104, 198-9, 200, 354, 356, 469

Jekyll/Hyde and Freud, 72, 89, 119, 122, 140, 144, 195 ff., 202, 204-7, 229, 391, 428, 452, 464, 468

Jesus and Freud (see Freud, S.), 76, 77, 96, 104, 107, 121, 140, 162, 166-7, 206, 172, 236, 256, 385, 392, 396, 404-5, 446, 452-3, 457-8, 462

Jones, Ernest, 8, 9, 20, 21, 23-5, 28, 36, 47, 48, 58, 61, 63, 75, 76, 140, 158, 203-5, 218, 220, 230, 242, 288, 324, 328, 349-50, 354-5, 365, 368-9, 372, 376-380, 382, 383-4, 386, 393-4, 400, 412-13, 416, 420, 429, 447, 465, 468, 474, 494, 501, Chap.11: on "administrative murder," 24, 172, 529-32; on censorship in three volumes, 2, 4, 23-5, 28, 58, 75-6, 140, 354, 411, 412, 504, 533; on claim that Jesus was a pervert, 518, 519; and free love doctrine, 505, 513-17, 521-5; on Freud's fears of death, 218 ff., 328; on his menage à trois, 521; on his sadism toward women, 520 ff.; on his sexual abuse of children, 510-514; on identification with rakish doctor, 506-7, 509, 516-7, 527; on incest with sister, 505-6; as "madman," per Riviere, 525-29; on name magic, Jones' 505-6; and patricidal man, 128 ff.; as seducer of engaged women, 508-9; on seducing his patient, Riviere, 517, 524-27, 534 ff.; on seducing his Toronto patient, 514-18, 520, 526; on seduction - try with Anna Freud, 378 ff., 503, 517, 522, 523; and smuggling escapade, 24, 374-5, 474, 528-9; as student of Otto Gross, 523-524; on voyeurism with actress, 507

Josef (Biblical), 85, 94 ff., 99 ff., 100, 113, 213, 274, 434-5: and Napoleon, 99 ff.

Jung, Carl, 8, 19-20, 52, 91-3, 106, 169, 176, 199, 203, 205, 209, 249, 253, 280, 348-50, 352-71, 373, 384n., 386, 412-13, 451, 533: cited sickness in Freud, 81; on murder plan against Jung, 154, 362, 364-5, 369-70; and sexual molestation of young Carl, 28, 354; on split-mind of Jung, 209, 498

Kann, Loe (Jones' mistress), 24, 379-80, 503-4, 514-15, 520-2, 526

Kanzer, Mark, 212-13, 326, 414, 436

Kremzer, Margit (suicide), 112, 162, 278, 284, 287, 291, 294, 311, 314, 319-21, 383

Krüll, Marianne, 2, 3, 14, 17, 28, 31, 34, 40-1, 44-6, 48, 104, 110, 165, 167, 173, 279, 330, 358, 360-1, 399-401, 408, 473: on Freud's mental crises, 163

Kushner, Martin: on Freud justifies patricide, 183; and justifies incest, 494

Laforgue, René, 204, 480

Lamarckian magic, 105 ff., 177-8, 359-60, 423-4, 426

Lecher, Dr., 237-8

Lina, (a mistress of E. Jones), 379, 520-23

Macbeth, 108-9, 286, 387, 537 ff.

Magical thinking, Freud's (see number magic; name magic; birthday magic), 216-17, 219, 222, 342, 423, 428-9, 431, 475, 497-8: and cigar magic, 247-8

Mann, Thomas, 98-99

Manson and Freud, 78

Marburg: Schiller's birthplace, 130; professor who exposed Freud's sex life, 135; business friend of Jacob Freud, 135

Masochistic identifications, Freud's 79-81

Masson, Jeffrey, 183, 236, 264, 299, 341, 411, 471-2

Masturbation, 173-4: on masturbation complex of Freud, 173

Mathilde: patient killed by Freud, 12, 75, 241

Maylan, Charles, 179, 449

McGrath, William, 80, 82 ff., 90-1, 94, 137 ff., 145-6

McGuire, W. 358

Megalomania (Freud's), 179-80, 207: and his admission of sexual megalomania, 180; and his king complex, 245

Mental crises of Freud (14), 64 ff., 163 ff.

Index

Meynert, Dora, 298

Meynert, Theodor, 251-2, 298

Militarism in Freud, 76, 82, 169, 279, 371, 372, 384, 387, 390, 413-14, 466-8: and conquistador image, 137, 372; and identification with military messiah, 137 ff.

Miller, Erick 11-17, 20, 23, 143, 285-6, 407, 409, 411

Moor, Franz and Karl, 119, 130, 229, 433-4

Moral insanity in Freud, 159-161, 208, 327, 392

Mosen, Julius (a"forgetting"), 124 ff., 133: on connection with Freud's murder complex 125 ff.; and connection with Moses and murder, 128; and Fanny Moser/Fra Moser, 126; on Fanny's estate (Au), 126; on Freud's desire to suppress, 125; as tied to loss of nanny, 126-7

Moser, Fanny (Emmy von N.), 122 ff., 235-6, 305: on claim she murdered rich husband, 123; on tie to Julius Mosen, 124 ff.; on hypnosis scam by Freud, 124; on notoriety sought by Freud, 123 ff.

Moses and Freud, 19, 20, 90 ff., 112, 198, 213, 368-9, 396-7, 399-405, 396, 398-405, 448, 467: on Julius Mosen (forgetting), 128, 481, 483

Moses and Monotheism, 10, 92 ff., 197, 465: as confession of Emanuel's murder, 177, 213, 402; on Moses' murder, as Freud's wish, 400, 402; on seven faces of Moses, 403 ff.

Muley Hassan (Moor of Tunis), 113 ff., 130, 229, 432n.,

Murder issues, 134-5, 142, 262, 389, 390: on acting-out murderous fantasies, 81 ff.; on fainting spells 362 ff.; on Freud's desire to destroy world, 262; on healthy murderous ego, 389 ff.; and Julius Mosen, 126; on many who claimed Freud murdered, 285; and ucs. predictions of murder, 155; and trains, 133, Chap. 8

Murderous identifications, Freud's, 72, Chap. 4

Myths about Freud, 184

Name magic, 25-6, 88, 95, 99, 100, 102-4, 111, 112, 116, 122, 138-40, 170, 171, 208-9, 211, Chap. 6; 379, 422, 443, 463-4: on Alhama and nanny 193; and attacks on name "Freud," 232-3; and Bergasse," 222; for coalescing identifications, 228; on concept of name magic 228; and Fliess' name, 149; and Freud's acting-out fantasy identifications 138; on Freud and name magic, 228 ff; on Freud's many names, 139, 233-4, 460; and Freud on Napoleon's name-compulsions 193; and golden fleece, 156; and golden Sigi, 126; on initial magic and Emanuel, 345; on introduction to Name Magic, 225 ff.; on Jones' name magic, 505-6; on Josef Poppers names, 272 ff.; on Moses and name magic 398, 401-2; on murderers and name magic, 228; and the names of Fliess and Schur, 253-5, 278; on name magic and Dora case, 309-10, 312-14; and name of Romain Rolland, 213-14; and name-series (see name-series, magical), 257-86; on relation to dwarf in "Freud," 171; on relation to Julius Mosen (forgetting), 126; in *The Robbers,* 121-2; on "roy" in "Freud" and "Breuer," 245; on Salomé and John Freud, 462-3; on sexuality and name "Freud," 233 ff.; on Sig and Sigi,

251 ff; on Sig as "Moor" and Moorish King, 193; on Stekel re name - compulsion, 225 ff.; and St. Sigismund (murderer), 137 ff. on "Weiss" and name magic, 221; on Woodrow Wilson's name magic, 459 ff.

Name Magic: In Murder Madness, and the Normal Mind, 26, 219, 228

Name-series, magical, 227 ff., 250, 257-286, 300: destructive name-series by Freud, 257; Dora's case and name-series, 294- 301; on Gisela/Gizella series, 77 ff.; and John Freud, 314; the K-initial series (Dora case), 316-321; on Napoleon's name-series, 258; on the Popper series, 266 ff.; as revenge factor, Freud, 228 ff.

Nasal neurosis theory, 173: and near death of Emma E., 174

Natenberg, Maurice, 179: Freud as charlatan and psychopath 179

Near-psychotic episodes, Freud, 10, 20, 134, 153-4, 290 ff., 372-3, 380-1, 418-9, 420-24, 426-9, 450, 456-9, 467, 478, 497

Non vixit dream, 12, 134, 215, 231, 346, 436-39, 442: and revenants, 215

Number magic, Freud and Fliess, 89 ff., 95, 103, 219 ff., 413-15, 421-2, 430-1, 490, 498, 500: and Acropolis episode, 187 ff.; on Freud"s fear of phone number, 414, 485, 488, 500; on periodicity theory, 89, 499, 500; and sphinx, 156 ff.

Number "2467," 95, 224, 344-5, 442, 485, 490-1, 499: as satanic pact, 484-5

Oedipal issues, 31, 63-4: on Freud as Oedipus, 68, 111; on Freud's imitation of hero's patricide, 155 ff.; and the name Sigismund, 138; on the sphinx and Freud, 156-7

Pálos, Gizella, 264 ff., 273, 277, 323, 416, 423: on her name-series, 259 ff.

Paneth, Josef, 232, 289, 298, 437

Paskauskas, R. Andrew, 533 ff.

Patricidal urges (Freud's, etc.) 12, 109-12, 113, 121-22, 126, 127, 144, 154-5, 183-4, 213, 275, 325, 330, 339-41, 347, 359-60, 364, 370-1, 387-8, 398-99, 400-1, 406, 433, 441: and Hollthurn patient, 131, 134; and patricidal man's legal expenses, 128, 395; on "Sigismund" as patricidal name, 138

Periodicity theory, 224: its "magic" endorsed by Freud, 125

Popper, Josef (Lynkeus), 101-2, 232, 267: dream theory plagiarized by Freud, 267 ff., 275 ff.; on life of Popper, 268 ff.; on name-series, 266 ff.

Project for a Scientific Psychology: created during cocaine madness, 176, 310, 392-3

Puner, Helen, 12, 205, 285, 347: on death of Freud's marriage, 118; on Freud's confession of sins, 13; on patricidal urges of Freud, 184, 482

Putnam, James, 493-96, 514-17, 526

Repetition compulsions, Freud's (see revenants), 173

Revenants, 210, 213-15, Chap. 6: on Adler and Stekel as revenants, 258; and name magic, 240-1, 272, Chap. 7, 415, 437-8

Index

Revenge motive (see *Interpretation of Dreams*, motto), 84-6, 184, 193, 205, 221, 266, 357-8, 373, 392, 406, 422, 457, 470: and Dora case, 301ff., 306, 312; and military messiah 136; and name-series, Freud, 228; on revenge and suicide (Dora), 314-16

Riviere, Joan: Jones' seduction of this patient, 524-27

Roazen, Paul, 2, 3, 13, 21, 139, 143, 181, 204, 278, 285, 404, 415, 447-51, 464-6, 467, 472, 530

The Robbers (Schiller), 119 ff., 313: and Fra Moser, 120, on Franz and Karl Moor, 119 ff., on name magic and Freud, 121; on play's profound effect on Freud, 120

Robert, Marthe, 82, 99, 100

Rolland, Romain, 10, 185 ff., 212, 213-4

Sadger, Isidor, 7, 21: on "administrative murder," 21, 24, 172, 179, 218, 474, 530-32

Salomé, Lou Andreas, 181, 356, 385-6, 462, 523

Sand-Man, 142-3

Sardou, Victorien, 300-1

Satan and anti-Christ (see Freud, S. on identification with Satan), 76-8, 87 ff., 112-13, 140, 143, 178, 196, 205-7, 404-5, 406, 446, Chap. 10: pacts with Satan, 89 ff., 111, 116, 166, 211, 224, 241, 345, 406, 477-9, 482, 484-92, 497-501

Schiller, Johann, 13, 113 ff., 132, 133: birthplace error re Freud's birthdate, 130

Schreber, Paul, 252-3

Schur, Max, 10, 13, 15, 20, 32, 38, 95, 97, 112, 163, 181, 205, 210, 214, 216, 219, 237, 255, 278, 285, 346, 354, 368, 405, 407-12, 473, 487-9

Scientific theories, as projected fantasies, 176 ff. 180, 359, 360, 448-50, 451-4, 456, 479: on wishes to murder Jung, Emanuel, etc., 177

Scipio (Africanus) 121-2

Screen Memory paper, 262 ff.

Secret Sex Lives, 17, 20, 23, 25, 72, 90, 106, 111, 135, 166, 175, 178, 261, 265, 352, 354-5, 379, 504, 515, 520, 524, 527, 530-3

Seduction theory, 174; abandoned by Freud, 174, 200, 471

Sexuality, notoriety, and fame, 173

Shakespeare, William, 178

Shengold, Leonard, 98, 245, 324-5, 437-8

Signorelli analysis, 127, 243: encodes lethal urges re nanny's loss, 127

Sphinx, as Fliess, 156 ff.

Spielrein, Sabina, 170, 425, 429, 523

Spitz, René, 73

Splitting of mind (see Freud, S.) 28-9, 78: on clinicians aware of Freud's split-mind, 201 ff.; on history of splitting, 198 ff.; on Jung's split-mind, 209; and origin of Devil, 206-7; and O.R.T. theory, 207; and sexual abuse by nanny, 207; on splits of Fliess and Jones, 209

Starr, Moses Allan, 135, 165-6, 355

Stein, Conrad, 325

Steiner, R. 534 ff.

Stekel, Wilhelm, 7, 8, 169-70, 234, 244, 257-8, 351-3, 359, 361: and name-compulsions, 225 ff., 230-1; and name - compulsion disputed by Freud, 230, 425, 531-2

Stepansky, Paul, 389-1, 394, 420, 424

Strachey, James: on shared psychosis of Freud and Fliess, 157, 182, 209, 343, 484

St. Sigismund and murder, 137 ff.

Suicide and murder, 20-1, 80 ff., 216, 218: in 1939, Freud's suicide, 172, 214; suicide and the K-initial series, 316-21

Suicide inducements by Freud (see Freud, suicide complex), 143, 415-6, on suicide of Weininger, 152, 162, 224; on Tausk's suicide (see Victor Tausk)

Sulloway, Frank, 82, 94-5, 100-1, 106, 147, 157, 178, 184, 200, 208, 255

Swales, Peter, 25, 31, 48, 82, 85, 87-8, 146-9, 150-2, 153-156, 207, 209, 234, 285, 288, 292 ff., 342, 412, 432, 434: on Freud's plan to murder Fliess, 146 ff., 155 ff.

Swaboda, Hermann: patient Freud used to assist plagiarism, 152, 293

Szasz, Thomas: called Ernest Jones "Great Falsifier," 23, 24

Talos (nephew of Daedalus), 189 ff., 435, 441: and Freud's intention to murder John, 189 ff.

Tausk, Victor, 12, 13, 143-4, 181-2, 284-5, 107, 423, 452, 472, 532: Freud induced suicide of Tausk, 143, 278, 412, 415, 451, 532; on Tausk's suicide, 13, 170, 177, 204

Teleky, Dora, 299

Thornton, E.M.: and Freud's cocaine psychosis, 182

Tilgner, Victor, 128, 218

Tomkins, Silvan: on Freud's paranoid trends, 181

Train dreams, 69, 335-41

Train phobia (anxiety) 18, 134, 197, 323, 324-35: death magic re trains, 332-3; and "double" (death) on train, 332; and sex fears, 334; and "slip" concerning train ride, 331-2; and train joke 330-1; and train suicide of Fliess' father, 342-44

Velikovsky, Emanuel, 87, 497

Vitz, Paul, 3, 4, 28-9, 31-4, 39, 44, 48, 56-7, 60, 69-71, 79, 82, 93, 107, 113, 143, 184, 200-1, 204, 206-7, 234, 244, 253, 497: on criminality in Freud family, 3, 4; on Freud's mental crises, like Schreber's, 163-4; on John molested by nanny, 50; on Satan identification (Freud's) 53 ff., 71, 87 ff., 184, 497; on splitting (Hebrew/Christian), 52 ff., 184

Weininger, Otto, 152 ff., 168-9, 188, 287, 293, 411: Freud responsible for suicide, 152, 246

Weiss, Edoardo, 283-5

Index

Weiss, Nathan, 221, 281-4, 289

Weiss, Simon: on Freud's criminality, 221, 281 ff., 320; on name-series re "Weiss", 280 ff.

Wilson, Woodrow, 9, 413: on connection of Wilson and John Freud, 447, 456-7; on destruction of Woodrow Wilson, 446-467; on Freud's identification with Wilson, 448-50, 458; on identifications with Jesus, 451-53, 455-7, 461-2, 467; name magic and Wilson, 459 ff.; Wilson's madness versus Freud's, 454-5

Winckelmann, Johann, 188-9

Windows (train), 133, 135

Wittek, Resi, 31, 295

Wittels, Fritz, 21, 172, 179, 207, 245, 269-73, 426-7, 451, 454, 481, 531

Wolf Man, 7, 382-4

Young-Bruehl, Elizabeth, 24, 368, 378-9, 380: on Anna Freud's "fictions," 409

Zajic, Monica (nanny), 5, 22, 30 ff., 36 ff., 38 ff., 47, 49, 55-6, 68, 70, 75, 77, 80, 83-4, 87, 95-6, 110, 111, 113, 132-3, 164-5, 168, 180, 193, 197, 201, 207-8, 214, 236, 247-8, 260-1, 287-8, 295-6, 313-14, 320, 329, 345, 347, 356, 381, 386, 389, 393, 397, 400, 411-12, 427, 429, 433-4, 438, 442-3, 458, 461, 471, 490-1, 502: on Anna and Monica, 243-4; on Emma E. and Monica, 75, 214, 248; on Minna and Monica, 57, 214, 222, 292; and revenants of nanny, 214, 261; on Sigi's secret baptism, 56-7; on tie with Julius Mosen, 127

Zeus and Freud, 129ff., 347: on patricide and Zeus, 129 ff., 347

Zilboorg, Gregory, 127, 163, 183, 204, 405

Zanuso, B., 201 ff.

HERE'S A UNIQUE CHRISTMAS GIFT FOR FRIENDS.

Order your copy now!

Pinewood Publishing Co., Dept PJ, P.O. Box 2417, Durham NC 27715 Allow 4 to 6 weeks for delivery.

(ORDER FORM)

Please send me ____ copies of DEADLY DR. FREUD at $30.00 each (price includes postage, handling, taxes), to:

Name _____

Address _____

City _____ State _____ Zip _____

☐ Check enclosed

HERE'S A UNIQUE CHRISTMAS GIFT FOR FRIENDS.

Order your copy now!

Pinewood Publishing Co., Dept PJ, P.O. Box 2417, Durham NC 27715 Allow 4 to 6 weeks for delivery.

(ORDER FORM)

Please send me ____ copies of DEADLY DR. FREUD at $30.00 each (price includes postage, handling, taxes), to:

Name _____

Address _____

City _____ State _____ Zip _____

☐ Check enclosed